Lessons 1-120

Keyboarding Essentials: Complete Course

MICROSOFT® WORD 2002 / MICROSOFT® WORD 2003

Susie H. VanHuss, Ph.D.
University of South Carolina

Connie M. Forde, Ph.D.
Mississippi State University

Donna L. Woo, Ph.D.
Cypress College, California

THOMSON

SOUTH-WESTERN

Australia · Canada · Mexico · Singapore · Spain · United Kingdom · United States

THOMSON

SOUTH-WESTERN

Keyboarding Essentials: Complete Course, Microsoft® Word 2002 / Microsoft® Word 2003, Lessons 1-120
Susie H. VanHuss, Connie M. Forde, Donna Woo

VP/Editorial Director:
Jack W. Calhoun

VP/Editor-in-Chief:
Dave Shaut

Senior Publisher:
Karen Schmohe

Acquisitions Editor:
Jane Phelan

Project Manager:
Dave Lafferty

Consulting Editor:
Mary Todd
Todd Publishing Services

Vice President/Director of Marketing:
Carol Volz

Marketing Manager:
Lori Pegg

Production Editor:
Kim Kusnerak

Production Manager:
Tricia Boies

Senior Print Buyer:
Charlene Taylor

Media Production Editor:
Mike Jackson

Design Project Manager:
Stacy Jenkins Shirley

Permissions Editor:
Linda Ellis

Copyeditor:
Gary Morris

Production House:
Peter Lippincott

Cover Designer:
Craig LaGesse Ramsdell
www.ramsdelldesign.com

Cover Images:
© PhotoDisc, Inc.

Internal Designer:
Craig LaGesse Ramsdell
www.ramsdelldesign.com

Printer:
Quebecor World, Dubuque
Dubuque, Iowa

TABLE OF CONTENTS

SUMMARY OF FUNCTIONS

THE LATEST WORD IN KEYBOARDING

Focus on the Essentials

Building a skill takes practice, and that's what you'll get with the *Keyboarding Essentials* series. More timed writings, five supplemental keyboarding lessons using the keyboarding software, and technique drills throughout.

Keyboarding Pro 4
Now with Web reporting and Spanish instruction!

Spice up your practice! *Keyboarding Pro 4* software uses graphics, games, progress graphs, videos, 3-D models for viewing proper posture and hand positions, and a full-featured word processor to keep learning fun and meaningful. Students also have the option of e-mail or the Web for transferring their assignments to you. Instruction available in Spanish.

Keyboarding Pro—Now with Web Reporting, especially designed for distance education

Extra skillbuilding lessons using Keyboarding Pro

The Latest Word
Microsoft® Word 2003 and Microsoft® Word 2002

The *Keyboarding Essentials* series teaches document formatting using the functions of Microsoft Word 2003 and 2002. Word processing commands are taught in the first lesson or two of each module and applied with simple drills. The remaining lessons provide extensive opportunities to apply the commands and reinforce new learning while extending keyboarding skills.

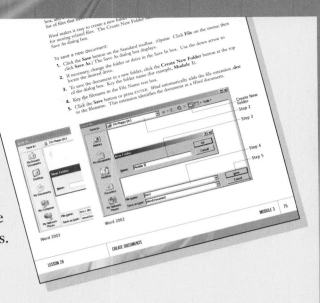

Up-to-Date Formats

New formats are explained and illustrated with callouts for proper placement.

Drills reinforce new functions.

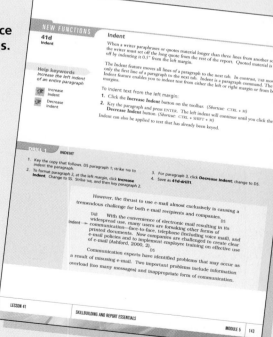

Model documents make it easy.

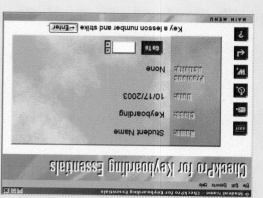

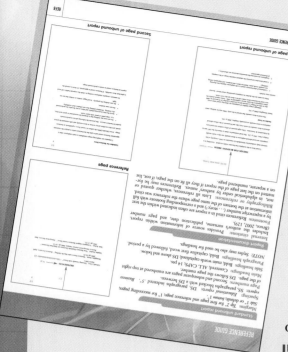

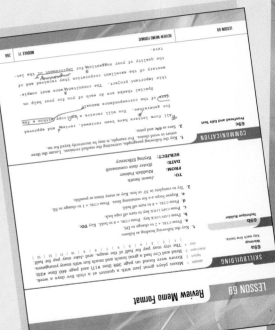

CheckPro for Keyboarding Essentials
Now with Web reporting for distance education!

Transferring student data between students and instructors just gets easier. *CheckPro for Keyboarding Essentials* is your answer to handling distance education with ease.

Reference Manual

provides easy access to model documents.

Document Processing

That's the focus of Lessons 61–120. Three new modules--18 lessons--address today's needs: Forms and Financial Documents, Promotional Document Formats, and Meeting Management.

Communication Skills

Proofreading, capitalization, composition, and other language arts skills are reinforced. Supplemental Communication Skill Builder pages provide extra practice.

CLEARLY FOCUSED ON YOUR NEEDS

THE LATEST WORD IN KEYBOARDING

Product Family

Formatting & Document Processing Essentials, Lessons 61–120
0-538-72774-8
Intensive document processing text that includes many document types: budgets, financial statements, a wide variety of forms, minutes, reports, agendas, itineraries, and merged documents. A Software Training Manual reviews functions learned in L1-60.

Keyboarding & Formatting Essentials, Lessons 1–60
0-538-72757-8

Instructor's Manual & Key, Lessons 1-60 (0-538-72758-6) and *Instructor's Resource CD, Lessons 1-60* (0-538-72759-4)
Solutions, data files, teaching tips, and tests—all in an easy-to-use format.

Technology Solutions

Keyboarding Pro 4
0-538-72802-7, Individual License. With Web reporting and Spanish.

CheckPro for Keyboarding Essentials
0-538-72798-5, Individual License. Now with Web reporting for your distance education needs.

MicroPace Pro, 2.0
0-538-72778-0, Individual License. Program software that correlates to *Keyboarding Essentials* and provides additional skillbuilding practice to increase technique and accuracy. Comprehensive error diagnostics.

KeyChamp, 2E
0-538-43390-6
Textbook and program software that builds speed by analyzing student's two-stroke key combinations and provides drills for building speed.

Instructor Approved

Lillie Begay
San Juan College
Farmington, New Mexico

Shirley Bennings
Augusta Technical College
Augusta, Georgia

Jane Clausen
Western Iowa Technical College
Sioux City, Iowa

Lucille Cusano
Tunxis Community College
Farmington, Connecticut

Claudia Fortney
Ramussen College
Mankato, Minnesota

Lucille Graham
San Antonio College
San Antonio, Texas

Cindy Moss
Appalachian Technical College
Jasper, Georgia

Janice Salles
Merced Community College
Merced, California

A Word from the Authors

Thank you for your support of our keyboarding texts over the past many years. We have designed this text especially for those who need a traditional keyboarding and document formatting approach. We hope our new series meets your needs.

Susie VanHuss
Connie Forde
Donna Woo

Keyboarding Pro 4 combines the latest technology for distance education with South-Western's superior method for teaching keyboarding.

Installing the Software

If you are using the Individual User version of *Keyboarding Pro 4* on your home computer, you must first install the software on your computer. Refer to the Individual User's Guide that accompanies *Keyboarding Pro 4*.

Getting Started with Keyboarding Pro

Click the **Start** button and then select **Programs**. Select the South-Western Keyboarding program group and click **Keyboarding Pro 4**. After a few seconds you will see the Log In dialog box.

The first time you use *Keyboarding Pro*, you must enter your user information and create a student record. You will create a student record *only once* so that the results of all lessons are stored in one file.

New User From the Log In dialog box, click the **New User** button to create a student record. A wizard will guide you through several screens.

Step 1: On the first screen, enter your first and last name and a password. Write the password in a safe place; you will need to enter it each time you log into the software. Then click the **Next** button.

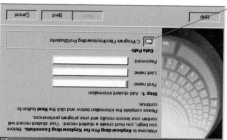

Notice that your default student record is C:\ **Program Files\ Keyboarding Pro 4\Students.** If you will be saving on drive A or if you have a subdirectory on the network, click the **Folder** icon and browse to identify the path.

Note: The graphic in the illustration above may be slightly different in your software.

Step 2: If you are *not a distance learning student*, do not enter anything on this screen, simply click the **Next** button.

If you are *a distance education student*, you must enter the data on this screen in order to send your files to the Keyboarding Pro Web server or to email your files to your instructor. Enter your instructor's email address and/or the course code your instructor has given you. Click the **Next** button.

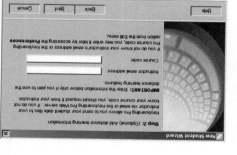

If you do not know this information, request it from your instructor and enter it at a later time by choosing **Preferences** from the **Edit** menu.

Step 3: Select your class from the list shown. If your class is not available, select **No Class Assigned.**

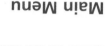

Step 4: From the final screen in the Wizard, click the **Finish** button.

Each time you enter *Keyboarding Pro* after the first time, the Log In dialog box displays (as in Step 3). Select your name and enter your password. If you do not see your name, click the **Folder** button to locate the drive where your student record is located (Drive A or your folder on the network).

Main Menu

The Main Menu provides access to the four main modules of the software, beginning with Alphabetic (Lessons 1–13). To access any module, click its name from the Main menu.

Alphabetic: Begin with this module to learn the alphabetic keys. Each lesson includes a variety of exercises. You will key from the software screen and from your textbook. In *Textbook Keying* and *Timed Writing*, the software directs you to key the exercise from the textbook.

Numeric and Skill: Activities focus on building skill and learning the top-row and symbol keys.

Skill Builder: After you know the alphabetic keys, use these 20 lessons to boost your keyboarding skill. Each lesson can be completed in both speed and accuracy mode.

Numeric Keypad: You will learn the numeric keypad operation by completing four lessons in this module.

Additional Features

Keyboarding Pro 4 includes several important features. Three of these features are described below.

 Open Screen: The Open Screen is a word processor; it has a timer option. You will be directed to key various exercises and timings in the Open Screen. These files may be saved and sent to your instructor.

 Diagnostic Writings: Numerous timed writings in the textbook can be keyed as Diagnostic Writings. This feature is available from either the Numeric and Skill Lesson menu or the Skill Builder Lesson menu. You will key each timing twice. Results are saved in your Summary Report (see Reports below).

Student Reports: *Keyboarding Pro 4* creates several reports. The two reports that you will use most frequently are the Lesson Report and the Summary Report. The Lesson Report shows your performance data for a specific lesson. The Summary Report provides an overview of your progress on each of the modules and your Diagnostic Writings (Timed Writings). To access all reports, select **Reports** from the Menu bar, and then choose the desired report. Reports can be printed.

Sending Files to Your Instructor

If you are a distance learning student, you can send files to your instructor through the Keyboarding Pro Web server or by email. Your instructor will advise you as to which method you should use. (*Note:* You must have entered your Course Code or instructor's email address. See Step 2 on the previous page.)

You can send three types of files; each file type has a different file extension:

- .swk Your student record that includes the results of all lessons completed and diagnostic writings.
- .kdw Diagnostic writings that were saved.
- .kos Documents or timings created and saved in the Open Screen.

Send Files to Keyboarding Pro Web Server:

1. Log in as a student with a valid course code.
2. Click the Send File button on the Main menu or the Lesson Report menu.
3. Your student data file is automatically selected. To attach additional files, click the **Attach Files** button and click the file you want to attach.

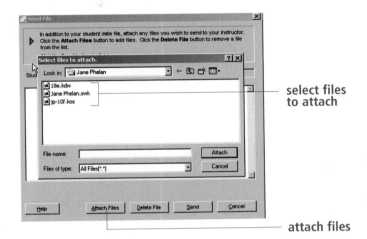

select files to attach

attach files

Send Files Using Email:

1. Log in as a student.
2. Click the Send File button on the Main menu or the Lesson Report menu.
3. The student data file is automatically attached. To attach additional files, click the **Attach Files** button and locate the files you wish to add.

Note: To use Send File, a MAPI-compliant email program must be installed and properly configured on your computer. (MAPI stands for *M*essaging *A*pplication *P*rogram *I*nterface, which is a Microsoft Windows program interface that enables the user to send email from within a Windows application and attach documents.) Microsoft Outlook is an example of a MAPI-compliant program.

If you are using an email program such as Hotmail or Yahoo that is not MAPI compliant, you will not be able to use the automatic Send File feature. However, you can still send your student files to your instructor using your email program by attaching the data files manually.

Create an email to your instructor in the usual manner. Use the attach function of your email program. Use the Browse or Attach function to navigate to the **C:\ Program\Keyboarding Pro\Students** folder on your hard drive. When you have located your Student Record (username.swk) in the Students folder, highlight it and click Open or Select.

CheckPro verifies the accuracy of the keystrokes in drills, timed writings, and selected documents that you key beginning in Module 4. The drill practice and timed writings features are built into the *CheckPro* program. For the document exercises, *CheckPro* works in conjunction with Microsoft *Word*. You will key documents using *Word* and then *CheckPro* error-checks your work.

Getting Started with CheckPro

To launch the program, click the **Start** button and then select **Programs**. Select the South-Western Keyboarding program group and click **CheckPro for Keyboarding Essentials.** Once the splash screen is removed, the Student Registration dialog box appears.

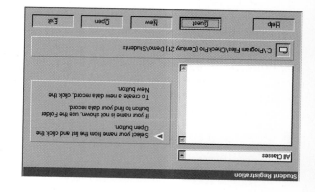

1. From the Student Registration dialog box, click **New.** This launches the New Student dialog box.

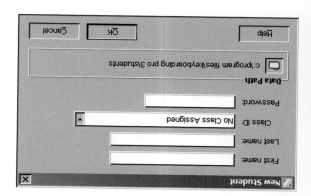

2. Enter your name and password and select your class if it is available on the drop-down list.

When you first use the *CheckPro* software, you must enter your user information and indicate where you will store your data. This process creates a student record. You will create a student record only once.

3. Specify the data location. The default storage path is **c:\Program Files\CheckProKE\Students.** If you will be storing on Drive A or if you have a student subdirectory on the network, set the path accordingly.

Each time you enter *CheckPro* after the first time, the Student Registration dialog box displays. Click your name and enter your password. If you do not see your name, click the folder icon and browse either Drive A or the folder on the network where your data is being saved to locate your data record.

Main Screen

After you start the program and log in, the program displays the *CheckPro* main screen. The main screen is the central navigation point for the entire program. From here you can select a lesson, e-mail a data file, or access the supplemental timings/documents. Supplemental timings refer to timed writings that are not located in a numbered lesson (for example, Skill Builders 2, 3, etc.). Supplemental documents include documents that cannot be accessed from numbered lessons (CheckPoints, projects, tests, and documents created by your instructor).

Choose a lesson by keying the lesson number or clicking on the arrows to the right of the Go To field. Then click on the **Go To** button or strike ENTER. You are now at a lesson screen, which will look *similar* to the example below.

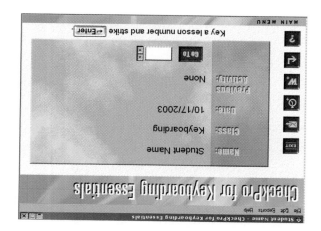

Lesson Screen

The lesson screen contains more activity options. Each activity corresponds directly with the activities for that lesson in your textbook. Click on the button next to an activity title to complete that activity. Drills and timed writings will be completed within the *CheckPro* software. *CheckPro* will launch *Word 2002* or *Word 2003* for you to complete documents or production tests.

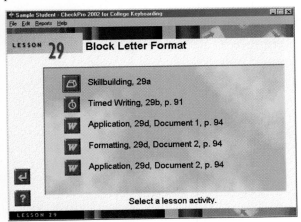

Drill Practice: For a drill practice activity, key each drill line as it appears on the screen. You can choose to repeat the activity when you finish the drill practice. A check mark appears next to the menu option on the lesson screen when you complete it.

Timed Writings: Click a **Timed Writing** button to take a timed writing. Then select the timing length and source. Key the timed writing from your textbook. The program shows the *gwam*, error rate, and actual errors when you finish the writing. You can print the timed writing report or save it to disk.

Documents and Production Tests: Select a document or assessment activity and choose **Begin new document**. You'll get a dialog box with important information, and then your word processor will be launched. *CheckPro* creates a document for you with the correct filename. The *CheckPro* toolbar will appear on top of the *Word 2002* document window. When you are finished proofreading the document, do not save the file. Instead, click on the check mark on the *CheckPro* toolbar. *CheckPro* will then save your document and open a checked version of it back in *CheckPro* for you to review your errors. To finish an exercise or revise a checked document, select the activity and choose **Open existing document**.

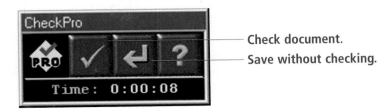

Reports

There are a number of reports available in *CheckPro*. Click on the **Reports** menu to see the selection. The Lesson Report provides a snapshot of your results for a specific lesson. Click on the **Activity Checklist** to see an overview of which activities have been completed. This report indicates the date each activity was completed, but provides no further information. Choose the **Reports** menu, **Summary Report** to view Drill, Timed Writing, Document, and Production Test summaries. All of the information for creating these reports is saved in your record file.

Special Features

CheckPro for Keyboarding Essentials makes it extremely easy to send your completed documents or student record to your instructor for evaluation. To learn more about using *CheckPro* for distance education, go to the website www.collegekeyboarding.com. A complete explanation is provided here.

The Supplemental Timed Writings button provides a way to check a timing located somewhere other than a numbered lesson (e.g. a timing located in a Skill Builder).

Select the Supplemental Documents button to complete any document exercise found in an unnumbered lesson (for example, an exercise from a project, a Communication Skill, or a document created by your instructor).

Microsoft® Windows® is an operating system, a program that manages all other software applications on your computer and its peripherals such as the mouse and printer. Software applications that run under *Windows* have many common features. Depending on the version of your operating system, some features may look, work, or be named slightly differently on your computer.

THE DESKTOP

When your computer is turned on and ready to use, a Welcome screen showing the names of every computer user on the computer will display. Click your user icon, key your password in the textbox, and then click the **Next** button to access the desktop. The illustration below shows a *Windows XP* **desktop**, which is the main working area. Your desktop will have many of the same features. Depending on what programs are on your computer and how the desktop has been arranged, it may look different.

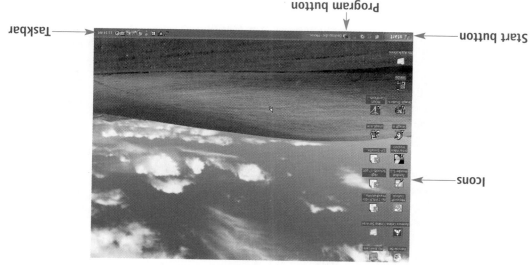

Icons   Start button   Program button   Taskbar

The desktop displays icons and a taskbar. Icons provide an easy way to access programs and documents that you frequently use. Desktop icons will vary. Two common icons are:

My Computer displays the disk drives, CD-ROM drives, and printers that are attached to your computer.

Recycle Bin stores files and folders that have been deleted from the hard drive. Documents in the Recycle Bin may be restored and returned to their folders. However, once you empty the Recycle Bin, the documents are deleted and cannot be restored.

The bar at the bottom of the desktop is the taskbar. **The taskbar** displays the Start button on the left, a button for each program or document that is open, and the system clock on the right (your taskbar may have additional icons). The taskbar enables you to open programs and navigate on your computer.

THE MOUSE

Windows requires the use of a mouse or other pointing device such as a touch pad built into your keyboard. The *Windows* software utilizes the left and right mouse buttons. The left button is used to select text or commands, to open files or menus, or to drag objects. The right button is used to display shortcut menus.

The pointer (arrow) ◄ indicates your location on the screen. To move the pointer, you must first move the mouse. If you have a touch pad on your keyboard, move the pointer by moving your finger on the touch pad. The mouse or touch pad is used to perform four basic actions.

Point: Move the mouse so that the pointer touches something displayed on the screen.

Click: Point to an item, quickly press the left mouse button once, and release it. You will always use the left mouse button unless directions tell you to right-click; which means click the right mouse button.

Double-click: Point to an item; quickly press the left mouse button twice, and release it.

Drag: Point to an item, then hold down the left mouse button while you move the mouse to reposition the item.

The mouse pointer changes in appearance depending on its location on the desktop and the task being performed.

| The *vertical blinking bar* indicates the current position of the cursor.

I   The *I-beam* indicates the location of the mouse pointer. To reposition the cursor at this point, you must click the mouse button.

▶   The *arrow* indicates that you can select items. It displays when the mouse is located outside the text area. You can point to a toolbar icon to display the function of that icon.

⧗   The *hourglass* indicates that *Windows* is processing a command.

↔   A *double-headed arrow* appears when the pointer is in the border of a window; it is used to change the size.

THE START BUTTON

start

The **Start** button opens the Start menu, which lists a variety of items from which to choose such as programs and documents.

The Start menu is divided into three sections and displays some of the programs and folders on your computer. The top of the menu displays the user icon and name. The middle section contains two columns of commands. The bottom section contains the Log Off and Turn Off Computer commands.

Let's take a closer look at the middle section of the Start menu. Separator lines divide sections of the Start menu. The section in the upper left is called the pinned items list, which contains an icon for your Web browser and your e-mail program. The next section below contains icons for your six most frequently used programs. The top right section contains commands to access various folders and My Computer. If your computer is connected to a network, the My Network Places command displays below My Computer. The next section contains commands to customize the computer and peripherals. The bottom section contains commands for Help, searching, and launching programs (Run).

If you do not see the program you need displayed, point to the All Programs arrow to display a full list of programs available on your computer. To open an item listed on the Start menu, point to the item and click the left mouse button. A right arrow beside a menu item indicates that a submenu with more options is available for that item. (*Note* If an icon is displayed on the desktop, you can double-click the icon to open the program, document, or folder that it represents.)

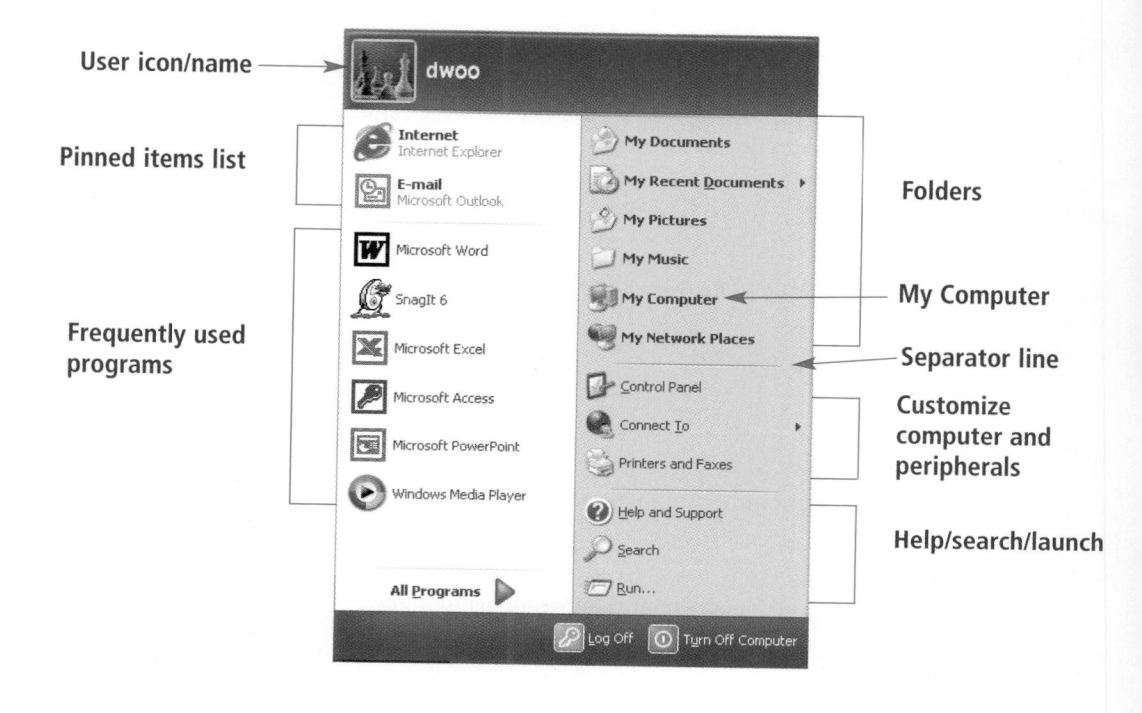

WINDOWS FEATURES

Windows displays folders, applications, and individual documents in windows. A **window** is a work area on the desktop that can be resized or moved. To resize a window, point to the border. When the pointer changes to a double-headed arrow, drag the window to the desired size. To move a window, point to the title bar, drag it to the new position, and release the mouse button.

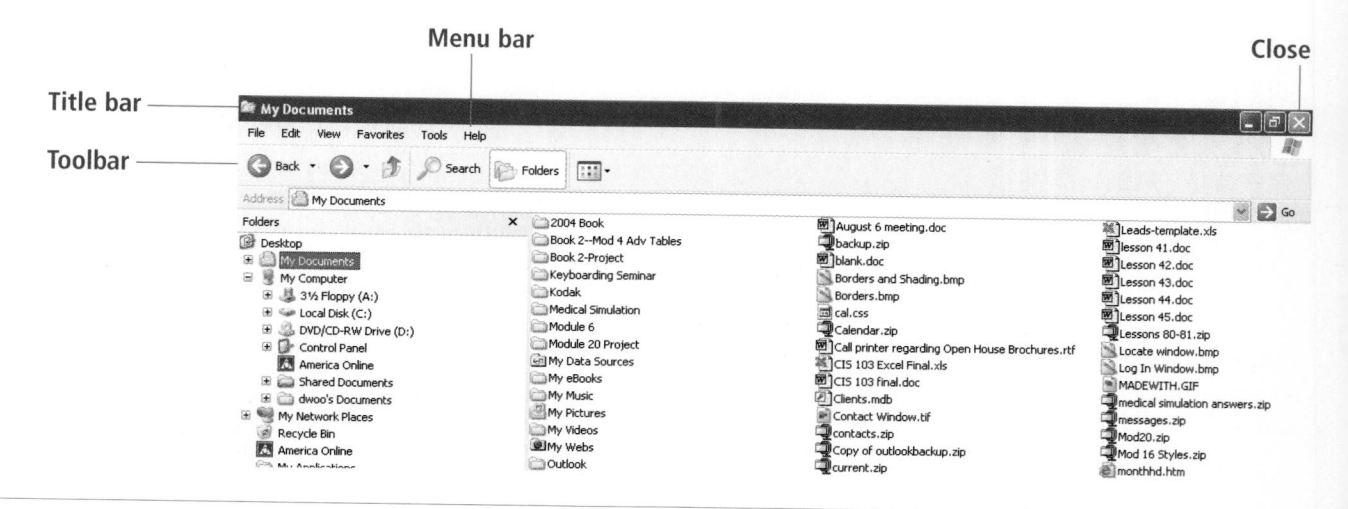

The basic features of all windows are the same. Each window contains the following:

Menu bar: Displays commands available in the software.

Toolbars: Display icons that offer a convenient way to access frequently used commands. Applications programs have different toolbars for different tasks.

Scroll bars: Enable you to see material that does not fit on one screen. You can click the arrows on the scroll bars or drag the scroll box to move through a document.

Title bar: Displays the name of the application that is currently open and the path (folder name). The Title bar also includes several buttons at the right.

> **Minimize button**: Reduces the window to a button on the taskbar. To restore the window, click the button on the taskbar.
>
> **Maximize button**: Enlarges a window to full-screen size.
>
> **Restore button**: When you maximize a window, the Maximize button is replaced with a Restore button that, when clicked, returns the window to its original size.
>
> **Close button**: Closes the application.

Minimize   Maximize   Close   Restore

HELP

Help is available for *Windows*. Help is also available with each software application that you use. Generally you will use the Help feature provided with the application. To access *Windows* Help, click the **Start** button, and then click **Help and Support**. You can choose from the list of Help topics displayed, or key your topic in the Search box and click the green arrow.

Index button —

Search — box

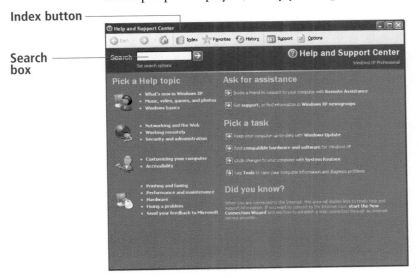

You can also click the **Index** button on the toolbar to display a list of specific items in alphabetical order. As you key the characters of the topic in the entry box, the program automatically moves to items beginning with the keyed letters. When the correct topic displays, highlight it and choose **Display**. If you prefer, you can scroll through the list of topics until you find what you are looking for.

DRILL 1

1. Click the **Start** button. Choose **Help and Support**.

2. Click **What's new in Windows XP** from the Help topics.

3. Click **Taking a tour or tutorial** in the left pane.

4. Choose **Take the Windows XP tour** in the right pane. Follow the directions on the screen to complete the *Windows XP* Tour. When finished, close the Help and Support Center.

FILE MANAGEMENT

File Management includes the processes of creating and managing the electronic files on your computer. You will learn to format a floppy disk, understand basic file structure, manage files and folders, and log off from the computer.

FORMAT A DISKETTE

Data that needs to be used again in the future must be saved on a storage device such as floppy diskettes, CD/DVD, zip disk, or the hard drive. Floppy diskettes are often used in school settings. A floppy diskette must be formatted before it can be used for storing data. Some diskettes are shipped from the manufacturer preformatted; they will not require additional formatting. If you purchase unformatted disks, they will need to be formatted before use. Formatting the disk means that the operating system will erase the disk, check for bad sectors, and place tracks and sectors on the disk so that files can be saved on the disk.

To format a disk:

The following steps will instruct you to format a high-density diskette in the A: drive. Ask your instructor what drive you are to use to format a diskette.

1. Insert the disk to be formatted in the disk drive (A:).
2. Double-click the **My Computer** icon to open the My Computer window.
3. Select the drive containing the disk to be formatted (A:).
4. Click the File menu and select **Format**; the Format dialog box displays.

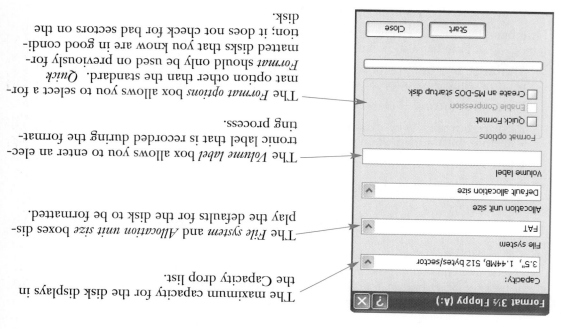

The maximum capacity for the disk displays in the Capacity drop list.

The *File system* and *Allocation unit size* boxes display the defaults for the disk to be formatted.

The *Volume label* box allows you to enter an electronic label that is recorded during the formatting process.

The *Format options* box allows you to select a format option other than the standard. *Quick Format* should only be used on previously formatted disks that you know are in good condition; it does not check for bad sectors on the disk.

5. Click the **Start** button to begin the formatting. A warning box displays so you do not format a disk that might contain data you need to keep.

6. Click **OK** when the warning box displays.

7. Click **OK** when the message box displays telling you the formatting is complete.

8. Click **Close** to close the Formatting dialog box.

9. Close the My Computer window.

DRILL 2

1. Format a 3½" floppy disk.   Use your name for the volume label on the disk.

2. Double-click **My Computer** to display the My Computer dialog box.

3. Right-click **3½" Floppy (A:)** and select **Properties** from the menu.

4. Click the **General** tab in the Properties dialog box. Your name should display in the text box at the top. Notice the amount of free space on your disk. Click **OK** to remove the Properties dialog box.

5. Close the My Computer window.

UNDERSTAND THE FILE SYSTEM

As with paper files, it is important to establish a logical and easy-to-use computer file management system to organize your files efficiently so that you can find them quickly and easily. You can manage files from the desktop or from My Computer or Windows Explorer.

Computer files are stored on **disks** specified by their location. The storage drives can be identified in My Computer.

The computer in this example has a hard disk drive (C), a floppy disk drive (A), and a DVD/CD drive (D).

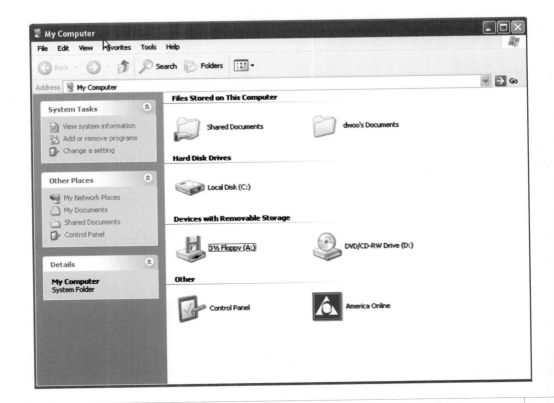

View Contents of a Drive

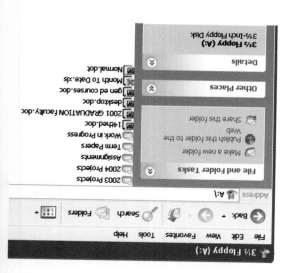

1. To view the contents of a drive through the **My Computer**, double-click the **My Computer** icon on the desktop. If the **My Computer** icon is not available, choose **My Computer** from the Start menu.

2. Double-click the desired disk drive to display the contents.

View Contents of a Folder

Folders are listed in numerical and alphabetical order. Folders with numerical names will be listed before those with alphabetic names, as shown in the figure above. To see the contents of a folder, double-click the folder. Folders may contain files, programs, and folders.

View Data and Arrange Files

Files and folders can be viewed in different ways: as Thumbnails, Tiles, Icons, List, and Details. The figure above shows the items in List View.

To change the view, click **View** on the menu; then choose a view. You may want to experiment with each of the views to decide which one you prefer.

As previously mentioned, folders are listed in alphabetical order. You can also arrange them in descending order by date, size, or type of file. To rearrange the order of files or folders, select **Details** from the **View menu**, and then click the heading displayed above the files or folders such as **Size**, **Type**, or **Date Modified**.

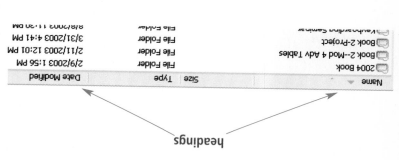

headings

DRILL 3

1. Insert your data CD in its drive. Use My Computer to display the contents of that CD.
2. Use the View menu to change to Thumbnails View.
3. Change the view to List View.
4. Change to Details View. Click the **Name** heading. Notice the files are displayed in ascending order.
5. Click the **Date Modified** heading to place the documents back in ascending order by date.
6. Double-click on a file folder to display the files in the folder.
7. Click the Up button on the toolbar to return to the previous level displaying the folders.
8. Click the **Back** button on the toolbar to return to the My Computer screen.

WORK WITH FOLDERS AND FILES

Folders are extremely important in organizing files. You will want to create and manage folders and the files within them so that you can easily locate them. Managing files and folders also involves renaming and deleting items.

Create Folder

Folders can be created in My Computer or in Windows Explorer.

1. To create a folder in My Computer, display the drive that is to contain the new folder.

2. Click **Make a new folder** in the left pane.

3. A new folder displays at the end of the list of files labeled **New Folder**. Delete the words *New Folder* and replace them with a new name.

4. Strike ENTER.

To create a folder in Windows Explorer, point to **All Programs** on the Start menu. Choose **Accessories**, and then choose **Windows Explorer**. Click the drive or folder that will contain the new folder. Select **New** from the File menu and choose **Folder**. Select and replace **New Folder** with the new name.

Name Files and Folders

Good file organization begins with giving your folders and files names that are logical and easy to understand. In the previous figure, a folder was created for Assignments, Term Papers, and Work in Progress. You may want create a folder named Module 3 to hold all work that you key in Module 3. You will save the files by the exercise name such as 26b-d1 or 26b-d2. A system like this makes finding files simple.

Rename Files and Folders

Occasionally, you may want to rename a file or folder. To do so, click the file or folder, choose **Rename this file** or **Rename this folder**, key the new name, and press ENTER. You can also rename files using the Windows Explorer menu; select the file or folder, and then choose **Rename** on the File menu.

Move and Copy Files and Folders

To move or copy files using My Computer, click the file/folder to be copied or moved.

1. To move or copy files using My Computer, click the file/folder to be copied or moved.

2. Click **Copy this file** or **Move this file** in the left pane. The Copy Items window displays.

3. Click the drive or the folder in which the copy is to be placed.

To copy or move files using Windows Explorer:

1. In the Windows Explorer screen, click the drive that contains the file or folder you want to move, then locate the item.

2. Be sure the place you want to move the file or folder to is visible. Press and hold down the left mouse button and drag the pointer to the new location.

To copy a file or folder, press and hold down CTRL while you drag.

Note: If you drag a file or folder to a location on the same disk, it will be moved. If you drag an item to a different disk, it will be copied. To move the item, press and hold down SHIFT while dragging.

If you wish to copy or move several items at once, click the first item; then hold down the CTRL key as you select each additional item. This allows you to copy or move all the files at one time. If the items you wish to copy or move are consecutive, click the first item, hold down SHIFT, and click the last item—now you can copy or move the entire list at once.

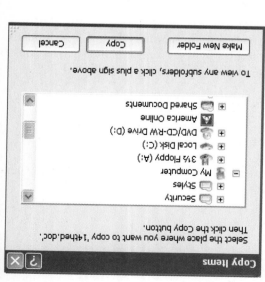

Copy Items

Select the place where you want to copy '14thed.doc'.
Then click the Copy button.

- Security
- Styles
- 🖥 My Computer
  - 3½ Floppy (A:)
  - Local Disk (C:)
  - DVD/CD-RW Drive (D:)
  - 📁 America Online
  - Shared Documents

To view any subfolders, click a plus sign above.

Make New Folder   Copy   Cancel

Delete Files and Folders

Files and folders can be deleted in My Computer or Windows Explorer. You can select and delete several files and folders at once, just as you select several items to move or copy. If you delete a folder, you automatically delete any files and folders inside it.

To delete a file or folder and send it to the Recycle Bin, right-click the item and choose **Delete.** Answer Yes to the question about sending the item to the Recycle Bin.

Restore Deleted Files and Folders

When you delete a file or folder, the item goes to the Recycle Bin. If you have not emptied the Recycle Bin, you can restore files and folders stored there. Items deleted from the A drive will be deleted permanently and do not go to the Recycle Bin.

To restore a file in the Recycle Bin:

1. Double-click the **Recycle Bin** icon on the desktop to open the Recycle Bin window.

2. Select the file you want to restore, right-click to display the shortcut menu, and choose **Restore.** You can also choose Restore from the File menu.

3. Close the Recycle Bin window. Click the folder where the file was originally located, and it should now be restored.

LOG OFF AND SHUT DOWN

Log Off

When you are finished using the computer, you should close your user account by logging off the computer. Logging off performs three functions: (1) any applications software left often will be closed; (2) you will be prompted to save any unsaved documents; and (3) you will end your *Windows* session and allow another person to use your computer. This procedure should always be followed if your computer has more than one user account listed in the Welcome screen. It is a good idea to log off, even if you are the sole user of the computer.

To log off, click the **Start** button and click the **Log Off** button on the Start menu. Confirm the log off in the dialog box that displays. The Welcome screen displays.

Shut Down

To shut down the computer after logging off, click the **Turn off computer** button on the Welcome screen, then click the **Turn Off** button in the Turn off computer dialog box.

DRILL 4

1. Using My Computer, create a new folder on Drive A called **XP Intro**.

2. Rename the folder **Win XP**.

3. Make a copy of this folder on Drive C. (If you cannot do this, ask your instructor for the location to which you can copy.)

4. Delete the folder you created on Drive A and the copy you made on Drive C.

DRILL 5

You will need to copy files from the data CD to your floppy diskette when you perform the exercises in this book. This exercise will walk you through the steps of copying a file folder and its contents from the CD to the diskette in Drive A. You will use Windows Explorer.

1. Insert your data CD in the CD Drive and a floppy diskette in Drive A.

2. Display the Windows Explorer window.

3. Click the + symbol to the left of My Computer to display the drives on the computer.

4. Double-click the CD drive to display the contents of the CD in the right pane.

5. Click the **View** menu and select **Details**.

6. Click a file folder, hold down the left mouse button, and drag the folder to Drive A. The folder and its contents will be copied to Drive A. Next, check to see that the folder and its contents were copied to Drive A, then delete the folder.

7. Double-click 3½" **Floppy (A:)** in the left pane under My Computer to display the contents of Drive A.

8. Double-click the file folder to view the files in the folder.

9. Click the **Up** button in the toolbar to display the higher level (file folders).

10. Select the file folder, click the **File** menu, and select **Delete**.

11. Click **Yes** to confirm the deletion of the folder.

12. Go back to your desktop. Ask your instructor if you should log off or shut down the computer.

Keyboard Arrangement

1. **Alphanumeric keys:** Letters, numbers, and symbols.

2. **Numeric keypad:** Keys at the right side of the keyboard used to enter numeric copy and perform calculations.

3. **Function (F) keys:** Used to execute commands, sometimes with other keys. Commands vary with software.

4. **Arrow keys:** Move insertion point up, down, left, or right.

5. **ESC (Escape):** Closes a software menu or dialog box.

6. **TAB:** Moves the insertion point to a preset position.

7. **CAPS LOCK:** Used to make all capital letters.

8. **SHIFT:** Makes capital letters and symbols shown at tops of number keys.

9. **CTRL (Control):** With other key(s), executes commands. Commands may vary with software.

10. **ALT (Alternate):** With other key(s), executes commands. Commands may vary with software.

11. **Space Bar:** Inserts a space in text.

12. **ENTER (RETURN):** Moves insertion point to margin and down to next line. Also used to execute commands.

13. **DELETE:** Removes text to the right of insertion point.

14. **NUM LOCK:** Activates/ deactivates numeric keypad.

15. **INSERT:** Activates insert or typeover.

16. **BACKSPACE:** Deletes text to the left of insertion point.

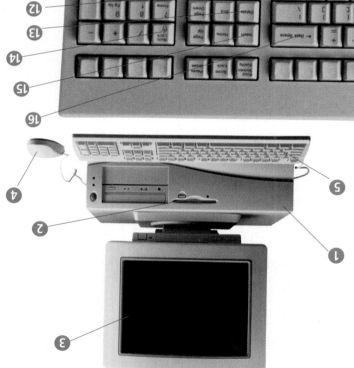

The numbered parts are found on most computers. The location of some parts will vary.

1. **CPU (Central Processing Unit):** Internal operating unit or "brain" of computer.

2. **Disk drive:** Reads data from and writes data to a disk.

3. **Monitor:** Displays text and graphics on a screen.

4. **Mouse:** Used to input commands.

5. **Keyboard:** An arrangement of letter, figure, symbol, control, function, and editing keys and a numeric keypad.

Developing Keyboarding Skill

OBJECTIVES

KEYBOARDING

To key the alphabetic and number keys by touch with good technique.
To key approximately 25 wam with good accuracy.

COMMUNICATION SKILLS

To apply proofreaders' marks and revise text.
To create simple documents in a basic word processor.

DRILL 6

SPECIFIC ROWS

Key each set of lines twice.

TIP

Reach to the first and third rows with a minimum of hand movement; keep hands quiet; don't bounce on the keys.

Key two 3' or one 5' writing; key with fluency and control.

 all letters

Rows 3, 2, 1

1 you we quip try pot peer your wire put quit wet trip power toy to
2 salad fad glad lass lag has gall lash gas lad had shall flag half
3 comb zone exam man carve bun oxen bank came next vent zoo van cab

4 we try to; you were; put up your; put it there; you quit; wipe it
5 Gail asked Sissy; what was said; had Jake left; Dana sold a flag
6 Zam came back; can Max fix my van? a brave man, Ben came in a cab

7 Peter or I will try to wire our popular reports to Porter or you.
8 Ada Glass said she is glad she had half a kale salad with Dallas.
9 Zack drove a van to minimize expenses; Ben and Max came in a cab.

Writing 41

	gwam	3'	5'

Sports are very big business today; that is, those sports competi- / 4 / 3 / 62
tions in which men participate are very big business. What about / 9 / 5 / 65
sports for women? At the professional level, women have made real / 13 / 8 / 67
progress in golf and tennis; they, as well as their sponsors, can / 18 / 11 / 70
make big money in both of these events. The other sports for women / 22 / 13 / 73
still are not considered to be major revenue sports. The future / 26 / 16 / 75
may be much better, however, because sports for women at all levels / 31 / 19 / 78
are gaining in popularity. Programs that are designed to help / 35 / 21 / 81
young girls develop their athletic skills and interest are having / 40 / 24 / 83
an impact. The result is that girls now expect to play for organ- / 44 / 26 / 86
ized clubs as well as in school programs just as boys do. Club / 48 / 29 / 88
sports often will lead to varsity teams. / 51 / 31 / 90

Many people wonder how much impact the current emphasis on / 55 / 33 / 92
gender equity will have on sports at the college level. Most / 59 / 35 / 95
people agree that this new emphasis is very positive for women. / 63 / 38 / 97
Some people feel, though, that it either has had or could have a / 68 / 41 / 100
negative impact on sports for men. They believe that resources / 72 / 43 / 103
that would have been spent on sports such as football, basketball, / 77 / 46 / 105
and baseball for men are now being spent on the Olympic sports for / 81 / 49 / 108
women. Overall, most people believe that both men and women who / 85 / 51 / 111
have the ability to excel in an athletic event as well as in the / 90 / 54 / 113
classroom should have the opportunity and should be encouraged to / 94 / 56 / 116
do so. Success for both women and men is better than success for / 98 / 59 / 118
either. / 99 / 59 / 119

3' | 1 | 2 | 3 | 4 |
5' | 1 | 2 | 3 |

Keyboarding Assessment/Placement

WARMUP

1. Open *Keyboarding Pro*. Create a student record. (see page xviii)
2. Go to the Open Screen.
3. Key the drill twice.
4. Close the Open Screen. Do not save or print the drill lines.

alphabetic
1 Zack quipped that Marny will get five or six jobs.
2 Quin Gaf's wax mock-up had just dazzled everybody.

Strike ENTER twice

figures
3 Room 2938 holds 50 people, and Room 1940 holds 67.
4 Call 803-555-0164 and then ask for extension 1928.

easy
5 Ken may go downtown now and then go to their lake.
6 Did he bid on the bicycle, or did he bid on a map?

gwam   1'   3'

Straight-Copy Assessment

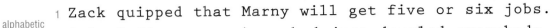

1. Go to Skill Builder. From the Lesson menu, click the **Diagnostic Writing** button.
2. Choose 3'. Select **pretest** from the Writings list. Press TAB to begin. Key from the text.
3. Take a second 3' timing. Click the Timer to begin.
4. Print your results.

I have a story or two or three that will carry you away	11	4
to foreign places, to meet people you have never known, to	23	8
see things you have never seen, to feast on foods available	35	12
only to a few. I will help you to learn new skills you want	47	16
and need; I will inspire you, excite you, instruct you, and	59	20
interest you. I am able, you understand, to make time fly.	71	24
I answer difficult questions for you. I work with you	11	27
to realize a talent, to express a thought, and to determine	23	31
just who and what you are and want to be. I help you to	35	35
know words, to write, and to read. I help you to comprehend	47	40
the mysteries of the past and the secrets of the future. I	59	44
am your local library. We ought to get together often.	70	47

```
1' |  1  |  2  |  3  |  4  |  5  |  6  |  7  |  8  |  9  |  10  |  11  |  12  |
3' |        1        |        2        |        3        |        4        |
```

gwam   1'   3'

Statistical Assessment

1. Follow the steps for the straight-copy assessment.
2. Take two 3' writings using the Diagnostic Writing feature. Choose the writing **placement2**.

Attention Wall Street! The Zanes & Cash report for the end	4	38
of the year (Report #98) says that its last-quarter income was up	8	42
26% from the record earnings of last year. The report also says	12	46
that it was caused by a rise in gross sales of just over 4 1/3%.	16	50
The increase is the 7th in a row for last-quarter earnings; and	20	54
the chief executive of this old firm—Paul Cash—has told at	24	58
least one group that he is sure to ask the board (it will meet on	28	62
the last day of the month) for an "increase of up to $1.50 a share	32	66
as its dividend for the year."	34	68

```
1' |  1  |  2  |  3  |  4  |  5  |  6  |  7  |  8  |  9  |  10  |  11  |  12  |
3' |        1        |        2        |        3        |        4        |
```

SPECIFIC FINGERS

Key each set of lines twice;
DS between groups.

1st
1 fun gray vent guy hunt brunt buy brunch much gun huge humor vying
2 buy them brunch; a hunting gun; Guy hunts for fun; try it for fun

2nd
3 cite decide kick cider creed kidded keen keep kit idea ice icicle
4 keen idea; kick it back; ice breaker; decide the issue; sip cider

3rd
5 low slow lax solo wax sold swell swollen wood wool load logs doll
6 wooden dolls; wax the floor; a slow boat; saw logs; pull the wool

4th
7 quip zap Zane zip pepper pay quiz zipper quizzes pad map nap jazz
8 zip the zipper; jazz at the plaza; Zane quipped; La Paz jazz band

1. Key three 1' writings on each paragraph.
2. Key one 5' or two 3' writings.

Option: Practice as a guided writing.

			gwam
1/4'	1/2'	3/4'	1'
8	16	24	32
9	18	27	36
10	20	30	40
11	22	33	44
12	24	36	48
13	26	39	52
14	28	41	56
15	30	45	60
16	32	48	64
17	34	51	68
18	36	54	72

 all letters

Writing 40

gwam 3' 5'

How much power is adequate? Is more power always better than less power? People often raise the question in many different instances. Regardless of the situation, most people seem to seek more power. In jobs, power is often related to rank in an organization, to the number of people reporting to a person, and to the ability to spend money without having to ask someone with more power. Most experts indicate that the power a person has should closely match the responsibilities (not just duties and tasks) for which he or she can be held accountable.

Questions about power are not limited to jobs and people. Many people ask the question in reference to the amount of power or speed a computer should have. Again, the response usually implies that more is better. A better approach is to analyze how the computer is to be used and then try to match power needs to the types of applications. Most people are surprised to learn that home computer buyers tend to buy more power than buyers in offices. The primary reason is that the computers are used to play games with extensive graphics, sound, and other media applications. Matching the needs of the software is the key.

3'	5'
4	2 50
8	5 52
12	7 55
17	10 57
21	13 60
25	15 63
30	18 65
34	20 68
37	22 70
41	25 72
45	27 75
50	30 77
54	32 80
58	35 82
62	37 85
67	40 87
71	43 90
75	45 93
79	47 95

3'   1   2   3   4
5'   1   2   3

Alphabetic Keys

- Key the alphabetic keys by touch.
- Key using proper techniques.
- Key at a rate of 14 gwam or more.

LESSON 1

Home Row, Space Bar, Enter, I

1a

Home Row Position and Space Bar

Practice the steps at the right until you can place your hands in home-row position without watching.

Key the drill lines several times.

Home Row Position

1. Drop your hands to your side. Allow your fingers to curve naturally. Maintain this curve as you key.

2. Lightly place your left fingers over the **a s d f** and the right fingers over the **j k l ;**. You will feel a raised element on the *f* and *j* keys, which will help you keep your fingers on the home position. You are now in **home–row position**.

Space Bar and Enter

Strike the Space Bar, located at the bottom of the keyboard, with a down-and-in motion of the right thumb to space between words.

Enter   Reach with the fourth (little) finger of the right hand to ENTER. Press it to return the insertion point to the left margin. This action creates a **hard return**. Use a hard return at the end of all drill lines. Quickly return to home position (over ;).

Key these lines

a s d f SPACE j k l ; ENTER
a s d f SPACE j k l ; ENTER

DRILL 2

ADJACENT KEYS

Key each set once; repeat entire drill.

Goal: To eliminate persistent errors on side-by-side keys.

as/sa
1 has sale fast salt was saw vast essay easy say past vast mast sap
2 We saw Sam; Sal was sad; Susan has a cast; as Sam said; as I said

er/re
3 were there tree deer great three other her free red here pert are
4 we were there; here we are; there were three; here are three deer

io/oi
5 point axiom prior choir lion boil toil billion soil action adjoin
6 join a choir; prior to that action; millions in a nation rejoiced

op/po
7 polo drop loop post hope pole port rope slope power top pony stop
8 rope the pony; drop the pole; power at the top; hope for the poor

rt/tr
9 trail alert train hurt tree shirt trap smart trim start tray dirt
10 trim the tree; start the train; dirt on the shirt; alert the trio

ew/we
11 few we stew were pew went dew web sew wept crew wear brew wet new
12 we were weak; few were weeping; the crew went west; we knew a few

gh/ui
13 sight quit laugh suit might ruin ghost guide ghastly guilt ghetto
14 a ghastly suit; quit laughing; recruit the ghost; might be guilty

DRILL 3

OUTSIDE REACHES

Key each set once. DS between groups.

Goal: To key with a maximum of one error per line. (Letters are often omitted in outside reaches—concentrate.)

a/p
1 tapioca actual against casual areas facial equally aware parallel
2 impower purpose people opposed compute pimple papyrus pope puppet
3 Perhaps part of the chapter page openers can appear on red paper.

s/w
4 class sash steps essential skills business discuss desks insisted
5 wow wayworn away awkward wrong awaits wildwood waterworks wayward
6 The snow white swan swayed as the waves swept the swelling shore.

z/l
7 hazard zip zero zeolite freezer zoom zealous z-axis zodiac sizing
8 likely indelibly, laurel finally leaflet regularly eloquently lily
9 A New Zealand zoologist was amazed as a zebra guzzled the zinias.

x/?
10 fax oxford exert excite examples xylan exercise oxygen exact taxi
11 When? Where? Which? For her? How much? What color? To whom?
12 After examining the x-rays, why did Dr. Ax exempt an exploratory?

DRILL 4

ALPHABETIC SENTENCES

Key each line once with good rhythm. Keep fingers curved and upright over the keys.

1 Judge McQuoy will have prizes for their next big track meet.
2 Jack may provide some extra quiz problems for the new group.

3 Gary Quazet mended six copies of books and journals we have.
4 Jack quibbled with a garrulous expert on Zoave family names.

5 Jake will study sixty chapters on vitamins for the big quiz.
6 Max asked Quin to provide a jewel box for the glossy zircon.

7 This judge may quiz the Iowa clerks about extensive profits.
8 Meg Keys packed and flew to Venezia to acquire her next job.

NEW KEYS

1b Procedures for Learning New Keys

Apply these steps each time you learn a new key.

STANDARD PLAN | for Learning New Keyreaches

1. Find the new key on the illustrated keyboard. Then find it on your keyboard.
2. Watch your finger make the reach to the new key a few times. Keep other fingers curved in home position. For an upward reach, straighten the finger slightly; for a downward reach, curve the finger a bit more.
3. Repeat the drill until you can key it fluently.

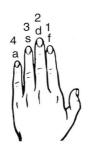

1c Home Row

1. Go to the Open Screen of *Keyboarding Pro.*
2. Key each line once. Press ENTER at the end of each line. Press ENTER twice to double-space (DS) between 2-line groups.
3. Close the Open Screen without saving your text.

Press Space Bar once.

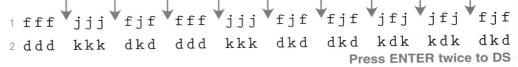

```
 1  fff   jjj   fjf   fff   jjj   fjf   fjf   jfj   jfj   fjf
 2  ddd   kkk   dkd   ddd   kkk   dkd   dkd   kdk   kdk   dkd
```
Press ENTER twice to DS
```
 3  sss   lll   sls   sss   lll   sls   sls   lsl   lsl   sls
 4  aaa   ;;;   a;a   aaa   ;;;   a;s   a;a   ;a;   ;a;   a;a

 5  ff  jj  ff  jj  fj  fj  fj  dd  kk  dd  kk  dk  dk  dk
 6  ss  ll  ss  ll  sl  sl  sl  aa  ;;  aa  ;;  a;  a;  a;

 7  f  j  d  k  s  l  a  ;
```
DS
```
 8  ff  jj  dd  kk  ss  ll  aa  ;;

 9  fff  jjj  ddd  kkk  sss  lll  aaa  jjj  ;;;
```

1d

i

1. Apply the standard plan for learning the letter *i.*
2. Keep fingers curved; key the drill once.

```
10  i ik ik ik is is id id if if ill i ail did kid lid
11  i ik aid ail did kid lid lids kids ill aid did ilk
12  id aid aids laid said ids lid skids kiss disk dial
```

Writing 37: 85 *gwam*

Business letters can be defined by their goals; for example, a letter of inquiry, a reply letter, a promotion letter, a credit letter, or other specialized letter. While you learn to compose these letters, just keep each letter's individual goals always in front of you. If you fix in your mind a theme, pattern, and ideal for your writing, composing good business letters may emerge as one of the best tricks in your bag.

	1'	3'
	12	4	60
	25	8	65
	38	13	69
	52	17	74
	64	21	78
	75	25	82
	85	28	85

Competent business writers know what they want to say—and they say it with simplicity and clarity. Words are the utensils they use to convey ideas or to convince others to accomplish some action. The simple word and the short sentence usually are more effective than the big word and the involved sentence. But don't be afraid of the long or unusual word if it means exactly what you intend to say in your business letter.

	12	32	89
	25	37	93
	38	41	98
	51	45	102
	64	50	106
	77	54	111
	85	57	113

Writing 38: 90 *gwam*

Although many of us are basically comfortable with sameness and appear to dislike change, we actually prize variation. We believe that we are each unique individuals, yet we know that we are really only a little different; and we struggle to find "sense of self" in how we think and act. Our cars, too, built on assembly lines are basically identical; yet when we purchase one, we choose model, color, size, and style which suits us individually.

	12	4	64
	24	8	68
	38	12	72
	50	16	76
	62	21	81
	75	25	85
	87	29	89
	90	30	90

Also many people expect to find security by buying things that are in keeping with society's "image" and "status." But what we think of as "status" always changes. The wise buyer will buy those items that give most in utility, comfort, and satisfaction. Status should just be a thing we create in ourselves, not a thing created for us. Common sense should guide us in making good decisions—and if our "status" is increased thereby, well, why not?

	12	34	94
	24	38	98
	37	42	102
	50	47	106
	63	51	111
	77	55	115
	90	60	120

Writing 39: 95 *gwam*

Normally, customers do not abandon a firm because of a mistake. All firms will make mistakes at one time or another. The way a problem is resolved is far more crucial than the fact that a problem existed. More customers leave a firm and take their business to a competitor because they get upset with an employee than for any other reason. The key qualifications for a customer service employee are superb human relations skills and knowledge of the product or service.

	13
	26
	38
	50
	63
	76
	89
	95

```
1' | 1 | 2 | 3 | 4 | 5 | 6 | 7 | 8 | 9 | 10 | 11 | 12 | 13 |
3' |     1     |         2         |         3         |     4     |
```

1. Read the information at the right. Then do Lesson 1 from *Keyboarding Pro.*

S T A N D A R D P L A N | **for Using Keyboarding Pro**

1. Select a lesson from Alphabetic by clicking the lesson number. (Figure 1-1)
2. The first activity is displayed automatically. In Figure 1-2, *Learn Home Row* is in yellow because this activity is active. Follow the directions on screen. Key from the screen.

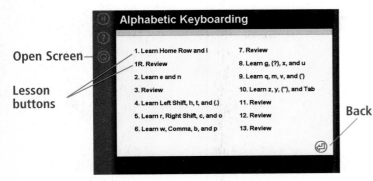

Figure 1-1 Alphabetic Keyboarding Lesson Menu

Figure 1-2 Alphabetic Keyboarding (Lesson 1: Learn Home Row and i)

3. Key the Textbook Keying activity from your textbook (lines 13–18 below). Press ESC or the **Stop** button to continue.
4. Figure 1-3 shows the Lesson Report. A check mark opposite an exercise indicates that the exercise has been completed.
5. At the bottom, click the **Print** button to print your Lesson Report. Click the **Send File** button to send your student record to your instructor. Click the **Graph** button to view the Performance Graph.
6. Click the **Back** button twice to return to the Main menu. Then click the **Exit** button to quit the program. Remove your storage disk if necessary. Clean up the work area.

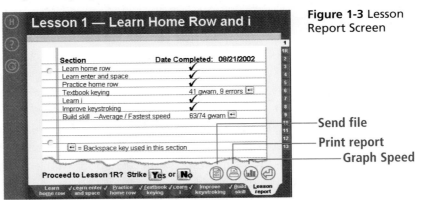

Figure 1-3 Lesson Report Screen

Textbook Keying

2. Key the lines at the right in Textbook Keying. Key each line once. Strike ENTER at the end of each line.
3. When you complete the lesson, print your Lesson Report (step 5 above) and exit the software.

```
13  a  a;  al  ak  aj  s  s;  sl  sk  sj  d  d;  dl  dk  dj
14  j  ja  js  jd  jf  k  ka  ks  kd  kf  l  la  ls  ld  lf
15  a;  sl  a;sl  dkfj  a;sl  dkfj  a;sldkfj  asdf  jk
16  a;  sl  a;sl  dk  fj  dkfj  a;sl  dkfj  fkds;a;  fj
17  f  ff  j  jj  d  dd  k  kk  s  ss  l  ll  a  aa  ;  ;;  fj
18  afj;  a  s  d  f  j  k  l  ;  asdf  jkl;  fdsa  jkl;
```

Writing 34: 70 *gwam*

Foreign study and travel take extra time and effort, but these two activities quickly help us to understand people. Much can be learned from other cultures. Today, business must think globally. Learning about the culture of others is not a luxury. Even the owner of a small business realizes that he or she cannot just focus on the domestic scene.

	1'	3'
	11	4	50
	24	8	55
	37	12	59
	50	17	63
	64	21	68
	70	23	70

Many examples can be used to show how a local business may be influenced by global competition. A hair stylist may be required to learn European styles because customers may want to try a style just like they saw on their travels. Or salons may want to offer other services such as facials that people have tried while they were traveling abroad.

	11	27	74
	24	31	78
	38	36	83
	51	40	87
	63	44	91
	70	47	93

Writing 35: 75 *gwam*

Getting a job interview is certainly a triumph for the job seeker. Yet anxiety quickly sets in as the applicant becomes aware of the competition. The same attention to details that was used in writing the successful resume will also be needed for the interview. Experts often say that the first four minutes are the most crucial in making a strong impact on the interviewer.

	12	4	54
	24	8	58
	37	12	62
	51	17	67
	64	21	71
	75	25	75

First, people focus on what they see. Posture, eye contact, facial expression, and gestures make up over half of the message. Next, people focus on what they hear; enthusiasm, delivery, pace, volume, and clarity are as vital as what is said. Finally, people get to the actual words that are said. You can make a good impression. But, realize, you have just four minutes.

	12	29	79
	26	33	84
	39	38	88
	51	42	92
	63	49	96
	75	50	100

Writing 36: 80 *gwam*

Would a pitcher go to the mound without warming up? Would a speaker go to the podium without practice? Of course not! These experts have spent many long hours striving to do their best. Similarly, the performance of business employees is rated. The manager's evaluation will include a record of actual performance and a list of new goals. A good mark in these areas will demand much hard work.

	12	4	57
	25	8	62
	38	13	66
	51	17	70
	64	21	75
	77	26	79
	80	27	80

Many work factors can be practiced to help one succeed on the job. Class attendance and punctuality can be perfected by students. Because work is expected to be correct, managers do not assign zeros. Thus, students must learn to proofread their work. A project must also be completed quickly. Students can learn to organize work and time well and to find ways to do their work smarter and faster.

	12	30	84
	24	35	88
	37	39	92
	49	43	96
	62	47	101
	75	52	105
	80	53	107

```
1' | 1 | 2 | 3 | 4 | 5 | 6 | 7 | 8 | 9 | 10 | 11 | 12 | 13 |
3' |     1     |       2       |       3       |       4       |
```

LESSON 1R

Review

WARMUP

1Ra Review home row

1. Open *Keyboarding Pro* software.
2. Click the ↓ next to *Class* and select your section. Click your name.
3. Key your password and click **OK**.
4. Go to *Lesson R1*.
5. Key each exercise as directed. Repeat if desired.

Note: All drill lines on this page may be keyed in the Open Screen. See 2d page 8 for instructions.

Fingers curved and upright

```
1 f j fjf jj fj fj jf dd kk dd kk dk dk dk
2 s ; s;s ;; s; s; s; aa ;; aa ;; a; a; a;

3 fj dk sl a; fjdksla; jfkdls;a ;a ;s kd j
4 f j fjf d k dkd s l sls a ; fj dk sl a;a

5 a; al ak aj s s; sl sk sj d d; dl dk djd
6 ja js jd jf k ka ks kd kf l la ls ld lfl

7 f fa fad s sa sad f fa fall fall l la lad s sa sad
8 a as ask a ad add j ja jak f fa fall; ask; add jak
```

SKILLBUILDING

1Rb Keyboard Review

Key each line once; repeat as time permits.

```
 9 ik ki ki ik is if id il ij ia ij ik is if ji id ia
10 is il ill sill dill fill sid lid ail lid slid jail

11 if is il kid kids ill kid if kids; if a kid is ill
12 is id if ai aid jaks lid sid sis did ail; if lids;

13 a lass; ask dad; lads ask dad; a fall; fall salads
14 as a fad; ask a lad; a lass; all add; a kid; skids

15 as asks did disk ail fail sail ails jail sill silk
16 ask dad; dads said; is disk; kiss a lad; salad lid

17 aid a lad; if a kid is; a salad lid; kiss sad dads
18 as ad all ask jak lad fad kids ill kill fall disks
```

Writing 31: 55 *gwam*

A crucial life skill is the ability to put things in proper perspective. Individuals often fail to realize that many things are just not worth fighting about. A quick way to know whether an issue is worth fighting for is to look at the situation from a long-term perspective.

	1'	3'
	12	4 41
	25	8 45
	38	13 50
	51	17 54
	55	18 55

If you will care five or six years from now that you defended an issue, it is a principle worth defending. If you will not even remember, the situation does not justify the effort required for defending it. The odds of winning are also important. Why fight a losing battle?

	1'	3'
	11	22 59
	24	26 63
	36	31 67
	49	35 72
	55	37 74

Writing 32: 60 *gwam*

Why do we remember some things and forget others? Often, we associate loss of memory with aging or an illness such as Alzheimer's disease. However, the crux of the matter is that we all forget various things that we prefer to remember. We tend to remember things that mean something special to us.

	1'	3'
	12	4 44
	24	8 48
	37	12 52
	50	17 57
	60	20 60

For many people, recalling dates is a difficult task; yet they manage to remember dates of special occasions, such as anniversaries. Processing requires one not only to hear but to ponder and to understand what has just been said. We recall things that we say and do longer than things we hear and see.

	1'	3'
	12	24 64
	25	28 68
	36	33 72
	49	37 77
	60	40 80

Writing 33: 65 *gwam*

Humor is very important in our professional and our personal lives. Fortunately, we realize that many things can and do go wrong. If we can learn to laugh at ourselves and with other people, we will get through the terrible times. Adding a little extra laughter can help put the situation in proper perspective much quicker.

	1'	3'
	12	4 47
	25	8 52
	37	12 56
	50	17 60
	63	21 64
	65	22 65

Maintaining our sense of humor lets us enjoy our positions to a greater degree. No one is perfect, and we cannot expect perfection from ourselves. However, the quality of our performance is greater when we do the things we like. We realize our prime time is devoted to work. Thus, it is important that we enjoy this time.

	1'	3'
	12	26 69
	24	30 73
	37	34 77
	50	38 82
	62	42 86
	65	43 87

1'	1	2	3	4	5	6	7	8	9	10	11	12	13
3'		1			2			3			4		

LESSON 2

E and N

WARMUP

2a

1. Open *Keyboarding Pro*.
2. Locate your student record.
3. Select Lesson 2.

```
1 ff  dd  ss  aa  ff  dd  ss  aa  jj  kk  ll  ;;  fj  dk  sl  a;  a;
2 fj  dk  sl  a;  fjdksla;  a;sldkfj  fj  dk  sl  a;  fjdksla;
3 aa  ss  dd  ff  jj  kk  ll  ;;  aa  ss  dd  ff  jj  kk  ll  ;;  a;
4 if  a;  as  is;  kids  did;  ask  a  sad  lad;  if  a  lass  is
```

NEW KEYS

2b E and N

Key each line once; DS between groups.

e Reach *up* with *left second* finger.

n Reach *down* with *right first* finger.

```
e
5 e  ed  ed  led  led  lea  lea  ale  ale  elf  elf  eke  eke  ed
6 e  el  el  eel  els  elk  elk  lea  leak  ale  kale  led  jell
7 e  ale  kale  lea  leak  fee  feel  lea  lead  elf  self  eke

n
8 n  nj  nj  an  an  and  and  fan  fan  and  kin  din  fin  land
9 n  an  fan  in  fin  and  land  sand  din  fans  sank  an  sin
10 n  in  ink  sink  inn  kin  skin  an  and  land  in  din  dink

all reaches learned
11 den  end  fen  ken  dean  dens  ales  fend  fens  keen  knee
12 if  in  need;  feel  ill;  as  an  end;  a  lad  and  a  lass;
13 and  sand;  a  keen  idea;  as  a  sail  sank;  is  in  jail;
14 an  idea;  an  end;  a  lake;  a  nail;  a  jade;  a  dean  is
```

2c Textbook Keying

Key each line once; DS between groups.

```
15 if  a  lad;
16 is  a  sad  fall

17 if  a  lass  did  ask
18 ask  a  lass;  ask  a  lad

19 a;sldkfj  a;sldkfj  a;sldkfj
20 a;  sl  dk  fj  fj  dk  sl  a;  a;sldkfj

21 i  ik  ik  if  if  is  is  kid  skid  did  lid  aid  laid  said
22 ik  kid  ail  die  fie  did  lie  ill  ilk  silk  skill  skid
```

> Reach with little finger; tap Enter key quickly; return finger to home key.

Skill Builders 5

Save each drill as a separate file. Save as **SB5-d1**, etc. (Skill Builders 5, Drill 1).

DRILL 1

PROGRESSIVE WRITINGS

1. Set the timer for 1'.
2. Practice each ¶ in a set until you can complete it in 1' with no more than one error.
3. Take a 3' writing; strive to maintain your 1' rate.
4. Move onto the next set. Notice that each set progresses by 5 words.

 all letters

Writing 28: **40** *gwam*

	gwam	1'	3'
"An ounce of prevention is worth a pound of cure" is really	12	4	31
based on fact; still, many people comprehend this statement more	25	8	35
for its quality as literature than on a practical, common-sense	38	12	39
philosophy.	40	13	40
Just take health, for example. We agonize over stiff costs	12	17	44
we pay to recover from illnesses; but, on the other hand, we give	25	22	48
little or no attention to health requirements for diet, exercise,	38	26	53
and sleep.	40	27	53

Writing 29: **45** *gwam*

	gwam	1'	3'
Problems with our environment show an odd lack of foresight.	12	4	34
We just expect that whatever we may need to support life will be	25	8	38
available. We rarely question our comforts, even though they may	38	13	43
abuse our earth, water, and air.	45	15	45
Optimism is an excellent virtue. It is comforting to think	12	19	49
that, eventually, anything can be fixed. So why should we worry?	25	23	53
A better idea, certainly, is to realize that we don't have to fix	38	28	58
anything we have not yet broken.	45	30	60

Writing 30: **50** *gwam*

	gwam	1'	3'
Recently, a friend of mine grumbled about how quickly papers	12	4	37
accumulated on her desk; she never seemed able to reduce them to	25	8	42
zero. She said some law seemed to be working that expanded the	38	13	46
stack today by precisely the amount she reduced it yesterday.	50	17	50
She should organize her papers and tend to them daily. Any	12	21	54
paper that needs a look, a decision, and speedy, final action	24	25	58
gets just that; any that needs closer attention is subject to a	37	29	62
fixed completion schedule. Self-discipline is the key to order.	50	33	67

1'	1	2	3	4	5	6	7	8	9	10	11	12	13
3'		1			2			3			4		

STANDARD PLAN for the Open Screen

The **Open Screen** is a word processor that includes many features and a timer. Exercises to be keyed in the Open Screen are identified with an Open Screen icon. These exercises give you an opportunity to build your keyboarding skills, key documents, or take a timed writing. Results are not recorded in the Lesson Report. Follow the instructions in the textbook when completing these exercises.

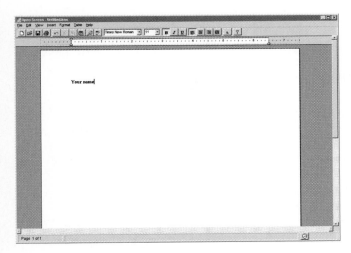

1. Click the **Open Screen** button on the Main Menu of *Keyboarding Pro*.
2. Key your name and strike ENTER twice.
3. Follow the directions in the textbook for the drill.
4. Print what you key in the Open Screen.
5. Click the **Close** button in the upper-right corner to exit the Open Screen. ✖

Note: Any exercise keyed in the Open Screen can be saved.

SKILLBUILDING

2e Reinforcement

1. In the Open Screen, key each line twice. DS between groups of two lines.
2. Print but do not save the exercise.
3. Close the Open Screen and you will return to Lesson 2 in the software.

TECHNIQUE TIP
Keep your eyes on the textbook copy.

i

23 ik ik ik if is il ik id is if kid did lid aid ails

24 did lid aid; add a line; aid kids; ill kids; id is

n

25 nj nj nj an an and and end den ken in ink sin skin

26 jn din sand land nail sank and dank skin sans sink

e

27 el els elf elk lea lead fee feel sea seal ell jell

28 el eke ale jak lake elf els jaks kale eke els lake

all reaches

29 dine in an inn; fake jade; lend fans; as sand sank

30 in nine inns; if an end; need an idea; seek a fee;

2f End the lesson

1. Print the Lesson Report.
2. Exit the software; remove the storage disk if appropriate.

Change left and right margins to 1"; arrange the document so that it fits on one page. Use the following heading lines. Signature line: **Respectfully submitted, Alice Liu, Secretary**. Save as 120c-d7.

Sterling Heights Community Hospital
August 10, 200-
Advisory Board Meeting Minutes

	words
	heading 17

Presiding: *bold*   Jacinto A. Campo, Administrator — 25

Participants: Shawn Hartman, Assistant Administrator; — 36
Terry Olson, Community Relations; John Kaplan, Director of — 48
Marketing; Ron Volson, Human Resources; Lisa Summons, — 59
Director of Education; Susan Phillips, Director of Nursing — 71

Board Members: *bold* Vincent Perez, City of Sterling Heights; — 82
Captain Wayne Anderson, Wayne County Sheriff Station; — 93
Robert Le, American Heart Association; Cynthia Cross, — 104
Buxton Medical Supplies; Nancy Ricardo, General Motors — 115
Corp. — 116

Administrator Jacinto Campo welcomed all new board members — 128
and guests to the first official advisory board meeting. — 140
~~Introductions were made around the table.~~ —

~~All advisory committee~~ *gave* members and participants *a* ~~toured~~ *of* — 155

the hospital ~~guided by~~ Jacinto Campo. Facility improve- — 162

ments *and* were discussed during the tour. Areas targeted for — 176

remodeling ~~this year were also pointed out.~~ —

Bylaws for the advisory board were distributed and — 186

discussed. Mr. Campo expressed the hospital*'s* *commitment* ~~desire~~ to ~~get~~ *being* — 200

involved in the community. *The advisory board input will be critical.* — 215

Bullet these items

Current hospital projects were discussed: Bears — 225

Program, MOMS, Hospital feedback methods. — 241

(Maternal Obstetrical Medical Services)

Plaques were presented to each of the advisory board — 250

members and pictures were taken. The next advisory board — 262

meeting is scheduled for . *October 16, 200-.* — 270

LESSON 3

Review

3a
Key each line at a steady pace; strike and release each key quickly. Key each line again at a faster pace.

home 1 ad ads lad fad dad as ask fa la lass jak jaks alas

n 2 an fan and land fan flan sans sand sank flank dank

i 3 is id ill dill if aid ail fail did kid ski lid ilk

all 4 ade alas nine else fife ken; jell ink jak inns if;

SKILLBUILDING

3b Rhythm Builder
Key each line twice.
Lines 5–8: Think and key words. Make the space part of the word.
Lines 9–12: Think and key phrases. Do not key the vertical rules separating the phrases.

easy words

5 if is as an ad el and did die eel fin fan elf lens

6 as ask and id kid and ade aid eel feel ilk skis an

7 ail fail aid did ken ale led an flan inn inns alas

8 eel eke nee kneel did kids kale sees lake elf fled

easy phrases

9 el el|id id|is is|eke eke|lee lee|ale ale|jill jill

10 is if|is a|is a|a disk|a disk|did ski|did ski|is a

11 sell a|sell a|sell a sled|fall fad|fall fad|did die

12 sees a lake|sees a lake|as a deal|sell a sled|all a

3c Technique Practice
Key each 2-line group twice; SS.

TECHNIQUE TIP
Reach with the little finger; tap Enter key quickly; return finger to home key.

home row: fingers curved and upright

13 jak lad as lass dad sad lads fad fall la ask ad as

14 asks add jaks dads a lass ads flak adds sad as lad

upward reaches: straighten fingers slightly; return quickly to home position

15 fed die led ail kea lei did ale fife silk leak lie

16 sea lid deal sine desk lie ale like life idea jail

double letters: don't hurry when stroking double letters

17 fee jell less add inn seek fall alee lass keel all

18 dill dell see fell eel less all add kiss seen sell

1. Change the left and right margins to .75". Create a 5-column, 7-row table.

2. Merge Row 1 and create a heading similar to the illustration. Row 1 contains all the copy from the top of the page through *This bill is due and payable within 21 days*.

3. Key the invoice shown below. Insert appropriate form fields (**ff**) to accommodate the type of information to be filled in.

4. Protect the form. Save as **120c-d5** and print.

*P*acific *N*ewport *M*edical *G*roup

3160 Redhill Ave. • Newport Beach, CA 90630 • (714) 555-0112

BILLING STATEMENT

This bill is due and payable within 21 days.

Date	Services Rendered	Charges	Insurance Payment	Balance Due
(ff-patient name) *(ff-street address)* *(ff-city, state, zip)*	Account # *(ff-acct. #)*	Balance Due Past Due Total Balance		

1. Open **120c-d5** and save it as **120c-d6**. Fill in the form with the name, address, and account number, as well as the services and charges shown below.

2. Unprotect the form to fill in the rest of the form.

3. Use the math feature to write a formula that will calculate Balance Due in Column E (Charges – Insurance Payment). Display the Balance Due with a dollar sign and two decimal places. Use the Sum Above feature to insert the Balance Due in Cell E7.

4. Insert decimal tabs to align the numbers. You will need to align the numbers manually in Cell E7.

5. Calculate Total Balance (Balance Due + Past Due). Save and print.

6-22-xx	Office visit	65.00	50.00
6-27-xx	Lab test/X-ray	185.00	160.00
7-06-xx	Consultation	200.00	125.00

Cheryl Bocanegra, 793 Haven Ln., Costa Mesa, CA 92626 Acct. # 09431   Past Due: $60.00

3d Textbook Keying

Key each line once; DS between groups of two lines.

TECHNIQUE TIP

Strike keys quickly.
Strike the Space Bar
Space Bar with down-and-in motion.
Strike Enter with a quick flick of the little finger.

LEFT FINGERS   4 3 2 1   1 2 3 4   RIGHT FINGERS

reach review

19 ea sea lea seas deal leaf leak lead leas fleas keas
20 as ask lass ease as asks ask ask sass as alas seas
DS
21 sa sad sane sake sail sale sans safe sad said sand
22 le sled lead flee fled ale flea lei dale kale leaf
DS
23 jn jn nj nj in fan fin an; din ink sin and inn an;
24 de den end fen an an and and ken knee nee dean dee

phrases (think and key phrases)

25 and and land land el el elf elf self self ail nail
26 as as ask ask ad ad lad lad id id lid lid kid kids

27 if if|is is|jak jak|all all|did did|nan nan|elf elf
28 as a lad| ask dad| fed a jak| as all ask| sales fad

29 sell a lead|seal a deal|feel a leaf|if a jade sale
30 is a|is as if|a disk|aid all kids|did ski|is a silk

d/e
31 den end fen ken dean dens ales fend fens keen knee
32 a deed; a desk; a jade; an eel; a jade eel; a dean

n/a
33 an an in in and and en end end sane sane sand sand
34 a land; a dean; a fan; a fin; a sane end; end land

nj
35 el eel eld elf sell self el dell fell elk els jell
36 in fin inn inks dine sink fine fins kind line lain

all reaches
37 an and fan dean elan flan land lane lean sand sane
38 sell a lead; sell a jade; seal a deal; feel a leaf

3e Reinforcement

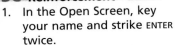

1. In the Open Screen, key your name and strike ENTER twice.
2. Key each line once. DS between groups of two lines.
3. Print the exercise.
4. Click the **X** box in the upper-right corner to close the Open Screen.
5. Print your Lesson Report and exit.

Body of letter:

Thank you for volunteering to be on the advisory committee for the County Medical Rescue Mission. I am sure that this will be a very rewarding experience for you and your company. The County Medical Rescue Mission served over 1,500 low income and homeless people during the past year.

I am enclosing a copy of the last advisory committee minutes to give you an idea of what was discussed at the last meeting. A copy of the agenda for the next meeting, scheduled for August 16, 200-, is also enclosed.

We look forward to seeing you on August 16th.

120c-d3
Name Badges

1. Use the mail merge feature to create name badges for the advisory committee members in **120c-d2**.

2. Use Avery 5883 Name Badge. Include the speaker's name, job title, and company name on each badge. Make the font large enough so that it is easily visible.

3. Save as **120c-d3**. Print.

120c-d4
Format Report with Styles and Footnotes

1. Open **Frogkick Island**. Save as **120c-d4**.

2. Format this document as a SS leftbound report. Change the spacing after the paragraphs to 6 points.

3. Main heading: Center, initial caps, Heading 1 style.

   Side headings: Heading 2 style.

   Paragraph headings: Place on line above ¶, make initial cap, remove period, and apply Heading 3 style.

4. **a.** Insert footnote 1 at the end of the first paragraph:

   International Government Publication, *2000 Census Report* **(Washington, D.C.: International Government Press, 2001) p. 92.**

   b. Insert footnote 2 at the end of the first paragraph under the side heading **Government**:

   ***Frogkick Island Ordinances* (New York: Majestic Publishing House, 2002) p. 1035, §2015.**

5. Insert a header that contains your name at the left margin and the page number at the right followed by a $3/4$-point line; the header will appear on all pages except the first.

   Student Name
                                                       2

6. Insert these references on the last page of the report; then save the report and print.

   Crane, Thomas B. *Unique Trips Around the World.* **London: Versaille Publishing Co., 2002.**

   Peterson, Angelica S. *Undiscovered Travel Adventures.* **Singapore: International Printing Association, 2002.**

LESSON 4

Left Shift, H, T, Period

WARMUP

4a

Key each line twice SS.
Keep eyes on copy.

home row	1	al as ads lad dad fad jak fall lass asks fads all;
e/i/n	2	ed ik jn in knee end nine line sine lien dies leis
all reaches	3	see a ski; add ink; fed a jak; is an inn; as a lad
easy	4	an dial id is an la lake did el ale fake is land a

NEW KEYS

4b Left `Shift` and `h`

Key each line once.

Follow the "Standard procedures for learning new keyreaches" on p. 4 for all remaining reaches.

left shift Reach *down* with *left fourth* (little) finger; shift, strike, release.

h Reach to *left* with *right first* finger.

left shift

5 J Ja Ja Jan Jan Jane Jana Ken Kass Lee Len Nan Ned
6 and Ken and Lena and Jake and Lida and Nan and Ida
7 Inn is; Jill Ina is; Nels is; Jen is; Ken Lin is a

h

8 h hj hj he he she she hen aha ash had has hid shed
9 h hj ha hie his half hand hike dash head sash shad
10 aha hi hash heal hill hind lash hash hake dish ash

all reaches learned

11 Nels Kane and Jake Jenn; she asked Hi and Ina Linn
12 Lend Lana and Jed a dish; I fed Lane and Jess Kane
13 I see Jake Kish and Lash Hess; Isla and Helen hike

4c **Textbook Keying**

Key the drill once: Strive for good control.

14 he she held a lead; she sells jade; she has a sale
15 Ha Ja Ka La Ha Hal Ja Jake Ka Kahn La Ladd Ha Hall
16 Hal leads; Jeff led all fall; Hal has a safe lead
17 Hal Hall heads all sales; Jake Hess asks less fee;

120c-d1
Agenda

1. Key the first line of the heading on approximately line 2". DS and bold the heading.
2. Set a left tab at .5" and a right leader tab at 6.0".
3. Key the agenda. Save as **120c-d1**. Print.

PACIFIC NEWPORT MEDICAL GROUP

ANNUAL BOARD OF DIRECTORS MEETING

July 15, 200-

Agenda

1. *Call to Order*...*Dr. Paul De La Rosa, President*
2. *Review of Previous Minutes*...*Melanie Leyda, Secretary*
3. *State of the Corporation Address*...*Richard Pham, Controller*
4. *Technology Update*..*Dr. Lisa Lee*
   Nuclear Medicine..*Dr. Steven Coast*
   Ultrasound Lab...*Dr. David Beem*
5. *Quality Assurance*..*Claire Zehner, RN*
6. *HIPAA Privacy Regulations* ....*Susan Smith, Director of Education*
7. *Goal Setting*...*Adam Rogers, Chief Operating Officer*

120c-d2
Mail Merge

1. Use mail merge to create the following letter. Supply all necessary letter parts. The letter is from you, Administrative Assistant.
2. Save the merged letters as **120c-d2**. Print the main document and the merged letters.

Recipients:

Mr. Jacinto Campo, Administrator, Sterling Heights Community Hospital, 5252 Hospital Rd., Newport Beach, CA 90630.

Ms. Betty Gross, Public Relations Coordinator, American Hospitals Association, 9754 Campus Dr., Buena Park, CA 90620

Ms. Loretta Pascua, Manager, Rehabilitation Specialist, 9217 Champion Way, Tustin, CA 92782

4d

t and **.** (period)
Key each line once.

Period: Space once after a period that follows an initial or an abbreviation. To increase readability, space twice after a period that ends a sentence.

t Reach *up* with *left first* finger.

. (period) Reach *down* with *right third* finger.

t

18 t tf tf aft aft left fit fat fete tiff tie the tin
19 tf at at aft lit hit tide tilt tint sits skit this
20 hat kit let lit ate sit flat tilt thin tale tan at

. (period)

21 .1 .1 1.1 fl. fl. L. L. Neal and J. N. List hiked.
22 Hand J. H. Kass a fan. Jess did. I need an idea.
23 Jane said she has a tan dish; Jae and Lee need it.

all reaches learned

24 I did tell J. K. that Lt. Li had left. He is ill.
25 tie tan kit sit fit hit hat; the jet left at nine.
26 I see Lila and Ilene at tea. Jan Kane ate at ten.

SKILLBUILDING

4e Reinforcement

Follow the standard directions for the Open Screen (page 8).

Lines 27–34: Key each line twice; DS between groups. Try to increase your speed the second time.

Lines 35–38: Key the lines once.

End the lesson

Print the lines keyed in the Open Screen and print your Lesson Report. Exit the software.

reach review
27 tf .1 hj ft ki de jh tf ik ed hj de ft ki 1. tf ik
28 elf eel left is sis fit till dens ink has delt ink

h/e
29 he he heed heed she she shelf shelf shed shed she
30 he has; he had; he led; he sleds; she fell; he is

i/t
31 it is if id did lit tide tide tile tile list list
32 it is; he hit it; he is ill; she is still; she is

shift
33 Hal and Nel; Jade dishes; Kale has half; Jed hides
34 Hi Ken; Helen and Jen hike; Jan has a jade; Ken is

enter
35 Nan had a sale.
36 He did see Hal.
37 Lee has a desk.
38 Ina hid a dish.

TECHNIQUE TIP
Strike Enter without pausing or looking up from the copy.

LESSON 120 | Assessment

SKILLBUILDING

120a
Warmup
Key each line twice SS;
DS between 2-line groups.

alphabet	1	Zack Q. Davis just left a very brief message with six nice poems.
figures	2	Jan bought 27 toys at $3.98 each, a total of $107.46 plus 5% tax.
adjacent reaches	3	We are going to build a store on a very quiet point west of here.
easy	4	Tod and I may visit the ancient chapel and then go to the island.

| 1 | 2 | 3 | 4 | 5 | 6 | 7 | 8 | 9 | 10 | 11 | 12 | 13 |

120b
Timed Writings
Key one 3' and one 5' writing. Strive for good accuracy.

 all letters

gwam   3' | 5'

	3'	5'
A successful organization tries to put the right employee in	4	2 51
the right job. The process of selecting employees raises many	8	5 53
questions that frequently are very perplexing. A key issue	12	7 56
that must be balanced deals with the rights of the individual	16	10 58
who is seeking a position and the rights of the organization that	21	12 61
is hiring a person to fill a position. Laws specify the types of	25	15 64
information that can be asked in the hiring process to ensure	29	18 66
that bias is not a factor in hiring. However, most firms do	33	20 69
strive to be fair in the hiring process. The issue that many	37	22 71
employers struggle with is how to determine who will be the	41	25 73
right employee for a particular job that is available.	45	27 76
The ability to predict an individual's performance on the	49	29 78
job is very important. Assessing an individual in the hiring	53	32 80
process to determine how he or she will perform on the job,	57	34 83
however, is a very difficult task. Most techniques measure the	61	37 85
potential or the way that a person can perform, but the way a	66	39 88
person can perform may differ drastically from the way the person	70	42 90
will perform when he or she is hired. Past performance on a job	74	45 93
may be the best measure of future performance, which is why firms	79	47 96
seek individuals with experience.	81	49 97

3' | 1 | 2 | 3 | 4 |
5' | 1 | 2 | 3 |

APPLICATIONS

120c
Assessment
Timed Production: 40'

On the signal to begin, key the documents in sequence. When time has been called, proofread all documents again and correct any errors you may have overlooked. Reprint if necessary.

LESSON 5

R, Right Shift, C, O

WARMUP

5a
Key each line twice.

home keys	1	a; ad add al all lad fad jak ask lass fall jak lad
t/h/i/n	2	the hit tin nit then this kith dint tine hint thin
left shift/.	3	I need ink. Li has an idea. Hit it. I see Kate.
all reaches	4	Jeff ate at ten; he left a salad dish in the sink.

NEW KEYS

5b r and Right Shift
Key each line once.

r Reach *up* with *left first* finger.

right shift Reach *down* with *right fourth* finger; shift, strike, release.

r

5 r rf rf riff riff fir fir rid ire jar air sir lair
6 rf rid ark ran rat are hare art rant tire dirt jar
7 rare dirk ajar lark rain kirk share hart rail tart

right shift

8 D D Dan Dan Dale Ti Sal Ted Ann Ed Alf Ada Sid Fan
9 and Sid and Dina and Allen and Eli and Dean and Ed
10 Ed Dana; Dee Falk; Tina Finn; Sal Alan; Anna Deeds

all reaches learned

11 Jane and Ann hiked in the sand; Asa set the tents.
12 a rake; a jar; a tree; a red fire; a fare; a rain;
13 Fred Derr and Rai Tira dined at the Tree Art Fair.

5c Textbook Keying
Key each line once; DS between groups of two lines.

14 ir ir ire fir first air fair fire tire rid sir
15 fir jar tar fir flit rill till list stir dirt fire
DS
16 Feral is ill. Dan reads. Dee and Ed Finn see Dere.
17 All is still as Sarah and I fish here in the rain.
DS
18 I still see a red ash tree that fell in the field.
19 Lana said she did sail her skiff in the dark lake.

Project, *continued*

Supplementary services. Meal and beverage services are frequently contracted, in addition to the transportation package. For example, box meals and cold drinks on the return flight after the game are usually a part of athletic charter flight packages. Equipment handling is also a part of the package. Tickets, convention packages, and other services provided usually are arranged through travel partners when they are part of a charter flight contract.

Market Analysis

The Southeast market was targeted first because of limited jet charter service available in the geographic area. Another determining factor was the intense interest in and support of athletics, particularly college football in the Southeast. Successful charters to games at other institutions created demand from those institutions for their travel schedule. The most profitable section of the market stems from the athletic connections.

Emerging markets. An emerging market is being created by women's athletic programs. This market is fueled by the current gender equity emphasis in college athletics. Court decisions and athletic regulations focus on equal treatment of men's and women's sports. Other emerging markets are the resort (particularly tennis, golf, beach, and ski resorts) and casino charters that are arranged by the resorts to bring in customers at a relatively low cost.

Competition. Only one other charter air service in the Southeast competes in the same niche market in which Pommery competes with all jet service. Several smaller charter air service companies try to compete with relatively large turboprop aircraft. The market clearly demands jet service. Pommery's market share is conservatively estimated to be 65 percent of the market in the Southeast.

Market expansion. The real challenge is to increase the size of this niche market through promotional activities and strategic alliances with travel partners. Pilot projects have produced promising results and are being evaluated as part of the growth strategy.

Pro Formas—2004–2006

Pro formas for 2004, 2005, and 2006 are based on the addition of two jet aircraft within the next 18 months. Revenue and expenses are in current dollars.

*(Insert Pro Forma Statement of Income from **117-d6**.)*

Ownership

Five million common shares have been authorized. Of the authorized shares, 2,802,654 shares have been issued. Common stock ownership is diverse as noted in the following groupings.

*(Insert the table from **117-d7** here.)*

5d

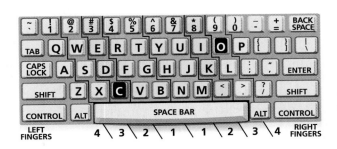

c and **o**
Key each line once.

c Reach *down* with *left second* finger.

o Reach *up* with right *third* finger.

c

20 c c cd cd cad cad can can tic ice sac cake cat sic
21 clad chic cite cheek clef sick lick kick dice rice
22 call acid hack jack lack lick cask crack clan cane

o

23 o ol ol old old of off odd ode or ore oar soar one
24 ol sol sold told dole do doe lo doll sol solo odor
25 onto door toil lotto soak fort hods foal roan load

all reaches learned

26 Carlo Rand can call Rocco; Cole can call Doc Cost.
27 Trina can ask Dina if Nick Corl has left; Joe did.
28 Case sent Carole a nice skirt; it fits Lorna Rich.

SKILLBUILDING

5e Keyboard Reinforcement
Key each line once SS; key at a steady pace. Repeat, striving for control.

TECHNIQUE TIP
Reach up without moving hands away from your body. Use quick keystrokes.

o/r
29 or or for for nor nor ore ore oar oar roe roe sore
30 a rose|her or|he or|he rode|or for|a door|her doll

i/t
31 is is tis tis it it fit fit tie tie this this lits
32 it is|it is|it is this|it is this|it sits|tie fits

e/n
33 en en end end ne ne need need ken ken kneel kneels
34 lend the|lend the|at the end|at the end|need their

c/o
35 ch ch check check ck ck hack lack jack co co cones
36 the cot|the cot|a dock|a dock|a jack|a jack|a cone

all reaches
37 Jack and Rona did frost nine of the cakes at last.
38 Jo can ice her drink if Tess can find her a flask.
39 Ask Jean to call Fisk at noon; he needs her notes.

Pommery Air Service, Inc.

Business Plan

Pommery Air Service, Inc. (Pommery), since it was founded as a Delaware corporation in January 1999, has operated as a niche player in the charter air segment of the airline industry.

Industry

Three distinct segments comprise the charter air service industry:

- Small, local charter operations designed to provide point-to-point transportation for groups of fewer than 20 people in turboprop aircraft.

- Occasional charter flights provided by major passenger airlines.

- Small niche markets that target specific types of clientele.

Pommery operates exclusively in the third segment of the industry, offering contract charter flights and event charter flights. The overall charter air service industry is highly competitive. The most intensive competition exists in the other two segments of the charter air service. Pommery's board of directors and management agree that Pommery cannot and should not try to compete with the major passenger airlines for numerous reasons. They also agree that Pommery cannot compete with the small, local charter services because of the cost structure involved in providing jet air service exclusively.

The Service

Pommery provides event charter flights and contract charter flights throughout the United States. About 85 percent of the flights originate east of the Mississippi River, and almost 65 percent of flights originate in the Southeast.

Event charter flights. These flights are called event charters because they exist to transport passengers to attend specific events that are occurring. The range of events spans from those that occur one time or once in a significant period of time to regularly scheduled events. Examples of one-time events include charters to attend Olympic events, Mardi Gras, or a world-class art exhibition or musical production.

Seasonal events are those that occur regularly during a specified period of time. Athletic events comprise a high percentage of seasonal events. Charter flights to a ski resort or to a nearby city on weekends during the season to watch professional football, basketball, or baseball games would be an example. The flight is made available to a number of participating travel agency partners who reserve a number of seats on these charter flights for their clientele.

Regularly scheduled charters include special packages (usually weekends) to fixed destinations such as Las Vegas, a Gulf Coast casino and resort, or a country music/golf weekend in Myrtle Beach. These events are generally marketed through participating travel agency partners.

Contract charter flights. Contract charter flights often overlap with event charter flights. The primary difference is that the contract charter flights are with specific organizations or individuals. For example, a contract may be issued with an athletic department to take its football team and band to a game. The contract is with that athletic department. On the other hand, an event charter flight may go to the same football game with passengers from several travel agency partners and an alumni group.

Companies also use charter flights to take groups to conventions, meetings, and other business activities. Travel agencies often contract for charter flights between destinations on vacation packages.

LESSON 6

W, Comma, B, P

6a
Key each line twice; avoid pauses.

home row	1	ask a lad; a fall fad; had a salad; ask a sad jak;
o/t	2	to do it; to toil; as a tot; do a lot; he told her
c/r	3	cots are; has rocks; roll cot; is rich; has an arc
all reaches	4	Holt can see Dane at ten; Jill sees Frank at nine.

NEW KEYS

6b w and , (comma)
Key each line once.

w Reach *up* with *left third* finger.

, (comma) Reach *down* with *right second* finger.

Comma: Space once after a comma.

LEFT FINGERS   4 \ 3 \ 2 \ 1 \ 1 \ 2 \ 3 \ 4   RIGHT FINGERS

w

5 w ws ws was was wan wit low win jaw wilt wink wolf
6 sw sw ws ow ow now now row row own own wow wow owe
7 to sew; to own; was rich; was in; is how; will now

, (comma)

8 k, k, k, irk, ilk, ask, oak, ark, lark, jak, rock,
9 skis, a dock, a fork, a lock, a fee, a tie, a fan,
10 Jo, Ed, Ted, and Dan saw Nan in a car lift; a kit

all reaches learned

11 Win, Lew, Drew, and Walt will walk to West Willow.
12 Ask Ho, Al, and Jared to read the code; it is new.
13 The window, we think, was closed; we felt no wind.

6c Textbook Keying
Key each line once.

14 walk wide sown wild town went jowl wait white down
15 a dock, a kit, a wick, a lock, a row, a cow, a fee
16 Joe lost to Ron; Fiji lost to Cara; Don lost to Al
17 Kane will win; Nan will win; Rio will win; Di wins
18 Walter is in Reno; Tia is in Tahoe; then to Hawaii

Document 8
Report

Key the Pommery Business Plan, shown on the following pages, according to the directions below. Save as **117-119-d8**.

1. Format the leftbound report as follows:
   a. Spacing—SS; set spacing at 6 points following the paragraph
   b. Main heading—Heading 1 style, centered, main words initial cap
   c. Side headings—Heading 2 style
   d. Paragraph headings—Place above the paragraph, make each word initial cap, remove period, and apply Heading 3 style

2. Tables: Insert tables from Documents 6 and 7 as indicated.

3. Headers: Insert the page number at the right, followed by a ¾-point graphic line (bottom border) header on all pages except the first.

4. Footers: Insert a ¾-point graphic line (top border) footer followed by *Pommery Air Service, Inc.* at the left margin and the current date at the right margin. Place on all pages. Example:

Pommery Air Service, Inc.   July 3, 2004

Document 9
Table of Contents

1. Key a Table of Contents for the Pommery Business Plan. Apply Heading 1 style to the main heading. Key side headings at the left margin; indent for the paragraph headings. Indent the main heading of each table.

2. Include leader tabs and page numbers. Center the page number *ii* in the footer.

3. Save as **117-119-d9** and print.

Table of Contents

Document 10
Title Page

Create an attractive title page using *WordArt*.

1. Insert the logo.

2. Insert a page border.

3. Use the current date.

4. Save as **117-119-d10**.

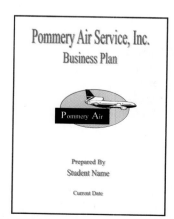

6d

b and **p**

Key each line once.

b Reach *down* with *left first* finger.

p Reach *up* with *right fourth* (little) finger.

b

19 bf bf bf biff fib fib bib bib boa boa fib fibs rob
20 bf bf bf ban ban bon bon bow bow be be rib rib sob
21 a dob, a cob, a crib, a lab, a slab, a bid, a bath

p

22 p; p; pa pa; pal pal pan pan pad par pen pep paper
23 pa pa; lap lap; nap nap; hep ape spa asp leap clap
24 a park, a pan, a pal, a pad, apt to pop, a pair of

all reaches learned

25 Barb and Bob wrapped a pepper in paper and ribbon.
26 Rip, Joann, and Dick were all closer to the flash.
27 Bo will be pleased to see Japan; he works in Oslo.

SKILLBUILDING

6e Keyboard Reinforcement

Key each line once; key at a steady pace.

reach review
28 ki kid did aid lie hj has has had sw saw wits will
29 de dell led sled jn an en end ant hand k, end, kin

s/w
30 ws ws lows now we shown win cow wow wire jowl when
31 Wes saw an owl in the willow tree in the old lane.

b/p
32 bf bf fib rob bid ;p p; pal pen pot nap hop cap bp
33 Rob has both pans in a bin at the back of the pen.

6f Speed Builder

1. Follow the standard Open Screen directions on page 8.
2. Key each line twice. Work for fluency.

all reaches
34 Dick owns a dock at this lake; he paid Ken for it.
35 Jane also kept a pair of owls, a hen, and a snake.

36 Blair soaks a bit of the corn, as he did in Japan.
37 I blend the cocoa in the bowl when I work for Leo.

38 to do|can do|to bow|ask her|to nap|to work|is born
39 for this|if she|is now|did all|to see|or not|or if

Document 6
Table with Formulas

1. Merge Row 1 and increase height to .45". Key the title in 12-point, all caps, and bold.
2. Write a formula to calculate Operating Profit / Loss = (Operating Revenue – Operating Expense).
3. Write a formula to calculate Net Income / (Loss) = (Operating Profit – Non-Operating Expense).
4. Apply 15% shading to Row 1. Save as **117-119-d6**.

2004, 2005, AND 2006 PRO FORMA STATEMENT OF INCOME			
	2004	**2005**	**2006**
Operating Revenue	$44,438,400	$61,466,400	$78,874,400
Operating Expenses	41,144,600	53,190,000	68,898,400
Operating Profit/(Loss)			
Non-Operating Expense	671,200	709,800	1,673,600
Net Income/(Loss)			
Cost Per ASM	.1019	.0721	.0868
Yield	.1647	.1621	.1575
Operating Margin	7.4%	13.5%	12.6%

Document 7
Table with Sum Above and Decimal Tab

1. Merge Row 1 and increase height to .45". Key title in 12-point, all caps, and bold.
2. Use Sum Above to obtain the totals in Row 8.
3. Use a decimal tab to align the numbers in Column C.
4. Apply Table List 7 format; do not apply special formats to the last column. Save as **117-119-d7**.

STOCK OWNERSHIP		
Group	**Shares**	**% of Stock Issued**
Employees	586,268	20.9
Senior officers	353,146	12.6
Outside directors	651,700	23.3
Business community	640,000	22.8
Founders	571,540	20.4
Total		

LESSON 7

Review

WARMUP

7a

Key each line twice; begin new lines promptly.

all	1	We often can take the older jet to Paris and back.
home	2	a; sl dk fj a;sl dkfj ad as all ask fads adds asks
1st row	3	Ann Bascan and Cabal Naban nabbed a cab in Canada.
3d row	4	Rip went to a water show with either Pippa or Pia.

SKILLBUILDING

7b Reach Mastery

Key each line once; DS between groups of three lines.

```
 5 ws ws was was wan wan wit wit pew paw nap pop bawl
 6 bf bf fb fb fob fob rib rib be be job job bat back
 7 p; p; asp asp pan pan ap ap ca cap pa nap pop prow
                                                    DS
 8 Barb and Bret took an old black robe and the boot.
 9 Walt saw a wisp of white water renew ripe peppers.
10 Pat picked a black pepper for the picnic at Parks.
```

7c Rhythm Builder

Key each line once; DS between groups of three lines

TECHNIQUE TIP

words: key as a single unit rather than letter by letter;

phrases: say and key fluently;

sentences: work for fluency.

words	11	a an pan so sot la lap ah own do doe el elf to tot
phrases	12	if it|to do|it is|do so|for the|he works|if he bid
sentences	13	Jess ate all of the peas in the salad in the bowl.
		DS
words	14	bow bowl pin pint for fork forks hen hens jak jaks
phrases	15	is for|did it|is the|we did a|and so|to see|or not
sentences	16	I hid the ace in a jar as a joke; I do not see it.
		DS
words	17	chap chaps flak flake flakes prow prowl work works
phrases	18	as for the|as for the|and to the|to see it|and did
sentences	19	As far as I know, he did not read all of the book.

Pommery Air

Pommery Facts

Pommery Air Service, Inc.

Headquarters
P.O. Box 8473
Hopkins, SC 29061-8473

(803) 555-0123
Fax (803) 555-0124

www.pommeryair.com

Mission Statement

Pommery Air Service Inc. is a charter air service headquartered in Hopkins, South Carolina. Pommery's mission is:

- To provide its charter customers with safe, reliable jet transportation, quality service, outstanding value, and low costs.

- To provide an environment for its employees that fosters teamwork and customer focus and rewards integrity and productivity.

- To deliver superior value to its shareholders.

The Company

Pommery Air Service, Inc., a Delaware corporation founded in January 1999, currently has a fleet of four 737 jet aircraft. Pommery provides air service to almost 60,000 passengers per month. The mix is almost equally divided among business trips, athletic functions, and leisure travel.

An experienced, highly competent management team leads Pommery Air Service, Inc. Management emphasizes teamwork, empowerment, and productivity. Employee stock options provide incentives to employees to focus on quality and profitability.

Pommery Air Service, Inc. became profitable in its tenth month of existence and continues to be profitable. The company operates as a lean, efficient organization. Costs per available seat mile (ASM) have dropped from 14 cents to 10 cents.

Yield per revenue passenger mile increased from 12 cents to 16 cents.

The Market

Pommery Air Service, Inc. provides charter flights to destinations throughout the United States. The primary market, however, is defined by origination point rather than destination point. Approximately 65 percent of all flights originate in the Southeast. The secondary market by origination point is the Northeast.

The Services

Pommery Air Service, Inc. provides two types of charter services: event charter flights and contract charter flights. Both event and contract charter flights include an array of services depending on the needs of the customer. Supplementary services available with both charter and event flights include: meal and beverage services; local transportation; event tickets; side trips; conference facilities, including logistical support; and a host of special activities.

The Strategy

Pommery Air Service, Inc. strives to become the dominant air charter service in the eastern United States. Pommery's core competencies involve providing safe, high-quality jet air services that are cost effective. All other services provided are designed to facilitate and enhance the continual development of the core competencies.

To implement this strategy, Pommery Air Service, Inc. must expand. Expansion requires the addition of two jet aircraft within 18 months.

7d Technique Practice

Key each set of lines once SS; DS between 3-line groups.

▼ Space once after a period following an abbreviation.

spacing: space *immediately* after each word

20 ad la as in if it lo no of oh he or so ok pi be we
21 an ace ads ale aha a fit oil a jak nor a bit a pew
22 ice ades born is fake to jail than it and the cows

spacing/shifting   ▼   ▼

23 Ask Jed. Dr. Han left at ten; Dr. Crowe, at nine.
24 I asked Jin if she had ice in a bowl; it can help.
25 Freda, not Jack, went to Spain. Joan likes Spain.

7e Timed Writings in the Open Screen

STANDARD PLAN for using the Open Screen Timer

You can check your speed in the Open Screen using the Timer. ⏱

1. In the Open Screen, click the **Timer** button on the toolbar.
   In the Timer dialog box, check **Count-Down Timer** and time; click **OK**.
2. The Timer begins once you start to key and stops automatically. Do not strike ENTER at the end of a line. Wordwrap will cause the text to flow to the next line automatically.
3. To save the timing, click the **File** menu and **Save as**. Use your initals (*xx*), the exercise number, and number of the timing as the filename. Example: **xx-7f-t1** (your initials, exercise 7f, timing1).
4. Click the **Timer** button again to start a new timing.
5. Each new timing must be saved with its own name.

7f Speed Check

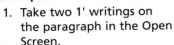

1. Take two 1' writings on the paragraph in the Open Screen.
2. Follow the directions in 7e. Do not strike ENTER at the ends of the lines.

Goal: 12 *wam*.

```
          .        4         .         8          .
It is hard to fake a confident spirit.  We will do
       12          .        16         .
better work if we approach and finish a job and
20        .        24         .        28          .
know that we will do the best work we can and then
        32
not fret.
| 1  | 2  | 3  | 4  | 5  | 6  | 7  | 8  | 9  | 10 |
```

7g Guided Writing

1. In the Open Screen, key each line once for fluency. Do not save your work.
2. Set the Timer in the Open Screen for 30". Take two 30" writings on each line. Do not save the timings.

Goal: to reach the end of the line before time is up.

gwam

26 Dan took her to the show.   12
27 Jan lent the bowl to the pros.   14
28 Hold the wrists low for this drill.   16
29 Jessie fit the black panel to the shelf.   18
30 Jake held a bit of cocoa and an apricot for Diane.   20
31 Dick and I fish for cod on the docks at Fish Lake.   20
32 Kent still held the dish and the cork in his hand.   20
   | 1 | 2 | 3 | 4 | 5 | 6 | 7 | 8 | 9 | 10 |

Document 4
Mail Merge

1. Insert the **letterhead** file and use mail merge to create a letter to each member of the board of directors. Sign the letter from you, Administrative Assistant. Supply necessary letter parts.

2. Print the main document and the merged letters. Save the merged letters as **117-119-d4**.

Members of the Board of Directors:

Natalie Bass, Airline Consultant, RTA and Associates, 3829 Quincy Ave., Denver, CO 80237-2756

Herman Davis, Chief Financial Officer, Financial Securities, Inc., 3979 El Mundo, Houston, TX 64506-2877

Betsy Burge, President, Associated Travel Services, 3958 Highland Dr., Sterling, CO 80751-1211

Joseph Perkins, Senior Vice President, River Industries, 7463 St. Andrews, Dallas, TX 75205-2746

Kimberly Hess, Professor, Business Administration, Central University, 3744 Main St., Oakdale, LA 71463-5811

Body of Letter:

A copy of the Pommery Air Service Business Plan is enclosed. Please review the plan carefully and be ready to vote on final approval at the board meeting next Friday. Note that this item appears on the agenda sent to you last week.

If you have any questions prior to the meeting, please call me. All of the changes recommended by the board at the last meeting have been implemented in the plan.

Document 5
Newsletter

1. In a new document, change the top and side margins to .6".

2. Insert the **logo** file, as shown on the next page. Use *WordArt* to key the banner heading. Insert the same graphic line that appears in the letterhead. Increase the width of the graphic line so that it stretches across the page.

3. Insert a continuous section break.

4. Use a three-column format with a line between columns for the newsletter. Set the width of the columns as follows: Column 1, **1.5"**; Columns 2 and 3, **2.4"**.

5. Key **Pommery Air Service, Inc.** in 12-point and bold. Key the remainder of the text in Column 1 in 10-point.

6. Key the text in Columns 2 and 3 in 11-point font; set the spacing to 6 points after paragraphs. Apply Heading 2 style to the headings. Use justify alignment.

7. Make adjustments to the banner heading, if needed to make the newsletter attractive; it should fit on one page.

8. Save as **117-119-d5**. Print.

LESSON 8

G, Question Mark, X, U

WARMUP

8a

Key each line twice. Keep eyes on copy.

all 1 Dick will see Job at nine if Rach sees Pat at one.
w/b 2 As the wind blew, Bob Webber saw the window break.
p/, 3 Pat, Pippa, or Cap has prepared the proper papers.
all 4 Bo, Jose, and Will fed Lin; Jack had not paid her.

NEW KEYS

8b **g** and **?**

Key each line once; repeat.

> **Question mark:** The question mark is usually followed by two spaces.

g Reach to *right* with *left first* finger.

? Left SHIFT; reach *down* with *right fourth* finger.

g

5 g g gf gaff gag grog fog frog drag cog dig fig gig
6 gf go gall flag gels slag gala gale glad glee gals
7 golf flog gorge glen high logs gore ogle page grow

?

8 ? ?; ?; ? ? Who? When? Where? Who is? Who was?
9 Who is here? Was it he? Was it she? Did she go?
10 Did Geena? Did he? What is that? Was Jose here?

all reaches learned

11 Has Ginger lost her job? Was her April bill here?
12 Phil did not want the boats to get here this soon.
13 Loris Shin has been ill; Frank, a doctor, saw her.

8c Textbook Keying

Key each line once; DS between groups.

reach review
14 ws ws hj hj tf tf ol ol rf rf ed ed cd cd bf bf p;
15 wed bid has old hold rid heed heed car bed pot pot

g
16 gf gf gin gin rig ring go gone no nog sign got dog
17 to go|to go|go on|go in|go in|to go in|in the sign

TECHNIQUE TIP
Concentrate on correct reaches.

?
18 ?; ?;? who? when? where? how? what? who? It is I?
19 Is she? Is he? Did I lose Jo? Is Gal all right?

Document 1
Create Logo

1. Use the Oval shape from the Drawing toolbar to draw an oval approximately 2" wide.

2. Fill the oval with Gold color.

3. Insert a clip art of an airplane. Size the airplane to look approximately like the illustration below.

4. Use the text box or the rectangle to key the box containing *Pommery Air*. Make the box black and the lettering white. Increase the size of the *P* and *A* to 20 point, bold.

5. Group the three items (hold down the CTRL key as you click each item; then select **Group** from the Draw menu).

6. Change the layout of the drawing canvas so that it is in back of the text. Do this by clicking the canvas border to select it; then click the **Format** menu and select **Drawing Canvas**. Click the **Layout** tab and select **Behind text**. Save as **logo** and print.

Document 2
Create Letterhead

1. In a new document, change the side margins to 1" and the top margin to .5".

2. Insert the file **logo** (**Insert, File, Logo, Insert**).

3. Key the letterhead as shown below; use 11-point font and italics.

4. Insert a graphic line below the logo. Change the width of the line to 6.5" so that it stretches across the entire letterhead. (Select the line; click **Format, Horizontal Line, Width** 6.5".)

5. Save as **letterhead** and print.

P.O. Box 8473, Hopkins, SC 29061-8473
(803) 555-0123   fax   (803) 555-0124
www.pommeryair.com

Document 3
Create Fax Cover Sheet

1. Open the Business Fax template. (In *Word 2003*, click **File** and then **New**, and then click **On my computer** in the Task Pane. Next, click the **Letters and Faxes** tab.)

2. Delete the picture of the facsimile machine (select the picture and press DELETE). Insert the Pommery logo in its place (**Insert, File, Logo, Insert**).

3. If a text box displays asking for the company name and address, delete it. Add the company address and phone number in the box.

4. Key the word **FACSIMILE** in a large bold print in the box. Arrange the logo, address, telephone number, and the word *FACSIMILE* attractively in the box.

5. Key the fax number in the From box at the right.

6. Save as **pommery business fax** and print.

8d

x and u

Key each line once; repeat.

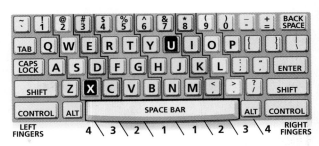

x Reach *down* with *left third* finger.

u Reach *up* with right first finger.

x

20 x x xs xs ox ox lox sox fox box ex hex lax hex fax
21 sx six sax sox ax fix cox wax hex box pox sex text
22 flax next flex axel pixel exit oxen taxi axis next

u

23 u uj uj jug jut just dust dud due sue use due duel
24 uj us cud but bun out sun nut gun hut hue put fuel
25 dual laud dusk suds fuss full tuna tutus duds full

all reaches learned

26 Paige Power liked the book; Josh can read it next.
27 Next we picked a bag for Jan; then she, Jan, left.
28 Is her June account due? Has Lou ruined her unit?

SKILLBUILDING

8e Reinforcement

Optional: In the Open Screen, key each line once; DS between groups. Repeat. Print.

29 nut cue hut sun rug us six cut dug axe rag fox run
30 out of the sun|cut the action|a fox den|fun at six
31 That car is not junk; it can run in the next race.

32 etc. tax nick cure lack flex walls uncle clad hurt
33 lack the cash|not just luck|next in line|just once
34 June Dunn can send that next tax case to Rex Knox.

8f Speed Check

In the Open Screen, take a 1' writing on each paragraph. Press ENTER only after you have keyed the entire paragraph. Save the timings as **xx8f-t1** and **xx8f-t2**, with *xx* being your **initials**.
Goal: 14 *wam*.

```
                 •         4         •         8
How a finished job will look often depends on how
          12          •        16         •        20
we feel about our work as we do it.  Attitude has
          •          24        •        28
a definite effect on the end result of work we do.
Press ENTER once
                 •         4         •         8
When we are eager to begin a job, we relax and do
          12          •        16         •        20
better work than if we start the job with an idea
          •          24        •        28
that there is just nothing we can do to escape it.
```

Pommery Air Service, Inc.

• Integrate formatting and word processing skills.

LESSONS 117–119 | Business Plan

117–119a
Timed Writing
Take one 3' and one 5' writing.

  all letters

	gwam	3'	5'

An effective job search requires very careful planning and a   3 | 2 | 42
lot of hard work. Major decisions must be made about the type of   8 | 5 | 45
job, the size and the type of business, and the geographic area.   13 | 8 | 48
Once all of these basic decisions have been made, then the com-   17 | 10 | 50
plex task of locating the ideal job can begin. Some jobs are   21 | 13 | 53
listed in what is known as the open job market. These positions   25 | 15 | 55
are listed with placement offices of schools, placement agencies,   30 | 18 | 58
and they are advertised in newspapers or journals.   33 | 20 | 60

The open market is not the only source of jobs, however.   37 | 22 | 62
Some experts believe that almost two-thirds of all jobs are in   41 | 25 | 65
what is sometimes called the hidden job market. Networking is   46 | 27 | 67
the primary way to learn about jobs in the hidden job market.   50 | 30 | 70
Employees of a company, instructors, and members of professional   54 | 32 | 72
associations are some of the best contacts to tap the hidden job   58 | 35 | 75
market. Much time and effort are required to tap these sources.   63 | 38 | 77
But the hidden market often produces the best results.   66 | 40 | 80

```
3' |    1    |    2    |    3    |    4    |
5' |      1      |      2      |      3      |
```

LESSON 9

Q, M, V, Apostrophe

WARMUP

9a
Key each line twice.

all letters	1	Lex gripes about cold weather; Fred is not joking.
space bar	2	Is it Di, Jo, or Al? Ask Lt. Coe, Bill; he knows.
easy	3	I did rush a bushel of cut corn to the sick ducks.
easy	4	He is to go to the Tudor Isle of England on a bus.

NEW KEYS

9b q and m
Key each line once; repeat.

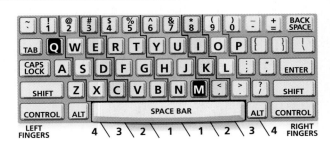

q Reach *up* with *left fourth* finger.

m Reach *down* with *right first* finger.

q

5 q qa qa quad quad quaff quant queen quo quit quick
6 qa qu qa quo quit quod quid quip quads quote quiet
7 quite quilts quart quill quakes quail quack quaint

m

8 m mj mj jam man malt mar max maw me mew men hem me
9 m mj ma am make male mane melt meat mist amen lame
10 malt meld hemp mimic tomb foam rams mama mire mind

all reaches learned

11 Quin had some quiet qualms about taming a macaque.
12 Jake Coxe had questions about a new floor program.
13 Max was quick to join the big reception for Lidia.

9c Textbook Keying
Key each line once for control. DS between groups of two lines.

m/x 14 me men ma am jam am lax, mix jam; the hem, six men
15 Emma Max expressed an aim to make a mammoth model.

q/u 16 qa qu aqua aqua quit quit quip quite pro quo squad
17 Did Quin make a quick request to take the Qu exam?

g/n 18 fg gn gun gun dig dig nag snag snag sign grab grab
19 Georgia hung a sign in front of the union for Gib.

Module 18: Checkpoint

Answer the questions below to see if you have mastered the content of this module.

1. Legal documents prepared for court are keyed on _____.
2. Legal documents contain a double ruling in the _____ margin and a single ruling in the _____ margin.
3. A(n) _____ form is completed by the person delivering the papers.
4. _____ contain information regarding the name, address, and purpose of the company, as well as the share structure.
5. Medical offices keep recorded notes of the patient's office visit called _____.
6. Patients sign a(n) _____, which allows a physician or medical facility to release information in their medical records.
7. A(n) _____ is a summary of your qualifications that is presented to potential employers.
8. A list of names, addresses, and telephone numbers of people who are willing to comment on you are called _____.
9. A letter indicating the job you are seeking, stating your key qualifications, and requesting an interview is called the _____ _____.
10. A(n) _____ letter should be sent to companies that have not responded to a resume that was mailed one month before.

Performance Assessment

Document 1
Create Lease Form

Document 2
Fill in Lease Form

1. Key the heading on line 2", DS. Insert form fields as indicated. Protect the form, and save it as **Checkpoint18-d1** and print.
2. Fill in the form with the following information: (1) **Molnar Inc.**; (2) **June 26, 200-**; (3) **4 Griffin Dr.**; (4) **Harbor City**; (5) **Wayne**; (6) **Michigan**; (7) **5**; (8) **July 1, 200-**; (9) **June 30, 200-**; (10) **11:59 p.m.**; (11) **60,000.00**; (12) **1,000.00**; (13) **July 1, 200-**; (14) **first**.
3. Save it as **Checkpoint18-d2** and print.

LEASE AGREEMENT BETWEEN
HUTTON PROPERTY MANAGEMENT, LESSEE
AND
(ff1), LESSOR

This lease agreement was entered into on (**ff2—date**), between Hutton Property Management, lessee, and (**ff1**), lessor.

Lessor leases to lessee the premises located at (**ff3—address**), (**ff4—city**), (**ff5—county**) County, (**ff6—state**).

The term of this lease agreement is (**ff7—number**) years, beginning on (**ff8—date**), and terminating on (**ff9—date**), at (**ff10—time**). The total rent under this lease agreement is $(**ff11—amount**). Lessee shall pay lessor the above-specified amount in installments of $(**ff12—amount**) each month, beginning on (**ff13—date**), with succeeding payments due on the (**ff14**) day of each subsequent month during the term of the lease agreement.

_____   _____
Lessor   Lessee

9d

V and **'** (apostrophe)

Key each line once; repeat.

Apostrophe: The apostrophe shows (1) omission (as Rob't for Robert or it's for it is) or (2) possession when used with nouns (as Joe's hat).

v Reach *down* with *left first* finger.

' Reach to ' with *right fourth* finger.

v

20 v vf vf vie vie via via vim vat vow vile vale vote
21 vf vf ave vet ova eve vie dive five live have lave
22 cove dove over aver vivas hive volt five java jive

' (apostrophe)

23 '; '; it's it's Rod's; it's Bo's hat; we'll do it.
24 We don't know if it's Lee's pen or Norma's pencil.
25 It's ten o'clock; I won't tell him that he's late.

all reaches learned

26 It's Viv's turn to drive Iva's van to Ava's house.
27 Qua, not Vi, took the jet; so did Cal. Didn't he?
28 Wasn't Fae Baxter a judge at the post garden show?

SKILLBUILDING

9e Reinforcement

1. Follow the standard Open Screen directions on page 8.
2. Key each line twice; DS between groups. Strive to increase speed.

v/?
29 Viola said she has moved six times in five months.
30 Does Dave live on Vine Street? Must he leave now?

q/?
31 Did Viv vote? Can Paque move it? Could Val dive?
32 Didn't Raquel quit Carl Quent after their quarrel?

direct reach
33 Fred told Brice that the junior class must depart.
34 June and Hunt decided to go to that great musical.

double letter
35 Harriette will cook dinner for the swimming teams.
36 Bill's committee meets in an accounting classroom.

9f Speed Check

In the Open Screen, take two 1' writings on the paragraph. Press ENTER only after keying the entire paragraph. Save the timings as **xx-9f-t1** and **xx-9f-t2**, substituting your initials for *xx*.

```
            .           4           .           8           .
We must be able to express our thoughts with ease
            12          .           16          .           20
if we desire to find success in the business world.
            .           24          .           28
It is there that sound ideas earn cash.
```

116c-d1
Pleading Form with Table List of Trial Exhibits

1. Activate the **Superior Court** Pleading Wizard. Click **Finish** to close the Wizard, and then fill in the following List of Trial Exhibits. Use the table feature; remove borders and underline column heads.

2. Save as **116c-d1** and print.

LEE & DURAND, LLP
ATTORNEYS AT LAW
James W. Lee, Esq.
State Bar Number 202256
8578 Main St., Suite 202
Huntington Beach, CA 92646-1801
Telephone: (714) 555-0174
Attorneys for Plaintiffs

Donald Hurt, et al., Plaintiffs   vs.   Susan Reckless, et al., Defendants.
Case No. 01 CC05144   PLAINTIFFS' LIST OF TRIAL EXHIBITS

Exhibit Number	Description	Date Identified	Date Admitted
1	City of Costa Mesa Police Department Accident Report dated February 15, 200-		

Dated this 19th day of June, 200-

By _____
    JAMES W. LEE
    Attorneys for Plaintiffs

116c-d2
SOAP Note

1. Open **Soap Note Form** and save it as **116c-d2**.

2. Fill in the form with the following information: **Lucas, Steve**; **# 22653**; age **42**; allergies: **None known**; Meds: **Nexium**; T: **99.0**; P: **80**; R: **15**; B/P: **118/76**; C/O: **Pain left elbow**; Date: **4-10-xx**.

S	Pt injured left elbow two days ago in fall from rollerblades. Complains of pain on outside of elbow, superficial.
O	No inflammation; slight hematoma; limited ROM on left elbow FLEXION.
A	Treatment: lateral epicondyle 15 minute hot pack every day for a week and help with passive ROM. Ask pt to apply a hot pack at home once a day. Diagnosis: Lateral epicondylitis on left.
P	Pt will return twice a week to reduce pain and increase ROM.

LESSON 10

Z, Y, Quotation Mark, Tab

WARMUP

10a
Key each line twice.

all letters	1	Quill owed those back taxes after moving to Japan.
spacing	2	Didn't Vi, Sue, and Paul go? Someone did; I know.
q/v/m	3	Marv was quite quick to remove that mauve lacquer.
easy	4	Lana is a neighbor; she owns a lake and an island.

NEW KEYS

10b z and y
Key each line once; repeat.

z Reach *down* with *left fourth* finger.

y Reach *up* with *right first* finger.

z

5 za za zap zap zing zig zag zoo zed zip zap zig zed
6 doze zeal zero haze jazz zone zinc zing size ozone
7 ooze maze doze zoom zarf zebus daze gaze faze adze

y

8 y yj yj jay jay hay hay lay nay say days eyes ayes
9 yj ye yet yen yes cry dry you rye sty your fry wry
10 ye yen bye yea coy yew dye yaw lye yap yak yon any

all reaches learned

11 Did you say Liz saw any yaks or zebus at your zoo?
12 Relax; Jake wouldn't acquire any favorable rights.
13 Has Mazie departed? Tex, Lu, and I will go alone.

10c Textbook Keying
Key each line once. DS between groups.

	14	Cecilia brings my jumbo umbrella to every concert.
direct reach	15	John and Kim recently brought us an old art piece.
	16	I built a gray brick border around my herb garden.

DS

	17	sa ui hj gf mn vc ew uy re io as lk rt jk df op yu
adjacent reach	18	In Ms. Lopez' opinion, the opera was really great.
	19	Polly and I were joining Walker at the open house.

LESSON 116 Assessment

SKILLBUILDING

116a
Warmup
Key each line twice SS.

alphabet 1 Di quickly won several junior prizes at the Foxburgh swim trials.
figures 2 From July 13 to 20, the extension numbers will be 45, 67, and 89.
shift/lock 3 Ms. Ing keyed the notations REGISTERED and CERTIFIED in ALL CAPS.
easy 4 Did he visit a city to handle the authentic enamel dish and bowl?

| 1 | 2 | 3 | 4 | 5 | 6 | 7 | 8 | 9 | 10 | 11 | 12 | 13 |

116b
Timed Writing
Key one 3' and one 5' writing.

	gwam	3'	5'

Individuals who conduct interviews often make snap judgments. In fact, the decision to hire or not to hire an applicant is usually made in the first five minutes of the interview. The rest of the time is used to verify that the decision made was the correct one. The wisdom of making a decision so early should be questioned. When a quickly made decision is analyzed, generally the result is that the decision is influenced heavily by the first impression the person makes.

4	2	41
8	5	43
12	7	46
17	10	49
21	13	51
25	15	54
30	18	56
32	10	58

You can learn to make a good first impression in an interview; all you have to do is be on time, dress appropriately, shake hands firmly, establish eye contact, relax, smile, and show that you have excellent communication skills. Doing all of this may seem very difficult, but it really is not. Making a good impression requires careful planning and many hours of practice. Practice gives you the confidence you need to be able to do the things that make an excellent impression.

36	21	60
40	24	62
44	26	65
48	29	68
53	32	70
57	34	73
61	37	75
64	38	77

3' | 1 | 2 | 3 | 4 |
5' | 1 | 2 | 3 |

APPLICATIONS

116c
Assessment

On the signal to begin, key the documents in sequence. Check spelling after keying each document. Preview before printing. When time has been called, proofread all documents again; identify errors.

10d

" **(quotation mark) and**
TAB

Key each line once; repeat.

" Shift; then reach to **"** with *right fourth* finger.

TAB Reach up with *left fourth* finger.

" (quotation mark)

20 "; "; " " "lingo" "bugs" "tennies"   I   like "malts."
21 "I am not," she said, "going."   I just said, "Oh?"

tab key

22   The tab key is used for indenting paragraphs
    and aligning columns.
23   Tabs that are set by the software are called
    default tabs, which are usually a half inch.

all reaches learned

24   The expression "I give you my word," or put another
25 way, "Take my word for it," is just a way I can say, "I
26 prize my name; it clearly stands in back of my words."
27 I offer "honor" as collateral.

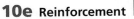

SKILLBUILDING

tab 28   Strike the tab key and begin the line without a pause
    to maintain fluency.
29   She said that this is the lot to be sent; I
    agreed with her.
30   Strike Tab before starting to key a timed
    writing so that the first line is indented.

gwam 1'

Tab → All of us work for progress, but it is not   8
always easy to analyze "progress."   We work hard   18
for it; but, in spite of some really good efforts,   28
we may fail to receive just exactly the response we   39
want.   40

Tab → When this happens, as it does to all of us,   9
it is time to cease whatever we are doing, have   18
a quiet talk with ourselves, and face up to the   28
questions about our limited progress.   How can we   38
do better?   40

| 1 | 2 | 3 | 4 | 5 | 6 | 7 | 8 | 9 | 10 |

10e Reinforcement

Follow the standard directions on page 8 for keying in the Open Screen. Key each line twice; DS between groups.

10f Speed Check

Take two 1' writings of paragraph 2 in the Open Screen, using wordwrap. Save as **xx-10f-t1** and **xx-10f-t2**.

Goal: 15 *wam*

TECHNIQUE TIP

Wordwrap: Text within a paragraph moves automatically to the next line. Press ENTER only to begin a new paragraph.

Follow-Up Letters

Successful job hunters understand the importance of writing winning resumes and application letters and the value of writing follow-up letters. Key these letters on quality paper, use an acceptable letter style, and proofread to ensure an error-free document. Applicants may also write any or all of the following letters:

- Follow-up letter to companies that have not responded to the resume (mailed two weeks to one month later).
- Thank-you letter after the interview (mailed the day of or the day after the interview).
- Thank-you letter to references.
- Job acceptance or job refusal letters.

APPLICATIONS

114–115b-d1
Application Letter

1. Open **fisher-lthd** from the data files. Save it as **114-115b-d1**.
2. Position the insertion point at the end of the document. Key Scott's application letter, which is shown on p. 444, block style with open punctuation. Remove the hyperlink within the letter (right-click and select **Remove Hyperlink**). Do not key any sentences in bold. Save and print.

114–115b-d2
Thank-You Letter
1. Use the **fisher-lthd** file to create the letter.
2. Save and print.

Thank you for taking time to talk with me about the position as a junior graphic designer at *Financial News*.

I appreciated the comprehensive tour and the information you provided about the Graphic Design Department. This group of professionals is very fortunate to be equipped with the most up-to-date hardware and software and an outstanding staff development program. Consequently, your subscribers are the real winners.

Mr. Stanberry, I would like the opportunity to work at *Financial News* and to contribute to the popularity and success of this outstanding newspaper. I am eager to receive a call from you.

Sincerely | Scott T. Fisher

114–115b-d3
Reference Letter
1. Use the **fisher-lthd** file to create the letter to Dr. Michael Jenkins.
2. Save and print.

Dr. Michael Jenkins, Academic Advisor | College of Arts and Communication | Cother University | Mobile, AL 36617-1001

Thank you for writing the letter of recommendation for my application to *Financial News*. Mr. Stanberry called today and offered me the position as a junior graphic designer.

I appreciate very much the time that was devoted to writing such a detailed letter listing my accomplishments. Thank you for encouraging me to compete in the National Collegiate Graphic Design Association contest. That early involvement in the profession and my success were edges in my selection.

Dr. Jenkins, I look forward to sharing with you my first experiences as a graphic designer. Sincerely | Scott T. Fisher

LESSON 11 | Review

WARMUP

11a
Key each line twice SS
(slowly, then faster).

alphabet 1 Zeb had Jewel quickly give him five or six points.
" (quote) 2 Can you spell "chaos," "bias," "bye," and "their"?
y 3 Ty Clay may envy you for any zany plays you write.
easy 4 Did he bid on the bicycle, or did he bid on a map?
| 1 | 2 | 3 | 4 | 5 | 6 | 7 | 8 | 9 | 10 |

SKILLBUILDING

11b Keyboard Reinforcement
Key each line once; repeat the drill to increase fluency.

5 za za zap az az maze zoo zip razz zed zax zoa zone
6 Liz Zahl saw Zoe feed the zebra in an Arizona zoo.

7 yj yj jy jy joy lay yaw say yes any yet my try you
8 Why do you say that today, Thursday, is my payday?

9 xs xs sax ox box fix hex ax lax fox taxi lox sixes
10 Roxy, you may ask Jay to fix any tax sets for you.

11 qa qa aqua quail quit quake quid equal quiet quart
12 Did Enrique quietly but quickly quell the quarrel?

13 fv fv five lives vow ova van eve avid vex vim void
14 Has Vivi, Vada, or Eva visited Vista Valley Farms?

TECHNIQUE TIP
Work for smoothness, not for speed.

11c Speed Builders
Key each balanced-hand line twice, as quickly as you can.

15 is to for do an may work so it but an with them am
16 am yam map aid zig yams ivy via vie quay cob amend

17 to do is for an may work so it but am an with them
18 for it|for it|to the|to the|do they|do they|do it

19 Pamela may go to the farm with Jan and a neighbor.
20 Rod and Ty may go by the lake if they go downtown.
| 1 | 2 | 3 | 4 | 5 | 6 | 7 | 8 | 9 | 10 |

DOCUMENT DESIGN

114–115a
Application Letters

The purpose of an application letter is to obtain an interview. Application letters vary, depending on how you learned of the position. You want to show that your skills match the position requirements. A good strategy for writing an application letter is to: 1) establish a point of contact if possible, 2) specify the job you are seeking, 3) convey your key qualifications, 4) interpret your major qualifications in terms of employer benefits, and 5) request an interview.

Plain paper or personal stationery—never an employer's letterhead—may be used for an application letter. Your application letter must include your return address. You can create your own letterhead or use the personal business letter format that places your address immediately above the date. Block or modified block format may be used.

Scott T. Fisher

1001 Hogan St., Apt. 216A ● Mobile, AL 36617-1001 ● (251) 555-0103 ● sfisher@cu.edu

Current date

Establish a point of contact if possible

Mr. Coleman Stanberry
Financial News
706 Kentwood St.
Honolulu, HI 96822-6218

Dear Mr. Stanberry

State the job you are applying for

My bachelor's degree with double majors in graphic design and information technology and my graphic design work experience in the United States and Japan qualify me as a **junior graphic designer for your international newspaper**.

Convey key qualifications

As a result of my comprehensive four-year program, I am skilled in the latest Office suite as well as the current versions of desktop publishing and graphics programs. In addition, my **excellent research and writing skills** played a very important role in the Cother University Design Award I received last month. **Being able to locate the right resources and synthesize that data into useful information for your readers** is a priority I have practiced in my positions at the Cother University College Alumni Office and the Cother University Library.

State how the employer will benefit from your qualifications

My technical and communication skills were applied as well as I worked as the assistant director and producer of the *Cother University Alumni News*. **I understand well the importance of meeting deadlines and also producing a quality product that will increase newspaper sales**. Additionally, my intern experience in Japan provides me with a global view of international business and communication.

Request an interview

After you have reviewed the enclosed resume as well as my graphic design samples located on my Web page at http://www.netdoor.com/~sfisher, **I would look forward to discussing my qualifications and career opportunities with you** at *Financial News*.

Sincerely

Scott T. Fisher

Enclosure

DOCUMENT DESIGN DOCUMENT DESIGN DOCUMENT DESIGN

11d Technique Builder

Key each line once; DS between groups.

 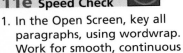
enter: key smoothly without looking at fingers

21 Make the return snappily
22 and with assurance; keep
23 your eyes on your source
24 data; maintain a smooth,
25 constant pace as you key.

space bar: use down-and-in motion

26 us me it of he an by do go to us if or so am ah el
27 Have you a pen? If so, print "Free to any guest."

caps lock: press to toggle it on or off

28 Use ALL CAPS for items such as TO: FROM: SUBJECT.
29 Did Kristin mean Kansas City, MISSOURI, or KANSAS?

11e Speed Check

1. In the Open Screen, key all paragraphs, using wordwrap. Work for smooth, continuous stroking, not speed.
2. Save as **xx-11e**. Substitute your initals for *xx*.
3. Take a 2' writing on all paragraphs.

Goal: 16 *gwam*

To determine gross-words-a-minute (*gwam*) rate for 2':

Follow these steps if you are *not* using the Timer in the Open Screen.

1. Note the figure at the end of the last line completed.

2. For a partial line, note the figure on the scale direcly below the point at which you stopped keying.

3. Add these two figures to determine the total gross words a minute (*gwam*) you keyed.

		gwam	2'
Have we thought of communication as a kind		4	31
of war that we wage through each day?		8	35
When we think of it that way, good language		12	39
would seem to become our major line of attack.		17	44
Words become muscle; in a normal exchange or in		22	49
a quarrel, we do well to realize the power of words.		27	54

11f Enrichment

1. Go to the Skillbuilding Workshop 1, Drill 1, page 31. Choose 6 letters that cause you difficulty. Key each line twice. Put a check mark beside the lines in the book so that you know you have practiced them.

2. Save the drill as **xx-11f**. Substitute your initials for *xx*.

SCOTT T. FISHER

Temporary Address (May 30, 200-)
1001 Hogan St., Apt. 216A
Mobile, AL 36617-1001
(251) 555-0103
E-mail: sfisher@cu.edu

Permanent Address
583 Post Oak Rd.
Savannah, GA 31418-0583
(912) 555-0171
Web page: http://www.netdoor.com/~sfisher

CAREER OBJECTIVE

To obtain a graphic position with an opportunity to advance to a management position.

SUMMARY OF ACHIEVEMENTS

Bachelor's degree with double major in graphic design and information technology; certified in major software applications and one programming language. Related work experience in two organizations.

EDUCATION

B.S. Graphic Design and Information Technology (double major), Cother University, Mobile, Alabama. May 200-. GPA: 8.8/4.0.

3.5" tab

SPECIAL SKILLS

Environments: Microsoft Windows and Macintosh
Software: Microsoft Office 2003, QuarkXpress, PhotoShop, Freehand, Dreamweaver
Certifications: C++ and MOS (Microsoft Office 2003 Suite)
Languages: Java, JavaScript, Visual Basic Script, C++
Keyboarding skills: 70 words per minute

EXPERIENCE

Cother University Alumni Office, Mobile, Alabama. Assistant editor and producer of the *Cother University Alumni News*, 2002 to present.
• Designed layout and production of six editions; met every publishing deadline.
• Received the "Cother University Design Award."
• Assisted editor in design of Alumni Office Web page (http://www.cu.edu/alumni/).

HONORS AND ACTIVITIES

Dean's Scholar (3.5 GPA or higher); President, Cother University Graphic Design Association; Recipient of "Cother University Leadership Award."

REFERENCES

Available upon request

LESSON 12   Review

WARMUP

12a
Key each line twice SS (slowly, then faster).

alphabet 1 Jack won five quiz games; Brad will play him next.
q 2 Quin Racq quickly and quietly quelled the quarrel.
z 3 Zaret zipped along sizzling, zigzag Arizona roads.
easy 4 Did he hang the sign by the big bush at the lake?
| 1 | 2 | 3 | 4 | 5 | 6 | 7 | 8 | 9 | 10 |

SKILLBUILDING

12b New Key Review
Key each line once; DS between groups; work for smoothness, not for speed.

b/f 5 bf bf fab fab ball bib rf rf rib rib fibs bums bee
6 Did Buffy remember that he is a brass band member?

z/y 7 za za zag zig zip yj yj jay eye day lazy hazy zest
8 Liz amazed us with the zesty pizza on a lazy trip.

q/u 9 qa qa quo qt. quit quay quad quarm que uj jug quay
10 Where is Quito? Qatar? Boqueirao? Quebec? Quilmes?

v/m 11 vf vf valve five value mj mj ham mad mull mass vim
12 Vito, enter the words vim, vivace, and avar; save.

all 13 I faced defeat; only reserves saved my best crews.
14 In my opinion, I need to rest in my reserved seat.

all 15 Holly created a red poppy and deserves art awards.
16 My pump averages a faster rate; we get better oil.

12c Textbook Keying
Key each line once; DS between groups. Work for smooth, unhurried keying.

de/ed 17 ed fed led deed dell dead deal sled desk need seed
18 Dell dealt with the deed before the dire deadline.

ol/lo 19 old tolls doll solo look sole lost love cold stole
20 Old Ole looked for the long lost olive oil lotion.

op/po 21 pop top post rope pout port stop opal opera report
22 Stop to read the top opera opinion report to Opal.

TECHNIQUE TIP
Keep fingers curved and body aligned properly.

we/ew 23 we few wet were went wears weather skews stew blew
24 Working women wear sweaters when weather dictates.

COMMUNICATION

113a
Creating Resumes

A **resume** is a summary of your qualifications; it is the primary basis for the interviewer's decision to invite you for an interview. Prior to preparing a resume, complete a self-analysis, identifying your career goals and job qualifications. Most resumes contain some or all of the following:

- **Identifying information:** Your name, telephone number, address, e-mail address, and Internet address. Students may need to list both a temporary and a permanent address.
- **Career objective:** The type of position you are seeking. Let the employer know you have a specific career goal.
- **Summary of achievements:** Summary of your most important achievements, strengths, or unique skills.
- **Education:** Diplomas or degrees earned, schools attended, and dates. Include majors and grade-point averages when it is to your advantage to do so.
- **Experience:** Job titles, employers, dates of employment, a brief description of the positions, and major achievements. Emphasize achievements rather than activities. Use active voice and concrete language; for example, *Handle an average of 200 customer orders a week*. List information in the same order for each position.
- **Honors and activities:** Specific examples of leadership potential and commitment.
- **References:** Generally do not include references on your resume. On a separate sheet of paper, list the names, addresses, and telephone numbers of several people who are willing to provide a reference for you. Use former employers, school advisors, former instructors, or a friend who is working in the field. Obtain their permission before you list them. Take the list with you to an interview.

Items within the sections of the resume are arranged in reverse chronological order (most recent experiences listed first). Which section is presented first? From your self-analysis, you will determine which one of your qualifications is the strongest. If work experience is stronger than education, present work experience first. A recent college graduate would present education first.

A major consideration in preparing an effective resume is the overall attractiveness of the resume. Use high-quality paper and print it on a laser printer using effective layout design that will allow your resume to appear professionally created.

Applicants may also submit resumes electronically by posting to corporate Web pages, personal Web pages, or job banks on the Internet. Saving the document as a Web page allows you to view your resume as it will appear in a Web browser.

APPLICATIONS

113b-d1
Resume

1. In a new document, change the side margins to 1" and key the resume on the following page.
2. Select Arial for the Identification section and the headings. Select Times New Roman for the body. Use 11-point font so that it will fit on one page.
3. Format the body as a 2-column table. Set a second tab in Column 2 for about 3.5".
4. Save as **resume**. Save it again as a Web page. View the resume using your browser.
5. Open the *Word* document **resume**. Remove the hyperlinks to the e-mail and Web page addresses since you will print this resume (right-click and select **Remove Hyperlink**). Save again and print.

113b-d2
Resume

Look for an ad or job description for a position for which you would qualify; then use the guidelines above to write a resume for the position. Save it as **113b-d2**.

12d Speed Builder

1. Key each line quickly to build stroking speed.
2. Save as **xx-L12**. (Substitute your initials for *xx*.)

TECHNIQUE TIP

Keep hands quiet; keep fingers curved and upright.

25 a for we you is that be this will be a to and well
26 as our with I or a to by your form which all would
27 new year no order they so new but now year who may

28 This is Lyn's only date to visit their great city.
29 I can send it to your office at any time you wish.
30 She kept the fox, owls, and fowl down by the lake.

31 Harriette will cook dinner for the swimming teams.
32 Annette will call at noon to give us her comments.
33 Johnny was good at running and passing a football.

| 1 | 2 | 3 | 4 | 5 | 6 | 7 | 8 | 9 | 10 |

12e Speed Check

1. In the Open Screen, key both paragraphs using wordwrap. Work for smooth, continuous stroking, not speed.
2. Save as **xx-12e**. Substitute your initials for *xx*.
3. Take a 1' writing on paragraph 1. Save as **xx-12e-t1**.
4. Repeat step 3 using paragraph 2. Save as **xx-12e-t2**.
5. Set the Timer for 2'. Take a 2' writing on both paragraphs. Save as **xx-12e-t3**.

 all letters

Goal: 16 *wam*

Copy Difficulty

What factors determine whether copy is difficult or easy? Research shows that difficulty is influenced by syllables per word, characters per word, and percent of familiar words. Carefully controlling these three factors ensures that speed and accuracy scores are reliable—that is, increased scores reflect increased skill.

In Level 1, all timings are easy. Note "E" inside the triangle at left of the timing. Easy timings contain an average of 1.2 syllables per word, 5.1 characters per word, and 90 percent familiar words. Easy copy is suitable for the beginner who is mastering the keyboard.

gwam 2'

| | | | | 4 | | | | 8 | | |
| There should be no questions, no doubt, about | | | | | | | | | 5 | 35 |

the value of being able to key; it's just a matter   10 40

of common sense that today a pencil is much too slow.   15 45

Let me explain. Work is done on a keyboard   19 49

three to six times faster than other writing and   24 54

with a product that is a prize to read. Don't you   29 59

agree?   30 60

2' | 1 | 2 | 3 | 4 | 5 |

1. Open **Release of Information Form**. Save it as **112c-d3**.
2. Fill in the form using the following information:

   I, **Hector Martinez**,

   ☒ receive information from

   NAME: **Dr. Phillip Simpson**

   AGENCY: **Blue River Medical Group**

   ADDRESS: **9062 Decanteur Ave.**

   CITY: **Sterling Heights, MI 48310**

   Information concerns 1. **Louisa Martinez, daughter**; 2. **Richard Martinez, son**

   Information requested is ☒ All of the above

   Release of information will terminate on (**insert a date that is approximately 60 days from the current date**)

3. Save and print.

TIP

It may be helpful to display the gridlines in the table when filling in the amounts (**Format, Borders and Shading, Borders** tab, **Grid**).

1. Open **Disclosure Statement** and save it as **112c-d4**.
2. Fill in the form using the following information:

   Patient: **Patricia Cheshire**

   Parents or Responsible Party: **Susana Cheshire, mother**

   Address: **67 Raven Ln., Irvine, CA 92623**

3. Unprotect the form and insert the following information in the table. Use a decimal tab to align the numbers in Column B. Use the math feature to calculate the total. The total should display with a dollar sign and two decimal places.

PROFESSIONAL FEE	
Limited Treatment:	$2,015.00
Phase I:	525.00
Phase II:	400.00
Full Treatment (Single Phase):	
Retainer Fee:	
Retainer Visit Fee:	
Finance Charge:	
Total	

4. Protect the form again and insert the following information in the ¶ below the table.

   Initial payment: **$1,440.00**; Balance: **$1,500.00**; payable at **$500.00** per month for **three** months. Retainer fee **$220.00** is due on debanding . . .

5. Check to see that the page breaks in an appropriate place. Save and print.

WARMUP

13a
Key each line twice SS (slowly, then faster).

alphabet 1 Bev quickly hid two Japanese frogs in Mitzi's box.
shift 2 Jay Nadler, a Rotary Club member, wrote Mr. Coles.
, (comma) 3 Jay, Ed, and I paid for plates, knives, and forks.
easy 4 Did the amendment name a city auditor to the firm?
| 1 | 2 | 3 | 4 | 5 | 6 | 7 | 8 | 9 | 10 |

SKILLBUILDING

13b Rhythm Builders
Key each line once SS.

word-level response: key short, familiar words as units

5 is to for do an may work so it but an with them am
6 Did they mend the torn right half of their ensign?
7 Hand me the ivory tusk on the mantle by the bugle.

letter-level response: key more difficult words letter by letter

8 only state jolly zest oil verve join rate mop card
9 After defeat, look up; gaze in joy at a few stars.
10 We gazed at a plump beaver as it waded in my pool.

combination response: use variable speed; your fingers will let you feel the difference

11 it up so at for you may was but him work were they
12 It is up to you to get the best rate; do it right.
13 This is Lyn's only date to visit their great city.
| 1 | 2 | 3 | 4 | 5 | 6 | 7 | 8 | 9 | 10 |

13c Keyboard Reinforcement
Key each line once; fingers well curved, wrists low; avoid punching keys with 3rd and 4th fingers.

p 14 Pat appears happy to pay for any supper I prepare.
x 15 Knox can relax; Alex gets a box of flax next week.
v 16 Vi, Ava, and Viv move ivy vines, leaves, or stems.
' 17 It's a question of whether they can't or won't go.
? 18 Did Jan go? Did she see Ray? Who paid? Did she?
. 19 Ms. E. K. Nu and Lt. B. A. Walz had the a.m. duty.
" 20 "Who are you?" he asked. "I am," I said, "Marie."
; 21 Find a car; try it; like it; work a price; buy it.

1. In a new document, change the side margins to 1" and top margin to .6" and insert the **letterhead** file.
2. Key the form shown below. Use text form fields (*tff*) as needed, and apply Table List 7 format to the table.
3. Change the height of Row 1 to .45" and center the heading. Change the height of Rows 2–9 to .3" and center the text vertically in the cells.
4. Place a heading at the top of the second page as follows:
   DISCLOSURE STATEMENT/CONSENT TO TREATMENT
   Page 2
   Insert current date code
5. Protect the form and save it as **Disclosure Statement**.

Insert medical letterhead file here

DISCLOSURE STATEMENT AND CONSENT TO TREATMENT

Federal law requires this disclosure statement pursuant to Regulation Z, Truth-in-Lending Act for Professional Services

Confirmation of arrangements for the orthodontic management of:

Patient: (*tff*)

Parents or Responsible Party: (*tff*)

Address: (*tff*)

FINANCIAL ARRANGEMENTS:

The undersigned hereby agrees to the following financial arrangements:

PROFESSIONAL FEE
Limited Treatment:
Phase I:
Phase II:
Full Treatment (Single Phase):
Retainer Fee:
Retainer Visit Fee:
Finance Charge:
Total

Initial payment of (*tff*) is due on the first treatment appointment. Balance of (*tff*) is payable at (*tff*) per month for (*tff*) months. Budgeting of the fee is for your convenience. Monthly remittance is not a monthly fee. Retainer fee of (*tff*) is due on debanding appointment.

A service charge of 5% per month will be made on all past due balances. If it becomes necessary to send your account to collection, the undersigned agrees to pay all costs and expenses including a reasonable attorney's fee.

I/We hereby certify we discussed the content of this contract with the physician and that I/we give INFORMED CONSENT for all necessary orthodontic treatment and related services.

Patient Signature	Parent Signature	Physician Signature	Date

13d Textbook Keying

Troublesome Pairs: Key each line once; DS between groups.

t 22 at fat hat sat to tip the that they fast last slat

r 23 or red try ran run air era fair rid ride trip trap

t/r 24 A trainer sprained an arm trying to tame the bear.

m 25 am me my mine jam man more most dome month minimum

n 26 no an now nine once net knee name ninth know never

m/n 27 Many men and women are important company managers.

o 28 on or to not now one oil toil over only solo today

i 29 it is in tie did fix his sit like with insist will

o/i 30 Joni will consider obtaining options to buy coins.

a 31 at an as art has and any case data haze tart smart

s 32 us as so say sat slap lass class just sassy simple

a/s 33 Disaster was averted as the steamer sailed to sea.

e 34 we he ear the key her hear chef desire where there

i 35 it is in tie did fix his sit like with insist will

e/i 36 An expression of gratitude for service is desired.

13e Speed Check

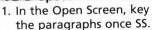

1. In the Open Screen, key the paragraphs once SS.
2. Save as **xx-13e**.
3. Take a 1' writing on paragraph 1. Save as **xx-13e-t1**.
4. Take a 1' writing on paragraph 2. Save as **xx-13e-t2**.
5. Print the better 1' writing.
6. Take a 2' writing on both paragraphs. Start over if time permits.

 all letters

Goal: 16 *gwam*

gwam 2"

    The questions of time use are vital ones; we   5

miss so much just because we don't plan.   9

    When we organize our days, we save time for   13

those extra premium things we long to do.   17

2' | 1 | 2 | 3 | 4 | 5 |

1. In a new document, change the side margins to 1", change the top and bottom margins to .5", and insert the **letterhead** file.

2. Key the form shown below. Use text form fields (*tff*) and checkboxes as needed. The form should fit on one page. Save as **Release of Information Form**; print.

Insert medical letterhead file here

CONSENT FOR RELEASE OF INFORMATION

I, (*tff*) , hereby authorize Christina Greene, Psy. D. to:

☐ disclose information to

☐ receive information from

NAME: (*tff*)

AGENCY: (*tff*)

ADDRESS: (*tff*)

CITY: (*tff*)   STATE: (*tff*)   ZIP CODE: (*tff*)

This information concerns myself or the following minors of whom I am parent or guardian:

1. (*tff*)

2. (*tff*)

The information to be disclosed/requested is to be used for professional purposes only.

The information to be disclosed/requested includes the following specific items:

☐ Treatment plan   ☐ Treatment progress notes

☐ Diagnosis   ☐ Other information

☐ Opinion & recommendation (specify) _____

☐ All of the above

I understand this information will be kept confidential and disclosed only to the persons named on this release or to law enforcement as required by law (Illinois Code 16-1619) or other applicable Illinois laws, or upon appropriate court order.

Consent termination date: This release of information will remain in effect for the duration of treatment or terminate on (*tff*), a date that has been mutually agreed upon by the psychologist and myself.

Client: _____   Witness: _____   Date: _____

Skill Builders 1

 Use the Option Screen for Skill Builders. Save each drill as a separate file.

DRILL 1

Goal: reinforce key locations

Key each line at a comfortable, constant rate; check lines that need more practice; repeat those lines.

Keep

- your eyes on source copy
- your fingers curved, upright
- your wrists low, but not touching
- your elbows hanging loosely
- your feet flat on the floor

A We saw that Alan had an alabaster vase in Alabama.
B My rubber boat bobbed about in the bubbling brook.
C Ceci gave cups of cold cocoa to Rebecca and Rocco.
D Don's dad added a second deck to his old building.
E Even as Ellen edited her document, she ate dinner.
F Our firm in Buffalo has a staff of forty or fifty.
G Ginger is giving Greg the eggs she got from Helga.
H Hugh has eighty high, harsh lights he might flash.
I Irik's lack of initiative is irritating his coach.
J Judge J. J. Jore rejected Jeane and Jack's jargon.
K As a lark, Kirk kicked back a rock at Kim's kayak.
L Lucille is silly; she still likes lemon lollipops.
M Milt Mumm hammered a homer in the Miami home game.
N Ken Linn has gone hunting; Stan can begin canning.
O Jon Soto rode off to Otsego in an old Morgan auto.
P Philip helped pay the prize as my puppy hopped up.
Q Quiet Raquel quit quoting at an exquisite marquee.
R As Mrs. Kerr's motor roared, her red horse reared.
S Sissie lives in Mississippi; Lissa lives in Tulsa.
T Nat told Betty not to tattle on her little sister.
U Ula has a unique but prudish idea on unused units.
V Eva visited every vivid event for twelve evenings.
W We watched as wayworn wasps swarmed by the willow.
X Tex Cox waxed the next box for Xenia and Rex Knox.
Y Ty says you may stay with Fay for only sixty days.
Z Hazel is puzzled about the azure haze; Zack dozes.
alphabet Jacky and Max quickly fought over a sizable prawn.
alphabet Just by maximizing liquids, Chick Prew avoids flu.

| 1 | 2 | 3 | 4 | 5 | 6 | 7 | 8 | 9 | 10 |

SKILLBUILDING

112a
Warmup
Key each line twice SS.

1 gait focal appendix bile colic pedal hernia dyspnea anorexia drug
2 test arid uria tissue benign adenitis renal jaundice sinus apical
3 cystitis dilate vital scan penicillin sputum pelvic saline tonsil
4 tubal flap aural chronic mucosa mitral nodes sputum codeine femur

| 1 | 2 | 3 | 4 | 5 | 6 | 7 | 8 | 9 | 10 | 11 | 12 | 13 |

DOCUMENT DESIGN

112b

Consent for Release of Information Form

Medical records are the property of the physician. He/she is legally and ethically obligated to keep them confidential unless a Release of Information form has been signed by the patient. In some cases, insurance companies and federal and state agencies are exceptions to the right of privacy and privileged communication. This means they may request medical information even without the consent of the patient.

Disclosure Statement

The Truth-in-Lending Act, also known as Regulation Z of the Consumer Protection Act, covers credit agreements that involve more than four payments. This act requires that the physician and patient discuss, sign, and retain copies of a disclosure statement, which is a written description of the agreed terms of payment.

Insert letterhead file here

CONSENT FOR RELEASE OF INFORMATION

I, (*tf*) , hereby authorize Christina Greene, Psy. D. to:

☐ disclose information to
☐ receive information from

NAME: (*tf*)
AGENCY: (*tf*)
ADDRESS: (*tf*)
CITY: (*tf*)   STATE: (*tf*)   ZIP CODE: (*tf*)

This information concerns myself or the following minors of whom I am parent or guardian:

1. (*tf*)
2. (*tf*)

The information to be disclosed/requested is to be used for professional purposes only.

The information to be disclosed/requested includes the following specific items:

☐ Treatment plan   ☐ Treatment progress notes
☐ Diagnosis   ☐ Other information
☐ Opinion & recommendation (specify) _____
☐ All of the above

I understand this information will be kept confidential and disclosed only to the persons named on this release or to law enforcement as required by law (Illinois Code 16-1619) or other applicable Illinois laws, or upon appropriate court order.

Consent termination date: This release of information will remain in effect for the duration of treatment or terminate on (*tf*), a date that has been mutually agreed upon by the psychologist and myself.

Client: _____   Witness: _____   Date: _____

Insert letterhead file here

DISCLOSURE STATEMENT AND CONSENT TO TREATMENT

Federal law requires this disclosure statement pursuant to Regulation Z, Truth-in-Lending Act for Professional Services

Confirmation of arrangements for the orthodontic management of:

Patient: (*tf*)

Parents or Responsible Party: (*tf*)

Address: (*tf*)

FINANCIAL ARRANGEMENTS:

The undersigned hereby agrees to the following financial arrangements:

PROFESSIONAL FEE
Limited Treatment:
Phase I:
Phase II:
Full Treatment (Single Phase):
Retainer Fee:
Retainer Visit Fee:
Finance Charge:
Total

Initial payment of (*tf*) is due on the first treatment appointment. Balance of (*tf*) is payable at (*tf*) per month for (*tf*) months. Budgeting of the fee is for your convenience. Monthly remittance is not a monthly fee. Retainer fee of (*tf*) is due on debanding appointment.

A service charge of 5% per month will be made on all past due balances. If it becomes necessary to send your account to collection, the undersigned agrees to pay all costs and expenses including a reasonable attorney's fee.

I/We hereby certify we discussed the content of this contract with the physician and that I/we give INFORMED CONSENT for all necessary orthodontic treatment and related services.

_____   _____   _____   _____
Patient Signature   Parent Signature   Physician Signature   Date

DRILL 2

Goal: strengthen up and down reaches

Keep hands and wrists quiet; fingers well curved in home position; stretch fingers up from home or pull them palmward as needed.

home position
1 Hall left for Dallas; he is glad Jake fed his dog.
2 Ada had a glass flask; Jake had a sad jello salad.
3 Lana Hask had a sale; Gala shall add half a glass.

down reaches
4 Did my banker, Mr. Mavann, analyze my tax account?
5 Do they, Mr. Zack, expect a number of brave women?
6 Zach, check the menu; next, beckon the lazy valet.

up reaches
7 Prue truly lost the quote we wrote for our report.
8 Teresa quietly put her whole heart into her words.
9 There were two hilarious jokes in your quiet talk.

DRILL 3

Goal: strengthen individual finger reaches

Rekey troublesome lines.

first finger
1 Bob Mugho hunted for five minutes for your number.
2 Juan hit the bright green turf with his five iron.
3 The frigates and gunboats fought mightily in Java.

second finger
4 Dick said the ice on the creek had surely cracked.
5 Even as we picnicked, I decided we needed to diet.
6 Kim, not Mickey, had rice with chicken for dinner.

third/fourth finger
7 Pam saw Roz wax an aqua auto as Lex sipped a cola.
8 Wally will quickly spell Zeus, Apollo, and Xerxes.
9 Who saw Polly? Zoe Pax saw her; she is quiet now.

DRILL 4

Goal: strengthen special reaches

Emphasize smooth stroking. Avoid pauses, but do not reach for speed.

adjacent reaches
1 Falk knew well that her opinions of art were good.
2 Theresa answered her question; order was restored.
3 We join there and walk north to the western point.

direct reaches
4 Barb Nunn must hunt for my checks; she is in debt.
5 In June and December, Irvin hunts in Bryce Canyon.
6 We decided to carve a number of funny human faces.

double letters
7 Anne stopped off at school to see Bill Wiggs cook.
8 Edd has planned a small cookout for all the troop.
9 Keep adding to my assets all fees that will apply.

| 1 | 2 | 3 | 4 | 5 | 6 | 7 | 8 | 9 | 10 |

1. Open **Soap Note Form** and fill in the form with the information for each document. NOTE: *Pt* is a common abbreviation for patient. Spell out the word "patient" when keying the notes.

2. Save Document 3 as **111b-d3** and Document 4 as **111b-d4**; print.

Field Names	Document 3	Document 4
Last Name	Jones	Pham
First Name	Sarah	Loriana
Patient No.	10680	31048
Age	20	27
Allergies	None	Bee stings
Meds	None	None
T	99.5	98.5
P	84	62
R	20	15
B/P	130/87	112/72
C/O	Cough	Pain in right knee
Date	6/9/--	6/21/--

DOCUMENT 3 SOAP NOTE BODY

S	Pt complains of cough and head congestion for the past 48 hours, shortness of breath, lethargy, and low appetite.
O	Pt coughing up green sputum. Lungs clear, ears clear. Lymph nodes enlarged bilateral neck. Bilateral tonsils enlarged. CXR-WNL, PPD negative. CBC—elevated white count.
A	Acute upper respiratory infection.
P	Pt is to take 333 Mg. E-Mycin, one tablet every 8 hours for one week. Increase fluids, increase rest. Pt is to remain off from work for 3 days. Recheck in one week or sooner, if needed.

DOCUMENT 4 SOAP NOTE BODY

S	Pt complains of pain in the right knee; tripped and fell 6/17/--.
O	Inflammation/hematoma on right anterior medial patella; decreased ROM right knee, with flexion, extension.
A	Diagnosis: Pre-patellar bursitis. Treatment: R.I.C.E. on right patellar anterior medial with ice pack twice a day for 4-6 weeks. Stay off right leg. ADL: rest knee; ice right anterior knee morn/night; elevate.
P	Stay off right leg. Rest; ice morn/night; elevate. Week 1: decrease pain; week 2: increase ROM.

Goal: improve troublesome pairs

Use a controlled rate without pauses.

1 ad add did does dish down body dear dread dabs bad
d/k 2 kid ok kiss tuck wick risk rocks kayaks corks buck
3 Dirk asked Dick to kid Drake about the baked duck.

4 deed deal den led heed made needs delay he she her
e/i 5 kit kiss kiln kiwi kick kilt kind six ribs kill it
6 Abie had neither ice cream nor fried rice in Erie.

7 fib fob fab rib beg bug rob bad bar bed born table
b/v 8 vat vet gave five ever envy never visit weave ever
9 Did Harv key jibe or jive, TV or TB, robe or rove?

10 aft after lift gift sit tot the them tax tutu tyro
t/r 11 for far ere era risk rich rock rosy work were roof
12 In Toronto, Ruth told the truth about her artwork.

13 jug just jury judge juice unit hunt bonus quiz bug
u/y 14 jay joy lay you your only envy quay oily whey body
15 Willy usually does not buy your Yukon art in July.

Goal: build speed

Set the Timer for 1'.
Key each sentence for 1'.
Try to complete each sentence twice (20 *gwam* or more).
Ignore errors for now.

1 Dian may make cocoa for the girls when they visit.
2 Focus the lens for the right angle; fix the prism.
3 She may suspend work when she signs the torn form.
4 Augment their auto fuel in the keg by the autobus.
5 As usual, their robot did half turns to the right.
6 Pamela laughs as she signals to the big hairy dog.
7 Pay Vivian to fix the island for the eighty ducks.

| 1 | 2 | 3 | 4 | 5 | 6 | 7 | 8 | 9 | 10 |

Goal: build speed

From the columns at the right, choose a *gwam* goal that is two to three words higher than your best rate. Set the Timer for **Variable** and then either **20"** or **30"**. Try to reach your goal.

	words	30"	20"
1 Did she make this turkey dish?		12	18
2 Blake and Laurie may go to Dubuque.		14	21
3 Signal for the oak sleigh to turn right.		16	24
4 I blame Susie; did she quench the only flame?		18	27
5 She turns the panel dials to make this robot work.		20	30

| 1 | 2 | 3 | 4 | 5 | 6 | 7 | 8 | 9 | 10 |

111b-d1

Letterhead

In the next two documents, you will create the form shown on the previous page. In Document 3, you will fill in the form.

1. In a new document, change the top margin to .6" and the side margins to 1".

2. Insert clip art that will be appropriate for a medical office. Change the height of the clip art to 1.25". Do not change the width; it will automatically reset in proportion to the height.

3. Change the layout of the picture to **In Front of Text** (select the picture, select **Picture** from the Format menu, and click the **Layout** tab).

4. Press TAB twice to move the insertion point to the right of the picture. Key **Quality Care Medical Center**, as shown on the previous page.

5. Arrange the address and telephone number (shown on the previous page) attractively in the letterhead.

6. Add a graphic line below the picture. Save as **medical letterhead**.

111b-d2

SOAP Note Form

1. In a new document, change the top margin to .6" and the side margins to 1", and then insert the **medical letterhead** file (**Insert, File**).

2. Create a field for each item in the SOAP note shown on the previous page. Make all fields text fields with unlimited length unless otherwise indicated in the table below.

Field Name	Field Type	Maximum Length	Format
Patient No.	number	5	0
Age	number	2	0
T	number	5	0.00
P	number	2	0
R	number	2	0
B/P	number	3/2	0
Date	date		m/d/yy

3. Insert a graphic line before beginning the body of the SOAP notes.

4. Create a table for the body of the SOAP notes. All rows will have a height of 1". Center text vertically in the cells. Set width of Column B to 6".

5. Center the letters *S O A P* in Column A. Apply a larger bold font to the letter *S* in SOAP. Use Format Painter to copy the formatting to the rest of the letters. Insert an unlimited text field in each row of Column B.

6. Key the physician signature line in the footer.

7. Apply Arial Black font to the heading (select only the heading letters and the colon that follows). Use Format Painter to apply the format to all the headings.

8. Use Times New Roman font when keying the fill-in information.

9. Protect the form, save it as **Soap Note Form**, and print.

These writings are available as Diagnostic Writings.

1. Go to the Numeric & Skill Lesson menu and click the **Diagnostic Writing** button in the lower-right corner.
2. Choose the writing and select the length of the timing (1', 3', or 5').
3. Key the writing. If you finish before time is up, begin again.
4. Review your results.
5. (Optional) Choose the **Practice Error Words** from the Edit menu to practice errors in the writing.
6. Click the Timer icon at the bottom of the screen to begin your second attempt. Results will be entered in your Summary Report.
7. Print or save the completed Diagnostic Writing. (Sample filename: xx-Writing 1-t1).
8. To return to the program, choose Exit Diagnostic Writings from the File menu.

Goal: build staying power
1. Key each paragraph as a 1' timing.
2. Key a 2' timing on both paragraphs.

Note: The dot above text represents two words.

 all letters

Writing 1: 18 gwam   gwam 2'

          •   4   •   8   •
Why spend weeks with some problem when just a few quiet   6
   12   •   16   •
minutes can help us to resolve it.   9

        •   4   •   8   •
If we don't take time to think through a problem, it will   15
   12   •   16   •
swiftly begin to expand in size.   18

Writing 2: 20 gwam

        •   4   •   8   •
We push very hard in our quest for growth, and we all   5
   12   •   16   •   20
think that only excellent growth will pay off.   10

        •   4   •   8   •
Believe it or not, one can actually work much too hard,   16
   12   •   16   •   20
be much too zealous, and just miss the mark.   20

Writing 3: 22 gwam

        •   4   •   8   •
A business friend once explained to me why he was often   6
   12   •   16   •   20
quite eager to be given some new project to work with.   11

        •   4   •   8   •
My friend said that each new project means he has to   16
   12   •   16   •   20
organize and use the best of his knowledge and his skill.   22

Writing 4: 24 gwam

        •   4   •   8   •
Don't let new words get away from you. Learn how to spell   6
   12   •   16   •   20   •   24
and pronounce new words and when and how finally to use them. 12

        •   4   •   8   •
A new word is a friend, but frequently more. New words   18
   12   •   16   •   20   •   24
must be used lavishly to extend the size of your own word power. 24

2' | 1 | 2 | 3 | 4 | 5 | 6 |

continued

DOCUMENT DESIGN

111a

Letterhead

Medical forms contain the name and address of the medical facility at the top of all the forms. In this lesson, you will follow the directions in 111b-d1 on p. 436 to create a letterhead that will be inserted at the top of all the medical forms.

SOAP Note Form

All medical offices keep recorded notes of the patient's office visit, which are commonly called SOAP notes. SOAP notes contain the patient's complaints, the physician's findings, and the physician's assessment and plan for treatment. The letters *S O A P* stand for:

S—SUBJECTIVE (what the patient tells the physician)

O—OBJECTIVE (the physician's findings as a result of a physical exam or evaluation)

A—ASSESSMENT (the physician's diagnosis or impression of the problem)

P—PLAN (the planned treatment for the patient)

Letterhead ———

Quality Care Medical Center

5252 Superior Rd.
Oak Park, IL 60301-7984
(708) 555-0186, fax (708) 555-0188

SOAP Note Form ———

Last Name:	**First Name:**		**Patient No.**
Age:	**Allergies:**		**Meds:**
T:	**P:**	**R:**	**B/P:** /
C/O:		**Date:**	

S	
O	
A	
P	

Physician: _____

DOCUMENT DESIGN

Writing 5: 26 *gwam*

gwam 2'

           •   4   •   8   •
We usually get best results when we know where we are   5
  12   •   16   •   20   •
going. Just setting a few goals will help us quietly see what   12
  24   •
we are doing.   13

           •   4   •   8   •
Goals can help measure whether we are moving at a good   19
  12   •   16   •   20   •
rate or dozing along. You can expect a goal to help you find   25
  24   •
good results.   26

Writing 6: 28 *gwam*

           •   4   •   8   •
To win whatever prizes we want from life, we must plan to   6
  12   •   16   •   20   •
move carefully from this goal to the next to get the maximum   12
  24   •   28
result from our work.   14

           •   4   •   8   •
If we really want to become skilled in keying, we must   19
  12   •   16   •   20   •
come to see that this desire will require of us just a little   26
  24   •   28
patience and hard work.   28

Writing 7: 30 *gwam*

           •   4   •   8   •
Am I an individual person? I'm sure I am; still, in a   5
  12   •   16   •   20   •
much, much bigger sense, other people have a major voice in   12
  24   •   28   •
thoughts I think and actions I take.   15

           •   4   •   8   •
Although we are each a unique person, we all work and   21
  12   •   16   •   20   •
play in organized groups of people who do not expect us to   26
  24   •   28   •
dismiss their rules of law and order.   30

2' | 1 | 2 | 3 | 4 | 5 | 6 |

110c-d2
Table on Pleading Form

Schedule A, illustrated below, is a portion of a long document prepared for court that shows the receipts, disbursements, and assets on hand for estates in probate. This document, like all documents prepared for court, is created on a pleading form.

1. Open the **Los Angeles County** pleading template you created in Lesson 109. When the Pleading Wizard dialog box displays, click the **Finish** button.

2. Schedules are placed at the back of legal documents; therefore, you will not need the information that is displayed on the first page of court documents. You will delete the text that is on the first page and use only the line numbering on the form. Choose **Select All** from the Edit menu, and then press the DELETE key to delete all the text from the pleading page.

3. Key the heading as shown.

4. Strike ENTER twice and create a 3-column, 6-row table. Key the table.

5. Use the math feature to insert the total. The total should display with a dollar sign and two decimal places, and it should be in bold print.

6. Set a decimal tab in Column C to align the numbers. Center and underline column heads.

7. Remove the table grid (**Format, Borders and Shading, Borders** tab, click **None** and **Apply to Table**).

8. Remove the page number from the footer and key **SCHEDULE A** in its place.

9. Save as **110c-d2** and print.

	SCHEDULE A	
	RECEIPTS	
Date	Item	Amount
03/22/--	Medical reimbursement from Medicare	$ 147.00
04/07/--	Accrued interest on savings account at People's Bank	225.00
04/28/--	Rent payment from Mazo property tenant	995.00
05/01/--	Dividend from Jefferson Electric Stock	89.00
05/15/--	Dividend from Alaska Oil Stock	116.50
05/30/--	Accrued interest from savings account at credit union	315.00
TOTAL RECEIPTS		

110c-d3
Fill in Articles of Incorporation

1. Open **110c-d1**. Fill in the form as follows: (1) **Quality Care Medical Center**; (2) **providing medical care**; (3) **Andrew Wainscott**; (4) **5561 Golden Lantern**; (5) **Laguna Niguel**; (6) **92677**; (7) **Ten Thousand (10,000)**; (8) **David M. Smith, Incorporator**.

2. Save as **110c-d3** and print.

Figure and Symbol Keys

- Key the numeric keys by touch.
- Use symbol keys correctly.
- Build keying speed and accuracy.
- Apply correct number expression.
- Apply proofreaders' marks.
- Apply basic Internet skills.

LESSON 14   1 and 8

WARMUP

14a
Key each line twice SS.
Line 2: Space once after a series of brief questions within a sentence.

alphabet	1 Jessie Quick believed the campaign frenzy would be exciting.
space bar	2 Was it Mary? Helen? Pam? It was a woman; I saw one of them.
3d row	3 We were quietly prepped to write two letters to Portia York.
easy	4 Kale's neighbor works with a tutor when they visit downtown.

| 1 | 2 | 3 | 4 | 5 | 6 | 7 | 8 | 9 | 10 | 11 | 12 |

SKILLBUILDING

14b
High-Frequency Words
The words at the right are from the 100 most used words.
Key each line once; work for fluency.

Top 100

5 a an it been copy for his this more no office please service

6 our service than the they up was work all any many thank had

7 business from I know made more not me new of some to program

8 such these two with your about and have like department year

9 by at on but do had in letter most now one please you should

10 their order like also appreciate that there gentlemen letter

11 be can each had information letter may make now only so that

12 them time use which am other been send to enclosed have will

1. In a new document, key **Name:** followed by 2 spaces. Click the **Text Form Field** button. Strike ENTER twice.

2. Key **Student Number:** followed by 2 spaces. Click the **Text Form Field** button. Click the **Form Field Options** button. Change the type of field to *Number* and the maximum length to 6. Strike ENTER twice.

3. Key **Gender:** followed by 2 spaces. Click the **Check Box Form Field** button followed by 2 spaces. Key **Male**. Press TAB twice. Click the **Check Box Form Field** button followed by 2 spaces. Key **Female**. Strike ENTER twice.

4. Key **Class Standing:** followed by 2 spaces. Click the **Drop Down Form** button. Click the **Form Field Options** button. In the Drop Down Item box, key **Freshman** and click the **Add** button. Add **Sophomore**, **Junior**, and **Senior** to the items in the Drop Down List. Click **OK**.

5. Click the **Protect Form** button. Test the form by filling in information about yourself. Press TAB to move to the next field.

6. Save as **110a-drill1**. Print.

DOCUMENT DESIGN

110b

Articles of Incorporation

Articles of Incorporation contain information regarding the name, address, and purpose of the company, as well as the share structure. The document may differ for medical, nonprofit, professional, and municipal corporations.

Key the Articles of Incorporation. DS between paragraphs. Leave a space about 3" square in the upper-right corner of the first page for the filing stamp of the Secretary of State. Use plain paper.

3" square space for filing stamp

ARTICLES OF INCORPORATION

I

The name of this corporation is (*ff1*).

II

The purpose of the corporation is to engage in the profession of (*ff2*) and any other lawful activities (other than the banking or trust company business) not prohibited to a corporation engaging in such profession by applicable laws and regulations.

III

The corporation is a professional corporation within the meaning of Part 4, Division 3, Title 1, California Corporation Code.

IV

The name and address in the State of California of this corporation's initial agent for service of process are:

Name: (*ff3*)

Street Address: (*ff4*)

City: (*ff5*)   California   ZIP: (*ff6*)

V

The corporation is authorized to issue only one class of stock; and the total number of shares which the corporation is authorized to issue is (*ff7*).

_____

(*ff8*)

APPLICATIONS

110c-d1
Articles of Incorporation

1. Strike ENTER to place the insertion point on approximately line 2.9".

2. Key the document shown above, inserting appropriate form fields (*ff*). Protect the form and save it as **110c-d1**.

NEW KEYS

14c 1 and 8

Key each line once SS.

Note: The digit "1" and the letter "l" have separate values on a computer keyboard. Do not interchange these characters.

1 Reach *up* with *left fourth* finger.

8 Reach *up* with *right second* finger.

Abbreviations: Do not space after a period within an abbreviation, as in Ph.D., U.S., C.O.D., a.m.

1

13 1 1a a1 1 1; 1 and a 1; 1 add 1; 1 aunt; 1 ace; 1 arm; 1 aye

14 1 and 11 and 111; 11 eggs; 11 vats; Set 11A; May 11; Item 11

15 The 11 aces of the 111th Corps each rated a salute at 1 p.m.

8

16 8 8k k8 8 8; 8 kits; ask 8; 8 kites; kick 8; 8 keys; spark 8

17 OK 88; 8 bags; 8 or 88; the 88th; 88 kegs; ask 88; order 888

18 Eight of the 88 cars score 8 or better on our Form 8 rating.

all figures learned

19 She did live at 818 Park, not 181 Park; or was it 181 Clark?

20 Put 1 with 8 to form 18; put 8 with 1 to form 81. Use 1881.

21 On May 1 at 8 a.m., 18 men and 18 women left Gate 8 for Rio.

SKILLBUILDING

14d Reinforcement

Key each line once; DS between groups. Repeat. Key with accuracy.

figures

22 Our 188 trucks moved 1881 tons on August 18 and December 18.

23 Send Mary 181 No. 188 panes for her home at 8118 Oak Street.

24 The 188 men in 8 boats left Docks 1 and 18 at 1 p.m., May 1.

25 pop was lap pass slaw wool solo swap Apollo wasp load plaque

26 Was Polly acquainted with the equipped jazz player in Texas?

27 The computer is a useful tool; it helps you to perform well.

14e Speed Builder

Set the timer for 1'. Key each sentence as many times as possible.

Goal: to complete each sentence twice in one minute.

28 Did their form entitle them to the land?

29 Did the men in the field signal for us to go?

30 I may pay for the antique bowls when I go to town.

31 The auditor did the work right, so he risks no penalty.

32 The man by the big bush did signal us to turn down the lane.

| 1 | 2 | 3 | 4 | 5 | 6 | 7 | 8 | 9 | 10 | 11 | 12 |

Legal Forms

110a
Creating Forms

Legal Forms

An online form can be created so that people can fill out the forms using *Microsoft Word*. You will key the **fixed text**; information that will be supplied by others will be keyed in **form fields**. There are three types of form fields. The table below explains them and when they are used. Display the Forms Toolbar (View, Toolbars, Forms) when working with forms.

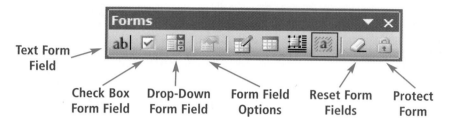

Text Form Field

Check Box Form Field   Drop-Down Form Field   Form Field Options   Reset Form Fields   Protect Form

Form Field Type	When It Is Used	Example
Text	You need the respondent to key the requested information.	Last name or telephone number
Checkbox	Respondent checks the box that applies.	❏ Male ❏ Female
Drop-down	User selects from a list of choices.	Mr. Mrs. Dr.

Form Field Options

After the field has been inserted, Form Field Options can be used to specify the parameters of the field, such as type of field and length. For example, if you are asking respondents for their social security number, you would insert a Text Form Field and then use Form Field Options to specify that the field be a number field and be limited to nine digits.

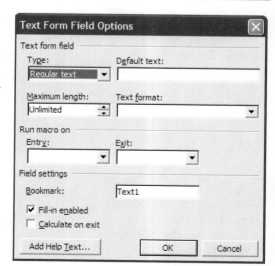

Protecting the Form

After creating the form, click the Protect Form button to prevent others from changing its contents. You cannot test the form until you protect it. If you need to edit the form, you must click the Protect Form button to unlock the form; make your changes and then click Protect Form again to lock it.

LESSON 15

5 and 0

WARMUP

15a

Key each line twice SS. For a series of capital letters, press CAPS LOCK with the left little finger. Press again to release.

alphabet	1	John Quigley packed the zinnias in twelve large, firm boxes.
1/8	2	Idle Motor 18 at 8 mph and Motor 81 at 8 mph; avoid Motor 1.
caps	3	Lily read BLITHE SPIRIT by Noel Coward. I read VANITY FAIR.
lock	4	Did they fix the problem of the torn panel and worn element?

| 1 | 2 | 3 | 4 | 5 | 6 | 7 | 8 | 9 | 10 | 11 | 12 |

15b Technique Reinforcement

Reach up or down without moving your hands. Key each line once; repeat drill.

adjacent reaches

5 as oil red ask wet opt mop try tree open shred operas treaty
6 were pore dirt stew ruin faster onion alumni dreary mnemonic
7 The opened red hydrants were powerful, fast, and very dirty.

outside reaches

8 pop zap cap zag wasp equip lazy zippers queue opinion quartz
9 zest waste paper exist parquet azalea acquaint apollo apathy
10 The lazy wasp passed the potted azalea on the parquet floor.

NEW KEYS

15c 5 and 0

Key each line once SS.

5 Reach *up* with *left first* finger.

0 Reach *up* with *right fourth* finger.

5

11 5 5f f5 5 5; 5 fans; 5 feet; 5 figs; 5 fobs; 5 furs; 5 flaws
12 5 o'clock; 5 a.m.; 5 p.m.; is 55 or less; buy 55; 5 and 5 is
13 Call Line 555 if 5 fans or 5 bins arrive at Pier 5 by 5 p.m.

0

14 0 0; ;0 0 0; skip 0; plan 0; left 0; is below 0; I scored 0;
15 0 degrees; key 0 and 0; write 00 here; the total is 0 or 00;
16 She laughed at their 0 to 0 score; but ours was 0 to 0 also.

all figures learned

17 I keyed 550 pages for Invoice 05, or 50 more than we needed.
18 Pages 15 and 18 of the program listed 150, not 180, members.
19 On May 10, Rick drove 500 miles to New Mexico in car No. 08.

TIP

When keying enumera-
tions, click **Undo
Automatic Numbering**
to restore numbering to
the format you keyed.

13. At the right, replace the case number with **No. SO C 87321**. Delete the words *PLEADING TITLE* and key **NOTICE OF DEPOSITION AND REQUEST FOR PRODUCTION OF DOCUMENTS AT DEPOSITION**.

14. Key **TO: ALL PARTIES AND THEIR ATTORNEYS OF RECORD** on line 17 and press ENTER twice.

15. Key the following paragraph beginning on line 19.

PLEASE TAKE NOTICE that defendants will take the deposition of plaintiff Henry Hurt on July 7, 200-, at 2:00 p.m., at the offices of Newton & Johnson, 15 Civic Center Dr., Suite 200, Santa Ana, CA 92701, before a notary public authorized to administer oaths in the State of California. The deposition will continue from day to day, excluding Saturdays, Sundays, and holidays, until completed.

16. Key **///** on numbered lines that do not contain text at the end of the page, such as on p. 1, line 26. This shows that the line was left blank by the writer.

17. On the second page of the pleading, key the following information, beginning on line 1:

PLEASE TAKE FURTHER NOTICE that plaintiff Henry Hurt is required to bring with him to the deposition the following records, documents, and things:

DS two times

1. Any and all documents which substantiate the claim for property damage.

DS two times

2. Any and all documents which substantiate the claim for loss of earnings.

DS two times

3. All photographs which in any way relate to the subject matter of this action.

18. Under the *By* line, key the following text:

BARBARA M. JOHNSON
Attorney for
Defendants JONATHAN
MOVERS and LAUREL
DELIVERIES

19. Save the document as **109b-d1** and print.

109b-d2
Create Pleading Form

1. Follow the Wizard steps in 109b-d1 to create a new pleading form for:

**SUPERIOR COURT OF THE STATE OF CALIFORNIA
FOR THE COUNTY OF LOS ANGELES**

2. Save the template as **Los Angeles County.dot**.

SKILLBUILDING

15d Textbook Keying
Key each line once; DS between 3-line groups.

improve figures

20 Read pages 5 and 8; duplicate page 18; omit pages 50 and 51.
21 We have Model 80 with 10 meters or Model 180 with 15 meters.
22 After May 18, French 050 meets in room 15 at 10 a.m. daily.

improve long reaches

23 Barb Abver saw a vibrant version of her brave venture on TV.
24 Call a woman or a man who will manage Minerva Manor in Nome.
25 We were quick to squirt a quantity of water at Quin and West.

15e Tab Review

1. Read the instructions to clear and set tabs.
2. Go to the Open Screen. Set a left tab at 4".
3. Practice the lines; strike TAB without watching your keyboard.

STANDARD PLAN for Setting and Clearing Tabs in the Open Screen

Preset or default tabs are displayed on the Ruler. If necessary, display the Ruler in the Open Screen. (Choose the **Show Ruler** option on the Format menu.) Sometimes you will want to remove or clear existing tabs before setting new ones.

To clear and set tabs:

1. On the menu bar, click **Format**, then **Clear All Tabs**.
2. To set tabs, select the type of tab you want to set (left, center, decimal, or right) shown at the lower-left side of the ruler.
3. Click the Ruler at the location where you want to set a tab.

Set tab 4"

	Tab	Keyboarding
has become	Tab	the primary
means of	Tab	written communication
in business and	Tab	in our personal lives.
Keyboarding is	Tab	used by persons
in every profession	Tab	and most job levels.

15f Speed Check

1. In the Open Screen, take two 1' writings on paragraph 2. Note your *gwam*. Do not save the timings.
2. Take two 1' writings on paragraph 1. Try to equal paragraph 2 rate.
3. Take one 2' writing on both paragraphs.

  all letters

gwam 2' | 3'

I thought about Harry and how he had worked for me for   6 | 4
10 years; how daily at 8 he parked his worn car in the lot;   12 | 8
then, he left at 5. Every day was almost identical for him.   18 | 12

In a quiet way, he did his job well, asking for little   23 | 15
attention. So I never recognized his thirst for travel. I   29 | 19
didn't expect to find all of those maps near his workplace.   35 | 23

109b-d1
Notice of Deposition and Request for Production of Documents at Deposition

Word's Pleading Wizard will assist in setting up the pleading form for you. Follow the steps below to create and complete a pleading template.

1. Select **New** from the **File** menu. In the Task Pane, select **General Templates** (*Word 2002*) or **On my computer** (*Word 2003*).

2. Select the **Legal Pleadings** tab in the Templates dialog box, click the **Pleading Wizard** icon, and click **OK**.

3. Click **Next** on the Pleading Wizard screen, select the option **Create a new pleading template for another court** if it is not already selected, and then click the **Next** button.

4. Key the following text in the text box on two lines:

   SUPERIOR COURT OF THE STATE OF CALIFORNIA
   FOR THE COUNTY OF ORANGE

5. Click the **Center** option, and then click **Next**. Choose **Courier New** (or another similar font). Set the line spacing for double and the lines per page to 26. Set the left margin for 1.25" and the right margin for 1". Click **Next**.

6. Set line numbers to appear on the pleading and to start the pleading at line **1**. Line numbers should start at **1** and the line numbers are to show in increments of **One**. Click **Next**.

7. Choose **Double** for the left border screen and **Single** for the right. Click **Next** to display the screen to choose the style. Select **Style 1** and then click the **Next** button.

8. Select the *Attorney and firm names* to display at the beginning of the pleading and the page numbers to display in the footer. Remove the check mark for *Summary of pleading title*. Click the **Next** button.

9. Select **Yes** for a signature block. Select **By** in the Sign With text box. Include the firm name and address above the attorney name. Include the date line before the signature.

10. Click the **Next** button and name the template **Superior Court.dot**. Click **Next** and then **Finish**. Click the **Finish** button again when the screen says that it will help you with the writing. The pleading form now displays.

11. Beginning on line 1, key the following exactly as shown. Press ENTER after each line unless otherwise specified.

    NEWTON & JOHNSON
    15 Civic Center Dr., Suite 200
    Santa Ana, CA 92701
    DS

    Telephone: (714) 555-0134   **This should start on line 3.**
    DS

    Attorneys for Defendants   **This should start on line 4.**
    JONATHAN MOVERS and
    LAUREL DELIVERIES

12. Strike ENTER as needed to place **Superior Court of the State of California** on line 8. Key **HENRY HURT, et. al.,** as the plaintiff on line 11 and key **JONATHAN MOVERS, et al.,** as the defendant on line 14.

(CONTINUED ON NEXT PAGE)

LESSON 16

2 and 7

WARMUP
16a
Key each line twice SS.

alphabet 1 Perry might know I feel jinxed because I have missed a quiz.
figures 2 Channels 5 and 8, on from 10 to 11, said Luisa's IQ was 150.
caps lock 3 Ella Hill will see Chekhov's THE CHERRY ORCHARD on Czech TV.
easy 4 The big dog by the bush kept the ducks and hen in the field.

| 1 | 2 | 3 | 4 | 5 | 6 | 7 | 8 | 9 | 10 | 11 | 12 |

NEW KEYS

16b 2 and 7
Key each line once SS.

2 Reach *up* with *left third* finger.

7 Reach *down* with *right first* finger.

2

5 2 2s s2 2 2; has 2 sons; is 2 sizes; was 2 sites; has 2 skis
6 add 2 and 2; 2 sets of 2; catch 22; as 2 of the 22; 222 Main
7 Exactly at 2 on August 22, the 22d Company left from Pier 2.

7

8 7 7j j7 7 7; 7 jets; 7 jeans; 7 jays; 7 jobs; 7 jars; 7 jaws
9 ask for 7; buy 7; 77 years; June 7; take any 7; deny 77 boys
10 From May 7 on, all 77 men will live at 777 East 77th Street.

all figures learned

11 I read 2 of the 72 books, Ellis read 7, and Han read all 72.
12 Tract 27 cites the date as 1850; Tract 170 says it was 1852.
13 You can take Flight 850 on January 12; I'll take Flight 705.

16c Number Reinforcement
Key each line twice SS (slowly, then faster); DS between 2-line groups.

8/1 14 line 8; Book 1; No. 88; Seat 11; June 18; Cart 81; date 1881
2/7 15 take 2; July 7; buy 22; sell 77; mark 27; adds 72; Memo 2772
5/0 16 feed 5; bats 0; age 50; Ext. 55; File 50; 55 bags; band 5005
all 17 I work 18 visual signs with 20 turns of the 57 lenses to 70.
all 18 Did 17 boys fix the gears for 50 bicycles in 28 racks or 10?

Legal, Medical, and Employment Applications

- Format legal office applications.
- Format medical office applications.
- Format employment application documents.

LESSON 109 — Legal Pleadings

DOCUMENT DESIGN

109a

Create Pleading Form

Legal documents that are presented for filing in court must follow specific guidelines and be keyed on pleading paper. Most documents today are keyed on standard $8\,{}^{1}/_{2} \times$ 11-inch paper; some lawyers may still use legal size paper ($8\,{}^{1}/_{2} \times 14$). Legal documents contain a double ruling, from top to bottom, at the left margin. The right margin is marked with a single ruling. The lines are numbered in the left margin. The margins for legal documents can be 1.25" on the left and 1" on the right. Some lawyers will use a 1.5" left margin and a .5" right margin. Top and bottom margins are usually 1".

SKILLBUILDING

16d Reach Review
Key each line once; fingers curved and relaxed; wrists low.

3d/4th
19 pop was lap pass slaw wool solo swap apollo wasp load plaque
20 Al's quote was, "I was dazzled by the jazz, pizza, and pool."

1st/2d
21 bad fun nut kick dried night brick civic thick hutch believe
22 Kim may visit her friends in Germany if I give her a ticket.

3d/1st
23 cry tube wine quit very curb exit crime ebony mention excite
24 To be invited, petition the six executive committee members.

16e Textbook Keying
Key each line once; DS between 3-line groups. Do not pause at the end of lines.

TECHNIQUE TIP
Think and key the words and phrases as units rather than letter by letter.

words: *think, say,* and *key* words

25 is do am lay cut pen dub may fob ale rap cot hay pay hem box
26 box wit man sir fish also hair giant rigor civic virus ivory
27 laugh sight flame audit formal social turkey bicycle problem

phrases: *think, say,* and *key* phrases

28 is it|is it|if it is|if it is|or by|or by|or me|or me|for us
29 and all|for pay|pay dues and|the pen|the pen box|the pen box
30 such forms|held both|work form|then wish|sign name|with them

easy sentences

31 The man is to do the work right; he then pays the neighbors.
32 Sign the forms to pay the eight men for the turkey and hams.
33 The antique ivory bicycle is a social problem for the chair.

| 1 | 2 | 3 | 4 | 5 | 6 | 7 | 8 | 9 | 10 | 11 | 12 |

16f Speed Check
1. Take two 1' writings on paragraph 1. Do not save.
2. Take two 1' writings on paragraph 2.
3. Take one 2' writing on both paragraphs.

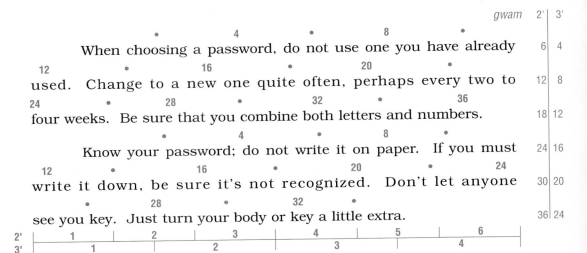

gwam 2' | 3'

When choosing a password, do not use one you have already   6 | 4
used. Change to a new one quite often, perhaps every two to   12 | 8
four weeks. Be sure that you combine both letters and numbers.   18 | 12

Know your password; do not write it on paper. If you must   24 | 16
write it down, be sure it's not recognized. Don't let anyone   30 | 20
see you key. Just turn your body or key a little extra.   36 | 24

2' | 1 | 2 | 3 | 4 | 5 | 6 |
3' | 1 | 2 | 3 | 4 |

Module 17: Checkpoint

Answer the questions below to see if you have mastered the content of this module.

1. A(n) _____ provides detailed travel and meeting information.

2. A document used to provide a record of a meeting is _____.

3. A document detailing the business to be covered in a meeting and the order in which it will be covered is a(n) _____.

4. A document saved to the Web is saved in _____ format.

5. To preview a document saved as a Web page, you must use your _____.

6. Minutes that capture only the key decisions made in a meeting are often called _____ minutes.

7. To create a variety of different kinds of labels from one data source that can be merged with other documents use the _____ Wizard.

8. To create labels, click _____ on the Tools menu.

9. To change to a different type of label, use the _____ feature.

10. To change the name of a default field or to add or delete a field on the data source, click the _____ button.

Performance Assessment

Document 1
Agenda

Use the information at the right to prepare an agenda. Save as **Checkpoint17-d1**.

Investment Oversight Committee Meeting; June 22, 200-; 10:00 a.m.

10:00	Welcome; approve minutes of May 24, 200- meeting Ralph Green
10:15	Review of portfolio performance: domestic equity; international equity; fixed income; alternative investments Bruce Diamond
10:45	General Discussion All members
11:00	Adjournment

Document 2
Action Minutes

Use the heading information from Document 1 above and the information at the right to create action minutes. Save as **Checkpoint17-d2**.

Ralph Green presiding; members attending: John Brennan; Sharon Brown; Lynn Barrow; Mark Houser; and Bruce Diamond, consultant

Ralph Green called the meeting to order at 10:00 and welcomed all attendees. The minutes were approved as presented.

Bruce Diamond reviewed the domestic and international equity portfolios, the fixed-income portfolio, and the alternative investment portfolio in detail. He expressed concern about the small-cap domestic equity portfolio and recommended that we continue to monitor it carefully. All other accounts were on target.

The members discussed the current status of the portfolio and recommended no changes in managers or asset allocation. Members were reminded that the next meeting of the Investment Oversight Committee is on July 21 at 10:00.

The meeting was adjourned at 10:50.

LESSON 17

4 and 9

alphabet 1 Bob realized very quickly that jumping was excellent for us.

figures 2 Has each of the 18 clerks now corrected Item 501 on page 27?

shift keys 3 L. K. Coe, M.D., hopes Dr. Lopez can leave for Maine in May.

easy 4 The men paid their own firms for the eight big enamel signs.

NEW KEYS

17b [4] and [9]
Key each line once SS.

4 Reach *up* with *left first* finger.

9 Reach *up* with *right third* finger.

4

5 4 4f f4 4 4 4; if 4 furs; off 4 floors; gaff 4 fish; 4 flags

6 44th floor; half of 44; 4 walked 44 flights; 4 girls; 4 boys

7 I order exactly 44 bagels, 4 cakes, and 4 pies before 4 a.m.

9

8 9 9l l9 9 9 9; fill 9 lugs; call 9 lads; Bill 9 lost; dial 9

9 also 9 oaks; roll 9 loaves; 9.9 degrees; sell 9 oaks; Hall 9

10 Just 9 couples, 9 men and 9 women, left at 9 on our Tour 99.

all figures learned

11 Memo 94 says 9 pads, 4 pens, and 4 ribbons were sent July 9.

12 Study Item 17 and Item 28 on page 40 and Item 59 on page 49.

13 Within 17 months he drove 85 miles, walked 29, and flew 490.

SKILLBUILDING

17c Textbook Keying
Key each line once.

14 My staff of *18* worked *11* hours a day from May *27* to June *12*.

15 There were *5* items tested by Inspector *7* at *4* p.m. on May *8*.

16 Please send her File *10* today at *8*; her access number is *97*.

17 Car *47* had its trial run. The qualifying speed was *198* mph.

18 The estimated score? *485*. Actual? *190*. Difference? *295*.

1. Prepare the following itinerary.
2. Save as **108c-d4** and print.

Itinerary for Tracy M. Westfield

July 14–17, 200–

Thursday, July 14	Boston to Bangor
8:15 a.m.	Leave Boston Airport on Coastline Flight 957 and arrive at Bangor Airport at 9:28 a.m.; Patriot Rental Car (Confirmation #218756).
10:30 a.m.	Meet with Rod Watson, Leigh Barber, Joe Coleman, and Mary Roszak of Round Rock Associates at their office—739 State St., Bangor, Maine.
4:00 p.m.	Drive to Bar Harbor (approximately 40 miles), Cliff View Hotel, 29 Eden St. (Confirmation #S536017).
Friday, July 15	Bar Harbor
10:30 a.m.	Meet with Richard Odom, Bar Harbor Medical Supply—527 West Highway 3.
2:30 p.m.	Conference for Medical Supply Professionals, Cliff View Hotel.
5:00 p.m.	Conference ends; no events scheduled for evening.
Saturday, July 16	Bar Harbor
10:30 a.m.	Conference for Medical Supply Professionals, Cliff View Hotel.
12:30 p.m.	Conference ends; no events scheduled for afternoon.
7:30 p.m.	Conference Awards Banquet
Sunday, July 17	Bar Harbor to Boston
1:30 p.m.	Drive to Bangor Airport
3:30 p.m.	Depart on Coastline Flight 648; arrive at Boston Airport at 4:28 p.m.

17d Technique Reinforcement

Key smoothly; strike the keys at a brisk, steady pace.

first finger

19 buy them gray vent guy brunt buy brunch much give huge vying
20 Hagen, after her July triumph at tennis, may try volleyball.
21 Verna urges us to buy yet another of her beautiful rag rugs.

second finger

22 keen idea; kick it back; ice breaker; decide the issue; cite
23 Did Dick ask Cecelia, his sister, if she decided to like me?
24 Suddenly, Micki's bike skidded on the Cedar Street ice rink.

third/fourth finger

25 low slow lax solo wax zip zap quips quiz zipper prior icicle
26 Paula has always allowed us to relax at La Paz and at Quito.
27 Please ask Zale to explain who explores most aquatic slopes.

17e Speed Builder

1. Key each paragraph in the Open Screen for a 1' writing.
2. Set the Timer for 2'. Take two 2' writings on all paragraphs. Reach for a speed within two words of 1' *gwam*.
3. Take a 3' writing on all paragraphs. Reach for a speed within four words of 1' *gwam*. Print.

all letters

	gwam	2'	3'
We consider nature to be limited to those things, such		6	4
as air or trees, that we humans do not or cannot make.		11	7
For most of us, nature just exists, just is. We don't		17	11
question it or, perhaps, realize how vital it is to us.		22	15
Do I need nature, and does nature need me? I'm really		28	19
part of nature; thus, what happens to it happens to me.		33	22

```
2' | 1    2    3    4    5    6
3' |   1       2       3       4
```

17f Speed Builder

TECHNIQUE TIP
Keep hands quiet and fingers well curved over the keys. Do not allow your fingers to bounce.

1. In the Open screen, key the information below at the left margin.

    Your name   ENTER
    Current date   ENTER
    Skillbuilders 1, Drill 2   ENTER ENTER

2. Key Drill 2, page 32 from your textbook. Concentrate as you practice on your own, working for good control. Save as **xx-17f**.

1. Prepare the following minutes.
2. Save as **108c-d3** and print.

Investment Committee Meeting
April 24, 200-
Action Minutes

Presiding:	Crystal Bingham
Participants:	Todd Berkley, Jane Kennemur, Bert Radcliff, Julie Markham, Jerold Bradshaw, Chris Pruitt, and Sandy Westfield
Consultant:	Bruce Diamond, Investment Evaluation Group (IEG)

Committee Chair Crystal Bingham called the meeting to order at 9:00, presented an overview of the meeting objectives, and introduced Bruce Diamond, who was representing our regular portfolio consultant, Fred Benjamin. She asked Bruce to summarize the results of the previous quarter. Bruce presented the written report including reports on domestic and international equity, fixed income, and alternative investments. He indicated that the portfolio results exceeded all benchmarks. The returns on the composite portfolio for the first quarter were 8.25%.

Jane Kennemur recommended that the portfolio structure be modified so that the core equity investments currently in index funds would be withdrawn and invested in actively managed funds. Bruce agreed that this move was prudent under market conditions. The committee concurred and requested that IEG complete the search for a core equity manager. Four managers need to be presented to the Committee before the final selection is made.

Jerold Bradshaw reported that the subcommittee reviewed the Investment Policy and recommended no changes. However, the change in the portfolio structure just approved would have to be incorporated in the policy. The updated policy will be sent to everybody.

James Wright reported that the Investment Oversight Committee had met monthly to monitor the investments carefully between Investment Committee meetings. The recommendation at each meeting during the past quarter had been to make no changes in the asset allocation of the portfolio or the investment managers. Monthly meetings have already been scheduled for the next quarter.

The meeting adjourned at 9:55.

LESSON 18

3 and 6

alphabet 1 Jim Kable won a second prize for his very quixotic drawings.

figures 2 If 57 of the 105 boys go on July 29, 48 of them will remain.

easy 3 With the usual bid, I paid for a quantity of big world maps.

| 1 | 2 | 3 | 4 | 5 | 6 | 7 | 8 | 9 | 10 | 11 | 12 |

NEW KEYS

18b 3 and 6
Key each line once SS.

3 Reach *up* with *left second* finger.

6 Reach *up* with *right first* finger.

3

4 3 3d d3 3 3; had 3 days; did 3 dives; led 3 dogs; add 3 dips

5 we 3 ride 3 cars; take 33 dials; read 3 copies; save 33 days

6 On July 3, 33 lights lit 33 stands holding 33 prize winners.

6

7 6 6j 6j 6 6; 6 jays; 6 jams; 6 jigs; 6 jibs; 6 jots; 6 jokes

8 only 6 high; on 66 units; reach 66 numbers; 6 yams or 6 jams

9 On May 6, Car 66 delivered 66 tons of No. 6 shale to Pier 6.

all figures learned

10 At 6 p.m., Channel 3 reported the August 6 score was 6 to 3.

11 Jean, do Items 28 and 6; Mika, 59 and 10; Kyle, 3, 4, and 7.

12 Cars 56 and 34 used Aisle 9; Cars 2 and 87 can use Aisle 10.

SKILLBUILDING

18c Keyboard Reinforcement
Key each line once; DS between groups of three.

> **TECHNIQUE TIP**
> Make the long reaches without returning to the home row between reaches.

long reaches

13 ce cede cedar wreck nu nu nut punt nuisance my my amy mystic

14 ny ny any many company mu mu mull lumber mulch br br furbish

15 The absence of receiving my umbrella disturbed the musician.

number review

16 set 0; push 4; Car 00; score 44; jot 04; age 40; Billet 4004

17 April 5; lock 5; set 66; fill 55; hit 65; pick 56; adds 5665

18 Her grades are 93, 87, and 100; his included 82, 96, and 54.

On the signal to begin, key the documents in sequence. When time has been called, proofread the documents again and correct any errors you may have overlooked. Reprint if necessary.

108c-d1
Agenda

1. Prepare the agenda shown below. Set decimal tabs at .3" (so times align properly) and .9" and set a left tab at .6". Tab before each time and before the en dash between the times. Position the heading at about 2". Set a left tab at 1.5" and a right tab with Leader 2 at 6".

2. Save as **108c-d1** and print.

Investment Committee Meeting

April 24, 200–

Agenda

9:00 – 9:10	Welcome	Crystal Bingham
	Overview of Meeting Objectives	
9:10 – 9:35	Quarterly Performance Report	Bruce Diamond
	Equity–Domestic	
	Equity–International	
	Fixed Income	
	Alternative Investments	
9:35 – 9:45	Investment Policy Review	Jerold Bradshaw
9:45 – 10:00	Oversight Committee Report	James Wright
10:00	Adjourn	

108c-d2
Save as Web Page

1. Save **108c-d1** as a Web page in the **Web Page** folder you set up in Lesson 104. Name the file **108c-d2**.

2. Preview in your browser and make any needed adjustments.

18d Textbook Keying

Key each line once; DS between 2-line groups; repeat.

word response: *think* and *key* words

19 he el id is go us it an me of he of to if ah or bye do so am

20 Did she enamel emblems on a big panel for the downtown sign?

stroke response: *think* and *key* each stroke

21 kin are hip read lymph was pop saw ink art oil gas up as mop

22 Barbara started the union wage earners tax in Texas in July.

combination response: vary speed but maintain rhythm

23 upon than eve lion when burley with they only them loin were

24 It was the opinion of my neighbor that we may work as usual.

18e Diagnostic Writing

Return to the Numeric Lesson menu. Click the **Diagnostic Writings** button. Key the paragraph as a 3' Diagnostic Writing.

Goals: 1', 17–23 *gwam*
2', 15–21 *gwam*
3', 14–20 *gwam*

  all letters

	gwam	2'	3'

I am something quite precious.   Though millions of people | 6 | 4

in other countries might not have me, you likely do.   I have | 12 | 8

a lot of power.   For it is I who names a new president every | 18 | 12

four years.   It is I who decides if a tax shall be levied. | 24 | 16

I even decide questions of war or peace.   I was acquired at | 30 | 20

a great cost; however, I am free to all citizens.   And yet, | 36 | 24

sadly, I am often ignored; or, still worse, I am just taken | 42 | 28

for granted.   I can be lost, and in certain circumstances I | 48 | 32

can even be taken away.   What, you may ask, am I?   I am your | 54 | 36

right to vote.   Don't take me lightly. | 58 | 39

2' | 1 | 2 | 3 | 4 | 5 | 6 |
3' | 1 | 2 | 3 | 4 |

COMMUNICATION

18f Composition

1. Go to the Open Screen.

2. Introduce yourself to your instructor by composing two paragraphs, each containing about three sentences. Use proper grammatical structure. Do not worry about keying errors at this time.

3. Save the document as **xx-profile**. It is not necessary to print the document. You will open and print it in a later lesson.

Assessment

SKILLBUILDING

108a
Warmup
Key each line twice; work for fluency.

alphabet 1 Jimmy Bond quickly realized we could fix the poor girl's vehicle.

adjacent reaches 2 Last autumn, Guy and Isadore loitered here as they walked to Rio.

easy 3 Eight neighbor girls and I wish to work in the cornfield by dusk.

| 1 | 2 | 3 | 4 | 5 | 6 | 7 | 8 | 9 | 10 | 11 | 12 | 13 |

108b
Timed Writing
Take two 5' timed writings.

gwam 3' | 5'

	3'	5'
Today, a huge number of white-collar workers use computers in	4	2
their daily work. Most of these workers also have access to the	8	5
Internet. Using the Internet for work purposes is becoming more	13	8
and more common and, most of the time, is quite effective. Some	17	10
organizations are finding, though, that a number of their workers	21	13
do abuse the Internet. The abuse tends to occur in two forms.	26	15
The first type of abuse they find is that a large number of	30	18
employees visit sites that are not related in any way to their work.	34	21
Some of the sites that workers visit contain material that is very	39	23
offensive to others. The problem is more serious when offensive	43	26
e-mails or material from Web sites are sent to other employees. In	48	29
some cases, the courts have found that these materials create a	52	31
hostile work environment. The second type of abuse is the waste of	56	34
work time. Employees who spend excessive amounts of time surfing	61	36
the Internet simply are not doing the work they are paid to do.	65	39
A number of large companies are trying to deal with this	69	41
problem by buying software that they use to track the sites that	73	44
workers access from their computers. These companies warn all of	78	47
their employees that visiting offensive sites at work can have major	82	49
consequences and might even result in job loss. They tend to be a	87	52
little more lenient on the time abuse issue and often treat the	91	54
Internet the same way that they deal with the telephone. Limited	95	57
personal use of the Internet or e-mail is not a major problem. If	100	60
the use becomes excessive, then action is taken.	103	62

3' | 1 | 2 | 3 | 4 |
5' | 1 | 2 | 3 |

LESSON 19

$ and - (hyphen), Number Expression

WARMUP

19a
Key each line twice SS.

alphabet 1 Why did the judge quiz poor Victor about his blank tax form?

figures 2 J. Boyd, Ph.D., changed Items 10, 57, 36, and 48 on page 92.

3d row 3 To try the tea, we hope to tour the port prior to the party.

easy 4 Did he signal the authentic robot to do a turn to the right?

| 1 | 2 | 3 | 4 | 5 | 6 | 7 | 8 | 9 | 10 | 11 | 12 |

NEW KEYS

19b $ and -
Key each line once SS;
DS between 2-line groups.

- = hyphen
-- = dash
Do not space before or after a hyphen or a dash.

$ Shift; then reach *up* with *left first* finger.

- (hyphen) Reach *up* with *right fourth* finger.

$

5 $ $f f$ $ $; if $4; half $4; off $4; of $4; $4 fur; $4 flats

6 for $8; cost $9; log $3; grab $10; give Rolf $2; give Viv $4

7 Since she paid $45 for the item priced at $54, she saved $9.

- (hyphen)

8 - -; ;- - - -; up-to-date; co-op; father-in-law; four-square

9 pop-up foul; big-time job; snap-on bit; one- or two-hour ski

10 You need 6 signatures--half of the members--on the petition.

all symbols learned

11 I paid $10 for the low-cost disk; high-priced ones cost $40.

12 Le-An spent $20 for travel, $95 for books, and $38 for food.

13 Mr. Loft-Smit sold his boat for $467; he bought it for $176.

SKILLBUILDING

19c Keyboard Reinforcement
Key each line once; repeat the drill.

e/d 14 Edie discreetly decided to deduct expenses in making a deed.

w/e 15 Working women wear warm wool sweaters when weather dictates.

r/e 16 We heard very rude remarks regarding her recent termination.

s/d 17 This seal's sudden misdeeds destroyed several goods on land.

v/b 18 Beverley voted by giving a bold beverage to every brave boy.

Mr. Russell Adams
Trapp, Inc.
2593 Fifth St.
Dallas, TX 75221-4768
Russ
russell.adams@trapp.com

Ms. Cynthia Busch
LeVan, Inc.
2986 Sky Way
Seattle, WA 05671-4342
Cyndi
cynthia.busch@levan.com

Mr. Bradley Tate
ATA Supplies, Inc.
2155 Mack Ave.
Los Angeles, CA 90155-2074
Brad
Bradley.tate@atasupplies.com

Ms. Judith Olson
Trapp, Inc.
2593 Fifth St.
Dallas, TX 75221-4768
Judy
judith.olson@trapp.com

Mr. Donald May
SDG, Inc.
9170 Glacier Dr.
Selden, NY 11784-3579
Don
donald.may@sdg.com

Ms. Elizabeth Roth
Ashcraft, Inc.
8265 Oregon Ave.
Arvada, CO 80002-3749
Liz
elizabeth.roth@ashcraft.com

107d-d2
Name Badge Labels

1. Prepare name badge labels for all of the Customer Service Seminar participants.
2. Use the same format you used in **107c-drill2**.
3. Select a name badge label of your choice from the Avery Standard list.
4. Save as **107d-d2** and print on plain paper.

107d-d3
File Folder Labels

1. Prepare file folder labels for all of the Customer Service Seminar participants.
2. Use the same format you used in **107c-drill3**.
3. Select a file folder label of your choice from the Avery Standard list.
4. Save as **107d-d3** and print on plain paper.

107d-d4
Portfolio Labels

1. Prepare portfolio labels for all of the Customer Service Seminar participants.
2. Select **5836-Portfolio-Mtg. Creator** label from the Avery Standard list.
3. Include the address block plus the e-mail address fields.
4. Format the label by placing a double-space between the address block and the e-mail address.
5. Save as **107d-d4** and print on plain paper.

19d Speed Builder

Key each line once, working for fluid, consistent stroking. Repeat at a faster speed.

easy words

19 am it go bus dye jam irk six sod tic yam ugh spa vow aid dug
20 he or by air big elf dog end fit and lay sue toe wit own got
21 six foe pen firm also body auto form down city kept make fog.

TECHNIQUE TIP

- Key the easy words as "words" rather than stroke by stroke.
- Key each phrase (marked by a vertical line) without pauses between words.

easy phrases

22 it is|if the|and also|to me|the end|to us|if it|it is|to the
23 if it is|to the end|do you wish|to go to|for the end|to make
24 lay down|he or she|make me|by air|end of |by me|kept it|of me

easy sentences

25 Did the chap work to mend the torn right half of the ensign?
26 Blame me for their penchant for the antique chair and panel.
27 She bid by proxy for eighty bushels of a corn and rye blend.

COMMUNICATION

19e Number Expression

1. Study the rules and examples at the right.
2. Key the sample sentences 28–33.
3. Change figures to words as needed in sentences 34–36.

Spell out numbers:

1. **First word in a sentence.** Key numbers ten and lower as words unless they are part of a series of related numbers, any of which are over ten.

   Three of the four members were present.
   She wrote 12 stories and 2 plays in five years.

2. The **smaller of two adjacent numbers** as words.

   SolVir shipped six 24-ton engines.

3. **Isolated fractions and approximate numbers.** Key as words **large round numbers that can be expressed as one or two words.** Hyphenate fractions expressed as words.

   She completed one-fourth of the experiments.
   Val sent out three hundred invitations.

4. **Preceding "o'clock".**

   John's due at four o'clock. Pick him up at 4:15 p.m.

28 **Six** or **seven** older players were cut from the **37**-member team.
29 I have **2** of **14** coins I need to start my set. Kristen has **9.**
30 Of **nine 24**-ton engines ordered, we shipped **six** last Tuesday.
31 Shelly has read just **one-half** of about **forty-five** documents.
32 The **six** boys sent well over **two hundred** printed invitations.
33 **One** or **two** of us will be on duty from **two** until **six** o'clock.
34 The meeting begins promptly at 9. We plan 4 sessions.
35 The 3-person crew cleaned 6 stands, 12 tables, and 13 desks.
36 The 3d meeting is at 3 o'clock on Friday, February 2.

CREATE NAME BADGE LABELS

1. Use the same procedures and data source to create Name Badge labels.

2. In Step 5 of 107c (p. 420), *Change document layout*, under Label Options, choose **5895-Name Badge**, and click **OK**.

3. In Step 6 under *Select recipients*, click **Use an existing list**, click **Browse**, and then select **Review Labels** from the drive on which you stored it.

4. Click **Next: Arrange your labels**.

5. Click **More Items** and use the following fields: Nickname, First Name, Last Name, and Company Name.

6. Format the first label block as follows: Select the first label, click **Center** and **Bold**. Then select **Nickname** and change font size to 36 point. Select the first and last names and company name and change font to 18 point.

7. Update all labels and preview.

8. Save as **107c-drill2 Name Badge** and print on plain paper.

CREATE FILE FOLDER LABELS

1. Use the same procedures and data source (**Review Labels**) to create file folder labels containing first and last name.

2. Use Label Option **5866-File Folder** labels.

3. When you select the recipients from the **Review Labels** data source, click the heading over Last Name so that the labels will be sorted in alphabetical order.

4. Save as **107c-drill3 Folder Labels** and print on plain paper.

APPLICATIONS

107d-d1
Address Labels

1. Prepare labels for all participants in a Customer Service training program.

2. Use the information below to prepare a data source for address labels. The same data source will be used for name badges, file folder labels, and e-mail addresses; therefore, include all of the information in the data source when you prepare it.

3. Name the data source **Customer Service**.

4. Select an address label of your choice from the Avery Standard list.

5. Save as **107d-d1** and print on plain paper.

Customer Service Seminar Participants

Mr. Alfred Carter
ATA Supplies, Inc.
2155 Mack Ave.
Los Angeles, CA 90155-2074
Al
alfred.carter@atasupplies.com

Mr. Edward Nix
LeVan, Inc.
2986 Sky Way
Seattle, WA 05671-4342
Ed
edward.nix@levan.com

Ms. Pamela Cox
Ashcraft, Inc.
8265 Oregon Ave.
Arvada, CO 80002-3749
Pam
pamela.cox@ashcraft.com

Ms. Janice Hill
SDG, Inc.
9170 Glacier Dr.
Selden, NY 11784-3579
Jan
janice.hill@sdg.com

(continued on next page)

LESSON 20

and /

WARMUP

20a
Key each line twice SS
(slowly, then faster).

alphabet 1 Freda Jencks will have money to buy six quite large topazes.

symbols 2 I bought 10 ribbons and 45 disks from Cable-Han Co. for $78.

home row 3 Dallas sold jade flasks; Sal has a glass flask full of salt.

easy 4 He may cycle down to the field by the giant oak and cut hay.

NEW KEYS

20b # and /
Key each line once SS.

= number sign,
pounds

/ = diagonal, slash

Shift; then reach *up*
with *left second* finger.

/ Reach *down* with *right
fourth* finger.

#

5 # #e e# # # #; had #3 dial; did #3 drop; set #3 down; Bid #3

6 leave #82; sold #20; Lyric #16; bale #34; load #53; Optic #7

7 Notice #333 says to load Car #33 with 33# of #3 grade shale.

/

8 / /; ;/ / / /; 1/2; 1/3; Mr./Mrs.; 1/5/94; 22 11/12; and/or;

9 to/from; /s/ William Smit; 2/10, n/30; his/her towels; 6 1/2

10 The numerals 1 5/8, 3 1/4, and 60 7/9 are "mixed fractions."

all symbols learned

11 Invoice #737 cites 15 2/3# of rye was shipped C.O.D. 4/6/95.

12 B-O-A Company's Check #50/5 for $87 paid for 15# of #3 wire.

13 Our Co-op List #20 states $40 for 16 1/2 crates of tomatoes.

SKILLBUILDING

gwam 30"

20c Keyboard Reinforcement
Key each line once; work for fluency.

Option: In the Open Screen, key 30" writings on both lines of a pair. Work to avoid pauses.

14 She did the key work at the height of the problem. 20

15 Form #726 is the title to the island; she owns it. 20

16 The rock is a form of fuel; he did enrich it with coal. 22

17 The corn-and-turkey dish is a blend of turkey and corn. 22

18 It is right to work to end the social problems of the world. 24

19 If I sign it on 3/19, the form can aid us to pay the 40 men. 24

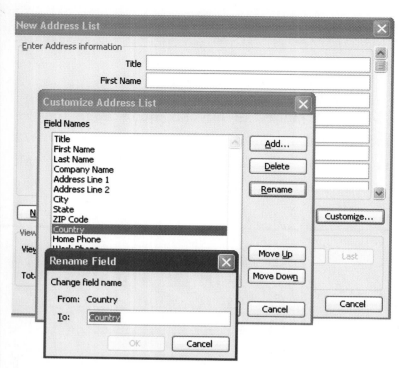

6. Under Select recipients, click **Type a New list** and then click **Create**. The New Address List box displays.

7. Click **Customize** to edit the default field names provided. For Drill 1, select **Country** and click **Rename**. Key **Nickname**.

8. Select each of the following fields and click the **Delete** button: **Address Line 2**, **Home Phone**, **Work Phone**, and **E-mail address**.

9. Key the variables for each record.

10. Click **Close** after keying all the records. The Save Address List dialog box displays. Enter the filename (**Review Labels**) in the File name box and click **Save**. (First select the correct drive to store the file; if you do not, it will be stored to the folder **My Data Sources** in the **My Documents** Folder.) Click **OK**; then **Next**.

11. Under Arrange your labels, click **Address block** (click **More items** if you prefer to select items individually).

12. Under Replicate labels, click **Update all labels** to replicate the address block merge field on each label across the page. Click **Next**.

13. From Preview your labels, click the arrows to preview labels; then click **Next**.

14. From Complete the merge, click **Edit individual labels**. Click **All**; then **OK**.

15. Resave the main document.

DRILL 1   CREATE LABELS

1. Create address labels for the records shown below.

2. Save the address list as **Review Labels**.

3. Save the labels as **107c-drill1 address** and print on plain paper.

Review Labels

Title	First Name	Last Name	Company Name	Address Line 1	City	State	ZIP Code	Nickname
Mr.	Reginald	McWhorter	Circle R, Inc.	1896 Lawndale Ave.	Salt Lake City	UT	84110-9365	Reggie
Ms.	Julie	Hartwell	Thomas General Hospital	2765 Sheridan Rd.	Chicago	IL	60650-7169	Julie
Dr.	Margaret	Wilson	Weeks Medical Center	957 W. Lake Dr.	Milwaukee	WI	53221-2956	Peggy
Mr.	William	Bass	Marcus, Inc.	830 Birch Cir.	Clinton	MS	39056-2864	Bill
Ms.	Rebecca	McGee	Circle R, Inc.	1896 Lawndale Ave.	Salt Lake City	UT	84110-9365	Becky
Mr.	Charles	Kapp	Marcus, Inc.	830 Birch Cir.	Clinton	MS	39056-2864	Chuck
Dr.	Henry	Wise	Weeks Medical Center	957 W. Lake Dr.	Milwaukee	WI	53221-2956	Hank
Ms.	Marjorie	Keene	Thomas General Hospital	2765 Sheridan Rd.	Chicago	IL	60650-7169	Margie

20d Number Usage Review

Key each line once. Decide whether the circled numbers should be keyed as figures or as words and make needed changes. Check your finished work with 19e, page 47.

20 Six or (7) older players were cut from the (37)-member team.

21 I have (2) of 14 coins I need to start my set.   Kristen has (9).

22 Of (9) 24-ton engines ordered, we shipped (6) last Tuesday.

23 Shelly has read just (1) half of about (45) documents.

24 The (6) boys sent well over (200) printed invitations.

25 (1) or (2) of us will be on duty from (2) until (6) o'clock.

20e Speed Builder

1. Go to the Open Screen.
2. Follow the procedures at the right for increasing your speed by taking guided writings.
3. Take a 3' writing without the guide on the complete writing.

 all letters

STANDARD PLAN | for Guided Writing Procedures

1. In the Open Screen, take a 1' writing on paragraph 1. Note your *gwam*.
2. Add four words to your 1' *gwam* to determine your goal rate.
3. Set the Timer for 1'. Set the Timer option to beep every 15".
4. From the table below, select from column 4 the speed nearest your goal rate. Note the ¼' point at the left of that speed. Place a light check mark within the paragraphs at the ¼' points.
5. Take two 1' guided writings on paragraphs 1 and 2.   Do not save.
6. Turn the beeper off.

			gwam
1/4'	1/2'	3/4'	1'
4	8	12	16
5	10	15	20
6	12	18	24
7	14	21	28
8	16	24	32
9	18	27	36
10	20	30	40

	gwam	2'	3'
Some of us think that the best way to get attention is		6	4	35
to try a new style, or to look quixotic, or to be different		12	8	39
somehow. Perhaps we are looking for nothing much more than		18	12	43
acceptance from others of ourselves just the way we now are.		24	16	47
There is no question about it; we all want to look our		29	19	50
best to impress other people. How we achieve this may mean		35	23	54
trying some of this and that; but our basic objective is to		41	27	58
take our raw materials, you and me, and build up from there.		47	31	62

2' | 1 | 2 | 3 | 4 | 5 | 6 |
3' | 1 | 2 | 3 | 4 |

LESSON 107 | Name Badges and Labels

SKILLBUILDING

107a
Warmup
Key each line twice SS.

alphabet	1	Paxton quoted Jay in an amazing article this week before leaving.
symbols	2	Take the 15% discount on the invoice (#4973280); then add 6% tax.
double letters	3	Bobby Lott feels that the meeting at noon will be cancelled soon.
fluency	4	Did Leigh visit the Land of Enchantment or a neighbor in Orlando?

| 1 | 2 | 3 | 4 | 5 | 6 | 7 | 8 | 9 | 10 | 11 | 12 | 13 |

DOCUMENT DESIGN

107b

Labels

Label options exist for a variety of purposes, such as address labels, name badges, file folders, CD-ROM labels, and many others. Many of these labels are useful in managing meetings effectively. Because all of these labels can be created from the same data source, it is important to capture all of the data that is needed in the data source. In this lesson, you will use the same data source to prepare address labels, name badges, and file folder labels.

Name badges for meetings and conferences are printed in large type so that they can be read easily. The tone for the conference is usually set by the way the name is printed on the badge. If a meeting is designed to be informal and interactive, the name badge usually features the individual's first name or nickname with the full name below it. A more formal meeting would include the full name. Rarely is a courtesy title (Ms., Mr., Mrs., or Dr.) used on a name badge. Professional titles and company or organization information may be included.

FUNCTION REVIEW

107c

Merge Labels

To create labels:

1. Open a new document and save with an appropriate filename. (For Drill 1, save as **107c-drill1 address**.)
2. Choose **Tools**, then **Letters and Mailings**, and then **Mail Merge Wizard**. Follow the steps of the Mail Merge Wizard to create labels. Click **Next** to move to the next step.
3. Under Select document type, select **Labels**. Click **Next**.
4. Under Select starting document, click **Change document layout**.
5. Under Change document layout, click **Label Options**. Choose **5922-address** from the Avery Standard Product number in the Label Options dialog box. Click **OK**.

(continued on next page)

LESSON 21

% and !

WARMUP

21a
Key each line twice SS.

alphabet 1 Merry will have picked out a dozen quarts of jam for boxing.

fig/sym 2 Jane-Ann bought 16 7/8 yards of #240 cotton at $3.59 a yard.

1st row 3 Can't brave, zany Cave Club men/women next climb Mt. Zamban?

easy 4 Did she rush to cut six bushels of corn for the civic corps?

NEW KEYS

21b % and !
Key each line once SS.

> **% = percent sign:** Use % with business forms or where space is restricted; otherwise, use the word "percent." Space twice after the exclamation point!

% Shift; then reach *up* with *left first* finger.

%

5 % %f f% % %; off 5%; if 5%; of 5% fund; half 5%; taxes of 5%

6 7% rent; 3% tariff; 9% F.O.B.; 15% greater; 28% base; up 46%

7 Give discounts of 5% on rods, 50% on lures, and 75% on line.

! reach *up* with the *left fourth* finger

8 ! !a a! ! ! !; Eureka! Ha! No! Pull 10! Extra! America!

9 Listen to the call! Now! Ready! Get set! Go! Good show!

10 I want it now, not next week! I am sure to lose 50% or $19.

all symbols

11 The ad offers a 10% discount, but this notice says 15% less!

12 He got the job! With Clark's Supermarket! Please call Mom!

13 Bill #92-44 arrived very late from Zyclone; it was paid 7/4.

SPACING TIP
▪ Do not space between a figure and the % or $ signs.
▪ Do not space before or after the dash.

21c Keyboard Reinforcement
Key each line once; work for fluency.

all symbols

14 As of 6/28, Jeri owes $31 for dinner and $27 for cab fare.

15 Invoice #20--it was dated 3/4--billed $17 less 15% discount.

16 He deducted 2% instead of 6%, a clear saving of 6% vs. 7%.

combination response

17 Look at my dismal grade in English; but I guess I earned it.

18 Kris started to blend a cocoa beverage for a shaken cowhand.

19 Jan may make a big profit if she owns the title to the land.

106c-d2
Revise Itinerary

1. Open **106c-d1** and save it as **106c-d2**.

2. Several plans have changed. Make the following modifications to Ms. Zachary's agenda.

   a. Brad Matthews cannot attend the 12:30 luncheon; he will meet with Ms. Zachary at the Mile High Hotel in Conference Room A at 2:30. June Wiley and Joseph Todd will be with him.

   b. Change the tour of the Azure Manufacturing Plant to 4:00.

   c. An earlier return flight was booked, Flight 482; depart at 2:45 and arrive at 5:40.

   d. Resave and print.

106c-d3
Itinerary

1. Use the same format as **106c-d1** and the following information to prepare an itinerary for Travelle Gortman who is attending and making a presentation at the Technology Summit in Washington, D.C. on June 1–3.

   a. Leave Mobile on Wednesday, June 1, on Freedom Flight 1475 at 7:00 a.m. and arrive in Atlanta at 7:35. Leave Atlanta on Freedom Flight 290 at 8:45 a.m. and arrive at Ronald Reagan Washington National Airport at 9:53; met by Executive Conference Service at baggage claim.

   b. Reservation on concierge level of the Hampton Hotel, 2300 Pennsylvania Ave., NW (Confirmation #527918).

   c. Conference (preregistration confirmation #S-963248); see conference program for schedule.

   d. Dinner on June 1 at 8:30 p.m. at Crystal's in Georgetown; reservations in your name for six (Anne Moore, Lee Roswell, Andy Cox, Leslie Kline, and Takisha Penn).

   e. Presentation at 10:00 a.m. on Thursday, June 2, in Ballroom A on the third floor of the Hampton Hotel; lunch with the Technology Summit Executive Committee at 12:30 in the Terrace Room.

   f. Depart at 6:30 p.m. for performance at Kennedy Center followed by dinner at Marbelle Estate with Larry Newman, president of the Technology Summit.

   g. Washington, D.C. to Mobile. Depart at 1:00 on Friday, June 3, for Ronald Reagan Washington National Airport (Executive Conference Service provides transportation) for return on Freedom Flight 861 at 2:45 p.m. and arrive in Atlanta at 3:51. Leave Atlanta on Freedom Flight 1683 at 4:45 p.m. and arrive in Mobile at 5:28.

2. Save as **106c-d3** and print.

SKILLBUILDING

21d Textbook Keying

Key each line once; DS between groups; fingers curved, hands quiet. Repeat if time permits.

1st finger

20 by bar get fun van for inn art from gray hymn July true verb
21 brag human bring unfold hominy mighty report verify puny joy
22 You are brave to try bringing home the van in the bad storm.

2d finger

23 ace ink did cad keyed deep seed kind Dick died kink like kid
24 cease decease decades kick secret check decide kidney evaded
25 Dedre likes the idea of ending dinner with cake for dessert.

3d finger

26 oil sow six vex wax axe low old lox pool west loss wool slow
27 swallow swamp saw sew wood sax sexes loom stew excess school
28 Wes waxes floors and washes windows at low costs to schools.

4th finger

29 zap zip craze pop pup pan daze quote queen quiz pizza puzzle
30 zoo graze zipper panzer zebra quip partizan patronize appear
31 Czar Zane appears to be dazzled by the apple pizza and jazz.

21e Speed Runs with Numbers

Take 1' writings; the last number you key when you stop is your approximate *gwam*.

1 and 2 and 3 and 4 and 5 and 6 and 7 and 8 and 9 and 10 and 11 and 12 and 13 and 14 and 15 and 16 and 17 and 18 and 19 and 20 and 21 and 22 and 23 and 24 and 25 and 26 and 27 and

21f Speed Check

Key a 1' and a 2' writing. Option: Key a 3' writing.

all letters

	gwam	1'	2'
Teams are the basic unit of performance for a firm.	11	5	42
They are not the solution to all of the organizational needs.	23	12	48
They will not solve all of the problems, but it is known	35	17	54
that a team can perform at a higher rate than other groups.	47	23	60
It is one of the best ways to support the changes needed for	59	30	66
a firm. The team must have time in order to make	71	36	72
a quality working plan.	74	37	74

```
1'  |  1  |  2  |  3  |  4  |  5  |  6  |  7  |  8  |  9  |  10  |  11  |  12  |
2'      |     1     |     2     |     3     |     4     |     5     |     6     |
```

ITINERARY FOR SUSAN C. ZACHARY

May 6-8, 200-

↑
14 point

Monday, May 6	**Dallas to Denver**
9:25 a.m.	Leave Dallas Fort Worth International Airport on Skyway Flight 498 and arrive at Denver International Airport at 10:28 a.m.; Bronco Rental Car (Confirmation #492084); Mile High Hotel, (Confirmation #360457) 3961 E. Louisiana Ave. (20 minutes).
12:30 p.m.	Luncheon meeting with Robert Jarworzky, Leigh Moreau, and Brad Matthews at Cherry Creek Eatery at 4827 Cherry Creek S. Dr.
3:00 p.m.	Tour of the Azure Manufacturing Plant; followed by meeting with the Quality Assurance team. Transportation: picked up at hotel by Dave S. Roane. Dinner arranged by Azure. Return to hotel by 10:00 p.m.

Tuesday, May 7	**Lakewood**
8:30 a.m.	Drive to Lakewood (map in Lakewood file).
9:30 a.m.	Full-day meeting with Lakewood Pharmaceuticals.
6:00 p.m.	Dinner with Christopher Davis, President of Lakewood Pharmaceuticals and Karen Davis. Return to hotel by 9:30 p.m.

Wednesday, May 8	**Denver**
9:30 a.m.	Meeting with the Gentry Group at the Mile High Hotel, Conference Center Board Room.
12:00 noon	Lunch for the Gentry Group in Skyview Room.
3:55 p.m.	Leave Denver International Airport on Skyway Flight 639; arrive Dallas/Fort Worth at 6:25 p.m.

LESSON 22

(and) and Backspace Key

22a
Key each line twice SS.

alphabet 1 Avoid lazy punches; expert fighters jab with a quick motion.

fig/sym 2 Be-Low's Bill #483/7 was $96.90, not $102--they took 5% off.

caps lock 3 Report titles may be shown in ALL CAPS; as, BOLD WORD POWER.

easy 4 Do they blame me for their dismal social and civic problems?

| 1 | 2 | 3 | 4 | 5 | 6 | 7 | 8 | 9 | 10 | 11 | 12 |

NEW KEYS

22b (and)
(parentheses)
Key each line once SS.

(Shift; then reach *up* with the *right third* finger.

) Shift; then reach *up* with the *right fourth* finger.

( ) = parentheses
Parentheses indicate offhand, aside, or explanatory messages.

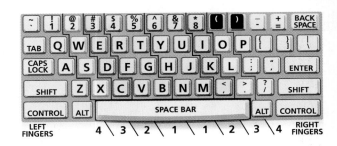

5 ((l l((; (; Reach from l for the left parenthesis; as, ((.

6)); ;))); Reach from ; for the right parenthesis; as,)).

( )

7 Learn to use parentheses (plural) or parenthesis (singular).

8 The red (No. 34) and blue (No. 78) cars both won here (Rio).

9 We (Galen and I) dined (bagels) in our penthouse (the dorm).

all symbols learned

10 The jacket was $35 (thirty-five dollars)--the tie was extra.

11 Starting 10/29, you can sell Model #49 at a discount of 25%.

12 My size 8 1/2 shoe--a blue pump--was soiled (but not badly).

22c Textbook Keying
Key each line once, keeping eyes on copy.

13 Jana has one hard-to-get copy of her hot-off-the-press book.

14 An invoice said that "We give discounts of 10%, 5%, and 3%."

15 The company paid Bill 3/18 on 5/2/97 and Bill 3/1 on 3/6/97.

16 The catalog lists as out of stock Items #230, #710, and #13.

17 Elyn had $8; Sean, $9; and Cal, $7. The cash total was $24.

LESSON 106 | Itineraries

SKILLBUILDING

106a
Warmup
Key each line twice SS.

alphabet	1	Rex Patey quickly moved to a new zone just before the group came.
figures	2	Vi paid $19.50 for Seats 7 and 8; Pat paid $26 for Seats 3 and 4.
1st/2nd fingers	3	Guy tried to come to my rescue before going to work this morning.
easy	4	Jay and I may go with eight girls to fish on the docks by a lake.

| 1 | 2 | 3 | 4 | 5 | 6 | 7 | 8 | 9 | 10 | 11 | 12 | 13 |

DOCUMENT DESIGN

106b

Itinerary

An **itinerary** is a detailed schedule prepared for individuals who are traveling or who are working away from their offices.   Normally when people are working in their offices, they have a variety of information available to them. When they are out of the office, a comprehensive itinerary provides a quick summary of all the logistical information needed to function effectively.   Itineraries for international travel typically require more information than for domestic travel. Types of information normally included in an itinerary include:

- Dates and times of meetings and events
- Transportation information—airline flight numbers and times, ticket information, passport or visa requirements, rental car or ground transportation
- Hotel information—name and address, confirmation number, special requests made
- Restaurant information—name and address, reservation information
- Meetings or appointments—individual and company names, times, addresses, transportation information if needed
- Leisure time activities and information

Most organizations use a list-type format so that the information is easy to read. Fragments are generally used rather than complete sentences. Position the heading for short itineraries about 2" from the top of the page and 1" to 1.5" for long itineraries. Set a hanging indent about 1.5" for the descriptive information. The itinerary shown on the next page illustrates a typical itinerary for a domestic business trip.

APPLICATIONS

106c-d1
Itinerary

1. Key the itinerary on the next page.
2. Position the heading at about 1.5" and format it in bold, 14-point type.
3. Use a default left tab of 1.5" and set a hanging indent at 1.5" for the second column.
4. Save as **106c-d1** and print.

22d BACKSPACE **Key**

Practice reaching to the BACK-SPACE key with your right little finger. Key the sentences, using the BACKSPACE key to correct errors.

22e **Speed Check**

1. Take two 1' timings on each paragraph.
2. Take a 3' timing on all paragraphs. Determine *gwam*.

Goal: 17 *gwam*

all letters

18 You should be interested in the special items on sale today.
19 If she is going with us, why don't we plan to leave now?
20 Do you desire to continue working on the memo in the future?
21 Did the firm or their neighbors own the autos with problems?
22 Juni, Vec, and Zeb had perfect grades on weekly query exams.
23 Jewel quickly explained to me the big fire hazards involved.

	1'	3'
	10	4	28
	22	7	32
	34	12	36
	38	13	37
	11	16	41
	12	21	45
	35	25	49

Most people will agree that we owe it to our children to pass the planet on to them in better condition than we found it. We must take extra steps just to make the quality of living better.

If we do not change our ways quickly and stop damaging our world, it will not be a good place to live. We can save the ozone and wildlife and stop polluting the air and water.

| 1' | 1 | 2 | 3 | 4 | 5 | 6 | 7 | 8 | 9 | 10 | 11 | 12 |
| 3' | | 1 | | | 2 | | | 3 | | | 4 | |

COMMUNICATION

22f **Number Expression**

1. Study the rules and examples at the right.
2. In the Open Screen, key the information below at the left margin. Press ENTER as shown.

   Your name ENTER

   Current date ENTER

   Skillbuilders 1, Drill 6

   ENTER ENTER

3. Key the sample sentences 24–28. Backspace to correct errors.
4. Save the file as **xx-22f**.

Express as figures

1. **Money amounts** and **percentages, even when appoximate.** Spell out cents and percent except in statistical copy.

   The 16 percent discount saved me $145; Bill, 95 cents.

2. **Round numbers expressed in millions or higher with their word modifier.**

   Ms. Ti contributed $3 million.

3. **House numbers** (Except house number One) and street names over ten. If a street name is a number, separate it from the house number with a dash.

   1510 Easy Street   One West Ninth Avenue   1592-11th Street

4. **Date followed by a month.** A date preceding the month or standing alone is expressed in figures followed by "d" or "th."

   June 9, 2001   4th of July   March 3d

5. **Numbers used with nouns.**

   Volume 1   Chapter 6

24 Ask **Group 1** to read **Chapter 6** of **Book 11** (**Shelf 19, Room 5**).
25 All **six** of us live at **One Bay Road**, not at **126--56th Street**.
26 At **9 a.m.** the owners decided to close from **12 noon** to **1 p.m.**
27 Ms. Vik leaves **June 9**; she returns the **14th or 15th of July**.
28 The **16 percent** discount saves **$115**. A stamp costs **35 cents**.

1. Key the following information to prepare minutes; then add the remaining part of the document from **minutes** in the data files.

2. Use the same format as **105c-d1**.

3. Number pages as a right-aligned header; do not show page number on the first page.

4. Preview to make sure that headings are not left alone at the bottom of the page.

5. Save as **105c-d2** and print.

Palmetto Children's Home / Meeting of Board of Directors / May 20, 200-

The Board of Directors of Palmetto Children's Home met on May 20, 200- at 8:00 in the Board Room. Mary Ott called the meeting to order and welcomed all participants.

Board members present were Allen Brown, Jeff Green, Steve Islam, Fred Jones, Jake Lee, Carol Marks, Mary Ott, Keith Price, Ann Ray, and Julie Wills. Staff members present were Nate Lipscomb, Wayne Simmons, Suzanne Reed, and Jack Washburn.

Mission Statement Review
Jake Lee reported that the Executive Committee reviewed the mission statement and recommended no changes in it. The Executive Committee also recommended that the mission statement be read at the beginning of each board meeting to ensure that all actions were focused on accomplishing the mission of the Palmetto Children's Home.

Development Update
Julie Wills reported on development activities since the last meeting. She provided an updated list of the major gift prospects and asked each board member to review the list and provide her with information about any of the prospects they knew. She reviewed the solicitation plan that was included in the meeting materials and on behalf of the Development Committee moved the acceptance of the plan. The motion was approved unanimously.

Financial Report
Jeff Green presented the actual revenues and expenditures year-to-date and compared them to the current budget. Revenues and expenditures were on target, and no budget revisions were recommended. He then reviewed the quarterly financial statements. The financial report was presented for information and no action was required until the audit report is presented.

Jeff Green then provided an update on the $6,000,000 proposed bond issue and moved on behalf of the Finance Committee that the transaction be finalized.   The motion was approved unanimously.

Insert **minutes** here.

LESSON 23

& and : (colon), Proofreaders' marks

WARMUP

23a
Key each line twice SS.

alphabet 1 Roxy waved as she did quick flying jumps on the trapeze bar.

symbols 2 Ryan's--with an A-1 rating--sold Item #146 (for $10) on 2/7.

space bar 3 Mr. Fyn may go to Cape Cod on the bus, or he may go by auto.

easy 4 Susie is busy; may she halt the social work for the auditor?

| 1 | 2 | 3 | 4 | 5 | 6 | 7 | 8 | 9 | 10 | 11 | 12 |

NEW KEYS

23b & and : (colon)
Key each line once SS.

& Shift; then reach *up* with *right first* finger.

: (colon) Left shift; then press key with *right fourth* finger.

> **& = ampersand:** The ampersand is used only as part of company names.
> **Colon:** Space twice after a colon except when used within a number for time.

LEFT FINGERS   4 \ 3 \ 2 \ 1 \   \ 1 \ 2 \ 3 \ 4   RIGHT FINGERS

& (ampersand)

5 & &j j& & & &; J & J; Haraj & Jay; Moroj & Jax; Torj & Jones

6 Nehru & Unger; Mumm & Just; Mann & Hart; Arch & Jones; M & J

7 Rhye & Knox represent us; Steb & Doy, Firm A; R & J, Firm B.

: (colon)

8 : :; ;: : : :; as: for example: notice: To: From: Date:

9 in stock: 8:30; 7:45; Age: Experience: Read: Send: See:

10 Space twice after a colon, thus: To: No.: Time: Carload:

all symbols learned

11 Consider these companies: J & R, Brand & Kay, Uper & Davis.

12 Memo #88-89 reads as follows: "Deduct 15% of $300, or $45."

13 Bill 32(5)--it got here quite late--from M & N was paid 7/3.

double letters

14 Di Bennett was puzzled by drivers exceeding the speed limit.

15 Bill needs the office address; he will cut the grass at ten.

16 Todd saw the green car veer off the street near a tall tree.

23c Keyboard Reinforcement

Key each line twice; work for fluency.

figures and symbols

17 Invoice #84 for $672.91, plus $4.38 tax, was due on 5/19/02.

18 Do read Section 4, pages 60-74 and Section 9, pages 198-225.

19 Enter the following: (a) name, (b) address, and (c) tax ID.

Position the main heading at about 1" to 2", depending upon the length of the document.

↓

CENTRAL UNIVERSITY MASTER PLAN FOR RESEARCH FACILITIES
Planning and Data Analysis Meeting Minutes
February 15, 200-

↑
14 point

The Central University Master Plan for Research Facilities team met on February 15, 200- in the Plaza Board Room.

Team members present were Shirley Marshall, Team Leader; Chuck Taylor, President, Taylor Properties; Scott Johnson, Architect; Jim Hendley, Vice President for Research; Toni Hess, Provost; Andy Maxwell, Chief Financial Officer; and Joyce Martin, Chief Executive Officer, Foundations.

Work Session

Shirley Marshall opened the meeting and indicated that all team members were present. The team devoted the first half hour of the meeting to a working session designed to review a series of concepts relating to the design of the Phase I building. Scott Johnson charted the pros and cons on each concept presented and will finalize the analysis that will guide the conceptual design of the Phase I building.

Project Goals and Process Review

Shirley Marshall reminded the team that the primary goal of this project was to complete the preliminary design work that Central University could use to develop state-of-the-art research laboratory and office facilities on the property designated as the research block. The team agreed that the highest and best use of the research block was for three separate buildings connected by an open plaza. All parking was moved from the research block to the block across the street on the east side. A 1,000-car parking deck was proposed for that site. All information collected to date has been processed and incorporated in the initial site plan options.

Site Plan Options

Chuck Taylor summarized the data collected and analyzed in the site evaluation. The topography of the site presents design challenges because there is a 50-foot difference in the highest and lowest points on the block. Slides detailing the four options were presented for the conceptual design of the team. The team selected the horseshoe terrace as the preferred option, but recommended some modifications in the conceptual design.

Architectural Image Concepts

A series of architectural image concepts for the first building were critiqued. The feedback provided on the concepts will be used in preparing the building design to be presented at the next meeting.

After a general discussion of the progress on the project, the meeting was adjourned at 3:55 p.m.

23d Textbook Keying
Key each line once; work for fluency.

20 Jane may work with an auditing firm if she is paid to do so.
21 Pam and eight girls may go to the lake to work with the dog.
22 Clancy and Claudia did all the work to fix the sign problem.
23 Did Lea visit the Orlando land of enchantment or a neighbor?
24 Ana and Blanche made a map for a neighbor to go to the city.
25 Sidney may go to the lake to fish with worms from the docks.
26 Did the firm or the neighbors own the auto with the problem?

| 1 | 2 | 3 | 4 | 5 | 6 | 7 | 8 | 9 | 10 | 11 | 12 |

 23e Speed Check

Key two 1' timed writings on each paragraph; then two 3' writings on both paragraphs; compute *gwam*.

Goals: 1', 20–27 *gwam*
3', 17–24 *gwam*

 all letters

	gwam	1'	3'

Is how you judge my work important? It is, of course; — 11 | 4 | 26
I hope you recognize some basic merit in it. We all expect — 23 | 8 | 30
to get credit for good work that we conclude. — 32 | 11 | 33

I want approval for stands I take, things I write, and — 11 | 14 | 36
work I complete. My efforts, by my work, show a picture of — 23 | 18 | 41
me; thus, through my work, I am my own unique creation. — 34 | 22 | 44

1' | 1 | 2 | 3 | 4 | 5 | 6 | 7 | 8 | 9 | 10 | 11 | 12 |
3' | | 1 | | 2 | | 3 | | 4 |

Proofreaders' marks are used to identify mistakes in typed or printed text. Learn to apply these commonly used standard proofreaders' marks.

  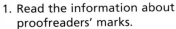 **23f** Edit Text

1. Read the information about proofreaders' marks.
2. In the Open Screen, key your name, class, and 23f at the left margin. Then key lines 27–32, making the revisions as you key. Use the BACKSPACE key to correct errors.
3. Save as **xx-23f** and print.

Symbol	Meaning	Symbol	Meaning
——	Italic	⟳ sp	Spell out
⁓⁓⁓	Bold	¶	Paragraph
Cap or ≡	Capitalize	#	Add horizontal space
∧	Insert	/ or *lc*	Lowerca
⸰⸰	Delete	⌣	Close up space
⊏	Move to left	⁓	Transpose
⊐	Move to right	*stet*	Leave as originally written

27 We miss 50% in life's rewards by refusing to new try things.

28 do it now--today--then tomorrow's load will be 100%% lighter.

29 Satisfying work--whether it pays $40 or $400-is the pay off.

30 Avoid mistakes: confusing a #3 has cost thousands.

31 Pleased most with a first-rate job is the person who did it.

32 My wife and/or me mother will except the certifi cate for me.

LESSON 105 Minutes

SKILLBUILDING

105a
Warmup
Key each line twice SS.

alphabet	1	Gayle just told them about five quick trips to Arizona next week.
figures	2	The system provides 168 majors to 39,475 students on 20 campuses.
direct reaches	3	Ned used their sled on cold days and my kite on warm summer days.
fluency	4	Sidney may go with us to the lake to fish with worms on the dock.

| 1 | 2 | 3 | 4 | 5 | 6 | 7 | 8 | 9 | 10 | 11 | 12 | 13 |

DOCUMENT DESIGN

105b

Minutes

Minutes provide a record of what occurred in a meeting. Two significantly different types of minutes may be prepared. Verbatim minutes provide a complete record of everything said in a meeting. Usually verbatim minutes are prepared only for very formal meetings or for meetings that have legal implications. Most organizations prefer to use minutes that capture the essential or very important information that needs to be recorded for future use. These minutes are often referred to as action minutes because they capture the decisions that are made and the actions that take place—such as assigning responsibilities to particular individuals and specifying deadlines for the responsibilities to be completed.

Typically minutes contain the following types of information:

1. Date, time, and place of the meeting
2. Name of the presiding officer or meeting leader
3. Names (may also include titles) of attendees
4. Meeting objectives
5. Summary of decisions made
6. Summary of action items
7. Handouts and meeting materials are often attached to the minutes so they become part of the record.

Minutes are formatted in basic report style. Shortened versions of agenda items are often used as headings in the minutes. Review the minutes illustrated on the next page; then review the agenda that you prepared in **104e-d1**. Note that the minutes summarize the actions that took place in the meeting. Note also that this meeting was a working and planning type meeting rather than one in which formal action was taken and recorded.

APPLICATIONS

105c-d1
Minutes

1. Key the minutes illustrated on the next page. Position the heading at about 1.5"; bold and single-space it.
2. Single-space the minutes with 6-point space after paragraphs.
3. Bold all headings.
4. Save as **105c-d1** and print.

LESSON 24

Other Symbols

WARMUP

24a
Key each line twice SS.

alphabet 1 Pfc. Jim Kings covered each of the lazy boxers with a quilt.
figures 2 Do problems 6 to 29 on page 175 before class at 8:30, May 4.
" 3 They read the poems "September Rain" and "The Lower Branch."
easy 4 When did the busy girls fix the tight cowl of the ruby gown?

| 1 | 2 | 3 | 4 | 5 | 6 | 7 | 8 | 9 | 10 | 11 | 12 |

NEW KEYS

24b Textbook Keying

Key each pair of lines once SS;
DS between 2-line groups.

Become familiar with
these symbols:

@   at
<   less than
>   greater than
*   asterisk
+   plus sign (use a
    hyphen for minus
    and x for "times")
=   equals
[ ] left and right
    bracket

@   shift; reach *up* with *left third* finger to @

5 @ @s s@ @ @; 24 @ .15; 22 @ .35; sold 2 @ .87; were 12 @ .95
6 You may contact Luke @: LJP@rx.com or fax @ (602) 555-0101.

<   shift; reach *down* with *right second* finger to <
>   shift; reach *down* with *right third* finger to >

7 Can you prove "a > b"? If 28 > 5, then 5a < x. Is a < > b?
8 E-mail Al ajj@crewl.com and Matt mrw10@scxs.com by 9:30 p.m.

*   shift; reach *up* with *right second* finger to *

9 * *k k8* * *; aurelis*; May 7*; both sides*; 250 km.**; aka*
10 Note each *; one * refers to page 29; ** refers to page 307.

+   shift; reach *up* with *right fourth* finger to +

11 + ;+ +; + + +; 2 + 2; A+ or B+; 70+ F. degrees; +xy over +y;
12 The question was 8 + 7 + 51; it should have been 8 + 7 + 15.

=   reach *up* with *right fourth* finger to =

13 = =; = = =; = 4; If 14x = 28, x = 2; if 8x = 16, then x = 2.
14 Change this solution (where it says "= by") to = bx or = BX.

[ ] reach *up* with *right fourth* finger to [and]

15 Mr. Wing was named. [That's John J. Wing, ex-senator. Ed.]
16 We [Joseph and I] will be in Suite #349; call us @ 555-0102.

Position the main heading 1" to 2", depending upon length of document.

CENTRAL UNIVERSITY MASTER PLAN FOR RESEARCH FACILITIES

Planning and Data Analysis Meeting Agenda

14 point

Left Tab 1"   **February 15, 200-**   Right Leader Tab 6"

DS

2:00 – 2:30   Work Session—Design Options . . . . Team

DS

2:30 – 2:50   Project Goals and Process Review. . . . . Shirley Marshall

Develop State-of-the Art Research Laboratories and
Offices
Develop Concept for "Highest and Best Use" for
Research Block
Create an Architectural Image for the Project
Process to Date

Left Tab 1.25" ⟶   Needs Assessment
Data Collection
Site Evaluation
Best Practices for Research Laboratories

2:50 – 3:20   Site Plan Options . . . . Chuck Taylor

Site Evaluation Conclusions
Options for Buildings on Block
     Central Courtyard
     Dense Linear Design
     Horseshoe Terrace
     Perimeter Buildings with Central Parking

3:20 – 3:50   Architectural Image Concepts . . . . Scott Johnson

3:50 – 4:00   General Discussion . . . . Team

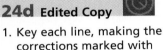

In the Open Screen, key each line twice; DS between 2-line groups.

```
                  17  feel pass mill good miss seem moons cliffs pools green spell
double letters    18  Assets are being offered in a stuffy room to two associates.

balanced          19  is if of to it go do to is do so if to to the it sign vie to
hand              20  Pamela Fox may wish to go to town with Blanche if she works.

                  21  date face ere bat lip sew lion rear brag fact join eggs ever
one hand          22  get fewer on; after we look; as we agree; add debt; act fast

                  23  was for|in the case of|they were|to down|mend it|but pony is
combination       24  They were to be down in the fastest sleigh if you are right.
                      |  1  |  2  |  3  |  4  |  5  |  6  |  7  |  8  |  9  | 10  | 11  | 12  |
```

24d Edited Copy

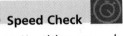

1. Key each line, making the corrections marked with proofreaders' marks.
2. Correct errors using the BACKSPACE key.
3. Save as **xx-24d**.

```
25  Ask Group 1 to read Chaᴾter 6 of Book 11 (Shelf 19,#Room 5).
                                 ^                           ^
         six
26  All 6 of us live at One Bay road, not at 126ₓ-56th Street.
        ^                           ⌐                ⌐
       lc
27  AT 9 a.m. the owners decided to close foᴩrm 12 noon to 1 p.m.
      ^
                                            th        th
28  Ms. Vik leaves June 9; she r⌒eturns the 14ₐor 15ₐof July.

29  The 16 per⌒cent discount saves $115.  A stamp costs 35 cents.
                                  $^
               $3 million    to charity
30  ⌐⌐⌐⌐⌐⌐Elin gave $̶3̶0̶0̶,̶0̶0̶0̶,̶0̶0̶0̶; our gift was only 75 cents.
                                  ^
```

24e Speed Check

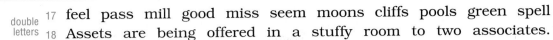

1. Key a 1' writing on each paragraph using wordwrap.
2. Key two 3' writings on both paragraphs. Save the timings if desired (**xx24e-t1** and **xx24e-t2**).

```
                                                          gwam   1'   3'

    Why don't we like change very much?  Do you think that   11   4 26
just maybe we want to be lazy; to dodge new things; and, as  23   8 30
much as possible, not to make hard decisions?                32  11 33
    We know change can and does extend new areas for us to   11  14 36
enjoy, areas we might never have known existed; and to stay  24  18 40
away from all change could curtail our quality of life.      34  22 44

1'|  1  |  2  |  3  |  4  |  5  |  6  |  7  |  8  |  9  | 10  | 11  | 12  |
3'|        1        |        2        |        3        |        4        |
```

COMMUNICATION

24f Composition Revision

1. In the Open Screen, open the file **xx-profile** that you created in Lesson 18.
2. Position the insertion point at the end of the last paragraph. Press ENTER twice.
3. Key an additional paragraph that begins with the following sentence:
   Thank you for allowing me to introduce myself.
4. Finish the paragraph by adding two or more sentences that describe your progress and satisfaction with keyboarding.
5. Correct any mistakes you have made. Click **Save** to resave the document. Print.
6. Mark any mistakes you missed with proofreaders' marks. Revise the document, save, and reprint. Submit to your instructor.

Agendas

Generally an **agenda** has four components:

1. Heading providing information about the meeting
2. List of the topics to be discussed at a meeting
3. Name of the person or group responsible for leading the discussion of each topic
4. Amount of time allocated for the topic

Attachments may be used to provide additional information about selected topics. The attachment number may be indicated in parentheses next to the agenda item (*See attachment 1*) or may just be attached without comment. Some organizations also like to include the primary objective of the meeting. Both the format and the level of detail vary depending on the organization. If an agenda is short, typically the heading will be positioned at about 2", and it will be double-spaced. If the agenda is long, it may be preferable to position the heading at about 1" or 1.5", and single-space it to fit the agenda on one page. An Agenda Wizard is also available in *Microsoft Word* to assist in the development of an agenda.

Review the agenda illustrated on the next page. This type of agenda was used in a client meeting by an architectural firm planning the development of research laboratories on an entire city block of property.

APPLICATIONS

104e-d1
Agenda

1. Key the agenda shown on the next page. Position the heading at approximately 2"; bold and double-space the heading.
2. Use an en dash for times (**Insert menu, Symbol, Special Characters**). *Hint:* Use copy and paste to insert the en dash the second through the fifth times.
3. Set left tabs at 1" and 1.25" and set a right tab with style 2 leader at 6".
4. Use spacing illustrated on the next page.
5. Save as **104e-d1** and print.

104e-d2
Save Agenda as Web Page

1. Open **104e-d1** and save it as a Web page.
2. Name the file **104e-d2** and save it in the **Web Page** folder you created.
3. Preview the Web page using your browser.

104e-d3
Agenda
(Challenge)

1. Open **104e-d1** and save it as **104e-d3**.
2. Add the following line as the first line of the agenda:

    12:30–2:00 Lunch and Presentation . . . . Team
3. Set decimal tabs at .3" and .75", left tabs at 1.25" and 1.5", and a right tab with style 2 leader at 6". You will need to tab before each time to make the times align correctly.
4. Resave and print.

LESSON 25

Assessment

25a

Key each line twice SS.

alphabet 1 My wife helped fix a frozen lock on Jacque's vegetable bins.

figures 2 Sherm moved from 823 West 150th Street to 9472--67th Street.

double 3 Will Scott attempt to sell his bookkeeping books to Elliott?
letters

easy 4 It is a shame he used the endowment for a visit to the city.

| 1 | 2 | 3 | 4 | 5 | 6 | 7 | 8 | 9 | 10 | 11 | 12 |

25b Reach Review

Key each line once; repeat.

TECHNIQUE TIP
Keep arms and hands quiet as you practice the long reaches.

n/y 5 deny many canny tiny nymph puny any puny zany penny pony yen

6 Jenny Nyles saw many, many tiny nymphs flying near her pony.

b/r 7 bran barb brim curb brat garb bray verb brag garb bribe herb

8 Barb Barber can bring a bit of bran and herbs for her bread.

c/e 9 cede neck nice deck dice heck rice peck vice erect mice echo

10 Can Cecil erect a decent cedar deck?   He erects nice condos.

n/u 11 nun gnu bun nut pun numb sun nude tuna nub fun null unit gun

12 Eunice had enough ground nuts at lunch; Uncle Launce is fun.

25c Speed Check

Key two 3' writings.
Strive for accuracy.
Goal: 3', 19–27 gwam

 all letters

gwam 3'

The term careers can mean many different things to   3 | 51

different people. As you know, a career is much more than a   8 | 55

job. It is the kind of work that a person has through life.   12 | 59

It includes the jobs a person has over time. It also involves 16 | 63

how the work life affects the other parts of our life. There 20 | 67

are as many types of careers as there are people.   23 | 71

Almost all people have a career of some kind. A career   27 | 74

can help us to reach unique goals, such as to make a living   31 | 79

or to help others. The kind of career you have will affect   35 | 83

your life in many ways. For example, it can determine where   39 | 87

you live, the money you make, and how you feel about yourself. 44 | 91

A good choice can thus help you realize the life you want.   47 | 95

3' | 1 | 2 | 3 | 4 |

Save a Word Document as a Web Page

To distribute a *Word* document on the World Wide Web, you must first convert the document to HTML format by saving it as a Web page document. *Word* automatically creates the HTML codes for the desired format. To view the new Web document as it will appear online, choose Web Layout View. After correcting any formatting problems, you may then preview the new Web document in your default Web browser.

To save a *Word* document as a Web page:

1. On the File menu, click **Save as Web Page.**

2. Select the drive and folder where you wish to save the file. (*Hint:* Save Web files in a folder created for that purpose. Storing these files in one location simplifies your work when you are ready to post the files to the Web.)

3. In the File name box, key the filename or accept the name provided. *Word* automatically adds the file extension .htm at the end of the document.

4. Click **Save.** (Click **Continue** if *Word* warns that the document has formatting not supported by the Web browser.)

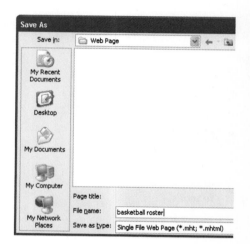

To view a document in Web Layout view:

1. On the View menu, click **Web Layout**. (*Shortcut:* Click the **Web Layout View** button on the status bar.)

2. Make any necessary formatting revisions (e.g., reposition graphics).

To preview the file in your browser:

On the File menu, click **Web Page Preview**. The file opens in your default Web browser. If the browser is not open, *Word* automatically opens it.

(*Note:* Web documents do not always display the same in all browsers. Using *Internet Explorer*, a *Microsoft*-compatible browser, will reduce these formatting differences.)

DRILL 1   SAVE AS WEB PAGE

1. Create a folder named *Web Page*. You will save the *Word* document used in this drill in this folder.

2. Open **orgchart** from the data files.

3. Save this *Word* document as a Web page to the *Web Page* folder created in Step 1. Name the file **104c-drill1**.

4. View the document in your browser.

   (*Note:* The file **104c-drill1** and a folder **104c-drill1_files** are created when you save a document as a Web page.)

SKILLBUILDING

25d Textbook Keying

Key each line once; DS between groups; repeat.

Key with precision and without hesitation.

13 is if he do rub ant go and am pan do rut us aid ox ape by is
14 it is | an end | it may | to pay | and so | aid us | he got | or own | to go
15 Did the girl make the ornament with fur, duck down, or hair?

16 us owl rug box bob to man so bit or big pen of jay me age it
17 it | it is | time to go | show them how | plan to go | one of the aims
18 It is a shame they use the autobus for a visit to the field.

| 1 | 2 | 3 | 4 | 5 | 6 | 7 | 8 | 9 | 10 | 11 | 12 |

25e Figure Check

In the Open Screen, key two 1' writings and two 3' writings at a controlled speed.

all letters/figures

Goal: 3', 16–24 gwam

```
                                                                    gwam  3'
            •            4            •            8            •
     Do I read the stock market pages in the news?  Yes; and       4  35
     12           •           16           •           20      •
at about 9 or 10 a.m. each morning, I know lots of excited         8  39
  24          •           28           •           32       •
people are quick to join me.  In fact, many of us zip right       12  43
  36          •           40           •           44       •
to the 3d or 4th part of the paper to see if the prices of        16  47
  48          •           52           •           56       •
our stocks have gone up or down.  Now, those of us who are        19  51
  60          •           64           •           68       •
"speculators" like to "buy at 52 and sell at 60"; while the       23  55
  72          •           76           •           80       •
"investors" among us are more interested in a dividend we         27  59
     84           •           88           •           92      •
may get, say 7 or 8 percent, than in the price of a stock.        31  62
3' |         1         |         2         |         3         |         4         |
```

COMMUNICATION

25f Edited Copy

1. Key the paragraphs and make the corrections marked with proofreaders' marks. Use the BACKSPACE key to correct errors.
2. Check all number expressions and correct any mistakes that may exist.
3. Save as **xx-25f**.

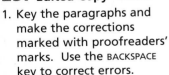

Last week the healthy heart foundation released the findings of a *significant* study that showed exercise diet and ~~if individuals don't~~ smoke are the major controllable factors that led to a healthy heart. Factors such as heredity can not be controlled. The study included 25 to 65 year-old males as well as females. The study also showed that just taking a walk ~~benefits our health~~. Those who walked an average of 2 to 3 hours a week were more then 30 percent less likely to have problems than those who did no exercise.

Meeting Management

- Build keyboarding skill.
- Format agendas.
- Format minutes.
- Format itineraries.
- Prepare labels and name badges.

LESSON 104 | Skillbuilding and Agendas

SKILLBUILDING

104a
Warmup
Key each line twice SS.

alphabet	1	Jeff and Gwen quickly analyzed the complex problem and solved it.
figures	2	Of the 20,473 square feet of office space, 16,598 is on Floor 16.
adjacent reaches	3	I saw her at an airport at a tropical resort leaving on a cruise.
easy	4	Andy and Blanche may make a map for a neighbor to go to the city.

| 1 | 2 | 3 | 4 | 5 | 6 | 7 | 8 | 9 | 10 | 11 | 12 | 13 |

104b
Timed Writing
Take two 3-minute timed writings.

gwam 3'

For many years, readers who had chosen a particular book had 4
just one question to answer. Do you want to purchase a hardcover 8
or a paperback book? It was assumed that books would be purchased 13
from a retail outlet, such as a bookstore. Currently, books are 17
being marketed and sold online. The book itself, however, is still 22
printed on paper. 23

With the technology that is on the market today, a third 27
alternative, the electronic or the so-called e-book, is emerging. 31
E-books are sold in digitized form. The book must be read from the 36
web site on a computer or on a special device designed for reading 40
e-books. 41

3' | 1 | 2 | 3 | 4 |

Skill Builders 2

 Use the Option Screen for Skill Builders 2. Save each drill as a separate file.

DRILL 1

OPPOSITE HAND REACHES

Key at a controlled rate; concentrate on the reaches.

i/e

1 ik is fit it sit laid site like insist still wise coil light
2 ed he ear the fed egg led elf lake jade heat feet hear where
3 lie kite item five aide either quite linear imagine brighter
4 Imagine the aide eating the pears before the grieving tiger.

w/o

5 ws we way was few went wit law with weed were week gnaw when
6 ol on go hot old lot joy odd comb open tool upon money union
7 bow owl word wood worm worse tower brown toward wrote weapon
8 The workers lowered the brown swords toward the wood weapon.

DRILL 2

PROOFREADERS' MARKS

Key each sentence. DS after each sentence. Make all the editing (handwritten) corrections. Print. Go on to Drill 3.

≡ Capitalize
/ Change letter
⊂ Close up space
⤬ Delete
∧ Insert
ℓⅽ Lowercase
Space
∪∩ Transpose

1. When a writer create the preliminary version of a document, they are concentrating on conveying the intended ideas.
2. This version of a preliminary document is called a rough.
3. After the draft is created, the Writer edits refines the copy.
4. Sometimes proofreader's marks are used to edit the draft.
6. The changes will them be make to the original. editing
7. After the changes have been made, then the Writer reads the copy.
8. Editing and proofreading requires alot of time and effort.
9. An attitute of excellance is required to produce error-free message.

DRILL 3

PROOFREADING

Compare your printout to this paragraph. How did you do? Then key the paragraph for fluency. Concentrate on keying as accurately as possible.

When a writer creates the preliminary version of a document, he or she is concentrating on conveying ideas. This preliminary version is called a rough draft. After the draft is created, the writer edits or refines the copy. Proofreaders' marks are used to edit the rough draft. The editing changes will be made to the original. Then the writer reads the copy again. Editing requires a lot of time and effort. An attitude of excellence is required to produce an error-free message.

«AddressBlock»

«GreetingLine»

For over fifty years, the Las Cruces community has enjoyed the magnificent concerts offered by the Las Cruces Symphony Association. Offering six concerts per year, including an outdoor concert and a special concert for children, the Association has drawn large audiences throughout the state and surrounding area.

All of this is made possible through the generosity of Las Cruces Symphony Association members who contributed more than $100,000 last year. Our plans for this season are even more ambitious, and we need your support in making these efforts possible. Please review the enclosed brochure detailing our "Plan for 2002" and consider becoming a supporter at one of the levels outlined below.

Membership Levels			
Patron	Over $5,000	Friend	$500 to $999
Benefactor	$2,500 to $4,999	Member	$50 to $499
Donor	$1,000 to $2,499	Contributor	Up to $50

Your membership in the Las Cruces Symphony Association is tax-deductible and can be mailed to the Las Cruces Symphony Association, P.O. Box 8390, Las Cruces, NM 88001. Join with other supporters of the fine arts in Las Cruces and contribute to the lives of the Las Cruces community and beyond.

Sincerely | Hung-Yueh Weng | xx | Enclosure

Document 2
Edit Data Source

1. **Ck16-d1merge** should be open.
2. Add the following record:

   Mr. and Mrs. Juan Rodriquez
   93 Maple Dr.
   Las Cruces, NM 88012

3. Change Dr. and Mrs. Sijansky's address to **P.O. Box 96396, ZIP 88001**.
4. Save the changes.
5. Sort by Last Name in ascending order.
6. Merge the data source and the main document and print the merged letters.
7. Save the merged letters as **Ck16-d2**.

Document 3
Mailing Envelopes

1. Prepare envelopes for the records stored in the data source **Ck16-d1data**.
2. Sort by Last Name in ascending order. Save as **Ck16-d3**.
3. Arrange each envelope with the appropriate letter. Be sure to keep in Last Name order.

ASSESS SKILL GROWTH:

 These writings are available as Diagnostic Writings in *Keyboarding Pro.* Access Diagnostic Writings from the Numeric & Skill menu.

OPEN SCREEN OPTION:

1. Key 1' writings on each paragraph of a timing. Note that paragraphs within a timing increase by two words.

   Goal: to complete each paragraph.

2. Key a 3' timing on the entire writing.

E all letters

To access writings on *MicroPace Pro,* key **W** and the timing number. For example, key **W8** for *Writing 8.*

gwam

	1'	3'

Writing 8

Any of us whose target is to achieve success in our professional 13 | 4
lives will understand that we must learn how to work in harmony 26 | 8
with others whose paths may cross ours daily. 35 | 12

We will, unquestionably, work for, with, and beside people, just 13 | 16
as they will work for, with, and beside us. We will judge them, 26 | 20
as most certainly they are going to be judging us. 38 | 24

A lot of people realize the need for solid working relations and 13 | 28
have a rule that treats others as they, themselves, expect to be 26 | 33
treated. This seems to be a sound, practical idea for them. 40 | 37

Writing 9

I spoke with one company visitor recently; and she was very much 13 | 4
impressed, she said, with the large amount of work she had noted 26 | 9
being finished by one of our front office workers. 36 | 12

I told her how we had just last week recognized this very person 13 | 16
for what he had done, for output, naturally, but also because of 26 | 21
its excellence. We know this person has that "magic touch." 38 | 25

This "magic touch" is the ability to do a fair amount of work in 13 | 29
a fair amount of time. It involves a desire to become ever more 26 | 34
efficient without losing quality--the "touch" all workers should 39 | 38
have. 40 | 38

Writing 10

Isn't it great just to untangle and relax after you have keyed a 13 | 4
completed document? Complete, or just done? No document is 25 | 8
quite complete until it has left you and passed to the next step. 38 | 13

There are desirable things that must happen to a document before 13 | 17
you surrender it. It must be read carefully, first of all, for 26 | 22
meaning to find words that look right but aren't. Read word for 39 | 26
word. 40 | 26

Check all figures and exact data, like a date or time, with your 13 | 31
principal copy. Make sure format details are right. Only then, 26 | 35
print or remove the work and scrutinize to see how it might look 39 | 39
to a recipient. 42 | 40

1'	1	2	3	4	5	6	7	8	9	10	11	12	13
3'		1			2			3			4		

Module 16: Checkpoint

Read the text in column A and match the correct term in column B. Enter the correct letter in the blank provided to the left of column A.

_____ 1. Contains the text and graphics that remain the same for each version of the merged document.

_____ 2. Inserted as placeholders at the place where the merge names, addresses, and other data will appear in a form letter.

_____ 3. To access the Mail Merge Wizard, select _____ from the Tools menu.

_____ 4. All the variables for one individual are called a _____.

_____ 5. A file that contains the names, addresses, and other variables to be merged with the main document is the _____.

_____ 6. The _____ button on the Mail Merge toolbar is used to edit the data source.

_____ 7. The _____ button on the Mail Merge toolbar is used to complete the merge so the merged letters appear as a new document.

_____ 8. Records sorted as A to Z or 1, 2, etc., are sorted in _____ order.

_____ 9. _____ allows the user to select a specific set of records to merge.

_____ 10. The _____ is the standard business envelope.

A. #8 landscape
B. #10 landscape
C. Ascending
D. Compare and Merge Documents
E. Customize
F. Data source
G. Descending
H. Filter
I. Letters and Mailings
J. Mail Merge Recipients
K. Main document
L. Merge fields
M. Merge to New Document
N. Merge to Printer
O. Record
P. Sort

Performance Assessment

Document 1
Mail Merge

1. Save a new document as **Ck16-d1merge**.
2. Create the data source. Save as **Ck16-d1data**.

Field names	Record 1	Record 2	Record 3
Title	Dr. and Mrs.	Mr. and Mrs.	Ms.
First Name	Hayden	Cory	Ruth
Last Name	Sijansky	Mandeville	Ikenberry
Address Line 1	1112 Woodview Dr.	135 N. Densbrook Ln.	P.O. Box 35329
City	Las Cruces	Las Cruces	Las Cruces
State	NM	NM	NM
ZIP Code	88012	88003	88012
Salutation	Dr. and Mrs. Sijansky	Mr. and Mrs. Mandeville	Ms. Ikenberry

3. Key the main document and insert the merge fields in it. Use open punctuation. Save the changes. The date should update automatically. Do not close this document; you will make changes indicated in Document 2.

Writing 11

ASSESS SKILL

To access writings on *MicroPace Pro*, key **W** and the timing number. For example, key **W11** for *Writing 11*.

The writings are available as Diagnostic Writings in *Keyboarding Pro*.

Anyone who expects some day to find an excellent job should begin now to learn the value of accuracy. To be worth anything, completed work must be correct, without question. Naturally, we realize that the human aspect of the work equation always raises the prospect of errors; but we should understand that those same errors can be found and fixed. Every completed job should carry at least one stamp; the stamp of pride in work that is exemplary.

```
4 | 34
8 | 38
13 | 43
17 | 47
20 | 51
26 | 56
30 | 60
```

Writing 12

No question about it: Many personal problems we face today arise from the fact that we earthlings have never been very wise consumers. We haven't consumed our natural resources well; as a result, we have jeopardized much of our environment. We excused our behavior because we thought that our stock of most resources had no limit. So, finally, we are beginning to realize just how indiscreet we were; and we are taking steps to rebuild our world.

```
4 | 34
8 | 38
13 | 43
17 | 47
20 | 51
26 | 56
30 | 60
```

Writing 13

When I see people in top jobs, I know I'm seeing people who sell. I'm not just referring to employees who labor in a retail outlet; I mean those people who put extra effort into convincing others to recognize their best qualities. They, themselves, are the commodity they sell; and their optimum tools are appearance, language, and personality. They look great, they talk and write well; and, with candid self-confidence, they meet you eye to eye.

```
4 | 34
8 | 38
13 | 43
17 | 47
20 | 51
26 | 56
30 | 60
```

3' | 1 | 2 | 3 | 4 |

Prepare form letters for your patients who are 45 days delinquent on their payments.

1. Save a new document as **103c-d2merge**.
2. Prepare the form letter below as the main document. Use block letter style, open punctuation. Send a copy of this letter to **Justin Langberg**.
3. Choose the file **103c-d2data** as the data source.
4. Sort the data source by ZIP Code in ascending order. Filter to select those patients past due 45 days.
5. Merge the main document and the data source. Save the merged letters as **103c-d2**.

«AddressBlock»

«GreetingLine»

Your unpaid balance of $«Unpaid_Balance» is now past due. We have requested payment from you on «No_Contacts_Made» occasions; however, we have received neither payment nor an explanation as to why payment has not been made.

Although we have no desire to cancel your credit privileges, we are forced to disallow any increase to your balance until payment of the past-due amount is paid. Future dental services for you and your family can be provided on a cash basis only.

Please call me at (305) 555-0135 and make arrangements for paying your overdue amount. If we do not hear from you regarding a revised payment schedule, please pay $«Minimum_Payment», a minimum payment. This payment must be received by March 20.

Sincerely | Paul Vanzandt | Office Manager | xx

Prepare cards for the individuals who have ordered bakery goods from your organization.

1. Save a new document as **103c-d3cards**. Use the file **103c-d3data** as the data source.
2. Prepare the note card below (**Avery 3259**) as the main document. Include the fields shown. Format the card attractively. Sort by Delivery date in ascending order.
3. Merge the main document and the data source. Save the merged cards as **103c-d3**.

«Name»

«Delivery_Location»
«Delivery_Date»

«Order_Item_1»
«Order_Item_2»

We appreciate your bakery order and wish you a happy holiday.

(662) 555-0090

Writing 14

These writings may be used as Diagnostic Writings

What do you expect when you travel to a foreign country? Quite a few people realize that one of the real joys of traveling is to get a brief glimpse of how others think, work, and live.

The best way to enjoy a different culture is to learn as much about it as you can before you leave home. Then you can concentrate on being a good guest rather than trying to find local people who can meet your needs.

	1'	3'
	12	4
	23	8
	36	12
	40	12
	11	16
	24	20
	36	24
	44	27

To access writings on *MicroPace Pro*, key **W** and the timing number. For example, key **W14** for *Writing 14*.

gwam

Writing 15

1' | 3'

What do you enjoy doing in your free time? Health experts tell us that far too many people choose to be lazy rather than to be active. The result of that decision shows up in our weight.

Working to control what we weigh is not easy, and seldom can it be done quickly. However, it is quite important if our weight exceeds what it should be. Part of the problem results from the amount and type of food we eat.

If we want to look fit, we should include exercise as a substantial part of our weight loss plan. Walking at least thirty minutes each day at a very fast rate can make a big difference both in our appearance and in the way we feel.

	1'	3'
	12	4
	24	8
	36	12
	37	13
	12	16
	24	21
	37	25
	44	27
	11	31
	23	35
	35	39
	47	42

gwam

Writing 16

1' | 3'

Doing what we like to do is quite important; however, liking what we have to do is equally important. As you ponder both of these concepts, you may feel that they are the same, but they are not the same.

If we could do only those things that we prefer to do, the chances are that we would do them exceptionally well. Generally, we will take more pride in doing those things we like doing, and we will not quit until we get them done right.

We realize, though, that we cannot restrict the things that we must do just to those that we want to do. Therefore, we need to build an interest in and an appreciation of all the tasks that we must do in our positions.

	1'	3'
	10	4
	23	8
	36	12
	41	14
	12	18
	25	22
	37	26
	47	29
	11	33
	23	37
	36	41
	44	44

1'	1	2	3	4	5	6	7	8	9	10	11	12
3'		1			2			3			4	

103c-d1
**Mail Merge and
Edit Data Source**

Prepare the main document and data source for a form letter to participants of a summer workshop. You will need to edit your data source after you create it.

1. Save a new document as **103c-d1merge**.
2. Create the data source. Save as **103c-d1data**.

Field names	Record 1	Record 2	Record 3
Title	Mr.	Ms.	Ms.
First Name	Phillip	Anele	Anna
Last Name	Lancaster	Nyiri	Skelton
Company Name	Fulton High School	Curtis Middle School	Curtis Middle School
Address Line 1	35 Wallace Cir.	16060 Aspen Rd.	1355 Palomino Dr.
City	Norfolk	Richmond	Richmond
State	VA	VA	VA
ZIP Code	23501	27173	27173
Date	June 15–16	June 23–24	June 23–24
Room	204	205	205

3. Move Ms. Skelton to the **June 15–16** workshop. Change Mr. Lancaster's address to **89 Castle Rd.**
4. Key the main document (mixed punctuation style) and insert the merge fields in it. Add notations as needed. Save the changes. Be sure the date updates automatically.

Date

«AddressBlock»

Dear «First_Name»:

I am delighted that you will be attending the Principles and Applications of Web Design Workshop on «Date» at Braswell Community College. Please arrive at Room «Room» of the Harper-Kock Union Building at 8 a.m. for registration and a brief orientation.

As the workshop title indicates, the objectives include learning principles of web design and applying these principles in realistic exercises. The first day is filled with outstanding assignments highlighting important principles of web design. During the second day, you will team with one of your colleagues to plan and design impressive web pages for «Company_Name». Do take time before coming to the workshop to locate materials from your office that you will need to create these web pages.

Directions to Hathorn Hall, the residence hall designated for summer workshop participants, are enclosed. You may check in at Hathorn from 8 a.m. to 10 p.m. Housing payment can be made at the residence hall.

«First_Name», should you have any questions about the workshop, please call me at 555-0234. I look forward to your being a part of our workshop series.

Sincerely | Jane D. Gunter | Workshop Coordinator

5. Merge the data source and the main document and print. Save as **103c-d1**.

Writing 17

gwam 1' | 3'

Many people like to say just how lucky a person is when   11 | 4 29
he or she succeeds in doing something well. Does luck play a   24 | 8 33
large role in success? In some cases, it might have a small   36 | 12 37
effect.   37 | 13 38

Being in the right place at the right time may help, but   11 | 16 41
hard work may help far more than luck. Those who just wait for   24 | 20 46
luck should not expect quick results and should realize luck   36 | 24 50
may never come.   39 | 26 51

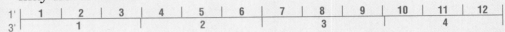

1' | 1 | 2 | 3 | 4 | 5 | 6 | 7 | 8 | 9 | 10 | 11 | 12
3' | | 1 | | 2 | | 3 | | 4

Writing 18

gwam 1' | 3'

New golfers must learn to zero in on just a few social   11 | 4 39
rules. Do not talk, stand close, or move around when another   23 | 8 44
person is hitting. Be ready to play when it is your turn.   35 | 12 47

Take practice swings in an area away from other people.   11 | 15 51
Let the group behind you play through if your group is slow.   24 | 20 55
Do not rest on your club on the green when waiting your turn.   36 | 23 59

Set your other clubs down off the green. Leave the green   12 | 27 63
quickly when done; update your card on the next tee. Be sure   24 | 31 67
to leave the course in good condition. Always have a good time.   37 | 36 72

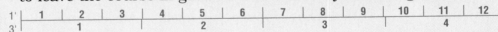

1' | 1 | 2 | 3 | 4 | 5 | 6 | 7 | 8 | 9 | 10 | 11 | 12
3' | | 1 | | 2 | | 3 | | 4

Writing 19

gwam 1' | 3'

Do you know how to use time wisely? If you do, then its   11 | 4 51
proper use can help you organize and run a business better.   24 | 8 55
If you find that your daily problems tend to keep you from   35 | 12 59
planning properly, then perhaps you are not using time well.   48 | 16 63
You may find that you spend too much time on tasks that are   60 | 20 67
not important. Plan your work to save valuable time.   70 | 24 70

A firm that does not plan is liable to run into trouble.   12 | 27 74
A small firm may have trouble planning. It is important   23 | 31 78
to know just where the firm is headed. A firm may have a   35 | 35 82
fear of learning things it would rather not know. To say   46 | 39 86
that planning is easy would be absurd. It requires lots of   58 | 43 90
thinking and planning to meet the expected needs of the firm.   70 | 47 94

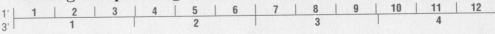

1' | 1 | 2 | 3 | 4 | 5 | 6 | 7 | 8 | 9 | 10 | 11 | 12
3' | | 1 | | 2 | | 3 | | 4

103a
Warmup
Key each line twice SS.

alphabet	1	Our unexpected freezing weather quickly killed Jo's mauve shrubs.
figures	2	Paula has moved from 8195 East 26 Street to 1730 West 148 Street.
double letters	3	Betty fooled Annabell by hitting a ball across the narrow valley.
easy	4	I fish for a quantity of smelt and may wish for aid to land them.

| 1 | 2 | 3 | 4 | 5 | 6 | 7 | 8 | 9 | 10 | 11 | 12 | 13 |

103b
Timed Writings
Key one 3' and one 5' writing at your control rate.

  all letters

gwam 3' 5'

	3'	5'
Most people today have become very health conscious. Some	4	2 52
individuals worry about the bad effects of a diet that contains	8	5 55
far too much fat and a life style that does not include very much	13	8 57
exercise. However, many of those people never get past the stage	17	10 60
of worrying. Others just try to find a quick solution to the	21	13 63
problem. They try zany diets and easy exercise programs. The	25	15 65
real solution is to get in the habit of eating correctly and doing	30	18 68
exercise on a regular basis. The results are well worth the effort.	34	21 70
The combination of exercising on a regular basis and eating	38	23 73
properly produces much better results than either of these activi-	43	26 76
ties can produce by itself. An effective diet includes food from	47	28 78
all of the major food groups. Eating food that has a very high	51	31 81
fiber content and a very low fat content can help to prevent a	56	33 83
number of diseases. Not eating a meal to save a few calories is	60	36 86
not a very good idea. A good exercise program has several important	65	39 89
characteristics. Each session lasts approximately twenty minutes	69	41 91
and occurs at least three times a week. Also, the activity should	73	44 94
be fast enough to increase your heart rate. Walking at a fast pace	78	47 97
is one of the best and one of the most desirable activities that	82	49 99
you can do.	83	50 100

3' | 1 | 2 | 3 | 4 |
5' | 1 | 2 | 3 |

103c
Assessment

On the signal to begin, key the documents in sequence. Correct errors. When time has been called, proofread all documents again and correct any errors you may have overlooked. Reprint if necessary.

Writings 20 and 21 are available as Diagnostic Writings.

To access writings on *MicroPace Pro*, key **W** and the timing number. For example, key **W20** for *Writing 20*.

Writing 20

If asked, most people will agree that some people have far more creative skills than others, and they will also say that these skills are in great demand by most organizations. A follow-up question is in order. Are you born with creative skills or can you develop them? No easy answer to that question exists, but it is worth spending a bit of time pondering.

If creative skills can be developed, then the next issue is how can you develop these skills. One way is to approach each task with a determination to solve the problem and a refusal to accept failure. If the normal way of doing a job does not work, just keep trying things never tried before until you reach a good solution. This is called thinking outside the box.

3'	5'
4	2 21
8	5 34
12	7 37
17	10 39
21	13 42
24	15 44
28	17 46
32	19 49
37	22 51
41	25 54
45	27 56
49	29 58

3' 1   2   3   4
5'   1   2   3

Writing 21

Figures are not as easy to key as many of the words we use. Balanced-hand figures such as 16, 27, 38, 49, and 50, although fairly easy, are slower to key because each one requires longer reaches and uses more time per stroke.

Figures such as 12, 45, 67, and 90 are even more difficult because they are next to one another and each uses just a single hand to key. Because of their size, bigger numbers such as 178, 349, and 1,220 create extra speed losses.

1'	3'
12	4 36
25	8 40
37	12 44
45	16 46
12	20 50
25	25 54
39	29 59
45	32 61

1' 1 2 3 4 5 6 7 8 9 10 11 12 13
3'   1   2   3   4

DRILL 5

SKILL TRANSFER

1. Set the timer for 2'. Take a 2' writing on paragraph 1. Do not save.
2. Set the timer for 2'. Take a 2' writing on paragraph 2. Do not save.
3. Take 2 or more 2' writings on the slower paragraph. Do not save.

Few people attain financial success without some kind of planning. People who realize the value of prudent spending and saving are those who set up a budget. A budget helps individuals determine just how much they can spend and how much they can save so that they will not squander their money recklessly.

Keeping records is a *vital* ~~crucial~~ part of *a* budget. *ing* A detailed ~~Complete~~ records *of all* income and expen*ditures* ~~ses~~ over a period of ~~a number of~~ *serveral* months *will* ~~can~~ help *to* determine what bills, *like utilities* ~~as water~~ or rent, are *fixed* ~~static~~ and which are flexible. To get the most out of your income, *focus* ~~pay~~ attention *on* ~~to~~ the items that *you* can *be changed* ~~modify~~.

1'	2'
11	6
24	12
36	18
49	24
61	31
12	6
24	12
37	18
49	25
61	30

1' 1 2 3 4 5 6 7 8 9 10 11 12
2'   1   2   3   4   5   6

The Holland Eye Center invites you to attend a special seminar sponsored for our patients who are potential candidates for laser vision correction. This seminar held at our clinic on «Date» at 7 p.m. will feature a panel of doctors and patients and a live laser vision correction procedure. A question/answer period will also provide an opportunity to have all your questions answered by these laser vision correction experts. You'll also have an opportunity to enter your name in a drawing for a complimentary laser vision correction procedure to be presented at the close of the seminar.

Would you like to join the millions of people who have chosen laser vision correction and be free of the daily hassles of glasses and contact lenses? Get started today by completing the enclosed reservation card indicating you will attend the seminar on «Date» and learn for yourself the details of laser vision correction.

Sincerely | Edward S. Vickery, M.D. | xx | Enclosure

4. Sort by ZIP Code in ascending order. Merge the data source and the main document and print. Save the merged document as **102c-d1**.

102c-d2
Edit Data Source

Several changes require you to edit the data source for the patients invited to the seminar on laser vision correction. Follow the directions below to make the edits and to print only those records with changes.

1. Open **102c-d1merge**. Edit the data source as follows:
   - Invite Dr. Jantz to the February 25 seminar.
   - Ms. Wiseman's new address is **235 N. Fifth St., Omak, WA 98841**.

2. Add two new records for the February 25 seminar.

   Mrs. Darlene Chism   Mr. James Lee
   830 Yorkville St.   332 Matilda Rd.
   Tonasket, WA 98855   Omak, WA 98841

3. Filter to select records of patients invited to the February 25 seminar. Merge to a new document; save the merged letters as **102c-d2**.

102c-d3
Envelopes

Prepare envelopes for all the patients invited to the laser vision correction seminar. (*Reminder*: Clear the filter used in **102c-d2** above.)

1. Prepare envelopes for the records stored in the data source **102c-d1data**.
2. Sort by ZIP Code in ascending order. Save the merged envelopes as **102c-d3**.

102c-d4
Name Badges

All the patients you invited to the laser vision correction seminar have agreed to attend the seminar. Prepare name badges for their use at the seminar.

1. Prepare name badges (**Avery 5095**) for the records stored in the data source **102c-d1data**. Include the first name and last name fields on the name badge. Sort by last name in ascending order. Format attractively (e.g., font, size, alignment, etc.).
2. Save the merged labels as **102c-d4**.

Internet Activities 1

Know your Browser

Knowing your browser includes opening the browser, opening a Web site, and getting familiar with the browser toolbar. You will also learn to set a bookmark at a favorite Web site.

Word users can quickly access the Internet while in *Word* by using the Web toolbar.

1. Display the Web toolbar by right-clicking on any toolbar and then choosing **Web** from the list of choices.

2. Open your Web browser by clicking the **Start Page** button on the Web toolbar. The Web page you have designated as your Home or Start Page displays.

Start Page

DRILL 1

1. Begin a new *Word* document.
2. Display the Web toolbar.
3. Click the **Start Page** button to open your Web browser.

Open Web Site

With the Web browser open, click **Open** or **Open Page** from the File menu (or click the **Open** button if it is available on your browser's toolbar). Key the Web address (e.g., http://www.weather.com) and click **Open**. The Web site displays.

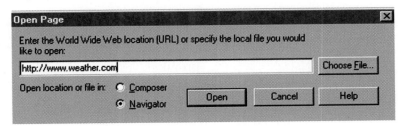

Shortcut: Click inside the Location or Address entry box, key the Web address, and press ENTER.

A **Web address** or site—commonly called the *URL* or *Uniform Resource Locator*—is composed of one or more domains separated by periods: http://www.house.gov/.

As you move from left to right in the address, each domain is larger than the previous one. In the Web address above, *gov* (United States government) is larger than *house* (House of Representatives). Other domains include educational institutions (.edu), commercial organizations (.com), military sites (.mil), and other organizations (.org).

A Web address may also include a directory path and filenames separated by slashes. In the address, the Web document named *index* provides various resources for students and faculty using Lessons 1–60 of the 15th edition of College Keyboarding. http://www.collegekeyboarding.com/fifteenth/lessons1-60/index.html

DRILL 3   MERGE LABELS

1. Follow the directions provided on the previous page to prepare address labels for the data source file **learn-data**.

2. Save the merged address labels as **102b-drill3**. (*Reminder:* Resave the main document **learn-labels** after all steps of the Mail Merge Wizard have been completed.)

DRILL 4   MERGE LABELS

1. Prepare file folder labels (**5066-File Folder**) for the records stored in data source **99d-d1data**. Open a new document and save it as **102b-drill4 Labels**. From the More items list, select the following merge fields and arrange as shown below:

    Last Name First Name Title
    Company Name

2. Sort by Last Name in ascending order. (*Note:* If desired, edit the merged labels to include uppercase according to standard record management procedures.)

3. Save the merged labels as **102b-drill4**.

APPLICATIONS

102c-d1
Mail Merge

The Holland Eye Center is hosting two seminars to inform their patients about laser vision correction. Prepare the form letters for the records shown below.

1. Save a new document as **102c-d1merge**.

2. Create the data source. Save as **102c-d1data**.

Field names	Record 1	Record 2	Record 3
Title	Mr.	Dr.	Ms.
First Name	Angelo	Karen	Mary
Last Name	Seay	Jantz	Wiseman
Address Line 1	P.O. Box 88	137 Sonoma Dr.	539 Swoope Ave.
City	Tonasket	Omak	Tonasket
State	WA	WA	WA
ZIP Code	98855	98841	98855
Date	January 31	January 31	February 25

3. Key the main document and insert the merge fields in it. Use open punctuation. Save the changes. (*Reminder:* The date should update automatically.)

«AddressBlock»

«GreetingLine»

Do you ever imagine being able to see the alarm clock when you wake up? Do you ever imagine no more hassles of daily contact lens maintenance? Perhaps you may have imagined playing your favorite sport with complete peripheral vision—no fogging or slipping glasses. Millions of people across the world have chosen laser vision correction as an alternative to glasses and contact lenses. They now are enjoying these freedoms that you have only imagined.

(continued on the next page)

Open the following Web sites. Identify the high-level domain for each site.

1. http://www.weather.com _____
2. http://fbla-pbl.org _____
3. http://www.army.mil _____
4. http://www.senate.gov _____

DRILL 3

Open the following Web sites and identify the filenames.

1. http://www.cnn.com/TRAVEL/ _____
2. http://sports.espn.go.com/ncaa/index _____
3. http://www.usps.com/buy/welcome.htm _____

Explore the Browser's Toolbar

The browser's toolbar is very valuable when surfing the Internet. Become familiar with your browser's toolbar by studying the screen. Browsers may vary slightly.

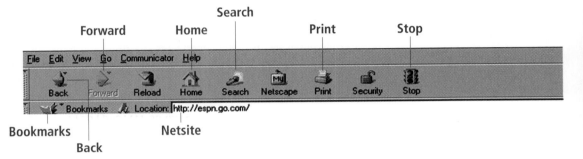

Netsite entry box	Displays the active URL or Web site address.
Back	Moves to Web sites or pages visited since opening the browser.
Forward	Moves forward to sites visited prior to using the Back button. (The Forward button is ghosted if the Back button has not been used.)
Print	Prints a Web page.
Home	Returns to the Web page designated as the Home or Start Page.
Stop	Stops computer's search for a Web site.
Search	Opens one of the Internet search engines.
Bookmarks	Moves to the list of Web sites marked for easy access.

DRILL 4

1. Open the following Web sites:
   a. http://nike.com
   b. http://realage.com
   c. http://mapquest.com
   d. A site of your choice
2. Click the **Back** button twice. The_____Web site displays.
3. Click the **Forward** button once. The_____Web site displays.
4. Print the active Web page.

1. Follow the directions provided on the previous page to prepare envelopes for the data source file **learn-data**.

2. Save the merged envelopes as **102b-drill1**. (*Reminder*: Resave the main document **learn-envelope** after all steps of the Mail Merge Wizard have been completed.)

1. Prepare envelopes for the records stored in data source **99d-d1data**. Open a new document and save as **102b-drill2 Envelope**. From the More items list, select the following merge fields and arrange as shown here:

Title First Name Last Name
Company Name
Address Line 1
City, State ZIP Code

2. Sort by ZIP Code in ascending order.
3. Save the merged envelopes as **102b-drill2**.

Merge Labels

help keywords
*Create and print labels
for a mass mailing*

Labels designed for printers are available in all sizes and for many purposes, including file folder labels, mailing labels, name badges, and business cards. The data source is often used for merging letters, registration forms, envelopes, and numerous types of labels. Merging labels is very similar to merging envelopes.

To create labels:

1. Open a new document and save with an appropriate filename. (For Drill 3, save it as **learn-labels**.)

2. Choose **Tools**, then **Letters and Mailings**, and then **Mail Merge Wizard**. Follow the steps of the Mail Merge Wizard. Click **Next** to move to the next step.

3. Under *Select document type*, select **Labels**. Click **Next**.

4. Under *Select starting document*, click **Change document layout**.

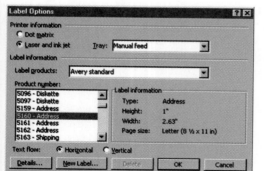

5. Under *Change document layout*, click **Label options**. Choose **5160-Address** from the Product number in the Label Options dialog box. Click **OK**.

6. Under *Select recipients*, click **Use an existing list**. Under *Use an existing list*, click **Browse**. From the appropriate disk drive, select **learn-data**, the data source created in Lesson 99. The Mail Merge Recipients dialog box displays the records. Click **OK**; then **Next**.

7. Under *Arrange your labels*, click **Address block**. (To select the merge fields individually for the address block, click **More items** and select each desired merge field.)

8. Under *Replicate labels*, click **Update all labels** to replicate the address block merge field on each label on the page. Click **Next**.

9. From *Preview your labels*, click the navigation buttons to preview envelopes if needed. (If changes in the data source are needed, click **Edit recipient list**.) Click **Next**.

10. From *Complete the merge*, click **Edit individual labels**. Click **All**; then **OK**. The merged labels will appear on the screen.

11. Resave the main document.

Bookmark a Favorite Web Site

When readers put a book aside, they insert a bookmark to mark the place. Internet users also add bookmarks to mark their favorite Web sites or sites of interest for browsing later.

To add a bookmark:

1. Open the desired Web site.
2. Click **Bookmarks** and then **Add Bookmark**. (Browsers may vary on location and name of Bookmark button.)

To use a bookmark:

1. Click **Bookmarks** (or **Communicator**, **Favorites**, or **Window Bookmarks**).
2. Select the desired bookmark. Click or double-click, depending on your browser. The desired Web site displays.

DRILL 5

1. Open these favorite Web sites and bookmark them on your browser.
   a. http://www.weather.com
   b. http://www.cnn.com
   c. http://ask.com
   d. Key the Web address of a city you would like to visit (destin.com)

2. Use the bookmarks to go to the following Web sites to find answers to the questions shown.
   a. The Weather Channel—What is today's temperature in your city? _____
   b. CNN—What is today's top news story? _____
   c. Ask Jeeves. Ask a question; then find the answer. _____
   d. City Web site you bookmarked—Find one attraction in the city to visit. _____

Activity 2

Set up E-mail Addresses

Electronic mail

Electronic mail or **e-mail** refers to electronic messages sent by one computer user to another computer user. To be able to send or receive e-mail, you must have an e-mail address, an e-mail program, and access to the Internet or an intranet (in-house network).

Many search engines such as Excite, Google, Lycos, Hotbot, and others provide free e-mail via their Web sites. These e-mail programs allow users to set up an e-mail address and then send and retrieve e-mail messages. To set up an account and obtain an e-mail address, the user must (1) agree to the terms of agreement, (2) complete an online registration form, and (3) compose an e-mail name and password.

DRILL 1

1. Click the Search button on the browser's toolbar. Click a search engine that offers free e-mail.
2. Click **Free E-mail** or **Mail**. (Terms will vary.)
3. Read the Terms of Agreement and accept.
4. Enter an e-mail name. This name will be the login-name portion of your e-mail address.
5. Enter a password for your e-mail account. For security reasons, do not share your password, do not leave it where others can use it, and avoid choosing pet names or birth dates.
6. Review the entire registration form and submit it. You will be notified immediately that your e-mail account has been established. (If your e-mail name is already in use by someone else, you may be instructed to choose a different name before your account can be established.)

LESSON 102

Merge with Envelopes and Labels

102a
Warmup
Key each line twice SS.

alphabet	1	Zan saw Jeffrey exit the park very quickly with a mean black dog.
figures	2	The stock price has increased 24.50 points to 189.75 in 36 weeks.
double letters	3	Pattie and Tripp meet at the swimming pool after football drills.
easy	4	Did the firm or their neighbor own the auto with signal problems?

| 1 | 2 | 3 | 4 | 5 | 6 | 7 | 8 | 9 | 10 | 11 | 12 | 13 |

NEW FUNCTIONS

102b

help keywords
Create and print envelopes for a mass mailing

Merge Envelopes

Envelopes can be merged from the data source. When printing envelopes, you will need to know the type of envelope feeder your printer uses. In this lesson, you will create #10 landscape envelopes (standard business envelopes).

To create envelopes:

1. Open a new document and save it with an appropriate name. (For Drill 1, save it as **learn-envelope**.)

2. Choose **Tools**, then **Letters and Mailings**, and then **Mail Merge Wizard**. Follow the six steps of the Mail Merge Wizard Task Pane explained below. Click **Next** to move to the next step.

3. Under *Select document type*, select **Envelopes**. Click **Next**.

4. Under *Select starting document*, click **Change document layout**.

5. Under *Change document layout*, click **Envelope options**. The Envelope Options dialog box displays. The Size 10 envelope is the default. Click **OK**; then **Next**.

6. Under *Select recipients*, click **Use an existing list**. Under *Use an existing list*, click **Browse**. From the appropriate disk drive, select **learn-data**, the data source created in Lesson 99. The Mail Merge Recipients dialog box displays the records. Click **OK**. Click **Next**.

7. In the envelope document at the left of the screen, position the insertion point in the letter address area.

8. Under *Arrange your envelope*, click **Postal bar code**. Click **OK** to accept the default merge fields for ZIP Code and Address 1.

9. Position the insertion point under the postal bar code. Click **Address block**. (If you prefer to select the merge fields individually for the address block, click **More items** and select each desired merge field.) Click **OK**; then **Next**.

10. From *Preview your envelopes*, click on the navigation buttons to preview envelopes. Click **Edit recipient list** to edit data source. Click **Next**.

11. From *Complete the merge*, click **Edit individual envelopes**. Click **All**; then **OK**. Merged envelopes will appear as a new document with a page break between each.

12. Save the document again (for Drill 1, save it as **learn-envelope**).

Send E-mail Message

To send an e-mail message, you must have the address of the computer user you want to write. Business cards, letterheads, directories, etc., now include e-mail addresses. Often a telephone call is helpful in obtaining e-mail addresses. An e-mail address includes the user's login name followed by @ and the domain (sthomas@yahoo.com)

Creating an e-mail message is quite similar to preparing a memo. The e-mail header includes TO, FROM, and SUBJECT. Key the e-mail address of the recipient on the TO line, and compose a subject line that concisely describes the theme of your message. Your e-mail address will automatically display on the FROM line.

DRILL 2

1. Open the search engine used to set up your e-mail account. Click **E-mail** or **Mail**. (Terms will vary.)

2. Enter your e-mail name and password when prompted.

E-mail Message 1

3. Enter the e-mail address of your instructor or another student. Compose a brief message describing the city you would like to visit. Mention one of the city's attractions (from Activity 1, Drill 5). Include a descriptive subject line. Send the message.

E-mail Message 2

4. Enter your e-mail address. The subject is **Journal Entry for March 29, 200-**. Compose a message to show your reflections on how keyboarding is useful to you. Share your progress in the course and your plan for improving this week. Send the message.

Respond to Messages

Replying to e-mail messages

Reading one's e-mail messages and responding promptly are important rules of netiquette (etiquette for the Internet). However, avoid responding too quickly to sensitive situations.

Forwarding e-mail messages

Received e-mail messages are often shared or forwarded to other e-mail users. Be sure to seek permission from the sender of the message before forwarding it to others.

DRILL 3

1. Open your e-mail account if it is not open.

2. Read your e-mail messages and respond immediately and appropriately to any e-mail messages received from your instructor or fellow students. Click **Reply** to answer the message.

3. Forward the e-mail message titled *Journal Entry for March 29, 200-* to your instructor.

4. Delete all read messages.

Attach a Document to an E-mail Message

Electronic files can be attached to an e-mail message and sent to another computer electronically. Recipients of attached documents can transfer these documents to their computers and then open them for use.

DRILL 4

1. Open your e-mail account if it is not open.

2. Create an e-mail message to your instructor that states your homework is attached. The subject line should include the specific homework assignment (**xx-profile**, for example).

3. Attach the file by clicking **Attach**. Use the browser to locate the homework assignment. (E-mail programs may vary.)

4. Send the e-mail message with the attached file.

FILTER DATA RECORDS

1. With **learn-merge** open, filter as follows:
   Field: **State**
   Comparison Phrase: **Equal to**
   Compare to: Illinois (**IL**)

2. Merge to a new document; save as **101b-drill5**.

FILTER DATA RECORDS

1. With **learn-merge** open, clear filters used in Drill 5.

2. Filter to select records of speakers who live in Chicago and are scheduled to speak at 8:30 a.m.

(*Hint:* Because both conditions must be met, select **and**; then key the requirements for the second condition.)

3. Merge to a new document; save as **101b-drill6**.

APPLICATIONS

101c-d1
Edit Data Source and Merge Letters

1. Open **99d-d1merge**. Edit data source as follows:
   - Mr. Bouchillon now works for **Prestage Technology Company**.
   - Ms. Vang's new address is **983 Old Cedar Pl.**; ZIP Code is **39704-0983**.

2. Add two new records. Print the selected records.

   Ms. Brenda Andres
   Gifts and More
   1456 W. 18 St.
   Starkville, MS 39759-1456
   Oktibbeha County

   Mr. Juan Seuffer
   Kubly and Ross Associates
   356 Airline Rd.
   West Point, MS 39773-0356
   Clay County

3. Add **Representative** as a new field.

4. Edit the records with the following data:

Record	Representative
Quarrels	Beth Stevens
Bouchillon	Kelly Cancienne
Vang	Patrick Konscak
Andres	Wade Sanford
Seuffer	Jennifer Fleming

5. Edit the main document to include the word *Representative* as the writer's title.

6. Sort by Last Name in ascending order and merge to a new document.

7. Save the merged document as **101c-d1**; print the merged letters. (*Reminder:* Save the main document, **99d-d1merge**.)

101c-d2
Filter Data Source

1. With **99d-d1merge** open, filter the data source to select records in Oktibbeha County.

2. Merge to a new document; save as **101c-d2**.

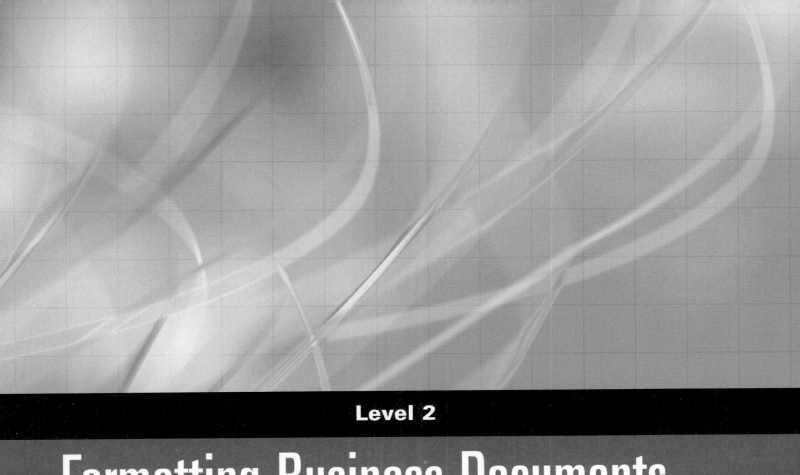

Level 2

Formatting Business Documents

OBJECTIVES

KEYBOARDING

To key about 40 *wam* with good accuracy.

DOCUMENT DESIGN SKILLS

To format accurately business letters, memos, reports, and tables.
To apply basic design skills to newsletters and announcements.

WORD PROCESSING SKILLS

To learn the basic word processing competencies.
To create, edit, and format documents efficiently.

COMMUNICATION SKILLS

To apply proofreaders' marks and revise text.
To compose simple e-mails and other documents.

To sort records by multiple fields:

1. Open the main document; click the **Mail Merge Recipients** button.

2. Click the arrow next to any column name, and then click **Advanced**.

3. From the Filter and Sort dialog box, select the **Sort Records** tab.

4. Click the down arrow by Sort by and select the first field to be sorted in the multiple sort.

   Click the arrow by Then by and select the second field, and so forth. Click **OK**.

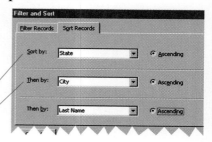

DRILL 2 SORT IN ASCENDING ORDER

1. With **learn-merge** open, sort by ZIP Code in ascending order and merge to a new document.

2. Save the merged document as **101b-drill2**. Close **learn-merge** without saving.

DRILL 3 SORT IN DESCENDING ORDER

1. With **learn-merge** open, sort by ZIP Code in descending order.

2. Merge to a new document; save as **101b-drill3**. Close **learn-merge** without saving.

DRILL 4 MULTIPLE SORT

1. With **learn-merge** open, sort in ascending order first by State, then by City, and then by Last Name.

2. Merge to a new document; save as **101b-drill4**. Close **learn-merge** without saving.

Filter Records

help keywords
Select recipients to include in mail merge

Filtering records before merging the main document and the data source allows you to select a specific set of records to merge. For example, you can create a target mailing to individuals in a specific state or ZIP Code area.

To filter data records:

1. Open the main document; click the **Mail Merge Recipients** button on the Mail Merge toolbar.

2. Click the arrow next to any column name, and then click **Advanced**.

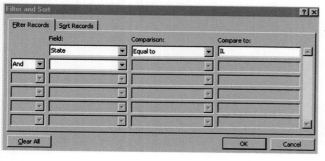

3. From the Filter and Sort dialog box, select the **Filter Records** tab.

4. Choose the appropriate data field (e.g., *State*); click a comparison phrase (e.g., *Equal to*); and key the text or data you will use for the comparison (e.g., *IL*). Click **OK**. (*Note:* Click down arrow for comparison and note the comparison phrases.)

5. Note the records displaying in the Mail Merge Recipients dialog box to determine if you have filtered correctly. Click **OK**.

To merge, click the **Merge to New Document** button on the Mail Merge toolbar.

(*Reminder:* Click the **Clear All** button in the Filter and Sort dialog box to remove filters before using the main document again to ensure all records will merge.)

Word Processing Basics

- Create documents.
- Save, preview, and print documents; use Help.
- Create and modify character and paragraph formats.
- Edit documents and apply communication skills.
- Build keyboarding skills.

LESSON 26   Create Documents

NEW FUNCTIONS

26a

Start Word

You are about to learn one of the leading word processing packages available today. At the same time, you will continue to develop your keyboarding skill. You will use *Microsoft Word*® to create and format professional-looking documents. *Word* will make keying documents such as letters, tables, and reports easy and fun.

When you first start *Word*, the screen appears with two windows. The left area is a blank document screen where you can enter text. The right area is called the **Task Pane**. The Task Pane provides options for opening current and and new files.

Study the illustration of the opening *Word* screen to learn the various parts of the screen.

CheckPro: If you are using *CheckPro*, it will launch or open *Microsoft Word* automatically when you choose the first activity to be done in *Word*. See instruction on page 79.

Changes to fields are made by editing the data source. Once the change is made, all of the records are revised.

To edit fields:

1. Click the **Customize** button on the Address List dialog box.
2. Edit as follows:
   a. *Add new field*: Click the **Add** button; key the field name. Use the move buttons to position correctly. (*Reminder*: Be sure to update the main document by inserting the new merge field.)
   b. *Delete field*: Select the field to be deleted. Click the **Delete** button.
   c. *Rename field*: Select the field to be renamed. Click the **Rename** button. Key new name.
3. Save your main document to update your data source.

DRILL 1 **EDIT RECORDS AND FIELDS**

1. Open **learn-merge**.

2. Add **Fax Number** as a new field after the ZIP Code field.

3. Update the records with the following fax numbers:

   Ms. Hershbarger (708) 555-0881

   Dr. Hodnett (414) 555-0094

   Mr. Zuber (708) 555-0692

4. Change Ms. Hershbarger's address to **206 Fourth Ave., Chicago, IL 60650-0206**.

5. Save edited records' main document and close it.

Sort Data Records

help keywords
Sort items in the list

Sorting records determines the order in which the records are merged. You might sort records in ZIP Code order, Last Name order, or City order. Occasionally, a multiple sort is needed to sort first by one field and then a second field, and so forth. For example, merged name badges or registration letters might be sorted first by state, then by city, and then by last name. Records are sorted either in **ascending order** (A to Z *or* 1, 2, etc.) or **descending order** (Z to A *or* 100, 99, etc.).

To sort records by one field:

1. Open the main document; click the **Mail Merge Recipients** button.
2. Click the column heading of the field to be sorted to display the data in ascending order. Click again to display data in descending order. Click **OK**.

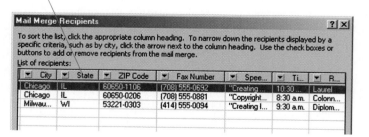

To merge, click the **Merge to New Document** button on the Mail Merge toolbar.

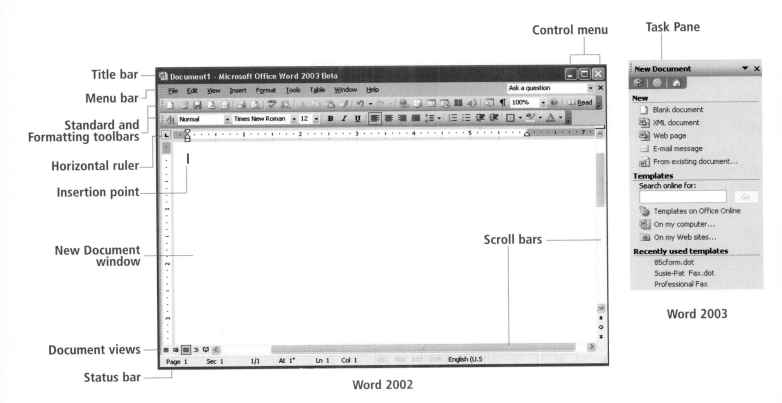

Control menu

Task Pane

Title bar

Menu bar

Standard and
Formatting toolbars

Horizontal ruler

Insertion point

New Document
window

Scroll bars

Document views

Status bar

Word 2003

Word 2002

Word 2003 standard toolbar

Start Reading
button

Title bar	Displays the names of the application and document that are currently open.
Control menu	Buttons that size (enlarge or shrink) and close a window. Buttons include Minimize, Restore, and Close.
Menu bar	Displays drop-down menus from which commands can be selected.
Standard and Formatting toolbars	Display buttons that provide access to common commands. The name of each button displays when you point to it.
Horizontal ruler	Displays the margins, tabs, and indents.
New Document window	A blank area on the screen where you can enter text.
Task Pane	Displays options for opening files and creating new documents.
Insertion point	Blinking vertical line that shows where the text you key will appear. Moving the pointer with the mouse does not move the insertion point until you click the mouse.
Document views	Display documents in four views: Normal, Print Layout, Outline, and Web Layout.
Scroll bars	Enable you to move rapidly through documents.
Status bar	Displays information about the document such as page number and position of the insertion point.
Taskbar	Displays the Start button and whatever programs are currently running.

LESSON 101 | Edit the Data Source

SKILLBUILDING

101a
Warmup
Key each line twice SS.

alphabet 1 Jacky was given a bronze plaque for the extra work he did for me.

fig/sym 2 Order 12 pairs of #43 skis at $75.59 each for a total of $919.08.

3rd/4th fingers 3 Zane, Sally, and Max quit polo to swim six laps and work puzzles.

easy 4 Claudia and I do handiwork at both the downtown and lake chapels.

| 1 | 2 | 3 | 4 | 5 | 6 | 7 | 8 | 9 | 10 | 11 | 12 | 13 |

NEW FUNCTIONS

101b

> **TIP**
> An alternate way to display the toolbar is to use **Tools, Letters and Mailings,** and **Show Mail Merge toolbar.**

Mail Merge Toolbar

After all the steps of the Mail Merge Wizard are completed, you may want to edit your data source. To do this, you may reopen the Mail Merge Wizard (**Tools, Letters and Mailings,** and **Mail Merge Wizard**) or use the Mail Merge toolbar.

The Mail Merge toolbar is accessed from the View menu (**Toolbars, Mail Merge**). Use the Insert Address Block, the Insert Greeting Line, and Insert Merge Fields buttons to create the placeholders for the merge fields in the main document. The Mail Merge Recipients button is used to edit the data source while the Merge to New Document button is used to complete the merge.

Mail Merge Recipients
Insert Address Block
Insert Greeting Line
Insert Merge Fields

Merge to New Document

Edit Data Source

Sometimes you will need to edit the data source (list of variables) by changing individual records or revising the fields for all records.

help keywords
About mail merge data sources

To edit records:

1. From the main document, click **Mail Merge Recipients** on the Mail Merge toolbar.

2. Click **Edit.** The Address List dialog box displays.

   a. Use the navigation buttons to move from record to record, or click **Find Entry** to locate a record quickly.

   b. Make the desired changes.

   c. Click **Delete Entry** to delete a record.

   d. Click **New Entry** to add a new record.

Navigation buttons

Wordwrap and Entering Text

When you key text, it is entered at the insertion point (the blinking vertical bar). When a line is full, the text automatically moves to the next line. This feature is called **wordwrap.** To begin a new paragraph, press ENTER. To indent the first line of a paragraph to the first default tab, press the TAB key.

To change or edit text, you must move the insertion point around within the document. You can move to different parts of the document by using the mouse or the keyboard. To use the mouse, move the I-beam pointer to the desired position and click the left mouse button. You can also use the arrow keys on the keyboard to move the insertion point to a different position.

DRILL 1   **ENTER TEXT**

1. Click the **Start** button at the bottom of the screen. Point to **All Programs**; then click **Microsoft Word**.

2. If the opening *Word* screen does not fill your entire screen, click the **Maximize** button.

3. Key the text that follows using wordwrap. Press ENTER twice only at the ends of paragraphs to DS between paragraphs. Ignore any red and green wavy lines that may appear under text as you key.

4. Using the mouse, move the insertion point immediately before the *S* at the beginning of the document.

5. Key your name. Press ENTER four times. Notice that paragraph 1 moves down four lines.

6. Keep the document on the screen for the next drill.

Use wordwrap.

Serendipity, a new homework research tool from Information Technology Company, is available to subscribers of the major online services via the World Wide Web. (**Press** ENTER **two times.**)

Offered as a subscription service aimed at college students, Serendipity is a collection of tens of thousands of articles from major encyclopedias, reference books, magazines, pamphlets, and Internet sources combined into a single searchable database. (**Press** ENTER **two times.**)

Serendipity puts an electronic library right at students' fingertips. The program offers two browse-and-search capabilities. Users can find articles by entering questions in simple question format or browse the database by pointing and clicking on key words that identify related articles. For more information, call 800-555-0174 or address e-mail to lab@serendipity.com.

Menu Bar Commands

The commands available in *Word* are listed in menus located on the menu bar at the top of your screen. The names of the menus indicate the type of commands they contain. You can execute all commands using the proper menu. When you click an item on the menu bar, a menu cascades or pulls down and displays the available commands. Note that common shortcuts including toolbar buttons and keyboard commands are provided when appropriate. The File menu that follows illustrates the main characteristics of pull-down menus.

100c-d1
Mail Merge

Prepare the main document and data source for a form letter to new members of the Jefferson City Chamber of Commerce.

1. Save a new document as **100c-d1merge**.

2. Create the data source. Save as **100c-d1data**.

Field names	Record 1	Record 2	Record 3
Title	Mr.	Ms.	Dr.
First Name	Dennis	Catherine	Stephanie
Last Name	Lamar	Bradberry	Wade
Company Name	Lamar Office Products, Inc.	ITC, Inc.	Jefferson City Medical Clinic
Address Line 1	P.O. Box 983	100 Jones Rd.	P.O. Box 3832
City	Jefferson City	Jefferson City	Jefferson City
State	MO	MO	MO
ZIP Code	65101	65111	65101

3. Key the main document (open punctuation style) and insert the merge fields in it. Add notations as needed. Save the changes. Be sure the date updates automatically.

Thank you for your continued support of the Jefferson City Chamber of Commerce. Your generous contributions made 2003 a great year for the Jefferson City Chamber. The enclosed *Annual Report* outlines just a few of our accomplishments.

A new membership decal and plaque for your business are enclosed. Please display those proudly on your car and in a prominent place in your business. We encourage you to promote the Chamber to fellow business colleagues and friends.

<<Title>> <<Last Name>>, again, we thank you for your support and invite you to join us the first Friday of each month at the Chamber Business Hour. Because we rotate locations among business members, be sure to watch the monthly newsletter for the specific location.

Sincerely | Your Name, Director | Jefferson City Chamber of Commerce | Enclosures

4. Merge the data source and the main document and print. Save as **100c-d1**.

100c-d2
Mail Merge

1. Consider the various form letters that are often used by businesses or organizations. Decide upon one effective use of form letters.

2. Save a new document as **100c-d2merge**.

3. Create the data source. Save as **100c-d2data**.

4. Key the main document and insert the merge fields in the main document.

5. Merge the data source and the main document and print. Save as **100c-d2**.

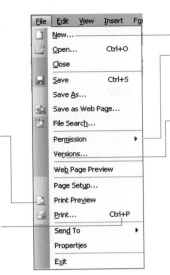

Ellipsis (...): indicates dialog box will display.

Arrow: indicates additional commands are available.

Bold: indicates the command can be used.

Dimmed command: indicates the command cannot be used.

Underlined letter: activates a command when keyed.

Files: List of files most recently opened.

Bottom chevrons ⍨: indicates additional commands are available.

Toolbar button: indicates button to click to activate a command.

Keyboard shortcut: activates a command when keys are pressed.

Toolbar Commands

Frequently used commands also can be accessed using the buttons on the Standard and Formatting toolbars. Whenever you use *Word*, make sure that both toolbars are displayed, with the Standard toolbar on top of the Formatting toolbar. If either toolbar is missing or other toolbars display, change the display following these steps. ✳ See Discover box at left.

Chevrons

To display or hide a toolbar:

1. Position the mouse pointer over any toolbar and click the right mouse button; a shortcut menu appears listing all of the toolbars that are available. (*Option:* Click **View** on the menu bar; then click **Toolbars**.)

2. Click to the left of **Standard** or **Formatting**, placing a check mark next to its name. The toolbar displays. If toolbars other than the Standard or Formatting toolbars are displayed, click the toolbar name to remove the checkmark and hide the toolbar.

3. To display the Task Pane, click **Task Pane** on the View menu: To close it, click the **Close** button at the upper-right corner of the Task Pane.

DRILL 2   COMMANDS

1. Check that the Standard and Formatting toolbars are the only ones that are displayed and that they each display on a separate row.

2. Point to several buttons on the Standard and Formatting toolbars. Notice the name of each button as it displays.

3. Click **File** on the menu bar. Point to the arrow at the bottom of the File menu, and click the left mouse button to display additional commands. If there is no arrow at the bottom of the File menu, then your entire menu is already displayed.

4. Click **Edit** on the menu bar. Note that *Cut* is dimmed. A dimmed command is not available; making it available requires another action.

5. Click **File** on the menu bar again. Note that the Save As command is followed by an ellipsis (...). Click **Save As** to display the Save As dialog box. Click **Cancel** to close the Save As dialog box.

6. Click each of the different View buttons on the status bar. Notice that a button is highlighted when that view is active. Return to Normal view.

100a
Warmup
Key each line twice SS.

alphabet	1	Dubuque's next track meet will have prizes given by forty judges.
fig/sym	2	Interest in 2000 climbed $346 (as the rates rose from 7% to 20%).
double letters	3	Ann and Buzz will carry my bookkeeping supplies to Judd's office.
easy	4	The auditor may laugh, but the penalty for chaotic work is rigid.

| 1 | 2 | 3 | 4 | 5 | 6 | 7 | 8 | 9 | 10 | 11 | 12 | 13 |

100b

Timed Writings
1. Key three 1' writings on each ¶.
2. Key one 5' writing or two 3' writings.

 all letters

gwam 3' | 5'

What do you think about when you hear individuals being called student athletes? Many people think only of the very visible football or basketball players who attract a lot of attention and often get special treatment on campus. Few people think about the large numbers of young men and women who put in long hours working and training to be the very best they can be in a wide variety of sports. These students may never receive any type of recognition in the news media, and they do not attract large crowds to watch them perform. They frequently excel in both academic and athletic performance.

What does a student athlete in one of the less visible sports with very little opportunity to become a professional athlete gain from the significant investment of time and effort in a sport? To be successful in a sport, a student must be organized, be an effective time manager, and have self-confidence. An athlete learns that teamwork, ethical conduct, and hard work are a major part of success in any type of endeavor. The skills do not apply just to sports; they also apply to jobs and to life. Most important of all, these individuals are doing what they really enjoy doing.

3'					
	1	2	3	4	
5'	1	2	3	

gwam values:
4 | 2 | 50
8 | 5 | 52
12 | 7 | 55
16 | 10 | 57
20 | 12 | 60
25 | 15 | 62
29 | 17 | 65
33 | 20 | 67
37 | 22 | 70
40 | 24 | 72
44 | 26 | 74
48 | 29 | 76
52 | 31 | 79
56 | 34 | 81
60 | 36 | 83
64 | 38 | 86
68 | 41 | 88
72 | 43 | 91
77 | 46 | 93
79 | 47 | 95

Save/Save As

Saving a document preserves it so that it can be used again. If a document is not saved, it will be lost once the computer is shut down. It is a good idea to save a document before printing. The first time you save a document, you must give it a filename. Filenames should accurately describe the document. In this course, use the exercise number as the filename (for example, **26b-drill4**).

The Save As command on the File menu is used to save a new document or to rename an existing document. The Save As dialog box contains a Save In list box, a File Name list box, and a Files of Type list box. The Save As dialog box may either be blank or display a list of files that have already been saved.

Word makes it easy to create a new folder when a file is saved. A folder would be created for storing related files. The Create New Folder button is located near the top of the Save As dialog box.

To save a new document:

1. Click the **Save** button on the Standard toolbar. (*Option:* Click **File** on the menu; then click **Save As.**) The Save As dialog box displays.
2. If necessary, change the folder or drive in the Save In box. Use the down arrow to locate the desired drive.
3. To save the document in a new folder, click the **Create New Folder** button at the top of the dialog box. Key the folder name (for example, **Module 3**).
4. Key the filename in the File Name text box.
5. Click the **Save** button or press ENTER. *Word* automatically adds the file extension **.doc** to the filename. This extension identifies the document as a *Word* document.

Word 2003

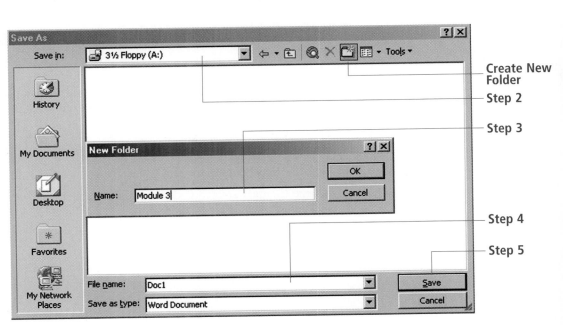

Create New Folder
Step 2
Step 3
Step 4
Step 5

Word 2002

TIP

If you are interrupted during your work on a mail merge and need to resume the merge at another time, you can save the main document and come back later. The Mail Merge Wizard keeps the data source and field information. It also remembers the step where you left off and opens to that step in the Task Pane.

3. Key the main document and insert the merge fields in the main document. Use open punctuation. Save the changes. (*Reminder:* The date should update automatically.)

Date

«AddressBlock»

«GreetingLine»

Thank you for submitting your proposal for enacting a more culturally diverse employment program for city workers to the American Studies Association.

The American Studies Association continually strives to work with city governments in three area counties to provide work environments that value diversity. The goal, of course, is to employ persons who reflect differences in age, lifestyle, and interests. Different people solve problems differently, and that leads to better decisions.

You may be contacted, «Title» «Last_Name», to represent «County» County on the special Council for Managing Diversity that is being established in our three-county region. Again, thank you for letting us know what you are doing to ensure diversity at «Company_Name».

Sincerely | Hunter Nyiri, Director | xx

4. Merge the data source and the main document and print. Save as **99d-d1**.

99d-d2
Mail Merge

1. Decide on a form letter that would be useful to you personally or to your class. Secure the names and addresses of the recipients of the form letter.

2. Save a new document as **99d-d2merge**.

3. Create the data source. Save as **99d-d2data**.

4. Key the main document and insert the merge fields in the main document.

5. Merge the data source and the main document and print. Save as **99d-d2**.

1. The document you keyed in Drill 1 should be displayed. If you are saving your files to a disk, insert a disk into Drive A or save to another location as directed by your instructor.

2. Click the **Save** button. The Save As dialog box displays.

3. Click the arrow in the Save In list box to locate the drive you will use. Point to Drive A to highlight it; then click the left mouse button to select it.

4. Click the **Create New Folder** button. The New Folder dialog box displays. Key the name **Module 3 Keys** in the text box; then click **OK**.

5. With the insertion point in the File Name text box, key **26a-drill3** as the filename.

6. Check to see that the default (*Word Document*) is displayed in the Files of Type list box. If not, click the down arrow and select **Word Document**.

7. Click the **Save** button or press ENTER to close the dialog box and return to the document window.

8. Keep the document on the screen for the next drill.

Print Preview

Print Preview enables you to see how a document will look when it is printed. Use Print Preview to check the layout of your document, such as margins, line spacing, and tabs, before printing.

To preview a document:

1. Click **Print Preview** on the Standard toolbar. A full-page version of the document displays. Print Preview displays the page where the insertion point is located.

2. Click **Close** to return to the document screen.

In Print Preview, a special toolbar displays with additional options for viewing the document. For example, when you click on the Magnifier button, the mouse pointer changes to a magnifying glass. When you click the magnifying glass on the page, you can see a portion of the document at 100%. Change the zoom percentage to view the document at a different size.

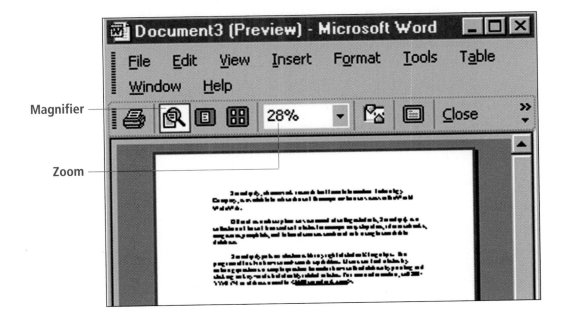

Magnifier

Zoom

6. Click **Save** on the Standard toolbar to update the changes you have made to the file **learn-merge**.

7. Click **Next: Preview your letters**.

Step 5: Preview your letters

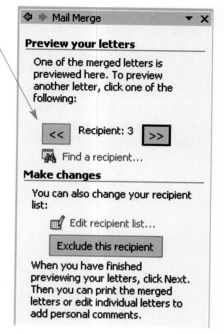

1. Click on the navigation buttons to preview each of your letters. (*Tip:* Should you need to edit one of the letters, click **Edit recipient list** and make the necessary changes to the data source file.)

2. Click **Next: Complete the merge**.

Step 6: Complete the merge

1. Click **Edit individual letters**. Click **All**; then **OK**. The merge letters will appear on the screen as a new document with a page break between each.

2. Save the merged file as **99c-drill1** and print.

APPLICATIONS

99d-d1
Mail Merge

1. Save a new document as **99d-d1merge**.
2. Create the data source. Save as **99d-d1data**.

Field names	Record 1	Record 2	Record 3
Title	Mrs.	Mr.	Ms.
First Name	Jessica	Allen	Paje
Last Name	Quarrels	Bouchillon	Vang
Company Name	Hendrix Plastics	Magnolia Chemicals	Faulkner Florists
Address Line 1	5689 Old Vinton Rd.	538 Hill St.	885 N. Third St.
City	Starkville	Columbus	West Point
State	MS	MS	MS
ZIP Code	39759-5689	39701-0538	39773-0885
County	Oktibbeha	Lowndes	Clay

Print

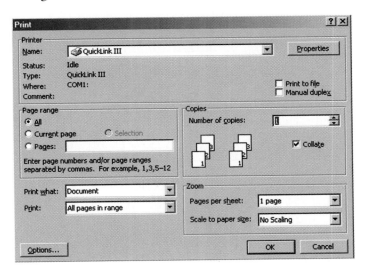 You can print a document by clicking Print on the File menu or by clicking the Print button on the Standard toolbar. Clicking the Print button immediately prints the document using all of the default settings. To view or change the default settings, click **Print** on the File menu or use the keyboard shortcut CTRL + P to display the Print dialog box.

DRILL 4   PREVIEW AND PRINT

1. The document **26a-drill3** should be displayed on your screen.

2. Click the **Print Preview** button to view your document.

3. Change the magnification to **75%**; then change it to **Whole Page**.

4. Click the **Close** button to return to Normal view.

5. Check to be sure that your printer is turned on and has paper.

6. Click **File** on the menu bar, and then click **Print**. Compare your dialog box with the one above. Your printer name may differ, but other choices should be the same. Verify that you will print one copy, and then click **OK**.

Close

 Close clears the screen of the document and removes it from memory. You will be prompted to save the document before closing if you have not saved it or to save your changes if you have made any to the document since the previous save. It is necessary to close each document that is open.

To close a document, do one of the following:

- Click **File** on the menu bar; then click **Close**.
- Click the **Close** button at the right side of the Menu bar.

4. Click **Greeting line** in the far right pane of the Mail Merge box (or click the **Insert Greeting Line** button on the Mail Merge toolbar). The Greeting Line dialog box displays. Business letters may use open or mixed punctuation (mixed punctuation includes a colon after the salutation and comma after the complimentary closing). This letter applies mixed punctuation; therefore, click the down arrow to the right of the comma. Select the colon and click **OK**. Press ENTER two times and continue keying the letter until you reach the merge field code for Speech.

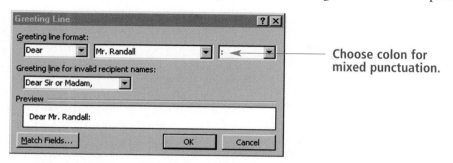

Choose colon for mixed punctuation.

5. Insert the merge field for Speech:

   a. Click **More Items** from the right pane (or click the **Insert Merge Fields** button on the Mail Merge toolbar).

   b. Select **Speech**, click **Insert**, and then click **Close**. (*Tip:* When necessary, strike the Space Bar to insert a blank space between fields. Insert punctuation as necessary between fields or at the end of a field.)

   c. Continue keying the letter. Insert the merge fields for Time and Room at the appropriate places.

(Date Code) (Enter 4 times)

«AddressBlock» (Enter 2 times)

«GreetingLine» (Enter 2 times)

Thank you for agreeing to present your paper titled «Speech» at the International Conference on Technology to be held at the Omni Hotel in San Francisco on May 12. Your presentation is scheduled for «Time» in the «Room». You may expect approximately 100 participants.

You are also invited to be our special guest at the annual awards luncheon on Friday at 11:45 a.m. in the Grand Ballroom. Your conference registration materials and a luncheon ticket will be held for you at the hotel registration desk. If you need assistance when you arrive at the hotel, please call conference headquarters at Extension 7532.

«Title» «Last_Name», we look forward to your presentation and to your outstanding contribution to our program.

Sincerely yours, (Enter 4 times) | Ms. Jacqueline VonKohn

Program Coordinator | xx

New

When all documents have been closed, *Word* displays a blank screen. To create a new document, click the **New Blank Document** button on the Standard toolbar.

Open

Any documents that have been saved can be opened and used again. When you open a file, a dialog box displays the names of folders or files within a folder. You can also select files saved on a disk.

To open a document:

1. Click the **File** menu. If the document name is shown in the list of files, click it to open the document. If it is not listed, click **Open** to display the Open dialog box. (*Option*: Click the **Open** button on the toolbar.)

2. In the Look In box, click the down arrow; then click the drive where your files are stored (Drive A).

3. If necessary, double-click the folder name to display the filenames. Click the desired filename; then click **Open**.

Exit

Exit saves all documents that are on the screen and then quits the software. When you exit *Word*, you close both the document and the program window. You will be prompted to save before exiting if you have not already saved the document or if you have made changes to it since last saving. Click the **Close** button in the title bar (top bar) to exit *Word*.

DRILL 5   **CLOSE AND OPEN A DOCUMENT**

1. Close the file **26a-drill3** that you saved in Drill 3.

2. Click **New Blank Document** on the Standard toolbar.

3. Close the blank document.

4. Click **Open** on the Standard toolbar, and open the file **26a-drill3**.

5. Click **Save As** on the File menu. In the Save As dialog box, save the file again as **26a-drill5**. Leave the document on the screen for the next drill.

---

4. Key the variables for Record 1. Click **New Entry** to begin a new record; key variables for Record 2. Repeat for Record 3.

TIP

To move within the New Address List dialog box:

SHIFT + TAB   Move to the previous field.

TAB   Move to the next field.

ENTER *after last field*   Move to new record.

Field names	Record 1	Record 2	Record 3
Title	Ms.	Dr.	Mr.
First Name	Alison	Lisa	Joseph
Last Name	Hershbarger	Hodnett	Zuber
Company Name	Hershbarger & Ward Attorneys	Columbia Hospital	First Bank of Chicago
Address Line 1	844 Locksley Way	303 Park Circle Rd.	1106 Whispering Pines Rd.
City	Salt Lake City	Milwaukee	Chicago
State	UT	WI	IL
ZIP Code	84110-0844	53221-0303	60650-1106
Speech	"Copyright Issues in the Digital Age"	"Creating Interactive Presentations"	"Creating a Web Presence for Your Organization"
Time	8:30 a.m.	9:30 a.m.	10:30 a.m.
Room	Colonnade Room	Diplomat Room	Laurel Suite

5. Click **Close** after keying all of the records. The Save Address List dialog box displays. Enter a filename (**learn-data**) in the File name box and click **Save**. (*Note*: By default, data files are saved to the folder My Data Sources under the My Documents folder.) In the Save in box, choose the appropriate folder for saving this file.

6. The Mail Merge Recipients dialog box shows the variables in table format. Click **OK** (or click **Edit** to view the data in the New Address List dialog box).

7. Click **Next: Write your letter** from the Mail Merge Task Pane.

Step 4: Write your letter

1. Begin keying the main document on approximately line 2.1". Insert the date as a field (**Insert menu, Date and Time**; click the **Update automatically box**). Press ENTER four times.

2. Click **Address block** from the right pane (or click the **Insert Address Block** button on the Mail Merge toolbar). The Insert Address Block dialog box displays. Click **OK** to accept the default settings for recipient's name, company name, and postal address.

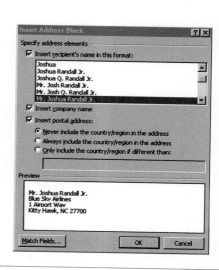

3. Press ENTER two times.

You may choose to use *CheckPro* for Lesson 26. To complete exercises in *CheckPro*, follow these steps:

1. Open *CheckPro* and choose Lesson 26.

2. Select the exercise to be completed from the Lesson menu. Whenever the exercise is to be completed in *Word*, *CheckPro* automatically opens *Word*.

3. Key the document as directed in your textbook.

4. When you are finished with the document, click the check mark button on the *CheckPro* toolbar in the upper-right corner. *CheckPro* will automatically check your document for speed and accuracy and save your document.

5. If you wish to save a document without checking it for accuracy, click the **Back** button. You will be able to open the document at a later time.

APPLICATIONS

26b-d1
Create a
New Document

1. Start *Microsoft Word*.

2. Key the paragraphs using wordwrap. Press ENTER twice between paragraphs to create a double space

3. Save the document as **26b-d1.** Print; then close the document.

In Lesson 26, I have learned the basic operations of my word processing software. Today I opened the word processor, created a new document, saved the document, printed the document, closed the document, and exited the software. This new document that I am creating will be named 26b-d1. I will save it so that I can use it in the next lesson to open an existing document.

(Press ENTER two times)

Learning basic word processing functions at the same time I improve my keyboarding skills is easy and fun. The toolbar functions provide a quick way to apply functions.

26b-d2
Create a
New Document

1. In a new document, key the text below using wordwrap. Press TAB to indent the first line of each paragraph. Double-space (DS) between paragraphs.

2. Save the document as **26b-d2** and print. Close the document. Then exit *Word*.

As the man says, "I have some good news and some bad news." Let me give you the bad news first. **(Press ENTER two times)**

Due to a badly pulled muscle, I have had to withdraw from the Eastern Racquetball Tournament. As you know, I have been looking forward to the tournament for a long time, and I had begun to hope that I might even win it. I've been working hard.

That's the bad news. The good news is that I have been chosen to help officiate, so I'll be coming to Newport News anyway. In fact, I'll arrive there a day earlier than I had originally planned.

So, put the racquet away, but get out the backgammon board. I'm determined to win something on this trip!

The Mail Merge Wizard is a straightforward way to produce a merged document such as the form letter you will create.

To start the Mail Merge Wizard:

1. Open a new document and save it with a meaningful name.
2. Select **Tools**, then **Letters and Mailings**, and then **Mail Merge Wizard**. The Mail Merge pane displays at the right of the screen.

DRILL 1   **MAIL MERGE WIZARD**

1. Follow steps 1 and 2 above to start the Mail Merge Wizard. In step 1, save the blank document as **learn-merge**.

2. Follow the six steps of the Mail Merge Wizard explained below and on the next few pages. To move from one step to the next, click **Next** located at the bottom of the pane. This drill will lead you through the steps for using the Mail Merge Wizard.

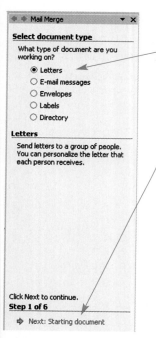

Step 1: Select document type

1. Choose **Letters** (or the type of document you will use for the main document).
2. Click **Next: Starting document** to go to Step 2 of the Wizard.

Step 2: Select starting document

1. Click **Use the current document** to create a new form letter in the active window (or choose **Start from a template** to use a *Word* template, or choose **Start from existing document** to use a form letter you have already created).
2. Click **Next: Select recipients**. (*Note:* You may click **Previous: Select document type** to return to the previous step.)

Step 3: Select recipients

1. Click **Type a new list** because the data source does not yet exist. (Choose **Select from Outlook contacts** to use the Outlook address book, or choose **Use an existing list** to use a file that you created previously.)
2. Under *Type a new list*, click **Create**. The New Address List dialog box displays.
3. Click **Customize** to edit the default field names provided in the Wizard. The Customize Address List dialog box displays.
   a. To delete a field name, select the field and click **Delete**. Click **Yes** to confirm the deletion of each field. For this drill, delete **Address Line 2**, **Country**, **Home Phone**, **Work Phone**, and **E-mail address**.
   b. To add a field name, click **Add**. The Add Field dialog box displays. Add three fields: **Time**, **Room**, and **Speech**.
   c. To position the new fields correctly, select the field to be moved. Click **Move Up** or **Move Down** as appropriate. Move the field names so they are positioned as shown at the left.

NEW FUNCTIONS

27a

Navigate in a Document

The document window displays only a portion of a page at one time. The keyboard, mouse, and scroll bars can be used to move quickly through a document to view it. To move to the end of a document, press CTRL + END. To move to the beginning of a document, press CTRL + HOME.

Scroll Bars

To move through the document using the mouse, use the scroll bars. The vertical scroll bar enables you to move up and down through a document. The horizontal scroll bar enables you to move left and right across a line. Scrolling does not change the position of the insertion point, only your view of the document.

To scroll	Click
Up or down	Scroll bar and drag or click Up and Down arrows
Up one screen	Above the scroll box
Down one screen	Below the scroll box
To a specific page	Drag the vertical scroll box and watch for page number
Left or right	Scroll bar and drag or click arrows

Select Text

To make any formatting changes to existing text, you must first select the text you want to change. Selected text is highlighted in black. An easy way to select text is to click at the beginning of the text and drag the mouse over the text. You can also double-click a word to select it or triple-click within a paragraph to select the whole paragraph. To deselect text, click anywhere outside of the selected text.

DRILL 1   NAVIGATE AND SELECT TEXT

1. Open the file you created in Lesson 26, **26b-d1.**

2. Move to the end of the document (CTRL + END).

3. Move to the top of the document (CTRL + HOME).

4. Select the first sentence; then deselect it.

5. Scroll down to the last sentence and select the word **Microsoft**.

6. Move to the top of the document (CTRL + HOME), and key your name followed by a DS.

7. Save the document as **27a-drill1**; then close it.

Mail Merge

Creating personal form letters, printing labels, and addressing envelopes to a large number of individuals are tasks done easily using the mail merge feature. **Mail merge** is creating a new (merged) document by combining information from two other documents—the main document and the data source.

The **main document** contains the text and graphics that remain the same for each version of the merged document. Within the main document, **merge fields** are inserted as placeholders in locations where you want to merge names, addresses, and other variable information that comes from the data source file.

The **data source** is a file that contains the names, addresses, and other variables to be merged with the main document. All the variables for one individual person are called a **record**. The separate variables for each record are called **fields**.

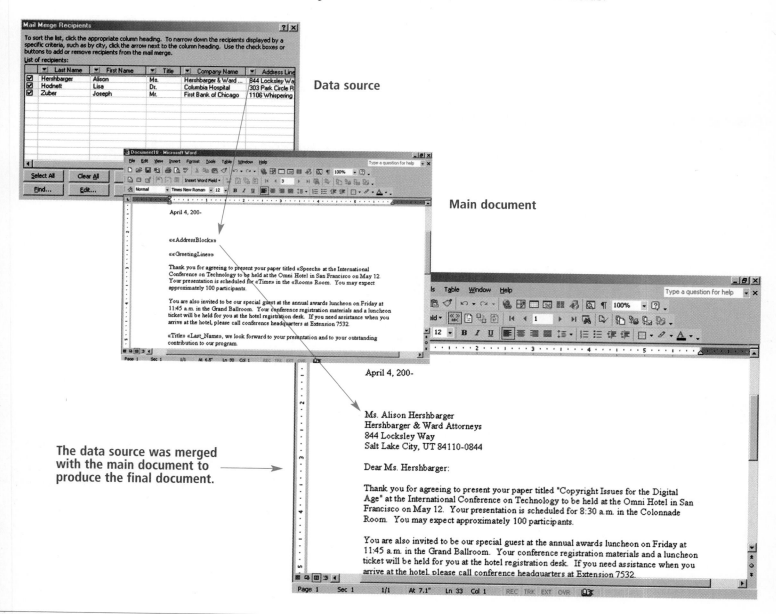

Data source

Main document

The data source was merged with the main document to produce the final document.

Character Formats

Character formats apply to letters, numbers, and punctuation marks and include such things as bold, underline, italic, fonts, and font sizes. The Formatting toolbar provides an efficient way to apply character formats. Formatting toolbar buttons also make it easy to align text.

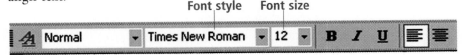

Font style   Font size

To apply character formats as you key:

1. Click the appropriate format button, and key the text to be formatted.

2. When you finish keying the formatted text, click the same button again to turn off the format. Notice that a format button is highlighted when the feature is on.

To apply character formats to existing text:

1. Select the text.

2. Click the appropriate format button.

Font Size and Styles

Word's default font is 12-point Times New Roman. Font size is measured in points. One vertical inch equals 72 points. Most text is keyed in a 10-, 11-, or 12-point font, although a larger font may be used to emphasize headings. *Word* has a variety of font styles available.

To change font size:

1. Select the text to be changed.

2. Click the **Font Size** down arrow.

3. Scroll through the list of available sizes, and click the desired font size.

To change font style:

1. Select the text to be changed.

2. Click the **Font** down arrow.

3. Scroll through the list of available styles, and click the desired style.

TIP
You can also change font size and formats by choosing **Format** on the menu bar, and then choosing **Fonts** to display the Font dialog box.

Mass Mailings

- Merge form letters.
- Merge envelopes and labels.
- Edit the data source and sort and filter records.

LESSON 99

Skillbuilding and Mail Merge

SKILLBUILDING

99a
Warmup
Key each line twice SS.

adjacent keys
1 Ty was going to see the trio perform at a junior college theater.
2 My class was starting to talk about tilling the soil in Freeport.

fig/sym
3 My mileage is 28,475 on 2 front tires and 39,610 on 2 rear tires.
4 Mark paid $230.49 plus 6% tax for 1.75# of pate & 1/8# of caviar.

fluency
5 The Orlando auditor did a formal audit of the firm on the island.
6 Jane may work as a tutor for eight girls; Ty may also tutor them.

| 1 | 2 | 3 | 4 | 5 | 6 | 7 | 8 | 9 | 10 | 11 | 12 | 13 |

99b
Technique Builder
Key each line twice SS.

balanced hand
7 pens turn fur slam pay rifle worn pan duck ham lap slap burn girl
8 Andy Clancy, a neighbor, may visit at the lake and at the island.

one hand
9 read ploy create kiln crate plum were pony cats jump severe hump
10 Phillip, as you are aware, was a reader on deferred estate cases.

combination
11 did you we spent pony street busy jump held severe pant exert due
12 Were profits better when we were on Main Street than Duck Street?

| 1 | 2 | 3 | 4 | 5 | 6 | 7 | 8 | 9 | 10 | 11 | 12 | 13 |

1. Open a new blank document.

2. Key your name, and press ENTER.

3. Key the document name **27a-drill2**, and press ENTER four times.

4. Key the first three sentences that follow, applying the formats as you key. Press ENTER after each sentence.

5. Key the last three sentences in normal style; then select the sentence and apply the formats.

6. Save the document as **27a-drill2**.

This sentence is keyed in bold. (Press ENTER.)

This sentence is keyed in italic.

<u>This sentence is underlined.</u> (Press ENTER two times.)

<u>This sentence is keyed in bold and italic and underlined.</u>

This sentence is keyed in 14-point Times New Roman.

This sentence is keyed in 12-point Arial.

Paragraph Formats

Paragraph formats apply to an entire paragraph and can be applied before or after a paragraph has been keyed. Each time you press ENTER, *Word* inserts a paragraph mark and starts a new paragraph. Thus, a paragraph may consist of a single line followed by a hard return (¶ mark) or several lines that wrap and are followed by a hard return. In order to apply paragraph formats such as line spacing or alignment, you must be able to see where paragraphs begin and end. Show/Hide displays hard returns as a paragraph mark (¶).

Show/Hide

¶   Click the **Show/Hide** button on the Standard toolbar to display all nonprinting characters such as paragraph markers (¶) and spaces (··). The Show/Hide button appears highlighted or depressed when it is active. To turn nonprinting characters off, click the **Show/Hide** button again.

Alignment

Alignment refers to the way in which the text lines up. Text can be aligned at the left, center, right, or justified (lined up with both margins). Use the Alignment buttons on the Formatting toolbar to quickly align paragraphs.

To align existing text:

1. Place the insertion point in the paragraph to be changed. If more than one paragraph is affected, select the paragraphs to be aligned.

2. Click the appropriate **Align** button.

To align text as you key:

1. Click the appropriate **Align** button.

2. Key the text. This alignment will remain in effect until you click the button again.

Module 15: Checkpoint

1. To wrap text around clip art, set the text wrapping style in the _____ dialog box.

2. To insert a picture that is available in your files, click **Picture** on the Insert menu and select _____.

3. Clip art size can be changed by holding the insertion point over the handle until the pointer turns to a _____ arrow and dragging a corner handle to increase or decrease it.

4. To wrap text around a graphic so that it is very close to the graphic, select _____ wrapping style.

5. AutoShapes, WordArt, and Rectangle can be accessed from the _____ toolbar.

6. A heading that spans two or more columns is called a masthead or a _____.

7. To balance columns so that they end at the same point on the page, insert a _____ break at the end of the text.

8. To force text to move to the next column, insert a _____ break.

9. To indicate that text is continued on the next page, insert a footer with the word _____ centered.

10. To indicate the end of a news release, key _____.

Performance Assessment

Document 1
Two-Column Newsletter

1. Open **cu news** from the data files.

2. Insert a continuous section break at the beginning of the body of the newsletter.

3. Format the document into two equal columns.

4. Check to see that the table is centered horizontally in the column.

5. Save the document as **Checkpoint15-d1**.

Document 2
Announcement

1. Format the document landscape with 1" margins on all sides.

2. Use keywords *buildings*, *house*, or *lake* to find appropriate clip art. Position it at top left margin with **Square** wrapping style and **left** alignment.

3. Use 36-point type and key to right of clip art: **Century Service Club / Picnic at the Lake House / 28 Lake Wateree Road**.

4. Center and key below clip art: **Club members and their immediate families / Saturday, June 10 from 12:30 to 6:30 p.m. / Make reservations by June 1 (555-0148) / Food and beverages provided / Bring lawn chairs or blankets**.

5. Save as **Checkpoint15-d2**.

Century Service Club
Picnic at the Lake House
28 Lake Wateree Road

Club members and their immediate families
Saturday, June 10 from 12:30 to 6:30 p.m.
Make reservations by June 1 (555-0148)
Food and beverages provided
Bring lawn chairs or blankets

1. Open a new blank document, and center **USING ALIGNMENTS** in 14 point and bold. Strike ENTER twice to create a DS.

2. Change to left alignment and 12 point to key the first paragraph. Apply wordwrap within a paragraph. Press ENTER twice between paragraphs to create a DS.

3. Apply the formatting and alignment as shown in the following document.

4. Save the document as **27a-drill3,** and print a copy. Leave the document on the screen for the next drill.

USING ALIGNMENTS

Left alignment is used for this first paragraph. When left alignment is used, each line in the paragraph begins at the same position on the left side. The right margin will be uneven.

Center alignment (ENTER)

Center titles and short lines.(ENTER)

Use for invitations, announcements, and other documents. (ENTER) (ENTER)

Right alignment is used for this third paragraph. When right alignment is used, each line in the paragraph ends at the same position on the right side. The left side will be uneven.

Justify is used for this fourth paragraph. When justification is used, all lines (except the last line of a paragraph) begin and end at the same position at the left and right margins. Extra spaces are automatically inserted to achieve this look.

Line Spacing

Word's default line spacing is single. When paragraphs are single spaced, the first line of the paragraph normally is not indented. However, a blank line is inserted between paragraphs to distinguish them and to improve readability. Double spacing leaves a blank line between each keyed line. Therefore, it is necessary to indent the first line of each double-spaced paragraph to indicate the beginning of the paragraph. To indent the first line of a paragraph, press the TAB key. The default indention is 0.5".

To change line spacing:

1. Position the insertion point in the paragraph in which you want to change the line spacing. If more than one paragraph is to be changed, select all the paragraphs.

2. Click **Format** on the menu bar; then click **Paragraph**.

3. Select the **Indents and Spacing** tab.

4. Click the arrow in the Line Spacing box; then click **Double.** Click **OK**.

Line spacing can also be changed using the Formatting toolbar. Place the cursor in the paragraph in which the spacing will be changed. Click the **Line Spacing** button; click the Down arrow; then click the desired line spacing. If the Line Spacing button is not displayed, click the chevrons at the right of the toolbar (>>) to display additional formatting options.

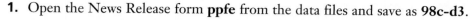

1. Open the News Release form **ppfe** from the data files and save as **98c-d3**.

2. Use the following information to key a one-page news release; double-space.

3. Resave, preview, and print.

Contact Person: Sherry Sinago

Current date

For Release: Immediately

CELEBRATION TO BENEFIT SCHOOLS

OKEMOS, MI—The Okemos Chapter of Parents' Partnership for Education will hold its annual Celebration of the Arts, Friday from 7:30 to 11 p.m. at the Talbert Hotel.

Participants will have an opportunity to enjoy an hors d'oeuvres buffet, see excellent musical and dramatic entertainment by students of Okemos Schools, view award-winning student artwork, and bid on artwork by locally and nationally known artists. An annual fundraising event for the Okemos Chapter of Parents' Partnership for Education, Celebration of the Arts serves several key purposes, according to organizers.

"The Celebration of the Arts provides an opportunity to showcase the superior quality of talent that is being nurtured in the Okemos Schools," said Chapter President Sherry Sinago. "It also provides an evening when people of the community can come together to socialize and share their support of the schools of Okemos. Also, this event enables our chapter to raise funds to carry out projects for the next school year," Sinago added.

The annual Celebration of the Arts is open to the public. Reservations may be made by calling 555-0134. Tickets will also be available at the door.

###

DRILL 4 — LINE SPACING

1. Document **27a-drill3** should be on your screen.
2. Click in the first paragraph and change the line spacing to double.
3. Click on **Center Alignment** in the second paragraph. Change the line spacing to 1.5. Note that the spacing change affects only paragraph 2—the paragraph where the insertion point is located.
4. Click in the third paragraph and change the line spacing to multiple. Save the document as **27a-drill4** and close it.

APPLICATIONS

27b-d1
Character Formats

1. Key the heading and the sentences in Group A applying the character formats shown as you key. DS between sentences.
2. Key the heading and the sentences in Group B, then select and apply the formats shown. DS between sentences.
3. Select all sentences in Group A and change the font to Arial 11 point. Select all sentences in Group B and apply a 14-point script font.
4. Save the document as **27b-d1**. Print the document.

Group A

I read a very inspirational book, <u>Turning Dreams into Reality</u>.

Use **Skill Builder** in *Keyboarding Pro* frequently to improve your skills.

Please meet the team at *Gate 4* of *Terminal A* at the airport **no later than 9:15 a.m.**

Group B

The Broadway play *Marching to My Own Drummer* lasted **three** hours.

We owe a total of <u>$1,597.26</u> for flights, hotel, and tickets.

Please make your check payable to ***LaShanda C. Bullock*** and deliver it Friday <u>morning</u>.

Pediatric News

PACIFIC NEWPORT MEDICAL GROUP

HEPATITIS B VACCINE

Hepatitis B is most commonly contracted in the teenage and adult years. It is highly recommended that all pre-teens and teenagers be vaccinated with the series of three Hepatitis B vaccines. The three shots are administered over a six-month period.

Hepatitis B can affect anyone—in fact, it is estimated that one in ten adults may acquire Hepatitis B at some time unless immunized. The most serious complications of Hepatitis B are a deterioration of liver function and development of liver cancer.

The vaccine is safe and has no side effects. We can administer the MMR or tetanus booster (if they are due) at the same time as the Hepatitis vaccine.

INSURANCE COVERAGE

All health insurance policies are required to cover your child's well child care visits as well as immunizations. Most insurance policies cover the cost of one well care visit each year.

PEDIATRIC ASTHMA

The number of cases of asthma in children under 18 years of age was reported as 2.7 million during this past year. At least one child with asthma was reported by 4.3 percent of households.

Similar to an overly sensitive car alarm, the cells that line the lungs of adults and children with asthma are often set off by the smallest disturbance. The trigger may be a bit of pollen, cat dander, dust, tobacco smoke, or some other pollutant. It may also be a draft of cold air, the common cold virus, or even the demands of exercise.

Many children do outgrow asthma, but that is not a reason to ignore treating it appropriately. If your child has problems with recurrent coughing, coughing with exercise, shortness of breath, nighttime coughing, or poorly controlled asthma, please discuss it with us. We have many treatment options to try to make your child as healthy as possible.

PHYSICAL EXAM FOR SCHOOL ENTRY

Call now to set up an appointment for a physical exam if your child will be entering kindergarten or first grade this year. We recommend vision and hearing screenings before school entry. There are a limited number of appointments allocated for physical exams each day, so call in advance to reserve your time.

27b-d2
Paragraph Formats

1. Center and bold the title, Commitment; apply Arial 14-point font.
2. Single-space the paragraphs and use wordwrap. Double-space between paragraphs. Do not indent paragraphs. Align paragraphs at the left.
3. Preview the paragraphs and print the document.
4. Change the format on all paragraphs to left alignment, double-spacing, and indented paragraphs.
5. Use right-alignment and single-spacing to add your name and the date on separate lines a double space below the last paragraph.
6. Save the document as **27b-d2**. Print the document.

Commitment

Commitment simply means that you will follow up on promises you make and do what you said you would do. The concept of commitment is a prerequisite for building credibility. It is extremely difficult to believe in or trust individuals who do not do what they committed to do. Many people think commitments are not valid unless they are written commitments. However, verbal commitments are just as important and should be honored in the same way that written commitments are honored.

On rare occasions, circumstances may make it impossible for you to honor a commitment. If it is impossible for you to keep a commitment, notify the individual to whom the commitment was made as quickly as possible. Explain why you cannot meet the commitment and try to give the individual as much time as possible so that other arrangements can be made. Letting people down at the last minute puts them in an awkward position

Your name
Today's date

SKILLBUILDING

27c
Skill Builder, Lesson A

Use the remaining class time to build your skills using the Skill Builder module within *Keyboarding Pro*. Complete these lessons as time permits.

1. Open *Keyboarding Pro*. Log on in the usual manner.
2. Click **Edit** on the menu bar and then **Preferences**. On the Preferences dialog box under Skill Builder, click the radio button for **Speed** and then **OK**. (You must choose your preference before entering Skill Builder.)
3. Open the Skill Builder module, and select Lesson A.
4. Beginning with Keyboard Mastery, complete as much of the lesson as time permits.
5. Exit the software. Remove your storage disk. Store your materials as directed.

98c-d1
Announcement

1. Set margins for 1" on all sides; use landscape orientation; use 48-point font.
2. Insert **andy** from the data file.
3. Select the picture; use **Square** wrapping and **left** alignment; select **Picture** tab; crop the picture .8" from the bottom, left, and top; size the picture 4.5" wide.
4. Position the picture at the top left margin.
5. To the right of the picture, key and center: **Lost Pet Named / Andy / Honey-Colored / Cairn Terrier.**
6. Below the picture and information in #5, center: **North Hopkins Neighborhood / $100 Reward / Call Pat at 555-0189**.
7. Save as **98c-d1**, preview to make sure the announcement fits on one page, and print.

98c-d2
Newsletter

1. Use .75" margins on all sides of the newsletter shown on the next page.
2. Use WordArt for banner; select the style in the fifth row of the fifth column. Put a double line below the banner using a color similar to the color of the WordArt.
3. Key **PACIFIC NEWPORT MEDICAL GROUP**; format using bold and same text color as the double line. Follow with a single line.
4. Insert a continuous section break about .5" below the single line and key the newsletter shown on the next page using two equal columns.
5. Format all headings using bold, ALL CAPS, and the same text color.
6. Insert clip art appropriate for pediatric medicine. Format clip art using a **Tight** wrapping style, **center** alignment, and size it about 2.5" wide. Position it near the center of the page.
7. Save as **98c-d2**, preview to make sure the newsletter fits on one page, and print.

NEW FUNCTIONS

28a

Spelling and Grammar

When you key, *Word* places a red wavy line under misspelled words and a green wavy line under potential grammar errors. Clicking the right mouse button in a marked word displays a shortcut menu with suggested replacement words that you can use to correct the error.

The Spelling and Grammar Status button on the status bar also informs you if there is an error in the document.

 To manually check a document, click the Spelling and Grammar button on the Standard toolbar to start the checking process.

When *Word* locates a possible error, the Spelling and Grammar dialog box displays. You can change words marked as errors or ignore them. You can click the **Add** button to add correct words not recognized by *Word* to the dictionary. If you choose Ignore All and Change All, the marked words will either be ignored or changed throughout the entire document.

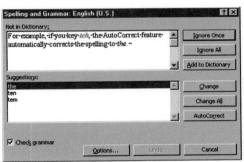

AutoCorrect

As you key, common errors are automatically corrected. For example, if you key *teh*, the AutoCorrect feature automatically corrects the spelling to *the*. When this feature is enabled, *Word* automatically replaces errors using the spell checker's main dictionary. You can customize or add words to the software's dictionary by accessing AutoCorrect Options on the Tools menu. Additional AutoCorrect options enable you to format text and automatically insert repetitive text as you key.

DRILL 1   **SPELLING AND GRAMMAR AND AUTOCORRECT**

1. On the Tools menu, select **AutoCorrect Options**. Note the available options, and then scroll through the list of replacement words (you can add additional words).

2. Key the following sentences exactly as they are shown; include the misspellings and abbreviations. Note that many errors are automatically corrected as you key.

3. In the last sentence, press ENTER to accept the AutoCorrect entry at the beginning of the sentence.

4. Right-click on the words marked with a wavy red line, and correct the errors.

5. Proofread the lines to find two unmarked errors.

6. Save the document as **28a-drill1**. Print and close the document.

i beleive a lot of dissatisfied customers will not return.

a seperate committee was formed to deal with the new issues.

please includ a self-addressed stampted envelope with you letter.

To Whom It May Concern: If you don't receive a repsonse to you e-mail messige, call Robbins and Assocaites at 555-0106.

SKILLBUILDING

98a
Warmup
Key each line twice SS.

alphabet	1	Mickey bought six lavender azaleas and quite a few nice junipers.
fig/sym	2	We gave a 15% discount on 3 invoices (#28574, #6973, and #12095).
3rd & 4th fingers	3	Pam was quick to zap Dex about a poor sample that was on display.
easy	4	Jan and six girls may go to the lake to sit on the dock and fish.

| 1 | 2 | 3 | 4 | 5 | 6 | 7 | 8 | 9 | 10 | 11 | 12 | 13 |

98b
Timed Writing
Take one 3' and one 5' writing. Work for control.

  all letters

gwam   3' | 5'

	3'	5'
Something that you can never escape is your attitude.	4	2 44
It will be with you forever. However, you decide whether your	8	5 47
attitude is an asset or a liability for you. Your attitude	12	7 49
reflects the way you feel about the world you abide in and	16	9 52
everything that is a part of that world. It reflects the way you	20	12 54
feel about yourself, about your environment, and about other peo-	25	15 57
ple who are a part of your environment. Oftentimes, people with	29	17 59
a positive attitude are people who are extremely successful.	33	20 62
At times we all have experiences that cause us to be	36	22 64
negative. The difference between a positive and a negative per-	41	24 66
son is that the positive person rebounds very quickly from a bad	45	27 69
experience; the negative person does not. The positive person is	49	30 72
a person who usually looks on the bright side of things and	53	32 74
recognizes the world as a place of promise, hope, joy, excite-	58	35 77
ment, and purpose. A negative person generally has just the	62	37 79
opposite view of the world. Remember, others want to be around	66	40 82
those who are positive but tend to avoid those who are negative.	70	42 84

3' | 1 | 2 | 3 | 4 |
5' | 1 | 2 | 3 |

APPLICATIONS

98c
Assessment

On the signal to begin, key the documents in sequence. Correct errors. When time has been called, proofread all documents again and correct any errors you may have overlooked. Reprint if necessary.

Undo/Redo

 To reverse the most recent action you have taken (such as inserting or deleting text, formatting in bold or underline, changing line spacing, etc.), click the **Undo** button. To reverse several actions, click the Down arrow beside Undo to display a list of recent actions. Then click the action you wish to reverse. Note, however, that all actions you performed prior to the action you select also will be reversed. Commands such as Save and Print cannot be undone this way.

Redo reverses the last Undo and can be applied several times to redo the past several actions. Click on the Down arrow beside Redo to view all actions that can be redone.

DRILL 2   **UNDO/REDO**

1. Key the following paragraph SS.

2. Bold and underline **Undo/Redo** in the first sentence.

3. Apply bold and italic to **Undo** in the second sentence and to **Redo** in the last sentence.

4. Change line spacing to DS.

5. Undo the underline in the first sentence.

6. Undo the double-spacing in the paragraph.

7. Redo the underline in the first sentence.

8. Undo the bold in the last sentence.

9. Redo the spacing to DS in the paragraph.

10. Save the document as **28a-drill2**.

Keying and formatting changes can be reversed easily by using the Undo/Redo function. If you make a change, one click of the Undo button can reverse the change. If you undo a change and decide that you really want to keep the change as it was originally made, you can go back to the original change by clicking the Redo button.

Help

Help provides you with quick access to information about commands, features, and screen elements. To access it, click **Help** on the menu bar, and then click **Microsoft Word Help**. This option includes Contents, Answer Wizard, and Index.

Contents displays a list of topics you can click on to display helpful information.

Answer Wizard enables you to ask a question. When you click **Search,** the Wizard displays a list of topics pertaining to your answer. Click on a topic to display additional information.

Index enables you to key a word or select a keyword to display a list of topics pertaining to the keyword. Click **Search** and then click on the topic to display the information in the right window.

Click outside the Help window to remove the window from the screen.

You can also access Help by clicking the Microsoft Word Help button or by keying a question in the Ask a Question box.

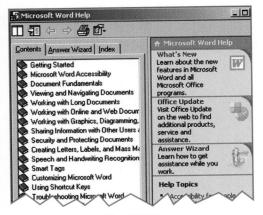

Word 2002

97c-d3
Two-Page News Release

1. Prepare the following news release on the Suarez news release form (**97c-d1**).

2. For the release date, use one week from today.

3. Add a footer with *–more–* positioned at the center.

4. On the second page, add the header **Suarez Scholarship Program/page number**. Click **Page Setup** and click **Different First Page**.

5. Key the text double-spaced.

6. At the end of the text, double-space and key **###**. Click the footer on the second page and remove *–more–* .

7. Save as **97c-d3**, preview, and print.

Suarez Corporation announced that the Suarez family has established the Suarez Scholars Foundation with a $25 million endowment and will begin the Suarez Scholars program immediately. The foundation will give 30 scholarships each year to outstanding graduating seniors from high schools throughout the ten-state region in which the company operates. Seniors from Alabama, Arkansas, Florida, Georgia, Kentucky, Louisiana, Mississippi, North Carolina, South Carolina, and Tennessee are eligible to apply to become a Suarez Scholar.

The 10 top students will be designated as Suarez All South Scholars and the remaining 20 students will be designated as Suarez Scholars. Suarez All South Scholars receive $7,500 per year for four years for a total scholarship value of $30,000. Suarez Scholars receive $2,500 a year for four years for a total scholarship value of $10,000.

Criteria for determining scholarship winners include academic achievement (rank in class, grade point average, and scores on standardized tests), leadership, and community service. Students who have overcome adversity to excel may be given additional consideration. A computer program selects the semifinalists and a panel of business and educational leaders from the ten states select the 30 finalists.

The Suarez All South Selection Panel—a group of leaders selected from across the region—will interview the 30 finalists in Memphis and select the ten Suarez All South Scholars. The remaining 20 finalists are named Suarez Scholars. An exciting program is planned for the three-day visit to Memphis to ensure that the event is a memorable one for all Suarez Scholars.

1. Click **Help** on the menu, then click **Microsoft Word Help.**

2. Click the **Contents** tab and note topics available.

3. Click the **Answer Wizard** tab and key: **Print a document.** Note the information provided.

4. Click the **Index** tab; key: **Print** in Box 1, Type Keywords or choose **Print** in Box 2, Choose Keywords. From the list of topics, choose **Print a document.**

5. Close Help.

6. Click the **Microsoft Word Help** button. Note that Help is accessed from the button in the same way it is accessed from the Help menu.

7. Key **Print a document** in the Ask A Question box; then click the **Print a document** option. Note that you access the same information in Help.

Edit Text

Once text is keyed, it often needs to be corrected or changed. The Insert and Delete functions are used to edit text.

To insert text: Click or move the insertion point where the new text is to appear and key the text. Existing text moves to the right.

To delete text: Select the text and press DELETE.

1. Open the document **26a-drill3**.

2. Edit the document as shown.

3. Change the line spacing to double. If necessary, delete any extra hard returns between paragraphs.

4. Tab to indent the first line of each paragraph.

5. Save the document as **28a-drill4** and print it.

6. Close the document.

Serendipity, a ~~new homework~~ research tool from Information Technology Company, is available to subscribers of ~~the major~~ online services via the World Wide Web.

Offered as a subscription service aimed at ~~college~~ students, Serendipity is a collection of tens of thousands of articles from ~~major~~ encyclopedias, reference books, magazines, pamphlets, and Internet sources combined into a single searchable database. *with just a computer and a modem*

Serendipity puts an electronic library right at students' fingertips. The program offers two browse-and-search capabilities. Users can find articles by entering questions in simple question format or browse the database by pointing and clicking on key words that identify related articles. For more information, call 800-555-0174 or address e-mail to lab@serendipity.com. *on just about any subject*

97c-d1
Formatting

1. Prepare the news release form shown below. Be sure to check update automatically in the date field. Add a top border below the telephone information line.

2. Save as a **document template** named **97c-d1**.

Insert date field; update automatically

18 point bold

Border

Contact person

97c-d2
One-Page News Release

1. Open **97c-d1** and save as a *Word* document named **97c-d2**.

2. Prepare the following news release; double-space the text.

3. Resave, preview, and print.

July 2, 200-

For Release: Immediately

SUAREZ MOVES HEADQUARTERS

MEMPHIS, TN—The Suarez Corporation announced today that it is consolidating its statewide offices and moving its headquarters to Memphis. The company has leased space in the Davenport Building until its Churchill Tower can be built.

Suarez employs 785 people. Of the 785 employees, 300 are expected to transfer to Memphis. During the next 15 months, Suarez expects to hire 500 employees in sales, administrative support, accounting, engineering, architectural, and management areas.

Suarez develops projects throughout the South. Its primary focus is commercial real estate development. Suarez has already developed 3 shopping centers in the Hammond area and 25 in the state.

###

28b-d1
Rough Draft

1. Key the following paragraphs DS, and make the revisions shown.
2. Save the document as **28b-d1**. Print the document.

The World Wide Web (www) and Internet Usenet News groups are electronic fan clubs that offers users a ways to exchange views and information on just about any topic imaginable with people all around the world.

World Wide Web screens contain text, graphic, and pictures *, and often audio and video*. Simple pointing and clicking on the pictures and links (underlined words) bring users to new pages or sites of information.

28b-d2
Revise a Document

1. Open the document **28a-drill4**. Select the entire document using the mouse, and change the font to Arial 12 point.
2. Center-align and bold your name.
3. Change the line spacing to 1.5.
4. Italicize Information Technology Company.
5. Undo center-align of your name.
6. Right-align your name.
7. Preview the document, print a copy, save as **28b-d2**, and close it.

SKILLBUILDING

28c
Key each line twice SS; DS between two-line groups.

one hand
1 A few treats were served as reserve seats were set up on a stage.
2 In my opinion, a few trees on a hilly acre created a vast estate.

balanced hand
3 Pam and Jake did go to visit the big island and may fish for cod.
4 Ken may visit the men he met at the ancient chapel on the island.

1/2 fingers
5 Kimberly tried to grab the bar, but she missed and hurt her hand.
6 My name is Frankie, but I prefer to be called Fran by my friends.

3/4 fingers
7 Zola and Polly saw us play polo at Maxwell Plaza; we won a prize.
8 Zack quickly swam past all six boys at a zoo pool on Saxony Land.

SKILLBUILDING

97a
Warmup
Key each line twice SS.

alphabet 1 Jack Voxall was amazed by the quiet response of the big audience.

fig/sym 2 Our #3865 clocks will cost K & B $12.97 each (less 40% discount).

shift 3 In May, Lynn, Sonia, and Jason left for Italy, Spain, and Turkey.

easy 4 It is the duty of a civic auditor to aid a city to make a profit.

| 1 | 2 | 3 | 4 | 5 | 6 | 7 | 8 | 9 | 10 | 11 | 12 | 13 |

DOCUMENT DESIGN

97b

News Release

A news release conveys information an organization wishes to publish. Organizations prepare news releases to send to newspapers, radio stations, television stations, and other media outlets. News releases that make preparing the story easy save news writers time and are more likely to get published provided the information contained in the release is newsworthy. Often space limits prevent news media from publishing all of the information provided. Therefore, a good news release states the most important information first and the least important information last so that it can be cut or shortened from the end.

Most organizations prepare news releases on letterhead or on specially prepared forms for news releases. The form includes contact information in case the writer wishes to verify information and the date the news can be released. It also includes a short subject line that could serve as a heading. Double-space the text. Use ### or -30- to indicate the end.

Two-Page News Release

If a news release is two pages long, add a footer with the word *more* centered to indicate that the release continues on the next page. On the second page, add a header (often called a *slug line*) with a very short heading and a slash plus the page number.

SUAREZ CORPORATION
1986 Briarwood Circle
Memphis, TN 38116-1986

(901) 555-0132   Barbara.Hatten@suarez.com   (901) 555-0148 Fax

NEWS RELEASE   **Contact Person:** Barbara Hatten

November 20, 2003

For Release: (one week from today)

Suarez Corporation announced that the Suarez family has established the Suarez Scholars Foundation with a $25 million endowment and will begin the Suarez Scholars program immediately. The foundation will give 30 scholarships each year to outstanding graduating seniors from high schools throughout the ten-state region in which the company operates. Seniors from Alabama, Arkansas, Florida, Georgia, Kentucky, Louisiana, North Carolina, South Carolina, and Tennessee are eligible to apply to become a Suarez Scholar.

The 10 top students will be designated as Suarez All South Scholars and the remaining 20 students will be designated as Suarez Scholars. Suarez All South Scholars receive $7,500 per year for four years for a total scholarship value of $30,000. Suarez Scholars receive $2,500 a year for four years for a total scholarship value of $10,000.

Suarez Scholarship Program/2

The Suarez All South Selection Panel—a group of leaders selected from across the region—will interview the 30 finalists in Memphis and select the 10 Suarez All South Scholars. The remaining 20 finalists are named Suarez Scholars. An exciting program is planned for the three-day visit to Memphis to ensure that the event is a memorable one for all Suarez Scholars.

###

DOCUMENT DESIGN   DOCUMENT DESIGN   DOCUMENT

Formatting Essentials

29a

Center Page

The **Center Page** command centers a document vertically on the page. Should extra hard returns (¶) appear at the beginning or end of a document, these are also considered to be part of the document. Be careful to delete extra hard returns before centering a page.

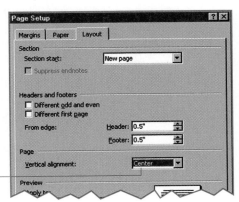

To center a page vertically:

1. Position the insertion point on the page to be centered.

2. From the File menu, select **Page Setup**. The Page Setup dialog box displays.

3. Click the **Layout** tab.

4. Click the **Vertical alignment** down arrow. Select **Center**; then click **OK**.

---

1. Open document **27b-d2**.

2. On the File menu, click **Page Setup**; then center the page vertically.

3. Click **Print Preview** to view the entire document, and check to ensure equal space exists at the top and bottom of the page.

4. Close Print Preview and save the document as **29a-drill1**. Close the document.

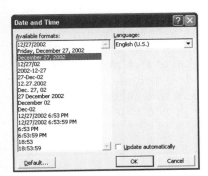

Date and Time

The current date and time can be inserted into documents using the **Date and Time** command from the Insert menu.

1. Choose **Date and Time** from the Insert menu.

2. Choose a format from the Available Formats box. Standard business format is the month-day-year format.

Note: The date is inserted as text and will not change. To update the date each time the document is opened, click the **Update Automatically** check box.

---

1. Open a new document.

2. Key your name on the first line and align it at the right.

3. Insert the date using month-day-year format a DS below your name.

4. Return to left alignment and key the following sentence: **The date shown above is in standard business format.**

5. Save the document as **29a-drill2** and close it.

Healthy Heart Trails

The county, the Coastal University Foundation, and the Healthy Heart Foundation announced today a joint venture to build and interconnect a series of walking and bike trails throughout the coastal area.

Healthy Heart Study

Last week the Healthy Heart Foundation released the findings of a significant study showing that exercise, diet, and not smoking are the major controllable factors that lead to a healthy heart. Factors such as heredity cannot be controlled. The study included both males and females aged 25 to 65.

Individuals over 45 are more likely to have heart problems, but the number of young people experiencing heart problems is increasing. Scientists believe that the increasing number of heart problems experienced by younger adults stems from a combination of diet, smoking, and leading a sedentary lifestyle.

Just Take a Walk

The study showed that women especially benefited from just taking a walk. Those who walked an average of two to three hours a week were more than 30 percent less likely to have heart problems than those who did no exercise. Those who walked briskly for five or more hours a week were more than 40 percent less likely to have heart problems.

Make Exercising Fun

The key to a successful exercise program is to enjoy it. Most people who find exercise boring or painful do not continue the program long enough to accomplish the desired benefits. Interesting walking routes take the boredom out of the exercise.

The Bike Trail

The proposed bike trail will feature over 100 miles of packed surface, coquina, and boardwalk bike paths along the coast for those who enjoy biking. The bike trail is designed so that riders can take short loops (1 to 10 miles) or go on extended rides for the entire trail.

Walking Trails

A leading nature trails designer has been retained to design environmentally sensitive trails that are both interesting and educational. The initial Healthy Heart Trails project features six trails ranging from one to five miles long. Each trail features a different type of educational node—ranging from endangered species such as red cockaded woodpeckers and loggerhead turtle nests to sustainability exhibits and pond restoration projects to enhance the habitat for waterfowl.

Healthy Heart Trails Project			
Project Component	Primary Sponsor	Estimated Time	Estimated Cost
Trail design and layout	Coastal University Foundation	4–6 weeks	$ 22,500
Highway work at trail head	County	6–8 weeks	30,000
Parking lot at entrance	Coastal University Foundation	3–4 weeks	26,000
Visitor's center	Healthy Heart Foundation	6–8 months	100,000
Walking trails	Coastal Univ./Healthy Heart	6–8 months	80,000
Bike trail	County	2 years	400,000
Total Project	All	2 years	$658,500

Tabs

Tabs are used to indent paragraphs and align text vertically. Pressing the TAB key aligns text at the **tab stop**. *Word* has five types of tabs, which are listed below. The left, right, and center tabs are similar to paragraph alignment types. In this lesson, you will work with left and right tabs.

L	**Left tab**	Aligns text at the left.
⅃	**Right tab**	Aligns text at the right.
⊥	**Center tab**	Aligns text evenly on either side of the tab stop.
⊥	**Decimal tab**	Aligns numbers at the decimal point.
❘	**Bar tab**	Aligns text to the right of a vertical bar.

Tabs can be set and cleared on the Horizontal Ruler. The numbers on the ruler indicate the distance in inches from the left margin. The small gray lines below each half-inch position are the default tab stops. The Tab Alignment button at the left edge of the ruler indicates the type of tab. To change the tab type, click the Tab Alignment button.

Tab alignment   **Left tab**   **Right tab**

To set a tab:	Click the Tab Alignment button, and choose the desired tab type. Click the Horizontal Ruler where you want to set the tab.
To delete a tab:	Click the tab marker, and drag it straight down off the ruler.
To move a tab:	Click the tab marker, and drag the tab to the new location.

Tabs can also be set in the Tab dialog box (**Format** menu, **Tabs**). The Tab dialog box provides more options and allows you to set precise settings.

DRILL 3   **SET AND MOVE TABS**

1. Display the Horizontal Ruler if necessary (**View** menu, **Ruler**).

2. Set a left tab at 1.5" and a right tab at 3.5".

3. Key the first three lines of the drill. Press TAB at the beginning of each line.

4. Move the left tab to 1" and the right tab to 3". Key the last three lines. Save as **29a-drill3**. Print and close.

	Left tab 1.5"	Right tab 3.5"
Tab ⟶	Schneider	5,000
	Langfield	17,200
	Almich	9,500
	Left tab 1"	Right tab 3"
	McCoy	12,000
	Buswinka	198,250
	Oritz	500

Newsletter with Graphics

96a
Warmup
Key each line twice SS.

alphabet 1 Joyce Wexford left my squad after giving back the disputed prize.
figures 2 Reply to items 4, 5, and 6 on page 39 and 1, 7, and 8 on page 20.
double letters 3 A committee supplied food and coffee for the Mississippi meeting.
easy 4 In Dubuque, they may work the field for the profit paid for corn.

| 1 | 2 | 3 | 4 | 5 | 6 | 7 | 8 | 9 | 10 | 11 | 12 | 13 |

96b
Timed Writings
Key two 3' timed writings.

	gwam	1'	3'

What do you like to do on a lazy, sunny weekend afternoon in | 12 | 4
spring or summer? Some people may prefer a quiet afternoon of | 25 | 8
watching television, while other people may want to wash the car | 38 | 13
or work in their gardens. Many others, however, agree that the | 51 | 17
very best way to enjoy a spring or summer afternoon is to attend | 64 | 21
a college or professional baseball game. In fact, that choice is | 77 | 26
so popular that the game is often said to be our national sport. | 90 | 30
Many people even hope for extra innings to extend the fun. Over | 103 | 34
the years, most baseball fans have shown excellent sportsmanship. | 116 | 39
However, today many people are concerned that the bad behavior of | 130 | 43
a few individuals may spoil the game for others. | 139 | 46

1' | 1 | 2 | 3 | 4 | 5 | 6 | 7 | 8 | 9 | 10 | 11 | 12 | 13 |
3' | 1 | | 2 | | 3 | | 4 |

96c-d1
Newsletter with Graphics

TIP
#5 Keywords: medicine or heart
#6 Keyword: bicycle
#7 Keywords: trails, backpacker, or nature

1. Key the following newsletter using three equal-sized columns with a line between.
2. Set left and right margins at 0.5".
3. Use WordArt of your choice and color for the banner heading; about two lines below the banner, insert a continuous section break.
4. Use Heading 3 for all headings.
5. In the Heart Health Study section, insert from clip art an image symbolic of a heart and/or medicine.
6. In the Bike Trail section, insert from clip art a bicycle or bicycle rider.
7. In the Walking Trails section, insert from clip art a bird watcher, backpacker, or someone walking in a natural area.
8. Adjust text and clip art above the table so that all text fits on one page.
9. At the end of the text, insert a next page section break.
10. On the second page, change to 1" left and right margins and one column; apply to this section only.
11. Format the table. Select an appropriate AutoFormat style.
12. Save as **96c-d1** and print.

29b-d1

Tabs, Date, and Center Page

1. Open a new document. Change spacing to DS. Center the title on the first line. Apply bold and change font to 16-point Times New Roman.

2. On the second line, insert the current date using day-month-date-year format. Apply same format as the first line.

3. Set a left tab at 1.5" and a right tab at 4.5".

4. Key the document shown below. Center the page.

5. Preview and print. Save as **29b-d1**.

Starting Lineup

Saturday, December 28, 200-

Power Forward	Shanze J. Penn
Small Forward	Christina U. Perovic
Center	Teresa C. Gortman
Shooting Guard	Tonisha J. Burgess
Point Guard	Kelly O. Reese

29b-d2

Tabs, Date, and Center Page

1. Open a new document. Change spacing to DS. Center the title in all caps on the first line. Apply bold and change font to 14-point Times New Roman.

2. On the second line, insert the current date using standard business format. Apply same format as the first line.

3. Set a left tab at 1" and a right tab at 5".

4. Key the document shown below. Center the page.

5. Preview and print. Save as **29b-d2**.

Internet Groups on Campus

December 28, 200-

Name	Description
webdes	Web page design topics
biz	Business administration—all majors
bioeng	Biomedical engineers
sprtmg	Sports management
marband	Marching band

29c

Use the remaining class time to build your skills using the Skill Builder module within *Keyboarding Pro*. Continue with the next lesson.

This typeface, Times, is a serif typeface.

This typeface, Arial, is a sans serif typeface.

𝕿𝖍𝖎𝖘 𝖙𝖞𝖕𝖊𝖋𝖆𝖈𝖊, 𝕺𝖑𝖉 𝕰𝖓𝖌𝖑𝖎𝖘𝖍 𝕿𝖊𝖝𝖙 𝕸𝕿, 𝖎𝖘 𝖆 𝖉𝖎𝖘𝖕𝖑𝖆𝖞 𝖙𝖞𝖕𝖊𝖋𝖆𝖈𝖊.

The units of measure for type size are picas and points. An inch is roughly 6 picas, and a pica contains 12 points or 72 points per inch. A good rule of thumb in creating styles is to use 10- to 12-point type for the body and 14- to 18-point type for headings. Larger type sizes may be used for banners.

Vertical distance between lines of type (the height of a line) is called *leading*. Leading is set automatically, but it can be adjusted. A rule of thumb is to use 2 points more than the type size for small type.

Color   second-level heading

Color helps convey vivid images and adds a new dimension to document design. Using color consistently gives a feeling of comfort and helps the reader locate information quickly. Color helps to link elements of a document. Special care needs to be used in selecting colors. The color that displays on a computer screen may look quite different when printed or projected. Often color is a part of a logo, and an exact match is critical.

The color scheme of a document should be simple. A good rule of thumb is to use a maximum of four colors in a document. Graphs with multiple bars or pie segments may require more than four colors and would be an exception. Consistency in the use of color is extremely important.

Tables and Graphic Elements   second-level heading

Tables and graphic elements should be used when they simplify and clarify information. Limit the use of graphics to those that contribute to the content of a document. A picture often gets the message across quickly and effectively. Too many graphic elements can be distracting and confusing, however. Another important consideration is matching the graphic elements with the tone of a document. A formal document must be matched with a sophisticated but simple graphic. Limited use of WordArt can be effective for informal documents such as employee newsletters. Effective design of all graphic elements is important.

Insert the file **Document Design** here.

95b-d2
Reformat Document

1. Open **95b-d1** and save it as **95b-d2**.

2. Reformat the document using three equal-size columns with .25" spacing between columns.

3. Resave, preview, and print.

SKILLBUILDING

30a
Warmup
Key each line twice SS.

alphabetic 1 Gay expected to solve the jigsaw puzzle more quickly than before.
figures 2 Jane opened Rooms 16, 20, and 39 and locked Rooms 48, 53, and 57.
shift 3 Ted and I spent April in San Juan and May in St. Paul, Minnesota.
easy 4 The island is the shape of a big sleigh.   Jake got clams for us.
| 1 | 2 | 3 | 4 | 5 | 6 | 7 | 8 | 9 | 10 | 11 | 12 | 13 |

30b
Technique Builders
Key each line twice SS.

Direct Reach words, phrases, and sentences
5 hung deck jump cent slope decide hunt serve polo brave cedar pump
6 no way | in tune | many times | jump in | funny times | gold plated | in sync
7 June and Cecil browsed in craft shops and found many funny gifts.

Adjacent Reach words, phrases, and sentences
8 Were pop safe sad quick column tree drew opinion excite guy point
9 We are | boil over | are we | few rewards | short trek | where are we going
10 Bert said he tries to shop where we can buy gas, oil, and treats.

30c
Speed Builders
Key each line twice; work for fluency.

11 Ken may go to the big lake to fish for sockeye and dig for clams.
12 Jan may go with us to visit the ancient chapel on the big island.
13 Their goal is to fix the bicycle or dismantle it to fit in a box.
14 A cow roams the cornfield, and fox, quail, and duck also roam it.
15 A neighbor bid by proxy for eighty bushels of corn and rye blend.

30d
Speed Check
Take two 3' timed writings.

I have a story or two or three that will transport you to   4
faraway places, to meet people you have never known, to see   8
things you have never seen, to feast on foods available only to a   12
few. I can help you to learn new skills you want and need; I can   17
inspire you, excite you, instruct you, and entertain you.   I   21
answer your questions. I work with you to realize a talent, to   25
express a thought, and to determine just who and what you really   29
are and want to be. I help you to know words, to write, and to   33
read. I help you to understand the mysteries of the past and the   38
secrets of the future. I am your library. I hope I shall see   42
you often. You might find me online.   45

3' | 1 | 2 | 3 | 4 |

Document Design—An Art and A Science   **WordArt**

A writer expects a document to communicate a message to a specific audience. Likewise, effective document design facilitates communication—it does not simply decorate or make a document look aesthetically pleasing. The science of document design refers to matching the design elements to the message that the document seeks to communicate. The art of document design refers to making a document sensitive to the needs of the audience—giving the document a feeling of being familiar, comfortable, and pleasing to read.

Design Standards   **first-level heading**

Design standards may vary depending on the formality of a document and the type of corporate identity an organization wishes to portray. Design standards for formal documents tend to follow the same standards that would be applied if the document were typeset by a professional printer. One space follows end-of-sentence punctuation. Spacing between paragraphs is controlled by the Spacing Before or Spacing After options on the Format Paragraph dialog box. Generally, six-point spacing is used to separate paragraphs. Special characters such as *en* and *em* dashes and special symbols such as copyright, trademark, and registered generally are used.

Design Objectives   **first-level heading**

Effective document design accomplishes a number of objectives, such as:

- Supports document content and adds organizational structure
- Provides a consistent image
- Denotes formality
- Enhances readability and provides a road map to lead the reader through the document
- Emphasizes important points and simplifies content presentation
- Compacts copy and optimizes space requirements

Document design requires careful planning to accomplish the objectives listed. Many organizations research design carefully and specify standards for all documents prepared both professionally and internally. They direct employees to apply specific predefined styles available in their software, or they create customized templates and styles and provide them to employees. Online styles frequently replace hard-copy style manuals. To these organizations, visual design is a key element in corporate identity and image.

Design Elements   **first-level heading**

Design elements consist of features used repeatedly and consistently in documents. Design elements include text, typeface, color, tables and graphic elements, white space, headings and layout, and paper.

Text   **second-level heading**

The amount of text, the nature of the text, and the purpose for which it is being used influence the design of documents. Long documents require more structure than short documents. Technical, statistical, and complex textual materials require significant amounts of illustration to simplify them. On the other hand, the rigid requirements for a formal report may not be appropriate for an informal newsletter to employees.

Text itself is often a design element. For example, a company analyzing 20 countries for potential export opportunities might use textual categories as repeated design elements. The analysis of each of the countries might have these segments: political climate, economic conditions, market potential, barriers to entry, and recommendations. Serif typefaces, such as Times or Times New Roman, have small lines that extend from the main portion of the character. Sans serif typefaces, such as Helvetica or Arial, do not have these extenders. Typefaces used for large type or headings, such as script or Zapf Chaucery, are generally called display typefaces. Script is often used for personal or informal documents and for invitations.

30e

Editing Review

DRILL 1 COMPOSE, PROOFREAD, AND EDIT

1. Key the ¶s filling in the information indicated.

2. Print the document; proofread it and mark any corrections needed using proofreaders' marks.

3. Correct the document and save it as **30e-drill1**.

4. Print a copy.

Review proofreaders' marks in 23f, page 55.

> My name is (*student's name*). I am a (*class level*) at (*school*) located on (*street*) in (*city, state*). In addition to (*name of this course*), I am also enrolled in (*names of other courses; modify sentence if you are not enrolled in any other courses*). My instructor in this course is (*title and name*).
>
> The reason I enrolled in this course is (*complete sentence*). What I like most about this course is (*complete sentence*). What I like least about this course is (*complete sentence*).

DRILL 2 EDIT SENTENCES AND PARAGRAPH

1. Key the text making the edits indicated by the proofreaders' marks.

2. Proofread and correct any errors.

3. Print the document and save it as **30e-drill2**.

16 Do you assess you~r~ writing skills as (average,) great, or mediocre?

17 You ~c~should also ask your instructor about *to assess* your writing skills.

18 Your instructor ~will know~ *may teach you* how to ~greatly~ improve your writing skills.

19 Do you ~always~ *take the time to* edit and proofread carefully things that you write?

20 ≡few people who do~#~not bother to edit the~i~re work are good writers.

21 Learning to edit effective*ly* may be just as important as writing well.

22 Another question to ~ask~ *answer* is: how important are writing skills?

23 ~G~*reat*ood writing skills are needed to be successful in most *any* careers.

24 You can improve your writing skills~;~ by making it a priority~e~. *to do so*

25 Judge your writing ~only~ *after* if you have proofread and edited your work.

Take the time to (carefully) evaluate your completed wor~t~k. Is the copy format~t~ed attractively? Does it read ~good~ *well*? have you~r~ corrected all grammar and spelling errors~?~ If your work does~#~not impress you, it will not impress any ⌢one else.

LESSON 95 — Newsletter with Columns

SKILLBUILDING

95a
Warmup
Key each line twice SS.

alphabet	1	Express mail requested at zone twelve gave finish to a rocky job.
figures	2	Check the area codes 304, 593, 281, and 763 before dialing calls.
combination	3	Typing business letters using a simple format is often suggested.
direct reaches	4	My cousin Ed brought my brown mums to school to delight me again.

| 1 | 2 | 3 | 4 | 5 | 6 | 7 | 8 | 9 | 10 | 11 | 12 | 13 |

APPLICATIONS

95b-d1
Document Format and Design

TIP
Continuous Break:
Insert, Break, Continuous

TIP
Bullets: Format, Bullets and Numbering, Bulleted tab; choose style

TIP
Shading: Format, Borders and Shading tab

1. In a new document, set 1" margins on all sides and 6 pt. spacing after paragraphs.

2. Create the main heading as a banner using WordArt. Select the design in the first row of the first column of the WordArt Gallery. Add blue fill. DS below the banner and enter a blue line. DS and insert a continuous section break.

3. Key the text as one column. Insert the file **Document Design** at the end of the document.

4. Apply Heading 1 style to all first-level headings and Heading 2 style to all second-level headings. Format all headings in blue. Format bullets in blue using this style: ❖

5. Format the three sentences shown in blue shading by applying the typeface indicated in the sentence. Then select all three sentences and apply blue shading to the paragraph. Change the font color of the sentences to white.

6. Format the body of the document as two equal columns with .5" spacing between. Add a blue page border. Save as **95b-d1**, preview, and print.

7. Read the document for content.

Document Design--An Art and a Science

A writer expects a document to communicate a message to a specific audience. Likewise, effective document design facilitates communication it does not simply decorate or make a document look aesthetically pleasing. The science of document design refers to matching the design elements to the message that the document seeks to communicate. The art of document design refers to making a document sensitive to the needs of the audience giving the docum ent a feeling of being familiar, comfortable, and pleasing to read.

Design Standards

Design standards may vary depending on the formality of a document and the type of corporate identity an organization wishes to portray. Design standards for formal documents tend to follow the same standards that would be applied if the document were typeset by a professional printer. One space follows end-of-sentence punctuation. Spacing between paragraphs is controlled by the Spacing Before or Spacing After options on the Format Paragraph dialog box. Generally, six-point spacing is used to separate paragraphs. Special characters such as en and em dashes and special symbols such as copyright, trademark, and registered generally are used.

❖ Denotes formality
❖ Enhances readability and provides a road map to lead the reader through the document
❖ Emphasizes important points and simplifies content presentation
❖ Compacts copy and optimizes space requirements

Document design requires careful planning to accomplish the objectives listed. Many organizations research design carefully and specify standards for all documents prepared both professionally and internally. They direct employees to apply specific predefined styles available in their software, or they create customized templates and styles and provide them to employees. Online styles frequently replace hard-copy style manuals. To these organizations, visual design is a key element in corporate identity and image.

Design Elements

Design elements consist of features used repeatedly and consistently in documents. Design elements include text, typeface, color, tables and graphic elements, white space, headings and layout, and paper.

Text

The amount of text, the nature of the text, and the purpose for which it is being used

formal report may not be appropriate for an informal newsletter to employees.

Text itself is often a design element. For example, a company analyzing 20 countries for potential export opportunities might use textual categories as repeated design elements. The analysis of each of the countries might have these segments: political climate, economic conditions, market potential, barriers to entry, and recommendations. Serif typefaces, such as Times or Times New Roman, have small lines that extend from the main portion of the character. Sans serif typefaces, such as Helvetica or Arial, do not have these extenders. Typefaces used for large type or headings, such as script or Zapf Chaucery, are generally called display typefaces. Script is often used for personal or informal documents and for invitations.

This typeface, Times, is a serif typeface.

This typeface, Arial, is a sans serif typeface.

This typeface, Old English Text MT, is a display typeface.

The units of measure for type size are picas and points. An inch is roughly 6 picas, and a pica contains 12 points or 72 points per inch. A good rule of thumb in creating styles is to use 10- to 12-point type for the body and 14- to 18-point type for headings. Larger type sizes may be used for banners.

Vertical distance between lines of type (the height of a line) is called leading. Leading is set automatically, but it can be adjusted. A rule of thumb is use 2 points more than the type...

quickly. Color helps to link elements of a document. Special care needs to be used in selecting colors. The color that displays on a computer screen may look quite different when printed or projected. Often color is a part of a logo, and an exact match is critical.

The color scheme of a document should be simple. A good rule of thumb is to use a maximum of four colors in a document. Graphs with multiple bars or pie segments may require more than four colors and would be an exception. Consistency in the use of color is extremely important.

Tables and Graphic Elements

Tables and graphic elements should be used when they simplify and clarify information. Limit the use of graphics to those that contribute to the content of a document. A picture often gets the message across quickly and effectively. Too many graphic elements can be distracting and confusing, however. Another important consideration is matching the graphic elements with the tone of a document. A formal document must be matched with a sophisticated but simple graphic. Limited use of WordArt can be effective for informal documents such as employee newsletters. Effective design of all graphic elements is important.

White Space

The natural tendency in designing documents is to try to save space. White space is not the place to economize, however. A key way to emphasize ideas is to isolate them from other ideas. White space provides the isolation needed to make things stand out on a page. A border is frequently used

wider than the text column they can extend into the blank space of the scanning column.

Documents packed with copy look cluttered and are difficult to read. White space provides an open, uncluttered look that is restful and that leads the reader to important copy that needs emphasis.

Headings and Layout

Headings follow the same structure as an outline. They are hierarchical and should be ranked from high to low. Headings with the most important content should be positioned above and in more prominent typestyle than headings with content of lesser importance. Heading styles follow this hierarchical style. Brief headings tend to be more effective than long headings. The key design consideration is consistency. Grammatical structure, as well as typeface and spacing elements, must be consistent for headings of the same level.

Layout refers to the careful positioning and spacing of the design elements on a page to

create the best visual effect. The number and width of columns influence layout significantly. Column layouts may vary on the same page. Some organizations provide templates and define layout rules for published documents so tightly that document design is purely a science. However, in most organizations, layout rules are not always hard and fast layout is an art. It is the product of careful experimentation to create the best way to communicate the information contained in a document.

Many trade-offs exist in designing the layout of a document. For example, consistency and flexibility often conflict. Certain graphic elements may not fit in the space that a consistent layout pattern provides. However, the importance of the consistent layout pattern dictates that the consistent layout pattern be modified to accommodate the content. Page size, weight, texture, and finish affect the design of a document.

30f-d1
Rough Draft

1. Open a new document and change spacing to DS.
2. On the first line, center the title: **You Are What You Eat.** Apply bold and 14-point Arial type.
3. Use default font and point size (Times New Roman 12 point) and left-align for the remainder of the document.
4. Key the document making all edits indicated by the proofreaders' marks.
5. Set a right-align tab at 5 3/4" and key your name a DS below the last line of the document.
6. Insert the date using standard business format directly below your name.
7. Proofread and correct all errors.
8. Center the page.
9. Save as **30f-d1**, preview, and print.

A speaker said, "you are what you eat"; the speaker didnot mean to imply that fast food makes fast people, or that an hearty meal makes a person hearty, or even that good food makes a person good? On the other hand, though, a healthfull diet does indeed make person healthier; and good health effects many things including performance, energy level, and attitude. Learning what to include in a healthful diet is the 1st step. The 2nd step is developing the discipline to apply that knowledge. The results are wellworth the effort. IN fact, good health may be one of the most often over looked treasures within human existance.

30f-d2
Rough Draft

1. Key the following document DS making all corrections indicated by the proofreaders' marks.
2. Add the following title on the first line: **Sportsmanship and Athletics—An Oxymoron?** Format it in bold and Times New Roman 14 point.
3. Proofread, correct errors, preview, print, and save as **30f-d2**.

An oxymoron is a figure of speech that involve words of opposite meaning, such as an honest thief. Today, many people are asking if sportsmanship in athletics is becoming an oxymoron. It fosters an attitude of honesty, ethical conduct, fair play, treating others with respect, and exhibition character worthy of emulation. Does this real describe the current state of intercollegiate athletics?

94d-d3
Announcement

1. Format the announcement using landscape and 1" margins on all sides.

2. Insert clip art appropriate for Valentine's Day at the top left side of the document. Format it with **Square** wrapping style, **left** alignment, and size it about 1.5" wide.

3. Add **Parents' Night Out** in WordArt; use a fill color that is compatible with the clip art.

4. Key the announcement text below using 18-point type. Bold the heading below the WordArt.

5. Save as **94d-d3**, preview, and print.

Saturday, February 14, is Valentine's Day. Make it special!

The Student Chapter of the Early Childhood Education Association (ECEA) invites you to enjoy an evening out without worrying about your children and to support the ECEA Scholarship Fund at the same time. The ECEA in cooperation with the University Child Development and Research Center is offering a fun night out for your children while you have a Valentine celebration without them. Your children will enjoy games, movies, crafts, snacks, and a variety of adventures.

The University Child Development Center accommodates up to 100 children in age ranges from infant to 12 years old. Students preparing to be early childhood educators will provide the babysitting services for the evening. Drop your children off at seven o'clock and pick them up at eleven. The rate for the evening is $25 for the first child and $10 for each additional child.

94d-d4
Announcement

1. Prepare the following announcement to be posted for the Fourth of July celebration.

2. Use .75" margins on all sides and landscape orientation.

3. Select clip art appropriate for the announcement.

4. Format the clip art so that it is approximately 2" wide; center it horizontally relative to the page and .75" below the top of the page.

5. Use WordArt for the title. Select appropriate colors.

6. Key the following text using Arial and as large a font size as you can and still fit the announcement on one page.

Fourth of July Celebration

Pack your lawn chairs or blankets and bring the entire family to join your friends and neighbors for the annual Fourth of July celebration at City Park. Music and festivities begin at 7:30 and end with a spectacular fireworks display at 10:30.

7. Save the document as **94d-d4** and print.

Fans, coaches, media, student athletes, parents, and administrators often have a win-at-all-cost attitude. Disruptive and destructive fans shout obscenities and harrass officials as well as fans of opponents, they also destroy property. Trash-talking has become commonplace *a way of life* for student athletes. Parents are willing to lie and cheat to get there children in athletic programs. Coaches and administrators cheat to recruit *or tolerate cheating* players and keep them academically eligible. Are these fair statements, or are they simply media ploys trying *designed* to sell newspapers and magazines and attract radio and television audiences?

Clearly, not all fans, student athletes, coaches, parents, and administrators exhibit unsportsmanlike conduct. How ever, numerous *stet* surveys indicate that most (70-80%) Americans believe that sportsmanship has significantly declined in recent years. Even if the figures are an exaggeration *ed*, intercollegiate athletics is in *still* trouble because of the public perception of poor sportsmanship.

Colleges offer expensive athletics program because of the educational value and the equal opportunity they provide all students. Other wise, they could not justify expending vast amounts of money on athletics. Despite the myth to the contrary, less *fewer* than 40 *sp* intercollegiate athletics programs breakeven *#* or make money.

94d-d1
Letterhead

1. Create letterhead for Global Travel Services, Inc. Use .7" top margin.
2. Search clip art and find a clip representative of a globe. Use **Square** wrapping and **left** alignment. Size the clip to approximately 1.5" width.
3. Center the address shown below to the right of the clip art.
4. Save as **94d-d1** and print.

Global Travel Services, Inc.
3975 Buckingham Road
Annapolis, MD 21403-6820
Telephone: 301 555-0146   FAX: 301 555-0183

94d-d2
Personal Letterhead

1. Use WordArt to create a letterhead for yourself. Use .7" top margin.
2. Use the design in the second row of the last column and key your initials. Change text color to match initials.
3. Center your address information:

   Your full name
   Street Address
   City, State, ZIP Code
   Telephone Number
   E-mail Address

4. Save as **94d-d2** and print.

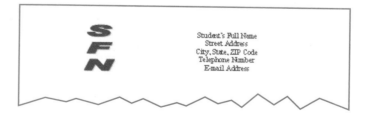

Module 3: Checkpoint

Self-Assessment
Evaluate your understanding of this project by answering the questions below.

1. The_____ feature automatically moves text to the next line when one line is full.

2. The _____ feature enables you to see how a document will look when it is printed.

3. The _____ keyboard shortcut can be used to move to the beginning of a document.

4. Before character formats can be applied to existing text, the text must be_____.

5. The alignment used to begin and end all lines at the same position on the left and right margins is_____.

6. Use the _____ function to format a one-page document with the same amount of space in the top and bottom margin.

7. Standard business format for the date is the _____-_____-_____ format.

8. A green wavy line under text indicates a potential _____ error.

9. A potential spelling error is indicated by a(n) _____wavy line.

10. The _____ function reverses changes made in formatting or keying text.

Performance Assessment

Document 1

Rough-draft

1. Key the text shown at the right; make all corrections noted by proofreaders' marks.

2. Add the title **The Hassles of Air Travel**; format it in bold, 14-point type and center it.

3. Right-align your name a DS below the last line of the document. Insert the date on the line directly below your name.

4. Center the page.

5. Print and save the document as **checkpoint3-d1**.

The disaster at the world trade center in NEW York resulted in a significant increase in the hassle factor in air travel. Passengers today must arrive at the airport early to allow addition time to go through enhanced security procedures. Those procedures range from walking through metal detectors to complete searches of individuals and luggage.

Some passengers are frustrated by these changes in security procedures that are both time-consuming and annoying. Most passengers however recognize that they are essential for our safety.

LESSON 94

Announcements and Letterheads with Graphics

94a
Warmup
Key each line twice SS.

alphabet 1 Who enjoyed traveling to Mexico after buying a quick dozen picks?

figures 2 Send mail to ZIP Code 48279 in January and 56031 before November.

1st/2nd fingers 3 Assessment is a term used by educators when they are testing you.

adjacent reaches 4 Sara stopped here, where her ruined art was stored for the month.

| 1 | 2 | 3 | 4 | 5 | 6 | 7 | 8 | 9 | 10 | 11 | 12 | 13 |

94b
Skillbuilding
Key each set of drills (one-hand lines and balanced-hand lines) twice.

one-hand lines

5 my wax jump dress pink fast limp crease hunk brace pool extra bat

6 link grace plump trace junk zebra you zest yolk vested opinion ax

7 tax only race join target union regret puppy graze hulk fewer him

8 Holly, a stewardess saw my test grade; Holly gave my Mom a treat.

9 In my opinion, Rebecca deserves a few extra rewards; Phil agrees.

10 Jimmy gave Phillip a great red sweater at a bazaar in West Texas.

balanced-hand lines

11 duck quake lake rigor prism proxy fix usual turkey right quake of

12 skeptic quantity problem mangy dogs handle ivory elbow cubicle six

13 augment burlap formal dismay kept mentor rigor social visit world

14 Claudia and Henry may work to fix a big problem with the bicycle.

15 Jane and Kent may want to go with a neighbor to the lake to fish.

16 The city auditor, Jake Hand, may fix the problems with the audit.

| 1 | 2 | 3 | 4 | 5 | 6 | 7 | 8 | 9 | 10 | 11 | 12 | 13 |

DOCUMENT DESIGN

94c

Design Letterhead and Announcements

Attractive letterhead can be designed using clip art, pictures, WordArt, and text formatting. Generally the letterhead should fit into 1.5" or 1.75" of space so that the letter can begin no lower than 2". The default top margin can be decreased to provide additional space for the letterhead.

The design of an announcement can vary depending on whether the announcement is being posted so that it can be read as people walk by or whether it is sent directly to individuals. If the announcement is posted, landscape print and large font sizes are normally used to make it more readable from a distance. Graphics may be used to enhance announcements.

DOCUMENT DESIGN

Business Correspondence

- Learn standard memorandum format.
- Format letters in block letter style.
- Format letters in modified block style.
- Modify tabs.
- Create envelopes.
- Improve keying speed and accuracy.

LESSON 31 — Interoffice Memo

SKILLBUILDING

31a
Warmup
Key each line twice SS.

alphabet 1 I quickly explained to two managers the grave hazards of the job.
figures 2 All channels—16, 25, 30, and 74—reported the score was 19 to 8.
shift 3 Maxi and Kay Pascal expect to be in breezy South Mexico in April.
easy 4 Did the man fight a duel, or did he go to a chapel to sign a vow?

| 1 | 2 | 3 | 4 | 5 | 6 | 7 | 8 | 9 | 10 | 11 | 12 | 13 |

31b
Timed Writing
Take two 3' timings.

LA all letters

gwam 3'

Hard work is required for job success. Set high goals and 4 | 43
devote time to the exact things that will help you succeed. Work 8 | 47
hard each day and realize you must be willing to make sacrifices. 13 | 51

Avoid being like the loser who says, "It may be possible, but 17 | 55
it's too difficult." Take on the attitude of the winner who says, 21 | 59
"It may be difficult, but it's possible." Count on working hard. 26 | 64

Also, seek mentors to pilot you in your long road to success. 30 | 69
They will encourage you and will challenge you to reach for higher 34 | 73
dreams even when you are very happy with where you are. 39 | 77

1' | 1 | 2 | 3 | 4 | 5 | 6 | 7 | 8 | 9 | 10 | 11 | 12 | 13 |
3' | 1 | 2 | 3 | 4 |

Crown Lake News and Views

Current date

Newsletter Staff

Eric Burge
    Editor

Nancy Suggs
Christopher Hess
Anne Reynolds
    Associate Editors

Wayne Martin
    Editorial Assistant

Crown Lake News and Views is a weekly newsletter compiled by the staff of the Human Resources Department, and it is sent to all employees.

New Development Project

Crown Lake won the bid to develop and construct the new multimillion-dollar Business Center adjacent to Metro Airport. Connie McClure, one of the three senior project managers, has been named as the Business Center project manager. The project is expected to take more than two years to complete. Approximately fifty new permanent employees will be hired to work on this project. All jobs will be posted within the next two weeks. The recruiting referral program is in effect for all jobs. You can earn a $100 bonus for each individual you recommend who is hired and remains with Crown Lake for at least six months. You may pick up your recruiting referral forms in the Personnel Office.

Blood Drive Reminder

The Crown Lake quarterly blood drive is set for Friday, April 4, in the Wellness Center. The Community Blood Bank needs all types of blood to replace the supplies sent to the islands during the recent disaster caused by Hurricane Lana. Employees in all divisions are being asked to participate this quarter because of the current supply crisis. All three donation sites will be used. Several volunteers will be needed to staff the two additional sites. The regular division rotation will resume next quarter.

Lee Daye Honored

The Community Foundation honored Lee Daye of the Marketing Department with the Eagle Award for outstanding service this year.

The Eagle Award is presented each year to three citizens who have made a significant impact on the lives of others. The Community Foundation recognized Lee for his work with underprivileged children, the Community Relations Task Force, the Abolish Domestic Violence Center, and the Community Transitional Housing Project. Congratulations, Lee. You made a difference in the lives of many citizens in our community. Your award was richly deserved.

New Training Program

The pilot test of the new Team Effectiveness training program was completed last month, and the results were excellent. Thanks to all of you who participated in the development and testing of the program. Your input is vital to its success.

Proofread and Finalize a Document

Before documents are complete, they must be proofread carefully for accuracy. Error-free documents send the message that you are detail oriented and capable. Apply these procedures when processing all documents:

1. Use Spelling and Grammar to check spelling when you have completed the document.
2. Proofread the document on screen to be sure that it makes sense.
3. Preview the document, and check the overall appearance.
4. Save the document, and then print it.
5. Compare the document to the source copy (textbook), and check that text has not been omitted or added. Revise, save, and print if necessary.

Interoffice Memorandums

Messages sent to persons within an organization are called **memorandums** (memos for short). A popular memo form is an e-mail, which is mailed electronically. Memos are printed on plain paper and sent in plain or interoffice envelopes. Memos consist of the heading, a body, and one or more notations.

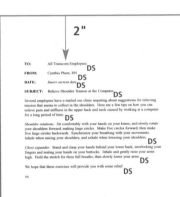

To format a memo:

1. Strike ENTER six times to position the first line of the heading at about 2".
2. Format the memo headings in bold and all caps. Turn off bold and all caps, and strike TAB once or twice after each heading to align the information. Generally, courtesy titles (Mr., Ms., etc.) are not used; however, if the memo is formal, the receiver's name may include a title.
3. Single-space the body of the memo. DS between paragraphs.
4. Add reference initials a DS below the body if the memo is keyed by someone other than the sender. Do not include initials when keying your own memo.
5. Items clipped or stapled to the memo are noted as attachments; items included in an envelope are enclosures. Key these notations a DS below the reference initials.

To format a distribution list:

When memos are sent to more than one person, list their names after TO:. Generally the names are listed in alphabetical order; some organizations, however, list the names in order of rank. For readability, key the names on separate lines. When sending the memo to many people, refer to a distribution list at the end of the memo. Example: TO: Task Force Members--Distribution Below. Indent the names on the distribution list to the first tab.

If you have any questions about these policies, please call me at any time.

xx

Distribution:
    Allen Bejahan
    Janet James
    Terry Johnson
    Ray Lightfoot

93d-d1
Newsletter with
Clip Art

1. Open **93b-drill1** and save as **93d-d1**.
2. Open **litter clip art** from the data files.
3. Select the first clip and format it using **Square** text wrapping and **left** alignment. Size the clip to approximately 2.5" width.
4. Copy the first clip and paste it between the first and second paragraphs of the first column of the newsletter.
5. Select the second clip in the **litter clip art** file and format it using **Square** text wrapping and **right** alignment. Size the clip to approximately 2.5" width.
6. Copy the second clip and paste it before the last paragraph of the second column of the newsletter.
7. Save again, preview, and print.

93d-d2
Newsletter with Clip Art

1. Key the newsletter shown on the next page as a 1-column document.
2. Set left and right margins of .75".
3. Use WordArt for the banner heading, and adjust the size so that the banner spans all columns. Leave 2 or 3 blank lines after the heading; then insert a continuous section break (**Insert, Break, Continuous**).
4. Use 14-point Times New Roman for headings within the document and 12-point Times New Roman for body text.
5. Format the document after the banner as a 3-column document with lines between the columns. Use the following settings in the Columns dialog box.

   First column: 1.5"

   Space between columns: .025"

   Second and third columns: 2.5"
6. Use the first column for editorial information as shown; then insert a column break.
7. Insert an Eagle from the Clip Art Gallery. Use **Square** text wrapping, size it appropriately to fit in the column, and center it after the Eagle Award is mentioned.
8. Save as **93d-d2**, preview, and print.

31e-d1
Memo

1. Strike ENTER to position the insertion point at about 2" on the status line; key the memo and save as **31e–d1**.

2. Follow "Proofread and Finalize a Document" on page 99.

  Interoffice Memo

2" **TO:** TAB TAB Loretta Howerton, Office Manager

FROM: TAB Lawrence Schmidt, OA/CIS Consultant

DATE: TAB Current date

SUBJECT: TAB Memorandums for Internal Correspondence

A memorandum is an internal communication that is sent within the organization. It is often the means by which managers correspond with employees and vice versa. Memos provide written records of announcements, requests for action, and policies and procedures.

Templates, or preformatted forms, are often used for keying memos. Templates provide a uniform look for company correspondence and save the employee the time of having to design and format each memo. Word processing software also has memo templates that can be customized. An example of a template is attached.

xx

Attachment

31e-d2
Memo

TIP
Use the Date command (**Insert** menu, **Date and Time**) to insert the current date.

TIP
If the first letter of your reference initials is automatically capitalized, point to the initial until the AutoCorrect options button appears. Click the button; then choose **Undo Automatic Capitalization**.

1. Key the memo and save as **31e-d2**.

words

TO:	Lonny Ashmyer DS	4
FROM:	Breton S. Vreede DS	9
DATE:	Current date	13
SUBJECT:	Wheelchair Access	19

Recently, I explained to you my efforts on a variety of projects to facilitate wheelchair entry into public buildings. I may have found a solution to one problem, Lonny; that is, how does someone open a large public door from a wheelchair?   35 50 64 67

The answer may lie in the installation of an electrical signal similar to a garage door opener that can be activated from the chair. All signals would be identical, of course, permitting universal application.   83 98 110

Please provide me with a rough estimate of the costs for conducting the necessary preliminary search, equipping a wheelchair, and tooling our factory to manufacture this item.   125 139 146

xx   146

1. Open **litter** from the data files. Save it as **93b-drill1**.

2. Click **Columns** and format the document in 3 even columns. Preview to see how it looks.

3. Format the same document in 2 columns. Preview to check the appearance.

4. Select the heading **Are You a Litter Bug?**; click **Columns** and select 1 column. Apply 36-point type. Center-align the heading. Add a hard return before column 1 to align the columns. Save again and close.

NEW FUNCTIONS

93c

To create columns of unequal width:

1. Select **Columns** from the Format menu to display the Columns dialog box.

2. Choose one of the Preset options, or click in the **Number of columns** box and key the number of columns.

3. *Word's* default is columns of equal width. To vary the column widths, click the box to remove the check mark.

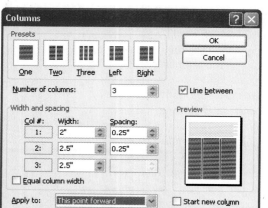

4. If you plan to vary the column widths, key the necessary information into the appropriate sections of the Width and spacing boxes.

5. If you want a vertical line between columns, click the **Line between** checkbox.

6. Click the down arrow beside the Apply to box, and choose one of the options. You can apply columns to the whole document, to one section, to selected sections, or from a particular point forward.

7. Use the Preview box to see what your layout will look like. In the dialog box shown here, the top portion of the document was formatted as a single column. At the end of that section, 3 unequal-width columns separated by lines were created. Note that in the Apply to box, **This point forward** has been selected.

To balance columns:

To balance columns so that all columns end at the same point on the page, position the insertion point at the end of the text to be balanced and insert a **Continuous section break (Insert, Break, Continuous, OK)**.

1. Open **litter** from the data files. Save it as **93c-drill2**.

2. Use the Columns dialog box to create 3 columns of equal width. Preview the document.

3. Select the heading and format it as a banner heading using 24-point bold type. Add a line between columns. Double-space below the heading. Save again and print.

4. Click in the body of the document. Display the Columns dialog box. Remove the check from the Equal Column Width checkbox and format the document in 2 columns. Decrease the size of the first column to 2". Preview the document, but do not save it.

1. Key both the memos below; both contain a distribution list.
2. Save as **31e-d3** and **31e-d4**.

TO: TAB TAB Manufacturing Team--Distribution Below

DS

FROM: TAB Mei-Ling Yee, Administrative Assistant

DS

DATE: TAB Current date

SUBJECT: TAB Enrichment Seminar

As was stated by Robert Beloz in the January newsletter, *Focus for the New Year*, Foscari & Associates will be offering a series of enrichment seminars for its employees in the year ahead. If you have suggestions for seminars that would be beneficial to your team, please let me know.

We are proud to announce our first seminar offering, *First Aid and CPR*. Participants will be awarded CPR Certificates from the American Heart Association upon successful completion of this eight-hour course. If you are interested in taking this seminar, please call me at ext. 702 or send me an e-mail message by April 25.

Mark your calendar for this important seminar.

First Aid and CPR Enrichment Seminar
May 16 and 17
1:00-5:00 p.m.
Staff Lounge

xx

Distribution:
 Eddie Barnett
 Steve Lewis
 Dinah Rice
 Amy Sturdivant

TO: Safety Officers--Distribution Below | FROM: Louis Cross | DATE: Current | SUBJECT: Safety Seminar

Mark your calendar for the *Safety Practices and Accident Prevention Seminar* that will be held on June 17, 200-, from 9:00 a.m. to 4:30 p.m. The seminar will be held at the Kellogg Center.

New OSHA regulations will be presented at this seminar, so it is extremely important for you as a safety officer to be in attendance. The seminar will be conducted by OSHA employees and professors from the University of New Mexico.

xx

Distribution:
 Lori Baker, Production
 George Markell, Maintenance
 Henry Otter, Human Resources

LESSON 93

Columns and Newsletters

93a

Warmup

Key each line twice SS.

alphabet	1	Judging each issue will quickly prove the magazine's flexibility.
figures	2	Check the inventory for items #782, #936, #351, and #405 at noon.
double letters	3	The little bookkeeper from Mississippi keeps all books for Tammy.
easy	4	Jo goes to town each day to open her mail box at the post office.

| 1 | 2 | 3 | 4 | 5 | 6 | 7 | 8 | 9 | 10 | 11 | 12 | 13 |

FUNCTION REVIEW

93b

Columns

Most text is formatted using one column; that is, the text extends from the left margin to the right margin. However, documents may also be formatted in two or more columns. Newsletters are usually formatted in columns similar to newspapers. These documents are normally designed with headings spanning the columns (called *banners* or *mastheads*) and are usually written in an interesting, conversational style and formatted with graphics and illustrations. Text flows down one column to the top of the next column. Columns may be of equal or unequal width.

Banner

Are You a Litter Bug?

Does the appearance of your campus, your neighborhood, your city, or your state make a difference? Appearance often creates the first impression a person has of a place he or she visits—and first impressions are usually lasting. When some people think of beautiful places, they think of lakes, rivers, oceans, mountains, countryside, firms, and forests. Others may think of suburban neighborhoods or of urban settings with modern, efficient buildings. The range of options is unlimited because beauty is in the eye of the beholder.

The beauty of many areas is marred by litter left by individuals who did not care about others who would follow them. One thing is certain—no matter how beautiful a place may be—if it is littered with trash or buildings are deteriorated, it will not make a good impression.

Litter creates two different types of costs for your campus, your city, and your state. One type of cost is *lost* business. Prospective students who visit campus with littered parking lots and vending

areas are often "turned off" by the appearance of the campus and search for a more appealing environment. Tourism is a major industry for most cities and states. Tourists are not likely to want to return to places that are littered and trashy.

The second type of cost is the clean-up cost. Picking up litter along highways, parks, waterways, and forests costs thousands of dollars every year. In addition, thousand of volunteers contribute huge amounts time to clean up public areas. Picking up litter improves the appearance for a short time, but it does not solve the problem because every soon after an area is cleared someone will come along and litter it again.

The real solution comes from not littering in the first place. Littering is not only expensive; it is wrong and against the law. Public awareness programs help. Teaching young people at home and in educational institutions to dispose of their trash properly may be our best solution for the future.

To create columns of equal width:

1. Click the **Columns** button on the Standard toolbar.
2. Drag to select the number of columns.
3. Using this method to create columns will format the entire document with columns of equal widths.

Column format may be applied before or after keying text. If columns are set before text is keyed, use Print Layout View to check the appearance of the text. Generally, column formats are easier to apply after text has been keyed.

Occasionally, you may want certain text (such as a banner or headline) to span more than one column.

Columns

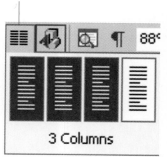

3 Columns

To format a banner:

1. Select the text to be included in the banner.
2. Click the **Columns** button, and drag the number of columns to 1.

LESSON 32 — Review Memo and E-Mail

SKILLBUILDING

32a
Warmup
Key each line twice SS.

alphabet 1 Extra awards given by my employer amazed Jo, the file clerk.
figures 2 I will be on vacation June 4-7, October 3, 5, 8, and December 6-9.
shift 3 Sue, May, Al, Tom, and Jo will meet us at the Pick and Save store.
easy 4 Ask the girl to copy the letter for all the workers in the office.

| 1 | 2 | 3 | 4 | 5 | 6 | 7 | 8 | 9 | 10 | 11 | 12 | 13 |

DOCUMENT DESIGN

32b

Electronic Mail

Electronic mail (or **e-mail**) is an informal message that is sent by one computer user to another computer user. To be able to send or receive e-mail, you must have an e-mail address, an e-mail program, and access to the Internet.

Heading: Accurately key the e-mail address of the receiver and supply a specific subject line. The date and your e-mail address will display automatically.

Attachments: Documents can be sent electronically by attaching the file to the recipient's e-mail message. The attached file can then be opened and edited by the recipient.

Body: SS the body of an e-mail; DS between paragraphs. Do not indent the paragraphs.

Formatting: Do not add bold or italic or vary the fonts. Do not use uppercase letters for emphasis. Use emoticons or e-mail abbreviations with caution (e.g., ;- for wink or BTW for by the way).

These addresses will receive a copy of the message.

You can enter multiple e-mail addresses.

E-Mail

| To: cryder@tech.com | cc: drowe@tech.com |
| | kforbes@tech.com |

Subject: March Staff Development

Attachment: Agenda.doc

Directions to attach will vary with e-mail software.

Message:

The March staff development session will be held on Thursday, March 5, at 2 p.m. in the fifth floor conference room. Please allow two hours in your schedule for this important program entitled "Appropriate Use of E-mail."

1. Open a new document and display the Drawing toolbar. Click the **Insert WordArt** button.

2. Select the first style from the second row of the WordArt Gallery.

3. Key the text **Happy Birthday to you!**

4. Select the text and click the **Format WordArt** button on the WordArt toolbar. Choose **Pale Blue** *Fill color*.

5. Save the document as **92d-drill5**.

APPLICATIONS

92e-d1
WordArt and Clip Art

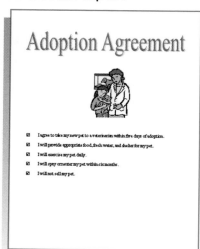

1. Open a new document. Insert WordArt; use the second WordArt style on the second row.

2. Key **Adoption Agreement.** Select *WordArt* and expand the size so that it spans the line of writing from the left margin to the right margin.

3. Use *animals* as the keyword and search for clip art. Insert a clip of an animal of your choice. Center the clip art.

4. Insert a checkbox from the symbol dialog box using a wingding font. Key the following statements DS. Save as **92e-d1** and print.

   ☑ I agree to take my new pet to a veterinarian within five days of adoption.

   ☑ I will provide appropriate food, fresh water, and shelter for my pet.

   ☑ I will exercise my pet daily.

   ☑ I will spay or neuter my pet within six months.

   ☑ I will not sell my pet.

92e-d2
Memo with AutoShapes

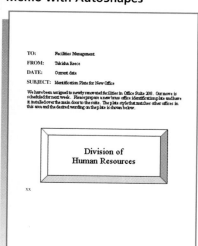

1. Open a new document and key the following memo:

   TO: Facilities Management | FROM: Takisha Reece | DATE: Current date | SUBJECT: Identification Plate for New Office
   We have been assigned to newly renovated facilities in Office Suite 208. Our move is scheduled for next week. Please prepare a new brass office identification plate and have it installed over the main door to the suite. The plate style that matches other offices in this area and the desired wording on the plate are shown below.

2. Insert a Bevel rectangle from the Basic Shapes category of AutoShapes.

3. Size the Bevel rectangle so that it is about 2" high and 5" wide.

4. Add the following text as shown at left: **Division of Human Resources**.

5. Center the text and use Bookman Old Style 24-point font.

6. Save as **92e-d2** and print.

Follow these directions for completing all documents in Lesson 32:

Without Internet access: Complete all documents as memos.

With an e-mail address: Complete the documents in your e-mail software and send them.

With Internet access but no e-mail address: Your instructor will assist you in setting up a free e-mail account and address.

32c-d1
E-mail Message

1. Key the following e-mail message to your instructor.
2. Key **Assignment 1 from (Your Name)** as the subject line.
3. Send the message.

Consider the following when choosing an appropriate e-mail password.

1. Do not choose a password that is named after a family member or a pet.
2. Do not use birth dates as a password.
3. Choose a combination of letters and numbers; preferably, use uppercase and lowercase letters, e.g., TLQ6tEpR.
4. Do not share your password with anyone.
5. Do not write your password on a piece of paper and leave it by your computer or in your desk drawer.

32c-d2
E-mail Message with Copy Notation

1. Key the following e-mail message to your instructor.
2. Copy the message to one student in your class.
3. Key **Assignment 2 from (Your Name)** as the subject line.
4. Send the message.

Follow these guidelines when composing e-mail.

1. Do not use bold or italic or vary fonts.
2. Do not use uppercase for emphasis.
3. Use emoticons or e-mail abbreviations with caution (e.g., :) for smile or BTW for by the way).
4. Write clear, concise messages that are free of spelling and grammatical errors.
5. Do not send an e-mail message in haste or anger. Think about the message carefully before clicking the Send button.

1. Click the **Rectangle** button; draw a rectangle about 2" wide. Key your name; use red color for text and lines.

2. Click the **Oval** button and draw an oval about 1" wide below the rectangle. Add blue fill.

3. Click the down arrow beside **AutoShapes**, select **Basic Shapes**, and draw a .75" smiley face below the rectangle; add yellow fill to the smiley face.

4. Save as **92d-drill4** and print.

WordArt

The WordArt Gallery provides a number of shapes and styles for WordArt. The first example shown below was created using the first design in the WordArt Gallery. The second example was created by adding a textured fill color and a 3-D effect to the first banner.

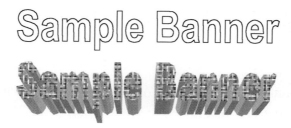

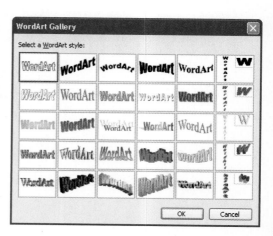

To use WordArt:

1. Display the Drawing toolbar, and click the **WordArt** button. The WordArt Gallery displays.

2. Select the desired style and click **OK** to display the Edit WordArt Text dialog box as shown at the right.

3. Key the text; change the font size or style in this textbox if desired. Click **OK**. Your text is now displayed as WordArt.

4. Select the text to display the WordArt toolbar. Format the WordArt text using the buttons on the WordArt toolbar. You may also use the buttons on the Drawing toolbar.

1. Key the memo below. Add your reference initials.

2. Indent the names on the Distribution List to the first tab.

   Distribution:
      Allen Bejahan
      Janet James
      Terry Johnson
      Ray Lightfoot

3. Save as **32c-d3**.

words

TO:	Team Leaders -- Distribution Below	8
	DS	
FROM:	J. Mac Chandler, Office Manager	15
DATE:	Current date	19
SUBJECT:	New Multimedia Lab Available June 12	29
	DS	

We are pleased to announce the opening of our new Multimedia Lab effec- 43
tive June 12. The lab is in the front office just beyond the Advertising 58
Department. The lab has four new computers with full multimedia capa- 72
bility, two laser disc players, a VCR, two presentation projection devices, 87
two scanners, and various color and laser printers. 97

Use this lab if your computer is too small for your job, too slow, or too 112
limited to handle a specific job. Just complete the sign-up sheet located 127
adjacent to the equipment. Projection equipment and two laptop com- 141
puters may be checked out for presentations. Please reserve this equipment 156
twenty-four hours in advance. 162

176

1. Key the memo; make changes as shown.

2. Use your reference initials.

3. Save as **32c-d4**.

TO: J. Ezra Bayh		4
FROM: Greta Sangtree		8
DATE: Current date		13
SUBJECT: Letter-Mailing Standards	DS	20

chk sp

Recently the post office delivered late a letter that *, because of the delay,* 35
caused us some embarassment. To avoid recurrence, please 47
ensure that all administrative assistants and mail person- 58
nel follow postal service guidelines. 67

U.S.

Perhaps a refresher seminar on correspondence guidelines is 79
~~in~~ in order. Thanks ~~or you~~ help. *for your* 86

1. Open a new document.

2. Key the heading **My New Pet**, at about 2"; center and bold; use 36 point.

3. Click below the heading; insert **Pet** from the data files.

4. Select the picture; use **Square** wrapping and **Center** alignment.

5. Select the **Picture** tab; crop the picture .8" from the bottom.

6. Save as **92d-drill3** and print.

My New Pet

Drawing Tools

A variety of drawing tools are available in *Word*. These tools can be accessed from the Drawing toolbar (**View, Toolbars, Drawing**). An easy way to become familiar with all of the tools is to display the Drawing toolbar and hold the mouse pointer over each object on the toolbar to display its function. Click the down arrow on each object that has one to display the available options for the tool. A canvas will display when you click a drawing tool to help with the formatting of the object.

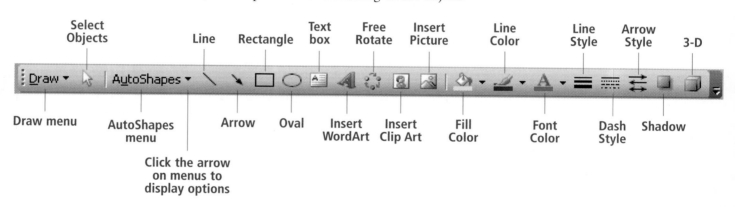

To insert a drawing tool object:

1. With the Drawing toolbar displayed, click on the desired object such as **Rectangle** or **AutoShapes**. If you choose AutoShapes, a list of various shapes displays. If a triangular arrow appears beside an object, click on it to display the available options.

2. When you choose the desired object, a "canvas" displays with the message "Create your drawing here." The mouse pointer turns into a crosshairs. Drag the mouse to create the object on the canvas.

3. Select the object and format it using the effects such as fill, lines, and 3-D that are available on the Drawing toolbar.

4. To add text to an object such as a rectangle or an oval, right-click the object and select **Add Text** from the drop-down menu. Then key your text.

SKILLBUILDING

33a
Warmup
Keep fingers curved, hands quiet as you key each line twice SS.

1st finger
1 My 456 heavy brown jugs have nothing in them; fill them by May 7.
2 The 57 bins are numbered 1 to 57; Bins 5, 6, 45, and 57 are full.

2d finger
3 Ed decided to crate 38 pieces of cedar decking from the old dock.
4 Mike, who was 38 in December, likes a piece of ice in cold cider.

3d finger
5 Polly made 29 points on the quiz; Wex 10 points. Did they pass?
6 Sall saw Ezra pass 200 pizza pans to Sean, who fixed 20 of them.

| 1 | 2 | 3 | 4 | 5 | 6 | 7 | 8 | 9 | 10 | 11 | 12 | 13 |

33b
Timed Writing
Take two 3' timings.

  all letters

gwam 3'

So now you are operating a keyboard and don't you find it amazing that your fingers, working with very little visual help, move easily and quickly from one key to the next, helping you to change words into ideas and sentences. You just decide what you want to say and the format in which you want to say it, and your keyboard will carry out your order exactly as you enter it. One operator said lately that she sometimes wonders just who is most responsible for the completed product—the person or the machine.

4 | 38
8 | 43
13 | 47
17 | 51
21 | 56
26 | 60
30 | 64
34 | 69

3' | 1 | 2 | 3 | 4 | 5 |

FUNCTION REVIEW

33c

Date and Time

The current date can be inserted into a document by using the Insert Date and Time feature.

To insert the date:

1. Place the cursor at the position the date is to be inserted.
2. Select **Date and Time** from the Insert menu.
3. Select the desired format from the Date and Time dialog box; click **OK**.

Center Page

Copy can be centered vertically on the page by using the Center Page command. To center the copy on the page, choose **Page Setup** from the File menu. Click the **Layout** tab, click the **Vertical Alignment** drop list arrow, and choose **Center**.

DRILL 1

INSERT DATE AND CENTER PAGE

1. Key your first and last name on the page; strike ENTER twice.
2. Insert the current date; select the format *March 5, 2003*.
3. Center the page and print. Do not save.

To move clip art:

1. Select the clip art.

2. Click the **Text Wrapping** button on the Picture toolbar. Then choose **Tight** (or one of the text-wrapping options) from the drop-down list. The sizing handles change to white squares.

3. Position the arrow pointer on the clip art until a four-headed arrow displays. Click and drag the clip art to the desired location.

To wrap text around graphics:

1. Insert the graphic; then place the insertion point over the graphic and right-click.

2. Select **Format Picture** to display the Format Picture dialog box.

3. Click the **Layout** tab and select the desired wrapping style (**Square**).

4. Click the desired alignment (**Left**) and then click **OK**.

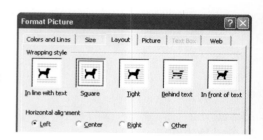

DRILL 2   WRAP TEXT

1. Key the paragraph at the right DS.

2. Insert clip art picturing a floppy disk.

3. Format the clip art using **Tight** *Wrapping style* and **Center** *Horizontal alignment* so the clip art will be centered and the text will wrap around it.

4. Print and save as **92c-drill2**.

> Most of us have grown accustomed to saving files on 3.5" disks. Today, however, 3.5" disks are rarely used to transport data. Technological advances make it possible to transport information over the Web, through the use of ftp sites, with zip disks, with CD-ROMs, with USB devices, and in a host of other ways, which explains why many leading computer manufacturers no longer supply 3.5" disk drives.

NEW FUNCTIONS

92d

To insert a picture from a file:

1. Click **Picture** on the Insert menu; then click **From File**.

2. Select the file, double-click or key the filename, and click **Insert**.

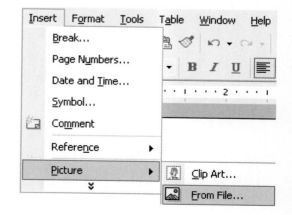

Business Letters

Business letters are used to communicate with persons outside of the business. Business letters carry two messages: one is the tone and content; a second is the appearance of the document. Appearance is important because it creates the critical first impression. Stationery, use of standard letter parts, and placement should convey that the writer is intelligent, informed, and detail minded.

Stationery

Letters should be printed on high-quality (about 24-pound) letterhead stationery. Standard size for letterhead is $8\frac{1}{2}$" x 11". Envelopes should match the letterhead in quality and color.

Letter parts

Businesspeople expect to see standard letter parts arranged in the proper sequence. The standard parts are listed below. Other letter parts may be included as needed.

Letterhead: Preprinted stationery that includes the company name, logo, address, and other optional information such as a telephone number and fax number.

Dateline: Date the letter is prepared.

Letter address: Complete address of the person who will receive the letter. Generally, the address includes the receiver's name, company name, street address, city, state (followed by one space only), and ZIP code. Include a personal title (*Mr.,* *Ms., Dr.*) with the person's name. Key the address four lines below the dateline, and capitalize the first letter of each word.

Salutation: Key the salutation, or greeting, a double space (DS) below the letter address. If the letter is addressed to an individual, include a courtesy title with the person's last name. If the letter is addressed to a company, use *Ladies and Gentlemen.*

Body: Begin the body, or message, a DS below the salutation. Single-space (SS) paragraphs and DS between paragraphs.

Complimentary closing: Begin the complimentary closing a DS below the body. Capitalize only the first letter of the closing.

Writer's name and title: Key the writer's name and job title four lines below the complimentary closing to allow space for the writer's signature. Key the name and title on either one or two lines, whichever gives better balance to the signature block. Separate the writer's name and title with a comma if they are on one line.

Reference initials: Key the initials of the typist in lowercase letters a DS below the typed name and title. If the writer's initials are also included, key them first in ALL CAPS followed by a colon (BB:xx).

Block Format

In block format, all letter parts are keyed at the left margin. For most letters, use open punctuation, which requires no punctuation after the salutation or the closing. For efficiency, use the default settings and features of your software when formatting letters.

Side margins: Default (1.25") or 1".

Dateline: Position the date at about 2" (strike ENTER six times) or at least 0.5" below the letterhead. If the letter is short, center the page vertically. To avoid interfering with the letterhead, do not center long letters or letters containing many extra parts.

Spacing: SS paragraphs; DS between them. Follow the directions for spacing between other letter parts provided above.

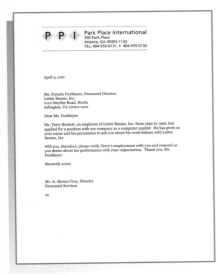

Block Letter

TIP
To center a page, click **File, Page Setup, Layout** tab, **Vertical Alignment,** and then **Center.**

Clip Art

Clip art, pictures, AutoShapes, WordArt, and other images are graphic elements that enhance documents such as announcements and newsletters. This lesson reviews inserting and formatting clip art and introduces inserting pictures from files, WordArt, and Drawing tools.

To insert clip art:

1. Click **Insert** on the menu bar, click **Picture**, and then click **Clip Art**.

2. In the Task Pane Search text box, key the type of clip art to search for such as *bicycle* and then click **Search**.

3. When the results display, select the desired clip, click the down arrow at the right of the image, and then click **Insert**.

To size clip art:

1. Select the clip art.

2. Position the insertion point over one of the handles. When the pointer turns to a double-headed arrow, drag the lower-right handle down and to the right to increase the size. Drag it up and to the left to decrease the size. Drag a corner handle to maintain the same proportion.

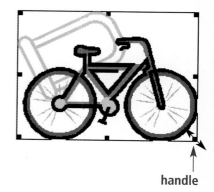

handle

DRILL 1   CLIP ART

1. Open a new document.

2. Search for a bicycle in the clip art gallery and insert it.

3. Increase the size of the clip art to approximately double the size.

4. Create the folder **Module 15 Keys**, and save the document as **92c-drill1** in this folder. Save all exercises for Module 15 in this folder.

2.1"

E-Market, Group
10 East Rivercenter Boulevard
Covington, KY 41016-8765

Dateline   Current date ↓4

Letter   Mr. Ishmal Dabdoub
address   Professional Office Consultants
1782 Laurel Canyon Road
Sunnyvale, CA 93785-9087 DS

Salutation
Dear Mr. Dabdoub DS

Body   Have you heard your friends and colleagues talk about obtaining real-time stock quotes? real-time account balances and positions? Nasdaq Level II quotes? extended-hours trading? If so, then they are among the three million serious investors that have opened an account with E-Market. DS

We believe that the best decisions are informed decisions made in a timely manner. E-Market has an online help desk that provides information for all levels of investors, from beginners to the experienced serious trader. You can learn basic tactics for investing in the stock market, how to avoid common mistakes, and pick up some advanced strategies. DS

Stay on top of the market and your investments! Visit our Web site at http://www.emarket.com to learn more about our banking and brokerage services. E-Market Group is the premier site for online investing. DS

Sincerely ↓4   **Complimentary Closing**

Margaritta Gibson

Writer's
name   Ms. Margaritta Gibson
Title   Marketing Manager DS

Reference   xx
initials

Graphic Enhancements

- Build keyboarding skill.
- Use clip art, drawing tools, and WordArt.
- Format announcements and newsletters with graphics.
- Format newsletters in columns.
- Format news releases.

LESSON 92 Skillbuilding and Graphics

SKILLBUILDING

92a
Warmup
Key each line twice SS.

alphabet	1	Viewing jungle dance experts from big cities quickly amazed them.
fig/sym	2	The yield of 18.469% on the 25-year, $730 million note was given.
3rd/4th fingers	3	Last spring was our good opportunity to zap poor display samples.
adjacent reaches	4	Where we build other stores in the west is a quiet concern of Jo.

| 1 | 2 | 3 | 4 | 5 | 6 | 7 | 8 | 9 | 10 | 11 | 12 | 13 |

92b
Timed Writings
1. Key a 1' writing.
2. Add 8 words to your base. Take three 1' writings; try to increase your rate by 8 words. Work for speed, not accuracy.

gwam 3'

Many people find that creative thinking can be nurtured with effort. One way to do this is to find multiple solutions to a problem. Alternatives to a problem should be sought out when there seems to be only one possible solution as well as when a solution has already been found. The more ideas generated, the more options there may be. If a person can identify the options that are available and experiment with them, then possibly he or she can come up with several other options. This approach fosters new ideas and stimulates the creative thinking process.

4	42
8	46
12	50
17	54
21	59
25	63
30	67
33	71
38	75

3' | 1 | 2 | 3 | 4 |

33e-d1
Block Letter

At 2.1"	Ln 7	Col 1

1. Key the model letter on page 107 in block format with open punctuation. Begin with the date.
2. Strike ENTER to position the dateline about 2.1" on the status bar. The position will vary depending upon the font size.
3. Insert the current date using the Date and Time feature.
4. Include your reference initials. If the first letter of your initials is automatically capitalized, point to the initial until the AutoCorrect Option button appears, click the button, and then choose Undo Automatic Capitalization.
5. Follow the proofreading procedures outlined in Lesson 31. Use Print Preview to check the placement.
6. Use Show/Hide to compare paragraph markers with the model at the left. Print the letter when you are satisfied. Create the folder **Module 4 Keys** and save the letter as **33e-d1** in this folder. Save all drills and documents for Module 4 in the **Module 4 Keys** folder.

33e-d2
Block Letter

1. Key the letter below in block format with open punctuation. Use Date and Time to insert the current date. Add your reference initials in lowercase letters.
2. Save the letter as **33e-d2**. Proofread and print the letter. Keep the document displayed for the next exercise.

↓2.1"
Current date ↓4

Ms. Alice Ottoman
Premiere Properties, Inc.
52 Ocean Drive
Newport Beach, CA 92747-6293 ↓2

Dear Ms. Ottoman ↓2

Internet Solutions has developed a new technique for you to market your properties on the World Wide Web. We can now create 360-degree panoramic pictures for your Web site. You can give your clients a virtual spin of the living room, kitchen, and every room in the house. ↓2

Call today for a demonstration of this remarkable technology. Give your clients a better visual understanding of the property layout—something your competition doesn't have. ↓2

Sincerely ↓4

Lee Rodgers
Marketing Manager ↓2

xx

33e-d3
Block Letter and Center Page

1. Document **33e-d2** should be displayed on your screen. Save it as **33e-d3**.
2. Replace the letter address with the one below in proper format.
   Ms. Andrea Virzi, J P Personnel Services, 2351 West Ravina Drive, Atlanta, GA 30346-9105
3. Supply the correct salutation. Turn on **Show/Hide (¶)**. Delete the six hard returns above the dateline. Align the page at vertical center (**File, Page Setup**). Proofread and save. Use Print Preview to view placement. Note that a short letter looks more attractive centered on the page rather than positioned at 2.1".

Level 4

Designing Specialized Documents

OBJECTIVES

DOCUMENT DESIGN SKILLS

To display graphics attractively in newsletters, letterheads, and announcements.

To produce mass mailings effectively using mail merge.

To format agendas, minutes, badges, and itineraries attractively.

To format legal, medical, and employment documents appropriately.

WORD PROCESSING SKILLS

To apply graphics, merge, and other commonly used word processing functions.

COMMUNICATION SKILLS

To produce error-free documents.

KEYBOARDING

To improve keyboarding speed and accuracy.

SKILLBUILDING

34a
Warmup
Key each line twice SS.

alphabetic	1	Buddy Jackson is saving the door prize money for wax and lacquer.
figures	2	I have fed 47 hens, 25 geese, 10 ducks, 39 lambs, and 68 kittens.
one hand	3	You imply Jon Case exaggerated my opinion on a decrease in rates.
easy	4	I shall make hand signals to the widow with the auditory problem.

| 1 | 2 | 3 | 4 | 5 | 6 | 7 | 8 | 9 | 10 | 11 | 12 | 13 |

34b
Rhythm Builder
Key lines 5–8 twice.
Take two 30" timings
on lines 9 and 10.

Balanced-hand words, phrases, and sentences.

5 am an by do go he if is it me or ox or so for and big the six spa
6 but cod dot dug eye end wit vie yam make also city work gage them

7 is it| is it| is it he| is it he| for it| for it| paid for it| it is she
8 of it| pay due| pay for| paid me| paid them| also make| such as| may end

9 Sue and Bob may go to the zoo, and he or she may pay for the gas.
10 Jim was sad; Ted saw him as we sat on my bed; we saw him get gas.

| 1 | 2 | 3 | 4 | 5 | 6 | 7 | 8 | 9 | 10 | 11 | 12 | 13 |

COMMUNICATION

34c

Letter Addresses and Salutations

The salutation, or greeting, consists of the person's personal title (*Mr.*, *Ms.*, or *Mrs.*) or professional title (*Dr.*, *Professor*, *Senator*, *Honorable*), and the person's last name. Do not use a first name unless you have a personal relationship. The salutation should agree in number with the addressee. If the letter is addressed to more than one person, the salutation is plural.

	Receiver	Salutation
To individuals	Dr. Alexander Gray	Dear Dr. Gray
	Dr. and Mrs. Thompson	Dear Dr. and Mrs. Thompson
To organizations	TMP Electronics, Inc.	Ladies and Gentlemen
Name unknown	Advertising Manager	Dear Advertising Manager

DRILL 1
PRACTICE LETTER PARTS

1. Review the model document on page 107 for correct placement of letter parts.
2. Key the letter parts for each activity, spacing correctly between parts. In the first exercise, strike ENTER six times to begin the dateline at 2.1"; use the Date and Time feature.
3. Press ENTER five times between drills. Do not save the drills.
4. Take a 2' timing on each drill. Repeat if you finish before time is up.

A Current date

Ms. Joyce Bohn, Treasurer
Citizens for the Environment
1888 Hutchins Ave.
Seattle, WA 98111-2353

Dear Ms. Bohn

B Please confirm our lunch date.

Sincerely yours

James D. Bohlin
District Attorney

xx

Module 14: Checkpoint

Self-Assessment

Answer the questions below to see if you have mastered the content of this module.

1. To create blank lines for a fill-in form, set an underline tab by using one of the _____ options.

2. To place a line around the perimeter of a page, select Box on the _____ tab of the Borders and Shading dialog box.

3. To enter text fields, checkbox, or drop-down fields, first display the _____ toolbar.

4. To create a list of alternatives in a Drop-Down form field, click the _____ button.

5. To activate a form and test it, you must first _____ the form.

6. A/an _____ form can be completed electronically and transmitted to the designer.

7. The excess of assets over liabilities on a personal financial statement is known as a person's _____.

8. On a balance sheet, liabilities and _____ must equal total assets.

9. A/an _____ statement shows the net profit or earnings of an organization.

10. A/an _____ is used to ensure that expenditures do not exceed the money available for operations or a project.

Performance Assessment

Document 1
Fill-In Form

1. Create a fill-in form for the Business Club to use for its members.

   - Position heading at about 2"; center it; and use 14-point bold font.

   - Provide lines for name, address, city, state, and ZIP Code, telephone number, e-mail, major, class, and committee. Put city, state, and ZIP Code on one line with a blank line for each item.

2. Save the document as **Checkpoint14-d1a**.

3. Put the same information on an online form. Use text boxes for everything except class and committee. Use drop-down boxes with **Freshman, Sophomore, Junior,** and **Senior** for Class options and **Membership, Finance,** and **Program** for Committee options. Move the committee options so that they are in alphabetical order.

4. Protect the form and save it as **Checkpoint14-d1b**.

Document 2
Budget

1. Prepare a budget for the Business Club Banquet.

2. Your estimated sources of revenue are ticket sales at $25 per person. You expect 40 people to attend. Business Club support will add $150 to help cover costs.

3. Your projected expenses are: Fixed costs: Decorations, $100; Entertainment, $125; and Gift for speaker, $25; Variable costs: Food, $20 per person; Program printing, $.50 per person. Any excess revenues over expenditures will be used for contingencies.

4. Save as **Checkpoint14-d2**.

Envelopes

The envelope feature can insert the delivery address automatically if a letter is displayed; postage can even be added if special software is installed. The default is a size 10 envelope (4⅛" by 9½"); other sizes are available by clicking the Options button on the Envelope tab. An alternative style for envelope addresses is uppercase (ALL CAPS) with no punctuation.

Ms. Alice Ottoman
Premiere Properties, Inc.
52 Ocean Drive
Newport Beach, CA 92747-6293

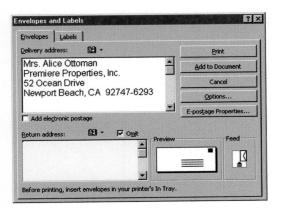

To generate an envelope:

1. With the letter you have created displayed, click **Tools** on the menu, and then **Letters and Mailings**. Click **Envelopes and Labels,** and if necessary, click the **Envelopes** tab. The mailing address is automatically displayed in the Delivery address box. (To create an envelope without a letter, follow the same steps, but key the address in the Delivery address box.)

2. If you are using business envelopes with a preprinted return address (assume you are), click the Return address Omit box. To include a return address, do not check the Omit box, click in the Return address box, and enter the return address.

   Note: To format a letter address on the envelope in all caps, click **Add to Document** to attach the envelope to the letter, and then edit the address.

Change Case

Change Case enables you to change the capitalization of text that has already been keyed.

Sentence case capitalizes the first letter of the first word of a sentence.

Lowercase changes all capital letters to lowercase letters.

Uppercase changes all letters to uppercase.

Title case capitalizes the first letter of each word.

Toggle case changes all uppercase letters to lowercase and vice versa.

To change case, select the text to be changed, choose **Change Case** from the Format menu, and then choose the appropriate option.

DRILLS 2–3

CREATE ENVELOPE

1. Create an envelope for the addressee in Drill 1 on page 109.

2. Attach the envelope to a blank document.

3. Save the document as **34d-drill2.**

4. Open **33e-d2**. Create and attach an envelope to the letter.

5. Select the entire address and convert it to uppercase. Delete the punctuation.

6. Save the document as **34d-drill3** and print it. Your instructor may have you print envelopes on plain paper.

91c-d2
Personal Financial Statement

Use the following information to prepare a personal financial statement for Tonisha C. Marcus, 3947 Keatley Ave., Huntington, WV 25755-9603. Set tabs: .5" left; 3.5" left with leader 2; 4.5" right; and 6" right tab. Use a 2" top margin.

1. Include the following assets: cash, $1,025; savings, $2,486; and automobile, $14,675. Show the total assets of $18,186.

2. Include the following liabilities: credit cards, $1,000; automobile loan, $4,279. Show the total liabilities of $5,279.

3. Show the net worth of $12,907. Double-underline the net worth.

4. Add a page border.

5. Save as **91c-d2** and print.

91c-d3
Balance Sheet

Use the following information to prepare a balance sheet. Position the following heading at about 2", centered, and 14-point bold font: **Saluda Gift Shop; Balance Sheet; As of December 31, 200-**. Set tabs: .5" left tab; 4.5" right tab; and 5.75" right tab. Add a page border; save as **91c-d3** and print.

Assets

Current Assets
Cash and equivalents $104,268
Receivables 26,493
Inventory 12,730
Total Current Assets $143,491

Long-Term Assets
Furniture and fixtures $14,862
Equipment 12,793
Total Long-Term Assets $27,619

Total Assets $171,110

Liabilities and Equity

Liabilities
Accounts payable $14,378
Accrued expenses 1,604
Total Liabilities $15,982

Equity
Owner's equity $155,128

Total Liabilities and Equity $171,110

34e-d1
Edit Letter

1. Open letter **33e-d1**, save it as **34e-d1**, and then make the changes shown below.
2. Center the letter vertically. Use **Show/Hide** to remove any extra paragraph markers (¶).
3. Change the date to the current date, preview the letter, and print one copy.

~~Mr. Ishmal Dabdoub~~ Dr. Arthur Goralsky
~~Professional Office Consultants~~ Global Enterprises, Inc.
~~1782 Laurel Canyon Road~~ 2000 Corporate Way
~~Sunnyvale, Ca 93785~~ Lake Oswego, OR 97035

Dear ~~Mr. Dabdoub~~ Dr. Goralsky

Have you heard your friends and colleagues talk about obtaining real-time stock quotes? real-time account balances and positions? Nasdaq Level II quotes? extended-hours trading? If so, then they are among the ~~three~~ *four* million serious investors that have opened ~~an~~ accounts with ~~E-Market~~ *E-Trade*.

E-Trade We believe that the best decisions are informed decisions made in a timely manner. ~~E-Market~~ has an online help desk that provides information for all levels of investors, from beginners to the experienced serious trader. You can
strategies learn basic ~~tactics~~ for investing in the stock market, how to ~~avoiding~~ common mistakes, and ~~picking~~ up some advanced strategies.

etrade Stay on top of the market and your investments! Visit our Web site at http://www. ~~emarket~~.com to learn more about our banking and brokerage services. ~~E-Market Group~~ *E-Trade* is the premier site for online investing.

Sincerely

~~Ms. Margaritta Gibson~~ Keisha Knight
Marketing Manager

xx

On the signal to begin, key the documents in sequence. When time has been called, proofread all documents again and correct any errors you may have overlooked. Reprint if necessary.

1. Prepare an online registration form with the heading **Central University Soccer Camp** formatted in bold, 14-point type.

2. Use the heading **Camper Information**, followed by text boxes for the following information:

   Full Name

   Date of Birth

   Name of Parent

   Street Address

   City, State, and ZIP Code

   Telephone Number

   E-Mail

3. Add borders to each text box.

4. Use a checkbox for ☐ **Boy**   ☐ **Girl**.

5. Use a drop-down list for t-shirt size with the following options:

   Small

   Medium

   Large

   X-Large

6. Use the heading **Camp Options**, followed by the two subheadings for camp selection and a drop-down list with the following options:

   Regular camp for boys and girls 6–15

   Options: Half-day; June 23–27; $99 or Full-day; July 11–15; $199

   Premier residential camps for ages 10–18

   Options: Boys; June 12–16; $400 or Girls; June 18–22; $400

7. Add the following notation at the bottom of the form: ***Note:*** **Checks must be received within 5 days to hold your reservation.**

8. Protect the form, save it as **91c-d1**, and print. (For *Word 2002*, use password *soccamp*.)

34e-d2
Block Letter

1. Use the Date feature to insert the current date.
2. Center the page vertically. Proofread and check the spelling. Preview the letter and check the placement. Save the letter as **34e-d2** and print one copy.

Current date | Mr. Trace L. Brecken | 4487 Ingram Street | Corpus Christi, TX 78409-8907 | Dear Mr. Brecken

We have received the package you sent us in which you returned goods from a recent order you gave us. Your refund check, plus return postage, will be mailed to you in a few days.

We are sorry, of course, that you did not find this merchandise personally satisfactory. It is our goal to please all of our customers, and we are always disappointed if we fail.

Please give us an opportunity to try again. We stand behind our merchandise, and that is our guarantee of good service.

Cordially yours | Mrs. Margret Bredewig | Customer Service Department | xx

34e-d3
Block Letter

1. Follow the directions for **34e-d2**. Save the letter as **34e-d3** and print one copy.

Current date | Mrs. Rose Shikamuru | 55 Lawrence Street |Topeka, KS 66607-6657 | Dear Mrs. Shikamuru

Thank you for your recent letter asking about employment opportunities with our company. We are happy to inform you that Mr. Edward Ybarra, our recruiting representative, will be on your campus on April 23, 24, 25, and 26 to interview students who are interested in our company.

We suggest that you talk soon with your student placement office, as all appointments with Mr. Ybarra will be made through that office. Please bring with you the application questionnaire the office provides.

Within a few days, we will send you a company brochure and more information about our offices; plant; salary, bonus, and retirement plans; and the beautiful community in which we are located. We believe a close study of this information will convince you, as it has many others, that our company builds futures as well as small motors.

If there is any other way we can help you, please write to me again.

Yours very truly | Miss Myrle K. Bragg | Human Services Director | xx

34e-d4
Envelopes

1. Open each of the following documents and create an envelope: **34e-d1**, **34e-d2**, **34e-d3**. Print each envelope; do not save.

SKILLBUILDING

91a
Warmup
Key each line twice SS.

alphabet	1	Gwen and Jackie both analyzed our five complex physics questions.
fig/sym	2	Room #1507 is 42'6" long and 38'9" wide; it can accommodate them.
home row	3	Jake said Sally and Klaus gladly did all I asked the staff to do.
fluency	4	Claudia and Clement may go with their neighbor to fish for smelt.

| 1 | 2 | 3 | 4 | 5 | 6 | 7 | 8 | 9 | 10 | 11 | 12 | 13 |

91b
Timed Writings
Take two 5' timed writings.

  all letters

	gwam	3'	5'
Most people find it amazing that mobile telephones can create a		4	3
number of etiquette and safety problems. The use of hand-held,		9	5
mobile telephones has increased dramatically in the past few years.		13	8
Just because a mobile telephone can be taken almost anywhere does		18	11
not mean that it is appropriate to use it in any place it can be		22	13
carried. Common sense and good manners seem to have been forgotten		26	16
when it comes to using a mobile telephone.		29	18
The major safety hazard of using a hand-held telephone results		33	20
from its use in moving automobiles. A significant percentage of		38	23
all accidents is the result of drivers being distracted. Of all the		42	25
distractions reported, the most frequent are those that occur while		47	28
a driver is holding a telephone in one hand and trying to drive		51	31
at the same time. A hands-free telephone is not as dangerous, but		56	33
it can still cause a driver to be distracted.		59	35
The etiquette problem is the result of a person speaking on		63	38
a telephone in a place that disturbs another person. Either the		67	40
individual doing this just does not care or does not realize how		71	43
rude he or she is being to another person. It is not unusual to		76	45
see signs that prohibit the use of a mobile telephone in meeting		80	48
rooms, restaurants, movie theaters, concert halls, and a number		84	51
of other places. What is most shocking is that these signs are		88	53
necessary. Except in rare cases, a telephone should not be used		93	56
in these places. What has happened to basic courtesy?		96	58

3'	1	2	3	4
5'	1	2	3	

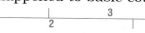

35a
Warmup
Key each line twice SS.

alphabet	1	Jacky Few's strange, quiet behavior amazed and perplexed even us.
figures	2	Dial Extension 1480 or 2760 for a copy of the 3-page 95-cent book.
double letters	3	Ann will see that Edd accepts an assignment in the school office.
easy	4	If I burn the signs, the odor of enamel may make a toxic problem.

| 1 | 2 | 3 | 4 | 5 | 6 | 7 | 8 | 9 | 10 | 11 | 12 | 13 |

35b

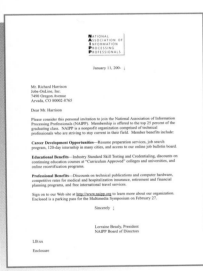

Modified Block Format

In modified block letter format, the dateline and the closing lines begin at the center point of the page. Paragraphs may be blocked or indented to the first tab stop; however, it is more efficient not to indent paragraphs. Set a tab at the center of the page to key the date and the closing lines. To determine the position of the tab, subtract the side margins from the center of the paper.

4.25"	Center of the paper
−1.25"	Margins
3"	Tab setting

Letter Parts

In Lesson 33 you learned the standard letter parts. Listed below are optional parts.

Enclosure notation: If an item is included with a letter, key an enclosure notation a DS below the reference initials. Press TAB to align the enclosures. Variations include:

Enclosures: Check #831
            Order form

Enclosures: 2

Copy notation: A copy notation c indicates that a copy of the document has been sent to the person listed. Key the copy notation a DS below the reference initials or enclosure notation. Press TAB to align the names.

       ┌─**Tab**
c ↓ Hillary Stevens
    David Schmidt
    Doug Overland

90c-d2
Project Budget

Prepare a budget for a seminar that Professional Development Seminars has scheduled. Use the following information to prepare the budget.

1. Use the heading **Professional Development Seminars, Inc./Effective Presentations Seminar/** and the current date. Position the heading at about 2"; center it and use 14-point bold font.

2. Set a left tab at .5" and right tabs at 4.5" and 5.75".

3. Key the data shown below.

4. Use capitalization, underlining, and bold as illustrated.

5. Add a page border to the document.

6. Save as **90c-d2** and print.

Projected Revenues
Number of participants projected	18	
Revenue per participant	$495	
Total Revenue Projected		$8,910

Projected Expenses
Fixed Costs
Instructor fees	$1,600	
Instructor expenses	150	
Training room/equipment rental	650	
Program marketing material	450	
Advertising and promotional costs	800	
Overhead allocation	400	
Coaches/mentors	400	
Total Fixed Costs		$4,450

Variable Costs
Seminar training manual ($15 each)	$270	
Meals/breaks ($30 each)	540	
Parking/other fees ($5 each)	90	
Total Variable Costs		$900
Total Projected Expenses		$5,350
Profit		$3,560

90c-d3
Project Budget

The same seminar whose budget you prepared in **90c-d2** above is being offered again one month from today. The projected number of participants is 30. The fixed costs are the same. The variable costs must be adjusted based on the number of participants. Prepare the budget for the seminar. Save as **90c-d3**.

NATIONAL
ASSOCIATION OF
INFORMATION
PROCESSING
PROFESSIONALS

Left tab 3"
Current date   ↓
                4

Mr. Richard Harrison
Jobs-OnLine, Inc.
7490 Oregon Avenue
Arvada, CO 80002-8765 DS

Dear Mr. Harrison
                DS

Please consider this personal invitation to join the National Association of Information
Processing Professionals (NAIPP). Membership is offered to the top 25 percent of the
graduating class. NAIPP is a nonprofit organization comprised of technical
professionals who are striving to stay current in their field. Member benefits include:
                                                                              DS

Career Development Opportunities—Resume preparation services, job search
program, 120-day internship in many cities, and access to our online job bulletin board.
                                                                              DS

Educational Benefits—Industry Standard Skill Testing and Credentialing, discounts on
continuing education courses at "Curriculum Approved" colleges and universities, and
online recertification programs. DS

Professional Benefits—Discounts on technical publications and computer hardware,
competitive rates for medical and hospitalization insurance, retirement and financial
planning programs, and free international travel services. DS

Sign on to our Web site at http://www.naipp.org to learn more about our organization.
Enclosed is a parking pass for the Multimedia Symposium on February 27.
                                                                    DS

                        Sincerely ↓
                                  4

                        Lorraine Beasly, President
                        NAIPP Board of Directors
                                                DS

LB:xx
     DS
Enclosure
       DS
c Adam Learner

Central University Foundation
Operational Budget for Unrestricted Funds
For Fiscal Year 200-

Estimated Revenues

Investment income	$1,025,000	
Annual fund—unrestricted portion	485,000	
Unrestricted gifts	1,275,500	
Unrestricted endowment income	487,300	
Endowment assessment income	1,720,000	
Total Revenues		$4,992,800

Projected Expenditures

Academic Expenditures

Scholarships	$1,075,325	
Graduate fellowships	448,950	
Distinguished professor supplements	484,975	
Administrative officer supplements	135,000	
Faculty research awards	25,000	
Faculty teaching awards	25,000	
Graduate and undergraduate student awards	25,000	
Faculty recruitment and retention	1,050,000	
Total Academic Expenditures		$3,269,250

Fundraising and Marketing Expenditures

Marketing	$145,000	
Gift acquisition and announcement costs	85,000	
Fundraising support	260,725	
Total Fundraising and Marketing Expenditures		$490,725

Operational Expenditures

Foundation operations	$775,250	
Board expenditures	35,000	
Total Operational Expenditures		$810,250
Total Projected Expenditures		$4,570,225
Excess Revenues over Expenditures[1]		$422,575

[1] Excess revenues are available as contingencies for this budget year. If they are not needed, excess revenues are added to the reserves for future use.

35c-d1
Modified Block Letter

1. Open a new document; set a left tab at 3". Insert the date at the top of the page at the tab. Key the letter on the previous page in modified block format. After keying the enclosure notation, strike ENTER twice and set a left tab at .5"; then key the copy notation.

2. Center vertically. Save as **35c-d1**, preview, and print.

35c-d2
Modified Block Letter

1. Add your reference initials and a copy notation to your instructor.

2. Proofread carefully, save the letter as **35c-d2**, and print.

Current date ↓4

Ms. Ana Gonzalez
One-Stop Printing Co.
501 Madison Road
Cincinnati, OH 45227-6398

Dear Ms. Gonzalez

Do you know that more and more people are opting to go on a shopping spree on the Internet rather than the mall? Businesses, ranging from small mom and pop stores to global multinational corporations, are setting up shop on the Web if they haven't already. They are selling goods, services, and themselves!

Consumers expect businesses to have a Web site. Those that don't will give their business to their competitor.

E-Business, Inc. has helped hundreds of businesses nationwide establish their business on the Internet. May we help you integrate your online and offline sales strategies? Call us today at 800-555-0100 and arrange for one of our consultants to analyze your e-commerce strategies to increase your volume. ↓2

Sincerely yours ↓4

Ellen Soey
Marketing Manager ↓2

35c-d3
Modified Block Letter

Key the letter in modified block format; center vertically. Save, preview before printing, and print.

	words
Current date | Dr. Burtram M. Decker | 800 Barbour Ave. |	10
Birmingham, AL 35208-5333 | Dear Dr. Decker	19
The Community Growth Committee offers you its sincere	30
thanks for taking an active part in the sixth annual Youth	41
Fair. We especially appreciate your help in judging the	53
Youth of Birmingham Speaks portion of the fair and for	64
contributing to the prize bank.	70
Participation of community leaders such as you makes this	81
event the annual success it has become. We sincerely hope	93
we can seek your help again next year.	101
Cordially | Grace Beebe Hunt | Secretary | HNJ:xx	110

Budget

SKILLBUILDING

90a
Warmup
Key each line twice SS.

alphabet 1 A huge crowd went from Jackson Square to the lively Plaza by six.

fig/sym 2 Our meal was very expensive—$137.95 + 18% tip ($24.85) = $162.80.

direct reaches 3 Celia and June are great friends who swam long hours for my team.

fluency 4 Jamale may own the bicycle, but a neighbor owns the antique auto.

| 1 | 2 | 3 | 4 | 5 | 6 | 7 | 8 | 9 | 10 | 11 | 12 | 13 |

90b
Technique Builder
Key each set of lines 3 times;
DS between 9-line groups;
work at a controlled rate.

direct reaches 5 red much brief hunt bred zany check jump decrease music many brat

6 polo excel munch brake junk swim wreck lunch curve kick dazed bed

7 Cec and Kim enjoy a great hunting trip in June after school ends.

adjacent reaches 8 were guy sad junior tree trio fast point rest joint walk gas join

9 opt crew going port backlog poster web suit few folder buy porter

10 Porter saw two important guys after we walked past Union Station.

double letters 11 bell look deed glass upper inn odd committee cabbage effect inner

12 add spell pool happy jazz mass scurry connect office fall setting

13 Debbie Desselle called a committee meeting at noon at the office.

| 1 | 2 | 3 | 4 | 5 | 6 | 7 | 8 | 9 | 10 | 11 | 12 | 13 |

APPLICATIONS

90c-d1
Operational Budget

Budgets are financial documents used to ensure that expenditures do not exceed the money available for a company or organization's operations. Budgets may be for the whole organization, for a department, or for a specific project or event. The budget illustrated for this activity is the budget for the year for the operation of a university foundation. Unrestricted money refers to money that the foundation can spend as its board of directors determines. Restricted money is spent according to the gift agreement of a donor.

1. Key the document shown on p. 355 using the format illustrated.
2. Center the heading at about 1" and use 14-point bold font.
3. Set the following tabs: .25" left tab, 4.5" right tab, and 6" right tab.
4. Use capitalization, underlining, and bold as illustrated.
5. Add a page border to the document.
6. Save as **90c-d1** and print.

36a
Warmup
Key each line twice SS.

alphabetic	1	Perhaps Max realized jet flights can quickly whisk us to Bolivia.
fig/sym	2	Send 24 Solex Cubes, Catalog #95-0, price $6.78, before April 31.
1st finger	3	The boy of just 6 or 7 years of age ran through the mango groves.
easy	4	The auditor did sign the form and name me to chair a small panel.

| 1 | 2 | 3 | 4 | 5 | 6 | 7 | 8 | 9 | 10 | 11 | 12 | 13 |

36b
Review Letter Parts
Arrange the letter parts correctly for a modified block letter. Ignore top margin requirements. Press ENTER five times between activities.

1 Sincerely yours | Manuel Garcia | Council President | MG:xx | c Ron N. Besbit

2 Yours truly | Ms. Loren Lakes | Secretary General | xx | Enclosure | c Libby Uhl

3 Ms. Mara Pena | 8764 Gold Plaza | Lansing, MI 48933-8312 | Dear Ms. Pena

36c

Modifying Tabs

Tabs can be added or moved in existing documents. When adding tabs to an existing document, you must first select all portions of the document where the new tab(s) will be applied; then set the additional tab(s). When moving a tab, first select all the text that will be affected. If you fail to select all the text, then only the tab that your cursor is on will be moved.

DRILL 1   ADDING TAB TO EXISTING DOCUMENT

1. Open **33e-d1**.

2. Select the entire letter by clicking the **Edit** menu and choosing **Select All**.

3. Set a left tab at 3.0".

4. Tab the appropriate lines to format this letter in modified block letter format.

5. Save as **36c-drill1**. Leave the document on the screen.

DRILL 2   MOVING A TAB

1. **36c-drill1** should still be displayed on the screen.

2. Select the entire letter (**Edit, Select All**).

3. Drag the tab on the ruler from 3.0" to 3.25".

4. Save as **36c-drill2**.

Pat's Promotions, Inc.
Balance Sheet
As of December 31, 200-

Assets

4" right tab

Current Assets

.25"—
left
tab

Cash and equivalents	$326,175	
Receivables	198,403	
Inventory	283,476	
Prepaid expenses	102,964	
Total Current Assets		$911,018

5.75" right tab

Long-Term Assets

Building and equipment (depreciated)	$209,685	
Furniture and fixtures	117,482	
Total Long-Term Assets		$327,167

Total Assets	$1,238,185

Liabilities and Equity

Current Liabilities

Accounts payable	$158,964	
Short-term debt	84,623	
Accrued expenses	42,701	
Total Current Liabilities		$286,288

Long-Term Liabilities

Long-term debt	$103,728	
Other liabilities	98,605	
Total Long-Term Liabilities		$202,333

Total Liabilities	$488,621

Equity

Owner's equity	$390,476	
Retained earnings	359,088	
Total Equity		$749,564

Total Liabilities and Equity	$1,238,185

36d-d1 and 36d-d2
Modified-Block Letter and
Envelopes

1. Format the letter in modified block format. Insert the current date at 2.1".
2. Supply the correct salutation, a complimentary closing, and your reference initials. Add an enclosure line and a copy notation to **Laura Aimes, Sales Representative**.
3. Proofread carefully. Preview for good placement. Save as **36d-d1**. Print.
4. Attach an envelope to the letter, and save it again as **36d-d2**.

Ms. Mukta Bhakta
9845 Buckingham Road
Annapolis, MD 21403-0314

Thank you for your recent inquiry on our electronic bulletin service. The ABC BBS is an interactive online service developed by All Business Communication to assist the online community in receiving documents via the Internet.

All Business Communication also provides a *Customer Support Service* and a *Technical Support Team* to assist bulletin board users. The Systems Administrators will perform various procedures needed to help you take full advantage of this new software.

For additional information call:

Customer and Technical Support
Telephone: 900-555-0112
9:00 a.m.-5:00 p.m., Monday-Friday, Eastern Time

Please look over the enclosed ABC BBS brochure. I will call you within the next two weeks to discuss any additional questions you may have.

Alex Zampich, Marketing Manager

36d-d3
Memo with Tab

1. Key the following memo in correct format (see Lesson 31).
2. After keying the second paragraph, strike ENTER twice. Set a tab at 2.5", and key the last several lines. Save the document as **36d-d3**.

TO:	All Sunwood Employees
FROM:	Julie Patel, Human Relations
DATE:	Current date
SUBJECT:	Eric Kershaw Hospitalized

We were notified by Eric Kershaw's family that he was admitted into the hospital this past weekend. They expect that he will be hospitalized for another ten days. Visitations and phone calls are limited, but cards and notes are welcome.

A plant is being sent to Eric from the Sunwood staff. Stop by our office before Wednesday if you wish to sign the card. If you would like to send your own "Get Well Wishes" to Eric, send them to:

Left tab 2.5" ———— Eric Kershaw
County General Hospital
Room 401
Atlanta, GA 38209-4751

89b-d3
Balance Sheet

Financial documents are used to show the financial condition of a business. Common financial documents include the balance sheet, income statement, and statement of cash flows. Financial statements can be formatted as a document using tabs to position columns of numbers, as a table, or as a spreadsheet. In this lesson, a balance sheet and an income statement are illustrated. Both of these documents are formatted by setting tabs. Different businesses vary the entries that are capitalized and the use of bold. Within a business, the format used for financial documents should be consistent.

1. Key the document shown on p. 353 using the format illustrated.
2. Center the heading using 14-point bold font.
3. Set the following tabs: .25" left tab, 4" right tab, and a 5.75" right tab.
4. Use capitalization, underlining, and bold as illustrated.
5. Add a page border to the document.
6. Save as **89b-d3** and print.

89b-d4
Balance Sheet

1. Use the same format and all headings as in **89b-d3** to prepare a balance sheet for The Pet Place as of December 31, 200-.
2. Substitute the following numbers for the various categories; total the amounts to determine the figures to be shown in the second column of the balance sheet.

Cash and equivalents	$125,000
Receivables	102,450
Inventory	150,975
Prepaid expenses	58,932
Building and equipment (depreciated)	183,206
Furniture and fixtures	98,065
Accounts payable	92,351
Short-term debt	23,074
Accrued expenses	18,649
Long-term debt	46,824
Other liabilities	12,706
Owner's equity	285,014
Retained earnings	240,010

3. Proofread all numbers carefully, print, and save as **89b-d4**.

36d-d4
Rough-Draft Letter
Block Format

1. Key the following letter in block format. Apply what you have learned about correct letter placement and letter parts.
2. Save the document as **36d-d4**, and print one copy.

Mr. John Crane
5760 Sky Way
Seattle, WA *05671-0321*

Would you like to invest in a company that will provide you with a 180% return on your investment? Consider investing in a ~~company~~ *firm* that specializes in importing and exporting with China. China's *gross* domestic product (GDP) is expected to be over a trillion dollars.

(bold & italic)
Ameri-Chinois has made a significant number of business arrangements with key organizations in China to source goods and to participate in global two-way trade. Trade between China and ~~other countries~~ *the rest of the world* is expected to grow over 20% this year. China's exports are expected to rise to $244 billion in the year 2004. Imports *are expected to* will grow to $207 billion.

Contact Lawrence Chen at Century Investments to learn how you can be an investor in the growing company of Ameri-Chinois. The current price is $0.52; the targeted price is $9.00. Call today! *per share*

800-555-0134

Sincerely

Lawrence Chen

36d-d5
Edit Modified Block Letter

1. Open **36d-d4**; and save it as **36d-d5**. Select the letter address, and then delete it.
2. Address the letter to: **Mr. Tom K. Onehawk, 139 Via Cordoniz, Evansville, IL 44710-3277.** Supply an appropriate salutation.
3. Add **Please study the enclosed portfolio and then** at the beginning of paragraph 3. Be sure to change the *c* in contact to lowercase.
4. Add an enclosure notation.

36d-d6
Move Tab

1. Open **36d-d3**.
2. Select the last four lines of the memo.
3. Move the tab from position 2.5" to 3.0". This moves the last four lines to 3.0".
4. Save as **36d-d6**.

Personal Financial Statement

Luiz C. and Sara R. Cortez
4935 Fifth St.
Dallas, TX 75221-8601

ASSETS

Cash	$ 24,375
Investments	273,287
Home and furnishings	330,500
Other real estate	196,250
Automobiles	62,920
Total Assets	$887,332

LIABILITIES

Credit cards	$ 13,869
Home mortgage	186,374
Other real estate	106,985
Automobile loans	36,425
Total Liabilities	$343,653
NET WORTH	$543,679

37a
Warmup
Key each line twice SS.

alphabetic	1	Johnny Willcox printed five dozen banquet tickets for my meeting.
fig/sym	2	Our check #389 for $21,460—dated 1/15/01—was sent to O'Neil & Co.
1st finger	3	It is true Greg acted bravely during the severe storm that night.
easy	4	In the land of enchantment, the fox and the lamb lie by the bush.

| 1 | 2 | 3 | 4 | 5 | 6 | 7 | 8 | 9 | 10 | 11 | 12 | 13 |

37b
Timed Writings
Take two 3' timings.

  all letters

gwam 3'

Many young people are quite surprised to learn that either lunch or dinner is included as part of a job interview. Most of them think of this part of the interview as a friendly gesture from the organization.

The meal is not provided just to be nice to the person. The organization expects to use that function to observe the social skills of the person and to determine if he or she might be effective doing business in that type of setting.

What does this mean to you if you are preparing for a job interview? The time spent reading about and learning to use good social skills pays off not only during the interview but also after you accept the job.

	4	48
	8	52
	13	56
	15	58
	18	62
	22	66
	27	71
	30	73
	33	77
	38	81
	42	86
	44	87

1' | 1 | 2 | 3 | 4 | 5 | 6 | 7 | 8 | 9 | 10 | 11 | 12 | 13 |
3' | 1 | | 2 | | 3 | | 4 |

37c
Assessment

 Continue button

 Check button

General Instructions: Format the letters in the style indicated; add additional letter parts if necessary. Use the Date and Time feature for the current date. Add a proper salutation and your reference initials for all letters. Position each letter at 2.1". Check spelling, preview for proper placement, and carefully proofread each letter before proceeding to the next document.

With CheckPro: *CheckPro* will keep track of the time it takes you to complete the entire production test, compute your speed and accuracy rate on each document, and summarize the results. When you complete a document, proofread it, check the spelling, and preview for placement. When you are completely satisfied with the document, click the Continue button to move to the next document. You will not be able to return and edit a document once you continue to the next document. Click the **Check** button when you are ready to error-check the test. Review and/or print the document analysis results.

Without CheckPro: On the signal to begin, key the documents in sequence. When saving documents, name them in the usual manner (for example, **37c-d1**). When time has been called, proofread all documents again, identify errors, and determine *g-pwam*.

$$g\text{-}pwam = \frac{\text{total words keyed}}{25'}$$

LESSON 89

Financial Documents

89a
Warmup
Key each line twice SS.

alphabet	1	Zack and Jimmy explored a quaint town and bought five neat gifts.
fig/sym	2	They got discounts (25% and 10%) on gifts priced $1,389 and $476.
adjacent reaches	3	We were going to walk to a new polo field with three junior guys.
fluency	4	Pamela and Jakken may go to town with a neighbor and eight girls.

| 1 | 2 | 3 | 4 | 5 | 6 | 7 | 8 | 9 | 10 | 11 | 12 | 13 |

APPLICATIONS

89b-d1
Personal Financial Statement

A personal financial statement often is used when individuals apply for loans or other types of credit. Financial documents are usually formatted in tabular form with leaders so that the data is easily readable. If the information contained in a financial document is complicated and contains multiple columns, the document may be formatted as a table or a spreadsheet. The financial documents in this lesson are relatively simple and formatted using tabs and leaders.

1. Key the document shown on p. 351 using the format illustrated.

2. Position the main heading at about 2"; center the heading using 16-point bold font; bold the names and address.

3. Set the following tabs: .5" left tab; 3.5" left tab with Leader 2; 4.5" right tab; and a 6" right tab.

4. Use all caps for the three main headings; double-underline the final net worth.

5. Add a page border to the document.

6. Print and save as **89b-d1**.

89b-d2
Personal Financial Statement

Use the following information to prepare a personal financial statement for Hayden S. Robinson, 3549 Woodview Dr., Las Cruces, NM 88012-9367.

1. Include the following assets: checking account, $1,975; savings account, $40,639; automobile, $28,910; apartment furnishings, $7,190; and art collection, $8,240. Show the total amount of assets.

2. Include the following liabilities: credit cards, $1,290; automobile loan, $2,073; college tuition loan, $6,539; and a personal loan, $1,496. Show the total amount of liabilities.

3. Determine the net worth by subtracting the total liabilities from the total assets; double-underline the net worth.

4. Add a page border to the document.

5. Save as **89b-d2** and print.

37c-d1
Enrichment
Block-Format Letter
Supply the salutation.

Current date | AMASTA Company, Inc. | 902 Greenridge Drive | Reno, NV   13
69505-5552   19

We sell your videocassettes and have since you introduced them. Several   33
of our customers now tell us they are unable to follow the directions on the   49
coupon. They explain that there is no company logo on the box to return to   64
you as you requested.   68

What steps should we take? A copy of the coupon is enclosed, as is a   82
Super D Container. Please read the coupon, examine the box, and then let   97
me know your plans for extricating us from this problem.   109

Sincerely yours | John J. Long | Sales Manager | Enclosures: 2   122

37c-d2
Modified-Block Letter
Supply the salutation.

Current date | Mr. John J. Long, Sales Manager | The Record Store | 9822   11
Trevor Avenue | Anaheim, CA 92805-5885   22

With your letter came our turn to be perplexed, and we apologize. When   36
we had our refund coupons printed, we had just completed a total redesign   51
program for our product boxes. We had detachable logos put on the   65
outside of the boxes, which could be peeled off and placed on a coupon.   79

We had not anticipated that our distributors would use back inventories   94
with our promotion. The cassettes you sold were not packaged in our new   108
boxes; therefore, there were no logos on them.   118

I'm sorry you or your customers were inconvenienced. In the future,   131
simply ask your customers to send us their sales slips, and we will honor   146
them with refunds until your supply of older containers is depleted.   160

Sincerely yours | Bruna Wertz | Sales and Promotions Dept. | xx   173

37c-d3
Memo with Distribution List

1. Key the memo to **Continuing Education Committee—Distribution List Below**. It is from **Alberto Valenzuela**; **May Seminar** is the subject line.
2. The distribution list is as follows: **John Patterson, Facilities Manager; Shawna Thompson, Regional Manager; Ed Vandenberg, Advertising Manager**

I have invited Lynda A. Brewer, P.H.D., Earlham   33
College, Richmond, Indiana, to be our seminar   42
leader on Friday afternoon, May 10.   50
    Dr. Brewer, a well-known psychologist who has   59
spent a lot of time researching and writing in the   69
field of ergonomics, will address "Stress Management."   80
    Please make arrangements for rooms, speaker accom-   90
modations, staff notification, and refreshments.   100
I will send you Dr. Brewer's vita for use in pre-   110
paring news releases.   114

closing lines   139

Pat's Catering Service
1947 First Ave.
Olympia, WA 99504-2863
Telephone: (360) 555-0103 Fax: (360) 555-0182

Credit Application

Applicant Information

Full Name: [   ]

Date of Birth: [   ]   Social Security No.: [   ]

Current Residence

Street Address: [   ]

City, State, and ZIP Code: [   ]

Telephone Number: [   ]   E-Mail: [   ]

Ownership Status: Own home   Length of time: Less than 1 year

Monthly Payment/Rent: [   ]

| Own home |
| Rent home |
| Rent apartment |

Previous Residence

Street Address: [   ]

City, State, and ZIP Code: [   ]

Telephone Number: [   ]

Ownership Status: Own home   Length of time: Less than 1 year

Monthly Payment/Rent: [   ]

| Less than 1 year |
| 1-3 years |
| More than 3 years |

Employment Information

Current Employer: [   ]

Employer Street Address: [   ]

City, State, and ZIP Code: [   ]

Telephone Number: [   ]

Position Held: [   ]   Length of Employment: [   ]

Compensation Status: Hourly

Hourly Rate: [   ]   Annual Salary: [   ]

Coapplicant: ☐ Yes ☐ No   If yes, complete a credit application form for coapplicant.

Module 4: Checkpoint

Answer the questions below to see if you have masterd the content of Module 4.

1. A(n) _____ is a form of written communication that is used primarily for internal communication.

2. _____ is a method of transmitting documents and messages via the computer system.

3. If several people are to receive a copy of a memo, key a(n) _____ list at the end of the memo.

4. When a business letter is addressed to a company, the correct salutation is _____.

5. Use 1.25" or _____ side margins for a business letter.

6. Letters are positioned vertically on the page by using the _____ command.

7. When keying a modified block letter, set a tab at the center point of the page, which is _____.

8. When an item is included with a letter, a(n) _____ notation is keyed a DS below the reference initials.

9. Use the _____ menu to create envelopes.

10. The _____ notation is used to indicate that a copy of the letter is being sent to another person.

Performance Assessment

Document 1
Modified Block Letter

1. Use the text at the right to create a modified block letter. Include letter parts as necessary.

2. The letter is to:
   Ms. Sharon Jens
   Western Regional
   Manager
   Acune, Inc.
   5450 Signal Hill Rd.
   Springfield, OH 45504-5440
   The letter is from **Troy Compton**.

Document 2
Memo

1. Key the same message as a memo to **Laura Riedel** from **Troy Compton**. Use the current date and **May Seminar** as the subject line.

2. Add a copy notation to **Jessica Smith**.

The keynote speaker for our annual sales conference this year will be Dr. Helen McBride, from the University of Southern California. She will be giving her opening speech at 2:00 p.m. on Tuesday, May 25, 200–.

Dr. McBride, a well-known psychologist who has spent a lot of time researching and writing on employee productivity, will address "Stress Management." I am sure you will find her speech to be both informative and entertaining.

A copy of Dr. McBride's resume is enclosed for use in preparing news releases and announcements for the sales conference.

88c-d2
Fill-In Form

1. Open the Breakeven Analysis Form you prepared in **88c-d1**. Save it as a *Word* document named **88c-d2**.

2. Complete the form, keying the handwritten data on the form illustrated on p. 347.

3. Resave the document.

88c-d3
Online Form

1. Create the online form shown on p. 349. Use .75" side margins and 1.5 spacing.

2. Use text boxes for all responses except the following:

   a. Ownership status: use three drop-down options—Own home, Rent home, Rent apartment

   b. Length of time: use three drop-down options—Less than 1 year, 1-3 years, More than 3 years

   c. Coapplicant: use checkboxes with Yes and No

3. Add a page border.

4. Protect the form and save it as **88c-d3**.

88c-d4
Fill in Online Form

1. Open **88c-d3** and save it as **88c-d4**.

2. Complete the form using your own information. Do not use your actual social security number; use 000-00-0000. If you do not know the current monthly payment of your residence, use $650 per month.

3. If you are not employed part-time or full-time, use your institution as the employer and an hourly wage of $10 per hour.

4. Resave the completed form.

88c-d5
Fill in Online Form

1. Open **88c-d3** and save it as **88c-d5**.

2. Complete the form for a coapplicant. As coapplicant, select a spouse, a parent, or any other relative. Do not use an actual social security number; use 000-00-0000. If you do not know the current monthly payment of your coapplicant's residence, use $800 per month.

3. If your coapplicant is not employed, use the name of a local bank and a salary of $35,000.

4. Resave the completed form.

Communication Skills 1

Capitalize:

1. **First word of a sentence and of a direct quotation.**

   We were tolerating instead of managing diversity.

   The speaker said, "We must value diversity, not merely recognize it."

2. **Proper nouns**—specific persons, places, or things.

   Common nouns: continent, river, car, street

   Proper nouns: Asia, Mississippi, Buick, State St.

   Exception: Capitalize a title of high distinction even when it does not refer to a specific person (e.g., President of the United States).

3. **Derivatives** of proper nouns and capitalize **geographical** names.

   Derivatives: American history, German food, English accent, Ohio Valley

   Proper nouns: Tampa, Florida, Mount Rushmore

4. **A personal or professional title** when it precedes the name; capitalize a title of high distinction without a name.

   Title: Lieutenant Kahn, Mayor Walsh, Doctor Welby

   High distinction: the President of the United States,

5. **Days of the week, months of the year, holidays, periods of history, and historic events.**

   Monday, June 8, Labor Day, Renaissance

6. **Specific parts of the country** but not compass points that show direction.

   Midwest   the South   northwest of town   the Middle East

7. **Family relationships** when used with a person's name.

   Aunt Carol   my mother   Uncle Mark

8. **A noun preceding a figure** except for common nouns such as line, page, and sentence.

   Unit 1   Section 2   page 2   verse 7   line 2

9. **First and main words of side headings, titles of books, and works of art.**
   Do not capitalize words of four or fewer letters that are conjunctions, prepositions, or articles.

   Computers in the News   *Raiders of the Lost Ark*

10. **Names of organizations and specific departments** within the writer's organization.

    Girl Scouts   our Sales Department

11. **The salutation of a letter and the first word of the complimentary closing.**

    Dear Mr. Bush   Ladies and Gentlemen: Sincerely yours,

    Very cordially yours,

Professional Development Seminars, Inc.
Seminar Breakeven Analysis

Program: Effective Presentations
Number of Days: 2

Fixed Costs:	Amount	Total Costs
Instructor fees	$1,600	
Instructor expenses	150	
Training room/equipment rental	650	
Program marketing material	450	
Advertising and promotional costs	800	
Overhead allocation	400	
Coaches/mentors	400	
Total Fixed Costs:		$ 4,450
Variable Costs:	Per Participant	
Seminar training manual	15	
Meals/breaks	30	
Parking/other fees	5	
Total Variable Costs:	$50 X 10	500
Total Costs		$4,950
Revenue Per Participant:	$495 X 10	$4,950
Breakeven Level:		10

CAPITALIZATION

Review the rules and examples on the previous page. Then key the sentences, correcting all capitalization errors. Number each item and DS between items. Save as **capitalize-drill 1.**

1. according to one study, the largest ethnic minority group online is hispanics.

2. the american author mark twain said, "always do right; this will gratify some people and astonish the rest."

3. the grand canyon was formed by the colorado river cutting into the high-plateau region of northwestern arizona.

4. the president of russia is elected by popular vote.

5. the hubble space telescope is a cooperative project of the european space agency and the national aeronautics and space administration.

6. the train left north station at 6:45 this morning.

7. the trademark cyberprivacy prevention act would make it illegal for individuals to purchase domains solely for resale and profit.

8. consumers spent $7 billion online between november 1 and december 31, 2003, compared to $3.1 billion for the same period in 2002.

9. new students should attend an orientation session on wednesday, august 15, at 8 a.m. in room 252 of the perry building.

10. the summer book list includes *where the red fern grows* and *the mystery of the missing baseball.*

DRILL 2

CAPITALIZATION

1. Open the file **capitalize2** from the data files and save it as **capitalize-drill2.**

2. Follow the specific directions provided in the data file. Remember to use the correct proofreaders' marks:

☰	Capitalize	sincerely	
lc	Lowercase	My Ðear Sir	

3. Resave and print. Submit the rough draft and final copy to your instructor.

DRILL 3

CAPITALIZATION OF LETTER PARTS

Key the letter parts using correct capitalization. Number each item and DS between each. Save as **capitalize-drill3.**

1. dear mr. petroilli
2. ladies and gentlemen
3. dear senator kuknais
4. very sincerely yours
5. dear reverend Schmidt
6. very truly yours
7. cordially yours
8. dear mr fong and miss landow
9. respectfully yours
10. sincerely
11. dear mr. and mrs. Green
12. dear service manager

DRILL 4

CAPITALIZATION

1. Open the file **capitalize4** from the data files. Save it as **capitalize-drill4.**

2. This file includes a field for selecting the correct answer. You will simply select the correct answer. Follow the specific directions provided in the data file.

3. Resave and print.

LESSON 88

Custom Forms

SKILLBUILDING

88a
Warmup
Key each line twice SS.

alphabet	1	Mickey bought six lavender azaleas and quite a few nice junipers.
figures	2	We gave a 15% discount on 3 invoices (#28574, #6973, and #12095).
shift key	3	Li, Jan, Al, and Carl went with Rod, Kay, and Oki to see Big Sky.
fluency	4	Jan and six girls may go to the lake to sit on the dock and fish.

| 1 | 2 | 3 | 4 | 5 | 6 | 7 | 8 | 9 | 10 | 11 | 12 | 13 |

88b
Timed Writings
1. Key two 3' writings.
2. Work for speed.

	gwam	1'	3'
Forms provide both a productive and an effective way to col-		12	4
lect data. Designing an effective form often is not accomplished		25	8
quickly, but the time spent can be justified easily. Creating a		38	13
form is productive because once the form is finished, it can be		51	17
used multiple times. Forms provide an effective way of collecting		64	21
data because they add structure. A form can be set up so that		77	26
the data is organized in exactly the way the designer wants to		89	30
collect it. Analyzing data can be simplified by the way the form		103	34
is structured. Online forms can even be designed to tabulate the		116	39
answers as they are entered.		121	40

1' | 1 | 2 | 3 | 4 | 5 | 6 | 7 | 8 | 9 | 10 | 11 | 12 | 13 |
3' | 1 | 2 | 3 | 4 |

APPLICATIONS

88c-d1
Breakeven Analysis Form

Custom forms are forms that are tailored to the specific needs of a business or an individual. Prepare the form illustrated on the next page that can be used to determine how many seminar participants must be enrolled in a program for it to break even. Note that fixed costs are expenditures that must be made regardless of the number of participants. Variable costs are dependent on the number of people enrolled in the program. Use a table to simplify the design of this form. Note that the blank lines in the form are available for special costs that might apply to some programs but not others.

1. Key the form on p. 347 as shown. Do not key the handwritten data shown filled in on the form.

2. Use Save As to save the form as a template named *Breakeven Analysis Form*. Click **Document Template** in the Save as type box.

File name:	Breakeven Analysis Form.dot		Save
Save as type:	Document Template (*.dot)		Cancel

Skill Builders 3

Skill Builder Lesson A

1. Open *Keyboarding Pro*, Skill Builder module. The Skill Builder section includes 20 lessons of increasing difficulty that will help you build keying speed and improve control.

2. You can choose to emphasize speed or accuracy as you complete a lesson. Choose **Speed**. Click on the Emphasis displayed at the bottom of the Lesson menu to toggle between Speed and Accuracy. (Not available if preferences are locked.) Or use the Preferences option before you choose a lesson to change the emphasis (choose **Edit** from the menu bar).

3. Complete Lesson A, or the first lesson that you have not completed. A red check mark will display to the left of any lesson completed.

4. Print your Lesson Report if requested by your instructor.

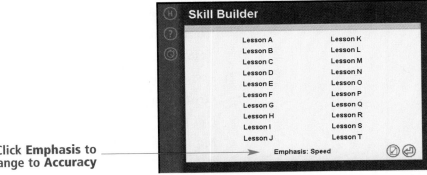

Click **Emphasis** to change to **Accuracy**

DRILL 1

SKILL TRANSFER PARAGRAPHS

1. Key a 1' writing on each paragraph. Compare your *gwam*. Type additional 1' writings on the slower timing.

2. Repeat these steps for 2'.

   To save timings in the Open Screen, use a filename that identifies the timing such as **xx-sb3-drill1-t1** (your initials, Skill Builder 3 Drill1-Timing1).

	gwam	1'	3'

There are many qualities which cause good employees to stand — 12 | 6
out in a group. In the first place, they keep their minds on the — 25 | 13
task at hand. Also, they often think about the work they do and — 38 | 19
how it relates to the total efforts of the project. They keep — 52 | 26
their eyes, ears, and minds open to new ideas. — 60 | 30

Second, good workers may be classed as those who work at a — 13 | 6
steady pace. Far too many people, work by fits and pieces. They — 25 | 13
begin one thing, but then they allow themselves to be easily taken — 39 | 19
away from the work at hand. At lot of people are good starters, — 52 | 26
but many less of them are also good finishers. — 60 | 30

1'	1	2	3	4	5	6	7	8	9	10	11	12	13
3'		1			2			3			4		

87c-d3
Online Form

1. Open **87c-d2** and save it as **87c-d3**.
2. Fill in the form using your last name + *Associates* as the company name. Use your address, telephone, and e-mail address.
3. Register as an individual using American Express, card number: 0000-000000-00000; Expiration: 10/07; and your name.
4. Resave the document.

87c-d4
Fill-In Form

Prepare a hotel reservation form that Professional Development Seminars, Inc. can use to mail to seminar participants in all seminars or group meetings held at The Inn at Central University.

1. Use the following heading information:

   The Inn at Central University

   1483 Pickens Street

   Columbia, SC 29201-7459

   Telephone: (803) 555-0193 Fax: (803) 555-0148

2. DS; set tabs to position information appropriately; add lines to fill in information:

   Group/Seminar:

   Name:

   Mailing Address:

   City: State: ZIP Code:

   Telephone: E-Mail:

   Arrival Date: Time:

   Departure Date: Time:

   Occupancy: ☐ $145 Double Room   ☐ $125 Single Room

   Room Type: ☐ Double beds   ☐ Queen bed   ☐ King bed

   Options: ☐ Nonsmoking   ☐ Smoking

   Share with:

3. Add same credit card information as used in **87c-d1**.
4. Save the form as **87c-d4**.

87c-d5
Online Form

1. Use the information in **87c-d4** to create an online hotel reservation form.
2. DS; use drop-down boxes for room information and credit card choice; add borders to text fields; move single rooms first in drop-down list.
3. Protect the form and save it as **87c-d5**.

Skill Builder Lesson B

1. Open *Keyboarding Pro*, Skill Builder module. Complete Lesson B with Speed Emphasis. If you have already completed Lesson B, go on to the next uncompleted lesson.

2. Print your Lesson Report if requested by your instructor.

DRILL 2

BALANCED-HAND COMBINATIONS

Practice the reaches for fluency.

```
1  to today stocks into ti times sitting until ur urges further tour
2  en entire trend dozen or order support editor nd and mandate land
3  he healthy check ache th these brother both an annual change plan
4  nt into continue want of office softer roof is issue poison basis

5  My brother urged the editor to have an annual health check today.
6  The manager will support the change to order our stock annually.
7  The time for the land tour will not change until further notice.
8  Did the letter mention her position or performance in the office?
```

| 1 | 2 | 3 | 4 | 5 | 6 | 7 | 8 | 9 | 10 | 11 | 12 | 13 |

DRILL 3

SKILL TRANSFER PARAGRAPHS

Follow the directions for Drill 2 on p. 124.

To save timings, use a filename that identifies the timing such as **xx-sb3-drill3-t1** (your initials, Skill Builder 3 Drill3-Timing1).

	gwam	1'	3'

Most of us, at some time, have had a valid reason to complain— 12 | 6

about a defective product, poor service, or perhaps being tired of 26 | 13

talking to voice mail. Many of us feel that complaining, however, 39 | 20

to a firm is an exercise in futility and don't bother to express 52 | 26

our dissatisfaction. We just write it off to experience and 64 | 32

continue to be ripped off. 70 | 35

Today more than at any time in the past consumers are taking some 12 | 6

steps to let their feelings be known—and with a great amount of 25 | 13

success. As a result, firms are becoming more responsive to 38 | 19

the needs of the consumer. complaints from customers alert firms 51 | 26

to produce or service defect and there by cause action to be taken 65 | 33

for their benefit. 70 | 35

| 1' | 1 | 2 | 3 | 4 | 5 | 6 | 7 | 8 | 9 | 10 | 11 | 12 | 13 |
| 3' | | 1 | | | 2 | | | 3 | | | 4 | | |

Professional Development Seminars, Inc.
Planning and Conducting Effective Meetings

April 28-30, 200-
The Inn at Central University
Columbia, SC 29201-7459

Company/Organization Name: _____

Mailing Address: _____

City: _____   ZIP Code: _____

First Team Member

Name: _____

Telephone: _____   E-Mail: _____

Second Team Member

Name: _____

Telephone: _____   E-Mail: _____

Third Team Member

Name: _____

Telephone: _____   E-Mail: _____

Seminar Registration Fees: Team of Three: $850

☐ Charge my: MasterCard

Individual:	$350
Team of Two:	$600
Team of Three:	$850

Card Number: _____

Expiration Date: _____

Name as it appears on card: _____

MasterCard
Visa
American Express

Skill Builder Lesson C

1. Open *Keyboarding Pro*, Skill Builder module. Complete Lesson C with the Speed Emphasis. If you have already completed Lesson C, go on to the next uncompleted lesson.
2. Print your Lesson Report if requested by your instructor.

DRILL 4

BALANCED-HAND COMBINATIONS
Practice the reaches for fluency.

1 an anyone brand spans th their father eighth he head sheets niche
2 en enters depends been nd end handle fund or original sport color
3 ur urban turns assure to took factory photo ti titles satin still
4 ic ice bicycle chic it item position profit ng angle danger doing

5 I want the info in the file on the profits from the chic bicycle.
6 The original of the color photo she took of the factory is there.
7 Assure them that anyone can turn onto the road to the urban area.
8 The color of the title sheet depends on the photos and the funds.

| 1 | 2 | 3 | 4 | 5 | 6 | 7 | 8 | 9 | 10 | 11 | 12 | 13 |

DRILL 5

TIMED WRITING
1. Take a 1' writing on each ¶.
2. Take a 3' writing on both ¶s.

Option: Key the timing as a Diagnostic Writing in *Keyboarding Pro 4* or from *MicroPace Pro:*

Filename **SB3-T5**

	gwam	1'	3'

Practicing basic health rules will result in good body condi- 12 4
tion. Proper diet is a way to achieve good health. Eat a variety 26 9
of foods each day, including some fruit, vegetables, cereal pro- 38 13
ducts, and foods rich in protein, to be sure that you keep a bal- 51 17
ance. Another part of a good health plan is physical activity, 64 21
such as running. 67 22

Running has become popular in this country. A long run is a 12 27
big challenge to many males and females to determine just how far 26 31
they can go in a given time, or the time they require to cover a 38 35
measured distance. Long runs of fifty or one hundred miles are on 52 40
measured courses with refreshments available every few miles. 64 44
Daily training is necessary in order to maximize endurance. 76 48

1' | 1 | 2 | 3 | 4 | 5 | 6 | 7 | 8 | 9 | 10 | 11 | 12 | 13 |
3' | | 1 | | 2 | | 3 | | 4 |

Professional Development Seminars, Inc.
Planning and Conducting Effective Meetings

April 28-30, 200-
The Inn at Central University
Columbia, SC 29201-7459

6.75" right
underline tab

Company/Organization Name:_____

Mailing Address: _____

_____

First Team Member

Name:_____

Telephone: _____ E-Mail _____

3.5" left underline tab

Second Team Member

Name:_____

Telephone: _____ E-Mail _____

Third Team Member

Name:_____

Telephone: _____E-Mail _____

Seminar Registration Fees:

5" left tab

Individual: $350; Team of Two: $600; Team of Three: $850 $ _____

☐ Check or purchase order payable to PDS, Inc. is enclosed.   PO# _____

Charge my ☐ MasterCard ☐ Visa ☐ American Express

Card Number: _____Expiration Date_____

Print name as it appears on card _____

Mail or fax to: Ms. Jennifer Jameson   Fax: (803) 555-0178
                       Professional Development Seminars, Inc.
                       P.O. Box 3947
                       Columbia, SC 29201-3947

1.5" left tab

Skill Builder Lesson D

1. Open *Keyboarding Pro*, Skill Builder module. Complete Lesson D with the Speed Emphasis.

2. Print your Lesson Report if requested by your instructor.

DRILL 6

ADJACENT KEY REVIEW

Key each row once; strive for accuracy. Repeat.

1 nm many enmity solemn kl inkling weekly pickle oi oil invoice join
2 iu stadium medium genius lk milk talk walks uy buy buyer soliloquy
3 mn alumni hymn number column sd Thursday wisdom df mindful handful
4 me mention comment same fo found perform info le letter flew files

5 The buyer sent his weekly invoices for oil to the group on Thursday.
6 Mindful of the alumni, the choirs sang a hymn prior to my soliloquy.
7 An inmate, a fogger, and a genius joined the weekly talks on Monday.
8 They were to join in the talk shows to assess regions of the Yukon.

| 1 | 2 | 3 | 4 | 5 | 6 | 7 | 8 | 9 | 10 | 11 | 12 | 13 |

DRILL 7

TIMED WRITINGS

1. Take a 1' writing on each ¶.
2. Take a 3' writing on both ¶s.

Option: Key the timing as a Diagnostic Writing in *Keyboarding Pro 4* or from *MicroPace Pro:*

Filename SB3-T7

gwam 1' | 3'

All people, in spite of their eating habits, have two major 12 | 4
needs that must be met by their food. They need food that 24 | 8
provides a source of energy, and they need food that will fill 37 | 12
the skeletal and operating needs of their bodies. Carbohydrates, 50 | 17
fats, and protein form a major portion of the diet. Vitamins and 63 | 21
minerals are also necessary for excellent health. 72 | 24

Carbohydrates make up a major source of our energy needs. 12 | 28
Fats also serve as a source of energy and act as defense against 25 | 32
cold and trauma. Proteins are changed to amino acids, which are 38 | 37
the building units of the body. These, in turn, are utilized to 51 | 41
make most body tissue. Minerals are required to control many 64 | 46
body functions, and vitamins are used for normal growth and aid 78 | 50
against disease. 79 | 51

1' | 1 | 2 | 3 | 4 | 5 | 6 | 7 | 8 | 9 | 10 | 11 | 12 | 13 |
3' | 1 | 2 | 3 | 4 |

SKILLBUILDING

87a
Warmup
Key each line twice SS.

alphabet	1	Jack Meyer analyzed the data by answering five complex questions.
fig/sym	2	On May 15, my ZIP Code will change from 23989-4016 to 23643-8705.
1st/2nd fingers	3	June Hunter may try to give Trudy a new multicolored kite to fly.
fluency	4	Pamela may risk half of the profit they make to bid on an island.

| 1 | 2 | 3 | 4 | 5 | 6 | 7 | 8 | 9 | 10 | 11 | 12 | 13 |

DOCUMENT DESIGN

87b

Online and Fill-In Forms

Both online forms and handwritten fill-in forms are used for a variety of purposes. Common uses of forms include registration and reservations for various events. A form may be distributed online, in printed materials, or it may be filled in by hand at the site of the event.

APPLICATIONS

87c-d1
Fill-In Form

1. Prepare the fill-in form illustrated on p. 343.
2. Set margins: Top: 1"; Right, Left, and Bottom: .75".
3. DS the fill-in portion of the form to allow room for handwriting.
4. *Tip:* After keying the fields for the first team member, copy them for the second and third team members.
5. Check to ensure that the form fits on one page; add a page border.
6. Save the form as **87c-d1**.

87c-d2
Online Form

1. Prepare the same form as an online form; see illustration on p. 344.
2. Use default margins for the online form.
3. *Tip:* After keying the fields for the first team member, copy them for the second and third team members.
4. Note that the option to pay by check or purchase order has been deleted.
5. After you prepare the form, select and add borders to each text box; then add a page border.
6. Protect the form and save it as **87c-d2**. (For *Word 2002*, use the password *pcem*.)

Skill Builder Lesson E

1. Open *Keyboarding Pro*, Skill Builder module. Complete Lesson E with the Speed Emphasis.
2. Print your Lesson Report if requested by your instructor.
3. Complete the Skill Builder lessons on your own or as directed by your instructor.

DRILL 8

WORD BEGINNINGS

In the Open Screen, key each row once; strive for accuracy. Repeat.

br
1 bright brown bramble bread breath breezes brought brother broiler
2 In February my brother brought brown bread and beans from Boston.

exe
3 exercises exert executives exemplify exemption executed exemplary
4 They exert extreme effort executing exercises in exemplary style.

bt
5 doubt subtle obtains obtrusion subtracts indebtedness undoubtedly
6 Extreme debt will cause more than subtle doubt among my creditors.

ny
7 tiny funny company nymph penny nylon many anyone phony any brainy
8 Anyone as brainy and funny as Penny is an asset to their company.

| 1 | 2 | 3 | 4 | 5 | 6 | 7 | 8 | 9 | 10 | 11 | 12 | 13 |

DRILL 9

TIMED WRITINGS

1. Take a 1' writing on each ¶.
2. Take a 3' writing on both ¶s.

Option: Key the timing as a Diagnostic Writing in *Keyboarding Pro 4* or from *MicroPace Pro:*

Filename **SB3-T9**

	gwam	1'	3'

Many people believe that an ounce of prevention is worth a   12 | 4
pound of cure. Care of your heart can help you prevent serious   25 | 8
physical problems. The human heart is the most important pump ever   38 | 13
developed. It constantly pushes blood through the body tissues.   51 | 17
But the layers of muscle that make up the heart must be kept in   64 | 23
proper working order. Exercise can help this muscle to remain in   77 | 26
good condition.   84 | 27

Another important way of keeping a healthy heart is just to   12 | 31
avoid habits which are considered detrimental to the body. Food   25 | 35
that is high in cholesterol is not a good choice. Also, use of   38 | 39
tobacco has quite a bad effect on the function of the heart. You   51 | 44
can minimize your chances of heart trouble by avoiding these bad   64 | 48
health habits.   67 | 49

1' | 1 | 2 | 3 | 4 | 5 | 6 | 7 | 8 | 9 | 10 | 11 | 12 | 13 |
3' | 1 | 2 | 3 | 4 |

86d-d1
Create and Protect
a Sales Form

1. Key **Weekly Flower Sales** in bold, 14 point at the top of the page. Press ENTER twice.

2. Create a table with three columns and 15 rows.

3. Key the following column headings in bold.

    Flowers   Number Ordered   Delivery Complete

4. Insert a **Drop-Down Form Field** box in cell A2 below the *Flowers* heading.

5. Key the following six choices in the Drop-down box: **Aster**, **Daisy**, **Gladiola**, **Iris**, **Orchid**, **Rose**. Copy this field to the 13 other cells in the first column.

6. Insert a **Text Form Field** in cell B2 below the *Number Ordered* heading. Copy this field to the 13 other cells in the second column.

7. Insert a **Check Box Form Field** in cell B3 below the *Delivery Complete* heading.

8. Copy this field to the 13 other cells in the third column.

9. Protect the form and save it as **86d-d1**.

86d-d2
Fill in Sales Form

1. Open **86d-d1**. Protect the form document using the password *flowers*.

2. Fill in the form using the following information. If the delivery is complete, place an *X* in the form. Save as **86d-d2**.

    | Iris | 112 | delivered |
    | Rose | 204 | delivered |
    | Orchid | 97 | not delivered |

86d-d3
E-Mail Form

1. Open **86d-d2**. Unprotect the form.

2. Reset, reprotect, and save the form as **86d-d3**.

3. Distribute an online copy of **86d-d3** to your instructor.

86d-d4
Handwritten Fill-In Form

1. Prepare the following form that will be handed out to students attending a basketball game. Set underline tab at 6" right, 3" right, and 4" left; 2" top margin; 14-point bold heading; DS.

2. Save the document as **86d-d4**.

Drawing for $1,000 Scholarship Given by Athletics Department

Name _____

Telephone_____

Address _____

City _____State_____ZIP Code _____

Simple Reports

- Format two-page reports with references and title pages.
- Indent long quotations and bibliography entries appropriately.
- Insert page numbers.
- Apply bullets and numbers.
- Insert and edit footnotes.

LESSON 38 — Skillbuilding and Report Basics

SKILLBUILDING

38a
Warmup
Key each line twice SS.

alphabetic 1 Dave Cagney alphabetized items for next week's quarterly journal.
figures 2 Close Rooms 4, 18, and 20 from 3 until 9 on July 7; open Room 56.
up reaches 3 Toy & Wurt's note for $635 (see our page 78) was paid October 29.
easy 4 The auditor is due by eight, and he may lend a hand to the panel.

| 1 | 2 | 3 | 4 | 5 | 6 | 7 | 8 | 9 | 10 | 11 | 12 | 13 |

38b
Timed Writings
Take two 3' timings.

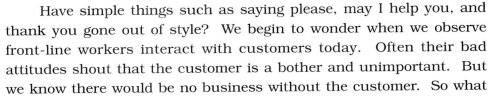
all letters

gwam 1' | 3'

Have simple things such as saying please, may I help you, and 12 | 4
thank you gone out of style? We begin to wonder when we observe 25 | 8
front-line workers interact with customers today. Often their bad 39 | 13
attitudes shout that the customer is a bother and unimportant. But 52 | 17
we know there would be no business without the customer. So what 66 | 22
can be done to prove to customers that they really are the king? 79 | 26

First, require that all your staff train in good customer 12 | 30
service. Here they must come to realize that their jobs exist for 25 | 35
the customer. Also, be sure workers feel that they can talk to 38 | 39
their bosses about any problem. You do not want workers to talk 51 | 43
about lack of breaks or schedules in front of customers. Clients 64 | 48
must always feel that they are kings and should never be ignored. 77 | 52

1' | 1 | 2 | 3 | 4 | 5 | 6 | 7 | 8 | 9 | 10 | 11 | 12 | 13 |
3' | 1 | 2 | 3 | 4 |

To protect a form:

1. Click **Protect Document** on the Tools menu to protect (lock) the document so that the user cannot alter the text or fields.

2. Select the **Forms** radio button in the Protect Document dialog box if not selected.

3. For *Word 2002*, key a password in the Password (optional) field. You will be asked to key the password a second time. If you do not add a password, the user will be able to change the document.

4. For *Word 2002*, to unprotect the form document later, choose **Tools, Unprotect Document**, and key the password.

TIP

The password is case-sensitive and must be keyed exactly as it was entered when the form was locked.

DRILL 7   **PROTECTING THE DOCUMENT**

1. Open **86c-drill6**.

2. Protect the document (**Tools, Protect Document**).

3. Click the **Forms** radio button if necessary and key the password **locked**.

4. Save as **86c-drill7**.

Distributing and Using Forms

When you make your form available for others to use, it is called **distributing the form**. The forms that you create in *Word* are designed to be filled in onscreen and can be used by anyone who has *Word* available. Send the form using any method that you normally use to send someone a file. You may physically send the file saved on a disk, save the file in a shared workplace, or e-mail it as an attachment. When the receiver opens the file in *Word*, information can be filled in and printed or returned to you.

In most cases, to use a form template, open it from the General tab in the Templates dialog box that is accessible from the Task Pane.

Word 2002

New from template

85c form

VanHuss Fax

General Templates...

Word 2003

Since you may have saved your templates in your working folder location, the template will not appear in the Templates dialog box.

To use a form that you receive:

1. Check to be sure that the Files of type field shows either All Files or Document Templates in the Open dialog box.

2. Open the form's template file from the list of files.

3. Fill in the form; use the TAB key to move from field to field.

IMPORTANT: Scan all files you receive for viruses before opening them.

DRILL 8   **OPEN AND FILL IN A FORM**

1. Open **86c-drill7**.

2. Use the following information to fill in the form: **Heather Malcolm, E-mail preferred, WV**.

3. Save as **86c-drill8a**. Do not close.

4. Use the following information to fill in the form: **Franklin Howard, Telephone preferred, KY**.

5. Save as **86c-drill8b**.

6. Close the document.

Bullets   ## Numbering

Numbered and bulleted lists are commonly used to emphasize information in reports, newspapers, magazine articles, and overhead presentations. Use numbered items if the list requires a sequence of steps or points. Use bullets or symbols if the list contains an unordered listing. *Word* automatically inserts the next number in a sequence if you manually key a number.

Help keywords:
Bullets, Numbering

Single-space bulleted or numbered items if each item consists of one line. If more than one line is required for any item, single-space the list and double-space between each item. Study the illustrations shown below.

- Word processing
- Spreadsheet
- Database
- Presentation
- Desktop publishing

1. Preheat oven to 350°.
2. Cream butter and sugar; add eggs.
3. Add flour.

To create bullets or numbers:

1. Key the list without bullets or numbers. Select the list and click the **Bullets** or **Numbering** button on the Formatting toolbar. If a double space is required between items, press SHIFT + ENTER at the end of each line.

2. To add or remove bullets or numbers, click the **Bullets** or **Numbering** button.

3. To convert bullets to numbers or vice versa, select the items to change and click either the **Bullets** or **Numbering** button.

DRILL 1   **BULLETS**

1. Key the text below as a single list; do not key the bullets.

2. Apply bullets to the list by selecting the text to be bulleted and clicking the **Bullets** button.

3. Convert the bullets to numbers. Select the bulleted items and click the **Numbering** button.

4. Add **Roll Call** as the second item.

5. Delete the number before *Next Meeting*.

6. Save the document as **38c-drill1** and print it.

- Call to Order
- Reading and Approval of the Minutes
- Announcements
- Treasurer's Report

- Membership Committee Report
- Unfinished Business
- New Business
- Adjournment
- Next Meeting: November 3, 200-

Testing the Form

During the design stage of a form, you cannot add text to text boxes or make choices from drop-down lists. As the designer of the form, you need to *protect the form* in order to activate the various field boxes that you want to test. When you protect the form, you change it so that the fields you have inserted and the text you have keyed cannot be changed while testing the fields.

To test the form:

help keywords
Protect forms, unprotect forms, reset forms

1. Click the **Protect Form** button on the Forms toolbar.
2. Enter text in text boxes, select or deselect checkboxes, and reveal drop-down boxes.
3. Click the **Protect Form** button again to deactivate the protection.
4. Click the **Reset Forms Field** button to remove any text that remains in the forms fields.

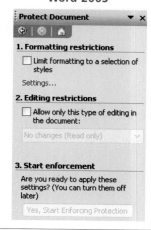

Reset Form Fields ⟶   ⟵ Protect Form

DRILL 6   FORM TEST

1. Open **86c-drill5**.
2. Click the **Protect Forms** button to enable testing.
3. Make changes to the form to test its functionality.

4. Click the **Protect Form** button to deactivate the protection.
5. Reset the form to clear any test changes.
6. Save as **86c-drill6**.

Protecting the Document

help keywords
Remove password

With *Word 2002*, even if you protect the form by clicking the Forms Protect button, the user can open the Forms toolbar and unprotect it. You need to prevent users from making changes to the form. Therefore, securely protect the form before distributing it by assigning a password with which to lock and unlock the form document. Without the password, the user cannot change the text and form fields that you have inserted.

Word 2002

Word 2003

DRILL 2   DATA FILES AND BULLETS

The CD-ROM in the back of your textbook contains extra files you will use in this course. This text refers to these files as **data files**. They are organized by module. A CD icon appears with the drill or application heading when a data file is used.

1. Ask your instructor how to access the files, or install the files on the hard drive following the instructions on the CD-ROM. When the files are installed, locate the data path or folder where these files are stored.

2. Double-click the **Module 5** folder to open it. Open the file **bullets**.

3. Select the bulleted items, and convert them to numbers.

4. Add a blank line between each numbered item without adding an additional number by pressing SHIFT + ENTER at the end of each item.

5. Save as **38c-drill2**.

Page Numbers

The Page Number command automatically inserts the correct page number on each page. Page numbers may be positioned automatically in the header position (0.5" at top of page) or in the footer position (bottom of page). To enable the number not to print on the first page, you will remove the ✓ before Show number on first page box.

Print Layout view is designed to view page numbers and other features as they will print. Select Print Layout from the View menu to view page numbers.

Help keywords:

Page numbers, Add page number, Add basic page numbers to headers or footers

To insert page numbers:

1. From the **Insert** menu, choose **Page Numbers**; the Page Numbers dialog box displays.

2. Select **Top of page (Header)** in the Position box.

3. Select **Right** in the Alignment box (default).

4. Remove the check (✓) in the **Show number on first page** box. Click OK.

5. Choose **Print Layout** from the **View** menu to view the page numbers.

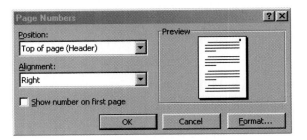

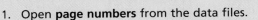

DRILL 3   PAGE NUMBERS

1. Open **page numbers** from the data files.

2. Use Page Numbers command to insert number at top of page. Remove the ✓ in Show number on first page box.

3. Use Print Layout view to verify page numbers (**View, Print Layout**).

4. Save as **38c-drill3**.

Drop-Down Form Field

This field allows the user to choose from a list created by the designer. Clicking the Drop-Down Form Field button creates a box that can be expanded (dropped down) to reveal a list of items from which the user can choose. For

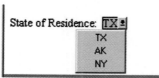

example, a drop-down box with state names included can be added to a form. The user clicks on the drop-down box, clicks on the appropriate state, and then that state appears in the box.

To add a Drop-Down Form field:

1. Open the Forms toolbar if it is not already displayed (**View**, **Toolbars**, **Forms**).

2. Place the insertion point where you want the drop-down box to appear.

3. Click the **Drop-Down Form Field** button.

Each time a Form field is placed in a document, the Form Field Options button is activated. This button allows the form's designer to make certain changes to the field. Specifically, the Form Field Options button allows the designer to add the list of choices to the Drop-Down Form Field box.

TIP

The Drop-Down Form Field Options dialog box can also be displayed by double-clicking the Drop-Down Form field placed in the document.

To add a list of drop-down choices:

1. Click the **Form Field Options** button to display the Drop-Down Form Field Options dialog box.

2. Key the user's first choice in the Drop-down item field. (For example, if the user is choosing from a list of state names, the first item listed might be Alabama.)

3. Click the **Add** button to move the text to the Items in the drop-down list box. Continue keying choices and clicking **Add** until all of the choices are entered.

4. Press ENTER one last time or click **OK** once you have entered all of the choices for the drop-down box.

TIP

To change the order of the entries in a drop-down list field, use the up and down arrows above and below the word *Move* that is found beside the Items in the drop-down list box.

DRILL 5   DROP-DOWN FORM FIELD

1. Open **86c-drill4** if it is not displayed on your screen.

2. Move the insertion point to the end of the document.

3. Key the text **State of Residence**: followed by two spaces.

4. Click the **Drop-Down Form Field** button.

5. Click the **Form Field Options** button.

6. Key **OH** in the Drop-down item field. Click **Add**. (The text will move to the Items in the drop-down list box.)

7. Key **KY** in the Drop-down item field. Click **Add**.

8. Key **WV** in the Drop-down item field. Click **Add**.

9. Click **OK**.

10. Save as **86c-drill5** and close the document. (*Note:* At this time the drop-down field choices are not active.)

Line and Page Breaks

help keywords

Format paragraph and line and page breaks.

TECHNIQUE TIP

You can also insert a page break by pressing CTRL + Enter or choosing **Page Break** from the Insert menu.

Pagination or breaking pages at the appropriate location can easily be controlled using two features: Widow/Orphan control and Keep with next.

Widow/Orphan control prevents a single line of a paragraph from printing at the bottom or top of a page. A check mark displays in this option box indicating that Widow/Orphan control is "on" (the default).

Keep with next prevents a page break from occurring between two paragraphs. Use this feature to keep a side heading from being left alone at the bottom of a page. To use Keep with next:

1. Select the side heading and the paragraph that follows.

2. Click **Format**; then **Paragraph**.

3. From the Line and Page Breaks tab, select **Keep with next**. Click **OK**. The side heading moves to the next page.

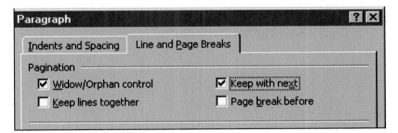

DRILL 4   **LINE AND PAGE BREAKS**

1. Open **keep with next** from the data files. Save as **38c-drill4**.

2. Select the heading **Friday, October 24** (include all lines of heading) and the paragraph that follows. Apply the **Keep with next** command.

3. Use the Insert command to insert number at the top of page. Suppress the page number on the first page.

4. Save and print.

APPLICATIONS

38d-d1
Report with Page Numbers, Bullets and Page Breaks

1. Open **report1** from the data files. Save it as **38d-d1**.

2. Key the following bulleted items just above the section *And the Final Report*.

    *   Italicize titles of complete publications.

    *   Use quotation marks with parts of publications.

    *   Months and certain locational words may be abbreviated.

3. Insert the number at the top of page. Suppress the page number on the first page.

4. Select the heading *In Conclusion* and the paragraph that follows. Apply the Keep with next command.

5. Change to Print Layout view to verify the page numbers and page breaks.

6. Save and print.

To add a Text Form field: ab|

1. Open the **Forms** toolbar if it is not already displayed (**View**, **Toolbars**, **Forms**).
2. Place the insertion point where you want the Text Form Field to appear.
3. Click the **Text Form Field** button.

DRILL 3 **INSERT A TEXT FORM FIELD**

1. Start a new blank document.
2. Save it in your designated work folder as a document template named **86c-drill3**.
3. Open the Forms toolbar if it is not already displayed.

4. Key the text **NAME**: followed by two spaces.
5. Click the **Text Form Field** button and then press ENTER twice to double-space.
6. Save **86c-drill3** without closing.

Check Box Form Field

Clicking the Check Box Form Field button creates a box ☐ for the user to click so that the box is filled with an X. For example, the user could place an X in a box to indicate an air-travel seating choice. If the user checks a box incorrectly, clicking on the box a second time will turn off the X.

Check your seating choice:

☐ 1st Class

☐ Business Class

☐ Coach

To add a Check Box Form field: ☑

1. Open the Forms toolbar if it is not already displayed (**View**, **Toolbars**, **Forms**).
2. Place the insertion point where you want the checkbox to appear.
3. Click the **Check Box Form Field** button.

DRILL 4 **INSERT A CHECK BOX FORM FIELD**

1. Open the document template named **86c-drill3** if it is not displayed on your screen.
2. Display the Forms toolbar if it is not displayed.
3. Press CTRL + END to move the insertion point to the end of the document if it is not already there (a double space below the Text Form Field line).
4. Key **Check the method of contact you prefer:** and press ENTER.

5. Click the **Check Box Form Field** button; then enter two spaces.
6. Key **E-mail** and press ENTER.
7. Insert a **Check Box Form Field**; enter two spaces; key **Parcel Post**; press ENTER.
8. Insert a **Check Box Form Field**; enter two spaces; key **Telephone**; press ENTER twice.
9. Save as **86c-drill4** without closing. (*Note*: At this time the checkboxes are not active.)

Unbound Report with Title Page

SKILLBUILDING

39a
Warmup
Key each line twice SS.

alphabetic 1 The explorer questioned Jack's amazing story about the lava flow.
fig/sym 2 I cashed Cartek & Bunter's $2,679 check (Check #3480) on June 15.
1st/2d finger 3 Hugh tried to go with Katrina, but he did not have time to do so.
easy 4 The eighty firms may pay for a formal audit of their field works.

| 1 | 2 | 3 | 4 | 5 | 6 | 7 | 8 | 9 | 10 | 11 | 12 | 13 |

39b
Troublesome Pairs
Key each line once; repeat if time permits.

t 5 it cat pat to top thin at tilt jolt tuft mitt flat test tent felt
r 6 fur bur try roar soar ram trap rare ripe true rear tort corral
t/r 7 The track star was triumphant in both the third and fourth heats.

m 8 me mine memo mimic named clam month maximum mummy summer remember
n 9 no snow ton none nine ninety noun mini mind minnow kennel evening
m/n 10 Men and women in management roles maximize time during commuting.

o 11 of one odd coil book oink cool polo crop soap yoyo option noodle
i 12 in it if did idea bike fix site with fill ilium indigo initiative
o/i 13 To know if you rock while giving a speech, stand on a foil sheet.

a 14 an as am is ask arm pass task team haze value salsa manage animal
s 15 so as sip spy must shape class shawl sister system second synergy
a/s 16 Assistants must find names and addresses for a class action suit.

e 17 he we me she they seal feel green there energy desire screensaver
i 18 is it in icon kite site tired unit limit feline service invisible
e/i 19 Initial triage services are limited to solely emergency patients.

TECHNIQUE TIP
Keep hands and arms still as you reach up to the third row and down to the first row.

39c
Timed Writings
1. Take two 1' timings; key as rapidly as you can.
2. Take one 2' timing. Try to maintain your 1' rate.

  all letters

	gwam	1'	2'
The value of an education has been a topic discussed many	12	6	48
times with a great deal of zest. The value is often measured in	25	12	54
terms of costs and benefits to the taxpayer. It is also judged	37	19	61
in terms of changes in the individuals taking part in the	49	24	67
educational process. Gains in the level of knowledge, the	61	30	72
development and refinement of attitudes, and the acquiring of	73	36	79
skills are believed to be crucial parts of an education.	84	42	84

1' | 1 | 2 | 3 | 4 | 5 | 6 | 7 | 8 | 9 | 10 | 11 | 12 | 13 |
2' | 1 | 2 | 3 | 4 | 5 | 6 |

Key the paragraph at the right. Then apply a ½-point red, double-line box border and pale blue shading to the paragraph. Save as **86c-drill2**.

> This paragraph is formatted with a ½-point red, double-line box border and pale blue shading.

Forms

Microsoft Word's **Forms** function is used to create forms that have places set aside called **fields** for the user to

- enter text (Text Form field)
- toggle a checkbox on or off (Check Box Form field)
- pick from a list of choices (Drop-Down Form field)

help keywords
Create forms, templates

The person who creates the form is called the **designer**. The person who fills in the form is the **user**.

Forms are created by inserting form fields into a document from the Forms toolbar. Shown below on the Forms toolbar are the three form fields that may be included in a document.

Text Form Field ———

Check Box Form Field ———   ——— **Drop-Down Form Field**

You as the designer of a form need to save it as a template.

To save a form as a template:

1. Choose **Save As** from the File menu.
2. Select **Document Template** in the Save as type field.
3. Name the file and save it in a location as you would any other file.

Note: You can define the area of a Text Form field by selecting the field and adding a border around it. This creates a box in which the user keys the information.

When you want to open a particular template from the folder in the location where you save your working files, be sure that the Files of type field is set to show either All Files or Document Templates in the Open dialog box.

Text Form Field

Clicking the Text Form Field button inserts a box where the user can key information. For example, you can insert this field in a form and the user can key a name, address, or whatever information is requested. Text Form Field boxes will expand as the user keys the information.

Name:

Address: 7777 Carter Falls

39d
Report Format Guides

Main heading

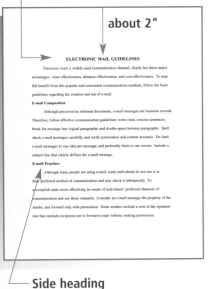

about 2"

Side heading

Unbound Report Format

Reports prepared without binders are called **unbound reports**. Unbound reports may be attached with a staple or paper clip in the upper-left corner.

Margins, Spacing, and Page Numbers

Margins: Margins are the distance between the edge of the paper and the print. Use the preset default top, side, and bottom margins on unbound reports. (Note: You will position the main heading by pressing ENTER.)

Font size and spacing: Use 12-point size for readability. Generally, educational reports are double spaced (DS) and business reports are single spaced (SS). Indent paragraphs 0.5" when the body of the report is DS. Begin the paragraphs at the left margin when the report is SS, and DS between paragraphs.

Enumerated items: Align bulleted or numbered items with the beginning of a paragraph. SS each item and DS between items.

Page numbers: The first page of a report is not numbered. The second and succeeding pages are numbered in the upper-right corner in the header position (0.5").

Headings

Headings have a hierarchy. Spacing and font size indicate the level of heading. The main heading informs readers of the report title. Side headings within the report break a lengthy report into smaller, easier-to-understand parts.

Main heading: Strike ENTER to position the main heading at about 2". The status bar will show at 2.1". Center and key the title in ALL CAPS. Use 14 point and bold.

At 2.1"	Ln 7	Col 1

Side headings: Key at left margin in bold. Capitalize the first letters of main words; DS above and below side headings if the report is SS.

Title Page

The cover or title page should have a concise title that identifies the report to the reader. A title page includes the title of the report, the name and title of the individual or the organization for which the report was prepared, the name and title of the writer, and the date the report was completed.

Center-align each line and center the page vertically. Allow near equal space between parts of the page (strike ENTER about eight times).

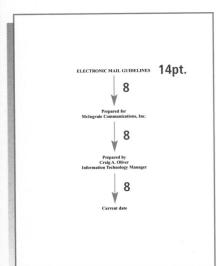

Underline Tabs

An option for leader tabs is an underline tab (Leader style 4), which produces a solid line. This type of leader is often used to create forms that will be filled in by hand.

FORM WITH UNDERLINE TABS

1. Format this document, setting a right underline tab at 6". Set DS; key the first two lines of the document.

2. On the third line of the document, set a right underline tab at 3" and a left tab at 3.5". (The right underline tab at 6" is still set.) Complete the document. Save it as **86c-drill1**.

Right underline tab 6" ⟶ ↓

Employee Name _____

Title _____

Reports to _____   Date _____

Review Period from _____   to _____

Right tab 3" ↗   ↖ Left tab 3.5"

Paragraph Borders and Shading

Borders and shading can be added to paragraphs, pages, or selected text. Various line styles, weights, and colors can be applied to borders. Shading can be applied in a variety of colors and patterns.

> This paragraph illustrates a block border with a 1-pt. black line. The shading for the paragraph is 10% gray fill.

To apply a paragraph border:

1. Click in the paragraph or select the text to be formatted with a border.
2. Click **Borders and Shading** on the Format menu, and then click the **Borders** tab.
3. Select the type of border, line style, color, and width; then click **Apply to Paragraph** and **OK**.

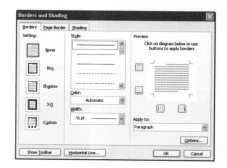

To apply shading:

1. Click in the paragraph or select the text to be shaded.
2. Click **Borders and Shading** on the Format menu, and then click the **Shading** tab.
3. Select the fill and pattern, and then apply them to the paragraph.

Set DS; Press ENTER 3 times

about 2"

ELECTRONIC MAIL GUIDELINES ← 14pt

Electronic mail, a widely used communication channel, clearly has three major advantages—time effectiveness, distance effectiveness, and cost-effectiveness. To reap full benefit from this popular and convenient communication medium, follow the basic guidelines regarding the creation and use of e-mail.

Side heading **E-mail Composition**

Default or 1" Although perceived as informal documents, e-mail messages are business records. Therefore, follow effective communication guidelines: write clear, concise sentences; break the message into logical paragraphs; and double-space between paragraphs. Spell check e-mail messages carefully, and verify punctuation and content accuracy. Do limit e-mail messages to one idea per message, and preferably limit to one screen. Include a subject line that clearly defines the e-mail message. **Default or 1"**

Side heading **E-mail Practices**

Although many people are using e-mail, some individuals do not use it as their preferred method of communication and may check it infrequently. To accomplish tasks more effectively, be aware of individuals' preferred channels of communication and use those channels. Consider an e-mail message the property of the sender, and forward only with permission. Some senders include a note in the signature line that reminds recipients not to forward e-mail without seeking permission.

Forms and Financial Documents

- Create forms.
- Protect forms.
- Use forms.
- Format financial documents.

LESSON 86

Skillbuilding and Forms

SKILLBUILDING

86a
Warmup
Key each line twice SS.

alphabet	1	Benji Vazquez was prepared for the very difficult marketing exam.
fig/sym	2	About 25% of my team (1,460) earned an average salary of $39,627.
adjacent reaches	3	Ty was the guy people wanted in government; he responded quickly.
fluency	4	My neighbor may tutor the eight girls on the theory and problems.

| 1 | 2 | 3 | 4 | 5 | 6 | 7 | 8 | 9 | 10 | 11 | 12 | 13 |

86b
Timed Writings
1. Key two 1' writings; work for speed.
2. Key one 3' writing; work for speed.

	gwam	1'	3'
Many people who attend a concert, sporting event, or another		12	4
function that attracts a large number of people rarely consider		25	8
the consequences of those people panicking if something unexpected		38	13
should happen. Just taking several minutes to locate one or more		52	17
nearby exits could result in your life and the lives of others		64	21
being saved if a fire alarm buzzer should go off. The location		77	26
at which you entered the facility might not be the most desirable		90	30
place to leave it in an emergency. The way you entered may not		103	34
even be a possible way to leave if it is blocked by individuals		116	39
who are rushing to leave the building.		123	41

1'	1	2	3	4	5	6	7	8	9	10	11	12	13
3'		1			2			3			4		

39e-d1
Unbound Report

1. Key the model report on the previous page. Change the line spacing to double. Strike ENTER three times to position the main heading at about 2". Use default side margins.

2. Key the main heading in ALL CAPS. Strike ENTER once. Select the heading; then change the font size to 14-point bold and center-align the heading. (*Tip:* Striking ENTER before formatting the main heading prevents the format of the heading from being applied to the body of the report.)

3. After keying and formatting the report, save it as **35e-d1**.

39e-d2
Unbound Report

1. Open **report2** from the data files.

2. Position the main heading at approximately 2.0"

3. Select the report and change the line spacing to double.

4. Correct the capitalization of the side headings and apply bold.

5. Make other edits shown in the report.

6. Save as **39e-d2**.

words

7

WHO CAN DESIGN A BETTER BROCHURE?

17

Producing a brochure with a professional appearance

29

requires careful creativity and planning. Not every one is

41

an accomplished paste-up artist who is capable of creating

50

a complex piece of printed art, but most skilled computer

62

users can create an attractive layout for a basic brochure.

66

Working with blocks

76

Work with copy and illustration in blocks. Type body

87

of text copy, leaving plenty of space for illustrations and

99

headlines. The blocks should then be arranged in an orderly

101

and eye appealing manner.

112

Using a small a small size type (or font) is not recommended.

122

In most cases, use a font that is 12 point or larger to

133

make the document easy to read. Copy that is arranged in

143

more than one column is also more attractive. Try not to key

147

copy across the full width of a page. Preferably break the

160

page into smaller columns of copy and intersperse with photos or

163

illustrations.

167

Module 13: Checkpoint

Answer the questions below to see if you have mastered the content of this module.

1. To increase the row height, click _____ on the Table menu.

2. The Table _____ feature enables you to apply preformatted styles to tables.

3. The _____ feature is used to align numbers at the decimal point.

4. To split one column into two columns, select the column and then click _____ on the Table menu.

5. A formula entered in the Formula text box must begin with _____.

6. Press the _____ key to recalculate an answer.

7. Access a complete list of available functions by clicking the _____ drop list arrow.

8. The _____ button allows you to rotate text from horizontal to vertical position.

9. _____ orientation positions the document horizontally on the paper.

10. Cells can be joined horizontally or vertically by selecting the cells and then choosing _____ from the Table menu.

Performance Assessment

Document
Draw Table and Calculate

1. Change the page to landscape orientation and key the table at the right.

2. Increase the height of row 1 to 1". Center headings in 14 point vertically and horizontally.

3. Calculate the total for columns C–F in row 8 (*Total Sales*). Calculate the total for rows 3–7 in column F (*Total per Person*).

4. Center the numbers in columns C–F.

5. Rotate the text in column A; center and bold the text in 20-point font.

6. Center the table vertically and horizontally on the page, save as **Checkpoint13-d**, and print.

First Quarter Sales	A-1 ELECTRONICS Eastern Division				
	Salesperson	January	February	March	Total per Person
	Cheryl Ignasio	17,000	11,000	15,000	
	Patrick Manning	21,500	19,000	23,000	
	Hillary Salinas	19,500	18,000	21,000	
	Alex Trombley	25,000	22,100	27,600	
	Van Pham	26,000	24,300	28,900	
	Total Sales				

Choosing a typeface

Typeface refers to the style of printing on the page. 167

Matching the style or "feeling" of the type with the purpose 178

of the finished product is very important. For example, 190

a layout *include* *of*
~~you~~ would not ~~want to~~ use a gothic or "old style" typeface 202

to promote a modern, high/tech product. Consider the bold- 215

ness or lightness of the style, the readability factor, *and* 227

the decorativeness or simplicity. ¶Mixing more than three 233

different typefaces on a page should also be avoided. Vary 251

the type sizes to give the effect of different type styles. 271

ital.
Bold and <u>italics</u> can also be added for emphasis and vari- 275

ety, especially when only one type style is being used. 286

297

39e-d3

Title Page

TIP
Center Page:
Choose File menu,
Page Setup, Layout tab,
Vertical alignment: Center

✳ DISCOVER

Click and Type—Switch to Print Layout View. Point to the center of the page to display centered text icon; double-click and key.

1. Prepare a title page for the unbound report completed in 39e-d1. See the illustration on page 134.
2. Use bold and 14 point for all lines.
✳ 3. Center-align each line using the Click and Type feature.
4. Center the page vertically. Save the document as **39e-d3**.

ELECTRONIC MAIL GUIDELINES

↓ 8

Prepared for
McIngvale Communications, Inc.

↓ 8

Prepared by
Craig A. Oliver
Information Technology Manager

↓ 8

Current date

85c-d3
Calculate and Format

1. Open **85c-d2**.
2. Write a formula that will calculate the amount of both regular and overtime earnings. Display the answer in the Amount columns with a dollar sign and two decimal places.
3. Decimal-align the Amount columns.
4. Add the Amount columns and place the answer in dollar format with two decimal places in the Total Earnings column.
5. Decimal-align the Total Earnings column.
6. Save as **85c-d3**.

85c-d4
SUM Function

1. Open **85c-d3**. Insert a row at the bottom of the table.
2. Key **Total** in cell A8. Use **SUM(ABOVE)** to place the total for the Amount columns and Total Earnings in row 8.
3. Save as **85c-d4**. Print.

85c-d5
Memo with Calculations in Table

1. Change the left and right margin to 1". Key the memo with the table.
2. Insert a column to the right of the table that will average the leads for each source. Label the column **Average**.
3. Insert a row at the bottom of the table that will total the leads for each day. Key **Total** in cell A6.
4. Apply **Tables Column 4** format to the table.

TO:	Cynthia Reed, Marketing Coordinator
FROM:	Ryan Ng
DATE:	Current Date
SUBJECT:	Lead Analysis

Please review the following statistics that were gathered the week of October 10–16. Let's meet next Monday at 9:00 a.m. in my office to do a cost analysis for the leads. Please bring a copy of the contracts with each source.

DAILY LEAD LOG

Source	Monday	Tuesday	Wednesday	Thursday	Friday
Daily Times	15	30	20	10	12
County Register	22	17	12	19	14
Internet	21	32	41	44	47
Yellow Pages	6	5	6	3	4

SKILLBUILDING

40a
Warmup
Key each line twice SS.

alphabetic	1	Jayne Cox puzzled over workbooks that were required for geometry.
figures	2	Edit pages 308 and 415 in Book A; pages 17, 29, and 60 in Book B.
shift	3	THE LAKES TODAY, published in Akron, Ohio, comes in June or July.
easy	4	The town may blame Keith for the auditory problems in the chapel.

| 1 | 2 | 3 | 4 | 5 | 6 | 7 | 8 | 9 | 10 | 11 | 12 | 13 |

40b
Technique Builder
Key at a controlled rate.

n/u	5	nun nut unbolt null unable nudge under nurture thunder numb shunt
	6	Uncle Hunter runs with me to hide under the bed when it thunders.
c/e	7	ecru cell echo ceil check cedar pecan celery secret receive price
	8	Once Cecilia checked prices for acceptable and special offerings.
b/r	9	brag barb brown carbon brain marble break herb brace gerbil brick
	10	Bradley will try to break the unbroken brown brood mare bareback.
n/y	11	many bunny irony grainy granny sunny phony rainy runny zany funny
	12	Aunt Nanny says rainy days are for funny movies and many candies.

COMMUNICATION

40c
Report Format Review

In Lesson 39 you learned the unbound report format. Check your understanding of the unbound report format by completing Drills 1 and 2 below. Refer to pp. 127–128 if you have questions.

DRILL 1   FORMAT REVIEW

Key each line below choosing the correct choice shown in parentheses. Use the numbering feature to number each statement. Save as **40c-drill1**.

1. The main heading that appears on the first page of a report is keyed approximately (1", 2") from the top of the page.
2. The main heading is keyed at the (center, left margin); the font size of the main heading is (14 point, 12 point).
3. The main heading is (bold, not bold); side headings are (bold, not bold).
4. Side headings are keyed at the (center, left margin); the font size of side headings is (14 point, 12 point).
5. Side margins of an unbound report are (default or 1", 1.5").

DRILL 2   PROOFREAD FOR CONSISTENCY

1. Open **Report3Key** from the data files and print; close this file.
2. Open **Report 3** and print. Proofread this report and mark any formats that are not consistent with the solution printed in

step 1. Use the proofreaders' marks shown on page 55 to mark all corrections.
3. Correct the errors you marked.
4. Save as **40c-drill2** and print. Submit the edited copy and the final copy to your instructor.

85c-d1
Rotate Text

1. Create the table below. Center the table vertically and horizontally on the page.
2. Key the main heading, **EMPLOYEE DATA**, in 14-point bold type vertically at the left of the table. Shade the cell 15%.
3. Center all text vertically in the cells.
4. Increase row 1 height to 1.3". Text in column B should fit on one line.
5. Save as **85c-d1**. Print.

EMPLOYEE DATA	Item	Fair Labor Standards Act	Social Security	Income Tax Withholding	Unemployment Tax
	Name	Yes	Yes	Yes	Yes
	Address	Yes	Yes	Yes	Yes
	Sex	Yes	—	—	—
	Social Security Number	Yes	Yes	Yes	Yes
	Withholding allowances claimed	—	—	Yes	—
	Occupation	Yes	Yes	Yes	Yes

85c-d2
Merge and Split Cells

1. Change the orientation to landscape.
2. Key the table below and format it using merged and split cells. Use decimal tabs to align the *Rate* columns. Center the *Hours* columns.
3. Save as **85c-d2**. Print.

PAYROLL REGISTER							
For Week Ending January 19, 200-							
Name	Regular Earnings			Overtime Earnings			Total Earnings
	Hours	Rate	Amount	Hours	Rate	Amount	
Oldfield, Carry	40	8.75					
Weingard, Susan T.	40	9.25		2	13.50		
Thompson, William	40	14.50		4	22.00		
Morrison, Carl	40	16.50		6	25.00		
Pham, Vo	38	12.00					

40d
Two-Page Reports

Report Format Guidelines

Reports are widely used in various environments. Study the information that follows:

Side margins: Default side margins for an unbound report. Set the left margin at 1.5" for a leftbound report.

Top margin: 2" for first page of report, preliminary pages, and Reference page; 1" on other pages.

Page numbers: Include page numbers for the second and succeeding pages of a report. Position at the top of the page (header), right alignment.

Single lines: Avoid single lines at the top or bottom of a report (called *widow/orphan lines*). Do not separate a side heading from the paragraph that follows between pages.

To format a report:

1. At the top of the document, change the line spacing to double. Strike ENTER three times to position the insertion point to leave an approximate 2" top margin.

2. Check that the font size is 12 point.

3. Insert page numbers. Suppress the page number on the first page.

4. Key the main heading in ALL CAPS. Strike ENTER twice, then select the heading and apply 14 point and bold. Center-align the heading.

5. Move the insertion point to below the heading, and begin to key the report.

6. Position the references on a new page. If necessary, insert a manual page break. Format the title REFERENCES in 14 point, bold, at approximately 2".

7. Protect side headings that may get separated from the related paragraph with the Keep with next feature.

8. View the report using Print Layout view.

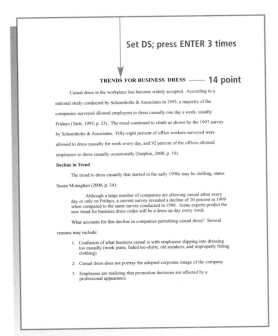

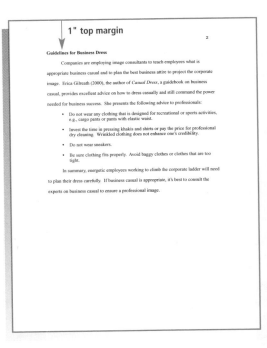

LESSON 85   Assessment

SKILLBUILDING

85a
Warmup
Key each line twice SS.

alphabet	1	Jacqueline Katz made extra money by singing with the five groups.
figures	2	I sold 27 roses, 10 irises, 68 lilies, 54 tulips, and 39 orchids.
space bar	3	If she may go with me to a lake, I may do all of the work and go.
easy	4	The girls got the bicycle at the land of enchantment at the lake.

| 1 | 2 | 3 | 4 | 5 | 6 | 7 | 8 | 9 | 10 | 11 | 12 | 13 |

85b
Timed Writing
Key one 5' writing.

gwam   3' | 5'

Employees who work together as a team are more effective   4   2 | 39
than those who work solo. This concept is known as synergy.   8   5 | 42
Synergy simply means that the joint action exceeds the sum of   12   7 | 44
individual actions. The results are not just in the quantity of   16   10 | 47
work; major gains in quality result when people work together as   21   12 | 49
a team. Teamwork is critical for success.   24   14 | 51

What characterizes an excellent team member? An excellent   28   17 | 53
team member understands the goals of the team and will place team   32   19 | 56
values above her or his individual objectives. An excellent team   36   22 | 59
member helps to determine the most effective way to reach the   40   24 | 61
goals that were set by the group and will help to make each   44   27 | 63
decision that affects the group. Above all, an excellent team   49   29 | 66
member will support a decision made by the team. Each member   53   32 | 68
must understand her or his role and respect the roles of others.   57   34 | 71
Every member of a team must share in both victory and defeat.   61   37 | 74

3' | 1 | 2 | 3 | 4 |
5' | 1 | 2 | 3 |

APPLICATIONS

85c
Assessment

Continue

Check

With CheckPro: When you complete a document, proofread it, check the spelling, and preview for placement. When you are completely satisfied, click the **Continue** button to move to the next document. You will not be able to return and edit a document once you continue to the next one. Click the **Check** button when you are ready to error-check the test. Review and/or print the document analysis results.

Without CheckPro: On the signal to begin, key the documents in sequence. When time has been called, proofread all documents again and identify errors.

DISCOVER

Insert file—Position insertion point where file is to be inserted. On the **Insert** menu, click **File**; select the desired file; click **Insert**.

1. Key the unbound report that follows. Position main heading at approximately 2". Set proper line spacing.

✳ 2. From the data disk, insert the file **writing** below the second paragraph. (*Note:* Be sure to position the insertion point where you want the text to appear before inserting the file.)

3. Format the first side heading *Researching* correctly.

4. Format the bulleted list SS with a DS between items.

5. Revise the side headings to make them parallel (grammatically consistent).

6. Insert page numbers; do not print the page number on page 1.

7. Apply Keep with next to protect side headings from being left alone at the bottom of a page.

8. Switch to Print Layout view to verify page numbers.

9. Save the report as **40e-d1**. Check the spelling, and print the document.

LEARN TO WIN AT WRITING

Being able to communicate effectively continues to be one of the most demanded work skills. Today's high demand for clear, concise, and logical communication makes it impossible for an employee to excuse himself or herself from writing by saying, "I'm just not a writer," or "I can't write."

Realizing you need to improve your writing skills is the first step to enhancing them. Then you must apply a systemized approach to writing as detailed in this report.

Insert the data file writing here.

The effective writer understands the importance of using technology to create an attractive document that adheres to correct style rules. Review the list below to determine your use of technology in the report writing process.

- Number preliminary pages of the report with small Roman numerals at the bottom center of the page.
- Number the report with Arabic numbers in the upper-right corner.
- Create attractive headers or footers that contain helpful information for the reader.
- Suppress headers, footers, and page numbering on the title page and on the first page of the report.
- Invoke the widow/orphan protection feature to ensure that no lines display alone at the bottom or top of a page.
- Use the block protection command to keep side headings from appearing alone at the bottom of the page.

continued

84d-d1
Landscape Form with Merged Cells

1. Change the page to landscape orientation. Create a 3-column, 9-row table.

2. Merge row 1 and key the main heading in 14-point bold. Increase the row height to .5" and center the heading vertically and horizontally in the row.

3. Merge row 2 and key the text.

4. Merge row 3; then split row 3 into 2 columns. Key **Payee Name:** and strike ENTER; key the remaining lines in the same format. Change the row height to .8", and then center the text vertically in the cells.

5. Key the remainder of the form. Center vertically and horizontally. Save as **84d-d1**.

RECEIPT OF PAYMENT		
Receipt Number:	Date:	
Payee Name: Address: City, State ZIP:	Payer Name: Address: City, State ZIP:	
Item No.	Description	Amount
	Subtotal	
	Tax	
Total		

84d-d2
Table with Math

Fill in the form you created in **84d-d1** and use the math feature to perform the calculations.

1. Open **84d-d1**. Save as **84d-d2**.

2. Fill in the form with the information shown below.

3. Calculate the subtotal by using the SUM above feature. Calculate the Tax by keying the formula **=c7*.05**. The tax is 5%. Calculate the Total by keying the formula **=c7+c8**.

4. Use a decimal tab to align column C. Save and print.

RECEIPT OF PAYMENT		
Receipt Number: 1452	Date: 6-15-04	
Payee Name: Amazon Electronics Address: 8360 Ortega Highway City, State ZIP: Houston, TX 77001	Payer Name: James Smith Address: 55 Alpine Road City, State ZIP: Houston, TX 77002	
Item No.	Description	Amount
4319	CPU Stand	41.00
4890	Side Extension Shelf	35.50
	Subtotal	
	Tax	
Total		

- Format references using the hanging indent feature.
- Use typographic or special symbols to enhance the report.

Writers also take advantage of the online thesaurus for choosing the most appropriate word and the spelling and grammar features to ensure spelling and grammar correctness. Additionally, electronic desk references and style manuals are just a click away.

Finally, all the report needs is the title page. Effective writers know that it pays dividends to create a custom title page that truly reflects the quality of the report that it covers. Use page borders and shading as well as graphics to create an attractive title page.

Two simple steps followed in a systematic order will assist you in your goal to learn to win at writing. Knowing the approach is the first step; the second step is to practice, practice, and practice.

40e-d2
Title Page

1. Prepare a title page for the unbound report prepared in **40e-d1**. Set the left margin at 1.5".
2. Prepare the title page for **XYZ Employees by Jennifer Schoenholtz, Office Manager**. Center the page.
3. Save the title page as **40e-d2**.

SKILLBUILDING
40f

Use the remaining class time to build your Skills using the Skill Builder module within *Keyboarding Pro*.

Landscape Orientation

Most documents are printed on standard 8.5" × 11" paper in portrait orientation. To print a wide document on a standard sheet of paper, you must choose landscape orientation. **Landscape** orientation positions the document horizontally on the paper (11" × 8.5").

To change the paper to landscape orientation:

1. From the File menu, choose **Page Setup**. Click the **Margins** tab.

2. Click the **Landscape** button in the Orientation section. Notice that the illustration in the Preview box changes from portrait to landscape. Click **OK**.

Change Text Orientation

Text is traditionally displayed horizontally in a cell. At times, you may wish to display the text vertically in the cell. You can rotate text in a cell by using the Change Text Direction button in the Tables and Borders toolbar or by selecting Text Direction in the Format menu.

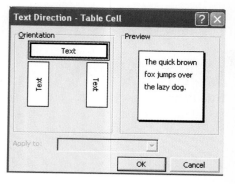

To Change Text Orientation:

Click the table cell that contains the text you want to change.

1. On the Format menu, click **Text Direction**.

2. Click the desired orientation.

CHANGE PAGE ORIENTATION AND TEXT DIRECTION

1. Open **83c-d3**. Change the page to landscape orientation.

2. Delete row 1. Insert a column to the left of the table. Merge the rows in the new column.

3. Key **CIS TEST SCORES** in the new column; apply 15% shading.

4. Rotate the text in the cell as shown. Center the text vertically and horizontally in the cell. Adjust column width.

5. Rotate heads in columns C–F.

6. Save as **84c-drill1**. Print.

CIS TEST SCORES	Student	Test 1	Test 2	Test 3	Test 4	Maximum Score
	Appleton, J.	81	74	83	86	86
	Carey, R.	87	92	93	91	93
	Palembo, T.	72	69	70	71	72
	Stover, A.	91	95	97	96	97
	Average per Test	83	83	86	86	

SKILLBUILDING

41a
Warmup
Key each line twice SS.

alphabetic	1	Jacki might analyze the data by answering five complex questions.
figures	2	Memo 67 asks if the report on Bill 35-48 is due on the 19th or the 20th.
shift	3	Plum trees on a hilly acre, in my opinion, create no vast estate.
easy	4	Did the foal buck? And did it cut the right elbow of the cowhand?

41b
Technique Builder
Key each line SS; DS between groups.

	5	you yes yelp year yeild yellow yule yours symbol pray grassy money
y/t	6	to at tent triek treat trestle tribute thirty match matter clutter
	7	Timothy printed a symbol, yacht, and yellowjacket for Mr. Forsyst.
	8	got get giggle gargle gargoyle gangway engage eagle magic peg piggy
g/h	9	he she her head harp hay heavy hearth homograph hyena high height
	10	Gail Hughes, a researcher, charted the height and weight of Hugh.

| 1 | 2 | 3 | 4 | 5 | 6 | 7 | 8 | 9 | 10 | 11 | 12 | 13 |

41c

Build Staying Power
Take two 3' writings on all ¶s.

  all letters

	gwam	1'	3'
In a recent show, a young skater gave a great performance.	12	4	69
Her leaps were beautiful, her spins were impossible to believe,	25	8	74
and she was a study in grace itself. But she had slipped during	38	13	78
a jump and had gone down briefly on the ice. Because of the high	51	17	82
quality of her act, however, she was given a third-place medal.	64	21	87
Her coach, talking later to a reporter, stated his pleasure	12	25	91
with her part of the show. When asked about the fall, he said	25	30	95
that emphasis should be placed on the good qualities of the per-	37	34	99
formance and not on one single blemish. He ended by saying that	50	38	104
as long as his students did the best they could, he would be	63	42	108
satisfied.	65	43	108
What is "best"? When asked, the young skater explained she	12	47	112
was pleased to have won the bronze medal. In fact, this perfor-	25	51	117
mance was a personal best for her; she was confident the gold	37	55	121
would come later if she worked hard enough. It appears she knew	50	60	125
the way to a better medal lay in beating not other people, but her	64	64	130
own personal best.	67	65	131

1'	1	2	3	4	5	6	7	8	9	10	11	12	13
3'		1			2			3			4		

Changing Page and Text Orientation

SKILLBUILDING

84a
Warmup
Key each line twice SS.

left hand
1 readers secrets dessert degrade cataracts abstracts basted create
2 barge adage beverages scarce assist trait area tea fast are dress
3 waves fatal taste zest craze star tear drawers garage grade trees

right hand
4 union poplin hookup hominy minimum onion link plump pool pink lip
5 million opinion pupil imply jolly knoll lymph yolk upon no nil on
6 nymph him hop hip ink mommy joy pin ply nip oil in poll oh pip my

both hands
7 work yams worn tutor vile slang shrug clams bogus slept me trains
8 blend sighs sign forks amend angle aisle visitor window if posted
9 tuck yield fowl cork duels roams tyrant clan soap rifle so jumped

| 1 | 2 | 3 | 4 | 5 | 6 | 7 | 8 | 9 | 10 | 11 | 12 | 13 |

84b
Timed Writings
Key a 3' and a 5' writing.

	gwam	3'	5'

Have you ever heard the saying "dress for success"? If you are going to a job interview, this is good advice to follow. Men should wear a good quality business suit, or at least a blazer. They should include a clean shirt, preferably white, and a nice tie. Clean dark shoes and dark socks will complete the outfit. Women should maintain a conservative look. A dark business suit with a medium-length skirt is most appropriate. A blouse in a modest color will help project a professional appearance.

Women's heels should be no more than two inches high. Both men and women should be sure that their hair is clean and neatly styled. Nails should be cut short and well groomed. Nail polish, if worn, should be clear or a pastel color; no black or flashy colors should be used. Little or no perfume is preferred, because some interviewers may be sensitive to fragrances. Jewelry should be kept to a minimum. Remember to devote extra effort to prepare for your interview; your future job may depend on it.

gwam	3'	5'
4	2	43
8	5	46
13	8	48
17	10	51
21	13	53
26	15	56
30	18	58
34	20	61
38	23	63
42	25	66
46	28	68
51	30	71
55	33	74
60	36	76
64	38	79
67	40	81

3' 1 2 3 4
5' 1 2 3

Indent

When a writer paraphrases or quotes material longer than three lines from another source, the writer must set off the long quote from the rest of the report. Quoted material is set off by indenting it 0.5" from the left margin.

The Indent feature moves all lines of a paragraph to the next tab. In contrast, TAB moves only the first line of a paragraph to the next tab. Indent is a paragraph command. The Indent feature enables you to indent text from either the left or right margin or from both margins.

To indent text from the left margin:

1. Click the **Increase Indent** button on the toolbar. (*Shortcut:* CTRL + M)

2. Key the paragraph and press ENTER. The left indent will continue until you click the **Decrease Indent** button. (*Shortcut:* CTRL + SHIFT + M)

Indent can also be applied to text that has already been keyed.

Help keywords
Increase the left indent of an entire paragraph

 Increase Indent

 Decrease Indent

DRILL 1   **INDENT**

1. Key the copy that follows. DS paragraph 1; strike TAB to indent the paragraph.

2. To format paragraph 2, at the left margin, click **Increase Indent**. Change to SS. Strike TAB, and then key paragraph 2.

3. For paragraph 3, click **Decrease Indent**; change to DS.

4. Save as **41d-drill1**.

> However, the thrust to use e-mail almost exclusively is causing a tremendous challenge for both e-mail recipients and companies. DS
>
> TAB   With the convenience of electronic mail resulting in its widespread use, many users are forsaking other forms of communication—face-to-face, telephone (including voice mail), and printed documents. Now companies are challenged to create clear e-mail policies and to implement employee training on effective use of e-mail (Ashford, 2000, 2). DS
>
> Communication experts have identified problems that may occur as a result of misusing e-mail. Two important problems include information overload (too many messages) and inappropriate form of communication.

Indent →

83c-d3
Paste MAX Function

1. Key the table below. Center it vertically and horizontally on the page.
2. Adjust the height of row 1 to 1". Center the headings vertically and horizontally in row 1.
3. Center columns B–F.
4. Calculate the average for each test and place in row 7. Display the answer as a whole number (Number Format, 0).
✳ 5. Use the MAX function to find the maximum score for each student. Place answers in column F.
6. Save as **83c-d3**. Print.

COMPUTER INFORMATION SYSTEMS Spring, 200-					
Student	**Test 1**	**Test 2**	**Test 3**	**Test 4**	**Maximum Score**
Appleton, J.	81	74	83	86	
Carey, R.	87	92	93	91	
Palembo, T.	72	69	70	71	
Stover, A.	91	95	97	96	
Average per Test	83	83	86	86	

83c-d4
Calculate Net Profits in Table

1. Key the table below. Adjust the height of row 1 to approximately 1". Center headings vertically and horizontally in row 1.
2. Insert totals for each column in row 7.
3. Insert Net Profits in column D (Gross Revenue – Expenses).
4. Right-align columns B–D.
5. Save as **83c-d4**. Print.

COMTEK INCORPORATED Western Region			
Quarter	**Gross Revenue**	**Expenses**	**Net Profits**
First	980,000	375,000	
Second	877,000	320,000	
Third	795,000	310,000	
Fourth	991,000	420,000	
Total			

Hanging Indent

Hanging indent places the first line of a paragraph at the left margin and indents all other lines to the first tab. It is commonly used to format bibliography entries, glossaries, and lists. Hanging indent can be applied before text is keyed or after.

Help keywords
Hanging indent; paragraph; about text alignment and spacing

To create a hanging indent:

1. Display the Horizontal Ruler (click **View**; then **Ruler**).

2. From the Horizontal Ruler, drag the hanging indent marker to the position where the indent is to begin. ———— Hanging Indent

3. Key the paragraph. The second and subsequent lines are indented beginning at the marker. (*Shortcut:* CTRL + T, then key the paragraph; or select the paragraphs to be formatted as hanging indents, and press CTRL + T.)

DRILL 2　　**HANGING INDENT**

1. Drag the Hanging Indent marker 0.5" to the right; then key the references that follow.

2. Turn Hanging Indent off by dragging the Hanging Indent marker back to the left margin.

3. Save the document as **41d-drill2**.

> Fowler, H. Ramsey and Aaron, Jane E. *The Little, Brown Handbook.* 6th ed. Boston: HarperCollins College Publishers, 1995.
>
> Osaji, Allison. "Know the Credibility of Electronic Citations." *Graduate Education Journal*, April 2000, 45–51.
>
> VandenBos, Gary R. "Software Helps Writers Conform to APA Style." *APA Monitor Online*, (1999) http://www.apa.org/monitor/jan99/soft.html (10 November 2000).
>
> Walters, Daniel S. dswalters2@umt.edu. "Final Report Available on Intranet." E-mail to Stephen P. Cobb, spcobb@umt.edu (14 September 2000).

DRILL 3　　**FORMAT TEXT WITH HANGING INDENT**

1. Open **references** from the data files, and save it as **41d-drill3**.

2. Select the references, and format them with a hanging indent. (*Hint:* Try the shortcut.) Save the file again.

DRILL 4　　**FORMAT TEXT WITH HANGING INDENT**

1. Open **glossary** from the data files, and save it as **41d-drill4**.

2. Select all the glossary entries, and format them with a hanging indent. Save the file again.

To paste a function:

1. Place the cursor in the cell where the calculation should be made.
2. Select **Formula** from the Table menu.
3. Delete the **SUM(ABOVE)**, but not the equal sign.
4. Click the **Paste** function drop list arrow.
5. Choose the new function, and then key between the parentheses the cell references (A1, D3, E4) or the direction (LEFT, RIGHT, etc) to which the function [formula] should apply. Click **OK**.

Note: If the same formula is to be applied repeatedly, use the Repeat Formula command on the Edit menu.

DRILL 5　　PASTE FUNCTION

1. Open **Data83b-drill5** and place the cursor in cell E1.
2. Click **Formula** on the Table.
3. Delete **SUM(LEFT)** from the Formula box. (Do not delete the equal sign.)
4. Click the **Paste** function drop list arrow.
5. Choose **COUNT** to total the number of cells that contain information.
6. Key **LEFT** between the parentheses ( ). Click **OK**.
7. Repeat for each row in column E. Save as **83b-drill5**.

APPLICATIONS

83c-d1
Format and Total

1. Key the following table and apply **Table Column 5** format. Center and bold the headings.
2. Decimal-align columns B through D.
3. In row 7, total the expenses for each month. Center vertically on the page. Save as **83c-d1**. Print.
4. Insert a column to the right of the table. Key **Monthly Average** in cell E1. Adjust width of columns so that all column heads fit on one line.

83c-d2
Average Calculation

5. Calculate the average for each expense and place the answers in column E. The average answers should contain a dollar sign and two decimal places. Save as **83c-d2**.

EXPENSES FOR JAMES STEWARD

First Quarter, 200-

Expense	January	February	March
Rent	$800.00	$800.00	$800.00
Food	270.50	255.25	290.00
Transportation	92.00	120.00	675.00
Clothing	90.75	95.50	80.25
Miscellaneous	50.00	75.00	83.00

Manual Page Break

When a page is filled with copy, the software automatically inserts a soft page break, which is indicated with a dotted line across the page when you are in Normal view.

You may need to begin a new page, however, before the page is filled. To insert a manual page break, press CTRL + ENTER. The software inserts a dotted line across the screen with the words "Page Break." The insertion point moves to the next page; the status line at the bottom of the screen indicates this change. A manual page break will not move as text is inserted or deleted.

To remove a manual page break, position the insertion point on the Page Break line and press DELETE.

DRILL 5   **MANUAL PAGE BREAK**

1. Key the text below.

2. Place the insertion point after the first set of goals. Insert a manual page break.

3. Continue keying page 2.

4. Use the Page Number command to insert number at the top of page. Do not print number on the first page.

5. Save as **41d-drill5**.

GOAL 1: MEMBERSHIP DEVELOPMENT

Objective: To increase membership.

Indent ⟶ **Plan**

      A. Review and evaluate membership benefits.
      B. Study avenues for additional membership benefits.
      C. Develop new membership markets.

·· Insert page break.

GOAL 2: STAFF DEVELOPMENT

Objective: To enhance performance and motivation of staff.

Indent ⟶ **Plan**

      A. Review and evaluate previous staff development programs.
      B. Survey staff to determine needs.
      C. Implement relevant staff development programs.

Increase Indent

Decrease Indent

Margins

Margins are the distance between the edge of the paper and the print. The default settings are 1.25" side margins and 1" top and bottom margins. Default margins stay in effect until you change them.

Help keywords:
Change page margins

To change the margins:

1. Click **File;** then **Page Setup**.

2. From the Margins tab, click the up or down arrows to increase or decrease the default settings.

3. Apply margins to the Whole document unless directed otherwise. Click **OK**.

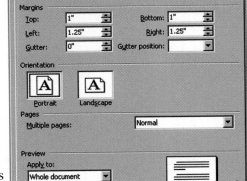

Recalculate

When a change is made to a number that was part of a calculation, *Word* can automatically recalculate the answer. To recalculate an answer, click on the number in the cell that contains the formula. Press F9; the new answer will display in the cell.

Number Format

You can specify the format in which your answer is to be displayed. To do so, select one of the choices listed in the Number format drop list found in the Formula box. For example, if you are calculating money amounts, you can choose to have the answer display with two decimal places, with or without a dollar sign, and with or without commas.

DRILL 3   **CALCULATE AND FORMAT**

1. Open **Data83b-drill3**, compare it to the illustration below, and make necessary changes.

2. Calculate Net Profits by subtracting Expenses from Income. Display the answer in $#,##0.00 format.

3. Change the height of row 1 to approximately 1". Center the headings in row 1 vertically and horizontally.

4. Change the height in rows 2–6 to .3 and center text vertically. Center the column headers horizontally.

5. Center column A. Decimal-align columns B, C, and D. Apply 15% shading to cells D2–D6.

6. Save as **83b-drill3**. Keep it open for Drill 4.

E-COMMERCE.COM

Income Summary

Year	Income	Expenses	Net Profits
2000	$129,050.00	$151,000.00	
2001	375,000.00	225,000.00	
2002	410,000.00	250,500.00	
2003	560,000.00	316,000.00	

DRILL 4   **RECALCULATE IN A TABLE**

1. Open **83b-drill3**, if necessary. Change the number in cell B3 to **165,000.00**.

2. Recalculate the answer in D3 by placing the insertion point in D3 and pressing F9.

3. Save as **83b-drill4**.

Paste Function

help keywords
Perform calculations

As you learned earlier, the default formula that displays in the Formula dialog box is SUM(ABOVE). Other functions are also available for use, such as AVERAGE, MIN, MAX, COUNT, etc. Click on the **Paste** function drop list arrow to display a complete list of available functions.

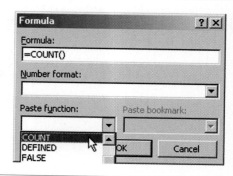

DRILL 6   MARGINS

1. Set 1" side margins. Key the paragraph below. Save as **41d-drill6**; then preview the document.

2. Position the insertion point at the beginning of sentence 4. Press ENTER twice.

3. With the insertion point in paragraph 2, change the top and side margins to 2". Preview the document.

4. At the end of sentence 4, press ENTER twice. Key and complete this sentence with the better response, (a) or (b).

The margin command affects the appearance of the (a) entire document (b) paragraph containing the insertion point.

5. Save the document again.

6. Change the left, right, and top margins to 1.5". Apply margin settings to the whole document.

7. Save the document as **41d-drill6b**.

Attractive document layout begins with margins set an equal distance from the left and right edges of the paper. When margins are equal, the document appears balanced. One exception to the equal-margin rule is in the formatting of reports bound at the left. To ensure the appearance of equal left and right margins in a leftbound report, you must add extra space to the left margin to allow for the binding.

DRILL 7   COMBINED PRACTICE

1. Set 1.5" side margins.

2. Key the text below following the directions in the text.

3. Insert a manual page break as shown.

4. Insert page number at the top right. Do not print number on the first page.

5. Save as **41d-drill7**.

Indent

Type the following paragraph indented 0.5" from the left margin.

> Long quotations of four lines or more are indented 0.5" from the left margin and single-spaced. A double-space or one blank line comes before and after the long quotation. The first line is indented an additional 0.5" if the quotation is the beginning of a paragraph.

··· Insert page break.

Hanging Indent

Key the following article as a reference in hanging indent style.

Falcon, Leah. "Reflections of an Echo Boomer." *Net Generation Magazine*, Vol. 2, No. 1, February 2003, 12–15.

DRILL 1   TABLE WITH SUM FUNCTION

1. Open **Data83b-drill1**, compare it to the illustration at the right, and make changes as instructed. **Save as 83b-drill1**.
2. Position the insertion point in the last cell and press TAB to add a row at the bottom. Key **TOTAL** in cell A8.
3. Use the SUM function to insert the total for column C in cell C8.
4. Use the SUM function to insert the total for column D in cell D8. Save again. Continue with Drill 2.

LAUREL CANYON ENTERPRISES

Employee	I.D.	Hardware	Software
Alexander, J.	R492	$105,134,384	$1,868,553,280
Courtenay, W.	R856	79,364,091	1,384,219,500
Holsonback, E.	C845	27,386,427	1,098,237,260
Palombo, L.	K511	44,296,101	971,360,515
Rajeh, C.	M451	82,665,900	1,052,564,100
Talbert, S.	P053	82,091,433	985,201,500
TOTAL			

DRILL 2   INSERT COLUMN AND SUM LEFT

1. Insert a column to the right of the table.
2. Key **Total per Employee** in cell E1, and then adjust the column to accommodate the header on one line.
3. Add the numbers in columns C and D, and place the total for each row in column E.
4. If =SUM(ABOVE) displays in the formula box, delete the word *ABOVE* and replace it with *LEFT*.
5. Save as **83b-drill2**.

---

help keywords
Formulas in tables; repeat a formula

Writing Formulas

You can write your own formulas directing *Word* to add, subtract, multiply, divide, or average numbers in a table. A formula always begins with an equal sign. It then includes identification of the cells and the math symbol. For example, =B2-C2 means "column B, row 2 minus column C, row 2."

To write a formula:

1. Place the insertion point in the cell that is to contain the calculation.
2. Choose **Formula** from the Table menu. The Formula dialog box displays.
3. Delete the **SUM** formula.
4. Enter the formula in the Formula text box, beginning with =.
5. Click **OK**. Repeat steps 1–4 for each formula.

Formula

Formula:

=B2-C2

The following symbols can be used in formulas. (Do not key the D2 and F2 as shown in the example column; your cursor will already be in that cell.)

Operation	Symbol	Example
Addition	+	D2=B2+C2
Subtraction	- (hyphen)	D2=B2-C2
Multiplication	*	D2=B2*C2
Division	/	D2=B2/C2
Average	Place parentheses ( ) around the part of the calculation to be performed first.	F2=(B2+C2+D2+E2)/4

LESSON 42

Two-Page Report with Long Quotations

SKILLBUILDING

42a
Warmup
Key each line twice SS.

alphabetic	1	Two exit signs jut quietly above the beams of a razed skyscraper.
figures	2	Send 345 of the 789 sets now; send the others on August 1 and 26.
direct reach	3	I obtain many junk pieces dumped by Marvyn at my service centers.
easy	4	Enrique may fish for cod by the dock; he also may risk a penalty.

| 1 | 2 | 3 | 4 | 5 | 6 | 7 | 8 | 9 | 10 | 11 | 12 | 13 |

42b
Timed Writings
Key a 1' timing on each paragraph, and a 3' timing on all paragraphs.

  all letters

gwam 1' | 3'

Does a relationship exist between confidence and success? If   12 | 4 42
you think it does, you will find that many people agree with you.   26 | 9 46
However, it is very hard to judge just how strong the bond is.   38 | 13 50

When people are confident they can do a job, they are very   12 | 17 54
likely to continue working on that task until they complete it   24 | 21 58
correctly. If they are not confident, they give up much quicker.   38 | 25 63

People who are confident they can do something tend to enjoy   12 | 29 67
doing it more than those who lack confidence. They realize that   25 | 34 71
they do better work when they are happy with what they do.   37 | 37 75

1' | 1 | 2 | 3 | 4 | 5 | 6 | 7 | 8 | 9 | 10 | 11 | 12 | 13 |
3' | 1 | | 2 | | 3 | | 4 |

FUNCTION REVIEW

42c

Review Indent

1. Open **indents** from the data files.
2. On page 1, increase the indent of paragraph 2.
3. On page 2, format the references with a hanging indent.
4. Save as **42c-drill1.**

DOCUMENT DESIGN

42d

Report Documentation

Reports must include the sources of all information used in the report. Documentation gives credit for published material, whether electronic or printed, that is quoted or closely paraphrased by the writer. The writer may document sources by using footnotes, endnotes, or internal citations. In this module, you will use internal citations and footnotes.

At the end of the report, the writer provides the reader with a complete alphabetical listing of all references. With this complete information provided in the references, the interested reader may locate the original source. You will learn to format a reference list in Lesson 43.

DOCUMENT DESIGN

83a
Warmup
Key each line twice SS.

1 it to the us me you so go now we my he two in can her by of do no
2 it is | it is the | is it | is it you | he can | can he | he can go | can he go
3 who is | who is it | is it you | you can go | can you go | you can go to it

4 car mail two you may just can lake ask sail sign his form her who
5 who can sail | you can sail | you may sign | can you sign | sign his form
6 sign the form | mail the form | sign and mail | sign and mail that form

7 it was | was it so | if she can go to | can he go to the | can she go to the
8 she can | she may not | she may not go | can you go to the | so we may go
9 sign the | sign the form | they may sign that | they may sign that form

83b

help keywords
*Perform calculations;
repeat last action*

TIP

Σ A quick addition method for totaling the numbers in a column or row is to first click the cell where you want the total to go. Next, click the **AutoSum** button on the Tables and Borders toolbar.

Formulas

Microsoft *Word* has the ability to perform basic mathematical calculations, such as addition, subtraction, multiplication, and division when numbers are keyed in a table. *Word* also can recalculate an answer when the numbers in a table change. While *Word* is excellent for working with basic formulas, more complex calculations are better performed in a spreadsheet, such as *Excel*.

Using the SUM Function

SUM is the default formula or function that displays in the Formula dialog box. Columns or rows of numbers can be quickly added by clicking OK or pressing ENTER.

Formulas can be repeated by placing the insertion point in the next cell to be calculated and choosing Repeat Formula from the Edit menu.

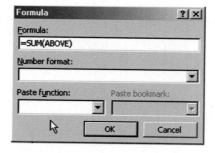

To total a column or row of numbers:

1. Position the insertion point in the empty cell that is to contain the answer.
2. Select **Formula** from the Table menu. *=SUM(ABOVE)* displays in the Formula box.
3. Click **OK** if you wish to add a column of numbers.
4. Change the word *ABOVE* to *LEFT* if you are adding numbers in a row; then click **OK**.

Internal Citations

Internal citations are an easy and practical method of documentation. The last name of the author(s), the publication date, and the page number(s) of the cited material are shown in parentheses within the body of the report (Crawford, 2002, 134). This information cues a reader to the name Crawford in the reference list included at the end of the report. When the author's name is used in the text to introduce the quotation, only the year of publication and the page numbers appear in parentheses: "Crawford (2002, 134) said that . . . ."

Short, direct quotations of three lines or fewer are enclosed within quotation marks. Long quotations of four lines or more are indented 0.5" from the left margin and SS. A DS or one blank line comes before and after the long quotation. The first line is indented an additional 0.5" if the quotation is the beginning of a paragraph.

If a portion of the text that is referenced is omitted, use an ellipsis (. . .) to show the omission. An ellipsis is three periods, each preceded and followed by a space. If a period occurs at the end of a sentence, include the period or punctuation.

deserves more attention that it gets. "Successful businesses have long known the importance of good verbal communication." (Catlette, 2000, 29).

Short Quotation

Probably no successful enterprise exists that does not rely for its success upon the ability

of its members to communicate:

> Make no mistake; both written and verbal communication are the stuff upon which success is built . . . . Both forms deserve careful study by any business that wants to grow. Successful businesspeople must read, write, speak, and listen with skill. (Schaefer, 1999, 28)

Long Quotation

APPLICATIONS

42e-d1
Two-Page Report with Long Quotations

1. Key the unbound report that follows.
2. Press ENTER to position the main heading at about 2". SS the two-line main heading as shown. DS the report.
3. Insert page number to display at the right; suppress page number on the first page.
4. Check for side headings alone at the bottom of the page.
5. Save the report as **42e-d1**.

COMPLETE AND ACCURATE DOCUMENTATION ESSENTIAL FOR EFFECTIVE REPORTS

Preparing a thorough and convincing report requires excellent research, organization, and composition skills as well as extensive knowledge of documenting referenced materials. The purpose of this report is to present the importance of documenting a report with credible references and the techniques for creating accurate citations.

Documenting with References

For a report to be credible and accepted by its readers, a thorough review of related literature is essential. This background information is an important part of the report and provides believability of the writer and of the report. When sharing this literature in the body of the report, the report writer understands the following basic principles of report documentation:

82b-d4
Merge/Split Cells
and Right Tab

1. Key the table as a 3-column, 8-row table. Save as **82b-d4**.

2. Increase the height of row 1 to .75". Center the headings vertically and horizontally in the row. Change the height of rows 2–7 to **.3**.

3. Merge cells A2 and A3; center *College* horizontally and vertically in the cell.

4. Center the table vertically and horizontally.

TIP

Split columns B and C by selecting the column; then click **Table**, click **Split Cells**, and change the number of columns to 2.

OREGON STATE COLLEGE 2004–2005 Enrollments				
College	Semester		Division	
	Fall	Spring	Upper	Lower
Business	1,043	677	120	1,600
Computer Science	750	322	63	1,095
Agriculture	43	12	2	53
Arts and Literature	68	21	3	86
Allied Health	875	192	191	873

82b-d5
Merge/Split Cells
and Adjust Row Height

1. Key the table as a 3-column, 7-row table; split columns B and C. Save as **82b-d5**.

2. Adjust the height of row 1 to **.8"**. Center and bold the headings. Center the headings vertically and horizontally in the row.

3. Center-align columns B and C. Decimal-align columns D and E.

4. Change the height of rows 2–6 to **.3**.

5. Center the table vertically and horizontally.

OUTPATIENT PROSPECTIVE PAYMENT SYSTEM Unadjusted National Medicare Reimbursement				
Description	Code		Insurance	
	CPT	APC	Medicare	Coinsurance
Immobilization	77341	0303	71.08	69.28
Basic Dosimetry	77300	0304	388.52	498.26
Daily IMRT Treatment	60174	0302	7,625.19	8,662.14
Continuing Physics	77336	0311	270.48	253.26

- All ideas of others must be cited so that credit is given appropriately.

- The reader will need to be able to locate the material using the information included in the reference citation.

- Format rules apply to ideas stated as direct quotations and ideas that are paraphrased.

- A thorough list of references adds integrity to the report and to the report writer.

Good writers learn quickly how to evaluate the many printed and electronic references that may have been located to support the theme of the report being written. Those references judged acceptable are then cited in the report. Writers of the *Publication Manual of the American Psychological Association* (1994, 174-175) share these simple procedures for preparing a reference list that correlates with the references cited in the report body:

Long quotation ———
> Note that a reference list cites works that specifically support a particular article. In contrast, a bibliography cites works for background or for further reading. . . . References cited in text must appear in the references list; conversely, each entry in the reference list must be cited in text.

Using a Style Manual

Three popular style manuals are the *MLA Handbook, The Chicago Manual of Style,* and the *Publication Manual of the American Psychological Association.* After selecting a style, carefully study the acceptable formats for citing books, magazines, newspapers, brochures, online journals, e-mail messages, and other sources. Visit Web sites such as http://www.wisc.edu/ writing/Handbook/DocChicago.html, http://www.mla.org, and http://www. apastyle.org/elecref.html for assistance in understanding these styles.

With the availability and volume of excellent electronic resources, writers are including a number of electronic citations along with printed journals, books, and newspapers. Electronic citations may include online journal articles or abstracts, articles on CD-ROM, e-mail messages, discussion list messages, etc. To format references for documents retrieved electronically, Lehman and Dufrene (2002, B-9) offer the following guidelines:

Long quotation ———
> The various referencing styles are fairly standardized as to the elements included when citing documents retrieved electronically. . . . Include the following items: author (if given), date of publication, title of article and/or name of publication, electronic medium (such as online or CD-ROM), volume, series, page, path (Uniform Resource Locator or Internet address), and date you retrieved or accessed the resource.

42e-d2
Title Page

Prepare a title page for report **42e-d1**. Save the document as **42e-d2**.

82b-d1
AutoFormat/Decimal Tab

1. Key the heading and create the table shown below.
2. Apply the **Table List 6** format.
3. Center column B; right-align columns C and D.
4. Center the table vertically and horizontally. Save as **82b-d1**.

LAUREL CANYON ENTERPRISES

Employee	I.D.	Hardware Sales	Software Sales
Alexander, J.	R492	$105,134,384	$1,868,553,280
Courtenay, W.	R856	79,364,091	977,219,500
Holson, E.	C845	9,987,120	81,003,367
Rajeh, C.	M451	82,665,900	1,052,564,100

82b-d2
Insert Rows

TIP
A quick way to insert a row at the end of the table is to click the insertion point in the last cell and press TAB.

1. Open **82b-d1**. Save as **82b-d2**.
2. Insert additional rows and key the names and accompanying information below in correct alphabetical order. Save again and print.

Palombo, L.	K511	44,296,101	971,360,515
Talbert, S.	P053	82,091,433	985,201,500

82b-d3
Delete Rows and Insert Column

TIP
To insert a column, select **Table, Insert**, and then choose **Columns to the Left** or **Columns to the Right**.

1. Open **82b-d2**. Save as **82b-d3**.
2. Delete the rows that contain ID numbers **R856** and **M451**.
3. Insert a new column to the left of the Employee column and key the following information. Center the column.

Team
Blue
Gold
Blue
Gold

4. Change the table to **Table List 3** format. Recenter the table and recenter the copy vertically in the cells.
5. Save again and print.

Two-Page Report with References

43a
Warmup
Key each line twice SS.

alphabetic	1	Melva Bragg required exactly a dozen jackets for the winter trip.
figures	2	The 1903 copy of my book had 5 parts, 48 chapters, and 672 pages.
direct reach	3	Olga, the French goalie, defended well against the frazzled team.
easy	4	Rodney and a neighbor may go to the dock with us to work for Ken.

| 1 | 2 | 3 | 4 | 5 | 6 | 7 | 8 | 9 | 10 | 11 | 12 | 13 |

43b
Timed Writings
Key one 3' timing; then key one 5' timing.

  all letters

gwam | 3' | 5'

Subtle differences exist among role models, mentors, and sponsors.   A role model is a person you can emulate, or one who provides a good example to follow.   A mentor is one who will advise, coach, or guide you when you need information about your job or your organization.   A sponsor is a person who will support you or recommend you for a position or a new responsibility.

One person may fill all three roles, or several people may serve as role models, mentors, or sponsors.   These individuals usually have higher ranks than you do, which means they will be able to get information that you and your peers may not have. Frequently, a mentor will share information with you that will enable you to make good decisions about your career.

	3'	5'
	4	2	32
	8	5	35
	12	7	37
	16	10	40
	21	12	42
	25	15	45
	30	18	48
	34	20	50
	38	23	53
	42	25	55
	46	28	58
	50	30	60

3' | 1 | 2 | 3 | 4 |
5' | 1 | 2 | 3 |

43c

Bullets, Page Break, Hanging Indent

In formatting a two-page report, you may need to use the Bullets and Page Break features. When formatting the references in a two-page report, you will also need to use the Hanging Indent feature.

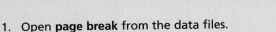

DRILL 1 **REVIEW BULLETS, PAGE BREAK, HANGING INDENT**

1. Open **page break** from the data files.
2. Format the last three paragraphs as numbered bullets.
3. Insert a hard page break to begin REFERENCES on a new page. Position insertion point at about 2.1" for references page.
4. Format references as a hanging indent.
5. Save as **43c-drill1**.

NEW FUNCTIONS

82a

Decimal Tabs

Numbers containing decimals are often more attractive if they are aligned with a decimal tab. The decimal tab allows you to center the numbers in the column and still have them aligned at the decimal point. Notice how the numbers in column B are easier to read than those in column A.

Right-align on Toolbar	Decimal Tab
1.2	1.2
39.45	39.45
678.3	678.3

To set a decimal tab in a column:

1. Select the column or cells to be aligned (do not include the column heading).

2. Click the tab marker at the far left of the Horizontal Ruler, and change the tab type to a decimal tab.

3. Click the Horizontal Ruler to set the tab. Repeat the process with each column that requires a tab.

DRILL 1   SET DECIMAL TABS

1. Key the table above. Use left alignment when keying rows 2–4.

2. Select rows 2–4 in column A and click the **Align Right** button.

3. Select rows 2–4 in column B; set a decimal tab in the column so the numbers automatically align with the decimal point.

4. Save as **82a-drill1**.

DRILL 2   MERGE CELLS AND ADJUST ROW HEIGHT

1. Key the table. Right-align column B. Set a decimal tab in column C.

2. Merge row 1 and increase height to .5". Center the title vertically and horizontally in the row.

3. Save as **82a-drill2**.

INVESTMENT PORTFOLIO		
Company	**Units Sold**	**Increase/ Decrease**
Aztec Printing	55,275	+4.85
Palomar Clothing	120,890	–.59
Quest Supplies	8,321	–10.5
Robles Framing	986	–39.1

References Page

References cited in the report are listed at the end of the report in alphabetical order by authors' last names. The reference list may be titled REFERENCES or BIB-LIOGRAPHY. Become familiar with the three types of references listed below:

1. A book reference includes the name of the author (last name first), work (italicized), city of publication, publisher, and copyright date.

2. A magazine reference shows the name of the author (last name first), article (in quotation marks), magazine title (italicized), date of publication, and page references.

3. A reference retrieved electronically includes the author (inverted), article (in quotation marks), publication (italicized), publication information, Internet address, and date the document was retrieved or accessed (in parentheses).

Begin the list of references on a new page by inserting a manual page break at the end of the report. Use the same margins as the first page of a report, and number the page at the top right of the page. The main heading (REFERENCES or BIBLIOG-RAPHY) should be approximately 2" from the top of the page. References should be SS in hanging indent format; DS between references.

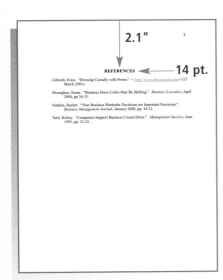

2.1"   3

REFERENCES ← 14 pt.

Gilreath, Erica. "Dressing Casually with Power." < http://www.dresscasual.com> (23 March 2001).

Monaghan, Susan. "Business Dress Codes May Be Shifting." *Business Executive*, April 2000, pp 34-35.

Sutphin, Rachel. "Your Business Wardrobe Decisions are Important Decisions." *Business Management Journal*, January 2000, pp. 10-12.

Tartt, Kelsey. "Companies Support Business Casual Dress." *Management Success*, June 1995, pp. 23-25.

1. Open **42e-d1**. Save it as **43e-d1**.

2. Position the insertion point at the end of the report. Press CTRL + ENTER to begin a new page. Key **REFERENCES** approximately 2" from the top of the page.

3. Key the references in hanging indent style. (*Hint:* Try the shortcut, CTRL + T.)

Lehman, C. M., and Dufrene, D. D. *Business Communication.* 13th ed. Cincinnati: South-Western/Thomson Learning, 2002.

Publication Manual of the American Psychological Association. 4th ed. Washington, D.C.: American Psychological Association, 2001.

1. Key the following unbound report DS. SS the long quote, and indent it 0.5".

2. Number the pages at the top right; suppress page number on the first page.

3. Key the references on a references page at the end of the report.

4. Switch to Print Layout view to verify the page numbers and ensure there are no widows or orphans.

5. Save the report as **43e-d2**.

81d-d1
Table with Shading

1. Key the heading, **LAUREL CANYON ENTERPRISES,** and create the table shown below. Save as **81d-d1**.

2. Apply 20% shading to row 1. Center the column headings. Center column B and right-align columns C and D. Center the table vertically on the page.

Employee	I.D.	Hardware	Software
Alexander, J.	R492	$105,134,384	$1,868,553,280
Courtenay, W.	R856	79,364,091	1,384,219,500
Holsonback, E.	C845	27,386,427	1,098,237,260
Palombo, L.	K511	44,296,101	971,360,515
Rajeh, C.	M451	82,665,900	1,052,564,100
Talbert, S.	P053	82,091,433	985,201,500

81d-d2
AutoFormat

1. Place the title, **SOFTWARE TRAINING SCHEDULE,** on Line 2.1". Apply **Table List 4** format. Center columns B and C. Save as **81d-d2**.

Software	Date	Time	Room
Microsoft Word	02-18-04	9:00	Ballroom A
WordPerfect	02-18-04	10:30	Ballroom A
Microsoft Excel	02-18-04	1:00	Red Lion
Lotus	02-19-04	9:00	Diamond
Microsoft Access	02-19-04	1:30	Emerald
Oracle	02-20-04	9:00	Emerald
Windows 2000	02-19-04	10:30	Ballroom A
Windows Me	02-20-04	1:30	Diamond
Windows 2000 Server	02-20-04	3:00	Emerald

81d-d3
Table

TIP

The Grid 8 style bolds the last column and the last row. Deselect the checkboxes for Last row and Last column so they will not be placed in bold print.

1. Key the table and add the title **GOLDEN HANDSHAKE CANDIDATES.** Apply the **Table Grid 8** style. Center the table vertically. Save as **81d-d3**.

Employee	Department	Hire Date
Thayer, Jeffrey	Information Systems	8/21/75
Stevenson, Allison	Human Resources	7/27/72
Lew, Richard	Marketing	6/15/76
Gore, Rajah	Information Systems	8/16/76
Castillo, Maria	Human Resources	10/23/74
Husaan, Miram	Information Systems	12/2/72
Nelson, Barbara	Marketing	3/16/74
Wallace, Reggie	Human Resources	8/10/75

TRENDS FOR BUSINESS DRESS

Casual dress in the workplace has become widely accepted. According to a national study conducted by Schoenholtz & Associates in 1995, a majority of the companies surveyed allowed employees to dress casually one day a week, usually Fridays (Tartt, 1995, 23). The trend continued to climb as shown by the 1997 survey by Schoenholtz & Associates. Fifty-eight percent of office workers surveyed were allowed to dress casually for work every day, and 92 percent of the offices allowed employees to dress casually occasionally (Sutphin, 2000, 10).

19
33
47
62
76
91
106
114

Decline in Trend

118

The trend to dress casually that started in the early 1990s may be shifting, states Susan Monaghan (2000, 34):

131
140

Although a large number of companies are allowing casual attire every day or only on Fridays, a current survey revealed a decline of 10 percent in 1999 when compared to the same survey conducted in 1998. Some experts predict the new trend for business dress codes will be a dress up day every week.

152
165
177
181
190

What accounts for this decline in companies permitting casual dress? Several reasons may include:

203
210

1. Confusion of what business casual is with employees slipping into dressing too casually (work jeans, faded tee-shirts, old sneakers, and improperly fitting clothing).

223
236
245

2. Casual dress does not portray the adopted corporate image of the company.

258
260

3. Employees are realizing that promotion decisions are affected by a professional appearance.

274
279

Guidelines for Business Dress

285

Companies are employing image consultants to teach employees what is appropriate business casual and to plan the best business attire to project the corporate image. Erica Gilreath (2000), the author of *Casual Dress*, a guidebook on business casual, provides excellent advice on how to dress casually and still command the power needed for business success. She presents the following advice to professionals:

297
316
327
342
357
367

- Do not wear any clothing that is designed for recreational or sports activities, e.g., cargo pants or pants with elastic waist.

381
393

- Invest the time in pressing khakis and shirts or pay the price for professional dry cleaning. Wrinkled clothing does not enhance one's credibility.

407
421
424

- Do not wear sneakers.

428

- Be sure clothing fits properly. Avoid baggy clothes or clothes that are too tight.

443
446

In summary, energetic employees working to climb the corporate ladder will need to plan their dress carefully. If business casual is appropriate, it's best to consult the experts on business casual to ensure a professional image.

458
472
488
492

TIP

Align Bullets
Select the bulleted items and click Increase Indent to align the bullets with the paragraphs.

Table Format Guides

1. Leave an approximate 2" top margin or center the table vertically on the page.

2. Center, bold, use 12-point font, and key the main heading in all caps. Key the secondary heading a DS below the main heading in bold, centered, and 12-point font; capitalize main words. Center and bold all column headings.

3. Adjust the column widths attractively, and center the table horizontally.

4. Increase the row height to .3" and center the text vertically in the cell.

5. Align text within cells at the left. Align numbers at the right. Align decimal number of varying lengths at the decimal point.

6. When a table appears within a document, DS before and after the table.

To center the table horizontally, increase the row height and center the text vertically in the cell:

1. Select only the table; be careful not to select any ¶ markers outside the table.

2. Select **Table Properties** from the Table menu. Click the **Table** tab, and then select **Center Alignment**.

3. Click the **Row** tab. Key the desired height in the Specify Height box.

4. Click the **Cell** tab. Choose Center Alignment and click **OK**.

Tables and Borders Toolbar

The Tables and Borders toolbar allows you to add shading, borders, patterns, and color to your tables. Table AutoFormat, which allows you to apply a variety of preformatted styles to your tables, can also be accessed from the toolbar.

Shading. Select the cells or the row, click the down arrow, and choose a color or shade of gray. *Option*: Choose **Borders and Shading** on the Format menu. Click the **Shading** tab. Under Style, click the down arrow to change *Clear* to **15%**; then click **OK**.

AutoFormat. Click the table, click the **AutoFormat** button, and select a style.

Key the table and shade row 1 15%. Key the text so that it fits on one line in each row. Save as **81c-drill1**.

Open **81c-drill1**. Remove the shading and apply **AutoFormat List 8** style. Recenter table and text in cells. Save as **81c-drill2**.

Agent	Sales $	Office
Jacqueline C. Zahradnik	3,869,451	Lakeshore Boulevard
Katherine Ann Harrington	2,564.081	Lexington Heights
Michael T. Wang	1,975,392	Center City

43e-d2
Continued

REFERENCES

494

Gilreath, Erica. "Dressing Casually with Power."   504
http://www.dresscasual.com (23 March 2001).   513

Monaghan, Susan. "Business Dress Codes May Be Shifting." *Business*   527
Executive, April 2000, 34–35.   533

Sutphin, Rachel. "Your Business Wardrobe Decisions Are Important   546
Decisions." *Business Management Journal*, January 2000, 10–12.   559

Tartt, Kelsey. "Companies Support Business Casual Dress."   571
Management Success, June 1995, 23–25.   578

43e-d3
Title Page

1. Prepare a title page for the unbound report completed in **43e-d2**. Assume the report is prepared for Donovan National Bank by you as Image Consultant. Use the current date.

2. Use bold and 14 point for all lines. Center the page vertically.

3. Save as **43e-d3**.

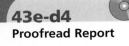

43e-d4
Proofread Report

1. Open **Report4** from the data files and print.

2. Proofread the report for consistency in the formatting of reports. Mark any errors you locate on the printed report. As an editor, you will want to use the proofreaders' marks shown on page 55 to mark the corrections. In the upper-right corner, write the following: **Your Name, Editor**.

3. Exchange reports with a classmate. Then make the corrections indicated on your classmate's edited report. If you do not agree with his/her edits, discuss the questioned items and reach an agreement. Make the final edits.

4. At the end of the corrected report, key the following:

   a. **Corrections made by: Your Name**

   b. **1st Editor: Your Classmate's Name**

5. Save as **43e-d4** and print. Submit the report you marked in step 2 and the report you corrected in step 3. (Team Goal: Correct all the errors.)

SKILLBUILDING

43f

Use the remaining class time to build your skills using the Skill Builder module within *Keyboarding Pro*.

Table Mastery

- Review create tables.
- Edit and format tables.
- Perform calculations in tables.
- Landscape tables.
- Rotate text in tables.

LESSON 81 Table Review

SKILLBUILDING

81a
Warmup
Key each line twice SS.

figures 1 The winning numbers for this week are 15, 27, 36, 48, 19, and 10.
2 Weekday show times are 12:30, 6:30, 7:15, 8:00, 9:45, and 10:15.
3 Take Highway 693 to Route 28 and exit 145th to get to 7th Avenue.
    | 1 | 2 | 3 | 4 | 5 | 6 | 7 | 8 | 9 | 10 | 11 | 12 | 13 |

81b
Timed Writings
Key a 3' and a 5' writing.

	gwam	3'	5'
A day planner can make your life easier by giving order to	4	2	38
chaos. It will organize the details of your week and notify you	8	5	40
when you should be somewhere. It will zealously remind you of	12	7	43
your duties and obligations. Just store the names and addresses	17	10	45
of your contacts, and it will quickly retrieve them for you.	21	12	48
You can enjoy life more when you are organized. You will	25	15	50
be able to remember all your usual classes, quizzes, projects,	29	17	53
and work responsibilities. You can also expect to know where you	33	20	55
need to go, arrive promptly, and not miss any important events.	37	22	58
Electronic planners are called "personal digital assistants"	42	25	60
or PDAs. A PDA can carry out all the functions of a day planner	46	28	63
and also let you send and receive e-mail. In addition, many PDAs	50	30	65
can share files with Word and Excel software; some allow you to	55	33	68
use the Internet. You can even use certain PDAs as telephones.	59	35	70

```
3' |      1      |      2      |      3      |      4      |
5' |         1         |         2         |         3         |
```

Leftbound Report with Footnotes

SKILLBUILDING

44a
Warmup
Key each line twice SS.

alphabetic	1	Jim Ryan was able to liquefy frozen oxygen; he kept it very cold.
double letters	2	Aaron took accounting lessons at a community college last summer.
one-hand	3	Link agrees you'll get a reward only as you join nonunion racers.
easy	4	Hand Bob a bit of cocoa, a pan of cod, an apricot, and six clams.

| 1 | 2 | 3 | 4 | 5 | 6 | 7 | 8 | 9 | 10 | 11 | 12 | 13 |

44b
Timed Writings
Key a 3' and a 5' writing.

 all letters

gwam 3' | 5'

	3'	5'	
The kinds of leisure activities you choose constitute	4	2	62
your life style and, to a great extent, reflect your personality.	8	5	65
For example, if your daily activities are people oriented, you	12	7	67
may balance this by spending your free time alone. On the other	17	10	70
hand, if you would rather be with people most of the time, your	21	13	72
socialization needs may be very high. At the other end of the	25	15	75
scale are people who are engaged in machine-oriented work and	29	18	77
also enjoy spending leisure time alone. These people tend to be	33	20	80
rather quiet and reserved.	35	21	81

3' | 1 | 2 | 3 | 4 |
5' | 1 | 2 | 3 |

44c
Troublesome Pairs
Key each line once; repeat if time permits.

d	5	do did dad sad faded daddy madder diddle deduced hydrated dredged
k	6	keys sake kicked karat kayak karate knock knuckle knick kilometer
d/k	7	The ten tired and dizzy kids thought the doorknob was the donkey.
w	8	we were who away whew snow windward waterway window webworm award
o	9	on to too onto solo oleo soil cook looked location emotion hollow
w/o	10	Those who know their own power and are committed will follow through.
b	11	be bib sub bear book bribe fiber bombard blueberry babble baboons
v	12	vet vat van viva have over avoid vapor valve seven vanish vanilla
b/v	13	Bo gave a very big beverage and seven coins to everybody bowling.
r	14	or rear rare roar saturate reassure rather northern surge quarrel
u	15	yours undue unity useful unique unusual value wound youth succumb
r/u	16	The truth of the matter is that only Ruth can run a rummage sale.

| 1 | 2 | 3 | 4 | 5 | 6 | 7 | 8 | 9 | 10 | 11 | 12 | 13 |

TECHNIQUE TIP
Keep hands and arms still as you reach up to the third row and down to the first row.

Module 12: Checkpoint

1. _____ are references at the bottom of a page; _____ are references at the end of the document.

2. To enter a section break, click _____ on the Insert menu.

3. To change page number format, select Page Numbers on the _____ menu.

4. To change to a different format for numbers in Section 2 of a document, you must first _____ _____ between sections.

5. A(n) _____ is a list of topics in a document and the page numbers on which they appear.

Performance Assessment

Document 1
Report

1. Open **Multimedia Artists** from the data files.
2. Insert page numbers at top right. Do not print on the first page.
3. Apply **Heading 1** style to the main and side headings.
4. Check that side headings are not alone at the bottom of the page.
5. Save as **Checkpoint12-d1**; print.

Document 2
Title Page

1. Create a title page for **Checkpoint12-d1**. Assume you are preparing for your instructor by you. Use the current date.
2. Save as **Checkpoint12-d2**. Do not close; you will use it in the next document.

   Option: You may create the title page in the same file as the report (**Checkpoint12-d1**).

Document 3
Table of Contents

1. The document **Checkpoint12-d2** should be open. Save as **Checkpoint12-d3**.
2. Create a table of contents. Set a leader tab at 5.5" and a right tab at 6.0".
3. Save and print. Assemble the report in the correct order.
4. Number the preliminary pages using lowercase Roman numerals at the bottom center. Do not print number on the first page.

   Option: You may create the table of contents in the same file with the title page and the report. You will need to use section breaks to number pages correctly.

Footnotes

References cited in a report are often indicated within the text by a superscript number (… story.[1]) and a corresponding footnote with full information at the bottom of the same page where the reference was cited.

Word automatically numbers footnotes sequentially with Arabic numerals (1, 2, 3), positions them at the left margin, and applies 10-point type. After keying footnotes, select them and apply 12-point type to be consistent with the report text. Indent the first line of a footnote 0.5" from the left margin. Footnotes are automatically SS; however, DS between footnotes.

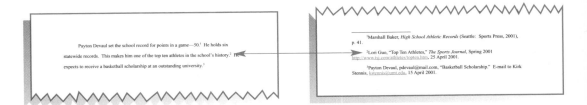

To insert and edit footnotes:

1. Switch to Normal view and position the insertion point where you want to insert the footnote reference.

2. On the menu, click **Insert**, **Reference**, and then **Footnote**. The Footnote and Endnote dialog box displays.

3. Be sure Footnotes is selected and Bottom of page (the default location) is displayed. Then click **Insert**.

4. The reference number and the insertion point appear in the Footnote Pane.

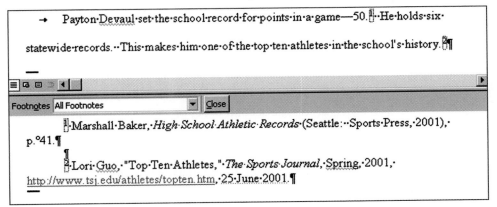

5. Move the insertion point before the reference number, and press TAB to indent it. Then move the insertion point beyond the number and key the footnote in 12-point font. (Note the default font is 10 point.) Click **Close** to return to the document text. (*Note*: If you are in Print Layout View, click anywhere above the footnote divider line to return to the document.)

6. To edit a footnote, double-click on the reference number in the text. Edit the footnote text in the Footnote Pane.

7. To delete a footnote, select the reference number in the text and press DELETE.

(Level 1 heading)   Web Site Development Costs

The projected costs of developing a Web site that is capable of handling a reasonably high volume of transaction type business and the associated advertising materials are expensive. The estimated cost of an in-house development team is $110,000; traditional agency, $225,000; and cyberagency, $275,000.

(Level 1 heading)   Recommendations

Pat's Place must enhance its Internet marketing. A number of strategies will be presented to the Executive Committee for accomplishing this objective. Considerable Web site work must be done before Pat's Place will be able to conduct a significant amount of business over the Internet. A team is developing a strategy to enhance the Web site and ways to increase the amount of business conducted on the site.

Footnote text:

1. Mark Levinson, "Benchmarking Internet Advertising," *The Small Business Journal* (March 2001), p. 49.

2. Mary Stackhouse, *Web Site Development* (Chicago: Seiver, Inc., 2002), pp. 86–92.

80c-d2
Title Page

1. Prepare a title page for the report in **80c-d1** and save it as **80c-d2**. Format in Arial 14 point.
2. Assume the report is prepared for **Meredith Ravennel** by you as Project Director.
3. Save. Do not close the document; you will use it in the next application.

80c-d3
Table of Contents

1. The document **80c-d2** should be open. Save as **80c-d3**.
2. As the second page, prepare a table of contents for **80c-d1**.
3. Number these preliminary pages appropriately. Do not print a page number on the title page.
4. Save; print and then assemble the report in the correct order.

80c-d4
(Challenge)
Section Breaks

1. Open **80c-d3**. Save as **80c-d4**.
2. Position insertion point at the end of the document. Insert the file **80c-d1**. You have inserted the title page and table of contents as the preliminary pages.
3. Insert section breaks appropriately and number pages appropriately.
4. Save and print. Assemble in correct order.

DRILL 1   **FOOTNOTES**

1. Key the paragraph in Drill 2 DS, and add the three footnotes.
2. Format footnotes in 12 point and DS between them.
3. Include all three sources on a separate references page in proper reference format. Select the title *References* and format it in 14 pt., bold, centered.
4. Save as **44d-drill1** and print.

DRILL 2   **DELETE FOOTNOTES**

1. Open **44d-drill1**. Delete the second footnote. Update the references page.
2. Save as **44d-drill2** and print.

Payton Devaul set the school record for points in a game—50.[1] He holds six statewide records. This makes him one of the top ten athletes in the school's history.[2] He expects to receive a basketball scholarship at an outstanding university.[3]

Footnotes

Book ——————— [1]Marshall Baker, *High School Athletic Records.* (Seattle: Sports Press, 2001), p. 41.

Online Journal ——————— [2]Lori Guo, "Top Ten Athletes," *The Sports Journal*, Spring 2001, http://www.tsj.edu/athletes/topten.htm, 25 June 2001.

E-mail ——————— [3]Payton Devaul, pdevaul@mail.com. "Basketball Scholarship." E-mail to Kirk Stennis, kstennis@umt.edu, 15 April 2001.

References

Baker, Marshall. *High School Athletic Records.* Seattle: Sports Press, 2001.

Devaul, Payton. pdevaul@mail.com. "Basketball Scholarship." E-mail to Kirk Stennis, kstennis@umt.edu. 15 April 2001.

Guo, Lori. "Top Ten Athletes." *The Sports Journal*, Spring 2001. http://www.tsj.edu/athletes/topten.htm (25 June 2001).

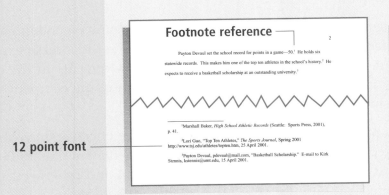

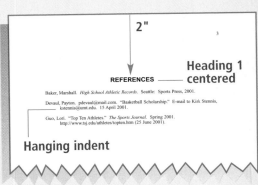

Firms using the Internet as one of their top five marketing strategies reported mixed results. Most of the firms indicated that the results over the past two years far exceeded the results of the earlier years. Many firms were still experimenting with alternatives for using the Internet. Most of them were using the equivalent of reprints of catalogs and other promotional materials.

(Level 1 heading) Site Development Strategies

Firms in the industry generally had developed their own Web site. Advertising experts interviewed believe that site development is critical to the success of cyberspace advertising and that the poor results some firms reported might be attributed to poorly developed Web pages. Benchmarking companies in a range of industries produces better results than using only the industry of a

(Insert footnote 1) company.

Three types of strategies for developing a Web site predominate: in-house development, the use of traditional full-service advertising agencies, and the use of the new cyberagencies that specialize in interactive marketing.

(Level 2 heading) In-House Development

The obvious advantage of in-house development is lower costs. The primary disadvantage is that most organizations have limited expertise in developing effective Web sites. A review of the literature indicates that about 45 percent of all Web sites currently in use were developed by company employees.

(Insert footnote 2)

(Level 2 heading) Traditional Full-Service Agencies

The key advantage of using the traditional advertising agency that handles other advertising for a company is that the Internet advertising can be an integral part of the company's total advertising plan. The primary disadvantage is that the traditional agency is not likely to have much expertise in cyberadvertising. About 25 percent of the Web sites in use were developed by traditional advertising agencies.

(Level 1 heading) Cyberagencies

These agencies specialize in interactive advertising on the Internet. The advantage they have over traditional agencies is the level of expertise in this new field. The disadvantages are lack of knowledge about the company and making interactive advertising an integral part of the company's total advertising.

Experts point out that cyberadvertising will be effective only when it is integrated into the mainstream advertising media such as radio, television, and print media. A joint venture of traditional and cyberagencies may offer the greatest promise for using the Internet effectively.

Leftbound report

The binding on a report usually takes about 0.5" inch of space. Therefore, when a report is bound on the left, set the left margin to 1.5" for all pages.

The same right, top, and bottom margins are used for both unbound and leftbound reports.

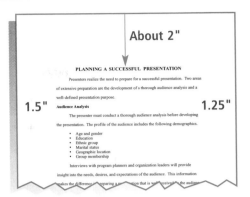

About 2"

PLANNING A SUCCESSFUL PRESENTATION

Presenters realize the need to prepare for a successful presentation. Two areas of extensive preparation are the development of a thorough audience analysis and a well-defined presentation purpose.

Audience Analysis

The presenter must conduct a thorough audience analysis before developing the presentation. The profile of the audience includes the following demographics.

- Age and gender
- Education
- Ethnic group
- Marital status
- Geographic location
- Group membership

Interviews with program planners and organization leaders will provide insight into the needs, desires, and expectations of the audience. This information makes the difference in preparing a presentation that is well received by the audience.

1.5"   1.25"

44f-d1
Leftbound Report

1. Key the leftbound report on page 158. Save the report as **44f-d1**.
2. To create the bulleted list, key the items; then select the items and apply bullets.
3. With the items selected, click the **Increase Indent** button to align the bullets with the paragraph indent.

44f-d2
Title Page

1. Create a title page for the leftbound report prepared in Document 1. Set the left margin at 1.5".
2. Prepare the title page for **John E. Swartsfager, Marketing Director**, by you as the **Information Technology Manager**.
3. Save the document as **44f-d2**.

44f-d3
Leftbound Report

1. Open **39e-d2** and format the document as a leftbound report.
2. Insert page numbers. Do not print page number on first page.
3. Add the last paragraph shown below, and save the document as **44f-d3**.

Summary

Remember to plan your page layout with the three basic elements of effective page design. Always include sufficient white space to give an uncluttered appearance. Learn to add bold when emphasis is needed, and do consider your audience when choosing typestyles. Finally, use typestyles to add variety to your layout, but remember, no more than two typestyles in a document.

44f-d4
Leftbound Report

1. Reformat report **43e-d2** as an unbound report.
2. Change the numbered list to a bulleted list.
3. Preview the document for correct pagination; then save it as **44f-d4**.

On the signal to begin, key the documents in sequence. When time has been called, proofread the documents again and correct any errors you may have overlooked. Reprint if necessary.

80c-d1
Leftbound Report with References Page

1. Open **business** from the data files. Format as a leftbound report with references page. Apply styles and other features as indicated on the copy below and on the following pages.
2. Single-space the report. Insert page numbers at top right. Do not show page number on first page.
3. Use Heading 1 style centered for titles, Heading 1 style for level-one headings, and Heading 2 style for level-two headings (paragraph).
4. Insert footnotes where shown. Create the references page.
5. Save the document as **80c-d1** and print.

(title) Conducting Business on the Internet

This study was conducted to determine the desirability of enhancing the current Web site to increase Internet advertising and to begin conducting business over the Internet. Several factors were considered:

(Bullet each factor and delete commas) Internet advertising by competitors, Level of business conducted by competitors, Site development strategies, Estimated cost of enhancing the Web site

(Level 1 heading) Competitive Internet Usage

Of the 1,000 randomly selected firms in the industry that were surveyed, 520 (52 percent) responded. Firms were asked to indicate if Internet advertising was one of their top five marketing strategies in each of three years (1998, 2000, and 2002). They were also asked to indicate if they conducted at least 15 percent of their business over the Internet.

Analysis of the data shows that firms in the industry have increased their usage of the Internet as one of their top five marketing strategies from 1998 to 2000. However, the growth in the percentage of firms in the industry that conduct at least 15 percent of their business on the Internet has not been as rapid.

Set DS; Press ENTER 3 times

About 2"

PLANNING A SUCCESSFUL PRESENTATION

Presenters realize the need to prepare for a successful presentation. Two areas of extensive preparation are the development of a thorough audience analysis and a well-defined presentation purpose.

Audience Analysis

1.5"   The presenter must conduct a thorough audience analysis before developing the presentation. The profile of the audience includes the following demographics.[1]   1.25"

- Age and gender
- Education
Align bullet ——→ • Ethnic group
with paragraphs • Marital status
- Geographic location
- Group membership

Interviews with program planners and organization leaders will provide insight into the needs, desires, and expectations of the audience. This information makes the difference in preparing a presentation that is well received by the audience.

Purpose of the Presentation

After analyzing the audience profile, the presenter has a clear focus on the needs of the audience and then writes a well-defined purpose of the presentation. With a clear focus, the presenter confidently conducts research and organizes a presentation that is on target. The presenter remembers to state the purpose in the introduction of the presentation to assist the audience in understanding the well-defined direction of the presentation.

12 point font ——→ [1]Susie Phelan, *Presentations*. (Indianapolis: King Press, 2002), p. 38.

SKILLBUILDING

80a
Warmup
Key each line twice SS.

adjacent keys
1 Jamie quickly apologized for submitting the complex reviews late.
2 Where were Mario, Guy, and Luis going after the water polo class?

fig/sym
3 Jay paid Invoice #2846 ($3,017.35) and Invoice #7925 ($8,409.16).
4 I caught 20 halibut (69.5# average) and 37 trout (4.81# average).

| 1 | 2 | 3 | 4 | 5 | 6 | 7 | 8 | 9 | 10 | 11 | 12 | 13 |

80b
Timed Writing
Key a 3' and a 5' writing.

	gwam	3'	5'

Just what does it mean to be young and when is a person young?   4 | 3 | 49
To be young is perhaps a feeling or disposition, a particular manner   9 | 5 | 51
of looking at things and responding to them. To be young is never   13 | 8 | 54
a chronological period or time of life, although it might be a young   18 | 11 | 57
person examining some material with fascination and pleasure or   22 | 13 | 59
the composer Verdi in his eighties writing his best opera. To be   26 | 16 | 62
young might be a person "hanging ten" on a surfboard or swinging   31 | 18 | 64
to a musical composition. To be young might be Einstein in his   35 | 21 | 67
seventies still working with his field theory, sailing his boat,   39 | 24 | 70
or playing his cherished fiddle.   41 | 25 | 71

To be young is never the monopoly of youth. It flourishes   45 | 27 | 73
everywhere visionaries have stimulated our thinking or amazed us.   50 | 30 | 76
To be young in nature is quite desirable whether you are a young   54 | 32 | 78
person, a middle-aged person, or a chronologically old person. To   59 | 35 | 81
be young should be respected whether the beard is soft and curly   63 | 38 | 84
or firm and gray. To be young has no color; it seems often trans-   67 | 40 | 86
lucent with its own imaginative light. There is no generation   71 | 43 | 89
space between the young of any age because they see things as they   76 | 46 | 92
ought to be.   77 | 46 | 92

3' | 1 | 2 | 3 | 4 |
5' | 1 | 2 | 3 |

LESSON 45 Assessment

SKILLBUILDING

45a
Warmup
Key each line twice SS.

one-hand 1 In regard to desert oil wastes, Jill referred only minimum cases.
sentences 2 Carra agrees you'll get a reward only as you join nonunion races.
3 Few beavers, as far as I'm aware, feast on cedar trees in Kokomo.
4 Johnny, after a few stewed eggs, ate a plump, pink onion at noon.
5 A plump, aged monk served a few million beggars a milky beverage.

| 1 | 2 | 3 | 4 | 5 | 6 | 7 | 8 | 9 | 10 | 11 | 12 | 13 |

45b
Timed Writings
Key one 3' timing and one 5' timing.

 all letters

gwam 3' | 5'

How is a hobby different from a business? A very common way to describe the difference between the hobby and the business is that the hobby is done for fun, and the business is done as work which enables people to earn their living. Does that mean that people do not have fun at work or that people do not work with their hobbies? Many people would not agree with that description.

Some people begin work on a hobby just for fun, but then they realize it has the potential to be a business. They soon find out that others enjoy the hobby as well and would expect to pay for the products or services the hobby requires. Many quite successful businesses begin as hobbies. Some of them are small, and some grow to be large operations.

	3'	5'
	4	2 32
	8	5 35
	13	8 38
	17	10 40
	22	13 43
	26	15 45
	30	18 48
	34	21 51
	39	23 53
	43	26 56
	48	29 59
	49	30 60

3' | 1 | 2 | 3 | 4 |
5' | 1 | 2 | 3 |

APPLICATIONS

45c
Assessment

 Continue

 Check

With CheckPro: *CheckPro* will keep track of the time it takes you to complete the entire production test and compute your speed and accuracy rate on each document and summarize the results. When you complete a document, proofread it, check the spelling, and preview for placement. When you are completely satisfied with the document, click the **Continue** button to move to the next document. You will not be able to return and edit a document once you continue to the next document.   Click the **Check** button when you are ready to error-check the test. Review and/or print the document analysis results.

Without CheckPro: On the signal to begin, key the documents in sequence. When time has been called, proofread all documents again; identify errors, and determine *g-pwam*.

$$g\text{-}pwam = \frac{\text{total words keyed}}{25'}$$

The new system has resulted in a 20 percent cost savings over the previous system. In addition, more than 80 percent of the employees indicated that the new system improved their efficiency and effectiveness.

79e-d2
Title Page

1. Open **79e-d1** and save as **79e-d2**.

2. At the top of the document, create a title page as the first page of the report. Assume the report is prepared for Hess and Glenn, Inc. and prepared by you as Consultant. Use the current date. Do not center vertically; position the main heading so title page is centered on the page.

3. Save. Keep this document open for use in the next application.

79e-d3
Table of Contents

1. Open **79e-d2** and save as **79e-d3**.

2. As the second page of the report, create a table of contents. Begin main heading at about 2".

3. Set tabs as follows: leader tab 5.5" and right tab 6.0".

4. Position insertion point at the end of the table of contents. Insert a next page section break. (*Note:* If you had already entered a hard page break so the report would print on the next page, delete the page break to avoid a blank page.)

5. In Section 1, insert lowercase Roman numeral page numbers centered at the bottom of the page. Do not show page number on the first page.

6. Position insertion point in Section 2. Display the Header/Footer toolbar and break the links between both the header and the footer. Delete the page number in the footer.

7. Switch back to the header and insert Arabic numeral page numbers at the top right. Do not print a page number on the first page.

8. Check that page numbers are positioned correctly and that the main heading is positioned at about 2". Save and print. Check the table of contents with the printed report.

79e-d4
(Challenge)
Generate Automatic
Table of Contents

1. Open **79e-d1** and save as **79e-d4**.

2. Apply **Heading 1** style to the main and side headings. Center the main headings and make them initial caps.

3. Position insertion point at the top of the document. Click **Insert, Reference, Index and Tables**. Choose the **Table of Contents** tab. Accept the defaults by clicking **OK**. The table of contents is automatically generated.

4. Open **79e-d2**. Copy the title page. Go to **79e-d4** and paste as the first page.

5. Insert a section break at the end of the table of contents. Insert page numbers for Section 1. Break the link between the two sections. Insert page numbers for Section 2.

6. Save and print the report. Check the table of contents page numbers with the printed report.

1. Key this leftbound report DS. Align bulleted items with the other paragraphs.
2. Number the pages at the top right; suppress the page number on the first page.
3. Insert the file **copyright** from the data files where indicated in the report.
4. Key the references on a separate references page at the end of the report.
5. Save the report as **45c-d1**.

words

COPYRIGHT LAW IN THE INTERNET AGE

7

Copyright owners continue to face copyright challenges as technology advances more rapidly than ever before. History shows us that copyright infringements occur at the introduction of each new invention or emerging technology. Examples include the phonograph and tape recorder and mimeograph and copy machines. Today, the Internet age provides Internet users the ease of copying and distributing electronic files via the Internet.

19
34
49
63
76
92
94

Copyright owners of content published on the Web, photographers who view their photographs on Web pages, and recording artists whose music is downloaded from the Internet are only a few examples of copyright issues resulting from the Internet age. Compounding the issue is that many Internet users may not be aware they are violating copyright law (Zielinski, 1999, 38). The following list shows actions taken daily that are considered copyright infringements:

107
121
134
148
163
179
187

- Copying content from a Web page and pasting it into documents.

200

- Reproducing multiple copies of a journal article that were printed from an online journal.

214
219

- Distributing presentation handouts that contain cartoon characters or other graphics copied from a Web page.

233
241

- Presenting originally designed electronic presentations that contain graphics, sound and video clips, and/or photographs copied from a Web page.

255
269
271

- Duplicating and distributing copies of music downloaded from the Web.

284
286

1. Open **79d-drill1** and save as **79d-drill2**.

2. Position insertion point in Section 1. Insert lowercase Roman numeral page numbers centered at the bottom of the page. Deselect **Show number on first page**.

3. Check page numbers in Section 1.

4. Position insertion point in Section 2. Display the Header/Footer toolbar, and break the links between both the header and the footer. Delete the page number in the footer.

5. Switch back to the header of Section 2. Insert Arabic numeral page numbers at the top right. Deselect **Show number on first page**, and click the **Format** button to start the numbers at 1.

6. Check page numbers in Section 2.

7. Switch back to header. Now that the link has been broken for both the header and footer, you can insert page numbers from the menu bar. Click **Insert, Page Numbers**, and **Right Alignment**. Do not show number on the first page.

8. Save and print the report.

APPLICATIONS

79e-d1
Report with Side Headings

1. Open **forms**. Save as **79e-d1**.

2. Key the remainder of the report. Check that side headings are not left alone at the bottom of the page.

3. Save and print. Keep this document open for use in the next application.

Forms Inventory

A perpetual forms inventory system was designed and maintained online for all company-wide forms. Employees were encouraged to add their individual or departmental forms to the inventory system so that they could be shared with others.

Goal of the System

The goal of the system was to convert 70 to 75 percent of the forms to an electronic format within a three-year time period. This goal was considered to be ambitious because a wide range of computers were used in the various departments, and some departments did not have access to the central network. During this same time frame, the company planned to upgrade computers and make the network available to all employees except warehouse and delivery personnel.

Follow-Up Study

This phase of the study was authorized to determine the effectiveness of the program that was implemented. The following chart shows the progress made since the program was instituted.

Results

Currently, 80 percent of all forms are in electronic format, and 20 percent are paper-based. The four forms that are currently purchased from vendors are being redesigned so that they can be made available electronically. The remaining paper-based forms are used primarily by warehouse and delivery personnel. However, the technology committee has recommended providing these employees with handheld computers to perform their work. As soon as this recommendation is implemented, the forms they use can be converted to electronic format.

Copyright Laws

To avoid copyright infringement, the Internet user must be
knowledgeable about copyright law. Two important laws include The Copyright
Law of 1976 and the Digital Millennium Copyright Act, which was enacted in
1998 to update the copyright law for the digital age. Zielinski (1999, 40)
explains that under the Copyright Law of 1976:

Copyright is automatic when an original work is first 'fixed' in a
tangible medium of expression. That means material is protected by
copyright at the point when it is first printed, captured on film, drawn,
or saved to hard drive or disk. . . . The farsighted statute covers fixed
works 'now known or later developed'.

Insert the file copyright here.

REFERENCES

Lee, John E. "Technology Aids in Stopping Copyright Offenders." *Hopper*
Business Journal, Fall 2000: http://www.hpj.edu/technologyaids.htm
(26 December 2000).

Zielinski, Dave. "Are You a Copyright Criminal?" *Presentations*, Vol. 13, No.
6, June 1999, 36-46.

45c-d2
Unbound Report

1. Open **present** from the data files. Save it as **45c-d2**.
2. Convert this leftbound report to an unbound report.
3. Format main and side headings correctly. Position the main heading on the correct line.
4. Number the pages at the top right; suppress page number on the first page.
5. Be alert to a widow line on page 1.

45c-d3
Title Page for Leftbound Report

1. Prepare a title page for the leftbound report prepared in **45c-d1**.
2. The report is prepared for **Webb & Morse Company Employees** by **Your Name, Information Technology Manager**.
3. Save the document as **45c-d3**.

4. Scroll to the bottom of the table of contents and check the page number in Section 1.

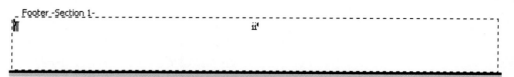

To break the link in Section 2:

5. Position the insertion point at the beginning of Section 2. Display the Header/Footer toolbar (**View**, **Header/Footer**). Click the **Same as Previous** button to break the link for the header. (Section 1 did not have a header; in Section 2 you want to add a header.)

6. Click the **Switch between Header and Footer** button to go to the footer, and click the **Same as Previous** button to break the link for the footer. Delete the page number that appears in the Footer box. (Section 1 had a footer with a centered lowercase Roman numeral; Section 2 will not have a footer.)

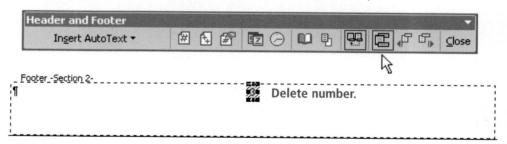

To insert page numbers in Section 2:

7. Switch back to the header. Click **Insert**, **Page Numbers**. Top of Page (Header) is already selected for you because you are still in the Header. For alignment, select **Right**. Do not show number on the first page.

8. Click the **Format** button. Choose the Arabic numeral (**1, 2, 3**). Start the page number at 1.

9. Close the Header/Footer toolbar.

10. Check the page numbers in Section 2. No number should appear on p. 1; a page number should display at the top right of the remaining pages.

Module 5: Checkpoint

Part A:

1. Margins for unbound reports are _____ side margins, _____ top margin (first page), _____ top margin (second page), and _____ bottom margin.

2. To set margins, choose _____ from the _____ menu.

3. Use ____ -point font for main headings. Use _____-point for side headings.

4. The _____ format displays the first line of text at the left margin and indents all other lines to the first tab.

5. To prevent a side heading from printing at the bottom of a page, apply _____.

6. To number the pages of a multipage report, choose _____ from the _____ menu.

7. Page numbers are positioned at the _____.

8. Long quotatons are _____-spaced and indented _____" from the left margin.

Part B: Study each format below. Circle the correct format.

9. Which of the following illustrates a hanging indent format?

    A Bruce, Lawrence A. The Report Guide: Selected Form and Style. Boise:
            State of Idaho Press, 2000.

    B   Bruce, Lawrence A. The Report Guide: Selected Form and Style. Boise:
        State of Idaho Press, 2000.

10. Which of the following illustrates correct formatting of main heading?

    A ELECTRONIC MAIL USAGE

    B Electronic Mail Usage

Performance Assessment

Document 1
Edit Report

1. Open **checkpoint5** from the data files. Make the edits below and save as **checkpoint5-d1**.
    a. Position the main heading and format it correctly.
    b. Format the side headings correctly.
    c. Format the report as a DS, unbound report.
    d. Format correctly the two long quotations that are displayed in red font.
    e. Format the references in hanging indent format. Begin references on a separate page. Position the first line correctly.
    f. Insert page numbers. Suppress the number on the first page.

Document 2
Prepare Title Page

1. Prepare a title page for **checkpoint5-d1**. Save as **checkpoint5-d2**.

    Prepared for
    Mr. Derrick Novorot, President
    Altman Corporation
    388 North Washington Street
    Starkville, MS 39759

    Prepared by
    Your Name, Communication Consultant
    Your Street Address
    Your City, State ZIP Code

In Normal View, section breaks appear as a dotted line with the type of break indicated. *Word* displays the current section number on the status bar.

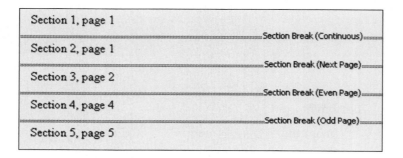

1. Open **sections** from the data files. Save as **79d-drill1**.
2. Insert a next page break after *Current date* on the title page.
3. Insert a next page section break after the table of contents.

4. Check that the table of contents and the first page of the report begin at approximately 2".
5. Save. Keep this document open for the next drill.

Insert Page Numbers and Break Link Between Sections

After learning to insert section breaks, you are ready to learn to insert page numbers with appropriate format in Section 1, break the link between Sections 1 and 2, and then insert the appropriate page format for Section 2.

To insert page numbers on preliminary pages:

1. Position the insertion point at the beginning of Section 1. Note that the status bar at the bottom left of the screen indicates *Sec 1*.

2. Click **Insert**, **Page Numbers**. For the position, choose **Bottom of page (Footer)** and for alignment, choose **Center**. Click **Show on first page** to deselect this option. Then click the **Format** button.

3. From the Format dialog box, choose lowercase Roman numerals for the number format (**i, ii, iii**). For Start at, key **1**. *Note:* You will not actually number the title page, but it still is considered p. 1. Click **OK** twice.

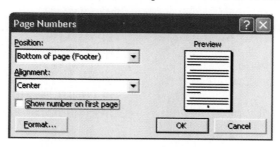

Communication Skills 2

Proofreading Guides

The final and important step in producing a document is proofreading. Error-free documents send the message the organization is detail-oriented and competent. Apply these procedures when producing any document.

1. Check spelling using the Spelling feature.

2. Proofread the document on the screen. Be alert for words that are spelled correctly but are misused, such as *you/your, in/on, of/on, the/then*, etc.

3. Check the document for necessary parts for correctness; be sure special features are present if needed—for example, in a letter, check for the enclosure or copy notation.

4. View the document on screen to check placement. Save and print.

These additional steps will make you a better proofreader:

5. Try to allow some time between writing a document and proofreading it.

6. If you are reading a document that has been keyed from a written draft, place the two documents next to each other and use guides to proofread the keyed document line by line against the original.

7. Proofread numbers aloud or with another person.

Proofreading for consistency is another important part of preparing documents. Consistency in style or tone, usage, facts, and format conveys an impression of care and attention to detail that reflects well on the writer and his or her organization. In contrast, lack of consistency gives an impression of carelessness and inattention to detail. Lack of consistency also makes documents more difficult to read and understand.

Proofreading statistical copy is extremely important. As you proofread, double-check numbers whenever possible. For example, verify dates against a calendar and check computations with a calculator. Remember these tips for proofreading numbers.

- Read numbers in groups. For example, the telephone number 618-555-0123 can be read in three parts: **six-one-eight, five five-five, zero-one-two-three**.

- Read numbers aloud.

- Proofread numbers with a partner.

Sections

Often long documents such as reports are formatted in **sections** so that different formats may be applied on the same page or on different pages using section breaks. Normally, the preliminary pages of a report are numbered at the bottom center with lowercase Roman numerals. The pages in the body of a report are numbered in the upper right with Arabic numerals. Page numbers are usually inserted as headers or footers. For convenience, you will want to save the report as one file and not two or more.

To use different page number formats within the same document, you must format the preliminary pages as one section and the remainder of the report as another section. *Word* continues to use the same format for headers and footers in a new section as it did in the previous section until you first break the link or connection between the sections.

Section 1

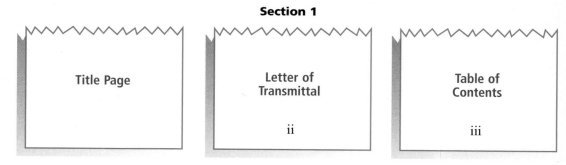

Title Page | Letter of Transmittal — ii | Table of Contents — iii

Section 2
(Break link before changing page format)

Body of Report First Page | Body of Report Second Page — 2 | Body of Report Third Page — 3

To enter a section break:

1. Select **Break** from the Insert menu.

2. Click the type of Section break desired, and then click **OK**.

   Next page: Begins a new page at the point the section break is entered.

   Continuous: Begins a new section on the same page.

   Even page: Begins a new section on the next even-numbered page.

   Odd page: Begins a new section on the next odd-numbered page.

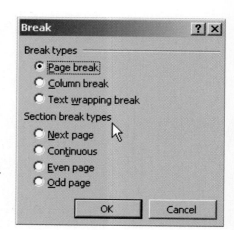

DRILL 2

**PROOFREADING
AND EDITING**

Key the drill making all
necessary corrections. Save
as **proofreading-drill2**.

First impressions does count, and you never get a second
chance to make a good first impression. This statement applys
too both documents and people. The minute you walk in to a
room you are judged by you appearance, your facial expressions,
and the way you present your self. As soon as a document is
opened, it is judged by it's appearance and the way it is
presented. First impressions are often lasting impressions
therefore you should strive to make a positive first impression for
yourself and for the documents you prepare. Learn to manage
your image and the image of your documents.

1. Open the data file **linger** from the Communication Skills folder.

2. Proofread the letter for consistency in usage, facts, and format (block letter style). Verify
information against the price list below. Make corrections. Use today's date for the
letter and your name for the writer's. Save the letter as **proofreading-drill3**.

COMPUTERS AND PRINTERS		
Product	**Manufacturer**	**Price**
Workstation 2010	**Chimera**	**$2,779**
550MHz processor, 19" monitor, 64GB RAM, 9.1GB hard drive, 7 x 24 dedicated workstation, 40X variable CD-ROM drive		
Vista XBT	**Chimera**	**2,299**
550MHz processor, 19" monitor, 128MB RAM, 9.1GB hard drive, Concord 2000 Office Suite, 40X variable CD-ROM drive		
Amina Optima	**Finn**	**2,199**
366MHz processor, 15" XGA active matrix display, 64MB RAM, 6.4GB hard drive, latest Capstone Office Suite, 20X variable CD-ROM/floppy drive		
Winger Laser Printer	**Primat**	**399**
600 dpi, 125-sheet input tray, 8 ppm		
Ink Jet Color Printer	**Primat**	**299**
Up to 600 dpi, 100-sheet input tray, 6 ppm, up to 16 million colors		
AZ Printer/Copier/Scanner	**Ventura**	**499**
600 dpi, 150-sheet input tray, 8 ppm, scans directly to e-mail, integrated desktop software for organizing scanned documents, OCR software for text editing		

SKILLBUILDING

79a
Warmup
Key each line twice SS. Work at a controlled rate.

1st/2nd fingers
1 dirt nut fun drum try buy been curt very hunt bunt rent cent jump
2 We think Julio may give Ruth a ring Sunday if she will accept it.
3 My name is Geoffrey, but I very much prefer Jeff on this nametag.

3rd/4th fingers
4 was pill look zoom loop west low loose quiz walk saw wax box zeal
5 Paul Velasquez was at a popular plaza quilt shop when he saw Sal.
6 Sal was at a Palawan zoo; he was also at Wuxi Plaza for six days.

| 1 | 2 | 3 | 4 | 5 | 6 | 7 | 8 | 9 | 10 | 11 | 12 | 13 |

79b
Technique Builder
Key each line once; fingers curved and relaxed; wrists low.

third row
7 query were pure wipe wept you tort twirp report rip tire weep tip
8 Perry required two types of paper, a protractor, and four rulers.

3rd/home
9 we tattle wayward pepper rattle eloped require your yellow queasy
10 Patty wrote poetry, took art, and worked two jobs this past year.

1st/3rd
11 minimum box zip zinc bomb ripen corner mine cure woven zoo winner
12 Merv and Robert were to turn a valve to terminate the water flow.

| 1 | 2 | 3 | 4 | 5 | 6 | 7 | 8 | 9 | 10 | 11 | 12 | 13 |

79c
Timed Writing
Key a 3' and a 5' writing.

	gwam	3'	5'

As you read copy for keyboarding, try to read at least a word or, better still, a word group ahead of your actual keyboarding point. In this way, you will be able to recognize the keystroking pattern needed as you learn to keyboard balanced-hand, one-hand, or combination word sequences. The adjustments you make in your speed will result in the variable rhythm pattern needed for expert keyboarding. It is easy to read copy correctly for keyboarding if you concentrate on the copy.

	3'	5'
	4	2 44
	8	5 46
	13	8 49
	17	10 51
	22	13 54
	26	16 57
	30	18 59
	32	19 60

When you first try to read copy properly for keyboarding, you may make more errors, but as you learn to concentrate on the copy being read and begin to anticipate the keystroking pattern needed, your errors will go down and your keyboarding speed will grow. If you want to increase your keyboarding speed and reduce your errors, you must make the effort to improve during each and every practice session. If you will work to refine your techniques and to give a specific purpose to all your practice activities, you can make the improvement.

	3'	5'
	36	22 63
	41	25 66
	45	27 68
	50	30 71
	54	33 74
	59	35 76
	63	38 79
	68	41 82
	69	41 82

3' | 1 | 2 | 3 | 4 |
5' | 1 | 2 | 3 |

Table Basics

- Create tables.
- Format tables using the Tables toolbar and AutoFormat.
- Edit table and cell structure.
- Build keying speed and accuracy.

LESSON 46   Create Tables

SKILLBUILDING

46a
Warmup
Key each line twice.

alphabetic   1   Jim Ryan was able to liquefy frozen oxygen; he kept it very cold.
figures   2   Flight 483 left Troy at 9:57 a.m., arriving in Reno at 12:06 p.m.
direct reaches   3   My brother served as an umpire on that bright June day, no doubt.
easy   4   Ana's sorority works with vigor for the goals of the civic corps.

| 1 | 2 | 3 | 4 | 5 | 6 | 7 | 8 | 9 | 10 | 11 | 12 | 13 |

NEW FUNCTIONS

46b

help keywords
tables; create a table

Create Tables

Tables consist of columns and rows of data—either alphabetic, numeric, or both.

Column: Vertical list of information labeled alphabetically from left to right.

Row: Horizontal list of information labeled numerically from top to bottom.

Cell: An intersection of a column and a row. Each cell has its own address consisting of the column letter and the row number (cell A1).

Use Show/Hide to display end-of-cell marks in each cell and end-of-row marks at the end of each row. End-of-cell and end-of-row markers are useful when editing tables. Use Print Layout View to display the table move handle in the upper left of the table and the Sizing handle in the lower right of the table.

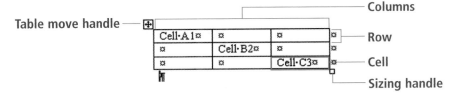

Use this information to prepare the Notes page.

[1]Cameron Maslin. cmaslin@ProdCon.com, "Enhancing Productivity: The Moss Springs Company." E-mail to Patrick Demetrio, pdemetrio@gwm.sc.edu. 15 April 2001.

[2]*Moss Springs Company Policy Manual.* (Chicago, 2001), p. 42.

[3]Scott Altig. *Effective Meetings.* (Philadelphia: Bay Publishing Co., 2001), pp. 74-86.

78d-d2
References Page

1. Prepare the references page for **78d-d1**. Position the title at approximately 2"; apply **Heading 1** style and center it.
2. Key the references that follow in alphabetical order; format with a hanging indent. Remove the hyperlinks.

Maslin, Cameron. cmaslin@ProdCon.com. "Enhancing Productivity: The Moss Springs Company." E-mail to Patrick Demetrio, pdemetrio@gwm.sc.edu (15 April 2001).

Moss Springs Company Policy Manual. Chicago, 2001.

Altig, Scott. *Effective Meetings.* Philadelphia: Bay Publishing Co., 2001.

3. Insert a page number at the top right on the references page; change the value to the appropriate starting number. All pages will now be numbered.
4. Save the document as **78d-d2** and print.

78d-d3
Table of Contents

1. Prepare a table of contents for **78d-d1**. List Notes and References as the last two side headings in the table of contents.
2. Save as **78d-d3** and print.

78d-d4
Title Page

1. Prepare a title page for the report in **78d-d1** and save it as **78d-d4**. Format in Arial 14 point.
2. Assume the report is prepared for Moss Springs Company and is prepared by you, Project Director.
3. Save; print; then assemble the report in the following order: title page, table of contents, report, notes, and references.

You can create tables using the Table menu or the Table button on the Standard toolbar. Either method produces the same results. Position the insertion point where you want the table to appear in the document before you begin.

To create a table using the Table menu:

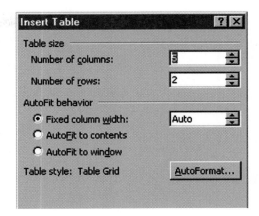

1. From the Table menu, choose **Insert**; then **Table**. The Insert Table dialog box displays. The default setting of AutoFit is set to create a table with a fixed width. The columns will be of equal width and spread across the writing line.

2. Click the up or down arrows to specify the number of rows and columns. Click **OK**. The table displays.

Notice that column widths are indicated by column markers on the Ruler.

To create a table using the Insert Table button:

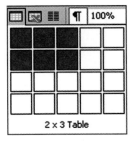

1. Click the **Insert Table** button on the Standard toolbar. A drop-down grid displays.

2. Click the left mouse button, and drag the pointer across to highlight the number of columns in the table and down to highlight the number of rows in the table. The table displays when you release the left mouse button.

Move Within a Table

When a table is created, the insertion point is in cell A1. To move within a table, use the TAB key or simply click within a cell using the mouse. Refer to this table as you learn to enter text in a table:

Press	Movement
TAB	To move to the next cell. If the insertion point is in the last cell, pressing TAB will add a new row.
SHIFT + TAB	To move to the previous cell.
ENTER	To increase the height of the row. If you press ENTER by mistake, press BACKSPACE to delete the line.

DRILL 1   **CREATE TABLES**

1. Create a two-column, five-row table using the Table menu.

2. Turn on **Show/Hide** and notice the marker at the end of each cell and each row. Hold down the ALT key, and click on one of the column markers on the ruler. Notice that the width of the column is displayed in inches (2.93").

3. Close the table without saving it.

4. Create a four-column, four-row table using the Table button on the Standard toolbar.

5. Move to cell B3. Move to cell B2.

6. Move to cell A1 and press ENTER.

7. Move to cell D4 and press TAB.

8. Close the table without saving it.

of the minutes within two weeks of the meeting. The minutes shall be a part of the permanent records of the Moss Springs Company. ②

Heading 1 style (Other Meetings)

Meetings ~~other than the annual meeting~~ will be held at the discretion of the Board of Directors and the appropriate company managers. Documentation for regular and "called" meetings of the Board ~~as~~ *is* described in the following paragraphs.

Heading 1 style (Support Documents)

Management

The Senior Committee require*s* that an agenda be distributed prior to all formal meetings of committees and of staff at the departmental level or higher. Minutes must be prepare*d* and distributed to all participants after the meeting.

Minutes

The Administrative Manager developed the following procedures to ~~to~~ implement the policy on maintaining ~~appropriate~~ minutes. The Senior Management Committee ~~met and~~ approved these procedures for immediate implementation.

Agenda

The agenda should contain the date, time, and place of the meeting. It also should contain a listing of all topic*s* to be discussed during the meeting. Distribution of the agenda should allow adequate time for ~~participants to prepare for the~~ meeting. *stet*

Heading 2 style

Verbatim Minutes. The Annual Meeting will be recorded, and a verbatim transcript of the meeting will be prepared by the Corporate Secretary. Verbatim minutes are costly ~~and~~ will be used only for the Annual Meeting. *, therefore, they*

Remember to delete period and place heading on separate line. Capitalize all important words in heading 2.

Action minutes. Action minutes, consisting of identifying information, *and* a brief summary of decisions made*,* and of key views expressed, will be used for most meetings. ③ The emphasis should be on decisions, assignment of responsibility, and action planned for the future.

Format Table, Rows, Columns, or Cells

If you wish to apply a format such as bold, alignment, or italics to the table, you must first select the table. Likewise, to format a specific row, column, or cell, you must select the table parts and then apply the format. Editing features such as delete and undo work in the usual manner. Follow these steps to select various parts of the table:

To select	Move the insertion point:
Entire table	Over the table and click the table move handle in the upper left of the table. (Option: **Table menu, Select, Table**). To move the table, drag the table move handle to a new location.
Column	To the top of the column until a solid down arrow appears; click the left mouse button.
Row	To the left area just outside the table until the pointer turns to an open arrow (⇗), then click the left mouse button.

Note: You can also select rows and columns by selecting a cell, column, or row, and dragging across or down.

DRILL 2   CREATE TABLES

1. Center-align and key the main heading in bold; press ENTER twice.

2. Change the alignment to left and turn bold off.

3. Create a three-column, four-row table.

4. Key the table shown below; press TAB to move from cell to cell.

5. Select row 1; then bold and center-align the column headings. Row 1 is called the **header row** because it identifies the content in each column.

6. Create the folder **Module 6 keys** and save the table as **46b-drill2** in this folder.

COLLEGE SPORTS PROGRAM

Fall Events	Winter Events	Spring Events
Football	Basketball	Golf
Soccer	Gymnastics	Baseball
Volleyball	Swimming	Softball

78d-d1
Leftbound Business
Report with Endnotes

1. Review the model on page 1 on the previous page. Notice that paragraphs are not indented. You're going to revise this rough draft and apply styles to the headings. Format the report as a leftbound report, single-spaced, and full justification. (*Remember*: 1.5" left margin for leftbound reports.)

2. The report includes three notations for endnotes. Indent the endnotes and change them to 12 point.

3. Apply **Heading 1** style to all side headings. Change all paragraph headings to side headings and apply **Heading 2** style. Remember to delete the period and place the heading on a separate line; capitalize all important words.

4. Insert page numbers at the top right; suppress the page number on the first page.

5. Prepare the notes page. Position the title at approximately 2", apply **Heading 1** style, and center it.

6. Preview the document to see that page numbers display correctly and to ensure that no headings are left alone at the bottom of a page. (Compare your document to the three illustrations on the previous page.)

7. Save as **78d-d1** and print.

Apply Heading 1 and center → Guides For Preparing Meeting Documentation

The procedures used to prepare support documents for meetings in the Moss Springs Company were review*ed* during the productivity analysis that was completed. ① The type of support documents used, *the format,* and the way in which they were prepared varied through out the company. The primary document*s* used were meeting notices, agendas, handouts, visual aids, and minutes. The following guides were compiled *as a result* ~~on the basis~~ of the productivity review.

Heading 1 **Annual Meeting**

The following quote from the Moss Spring*s* Company Policy Manual *italic* contains the policy for the documentation of the Annual Meeting:

Indent and SS — The annual Meeting of the Moss Springs Company shall be held within ③ *sp* months of the end of the fiscal year. The Corporate Secretary shall mail to all who are eligible to attend the meeting a notice and agenda ~~thirty~~ *30* days prior to the meeting. The Corporate Secretary shall prepare a verbatim record of the meeting and provide each member of the Board of Directors with a copy

46c-d1
Table

1. Position the main heading at about 2". Key the heading using center alignment and bold; press ENTER twice. Change the alignment to left, and turn bold off.
2. Create the table using the Table button and key the information in the cells.
3. Select row 1. Bold and center-align the column headings. Center-align cells C2–C7.
4. Save the document as **46c-d1**.

KEY CONTACTS FOR BUILDING PROJECT

Contact	Title	Telephone Number
Lara G. Elkins	Architect	(420) 555-0167
James C. Weatherwax	Contractor	(317) 555-0190
Peggy R. Lancaster	Site Supervisor	(513) 555-0164
Joanna B. Breckenridge	Interior Designer	(624) 555-0137
Marshall C. Dinkins	Kitchen Consultant	(502) 555-0126
Charles Wong	Engineer	(812) 555-0171

46c-d2
Table

TIP

Text is keyed left aligned, unless all the items are the same length (column A); then it can be center-aligned.

Numbers are right-aligned (column C).

1. Key the heading using center alignment and bold; press ENTER twice. Change the alignment to left, and turn bold off.
2. Create the table using the Insert command on the Table menu and key the information in the cells.
3. Select row 1. Bold and center-align the column headings. Center-align cells A2–A6. Right-align cells C2–C6.
4. Key the note DS below the table.
5. Center the table vertically on the page. Save the document as **46c-d2**.

PERSONAL COMPUTER ACCESSORIES

Stock Number	Description	Units Available
JGC2144	4mm Transporter	5,745,000
JGC9516	DLT/TK 20-pack Transporter	19,034,100
TMA3252	Mobile Base Storage System	3,972,155
CDS4971	Casa Multimedia Storage	9,734,250
LGT8920	Optical Keyboard and Mouse	10,457

Note: Inventory as of December 31, 200-

Notes Page

78c

When endnotes are used to cite references, the endnotes are placed on a separate page titled *Notes* at the end of the document.

To create the notes page:

1. After all endnotes are keyed, delete the endnote divider line.

2. Insert a page break below the last line of the report to position the endnotes on a separate page.

3. Position the insertion point at approximately 2"; key **Notes**; apply **Heading 1** style and center it; press ENTER.

4. Endnotes should be single-spaced with a double space between them. Remember to change the font to 12 point.

Note: You will still need to create a separate references page to include a complete listing of references.

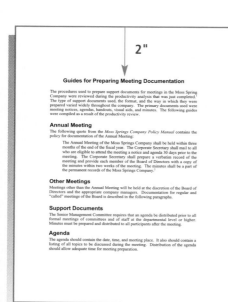

First Page

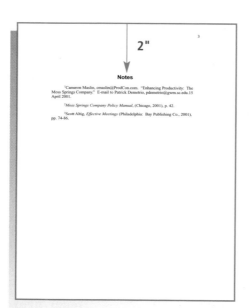

Notes Page

References Page

DRILL 3 — NOTES PAGE

1. Open **78b-drill1**, save it as **78c-drill3**, and create the notes page.

2. Delete the divider line between the report text and the endnotes.

3. Follow Steps 2–4 in section 78c.

4. Save the document again and print.

46c-d3
Table

1. Create a 3-column, 4-row table. Key the text in the table.
2. Place the cursor in cell C4; press the TAB key to create another blank row. Key the last row.
3. Center table vertically on the page. Save as **46c-d3**.

POMMERY SPRINGS PROJECT STATUS   *Center and Bold*

Job	Description	Date Completed
Road work	Building and grading	February 10, 200-
Drain	Adding french drain	February 25, 200-
Lot prep~aration~	Clearing and leveling	March 12, 200-

Pond   Adding silt fence   March 15, 200-   *add row*

46c-d4
Table

1. Position the main heading at about 2". Center main heading in all caps and bold. Key the secondary heading in title case, bold, and center.
2. Center column heads. Save as **46c-d4**. Print.

OFFICIAL BIRDS AND FLOWERS
For Selected States

State	Official Bird	Official Flower
Alaska	Willow ptarmigan	Forget-me-not
Arkansas	Mockingbird	Apple blossom
California	California valley quail	Golden poppy
Connecticut	American robin	Mountain laurel
Delaware	Blue hen chicken	Peach blossom
Georgia	Brown thrasher	Cherokee rose
Idaho	Mountain bluebird	Syringe
Illinois	Cardinal	Native violet
Louisiana	Eastern brown pelican	Magnolia
Maryland	Baltimore oriole	Black-eyed Susan
Massachusetts	Chickadee	Mayflower
Nebraska	Western meadowlark	Goldenrod
New Jersey	Eastern goldfinch	Purple violet
New Mexico	Roadrunner	Yucca
North Carolina	Cardinal	Dogwood

5. The Endnote Pane displays with the reference number and the insertion point in the Endnote Pane.

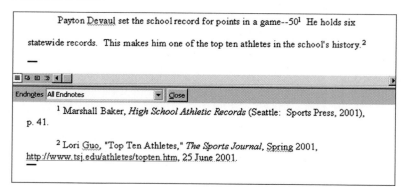

Payton Devaul set the school record for points in a game--50[1] He holds six

statewide records. This makes him one of the top ten athletes in the school's history.[2]

Endnotes All Endnotes ▾ Close

[1] Marshall Baker, *High School Athletic Records* (Seattle: Sports Press, 2001), p. 41.

[2] Lori Guo, "Top Ten Athletes," *The Sports Journal*, Spring 2001, http://www.tsj.edu/athletes/topten.htm, 25 June 2001.

6. Position the insertion point before the reference number, and press TAB to indent it. Then move the insertion point beyond the number and key the endnote.

7. DS between endnotes and remember to change the font to 12 point.

8. To edit an endnote, double-click on the reference number in the text. To delete an endnote, select the reference number in the text and press DELETE.

Word inserts a line between the report text and the endnotes. Because endnotes will appear on a separate Notes page, remove the line.

To delete the divider line: Click the down arrow to the right of the Endnotes box at the top of the Endnote Pane, and then choose **Endnote Separator**. Select the line, press DELETE, and click **Close**.

DRILL 1   ENDNOTES

1. Open **endnotes** from the data files. Save it as **78b-drill1**.

2. Insert as endnotes the three footnotes shown in Lesson 77 Drill 1, p. 294.

3. Select the endnotes and format them in 12 point.

4. Save and print.

help keywords
page numbers, specify

Change Page Number Value

Occasionally it may be necessary to start numbering pages at a number other than the default of 1.

To change the starting number value:

1. Select **Page Numbers** from the Insert menu. Select the desired position for the page numbers.

2. Click the **Format** button. Click **Start at,** enter the page number, and click **OK**.

DRILL 2   CHANGE PAGE NUMBERS

1. Open **78b-drill1** and prepare the references page for this document.

2. Copy all text on the references page and paste it to a new document.

3. Position the main heading at 2", apply **Heading 1** style, and center it.

4. Insert page numbers at top right; change the value to 3. Save as **78b-drill2**.

Note: The references page could not be keyed after the Notes page because the endnote feature does not allow a hard page break at the end of the endnotes.

SKILLBUILDING

47a
Warmup
Key each line twice.

alphabet	1	Dixie Vaughn acquired that prize job with a firm just like yours.
figures	2	By May 15 do this: Call Ext. 4390; order 472 clips and 168 pens.
easy/figures	3	The 29 girls kept 38 bushels of corn and 59 bushels of rich yams.
easy	4	The members paid half of the endowment, and their firm paid half.

| 1 | 2 | 3 | 4 | 5 | 6 | 7 | 8 | 9 | 10 | 11 | 12 | 13 |

47b
Timed Writings
Key a 3' or a 5' timing at your control rate.

  all letters

gwam 3' | 5'

	3'	5'
You may be familiar with the expression that we live in an	4	2
information age now. People interpret this expression in a host of	8	5
diverse ways, but most people agree on two key things. The first	13	8
thing is that a huge amount of information exists today; some even	17	10
think we suffer from information overload. The second thing is that	22	13
technology has changed the way we access that huge pool of data.	26	16
Some people are quick to point out that a big difference exists	30	18
between the quantity and the quality of information. It is very	35	21
critical to recognize that anyone who has access can simply post	39	23
information on the Internet. No test exists to screen for junk	43	26
before something is posted. Some of the data may be helpful and	48	29
valid. However, much of it must be analyzed quite carefully to	52	31
judge if it is valid.	53	32
Just how do you judge if the data you have accessed is valid?	58	35
Some of the same techniques that can be used with print media can be	62	37
applied with electronic media. A good way to assess material is to	67	40
examine its source carefully. What do you know about the people who	71	42
provided this information? Is the provider ethical and qualified	75	45
to post that information? If you cannot unearth the answer to this	80	48
question, you should be wary of trusting it.	83	50

3'	1	2	3	4
5'	1	2	3	

LESSON 78 — Leftbound Report with Endnotes

SKILLBUILDING

78a
Warmup
Key each line twice SS. Concentrate on keying the reach correctly.

```
i    1   sit in said did dirk city did fin its lit iris wit hit ilk simmer
e    2   gem ewe men eke ever me le hen cede key led fen eye be pen leader
i/e  3   pie lei piece feign mein feint neigh lie reign die veil vein diem
i/e  4   Either Marie or Liem tried to receive eight pieces of cookie pie.

w    5   new jaw awe win we was awe away hew saw flaw law wan pew wit wavy
o    6   to onto rot job coho sox box oboe wok roe out oil dot tote oriole
w/o  7   ow wows how won worn now woe wool mow row work cow woke flows low
w/o  8   Women won't want to work now; we are worn out after woeful worry.

s    9   sans is ants sons has sun spas his six bus asps skis its spy sobs
l    10  el let la alp lot lilt led elk lab old lily fly lip ilk loll milk
s/l  11  also slow else sly false slaw sells slag sails sly sled slip slam
s/l  12  Slater tells us Elsie is also slightly slow to slip off to sleep.
         |  1  |  2  |  3  |  4  |  5  |  6  |  7  |  8  |  9  | 10  | 11  | 12  | 13  |
```

NEW FUNCTIONS

78b

help keywords
endnote

Endnotes

An **endnote** consists of two linked parts—the endnote reference in the text and the corresponding endnote with full information at the end of the report. Create endnotes in Normal view; an endnote pane displays for keying the endnote text.

Word automatically numbers endnotes with small Roman numerals (i, ii, iii), positions them at the end of the document, and applies 10-point type. After keying endnotes, select them and apply 12-point type to be consistent with the report text.

To insert and edit endnotes:

1. Switch to Normal view and position the insertion point where you want to insert the endnote reference.

2. On the menu, click **Insert**, **Reference**, **Footnote**. The Footnote and Endnote dialog box displays.

3. Select **Endnotes**. The default location for endnotes is after the last line of document text.

4. Change the Number format to Arabic numerals (1, 2, 3). Click **Insert**.

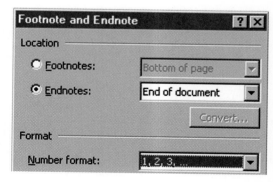

Table AutoFormat

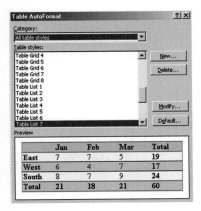

AutoFormat enables you to apply one of *Word*'s many preformatted styles to tables. You can view those styles in the Preview box. Choose a style based on the information in the table. For example, a style with shading in the last row is well suited to a table with totals.

To use AutoFormat:

1. Create the table and key the table data without formats.
2. Click the insertion point in the table, and then click the **AutoFormat** button on the Tables and Borders toolbar.
3. In the Table AutoFormat dialog box, check to see that All table styles is displayed in the Category list box; then choose a style from the Table styles list box.
4. Click **Apply** to apply the style, and return to the table.

Option: Choose Table AutoFormat from the Table menu. Continue with Step 3 above.

DRILL 1   **AUTOFORMAT**

1. Open **46b-drill2**.
2. Apply the Table List 4 format.
3. Save the document as **47c-drill1**.
4. Print.

APPLICATIONS

47d-d1
Table with Center Page

1. Key the table below and center it vertically on the page.
2. Save as **47d-d1**. Print.

MAJOR METROPOLITAN AREAS OF CANADA

City	Province	Population	
			7
			12
Toronto	Ontario	3,427,250	17
Montreal	Quebec	2,921,375	22
Vancouver	British Columbia	1,380,750	30
Ottawa	Ontario	819,275	34
Winnipeg	Manitoba	625,325	40
Quebec	Quebec	603,275	44
Hamilton	Ontario	557,250	49

6. Do you tilt your neck backward to see the computer screen? (No)

7. Do you take two 5-minute breaks and one 15-minute break in the morning and afternoon? (Yes)

8. Do you vary your activities to break the repetitive motion? (Yes)

9. Do you drink plenty of water to lubricate your joints? (Yes)

For each of your responses that do not match the desired response, please accept the challenge today to correct the undesired practice and avoid computer-related stress injuries.

Footnote text:

[1]"Repetitive Strain Injuries—The Hidden Cost of Computing," http://www.webreference.com/rsi.html, (8 March 2001).

[2]Jonathan Lee, *Comfortable Computing for Your Hands and Wrists* (Liberty Insurance Company, 2001), p. 53.

[3]Mason E. Gentry, "Workplace Ergonomics," *Computing,* March 2001, p. 46.

References text:

Lee, Jonathan. *Comfortable Computing for Your Hands and Wrists.* Liberty Insurance Company, 2001.

Gentry, Mason E. "Workplace Ergonomics." *Computing.* March 2001.

"Repetitive Strain Injuries—The Hidden Cost of Computing." http://www.webreference.com/rsi.html (8 March 2001).

TIP

When e-mail or Internet addresses appear in a printed report, remove the hyperlink (right-click the hyperlink; then click **Remove Hyperlink**).

77d-d2
Table of Contents

1. Prepare a table of contents for **77d-d1**. List **References** as a side heading in the table of contents.

2. Save as **77d-d2** and print.

77d-d3
Title Page

1. Prepare a title page for the report in **77d-d1** and save it as **77d-d3**. Assume the report is prepared for your course (include course number and title) and is prepared by you.

2. Save and print; then assemble the report in the following order: title page, table of contents, and report.

77d-d4
Edit Report with Styles

1. Open **77d-d1** and save as **77d-d4**. Reformat the report using styles.

2. Change the main headings to initial caps and to Heading 1 style. (*Note:* When styles are applied, titles are easier to read in initial caps.)

3. Change side headings to Heading 1 style.

4. Change paragraph headings to side headings and apply **Heading 2** style. Delete the period after the heading, position the text at the left margin, and capitalize the main words in each heading.

5. Save and print.

47d-d2
Table with AutoFormat

1. Key and format the table. Position the main heading at about 2".
2. Right-align columns B, C, and D.
3. Apply **Table 3D Effects 2** style.
4. Save as **47d-d2**. Print.

words

ESTIMATES ON KITCHEN CABINETRY

Kitchen Component	VSP Kitchens	Designs by Pat	Euro Image	
Cabinetry	$34,475	$22,100	$38,350	24
Granite countertops	8.150	7,950	10,275	32
Halogen lighting	1,450	1,600	1,800	39
Appliances (allowance)	12,000	12,000	12,000	48
Total	$56,075	$43,650	$62,425	54

6
18

47d-d3
Table with AutoFormat

1. Key the table. Right-align column C.
2. Apply the **Table List 8** style.
3. Center the table vertically on the page.
4. Save as **47d-d3**. Print.

words

CANADIAN PROVINCES

Province	Capital	Population	
Alberta	Edmonton	2,375,300	15
British Columbia	Victoria	2,889,200	22
Manitoba	Winnipeg	1,071,250	28
New Brunswick	Fredericton	710,450	34
Newfoundland	St. John's	568,350	41
Northwest Territories	Yellowknife	52,250	49
Nova Scotia	Halifax	873,200	55
Ontario	Toronto	9,113,500	60
Prince Edward Island	Charlottetown	126,650	68
Quebec	Quebec	6,540,300	73
Saskatchewan	Regina	1,010,200	79
Yukon	Whitehorse	23,500	84

4
9

LESSON 47   SKILLBUILDING AND AUTOFORMAT   MODULE 6   172

77d-d1
Report with Footnotes

TIP

When e-mail or Internet addresses appear in a printed report, remove the hyperlink (right-click the hyperlink; then click **Remove Hyperlink**).

1. Key the unbound, educational report that follows with DS.
2. Indent the footnotes and change the font to 12 point.
3. Position the main heading at approximately 2". Format the headings appropriately.
4. Align the bullets with the beginning of the paragraph. (Click the **Increase Indent** button on the Formatting toolbar.)
5. Number the pages at the top right; suppress the page number on the first page.
6. Prepare the references page. Position the title at approximately 2"; apply Heading 1 style and center it. Key the references in alphabetical order; format as a hanging indent. Remove the hyperlinks.
7. Preview the document to see that page numbers display correctly and that no headings are left alone at the bottom of a page. If any headings appear at the bottom of a page, use **Keep with next** to keep the heading with the paragraph that follows.
8. Save the report as **77d-d1** and print.

Avoid Computer-Related Injuries

In the business environment, repetitive stress injuries (RSI), cumulative trauma disorder (CTD), and carpal tunnel syndrome (CTS) have mushroomed to afflict everyone from secretaries to executives with hurting muscles, tendons, and nerves. The Bureau of Labor Statistics reports that 70 percent of all occupational illnesses reported in the United States will be cases of repetitive stress injuries. Medical expenses and lost work for U.S. businesses are totaling $20 billion.[1]

The center of keyboard repetitive stress injuries is hand-arm alignment. Misalignment causes muscles to become overworked, causing stress and fatigue in the hands, arms, neck, and shoulders. Also, with the rapid rise of mouse-driven software and the large number of people surfing the Internet via a mouse, new ergonomic issues related to the use and the location of the mouse must be studied. To avoid computer-related injuries, all computer users can benefit from understanding basic guidelines for proper positioning at the computer and effective workstation design.

Position Yourself Properly

Preventing tired wrists and hands is really a matter of taking charge of your posture and computer work environment. Awkward posture while keying and failure to change your keying or sitting position can add to wear and tear on your wrists and hands.

Hand position. Keep your wrists and hands straight. When you work with straight wrists and fingers, the nerves, muscles, and tendons stay relaxed and comfortable. Therefore, they are less likely to develop the strains and pains that are often associated with keying.

Insert file **injuries**; format like the rest of the report.

Format Tables

48a
Warmup
Key each line twice SS.

direct reaches

1 June and my brother, Bradly, received advice from junior umpires.
2 My bright brother received minimum reward for serving many years.

adjacent reaches

3 Clio and Trey were sad that very few voters were there last week.
4 Western attire was very popular at the massive auction last week.

double letters

5 Tommie Bennett will go to a meeting in Dallas tomorrow afternoon.
6 Lee will meet Joanne at the swimming pool after accounting class.

NEW FUNCTIONS

48b

Change Row Height

The tables that were created in Lesson 46 can be made more attractive and easier to read by inserting some blank space above and below the text; this can be done by increasing the row height. Center the text vertically in the cell after increasing the row height.

Default row height	
This illustrates	A table created
Using default	Row height

Increased row height	
This illustrates	A table created
With increased	Row height

To increase the row height and center the text vertically in the cell:

1. Create and key the table. Turn on Show/Hide.

2. Select only the table; be careful not to select any ¶ markers outside the table. Select **Table Properties** from the Table menu.

3. Click the **Row** tab. Click the **Specify Height** checkbox. Use the spin arrows to select a row height. (See Figure 1.)

4. Click the **Cell** tab. Choose **Center Alignment** so the text will display in the middle of the cell. (See Figure 2.) Click **OK**.

Row height set at .3"

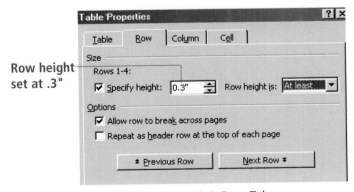

Figure 1-1 Row Tab

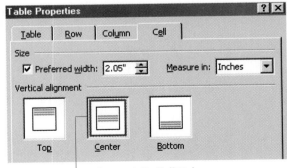

Figure 1-2 Cell Tab

Center alignment

1. Key the paragraph in Drill 2 DS, and add the three footnotes. Insert a nonbreaking space to keep p. and the number on the same line in footnote 1 (**Insert, Symbol, Special Characters**).
2. Format footnotes in 12 point and DS between them.
3. Include all three sources on a separate references page in proper reference format. Select the title *References* and apply the **Heading 1** style and center.
4. Save as **77c-drill1** and print.

1. Open **77c-drill1**. Delete the second footnote. Update the references page.
2. Save as **77c-drill2** and print.

Payton Devaul set the school record for points in a game—50.[1] He holds six statewide records. This makes him one of the top ten athletes in the school's history.[2] He expects to receive a basketball scholarship at an outstanding university.[3]

Footnotes

Book ———— [1]Marshall Baker, *High School Athletic Records.* (Seattle: Sports Press, 2001), p. 41.

Online Journal ———— [2]Lori Guo, "Top Ten Athletes," *The Sports Journal*, Spring 2001, http://www.tsj.edu/athletes/topten.htm, 25 June 2001.

E-mail ———— [3]Payton Devaul, pdevaul@mail.com. "Basketball Scholarship." E-mail to Kirk Stennis, kstennis@umt.edu, 15 April 2001.

References

Baker, Marshall. *High School Athletic Records.* Seattle: Sports Press, 2001.

Devaul, Payton. pdevaul@mail.com. "Basketball Scholarship."
        E-mail to Kirk Stennis, kstennis@umt.edu. 15 April 2001.

Guo, Lori. "Top Ten Athletes." *The Sports Journal*, (Spring 2001).
        http://www.tsj.edu/athletes/topten.htm (25 June 2001).

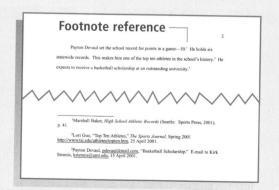

Report with footnote

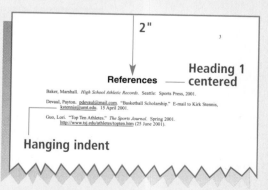

References page

Adjust Column Widths

Tables extend from margin to margin when they are created, regardless of the width of the data in the columns. Some tables, however, would be more attractive and easier to read if the columns were narrower. Column widths can be changed manually using the mouse or automatically using AutoFit. Using the mouse enables you to adjust the widths as you like. Once you change the width of a table, you will need to center it horizontally.

Column marker

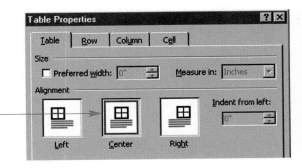

To adjust column widths using the mouse:

1. Point to the column border between the first and second columns in the table.

2. When the pointer changes to ✛, drag the border to the left to make the column narrower or to the right to make the column wider.

3. Adjust the column widths attractively. Leave approximately 0.5" to .75" between the longest line and the border. Use the Horizontal Ruler as a guide.

4. You can display the width of the columns by pointing to a column marker on the ruler, holding down the ALT key, and clicking the left mouse button.

To center a table horizontally:

1. With the insertion point in the table, choose **Table Properties** from the Table menu.

2. Click the **Table tab**, if necessary.

3. Choose the **Center** option in the Alignment box, and click **OK**.

DRILL 1   CHANGE ROW HEIGHT, CENTER TEXT IN CELL, AND ADJUST COLUMN WIDTH

1. Open **46c-d1**.

2. Select the table. (Do not select the title or any ¶ markers outside the table.)

3. Change the row height to .3" and center the text vertically in the cell.

4. Use the mouse to manually adjust the column width of each column. Leave approximately 0.5" of blank space to the right of the longest line in each column.

5. Center the table horizontally.

6. Save as **48b-drill1** and print.

DRILL 2   CHANGE ROW HEIGHT, CENTER TEXT IN CELL, AND ADJUST COLUMN WIDTH

1. Open **46c-d2**. Change the row height to .3" and center the text vertically in the cell. Adjust the column width and center the table horizontally. Save as **48b-drill2a**.

2. Open **46c-d3** and apply the directions in step 1. Save as **48b-drill2b**.

3. Open **46c-d4** and apply the directions in step 1. Save as **48b-drill2c**.

Footnotes

References cited in a report are often indicated within the text by a superscript number (… story.[1]) and a corresponding footnote with full information at the bottom of the same page where the reference was cited.

Word automatically numbers footnotes sequentially with Arabic numerals (1, 2, 3), positions them at the left margin, and applies 10-point type. After keying footnotes, select them and apply 12-point type to be consistent with the report text. Indent the first line of a footnote 0.5" from the left margin. Footnotes are automatically SS; however, DS between footnotes.

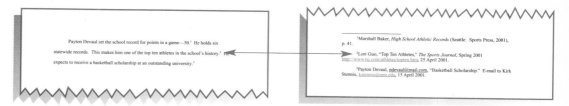

To insert and edit footnotes:

1. Switch to Normal view and position the insertion point where you want to insert the footnote reference.

2. On the menu, click **Insert**, **Reference**, and then **Footnote**. The Footnote and Endnote dialog box displays.

3. Be sure Footnotes is selected and Bottom of page (the default location) is displayed. Then click **Insert**.

4. The reference number and the insertion point appear in the Footnote Pane.

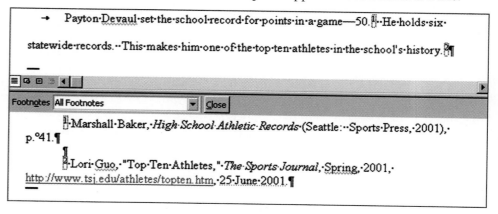

5. Move the insertion point before the reference number, and press TAB to indent it. Then move the insertion point beyond the number and key the footnote. Click **Close** to return to the document text. (*Note:* If you are in Print Layout View, click anywhere above the footnote divider line to return to the document.)

6. To edit a footnote, double-click the reference number in the text. Edit the footnote text in the Footnote Pane.

7. To delete a footnote, select the reference number in the text and press DELETE.

TIP
To insert a nonbreaking space, click **Insert, Symbol, Special Characters, Nonbreaking Space**.

Tables and Borders Toolbar

You can change the appearance of tables by adding shading, borders, patterns, and color. You can use Table AutoFormat to apply a preformatted design to the table, or display the Tables and Borders toolbar, which provides you with many formatting options. To display this toolbar, click **View** on the menu; then click **Toolbars**, **Tables and Borders**.

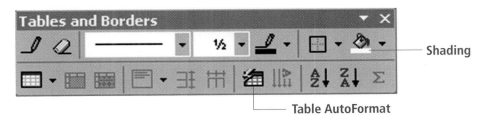

Shading

Table AutoFormat

Shading Cells

  Shading can be applied to cells for emphasis. Normally, shading is applied to emphasize headings, totals, or divisions and sections of a table.

To add shading to cells:

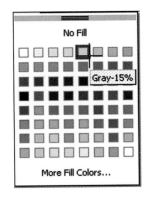

1. Select the cells to be shaded, and click the **Shading** button on the Tables and Borders toolbar.

2. Click the down arrow, and choose a color or shade of gray. For class assignments, choose 15% gray (row 1, item 5).

Option: Choose **Borders and Shading** on the Format menu. Click on the **Shading** tab. Under Style, click the down arrow to change *Clear* to 15%; then click **OK**.

DRILL 3   SHADING

1. Open **48b-drill1**.
2. Apply 15% shading to row 1.
3. Save as **48b-drill3a** and print.

4. Open **48b-drill2a**.
5. Apply 20% shading to row 1.
6. Save as **48b-drill3b** and print.

DOCUMENT DESIGN

48c

Table Format Guides

1. Position the table (or main heading) at about 2", or center the table vertically on the page.

2. **Headings:** Center, bold, use 12-point font, and key the main heading in all caps. Key the secondary heading a DS below the main heading in bold, centered and 12-point font; capitalize main words. Center and bold all column headings.

3. Adjust column widths attractively, and center the table horizontally.

4. Increase the row height to .3" and center text vertically in the cell.

5. Align text within cells at the left. Align numbers at the right. Align decimal numbers of varying lengths at the decimal point.

6. When a table appears within a document, DS before and after the table.

DOCUMENT DESIGN

LESSON 77 | Unbound Report with Footnotes

SKILLBUILDING

77a
Warmup
Key each line twice SS.

1 Oak Road; Ninth Blvd; Union Avenue; Main Court; High Circle
shift 2 Wade and Jeff; Randy and Paul; Carl and Nan; Teresa and Jane
3 Mr. and Mrs. Brian Nunn's grandson is Andrew Michael Quincy.

4 Keep your fingers curved.
5 Keep your eyes on the copy.
ENTER 6 Use quick and snappy keystrokes.
7 Strike Enter without pausing.

77b
Timed Writing
Key a 3' and a 5' writing.

  all letters/figures

	gwam	3'	5'

Now and then the operation of some company deserves a closer ... 4 | 2 | 41
look by investors. For example, Zerotech Limited, the food, oil, ... 8 | 5 | 44
and chemical company, says in its monthly letter that it will be ... 13 | 8 | 46
raising its second-quarter dividend to 85 cents a share, up from ... 17 | 10 | 49
79 3/4 cents a share, and that a dividend will be paid July 12. ... 21 | 13 | 51

This fine old area firm is erecting an enviable history of ... 25 | 15 | 54
dividend payment, but its last hike in outlays came back in 1987, ... 30 | 18 | 56
when it said a share could go above 65 cents. Zerotech has, how- ... 34 | 21 | 59
ever, never failed to pay a dividend since it was founded in ... 38 | 23 | 61
1937. The recent increase extends the annual amount paid to ... 42 | 25 | 64
$5.40 a share. ... 43 | 26 | 65

In this monthly letter, the firm also cited its earnings for ... 47 | 28 | 67
the second quarter and for the first half of this year. The net ... 52 | 31 | 70
revenue for the second quarter was a record $1.9 billion, up 24.2 ... 56 | 34 | 72
percent from a typical period just a year ago. Zerotech has its ... 61 | 36 | 75
main company offices at 9987 Nicholas Drive in Albany. ... 64 | 38 | 77

3' | 1 | 2 | 3 | 4
5' | 1 | 2 | 3

1. Follow the Table Format Guides on page 175 when keying the tables.
2. Center each table vertically on the page.
3. Save and print.

48d-d1
Table with Shading

1. Key the table. Adjust column width so that each entry fits on one line.
2. Apply 20% shading to row 1. Center the table on the page.

MAJOR SPORTS TEAMS

City	Baseball	Basketball	Football	Hockey
Detroit	Tigers	Pistons	Lions	Red Wings
Chicago	Cubs— White Sox	Bulls	Bears	Black Hawks
New York	Yanks— Mets	Knicks— Mets	Giants— Jets	Rangers
Boston	Red Sox	Celtics	Patriots	Bruins
San Francisco	Giants	Warriors	49'ers	Seals

48d-d2
Table with Indented Lines

1. Key the table below; press CTRL + TAB to indent lines. Adjust column width so each entry fits on one line.
2. Apply 20% shading to row 1; apply 10% shading to rows 2 and 5.

EFFECTS OF CRONIX ON PATIENTS

Body Systems	Cronix + Aspirin	Placebo + Aspirin
Central nervous system		
Headache	867	402
Dizziness	1,084	839
Gastrointestinal system disorders		
Abdominal pain	317	130
Dyspepsia	62	1,017
Diarrhea	64	9

48d-d3
Table with Adjusted Column Width

1. Key the table below; adjust column width so all items fit on one line.
2. Apply 15% shading to row 1.

FREQUENTLY PRESCRIBED MEDICATIONS

Brand Name	Generic Name	Treatment
Actifed	Tripolidene-Pseudoephedrine	Decongestant
E-Mycin	Erythromycin	Antibiotic
Lanoxin	Digoxin	Abnormal heart rhythm or CHF
Prostep	Nicotine patch	Smoking addiction
Prozac	Fluoxetine	Depression

76e-d1
Unbound Report with Styles

(thumbnail of report titled "Nutrition and Health")

1. Open **nutrition** from the data files. Format the unbound report SS.
2. Position the main heading at approximately 2".
3. Apply the **Heading 1** style to the main heading and to the two level-two headings. Center the main heading. Apply the **Heading 2** style to the three level-three headings (shown in italics in the data file).
4. Number the pages at the top right; suppress the page number on the first page.
5. Key the paragraph below at the end of the document.
6. Save the document as **76e-d1** and print.

Food Preparation   Heading 2
Foods should be prepared in a manner that does not add fat to the food. Baking, steaming, poaching, roasting, and cooking in a microwave are the best ways to prepare foods.

76e-d2
Table of Contents

1. Prepare a table of contents for **76e-d1**.
2. Save as **76e-d2** and print.

76e-d3
Title Page

1. Prepare a title page for the report in **76e-d1** and save it as **76e-d3**. Format in Arial 14 point.
2. Assume the report is prepared by you for your instructor (include title and full name).
3. Print; then assemble the report in the following order: title page, table of contents, and report.

76e-d4
Edit Report

TIP

Change Case: Select the text to be changed. Choose **Format, Change Case**, and then the desired option.

1. Open the report keyed in **75d-d1**. Save as **76e-d4**.
2. Follow the directions below to change to a single-spaced report with styles.
   a. Select the entire report. Change to SS.
   b. Delete the paragraph indent since SS reports are formatted with block paragraphs.
   c. Apply **Heading 1** style to the main heading; press ENTER once after the main heading. Change the format to initial caps (Title Case).
   d. Apply **Heading 1** style to the side headings.
   e. Edit the paragraph headings to display on a separate line and delete the period. Apply **Heading 2** style.
3. Save.

LESSON 49

Revise Tables

49a

Warmup

Key each line twice at a controlled rate.

adjacent key
1 her err ire are cash free said riot lion soil join went wean news
2 sat coil riot were renew forth weed trade power grope owner score

one hand
3 him bear joy age kiln loup casts noun loop facet moon deter edges
4 get hilly are fear imply save phony taste union versa yummy wedge

balanced hand
5 oak pay hen quay rush such burp urus vial works yamen amble blame
6 cot duty goal envy make focus handy ivory lapel oriel prowl queue

| 1 | 2 | 3 | 4 | 5 | 6 | 7 | 8 | 9 | 10 | 11 | 12 | 13 |

49b

Timed Writing

Take two 2' timings; count errors. Take two more 2' timings. Try to reduce errors with each timing.

  all letters

gwam 2'

Little things do contribute a lot to success in keying. Take our work attitude, for example. It's a little thing; yet, it can make quite a lot of difference. Demonstrating patience with a job or a problem, rather than pressing much too hard for a desired payoff, often brings better results than we expected. Other "little things," such as wrist and finger position, how we sit, size and location of copy, and lights, have meaning for any person who wants to key well.

6	53
12	59
18	66
25	72
31	79
38	85
44	91
47	94

2' | 1 | 2 | 3 | 4 | 5 | 6 |

NEW FUNCTIONS

49c

help keywords
cell

Merge Cells

Cells can be joined horizontally or vertically by selecting the cells and then choosing the **Merge Cells** command on the Table menu or the Tables and Borders toolbar. Frequently, main and secondary headings are included in the table by merging cells in row 1 and centering the headings in the row.

To merge cells:

Select the cells to be merged. Choose **Merge Cells** from the Table menu, or click the **Merge Cells** button on the Tables and Borders toolbar.

DRILL 1 — MERGE CELLS

1. Create a four-column, six-row table.

2. Select row 1 and merge the cells.

3. Key the table. Center and bold the headings.

4. Center-align column B. Right-align columns C and D.

5. Save as **49c-drill1**. Print.

EMPLOYEE RATINGS			
Employee	**Position**	**Identification**	**Rating**
Janice Goodman	Manager	3495075	8.7
Dinh Lee	Manager	732	9.1
Ralph Marshall	Associate	486028776	9.5
Frank Wiley	Associate	9376	7.6

Unbound Report with Styles

76a
Warmup
Key each line twice SS.

alphabet	1	Jim Winnifred, the proud quarterback, got criticized excessively.
fig/sym	2	Pat paid $85.90 each ($171.80) for 2 tickets in Row #34 on May 6.
double letters	3	Will the committee have access to all the books at noon tomorrow?
easy	4	Jake, their neighbor, paid for the right to fish on the big dock.

| 1 | 2 | 3 | 4 | 5 | 6 | 7 | 8 | 9 | 10 | 11 | 12 | 13 |

76b
Technique Builder
Key each line twice SS (slowly, then faster); DS between 2-line groups.

8/2	5	Row 2; Show 8; Page 82; Seat 28; Line 8228; Part 2822; Level 2882
1/7	6	1 second; 7 hours; 17 months; 717 seconds; 717 minutes; 1771 days
3/5	7	bake 3; take 5; give 53; grade 35; skip 535; call 5335; join 3535
4/6	8	Test 4; Pack 6; Troop 64; team 66; Tract 464; Ext. 664; memo 4466
9/0	9	0 errors; 9 cats; 0 dogs; 90 cows; 99 hooks; 990 words; 9009 laws
All	10	Call Ext. 3819 and ask Inspector 521 to explain Rules 50 and 467.

| 1 | 2 | 3 | 4 | 5 | 6 | 7 | 8 | 9 | 10 | 11 | 12 | 13 |

76c
Review Styles

1. Open **75d-d1** and save as **76c**.
2. Apply the **Heading 1** style to the main and side headings. Center the main heading and make it initial caps. Press ENTER one time after the main heading.
3. Edit the paragraph headings to display on a separate line; delete the period. Capitalize all important words, and apply the **Heading 2** style.
4. Preview the document to ensure no headings are left alone at the bottom of the page.
5. Print.

76d

Report Formatted with Styles

Reports are often formatted using predefined styles or by creating a custom style. Study the illustration on page 283. Only the first page is shown as an example. Note the main heading and the second-level heading are formatted with the Heading 1 style. When styles are applied, main headings are easier to read in initial caps rather than all capital letters. When a third-level heading (or a paragraph heading) is required, key the third-level heading on a separate line, capitalize in initial caps, and apply the Heading 2 style, as shown in the illustration.

The spacing before and after the headings is automatically determined by the style. Be cautious not to insert an additional ENTER before or after the heading.

Insert and Delete Columns and Rows

Columns can be added to the left or right of existing columns. Rows can be added above or below existing rows. A row also can be added at the end of the table by clicking the insertion point in the last cell and pressing TAB.

To insert rows or columns in a table:

1. Click the insertion point where the new row or column is to be inserted. If several rows or columns are to be inserted, select the number you want to insert.
2. Choose **Insert** from the Table menu.
3. Choose **Rows Above** or **Rows Below** to insert rows. Choose **Columns to the Left** or **Columns to the Right** to insert columns.

To delete rows or columns in a table:

1. Click the insertion point in the row or column to be deleted. If you want to delete more than one row or column, you must first select them.
2. Choose **Delete** from the Table menu, and then choose **Rows or Columns**.

DRILL 2   INSERT AND DELETE ROWS AND COLUMNS

1. Open **49c-drill1**. Insert the information at the right so that the employees' names are in alphabetical order.

2. Delete the row containing Janice Goodman.

3. Save as **49c-drill2a**; print.

4. Delete row 1, and then place the cursor in cell B1 and insert a column to the right.

5. Key the text at the right in the new column. Left-align the text in the column. Center the text vertically in the cells.

6. Save as **49c-drill2b** and print.

| Ed Baker | Associate | 87321 | 9.3 |
| Susan Torres | Manager | 5611 | 9.8 |

Office

Wilshire

Toledo

Lake Forest

Tampa

Seattle

APPLICATIONS

49d-d1
Create Table

1. Key the table below; right-align column C. Center vertically on the page.
2. Save as **49d-d1** and print.

SAFETY AWARDS

Award Winners	Department	Amount
Lorianna Mendez	Accounting	2,000
William Mohammed	Marketing	800
Marjorie Adams	Engineering	1,500
Charles Drake	Purchasing	1,000

Pagination. The way a report is paginated depends on the binding and the preference of the writer. Usually, leftbound and unbound reports are paginated at the top right margin, and topbound reports are paginated at the center bottom margin. However, other positions are acceptable. Arabic numerals (1, 2, 3) are used for the body of the report and the appendix; lowercase Roman numerals (i, ii, iii) are used for preliminary pages. The body of the report starts with page 1, but it is not numbered.

Headings

Topical headings or captions introduce the material that follows and provide structure in a report. Position, capitalization, font size, and attributes, such as bold and italic, indicate levels of importance. Headings also set segments of copy apart and make the copy easier to read. The spacing before and after headings depends on the font and attributes used.

75d-d2
Table of Contents

1. Key the table of contents for the report prepared in **75d-d1**. Refer to the illustration on page 289 to assist you.
2. Key the main heading at the center; format bold, 14-point font.
3. In the Tabs dialog box, set a left tab at 0.5" to indent for the paragraph heading, a leader tab at 5.5" for the dot leaders, and a right tab at 6.0" for the page number.
4. Key the side headings at the left margin. Press TAB and key the paragraph headings indented ¹/₂" from the left margin. After keying the heading, press TAB to display the dot leaders; press TAB again to move to the right tab. Key the page number. DS between the side headings to show the report division.
5. Save as **75d-d2** and print.

75d-d3
Title Page

1. Prepare a title page for the report in **75d-d1** and save it as **75d-d3**.
2. Use the following information: key the title in 14-point font and insert the current date. Use bold for all text on the title page.
3. Print; then assemble the report in the following order: title page, table of contents, and report.

Prepared for
Phoenix Technology, Inc.

Prepared by
Student Name, Information Manager
Phoenix Technology, Inc.

75d-d4
Table of Contents

1. Prepare a table of contents for **74c-d1**, the report prepared in Lesson 74.
2. Save as **75d-d4** and print.

49d-d2

Insert Column and Row; Merge Cells

1. Save **49d-d1** as **49d-d2**.
2. Click the insertion point in cell B1 and insert a column to the right.
3. Add the following text left-aligned in the column. Resave and print.

   Division
   Commercial
   Space Shuttle
   Military
   Commercial

4. Insert a blank row above row 1. Merge the cells in the new row 1.
5. Cut the title SAFETY AWARDS and paste it in row 1. Apply 15% shading. Save as **49d-d2b**; print.

49d-d3

Insert and Delete Rows

1. Save **49d-d2** as **49d-d3**.
2. Insert a row after Lorianna Mendez, and add the following information.
   Robert Ruiz, Research, Military, 2,250
3. Insert a row at the end of the table, and add the following information:
   Franklin Cousins, Security, Space Shuttle, 500
4. Delete the row for William Mohammed. Resave and print.

49d-d4

Table with Merge Cells

1. Create a 6-column, 10-row table. Merge the cells in rows 1 and 2 as needed.
2. Center the table vertically. Save as **49d-d4**; print.

CANADA GEOGRAPHICAL INFORMATION					
Key Islands		Key Mountains		Key Lakes	
Island	Sq. Miles	Mountain	Height	Lake	Sq. Miles
Baffin	195,928	Logan	19,524	Superior	31,700
Victoria	83,897	St. Elias	18,008	Huron	23,000
Ellesmere	75,767	Lucania	17,147	Great Bear	12,095
Newfoundland	42,031	Fairweather	15,300	Great Slave	11,030
Banks	27,038	Waddington	13,104	Erie	9,910
Devon	21,331	Robson	12,972	Winnipeg	9,416
Melville	16,274	Columbia	12,294	Ontario	7,540

75d-d1
Multipage Unbound Report

1. Key the unbound report that follows with DS. Pay particular attention to the content that gives guides for formatting reports.

2. Key the main heading; position at about 2.1", and format appropriately. Key the side headings at the left margin and bold.

3. Indent the paragraph headings as shown. Bold and capitalize only the first word. Follow paragraph headings with a period.

4. Number the pages at the top right; suppress the page number on the first page.

5. Preview the document before printing to see that the page numbers display on the second and succeeding pages. If any headings are left alone at the bottom of the page, use the **Keep with next** function to position the heading with the paragraph that follows.

6. Save the document as **75d-d1**; print.

FORMATTING GUIDES FOR REPORTS

Business reports are used internally and externally. Managers often delegate the preparation of internal reports to subordinates; therefore, most reports go up to higher ranks in the organization. External reports often are used to secure business or to report on business that has been conducted for a client. Since reports can have a significant impact on an organization's business and on an individual's upward career mobility, they are usually prepared with care. Two important factors to be considered in formatting reports are placement and headings.

Placement

Effective report design requires many decisions about each of the factors just listed. A few basic guides can be applied to assist in making good formatting decisions.

Spacing. Reports may be formatted using either single or double spacing. Commercially prepared reports are generally single-spaced using many typesetting features. The desktop publishing capabilities of word processing software enable employees to prepare reports similar to those prepared professionally. Therefore, the trend is to single-space reports, to use full justification, and to incorporate desktop publishing features in the report.

Margins. Reports may be formatted with a default or 1" top, side, and bottom margins. An inch of extra space is provided in the top margin (2") for the first page of the report and for major sections that begin a new page. Extra space is required for binding. Most reports are bound at the left (1.5" left margin); a few are bound at the top (1.5" top margin).

Tables within Documents

50a
Warmup
Key each pair of lines twice at a controlled rate.

1st and 2d fingers
1 Mickey teaches golf three times this month to young children.
2 Jenny might meet her husband at the new stadium before the match.

3d and 4th fingers
3 Wallace was so puzzled over the sizable proposal due in six days.
4 Paula will wash, wax, and polish Polly's old, aqua car quite soon.

direct reach
5 Kilgore, located in a low-lying area, was destroyed by the flood.
6 Dennie framed the ball to help the Jupiter pitcher earn a strike.

| 1 | 2 | 3 | 4 | 5 | 6 | 7 | 8 | 9 | 10 | 11 | 12 | 13 |

APPLICATIONS

50b-d1
Table Report

The table structure can be used to create an attractive report. Create the report using a 2-column, 5-row table. Print the report without borders to achieve this look.

1. Key the title at about 2". Change the width of column A to approximately 2" and bold the text. Wrap the text in Column B. Do not change the row height.

2. After keying the table, insert a blank row after each row except the last.

3. Remove the table borders (**Format, Borders and Shading, Borders** tab, *Setting*: **None,** *Apply to:* **Table, OK**). Save as **50b-d1**. Print.

NOTEBOOK SECURITY GUIDELINES

Choose an easy-to-use security system.	Select a security system that is easy to use. If the security system is difficult to use and requires complicated steps, users will either not use it or look for ways to defeat it.
Assign someone to be in charge of notebook security.	One or more persons in the company should be responsible for monitoring the hardware and software on notebook computers. This person needs to be in charge of disseminating security rules and making sure that the rules are followed.
Apply several levels of security.	Different levels of security should be applied to different levels of employees. A CEO or an engineer working in the company's R & D department may be working with data that will require a higher level of security than someone in the art department. Don't bog down the artist with the high level of security needed for the CEO.
Most laptop/notebook thefts are opportunistic.	Train users to be alert and to keep an eye on their computers at all times. Remind them to use extra caution when passing through airports and staying in hotels.
Hold users responsible for their computers.	Encourage users to take precautions, and punish those who are careless by taking away laptop privileges.

LESSON 75 — Unbound Report with Table of Contents

SKILLBUILDING

75a
Warmup
Key each line twice.

alphabet	1	Chris Zweig quickly examined the job analysis forms we developed.
fig/sym	2	The trip cost $545.68 (1,859 miles at $.32 + $136.70 for a room).
double letter	3	Ann called a committee meeting at noon to discuss several issues.
easy	4	Claudia and my neighbor got fishbowls by the docks on the island.

| 1 | 2 | 3 | 4 | 5 | 6 | 7 | 8 | 9 | 10 | 11 | 12 | 13 |

FUNCTION REVIEW

75b
Leader Tabs

1. In the Tabs dialog box, set a left tab at 0.5", a leader tab at 5.5", and a right tab at 6.0".
2. Key the table of contents at the bottom of this page. Save as **75b**.

DOCUMENT DESIGN

75c

Table of Contents

A **table of contents** contains a list of the headings in a document along with the page number on which each heading appears. The table of contents is created after the document has been completed. In a report, the table of contents is placed at the beginning of a document and is considered one of the preliminary pages. The table of contents (and other preliminary pages) is numbered with lowercase Roman numerals positioned at the bottom center of the page.

To create a table of contents, set three tabs: 0.5" left tab, 5.5" leader tab, and 6.0" right tab. Key the side headings at the left margin. Press TAB to indent the paragraph headings at the first tab. Press TAB again to display the dot leaders; then press TAB to move to the right tab to key page numbers.

Position heading at about 2.1".
Bold, 14-point font → **TABLE OF CONTENTS**   default margin

DS

Organization 1
.5" → Audience Analysis.. 1
left tab   Clear Purpose... 2
            Organizational Pattern.. 3

DS

Delivery... 4
    Gestures.. 4
    Posture.. 5

Number preliminary pages with → ii   5.5"   6.0"
lowercase Roman numerals.   leader tab   right tab

DOCUMENT DESIGN   DOCUMENT DESIGN

1. Key the following memo to **Robert May**, from **Marcia Lewis**. The subject is **Purchase Order 5122**.
2. Center the data in column A, right-align column C, apply 15% shading to row 1, adjust the column widths, and center the table horizontally.
3. DS after the table, and add your reference initials. Save it as **50b-d2**.

The items that you requested on Purchase Order 5122 are in stock and will be shipped from our warehouse today. The shipment will be transported via Romulus Delivery System and is expected to arrive at your location in five days.   ↓ 2

Item Number	Description	Unit Price
329	Lordusky locking cabinet	212.00
331	Anchorage heavy duty locking cabinet	265.00
387	Lordusky locking cabinet (unassembled)	175.00

↓ 2

1. Key the following letter in modified block format. Supply all necessary letter parts. All column heads in the table should fit on one line.
2. Apply the **Table Contemporary** format to the table. Right-align numbers in column D. Save as **50b-d3**.

Ms. Beatrice Snow | Collection Manager | Precision Office Products | 2679 Orchard Lake Road | Farmington Hills, MI 48297-5534

Thank you for allowing International Financial Systems to assist you in managing your delinquent accounts. We provide you with the fastest interface to International Systems Collection Services. The activity report for last month is shown below.

Client Number	Last Name	First Name	Current Balance
1487	Jones	Alice	1,576.00
1679	Kim	Lisa	954.35
1822	Batavia	Roger	1,034.21
1905	Vokavich	Kramer	832.09

Please verify the accuracy of the names transmitted by your billing office. If you find any transmission errors, please contact Joseph Kerning at (888) 555-0134 immediately.

Sincerely | Sandra McCulley | Information Systems Specialist

ability to be an active listener. These annoyances may be loud noises near the speaker or a room that is too cold or too warm (Watts, 2002).

Poor Listening Habits

The poor listening habits presented here by Lehman and Dufrene (1999) and the International Listening Association (2001) are quite common among listeners. Being aware of the most common poor listening habits will aid in overcoming them.

SS each item.

DS between items.

Indent to paragraph point.

1. Pretending to listen is easy to do. By nodding, saying yes, and looking directly at the speaker, listeners can fake listening.

2. On the other hand, not looking at the speaker also results in poor listening as facial expressions and gestures are not communicated to the listener.

3. A listener's commitment to recording detailed notes often results in poor listening or overlistening.

4. Judgments by the listener about the speaker or the topic result in poor listening.

5. Rushing the speaker causes the speaker to think the listener's time is being wasted.

6. Interrupting the speaker is rude and does not enhance listening.

7. Showing interest in something other than the conversation and allowing any distractions to obtain the listener's attention result in poor listening.

Summary

Understanding that listening is not easy is a first step in becoming a better listener. Identifying individual habits that do not enhance effective listening is the next step. The first session of the Listening Skills Training Program will focus on the poor listening habits listed here and others.

1. Key the report in unbound format.
2. DS before and after the table. Apply **Table List 7** format to the table.
3. Save as **50b-d4**.

MALICIOUS INTRUDERS

We previously only worried about getting a virus by booting the computer from an infected floppy disk or by downloading and running programs from a BBS, a computer bulletin board system. Today, the majority of the viruses are obtained through the Internet. Downloading files from the Internet or opening e-mail containing a virus is the primary means by which malware spreads.

"Malware" is defined as getting your system infected by malicious software. Malware is usually classified according to two traits: where it hides and how it spreads. The table below will help you understand the categories of malicious software.

Type	Description
Boot sector viruses	This virus is obtained from booting an infected floppy disk.
File infectors	This virus modifies the programs you use, inserting code that runs when you execute programs.
Macro viruses	This is a file infector that hides inside macros. The virus is activated when the macro is opened.
Worm	This malware propagates from machine to machine without human intervention.

Load antivirus software on your computer to help screen out viruses. You will also want to carefully scrutinize all e-mail attachments and download programs from trusted sources only. Protect your computer, files, and software from dangerous intruders.

2.1"

Main heading **BARRIERS TO EFFECTIVE LISTENING** 14 point

1.25" In the initial phase of study of customer service operations, Fleming Communications, Inc., determined that listening is the communication task that our customer representatives spend almost 50 percent of their time doing. This report is the first in a series of reports. The purpose of this report is to explain a major barrier to effective listening and to present poor listening habits. 1.25"

Side heading **Issues in Listening**

Contrary to common belief, listening is not an easy task. Two issues to consider are the rate that listeners can process words and barriers to listening.

Paragraph heading **Rate.** Studies show that listeners can recognize words at a rate of 500 words per minute while speakers speak from 100 to 150 words per minute. A very important question to consider is at what rate does the mind process these words? With the mind processing information at over 1,000 words per minute, the listener is challenged to listen actively (Lehman and Dufrene, 1999).

Listening barriers. Listeners are also confronted with various other barriers to effective listening. These might include assumptions already made about the topic, about the speaker, about what the speaker will say, or about the specific setting. All of these assumptions will lead the listener to tune out what the speaker is actually saying. Another barrier to listening may be simply fatigue--the listener is too tired or perhaps too hungry or too busy to listen. Distractions often influence the listener's

1"

LESSON 51 Table Assessment

SKILLBUILDING

51a
Warmup
Key each line twice SS.

alphabet	1	Jacob Kazlowski and five experienced rugby players quit the team.
figures	2	E-mail account #82-4 is the account for telephone (714) 555-0108.
double letters	3	Anne will meet with the committee at noon to discuss a new issue.
easy	4	The men may pay my neighbor for the work he did in the cornfield.

| 1 | 2 | 3 | 4 | 5 | 6 | 7 | 8 | 9 | 10 | 11 | 12 | 13 |

51b
Timed Writing
Take two 3' timings. Strive to key with control and fluency.

  all letters

gwam 3' | 5'

Whether any company can succeed depends on how well it fits into the economic system. Success rests on certain key factors that are put in line by a management team that has set goals for the company and has enough good judgment to recognize how best to reach these goals. Because of competition, only the best-organized companies get to the top.

A commercial enterprise is formed for a specific purpose: that purpose is usually to equip others, or consumers, with whatever they cannot equip themselves. Unless there is only one provider, a consumer will search for a company that returns the most value in terms of price; and a relationship with such a company, once set up, can endure for many years.

Thus our system assures that the businesses that manage to survive are those that have been able to combine successfully an excellent product with a low price and the best service—all in a place that is convenient for the buyers. With no intrusion from outside forces, the buyer and the seller benefit both themselves and each other.

	3'	5'
	4	2
	8	5
	13	8
	17	10
	21	13
	23	14
	27	16
	31	19
	36	21
	40	24
	43	27
	47	28
	51	31
	56	33
	60	36
	64	39
	69	41
	70	42

3' | 1 | 2 | 3 | 4 |
5' | 1 | 2 | 3 |

APPLICATIONS

51c
Assessment

 → Continue

 ✓ Check

With CheckPro: When you complete a document, proofread it, check the spelling, and preview for placement. When you are completely satisfied with the document, click the **Continue** button to move to the next document. You will not be able to return and edit a document once you continue to the next document. Click the **Check** button when you are ready to error-check the test. Review and/or print the document analysis results.

Without CheckPro: On the signal to begin, key the documents in sequence. When time has been called, proofread all documents again and identify errors.

References

A references page or bibliography includes a complete listing of references cited in the report. Position the title References or Bibliography approximately 2" from the top of the page. If styles are used, format the title using the Title style or use Heading 1 style and center-align it. List references alphabetically by author surname. Use hanging indent format to position the first line at the left margin and indent all other lines 0.5". Double-space between entries. Number the references page sequentially with the body of the report.

Title Page

The title page of a report includes a concise title of the report, name and title of the individual or the organization for whom the report was prepared, name and title of the individual preparing the report, and the date.

Center each line; leave approximately 8 lines between parts. Center the page vertically. Use the same side margins as the report. A page number is not printed on the title page.

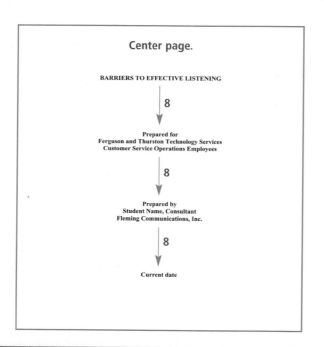

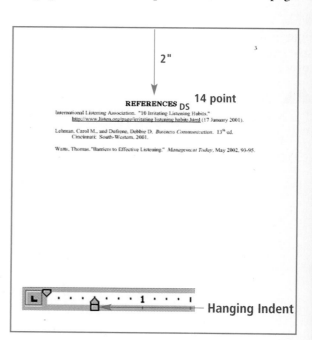

APPLICATIONS

74c-d1
Multipage Unbound Report with References Page

1. Key the model unbound report on pp. 287–288.
2. Insert a page number at top right; suppress the page number on the first page.
3. Use the information in the data file **references** to create a separate references page at the end of the report; format appropriately.
4. Switch to Print Layout View to verify page numbers and ensure that side headings are not alone at the bottom of the page.
5. Save the report as **74c-d1** and print.

74c-d2
Title Page

1. Prepare a title page for the report in **74c-d1** and save it as **74c-d2**.
2. Use the information shown above in the illustration, add the title in 14-point font, and insert the current date. Use bold for all text on the title page.

1. Key the table below.
2. Center column B; right-align columns C and D.
3. Format the table and apply Table List 4 format.
4. Center the table vertically. Save as **51c-d1**. Print.

LARSON LEARNING

Book Title	Publications	Sales	Unit Price
Adventures of Sally Boyer	2003	478,769.00	9.95
Tale of Five Cities	2002	91,278.00	32.50
New York, New York	2003	32,829.00	28.75
Horrell Hill Adventures	2003	89,412.00	29.00
Pommery Mountain	2003	194,511.00	33.75
Tom Creek's Adventures	2002	105,750.00	27.50

1. Key the memo.
2. Right-align column D and center columns B and C.
3. Save as **51c-d2**. Print.

TO: Brenda Cook | FROM: Mark Olson | SUBJECT: Sales Report

A comparison of the sales figures for 2003 and 2004 are shown below. Figures look pretty good for all the regions except the Northern region. I am concerned about the decrease in sales for the Northern region; this has always been a high-growth area.

Region	2003 Sales	2004 Sales	% of Change
East	53,256	72,002	+18.55%
North	41,899	37,576	–4.07%
West	62,965	64,211	+2.88%
South	27,894	29,031	+3.55%

Please research the cause in the drop of sales for the Northern area. Let's get together next week and discuss how we can improve Northern sales for next year.

Unbound Report with Title Page and References Page

74a
Warmup
Key each line twice.

alphabet	1	Jack won five or six pan pizzas after the racquetball game today.
fig/sym	2	My $5,406 of stock (102 shares at $53/share) is now worth $7,489.
adjacent reaches	3	Klaus and Opal were going to try hard to prepare the guide today.
easy	4	Alan, a neighbor, may fix a clam or lamb dish for us at the lake.

| 1 | 2 | 3 | 4 | 5 | 6 | 7 | 8 | 9 | 10 | 11 | 12 | 13 |

DOCUMENT DESIGN

74b

Unbound Reports

Reports generally include the report body, title page, and often a table of contents. Follow the information and models shown to format these pages.

Body of the Report

Margins: Use default side margins, top margin, and bottom margin in an unbound report. In a leftbound report, set the left margin at 1.5, allowing $1/4$" for binding.

Page numbers: Create a header to number pages at the top right. Suppress the Number pages so that the number prints at the top right. Suppress the page number so that it does not print on the first page of the report. Use either the Page Number or the Header command to position the page number $1/2$" from the edge of the page.

Preliminary pages include the Title Page and Table of Contents. These pages are numbered with Roman numerals at the bottom center. The page number should be suppressed, however, on the Title Page.

Headings: Headings should reflect a hierarchy, with main headings being most important. To create this hierarchy, follow these guidelines:

Main heading (Level 1 heading): Strike ENTER to position the main heading about 2" from the top edge of the paper. Center-align in all caps, bold, and 14 point.

Side headings (Level 2 heading): Key at the left margin in bold. Capitalize all main words. Use Keep with next when headings appear close to the bottom of the page to keep the side headings with at least two lines of the paragraph. If Styles are applied, use Heading 2.

Paragraph headings (Level 3 heading): Indent paragraph headings 0.5" and bold. Capitalize the first word and follow the heading with a period.

Styles: Headings may also be formatted with styles. Although various styles may be applied, as a general rule, format the main heading using either the Title Style or Heading 1 (capitalize only the main words and center it), side headings (Heading 1), and paragraph headings (Heading 2). All headings, including paragraph headings, must be freestanding (on separate lines) when styles are applied.

Spacing: Single-space business reports and block paragraphs. Double-space educational reports and indent paragraphs 0.5".

Single lines: Avoid single lines at the top or bottom of a page (called widow/orphan lines).

1. Key the table below. Make column A approximately 2" wide. Apply bullets to column B. Align bullets at the left; DS between bullets.

2. Bold column A. Align the text at the left.

3. Center the main heading in bold. Shade row 1 15%.

4. Select the entire table. Center the text vertically in the cells.

5. Set the row height for each of the rows as follows: row 1—.65", row 2—1.5", row 3—1.9", and row 4—1.4".

6. Center the table vertically. Save as **51c-d3**.

BENEFITS OF DSL SERVICE	
Improves productivity and eliminates frustration	• Always on; ends busy signals and dropped calls. • High-speed Internet access; greatly reduces wait time when uploading or downloading files.
Saves money	• Unlimited Internet access for one affordable flat rate. • One dedicated connection; no extra costs for network or multiple users. • No additional telephone company fees or usage charges.
Maximizes growth potential	• Increased bandwidth enables you to fully take advantage of the Internet. • Scalable enhanced services and applications that can accommodate change and growth with your business needs.

1. Open **51c-d1** and insert the columns and rows as directed.

2. Key the data below in a new column B; then adjust column widths.

Publisher
Bodwin
American
TWSS
Bodwin
TWSS
American

3. Insert a new row above Pommery Mountain and add the following information. Save as **51c-d4**. Print.

The Lion and the Mouse   American   2003   63,500.00   9.95

Forms Design, Management, and Control

In 2003, a survey of the forms used by Hess and Glenn, Inc. indicated that 74 percent of all forms were paper based, and only 26 percent were in electronic format. Forms were produced both internally and externally. However, the majority of the forms were created internally. The following table shows the source of the forms used at that time.

5.5" leader tab   6.0" right tab

Employee—Paper	26%
Company—Paper	35%
Vendor—Paper	9%
External—Paper	4%
Company—Electronic	17%
Employee—Electronic	9%

The bulk of the paper-based forms were created either by individual employees to simplify their work or as standard forms used throughout the company. These forms were targeted for conversion to electronic format.

Existing System

No centralized forms management or control system existed at the time of the 2003 study. The responsibility for managing each form rested with the individual who created it. The cost, quality, and effectiveness of forms that were in use varied widely. Many forms were poorly designed and were ineffective. An analysis of the forms indicated that a significant number of them could be put online. Taking this action would reduce the cost and increase the effectiveness of all forms used by Hess and Glenn, Inc.

New System

A new system was recommended to the Executive Committee. The Executive Committee approved the recommendation and authorized the consultant to develop the implementation plan. The office manager was made responsible for the design, management, and control of all forms. Three components comprised the system.

Forms Analysis and Design

A checklist was created to evaluate each form. Because of the large inventory of forms, it was determined that the stock of forms should be used until the supply was depleted. However, before a form was reprinted, it would be analyzed for effectiveness. New forms could be designed by departments and submitted for review, or they could be designed by a forms designer on the office manager's staff.

Conversion from Paper to Electronic Forms

The primary goal of the program was to convert as many of the paper-based forms as possible to electronic forms. Forms that were used by or at the request of external customers were exempt from the mandate to convert paper forms to electronic forms. Forms that were filled in using pen or pencil would be considered on a case-by-case basis.

Module 6: Checkpoint

Answer the questions below to see if you have mastered the content of Module 6.

1. A vertical list of information within a table is referred to as a(n) _____.
2. To move to the next cell in a table, press the _____ key.
3. A quick way to select an entire table is by clicking the _____ .
4. To center a table horizontally on the page, use the _____ option.
5. Preformatted styles can be applied to tables by using the _____ feature.
6. A row can be added at the end of the table by clicking the insertion point in the last cell and pressing _____.
7. The Table feature that allows you to join cells is referred to as _____ Cells.
8. Increase row height by selecting the rows and clicking _____ on the Table menu.
9. Whole numbers are generally aligned at the _____ in columns.
10. Text is generally aligned at the _____ in columns.

Performance Assessment

Document 1
Create Table

1. Format the main and secondary headings. Increase row 1 height to 1" and apply 15% shading.
2. Right-align columns B and C.
3. Change row height of rows 2–9 to .3". Adjust column widths, and center the table horizontally and vertically.
4. Save as **checkpoint6-d1**. Print but do not close.

UNIVERSITY OF NEVADA		
College of Business		
Department	Majors	Growth Rate
Accounting	945	3.65%
Banking, Finance, and Insurance	1,021	2.17%
Communications	326	-2 .5%
Economics	453	1.4%
International Business	620	14.74%
Management Science	1,235	11.8%
Marketing	1,357	10.38%

Document 2
Edit Table

1. Save the table as **checkpoint6-d2**.
2. Add the row at the right in alphabetical order.

Information Technology   8,756   14.5%

1. Open **Styles** from the data files.

2. Select the first heading (**Styles**), and apply the style **Heading 1**. Then center-align the heading and position it at about 2".

3. Select the next heading (**Built-in Styles**), and apply the style **Heading 1**.

4. Apply the style **Heading 2** to the next two headings (**Paragraph Style** and **Character Style**).

5. Apply the style **Heading 1** to the last heading (**Style Usage**).

6. Save it as **73d-drill6**. Your document should be similar to the one shown below. Print the report.

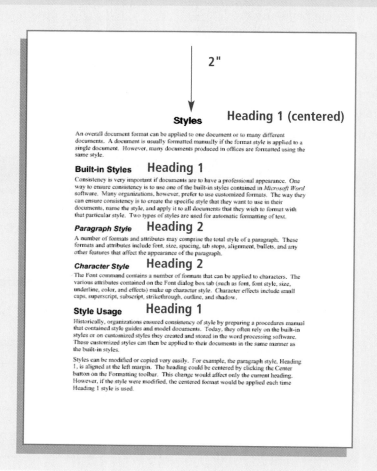

APPLICATIONS

73e-d1
Report

1. Key the report on page 284 SS.

2. For the tab, set tabs as follows: leader tab at 5.5" and right tab at 6.0".

3. Apply **Keep with next** feature to the side heading left alone at the bottom of the first page.

4. Insert page numbers at the top right; suppress page number on the first page.

5. Apply **Heading 1** style to the main and side headings.

6. Position main heading at approximately 2" and center it. Check side headings again.

7. Save as **73e-d1**.

Communication Skills 3

Use a singular verb

1. With a **singular subject**. (The singular forms of *to be* include: am, is, was. Common errors with *to be* are: you was, we was, they was.)

> She monitors employee morale.
> You are a very energetic worker.
> A split keyboard is in great demand.

2. With most **indefinite pronouns**: *another, anybody, anything, everything, each, either, neither, one, everyone, anyone, nobody.*

> Each of the candidates has raised a considerable amount of money.
> Everyone is eager to read the author's newest novel.
> Neither of the boys is able to attend.

3. With singular subjects joined by *or/nor, either/or, neither/nor.*

> Neither your grammar nor punctuation is correct.
> Either Jody or Jan has your favorite CD.
> John or Connie has volunteered to chaperone the field trip.

4. With a **collective noun** (*family, choir, herd, faculty, jury, committee*) that acts as one unit.

> The jury has reached a decision.
> The council is in an emergency session.
> But:
> The faculty have their assignments. (Each has his/her own assignments.)

5. With words or phrases that express **periods of time, weights, measurements**, or **amounts of money**.

> Fifteen dollars is what he earned.
> Two-thirds of the money has been submitted to the treasurer.
> One hundred pounds is too much.

Use a plural verb

6. With a **plural subject**.

> The students sell computer supplies for their annual fundraiser.
> They are among the top-ranked teams in the nation.

7. With **compound (two or more) subjects** joined by *and*.

> Headaches and backaches are common worker complaints.
> Hard work and determination were two qualities listed by the references.

8. With *some, all, most, none, several, few, both, many*, and *any* when they refer to more than one of the items.

> All of my friends have seen the movie.
> Some of the teams have won two or more games.

Styles

The **Styles** feature enables you to apply a group of formats automatically to a document. A new *Word* document opens with the following styles attached to it: Normal, Heading 1, Heading 2, and Heading 3. Normal is the default style of 12-point Times New Roman, left alignment, single spacing, and no indent. Text that you key is formatted in the Normal style unless you apply another style.

Styles include both character and paragraph styles. The attributes listed in the Font dialog box make up the character styles. **Character styles** apply to a single character or characters that are selected. To apply character styles using the Formatting toolbar, select the characters to be formatted and apply the desired font.

Paragraph styles include both the character styles and other formats that affect paragraph appearance such as line spacing, bullets, numbering, and tab stops. The illustration below shows a list of styles that have been applied within a particular document. Character styles are listed; paragraph styles are indicated with the paragraph marker.

To apply paragraph styles using the Formatting toolbar:

1. Select the text to which you want to apply a style.

2. Click the down arrow on the Style box on the Formatting toolbar.

3. Select the desired style.

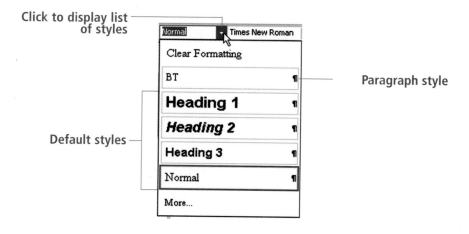

DRILL 5   **STYLES**

1. Open a new document. Display the styles list box. Notice the default styles that are available.

2. Key your name on one line and your address below it. Select your name and apply Heading 1 style. Select your address and apply Heading 2 style.

3. Select your name again and apply Normal. Then select your name and italicize it. Display the styles list. Notice that Italic has been added as a character style.

4. Close the document without saving.

5. Open **Body Text** from the data files.

6. Apply the style **Body Text** to the document. Since there is only one paragraph, simply click anywhere within the paragraph and apply the style. The entire paragraph changes to the new style.

7. Save the document as **73d-drill5**.

DRILL 1

SUBJECT-VERB AGREEMENT

1. Review the rules and examples on the previous page.
2. Open **subjectverb1** from the data files. Save it as **subjectverb-drill1**.
3. Follow the specific directions provided in the data file.
4. Save again and print.

DRILL 2

SUBJECT-VERB AGREEMENT

1. Open **subjectverb2** from the data files. Save it as **subjectverb-drill2**.
2. Follow the specific directions provided in the data file.
3. Save and print.

DRILL 3

SUBJECT/VERB AND CAPITALIZATION

1. Key the ten sentences at the right, choosing the correct verb and applying correct capitalization.

2. Save as **subjectverb-drill3** and print.

1. both of the curies (was/were) nobel prize winners.
2. each of the directors in the sales department (has/have) given us approval.
3. mr. and mrs. thomas funderburk, jr. (was/were) married on november 23, 1936.
4. my sister and her college roommates (plan/plans) to tour london and paris this summer.
5. our new information manager (suggest/suggests) the following salutation when using an attention line: ladies and gentlemen.
6. the body language expert (place/places) his hand on his cheek as he says, "touch your hand to your chin."
7. the japanese child (enjoy/enjoys) the american food her hosts (serve/serves) her.
8. all of the candidates (was/were) invited to the debate at boston college.
9. the final exam (cover/covers) chapters 1-5.
10. turn south onto interstate 20; then take exit 56 to bossier city.

DRILL 4

EDITING SKILLS

Key the paragraph. Correct all errors in grammar and capitalization. Save as **editing-drill4**.

This past week I visited the facilities of the magnolia conference center in isle of palms, south carolina, as you requested. bob bremmerton, group manager, was my host for the visit.

magnolia offers many advantages for our leadership training conference. The prices are reasonable; the facilities is excellent; the location is suitable. In addition to the beachfront location, tennis and golf packages are part of the group price.

1. Open **73d-drill1** and save as **73d-drill3**.
2. Apply the **Keep with next** feature to the side heading left alone at the bottom of the first page.

3. Verify that Widow/Orphan control is on (✓ appears in box).
4. Save and print.

Leader Tabs

A **leader tab** displays a series of dots that lead the eye to the next column. Leaders can be combined with a left, center, right, or decimal tab. Leaders are often used in documents such as table of contents, agendas, and financial statements. Leader tabs can only be set from the Tab dialog box.

To set a leader tab:

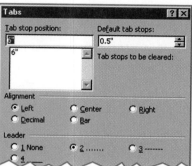

1. Click **Tabs** on the Format menu to display the Tab dialog box.
2. Enter the position of the tab in the Tab Stop Position box.
3. Choose the **Alignment** type.
4. Choose the **Leader** style, for example 2; click **Set**; then click **OK**.

1. In the Tabs dialog box, set a right leader tab at 6" using Leader style 2.
2. Key the first name at the left margin and press TAB. Note that the leaders extend to the right margin.

3. Key the title (*President*). Notice that it aligns at the right tab stop.
4. Complete the drill and save it as **73d-drill4**.

6.0" right leader tab

John Sneider . . . . President

JoAnn Rouche . . . . Vice President, Education

Janice Weiss . . . . Vice President, Membership

Lotus Fijutisi . . . . Chief Financial Officer

Loretta Russell . . . . Recording Secretary

Skill Builders 4

Save each drill as a separate file. Save as SB4-d1, etc. (Skill Builder 4, Drill 1).

DRILL 1

KEYSTROKING PATTERNS

Key each line twice SS.

3d row

1 it we or us opo pop you rut rip wit pea lea wet pit were quiet
2 pew tie toe per rep hope pour quip rope your pout tore rip quirk.

Home row

3 ha has kid lad led last wash lash gaff jade fads half sash haggle
4 as dad had add leg jug lads hall lass fast deal fall leafs dashes

1st row

5 ax ban man zinc clan bank calm lamb vain amaze bronze back buzzer
6 ax sax can bam zag cab mad fax vans buzz caves knack waxen banana

Standard Plan for Guided Writing Procedures

1. Take a 1' writing on paragraph 1. Note your *gwam*.
2. Add four words to your 1' *gwam* to determine your goal rate.
3. In the Open screen, set the timer for 1' and the Timer option to beep every 15" (*MicroPace Pro* or *Keyboarding Pro*).
4. From the table below, select from Column 4 the speed nearest your goal rate. Note the ¼' point at the left of that speed. Place a check mark at each ¼' goal.
5. Take two 1' guided writings on paragraphs 1 and 2 striving to meet your ¼' goal. Do not save.

A all letters

1. Key two 1' writings on each paragraph.
2. Key one 3' or one 5' writing.

Optional: Practice as a guided writing.

			gwam
1/4'	1/2'	3/4'	1'
8	16	24	32
9	18	27	36
10	20	30	40
11	22	33	44
12	24	36	48
13	26	39	52
14	28	41	56
15	30	45	60
16	32	48	64
17	34	51	68
18	36	54	72

Writing 22

gwam 3' | 5'

Who is a professional? The word can be defined in many ways. Some may think of a professional as someone who is in an exempt job category in an organization. To others the word can denote something quite different; being a professional denotes an attitude that requires thinking of your position as a career, not just a job. A professional exerts influence over her or his job and takes pride in the work accomplished.

Many individuals who remain in the same positions for a long time characterize themselves as being in dead-end positions. Others who remain in positions for a long time consider themselves to be in a profession. A profession is a career to which you are willing to devote a lifetime. How you view your profession is up to you.

gwam 3' | 5'
4 | 2 | 32
8 | 5 | 35
12 | 7 | 37
17 | 10 | 40
21 | 13 | 43
25 | 15 | 45
28 | 17 | 47
32 | 19 | 49
36 | 22 | 52
40 | 24 | 54
45 | 27 | 57
49 | 29 | 59
50 | 30 | 60

3' | 1 | 2 | 3 | 4
5' | 1 | 2 | 3

Change Number Format

help keywords
number format

Preliminary pages of reports may include a title page, a transmittal letter or memo, a list of tables, a list of figures, a table of contents, and an executive summary. These preliminary pages are numbered with lowercase Roman numerals at the bottom of the page. Title pages are numbered, but the page number is suppressed. To number these pages, you will need to change the number format.

To change number format:

1. Select **Page Numbers** from the Insert menu.
2. Select **Bottom of page (Footer)** in the Position box, and **Center** in the Alignment box.
3. Click the **Format** button; click the down arrow beside Number format; select **i, ii, iii**.
4. Click **Start at,** enter the page number, and click **OK**.

DRILL 2   **FORMAT PAGE NUMBERS**

1. Open **preliminary** from the data files.
2. Insert the correct page numbers in the appropriate position for these preliminary pages.

3. Save as **73d-drill2** and print.

Note: In a later lesson, you will learn to use section breaks to insert page numbers for both preliminary pages and report pages in the same document file.

Line and Page Breaks

help keywords
Format paragraph and line and page breaks

Pagination or breaking pages at the appropriate location can easily be controlled using two features: Widow/Orphan control and Keep with next.

Widow/Orphan control prevents a single line of a paragraph from printing at the bottom or top of a page. A check mark displays in this option box indicating that Widow/Orphan control is "on" (the default).

Keep with next prevents a page break from occurring between two paragraphs. Use this feature to keep a side heading from being left alone at the bottom of a page. To use Keep with next:

1. Select the side heading and the paragraph that follows.
2. Click **Format**; then **Paragraph**.
3. From the Line and Page Breaks tab, select **Keep with next**. Click **OK**. The side heading moves to the next page.

> **TIP**
>
> You can also insert a page break by pressing CTRL + ENTER or choosing **Page Break** from the Insert menu.

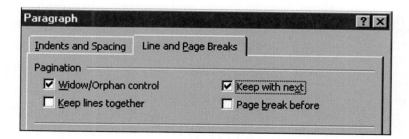

KEYBOARDING TECHNIQUE

Key each line twice, SS.

1st 1 Zam and six lazy men visited Cecil and Bunn at a bank convention.
2 Zane, much to the concern of Bev and six men, visited their zone.

2d 3 Jill said she wished that she had fed Dale's dog a lot less food.
4 Jake Hall sold the glass flask at a Dallas "half-off" glass sale.

3d 5 Did either Peter or Trey quip that reporters were out to get you?
6 Either Trey or Peter tried to work with a top-quality pewter toy.

4th 7 18465 97354 12093 87541 09378 34579 74629 45834 28174 11221 27211
8 02574 29765 39821 07623 17659 20495 39481 10374 32765 77545 22213

Writing 23

gwam 3' 5'

 all letters

1. Key three 1' writings on each ¶.
2. Key one 5' writing or two 3' writings. Proofread; circle errors; determine *gwam*.

Option: Practice as a guided writing.

			gwam
1/4'	1/2'	3/4'	1'
8	16	24	32
9	18	27	36
10	20	30	40
11	22	33	44
12	24	36	48
13	26	39	52
14	28	41	56
15	30	45	60
16	32	48	64
17	34	51	68
18	36	54	72

Students, for decades, have secured part-time jobs to help pay for college expenses. Today, more students are gainfully employed while they are in college than ever before. Many of them are employed because their financial situation requires that they earn money. Earnings from jobs go to pay for tuition, books, living costs, and other necessities. Some work so that they can own cars or buy luxury items; others seek jobs to gain skills or to build their vitas. These students are aware that many organizations prefer to hire a person who has had some type of work experience than one who has had none.

Students often ask if the work experience has to be in exactly the same field. Obviously, the more closely related the experience, the better it is. However, the old adage, anything beats nothing, applies. Regardless of the types of jobs students have, they can demonstrate that they get to work regularly and on time, they have good human relations skills, they are organized and can manage time effectively, and they produce good results. All of these factors are very critical to employers. The bottom line is that employers like to use what you have done in the past as a predictor of what you will do in the future.

3' gwam columns: 4 2 52 / 8 5 54 / 12 7 57 / 17 10 59 / 21 12 62 / 25 15 64 / 29 17 67 / 33 20 69 / 38 23 72 / 41 24 74 / 44 27 76 / 49 29 78 / 53 32 81 / 57 34 84 / 62 37 86 / 66 40 89 / 70 42 91 / 75 45 94 / 79 47 97 / 82 49 99

3' | 1 | 2 | 3 | 4 |
5' | 1 | 2 | 3 |

73c

Timed Writing

Take one 3' and one 5' timed writing; determine *gwam*; proofread and circle errors.

What characterizes the life of an entrepreneur? Those who   4 | 2 43
have never owned their own businesses may think owning a business   8 | 5 46
means being your own boss, setting your own hours, and making a   13 | 8 48
lot of money. Those who have run their own businesses are quick   17 | 10 51
to report that owning a business may be exciting and challenging,   21 | 13 54
but it also requires hard work, long hours, and personal sacri-   26 | 15 56
fice. A good idea is not the only prerequisite for a successful   30 | 18 59
business. A little luck even helps.   32 | 19 60

Many small businesses are operated as businesses from the   36 | 22 63
initial stages. However, some small businesses that turn out to be   41 | 24 65
successful are just hobbies in the early stages. The entre-   45 | 27 68
preneur has a job and uses the income from it to support the   49 | 29 70
hobby. When the hobby begins to require more and more time, the   53 | 32 73
entrepreneur has to choose between the job and the hobby. The   57 | 34 75
decision is usually based on finances. If enough money can be   62 | 37 78
made from the hobby or can be obtained from another source, the   66 | 39 80
hobby is turned into a business.   68 | 41 82

```
3' |----------1----------|----------2----------|----------3----------|----------4----------|
5' |---------------1---------------|---------------2---------------|---------------3---------------|
```

FUNCTION REVIEW

73d

help keywords
page numbers

Page Numbers

In Module 5, you learned to number pages in simple reports. If you need to review how to insert page numbers at the top right, study the instructions below.

To insert page numbers:

1. Select **Page Numbers** from the Insert menu.
2. Select **Top of page (Header)** in the Position box.
3. Select **Right** in the Alignment box.
4. Remove the check mark from the Show number on first page box.

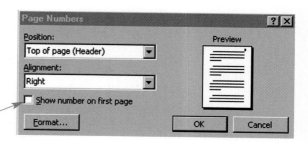

DRILL 1   PAGE NUMBERS

1. Open **benefits** from the data files. Save as **73d-drill1**.
2. Insert page numbers at the top right; do not number the first page.
3. Save and print.

NUMBER REACHES

Key each line at a comfortable rate; practice difficult lines.

1 My staff of 11 worked 11 hours a day from May 11 to June 11.
2 Her flight, PW 222, lands at 2:22 p.m. on Thursday, June 22.
3 We 3, part of the 333rd Corps, marched 33 miles on August 3.
4 Car 444 took Route 4 east to Route 44, then 4 miles to Aden.
5 The 55 wagons traveled 555 miles in '55; only 5 had trouble.
6 Put 6 beside 6; result 66. Then, add one more 6 to get 666.
7 She sold 7,777 copies of Record 77, Schubert's 7th Symphony.
8 In '88, it took 8 men and 8 women 8 days to travel 88 miles.
9 The 9 teams, 9 girls and 9 boys, depart on Bus 999 at 9 a.m.
10 Million has six zeros; as, 000,000. Ten has but one; as, 0.

| 1 | 2 | 3 | 4 | 5 | 6 | 7 | 8 | 9 | 10 | 11 | 12 | 13 |

  all letters

To access the timing in *MicroPace Pro*, key **W** and the timing number. For example, key **W24** for *Writing 24*.

Writing 24

gwam 3' | 5'

	3'	5'
Planning, organizing, and controlling are three of the	4	2	65

Planning, organizing, and controlling are three of the functions that are familiar to all sorts of firms. Because these functions are basic to the managerial practices of a business, they form the very core of its daily operations. Good managerial procedures, of course, do not just occur by accident. They must be set into motion by people. Thus, a person who plans to enter the job market, especially in an office position, should study all of the elements of good management in order to apply those principles to her or his work.

Leadership is another very important skill for a person to develop. Leaders are needed at all levels in a business to plan, organize, and control the operations of a firm. A person who is in a key position of leadership usually is expected to initiate ideas as well as to carry out the goals of a business. Office workers who have developed the qualities of leadership are more apt to be promoted than those without such skills. While leadership may come naturally for some people, it can be learned as well as be improved with practice.

Attitude is an extremely important personality trait that is a big contributor to success in one's day-to-day activities. Usually a person with a good attitude is open-minded to the ideas of others and is able to relate with others because he or she has an interest in people. Thus, one's attitude on the job often makes a great difference in whether work gets done and done right. Because teamwork is a part of many jobs, developing a good attitude toward work, people, and life seems logical.

gwam values (3' | 5'):
4 | 2 | 65
8 | 5 | 68
12 | 7 | 71
17 | 10 | 73
21 | 13 | 76
25 | 15 | 78
30 | 18 | 81
34 | 20 | 83
36 | 22 | 85
40 | 24 | 87
44 | 26 | 89
48 | 29 | 92
52 | 31 | 95
57 | 34 | 97
61 | 37 | 100
65 | 39 | 102
70 | 42 | 105
72 | 43 | 106
76 | 46 | 109
80 | 48 | 111
85 | 51 | 114
89 | 53 | 117
93 | 56 | 119
97 | 58 | 122
101 | 61 | 124
105 | 63 | 126

3' | 1 | 2 | 3 | 4
5' | 1 | 2 | 3

Report Mastery

• Format reports with title page and table of contents.
• Format reports with notes page and references page.
• Format reports with styles, footnotes, and endnotes.
• Change number format of preliminary pages.
• Insert section breaks.

LESSON 73

Skillbuilding and Word Processing Basics

SKILLBUILDING

73a
Warmup
Key each line twice SS.

direct reaches	1	June and my brother, Bradly, received advice from junior umpires.
	2	My bright brother received minimum reward for serving many years.
adjacent reaches	3	Clio and Trey were sad that very few voters were there last week.
	4	Western attire was very popular at the massive auction last week.
double letters	5	Tommie Bennett will go to a meeting in Dallas tomorrow afternoon.
	6	Lee will meet Joanne at the swimming pool after accounting class.

| 1 | 2 | 3 | 4 | 5 | 6 | 7 | 8 | 9 | 10 | 11 | 12 | 13 |

73b
Technique Builder
Key each group 3 times; work at a controlled rate.

b	7	be bib bribe bubble baby baboon bobble cobble bonbon bogie bobbin
n	8	no nun new none noon napkin nanny ninth nonsense nothing national
b/n	9	Benny and Nate have been told to begin with bends before running.

j	10	jet joy join joke jelly jacket jackel jewel rejoice judge jonquil
f	11	of fast fief fanfare fearful fifteen flora forefoot format buffer
j/f	12	Join Jon Fondren and his staff for a fun-filled five-day journey.

y	13	yes you your yield yokes yellow yesterday phyloid reply navy away
t	14	twin total trinket triplet title ticket token meant impact tattle
y/t	15	Tom, Timothy, and Tony are triplets; Yvonne and Yvette are twins.

| 1 | 2 | 3 | 4 | 5 | 6 | 7 | 8 | 9 | 10 | 11 | 12 | 13 |

DRILL 4

IMPROVE RESPONSE PATTERNS

Key lines 5–16 once; DS between 4-line groups; work at a controlled rate; repeat drill.

  all letters

To access the timing in *MicroPace Pro*, key **W** and the timing number. For example, key **W25** for *Writing 25*.

direct reaches: reaches with the same finger; keep hands quiet

1 brand much cent numb cease bright music brief jump special carved
2 create mumps zany mystic curve mummy any checks brag brunch after
3 Bradley broke his left thumb after lunch on a great hunting trip.
4 After having mumps, Cecil once saw June excel in a funny musical.

adjacent reaches: keep fingers curved and upright

5 were junior sad yuletide trees polo very join safe property tweed
6 tree trio trickle tripod quit excess was free easy million option
7 Gwen and Sumio are going to be quite popular at the Western Club.
8 Fred said we were going to join the guys for polo this afternoon.

double letters: strike keys rapidly

9 dill seem pool attic miss carry dragged kidded layoff lapped buzz
10 commend accuse inner rubber cheer commission football jazz popper
11 Tammy called to see if she can borrow my accounting book at noon.
12 Lynnette will meet with the bookseller soon to discuss the issue.

Writing 25

gwam

	1'	5'
	12	2	47

Working at home is not exactly a new phenomenon, but the concept is growing quite rapidly. For many years, people have worked at home. In most instances, they were self-employed and operated a business from their homes. Today, the people who work at home fit into a variety of categories. Some own their own businesses; others bring extra work home after the workday ends. A key change is the large group of people who are employed by huge organizations but who work out of home offices. These employees are in jobs that include sales, creative, technical, and a host of other categories.

1'	5'
12	2 47
26	5 50
39	8 52
52	10 55
65	13 58
79	16 60
92	18 63
106	21 66
120	24 69

The real change that has occurred is not so much the numbers of people who are working at home and the variety of jobs, but the complex tools that are now available for doing the job. Technology has truly made the difference. In many cases, clients and customers are not even aware that they are dealing with individuals working at home. Computers, printers, fax machines, telephone systems, and other office equipment enable the worker in the home to function in the same way as workers in a typical business office.

1'	5'
12	26 71
26	29 74
39	32 76
53	35 79
66	37 82
79	40 84
93	42 87
104	45 89

| 1' | 1 | 2 | 3 | 4 | 5 | 6 | 7 | 8 | 9 | 10 | 11 | 12 | 13 |
| 5' | | 1 | | | 2 | | | | 3 | | |

Module 11: Checkpoint

1. What is the correct salutation written to the attention of Ms. Sarah Gray at Mountain Inn Resort?

    a. Dear Ms. Gray
    b. Ladies and Gentlemen

2. For a–f below, circle the letter part that appears first.

    a. reference line or attention line
    b. subject line or reference line
    c. reference initials or enclosure
    d. salutation or subject line
    e. mailing notation or dateline
    f. attention line or reference line

3. A _____ notation shows that a copy of the document was sent to the person(s) named without the recipient's knowledge.

Performance Assessment

Document 1
Modified Block Letter

1. Key the modified block letter with mixed punctuation for **Alberto Valenzuela, Conference Planner**, to the following address:

    Ms. Shawna Olson
    Western Regional Manager, Acune, Inc.
    5450 Signal Hill Rd., Springfield, OH 45504-5450

2. Supply an appropriate subject line. Send a copy to Susan Reading.

3. Save as **Checkpoint11-d1**; print.

Thank you for agreeing to exhibit at the National Technology Conference on May 10-12 at the Earlham Hotel in Memphis, Tennessee. We are very excited about your first-time attendance at our conference. We know our over two thousand participants will be equally as excited about the outstanding products you will have to offer them.

The exhibit hall will be available to you from 8-12 on Wednesday, May 10, for setup. You will be provided a large table with drape, two folding chairs, power supply, and a garbage can. Should you need additional assistance during the conference, please call me at my cell phone, (901) 555-0124.

Document 2
Block Letter

1. Open **Checkpoint11-d1**. Reformat as a block letter with open punctuation.

2. Add a **SPECIAL DELIVERY** mailing notation. Add the reference line **Stress Management Session**.

3. Save as **Checkpoint11-d2**.

4. Generate an envelope. Save as **Checkpoint11-d2a**.

Document 3
Memo

1. Key the message in Document 1 as a memo to **Sandra Habek** from **Alberto Valenzuela**.

2. Save as **Checkpoint11-d3**.

DRILL 5

IMPROVE CONCENTRATION

Set a right tab at 5.5" for the addresses. Key the Internet addresses in column 2 exactly as they are listed. Accuracy is critical.

A all letters

The paperless guide to New York City	http://www.mediabridge.com/nyc
A trip to outer space	http://spacelink.msfc.nasa.gov
Search engine	http://webcrawler.com
Government Printing Office access	http://www.access.gpo.gov/index.html
MarketPlace—corporate information	http://www.mktplace.com
Touchstone's PC-cillin virus scan	http://www.antivirus.com

Writing 26

gwam 3'

Many small businesses fail. Surprisingly, though, many   4
people are still willing to take a chance on starting one of   8
their own. A person who is willing to take the risks necessary   12
to manage a business in order to receive the potential rewards is   17
called an entrepeneur. In a sense, such individuals are pio-   21
neers who enjoy each step on the way to achieving objectives that   25
they have determined to be important. This type of person has   29
had a profound impact on shaping our economy and our quality of   34
life.   34

What does is take to start a business venture, and what   38
kinds of people make it work? Obviously, the desire to make   42
money and to be one's own boss are two basic incentives, but   40
these alone are not enough to guarantee success. Two qualifica-   50
tions common to most successful entrepeneurs, whatever field   54
they are in, are an attentiveness to detail and a knack for   58
solving day-to-day problems without losing sight of long-range   62
goals.   63

While there is a high risk in organizing any new business,   67
the entrepeneur who is successful is seldom someone who could be   71
considered a gambler. Most gamblers expect to have the odds   75
against them. On the other hand, a clever businessperson sees to   80
it that the odds are as good as possible by getting all of the   84
facts and planning carefully before going ahead. Luck helps, to   88
be sure, but a new business enterprise depends far more on good   92
ideas and detailed plans.   94

| 3' | 1 | 2 | 3 | 4 |
| 5' | 1 | 2 | 3 |

72c-d3
Memo

1. Key the memo and save as **72c-d3**.

words

TO: Technology Task Force|**FROM:** Clifford F. McCrory, Chair|**DATE:**   14
October 20, 200-|**SUBJECT:** School Board Recommendations   25

Our professional staff finalized the Technology Task Force report request-   40
ing approval of four major technology enhancements for K-14. A draft copy   55
is enclosed for your review. Please make any corrections and return the   69
draft to us within one week so that the final report can be prepared.   83

The report will be sent special delivery to each school board member no   98
later than Monday. This deadline must be followed if the item is to appear   113
on the November 15 agenda. If we do not hear from you within one week,   127
we will assume that you accept the draft as submitted.|xx|Enclosure   141

72c-d4
Memo from Template

1. Key the memo using the Professional Memo template.
2. Key **Investments, Inc.** as the company name.
3. Save as **72c-d4**.

TO: All Employees|**FROM:** Cory Johnson|**DATE:** (Insert next Monday's   12
date)|**SUBJECT:** Guidelines for Voice Mail Greeting   21

Recording an appropriate voice mail greeting is very important as we pro-   36
vide our clients with excellent and friendly service. Please study the fol-   51
lowing essential parts of an effective voice mail greeting and then study the   67
sample greeting shown below: 73

1. State your name.   77
2. Include the day and date you are recording the greeting.   89
3. Describe why you are not available to take the call.   101
4. Request caller to leave a message or directions for obtaining personal   115
   assistance.   118
5. Provide an approximate time when the call will be returned.   131

Hello, this is Cory Johnson's voice mail. It's Monday, (Insert date), and I am   147
in a meeting until 3:30. After the tone, please leave your name, phone num-   162
ber, and a detailed message. I will return your call before 5 p.m. today. For   178
immediate assistance, press 0 now. Thank you.   188

In addition to recording an appropriate message, it is equally important   203
that you update the greeting each day. Also check for voice mail messages   218
throughout the day and remember to return calls as promised in the   232
greeting.   234

72c-d5
E-Mail Message

1. Send an e-mail to your instructor that introduces yourself. Include why you are taking
   this class and what you hope to achieve. Create a subject line.
2. Copy the e-mail to yourself.

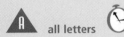
all letters

y/t
1 yj my say may yes rye yarn eye lye yap any relay young berry
2 tf at it let the vat tap item town toast right little attire
3 Yesterday a young youth typed a cat story on the typewriter.

b/n
4 bf but job fibs orb bow able bear habit boast rabbit brother
5 nj not and one now fun next pony month notice runner quicken
6 A number of neighbors banked on bunking in the brown cabins.

g/h
7 gag go gee god rig gun log gong cog gig agog gage going gang
8 huh oh hen the hex ash her hash ah hush shah hutch hand ache
9 Hush; Greg hears rough sounds. Has Hugh laughed or coughed?

r/u
10 row or rid air rap par rye rear ark jar rip nor are right or
11 cut us auk out tutu sun husk but fun cub gun nut mud tug hug
12 Ryan is sure you should pour your food from an urn or cruet.

| 1 | 2 | 3 | 4 | 5 | 6 | 7 | 8 | 9 | 10 | 11 | 12 |

Writing 27

gwam 3' | 5'

Most people think traveling is fun because they associate travel with exciting vacations. People who have to travel as part of their jobs have a very different view of travel. They are more prone to view business travel as a hassle than a pleasure. Business travelers often have to work under less than ideal circumstances. While they are away from the office, regular work tends to pile up; and they often return to find stacks of work waiting for them. Many business travelers learn to utilize wisely the waiting time that is a part of most travel.

A successful business trip requires careful planning. The typical business traveler tends to think of a trip as a success if two conditions are met. The business goals must be achieved, and the trip must be totally free of headaches. The person making the trip has to worry about achieving the business goals, but a good travel agent can relieve the traveler of many of the worries of making travel arrangements. A good checklist can help to ensure that all the personal items as well as business items needed for the trip will be handy when they are needed.

4 | 2
8 | 5
12 | 7
16 | 10
21 | 12
25 | 15
29 | 17
33 | 20
37 | 22
41 | 25
45 | 27
50 | 30
54 | 32
58 | 35
63 | 38
67 | 40
71 | 43
75 | 45

gwam 3' | 1 | 2 | 3 | 4 |
5' | 1 | 2 | 3 |

72c-d1
Modified Block Letter

1. Key the modified block letter with mixed punctuation for Michael Taylor, President.
2. Add the mailing notation **CONFIDENTIAL** and the subject line **Invitation to Honor Society**. Send a copy to Dr. Zimiko Tayyar. Provide the appropriate complimentary close and other notations. Center vertically on the page. Save as **72c-d1**.
3. Generate an envelope. Save as **72c-d1a**.

	words
January 30, 200- | Miss Shea Patterson | 43 University Dr. | Lacombe, LA	10
70445-2536 | Dear Shea	18

Congratulations! Because of your outstanding academic record and lead-	32
ership potential in your teaching profession, you have been selected for	47
membership in Pi Omega Pi, the honorary society for undergraduate busi-	61
ness education majors. Being selected for membership in Pi Omega Pi is	75
the highest honor that a student of business education can achieve.	89

A formal initiation ceremony will be held on Tuesday, February 13, at	103
4 p.m. in Room 252 of the T. S. McKinney Building. Please complete	117
the enclosed form and return it to me by Friday, February 9. A one-time	132
initiation fee of $40 is also due by the initiation.	142

Shea, I am delighted that you have been selected as a Pi Omega Pi mem-	156
ber and look forward to your initiation on February 13.	168

72c-d2
Two-Page Block Letter

1. Open **72hightower**. Save as **72c-d2**.
2. Use the date command and position appropriately on the page.
3. Include **CERTIFIED** as the mailing notation, and add **Account USC3828GB** as the reference line.
4. Key the remainder of the letter shown below for Ms. Kathy Hossain, Manager. Provide the appropriate complimentary close and other notations. Create an appropriate second-page header. Key the last sentence as a postscript.

Our market tests indicate a great deal of interest in a tailgating package.	12
The cost for a box lunch for four is $20. The lunch will include chicken,	24
potato salad, corn on the cob, rolls, and a brownie. We could add High-	36
tower napkins, plates, plastic utensils, and souvenir mugs and sell the	45
package for $30.	55

Please review our preliminary design sketches. We will contact you in a	65
few days for your reaction to the design samples. By then, we should have	77
the final results of our marketing tests.	85

We plan to visit with you three weeks prior to the game to provide an	99
update on all of our marketing activities.	106

This game will be a bright spot for your team and your financial standing.	132
(header and notations)	150

Edit Business Documents

- Build keying skill.
- Build editing skills.
- Edit letters.
- Edit memos and e-mail.
- Edit tables and reports.

LESSON 52

Skillbuilding, Editing, and Reference Tools

SKILLBUILDING

52a
Warmup
Key each line twice SS.

alphabet	1	Jim Daley gave us in that box the prize he won for his quick car.
figures	2	At 7 a.m., I open Rooms 18, 29, and 30; I lock Rooms 4, 5, and 6.
adjacent reaches	3	As Louis said, few questioned the points asserted by the porters.
easy	4	Did he vow to fight for the right to work as the Orlando auditor?

| 1 | 2 | 3 | 4 | 5 | 6 | 7 | 8 | 9 | 10 | 11 | 12 | 13 |

52b
Technique Builder
Key each line twice SS.

caps	5	James Carswell plans to visit Austin and New Orleans in December.
	6	Will Peter and Betsy go with Mark when he goes to Alaska in June?
	7	John Kenny wrote the book Innovation and Timing—Keys to Success.

double letters	8	Jeanne arranges meeting room space in Massey Hall for committees.
	9	Russell will attend to the bookkeeping issues tomorrow afternoon.
	10	Todd offered a free book with all assessment tools Lynette sells.

balanced hand	11	Jane, a neighbor and a proficient auditor, may amend their audit.
	12	Blanche and a neighbor may make an ornament for an antique chair.
	13	Claudia may visit the big island when they go to Orlando with us.

72a
Warmup
Key each line twice SS.

alphabet	1	Jamie quickly apologized for submitting the complex reviews late.
figures	2	Those 1,863 bars cost $27.05 each for a total cost of $50,394.15.
easy	3	I may go to the zoo or to see you if I do not go to the new pool.
easy	4	The men may be busy, but they go to the lake to work on the dock.

| 1 | 2 | 3 | 4 | 5 | 6 | 7 | 8 | 9 | 10 | 11 | 12 | 13 |

72b
Timed Writing
Key one 3' writing and one 5' writing.

gwam   3' | 5'

How are letters and other documents produced in the modern office? They are prepared in a number of ways. Just a few years ago, with rare exceptions, a document was composed by a manager who either wrote it in longhand or dictated it. Then, one of the office staff typed it in final form. Today, the situation is quite different. Office staff may compose and produce various documents, or they may finalize documents that were keyed by managers. In some cases, managers like to produce some or all of their documents in final form.

Many people question how this dramatic change in the way documents are prepared came about. Two factors can be cited as the major reasons for the change. The primary factor is the extensive use of computers in offices today. A manager who uses a computer for a variety of tasks may find it just as simple to key documents at the computer as it would be to prepare them for office personnel to produce. The other factor is the increase in the ratio of office personnel to managers. Today, one secretary is very likely to support as many as six or eight managers. Managers who share office staff find that they get much quicker results by finalizing their own documents when they compose them.

| 3' | | 1 | | 2 | | 3 | | 4 | |
| 5' | | | 1 | | | 2 | | | 3 | |

gwam values (3' | 5'):
4 | 2 | 52
8 | 5 | 54
13 | 8 | 57
17 | 10 | 60
21 | 13 | 62
25 | 15 | 65
29 | 18 | 67
34 | 20 | 70
36 | 22 | 71
40 | 24 | 73
44 | 26 | 76
48 | 29 | 78
52 | 31 | 81
57 | 34 | 83
61 | 37 | 86
65 | 39 | 89
70 | 42 | 91
74 | 44 | 94
78 | 47 | 96
82 | 49 | 99

72c
Assessment

 Continue

 Check

With CheckPro: When you complete a document, proofread it, check the spelling, and preview for placement. When you are completely satisfied with it, click the **Continue** button to move to the next document. You will not be able to return and edit a document once you continue to the next one. Click the **Check** button when you are ready to error-check the test. Review and/or print the document analysis results.

Without CheckPro: On the signal to begin, key the documents in sequence. When time has been called, proofread all documents again and identify errors.

Character Effects

Character effects include a number of special attributes that enhance the appearance of text. Commonly used character effects include superscript, subscript, small caps, strikethrough, shadow, and outline. Character effects are accessed from the Font dialog box (Format menu, Font). Color and underline style are also available on the Font tab. Select existing text and click the appropriate effect to apply it, or turn the effect on before keying and off after keying.

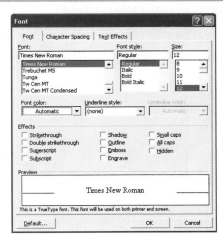

CHARACTER EFFECTS

1. Key the text at the right applying the character effects shown.
2. Apply blue color to SMALL CAPS in line 1.
3. Apply double underline to the formula in line 3.
4. Create the folder **Module 7 Keys** and save the document as **52c-drill1**. Save all documents for Module 7 in this folder.

Apply SMALL CAPS to this text.
The symbol for water, H_2O, contains a subscript.
Formulas often use superscripts, such as $\underline{\underline{X^2 + Y^3}}$.
~~Strikethrough~~ is a useful effect in editing text.
Outline and shadow change the appearance of text.

Insert a symbol;
Insert a special character

Symbols and Special Characters

Symbols and special characters not available on the keyboard can be inserted using the symbol function. Examples of symbols and special characters include:

Em dash —   En dash –   Copyright ©   Registered ®   Trademark™

To insert symbols or special characters:

1. Position the insertion point where the symbol or special character is to be inserted.
2. Click **Insert** on the menu, and then click **Symbol**.
3. Click the **Symbols** tab to insert symbols or the **Special Characters** tab to insert special characters.
4. For symbols, select a font such as Symbol, Wingdings, Wingdings2, or Wingdings3, and then select the desired symbol. For special characters, select the character desired.
5. Click **Insert** and then click **Close**.

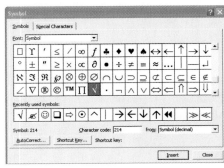

71d-d1
E-Mail Message

1. Key the e-mail message below to your instructor.
2. Key the subject line as **Assignment 3**.
3. Send the message.

Task 1: List five things to consider when choosing an appropriate e-mail password.

1. Do not choose a password that is named after a family member or a pet.
2. Do not use birth dates as a password.
3. Choose a combination of letters and numbers; preferably, use UPPERCASE and lowercase letters, e.g., TLQ6tEpR.
4. Do not share your password with anyone.
5. Do not write your password on paper and leave by your computer.

Task 2: List five things to consider when composing e-mail.

1. Do not use bold or italic or vary fonts.
2. Do not use UPPERCASE for emphasis.
3. Use emoticons or e-mail abbreviations with caution (e.g., :) for smile or BTW for by the way).
4. Write clear, concise messages that are free of spelling and grammatical errors.
5. Do not send an e-mail in haste or anger. Think about the message carefully before pressing the Send button.

71d-d2
E-Mail Message with
Attachment

1. Key the e-mail message below to your instructor and one student in your class.
2. Key the subject line as **Activity Report**.
3. Attach the data file **activity** (optional). Send the message.

I have completed the Activity Report required for this year's competitive events. The file Activity.doc is attached to this e-mail for your review. Please add the names of the members initiated at the February meeting and review the listing of awards received by our members. Revise the file as needed.

After you have proofread the report, please print a laser copy and give to Brenda Jones for inclusion in the national project notebook. I would also appreciate your e-mailing me the revised file for my historian records.

Remember, the reports must be postmarked by March 1.

71d-d3
E-Mail Message

1. Send an e-mail to your instructor.
2. Copy the e-mail to yourself.
3. Use the subject line and message given in **70c-d2**. (Simplify the process by opening **70c-d2** and copying the message to the e-mail screen.)

1. Key the following lines as a numbered list.
2. Insert the symbols and special characters shown.

3. Save it as **52c-drill2** in the folder **Module 7 Keys**.

Special Characters
1. Parker House—Best Dining (em dash)
2. Pages 13–25 (en dash)
3. July 20 (nonbreaking space)
4. 92° F (degree and nonbreaking space)
5. Revise ¶3.

Symbols
6. ☺ Have a nice day.
7. ⇨ Room 253.
8. ✎ Sign here.
9. ✓ Yes, send today.
10. ❑ Yes ❑ No

Cut, Copy, and Paste

The **Cut** feature removes text or an image from a document and places it on the Office Clipboard. The **Copy** feature places a copy of text or an image from a document on the Clipboard. The **Paste** feature transfers a copy of the text or image from the Clipboard to a document.

help keywords
move or copy text; cut; copy; paste

To move text to a new location:

1. Select the text to be copied. Click **Cut** on the Standard toolbar.
2. Move the insertion point to the new location. Click **Paste** on the Standard toolbar.

To copy text to a new location:

1. Select the text to be copied. Click **Copy** on the Standard toolbar.
2. Move the insertion point to the new location. Click **Paste** on the Standard toolbar.

1. Open **Cut and Paste** from the data files.
2. Select **Cut and** in the first heading and cut it so the heading is **Paste**.
3. Select the heading **Paste** and the paragraph that follows it.
4. Move the selected copy below the last paragraph.
5. Key a line across the page.
6. Copy both paragraphs, and paste them below the line.
7. Save the document as **52c-drill3**.

71a
Warmup
Key each line twice SS.

alphabet	1	Liz Page quickly found six major errors in the book she reviewed.
figures	2	Chapters 7, 18, 19, and 23 had 65 pages; the others had 40 pages.
space bar	3	Ty saw us as we got in a new car to go to the zoo; he did not go.
easy	4	Is the problem with the ancient chapel or the chapel at the lake?

| 1 | 2 | 3 | 4 | 5 | 6 | 7 | 8 | 9 | 10 | 11 | 12 | 13 |

71b
Technique Builder

	5	to kite flat byte joyful hitter night vacuum tab yummy vague earn
first finger	6	Babbs hung a gorgeous hanging on the first floor by the fountain.
	7	Annabelle gave her baby daughter big hugs and put her in the bed.

	8	dike kind cider insider decided child creek cracked deadlock kite
second finger	9	Dicky screamed and cried as Mickey cracked the huge chicken eggs.
	10	Tired divers tried to no avail to rescue the sinking cargo liner.

	11	sap soap spots salsa poppy squares people wool swoosh assess pass
fourth finger	12	Sally knew pool, zymoscope, x-axis, wassail, Lallan, and swallow.
	13	Palisade apologized to sloppy Wally for the lollipops and apples.

71c

E-Mail Review

Memorandums sent electronically are called **e-mail**. Accurately key the recipient's e-mail address and supply a specific subject line. The sender's name and date are automatically added by the e-mail software.

The following three examples of commonly used e-mail software screens illustrate that while each is different, they all have locations for the recipient's address, the subject line, and the message.

Attachments: Documents can be sent electronically by attaching the document files to the email. The attachment can be saved and opened. To attach a file, click the Attach button or icon browse to locate the file. A window will open to search for the file. When you locate the file, click on the file name. Click Open, Insert, or Attach to attach the document; procedures will vary depending on the e-mail service.

Formatting: Do not add bold or italic or vary the fonts. Do not use uppercase letters for emphasis. Use emoticons or e-mail abbreviations with caution (e.g., ;- for wink or BTW for by the way). SS the body of an e-mail. DS between paragraphs.

America Online

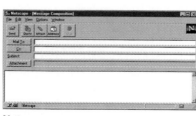

Netscape

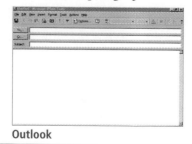

Outlook

DOCUMENT DESIGN DOCUMENT

Office Clipboard

The **Clipboard** can store up to 24 items that have been cut or copied. The Clipboard displays in the side pane. If it is not displayed, click **Edit** on the menu bar and then **Office Clipboard** to display it. Note that each item on the Clipboard is displayed for easy reference. All items on the Clipboard can be pasted at once by clicking **Paste All**. A single item can be pasted by clicking on the item and selecting **Paste** from the drop-down menu.

All items on the Clipboard can be removed by clicking the **Clear All** button. A single item can be removed by clicking the item and selecting **Delete** from the drop-down menu.

When an item is pasted into a document, the Paste button smart tag provides options for formatting the text that has been pasted.

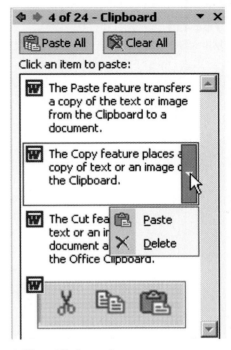

Office Clipboard

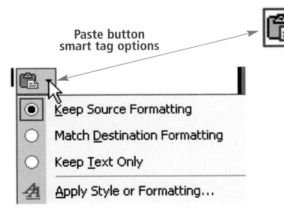

Paste button
smart tag options

To format the text using the same format as the new document, click **Match Destination Formatting**. To format the text using the same format as the document from which the text was copied, click **Keep Source Formatting**.

DRILL 4   **CLIPBOARD**

1. Open **Effective Pres** from the data files.
2. Display the Office Clipboard (**Edit**, **Office Clipboard**) and clear all items from the Clipboard.
3. Select the heading *Opening* and the paragraph that follows, and cut them.
4. Select the heading *Presentation Body* and the paragraph that follows, and cut them.
5. Select the heading *Closing* and the paragraph that follows, and cut them.
6. Place the insertion point a double space below the paragraph with the heading *Planning and Preparing Presentations* and paste all items on the Clipboard at once; adjust line spacing if necessary.
7. Save as **52c-drill4** and print the document.

70c-d1
Memo

1. Create the following memo using the Professional Memo (do not use the Memo Wizard).
2. Add the company name **Ocean Springs, Inc.**
3. Save as **70c-d1**; print.

To: Richard M. Taylor | From: Student Name | CC: Bruce Diamond | Date: Current date | Re: Trail Design

Last week, Madilyn signed the contract for the trail design for Phase 1 of our Georgetown property. NatureLink was selected as the contractor. This firm was chosen because of its extensive experience in selecting interpretative sites, designing trails, and installing boardwalks to protect wetlands and environmentally sensitive areas.

The first onsite meeting is scheduled for November 10. We plan to meet at the main entrance at 10:30 a.m. to tour the property and review the procedures that NatureLink plans to use in designing the trails near the red cockaded woodpecker (RCW) habitat. Since the RCW is an endangered species, we want to balance the desires of ecotourists to observe these birds and the need to protect them.

Please let me know if you plan to participate in the initial meeting with NatureLink.

70c-d2
Memo

1. Create the following memo using the Contemporary Memo.
2. Include the following in the heading: **TO: Marvell Hodges; FROM: Student Name, Coordinator; DATE: Current date; CC: Jacob White, Human Resources Manager; SUBJECT: August 8-9 Workshop**
3. Save as **70c-d2**; print.

Over seventy-five teachers have preregistered to participate in the Electronic Presentation Workshop scheduled for August 8-9 at Ferguson Community College. We are very pleased with the overwhelming response to this offering.

The workshop will begin at 8 a.m. and conclude by 5 p.m. each day. Please come to Room T38 of the Continuing Education Building. You may make your housing reservation today by calling (601) 555-0142. I look forward to an outstanding learning experience.

Drag-and-Drop Editing

Another way to edit text is to use the mouse. With **drag and drop**, you can move or copy text using the mouse. To move copy, you must first select the text, then hold down the left mouse button, and drag the text to the desired location. The mouse pointer displays a rectangle indicating that copy is being moved. Release the mouse button to "drop" the text into the desired location.

Follow a similar procedure to copy (or duplicate) text. Hold down the left mouse button and the CTRL key, and drag the text to the desired location. A plus sign indicates the text is being copied.

Copy and Paste Between Documents

Multiple documents can be opened at the same time. Each document is displayed in its own window. To move from one document to another, click **Window** on the menu; then click the document name. You may also just click the document name on the Windows taskbar. Text can then be copied and pasted between documents.

DRILL 5   **DRAG AND DROP**

1. Open **Effective Pres** from the data files.
2. Use drag-and-drop editing to make the same changes you made in **52c-drill4**.

3. Save the document as **52c-drill5**; print and close it.

Find and Replace

Find is used to locate text, formatting, footnotes, graphics, or other items within a document. **Replace** is used to find text, formatting, or other items within a document and replace them with different text, formatting, or items.

Clicking the More button on the Find or Replace tab displays a list of search options such as *Match case* or *Find whole words only*, as shown in the illustration below. The Format and Special buttons in the extended dialog box provide options for searching for formatting features or for special elements.

help keywords
find, replace

To find text:

1. Click **Edit** on the menu bar; then click **Find**.
2. Enter the text you wish to locate in the Find what box.
3. Click **Find Next** to find the next occurrence of the text.

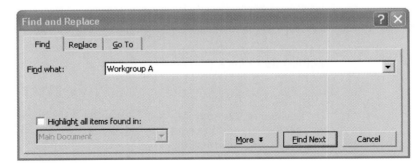

70a
Warmup
Key each line twice SS.

alphabet	1	Maxwell paid just a quarter for a very big cookie at the new zoo.
fig/sym	2	Lunches for the 14 customers cost $77.37 ($67.28 x 15% = $10.09).
3rd/4th fingers	3	Quinn will oppose an opinion of Max about a jazzy pop show we saw.
easy	4	Angie, the neighbor, paid to go to the island and fish for smelt.

| 1 | 2 | 3 | 4 | 5 | 6 | 7 | 8 | 9 | 10 | 11 | 12 | 13 |

70b

help keywords
templates

Templates

A **template** is a master copy of a set of predefined styles for a particular type of document. Templates are available for formatting documents such as a memo, fax, or letter. A template can be used exactly as it exists, or it can be modified or customized and saved as a new template. The tabs on the Templates dialog box indicate the variety of templates that *Word* has available. You can also attach a template to a document.

To use an existing template:

1. Click **New** on the File menu.

2. In the New Document pane, under New from template, click **General Templates**.

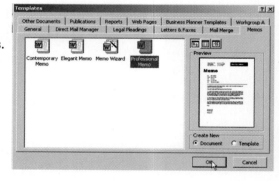

3. In the Templates dialog box, click the desired tab, such as **Memos**.

4. Select the desired memo style, such as **Contemporary, Elegant,** or **Professional**.

5. If necessary, click **Document** under Create New.

6. Click **OK**. Follow the directions on the template to key the desired document.

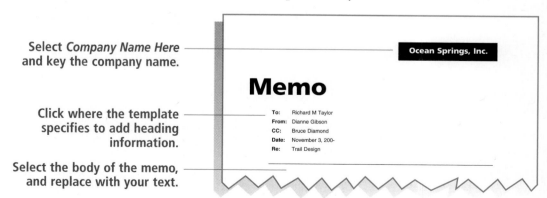

Select *Company Name Here* and key the company name.

Click where the template specifies to add heading information.

Select the body of the memo, and replace with your text.

Ocean Springs, Inc.

Memo

To:	Richard M Taylor
From:	Dianne Gibson
CC:	Bruce Diamond
Date:	November 3, 200-
Re:	Trail Design

To replace text:

1. Click **Edit** on the menu bar; then click **Replace**.

2. Enter the text you wish to locate in the Find what box.

3. Key the replacement text in the Replace with box.

4. Click **Find Next** to find the first occurrence of the text.

5. Click **Replace** to replace one occurrence, or click **Replace All** to replace all occurrences of the text.

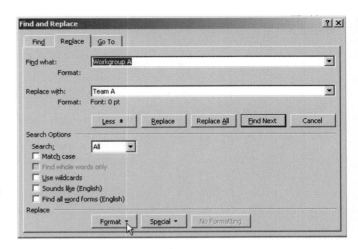

DRILL 6   **FIND AND REPLACE**

1. Open **Restructure** from the data files.
2. Find the word *restructuring* the first place it appears.
3. Find the second and third occurrences of *restructuring*.
4. Find *Workgroup A* and replace it with *Team A*.

5. Edit the document so that the letter is formatted correctly as a block-style letter.
6. Save the document as **52c-drill6**.

Thesaurus

TIP

An alternative way to use the Thesaurus is to position the insertion point in a word and right-click the mouse. Select **Synonyms** and then the desired word or **Thesaurus** for more information.

The Thesaurus is a tool that enables you to look up words and replace them with synonyms, antonyms, or related words.

To use the Thesaurus:

1. Position the insertion point in the word you wish to replace.

2. Click **Tools** on the menu, click **Language**, and then click **Thesaurus**.

3. If more than one meaning appears, select the appropriate meaning.

4. Select the desired synonym or antonym, and click **Replace**.

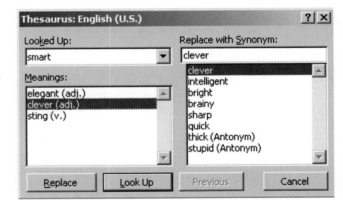

DRILL 7   **THESAURUS**

1. Key the following words on separate lines:
       generous   **data**   **smart**   **profit**
2. Replace *generous* and *data* with synonyms.
3. Replace *smart* (meaning clever) with a synonym.

4. Key **smart** again (meaning elegant), and replace it with an antonym.
5. Replace *profit* with an antonym.
6. Save the document as **52c-drill7**.

---

1. Key the two-page memo. Use the following information for the heading:

   TO: Electronic Presentations Class; FROM: Linda T. Walters, Instructor; DATE: Current date; SUBJECT: Library Research

2. DS between numbered items.

3. Add an appropriate second-page header. Save as **69e-d2** and print.

The library research assignment described in this memo comprises 10 percent of your total grade. Read the directions carefully, follow the enclosed format, and mark the deadline on your calendar. If you have questions about this assignment, please call me at my office or e-mail me via the class Web page.

Prepare a critical review of five recent (2000 to present) journal articles (not the popular press) related to the following electronic presentation issues.

1. What design rules should be considered in creating electronic presentations?

2. What delivery skills are needed when using electronic presentation software?

3. What copyright issues should be considered when creating electronic presentations?

4. What advanced features of *PowerPoint* are available to make a powerful electronic presentation?

5. What speaking skills are necessary when delivering a presentation (with or without visual aids)?

6. What helpful advice would be given to new presenters who will design their own presentations?

7. What resources are available to assist the presentation designer?

See the Web sites provided in the syllabus. Your online databases at the University Library are excellent. For many articles, you are able to choose full- text articles with full citations. Be sure to choose a combination of journals and magazines. Beware of Web sites that are not scholarly but rather someone's opinion.

Discuss, summarize, and evaluate each article separately. Submit this assignment in a three-ring folder—not notebook. Be sure you have labeled the outside of the folder with your name and the title *Library Research.* Mail to Linda T. Walters, 307 Springdale Drive, Ellisville, MS 39437. This assignment must be postmarked Monday, March 17. You are also required to post the electronic file to the drop box labeled *Library Research.* Remember when naming your file, use one word. The drop box will be open only up to the deadline—March 17 at 11 p.m.

The required format is enclosed. Be sure to read it carefully and follow it.

Good luck on this project. I look forward to reading outstanding research in these areas of electronic presentations.

Space After Paragraphs

Double-spaced documents do not need additional space between paragraphs. However, to make single-spaced documents more readable, add additional space after each paragraph. You can add additional space automatically by setting the space after paragraphs to 6 points, the equivalent of one line. Each time you press ENTER, an additional line is added.

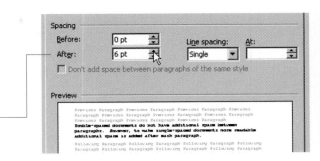

To set spacing after paragraphs:

1. Click **Paragraph** on the Format menu.
2. Select the **Indents and Spacing** tab.
3. In the Spacing section of the dialog box, increase spacing *After* from 0 to 6 pt. Click **OK**.

DRILL 8   **PARAGRAPH SPACING**

1. Open **Preview** from the data files.
2. Select all of the single-spaced paragraphs.

3. Increase the space after the paragraphs to 6 points.
4. Save the document as **52d-drill8** and print.

APPLICATIONS

52e-d1
Edit Report

1. Open **Punctuality** from the data files and save it as **52e-d1**.
2. Center the title. Change the font size to 14 point and apply bold and shadow effect.
3. In the sentence *Punctuality-Not Performance-Determines Outcome!*, change the hyphens to em dashes.
4. In the sentence that follows, replace the commas around *and by all accounts one who was unbeatable and assured to repeat the title* with em dashes.
5. Select *Punctuality—Not Performance—Determines Outcome!* in paragraph 1 and apply italic format.
6. Change spacing after paragraphs to 6 pt.
7. Move paragraph 3 between paragraphs 1 and 2.
8. Find *weak* and replace it with *lame*.
9. Select the last sentence and change the text color to red.
10. Add the following below the last paragraph: © 2003 by (*student's name*).
11. Center the page vertically.
12. Preview, print, and resave the document.

69e-d1
Memorandum with Distribution List

1. Key the following memo, but do not key the letterhead. Save as **69e-d1**.

2. Print a copy for each person on the list. Place a check mark next to the name of each person who will receive the memo. (*Example*: Place a check mark next to Samuel Gibbs on the first copy, next to Angela Sansing on the second copy, etc.)

2" top margin

Acme Technologies

Interoffice Memo

TO: Distribution List
                                    DS
FROM: Acme Mexican-American Achievers Committee
                                    DS
DATE: April 15, 200-
                              DS
SUBJECT: Mexican-American Achievers
                              DS

Default
side
margins

For the past three years Acme has nominated a deserving Mexican-American staff member to be honored as a Mexican-American Achiever. This career development program seeks to expose, educate, and enlighten young adults to various opportunities found in the corporate sector. Adult Mexican-American Achievers serve as volunteer counselors, tutors, confidants, and advisors to youth.

Mara Pena was the first recipient for Acme. Lydia Valquez was the recipient the second year, and last year Acme sponsored an At Large participant chosen by the Youth in Business Association (YBA).   This year we should like to nominate an Acme staff member.

The nominating criteria established by the YBA are as follows:

• A current Acme employee who has been employed for at least two years.

• An individual who is willing to volunteer at least one year of service to the program.

• An individual recently completing a special leadership role by representing our company on a community service project.

Please make your nomination on the attached form and forward it to Human Resources by **Thursday, April 20**.
                                    DS
xx
   DS
Attachment

Distribution List:
Tab → Samuel Gibbs
      Angela Sansing
      Collin Sheridan
      Joan Wang

SKILLBUILDING

53a
Warmup
Key each line twice SS.

alphabet	1 Jakob will save the money required for your next big cash prizes.
fig/sym	2 I saw Vera buy 13 7/8 yards of #240 cotton denim at $6.96 a yard.
3d/4th	3 Zone 12 is impassable; quickly rope it off. Did you wax Zone 90?
easy	4 Did an auditor handle the formal audit of the firms for a profit?

| 1 | 2 | 3 | 4 | 5 | 6 | 7 | 8 | 9 | 10 | 11 | 12 | 13 |

53b
Technique Builder
Key each line twice SS.

1/2 fingers
5 Did bedlam erupt when they arrived after my speech ended quickly?
6 Joyce bought me a new bright red jacket for my birthday tomorrow.
7 Did Rebecca make the needlepoint cushion for the club room couch?
8 Much to the concern of our teacher, I did my homework on the bus.

3/4 fingers
9 Zam saw six small poodle puppies playing in the meadow last week.
10 Paxton saw a lazy lizard on the old wooden oar at Pawley's Plaza.
11 Zam Velasquez sells squid in six stores near the pool at the zoo.
12 Paul quizzed a shop owner about a patchwork quilt we saw in Waco.

all fingers
13 Jarvis Zackery played quarterback with six teams before retiring.
14 Jan Weitzel made grave errors, but he quickly fixed the problems.
15 Quinn Zack wrote just six poems and a short story before leaving.
16 Maxey Czajka will quit swimming because he performed very poorly.

53c
Timed Writings
Key two 1' timings on each ¶.
The second and third ¶s each
contain 2 more words than the
previous ¶. Try to complete
each ¶ within 1'.

 all letters

	gwam	1'	3'

Have you thought about time? Time is a perplexing commod- | | 12 | 4 | 40
ity. Frequently we don't have adequate time to do the things we | | 25 | 8 | 45
must; yet we all have just the same amount of time. | | 35 | 12 | 48

We seldom refer to the quantity of time; to a great extent, | | 12 | 16 | 52
we cannot control it. We can try to set time aside, to plan, | | 24 | 20 | 56
and therefore, to control portions of this valuable asset. | | 37 | 24 | 60

We should make an extra effort to fill each minute and hour | | 12 | 28 | 64
with as much quality activity as possible. Time, the most pre- | | 25 | 32 | 68
cious thing a person can spend, can never be realized once it | | 37 | 36 | 72
is lost. | | 39 | 36 | 73

1'	1	2	3	4	5	6	7	8	9	10	11	12	13
3'		1			2			3			4		

Memorandums

Memos, which are less formal than letters, are used for correspondence within an organization. Memos are generally prepared on plain paper and sent in plain or interoffice envelopes.

To format a memo:

1. Begin the heading approximately 2" from the top of the page. DS the heading lines and key the heading words in all caps and bold.

2. Press TAB once or twice after each heading to align the text that follows each item.

3. Press ENTER once after the last heading, change the line spacing to single, and key the body of the memo with a double space between paragraphs.

4. Press ENTER twice after the last line of the body and key the reference initials and any other notations such as attachment, enclosure, or copy notation.

Distribution Lists

When memos are sent to more than one person, key the names separated by commas after the word **TO:** or in a list. Generally, names should be in alphabetical order by last name. Some organizations prefer the names in order of rank.

TO: Maxine Cagiano, Benjamin Morgan   or   **TO:** Maxine Cagiano
                                                             Benjamin Morgan
                                                             CynthiaYost

When the memo is being sent to a large number of people, use a distribution list.

1. After the heading word **TO:**, key a reference to a distribution list at the end of the memo.

2. At the end of the memo, key the words **Distribution list** or the name of the group (for example, *Project Managers*) followed by a colon.

3. TAB to begin the first name. Key each name on a separate line (aligned at the tab) in alphabetical order.

    Distribution list:
        Maxine Cagiano
        Benjamin Morgan
        Naomi Peyton
        Heather Lewis
        Cynthia Yost

Two-Page Memorandums

If a memo is more than a single page, follow the same guidelines for long letters.

1. Leave a 1" top margin on second and succeeding pages.

2. Create a header that includes the recipient's name, page number, and date on separate lines, and suppress the header on the first page.

3. Press ENTER once after the date to leave a blank line between the header and the body of the memo.

53d
Composing and Editing

1. Compose a paragraph with at least two or three complete sentences to complete the three statements listed below.

2. Double-space the answers and indent each paragraph.

3. Print the paragraphs; use proofreaders' marks to edit the paragraphs carefully to improve your writing. Make the corrections.

4. Save as **53d** and print.

1. **Currently, I live in** (name and describe the city, town, or area in which you live—indicate if it is a large city, small town, or rural area and provide other descriptive information about the locale).

2. **When friends from other locations come to visit me, the places I enjoy taking them are** (describe two or three places in your area that would be interesting to show to visitors).

3. **If I could pick one place in the United States to visit, it would be** (describe one place you would like to visit and explain why you would like to go there and what you would like to see and do while you are there).

53e-d1
Letter from Rough Draft

1. Key the letter below making all of the corrections noted.

2. Use the current date and the address and closing lines shown below. Format the letter in block style. Add an enclosure notation. Center the page.

3. Proofread, preview, save as **53e-d1**, and print.

Ms. Karen Bradley
228 High Ridge Road
Irmo, SC 29063-4187

Dear Ms. Bradley

giving Todd Travel associates Thank you for the opportunity to plan an exciting vacation for you and your family. *and arrange* We are certain that this trip will be one *a memorable* all of you will remember. The Greek Isles *delightful* are a fun destination and you have selected outstanding pre- and post-cruise tours in Athens and Istanbul.

All of the travel arrangements have been confirmed, *stet* and a detailed itinerary and cruise brochure are enclosed. Please carefully review the itinerary to make certain *ensure* that we have followed all of your instructions correctly. If any changes need to be made, please call us soon. *within ten days.*

Your travel documents will be sent to you 2 weeks prior to departure. *SP* Please let us know if we can provide additional information for you.

Sincerely

Jane R. Todd
President

LESSON 69 | Review Memo Format

SKILLBUILDING

69a
Warmup
Key each line twice.

alphabet	1	Mixon plays great jazz with a quintet at a club five days a week.
fig/sym	2	Errors were found on page 389 (line #17) and page 460 (line #25).
direct reach	3	Brad and Cec had a great lunch and much fun with many youngsters.
easy	4	The city may pay for half of the maps, and Jake may pay for half.

| 1 | 2 | 3 | 4 | 5 | 6 | 7 | 8 | 9 | 10 | 11 | 12 | 13 |

69b
Technique Builder

1. Key the following heading as follows:
   a. Press CTRL + 2 to change to DS.
   b. Press CAPS LOCK key. Press CTRL + B to bold. Key **TO:**.
   c. Press CAPS LOCK key to turn off caps lock.
   d. Press CTRL + B to turn off bold.
   e. Repeat Steps a-e for remaining lines. Press CTRL + 1 to change to SS.

2. Try to complete in 30" or less. Key as many times as possible.

TO:	Jason Smith
FROM:	Khalilah Palmer
DATE:	(Enter date command)
SUBJECT:	Keying Efficiency

COMMUNICATION

69c
Proofread and Edit Text

1. Key the following paragraphs, correcting the marked revisions. Locate the three errors in word choice. For example, *to* may be incorrectly keyed for *too*.

2. Save as **69c** and print.

¶All form letters have been reviewed, revised, and approved for general use. You will receive a (ewn) copy within a few days of the correspondence manual.

Special thanks are do each of you for your help on this important project. The consultants were most complementary of the excellent corporation they received and of the quality of your suggestions for improving the letters.

53e-d2
Letter

1. Open **Brady** from the data files. Save it as **53e-d2**. Make the following edits:
   - Revise the letter so that it will be formatted correctly as a modified block letter.
   - Search for the name *Debauche*; each time it appears, replace it with *DeBauche*.
   - Use the Thesaurus to find a synonym for *statistics*. Replace *statistics* with the second synonym listed.
   - Make the following correction in the first sentence of paragraph 2:
     Brad Swinton, our new vice president of Marketing, indicated. . .
   - Cut the following sentence from paragraph 2:
     I hope this will not be a problem for you.
2. Save the document again and print it.

53e-d3
Letter

1. Open document **53e-d2** that you completed in the previous activity.
2. Reformat the document as a block style letter.
3. Save it as **53e-d3** and print.

53e-d4
Letter

1. Prepare another letter for Ms. DeBauche using the same address, salutation, and closing lines that were used in **53e-d3**. Note that this letter does not contain an enclosure.
2. Key the letter below in block style format.
3. Search for *section*, and replace it each time it appears with *phase*.
4. Use the Thesaurus to find a synonym for *prolific*. Select the first option.
5. Save as **53e-d4** and print.

October 11, 200-

Our team completed its preliminary review of your proposal today. Overall, we are very pleased with the approach you have taken.

Please plan to provide the following information at our meeting on October 18:

1. Please provide a more detailed pricing plan. We would like to have each section of the project priced separately specifying hourly rate and expenses rather than the one total sum quoted.

2. How many hours do you estimate will be necessary to complete each section of the project? When would your firm be able to begin the project?

We look forward to a very prolific meeting on October 18.

68d-d1
Two-Page Letter

1. Key the following two-page letter in block style.

2. Add the necessary letter parts. Create a header for the second page; use the Search Committee name in the header. Add the subject line **Assistant Professor of Curriculum Position**.

3. Save the letter as **68d-d1** and print.

Current Date | Attention Chairperson | College of Education Search Committee | Lynn State University | 323 University Ave. | Albuquerque, NM 87105-1742

It is my pleasure to apply for the position of Assistant Professor as advertised in the *Bulletin of Educational Positions*. As you can see from my enclosed resume, I have extensive experience in the area of curriculum design and instruction. I am excited about the prospect of using my knowledge and experience in this area to strengthen your program.

In my current position with the State Board of Education, I am responsible for overseeing the curriculum development for all Business Education programs at the secondary level throughout the state. I meet regularly with secondary teachers, content specialists, advisory boards, industry representatives, and state legislators. These contacts provide me with a variety of viewpoints concerning the construction of curriculum. Without considering all of the available sources of input, it would be impossible to develop a curriculum that would address the needs of today's workforce.

In addition to supervising curriculum development, during the past five years I have been loaned to three other states to help with their curriculum development. Each assignment gave me the opportunity to use and expand my expertise in my field. These experiences in particular are significant when considering the knowledge base that I can bring to the classroom.

I also have classroom experience at the secondary level. After obtaining my bachelor's degree, I taught Business Education for Finton Public Schools. During the five years that I held this position, I completed both my master's and doctorate degrees. After completing these degrees, I taught for two years at Shadowland Community College. These invaluable experiences of developing curriculum for and teaching in both secondary and postsecondary schools will make it possible for me to personally guide the future teachers being trained by Lynn State University to a point where they are prepared to excel at whatever teaching level they seek.

I look forward to hearing from you to discuss your faculty needs. I can be reached at 505-555-0199 Monday through Friday. Your advertised position and my curriculum development experiences certainly appear to be a good fit. | Sincerely yours | Ms. Betheny Isner | Enclosure

SKILLBUILDING

54a
Warmup
Key each line twice SS.

1 Sandra quickly gave the boy a major prize for his excellent work.
2 Invoice #758 for $294 is due 2/14/03 and #315 for $67 is due now.
3 Todd and Ann meet with a committee at noon to discuss all issues.
4 He may sign both of the forms for the amendment to the endowment.

| 1 | 2 | 3 | 4 | 5 | 6 | 7 | 8 | 9 | 10 | 11 | 12 | 13 |

54b
Technique builder
Key each group of 3 lines twice.

5 Lou kicked the gray umbrella Fred gave me and broke it in pieces.
6 Cecilia jumped in the pool, kicked the side, and fractured a toe.
7 Bunny browsed in the library while June served the healthy lunch.

8 Teresa was there to operate the projection equipment on Saturday.
9 Walker sang three hymns, and Louisa taught everyone how to polka.
10 Guy and Teresa were going to buy ice cream after the polo match.

APPLICATIONS

54c-d1
Composing and Editing

1. Use the information below to compose and send an e-mail to your instructor.
2. Use the subject line **Extra Credit Assignment**.
3. Read the second bullet carefully. Select one of the 3 topics, create a new document, and save it as **54c-drill1-attach**. Key the title of your topic on the first line of this document. Close the file.
4. Proofread and edit the e-mail carefully before sending it.
5. Print a copy of your e-mail.

■ Thank your instructor for providing the opportunity to complete an extra-credit assignment.

■ Indicate which of the three topics available (E-Mail Etiquette, First Impressions Count, and Developing a Professional Attitude) you selected. Add a sentence indicating why you selected that topic for the three-page paper.

■ Indicate that an electronic copy of your paper is attached to this e-mail and that a printed version has been placed in the appropriate assignment folder. Attach the file **54c-d1-attach** to your e-mail.

Two-Page Letters

Letters that are more than one page in length require special layout considerations. Use letterhead paper only for the first page. For additional pages, use plain paper that matches the letterhead in quality and color. Be sure that there are at least two lines of text from the final paragraph of the body of the letter on the last page with the closing lines.

Follow these steps to format multipage letters:

1. Position the date on the first page approximately 2" from the top of the page or 0.5" below the letterhead.

2. On the second and following pages, use a 1" top margin and the same side margins as the rest of the letter.

3. Create a header for the second and following pages (suppress the header on the first page, click the **Page Setup** button on the Header and Footer toolbar, and select **Different first page** in the Page Setup dialog box).

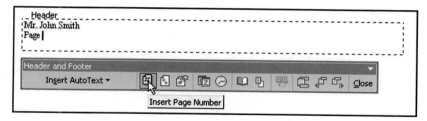

4. At the left margin of the header box, key the name of the recipient and press ENTER.

5. Key the word **Page** and space; then use the automatic page numbering feature on the Header and Footer toolbar to insert the page number and press ENTER.

6. Insert the date and press ENTER to leave a blank line between the header and the body of the letter.

> Mr. Jay Bloss
> Page 2
> October 10, 200-
>
> a reply by the end of the week will give us ample time to process your request.

Correct style. At least two lines of the last paragraph are on the page.

DRILL 1   TWO-PAGE LETTER

1. Open **68Collins** from the data files.

2. Add standard letter parts and adjust spacing as needed. Position the date at approximately 2". Change the font to 12-point Times New Roman.

3. Add an appropriate header for the second page and suppress it on the first page. Be sure the font matches the letter.

4. Add a copy notation to **Susan Wyman**. Note that the letter ends with a postscript.

5. Save the letter as **68c-drill1**.

54c-d2
Composing and Editing

1. Use the information from **54c-d1** to prepare a traditional memo to your instructor.
2. Modify the third bulleted instruction above to indicate that you have attached the printed version of your paper to this memo. Ignore the information about the electronic copy.
3. Add an attachment notation to the memo.
4. Proofread and edit the memo carefully.
5. Save the document as **54c-d2** and print it.

- Modify the third instruction above to indicate that you have attached the printed version of your paper to this memo.

- Ignore the information about the electronic copy.

54c-d3
Memo

1. Key the memo below.
2. Position the heading at about 2" and DS between paragraphs.
3. Move ¶2 so that it will be the last ¶.
4. Search for *NatureDesigns* and replace it with *NatureLink* each time it appears.
5. Use the Thesaurus to find another option for *wide-ranging* in the third sentence; select the first option.
6. Change the date in the memo from *November 10* to two weeks from today.
7. Proofread carefully, preview, save as **54c-d3**, and print.

To: Richard M. Taylor | From: Dianne Gibson | Date: Current | Subject: Trail Design

Last week, Madilyn signed the contract for the trail design for Phase 1 of our Georgetown property. NatureDesigns was selected as the contractor. This firm was chosen because of its wide-ranging experience in selecting interpretative sites, designing trails, and installing boardwalks to protect wetlands and environmentally sensitive areas.

Please let me know if you plan to participate in the initial meeting with NatureDesigns.

The first onsite meeting is scheduled for November 10. We plan to meet at the main entrance at 10:30 a.m. to tour the property and review the procedures that NatureDesigns plans to use in designing the trails near the red cockaded woodpecker (RCW) habitat. Since RCW is an endangered species, we want to balance the desires of ecotourists to observe these birds and the need to protect them.

xx | c Bruce Diamond

68a
Warmup
Key each line twice SS.

alphabet 1   Frances Zwanka exited very quietly just prior to the big seminar.
figures 2   Please call 235-9167 or 294-3678 before 10:45 a.m. on January 18.
adjacent reaches 3   Louis, Sadi, Art, and a few other people were going to a concert.
easy 4   Vivian may go with a neighbor or with me to work on an amendment.

| 1 | 2 | 3 | 4 | 5 | 6 | 7 | 8 | 9 | 10 | 11 | 12 | 13 |

68b
Proofreading

1. Open **68b** from the data files and print.

2. Compare the printed letter to the source copy shown below. Mark any errors using the proofreaders' marks on page REF3.

3. Make the marked corrections; save as **68b-revised** and print. Submit the marked copy and the corrected printout to your instructor.

January 23, 200-

                Press ENTER 4 times

Ms. Audra Meaux
2689 Marsalis Ln.
Hot Springs, AR 71913-0345

Dear Ms. Meaux

Thank you for agreeing to serve as chair of the Hospitality Committee for the National Technology Association Convention on April 3-6 in Phoenix, Arizona.

The enclosed guidelines outline the responsibilities and timelines of the Hospitality Committee. Please read them carefully and call me at (602) 555-0137 if you have any questions. You will need about 25 individuals to work with you on this committee. After you have organized this group, please mail me a complete roster including names, addresses, phone and fax numbers, and e-mail addresses.

Ms. Meaux, thank you for your professionalism and willingness to serve.

Sincerely

            Press ENTER 4 times

Ryan Messamore
Vice President of Sales

xx

Enclosure

1. Key the memo below. Make all of the corrections noted by proofreaders' marks.
2. Send the memo to **David C. Kline** from **Carolyn M. Pastides**; use the current date and the subject **Economic Development Project**.
3. Search for *Department of Commerce* and replace it with *Board of Economic Development* each time it appears.
4. Proofread carefully, preview, save as **54c-d4**, and print.

TIP

To insert a nonbreaking hyphen, click Insert, Symbol, and then Special Characters.

The meeting with ^several^ representatives of the department of commerce and the

representatives ^of the Company^ being recruited to move here ^to this area^ provided a very interesting perspective

on the changing approach of recruiting small, knowledge-based companies rather

than large manufacturing operations. The company being recruited is a recent spin- ^nonbreaking hyphen^

off form a research project at a major university. It's stage of development could

best be described as developmental.

We signed non-disclosure forms, and the Department of Commerce provided us

with ^a set of^ financials provided ^prepared^ by the company's auditor. However, the audit was not

signed, ^nor was^ and the management letter was not included. I have requested that the (CFO) ^chief financial officer^

bring to the meeting tomorrow a complete copy of the audit and proformas for two

years forward.   My guess is that the audit will contain a "going concern" clause. The

company currently has a stockholders' deficit of approximately $15,000,000. ^million^

Unless ^additional^ financing is obtained, it is unlikely that the company can continue to

operate. I ^also^ requested copies of contracts (are) ^or^ agreements that would support the

revenue projections in the proformas.

The technology developed by the company is exciting, and the upside potential of

the joint venture appears to be very good. Documentation of prototype orders was

provided. Because of the risk involved in a company at this early stage of

development, it is imperative that we do a lot of ^extensive^ due diligence before investing in

this company.

67e-d3
Block Letter with Special Features

1. Format the block letter; use open punctuation.
2. Compose an appropriate subject line and correct salutation.
3. Send a blind copy to the intern mentioned in the letter. Save as **67e-d3**.
4. Generate an envelope with the special notation. Save as **67e-d3a**.

	words
Current date | CONFIDENTIAL | Merritt College | Attention Ms.	16
Louise Brown, Director | 750 East Wolfe Rd | Vienna, Wv	22
26105-0750	25

Thank you for the opportunity to participate as an [one of your technology majors] 38

employer in your internship program. Paul Zieger worked 90 56

hours this summer, and was an excellent ~~edition~~ *addition* to our 67

department. His final project was a*n* interactive tutorial of 80

the Merritt College library. This tutorial provides an 91

electronic tour of the library, including the layout of the 103

library, *its holdings,* and specific directions on locating certain materials. 119

¶ Paul has agreed to work (for us part-time) during the fall 130

semester. Our initial plans ~~is~~ *are* for him to work with faculty 143

in setting up and conduct*ing* private demonstrations for classes. 156

In addition, he will write a second tutorial for the graduate 168

library. ¶ *Please send another excellent intern next semester.* 181

Sincerely \| Daniel E. Romano, Director \| Library Services \| xx 192

67e-d4
Edit Letter

1. Open **67e-d3** and save it as **67e-d4**.
2. Reformat as a modified block letter with mixed punctuation.
3. Reformat the last paragraph as a postscript.
4. Save and print the letter.

67e-d5
Compose Letter

1. Compose a letter for **Paul Zieger** to **Merritt College** to the attention of **Registrar** requesting an official copy of his transcript. The transcript should be sent to **Mr. Daniel E. Romano, Director, Library Services, Merritt College**. See the address in Document 3. Paul was enrolled from June 2001 to present. Enclose $5 for the transcript.
2. Format the letter in block letter style with open punctuation. Center this short letter vertically on the page and add the special notation **FACSIMILE**.
3. Add the reference line **Re: Paul Zieger ID No. 55-43-2001**.

Edit Tables and Reports

SKILLBUILDING

55a
Warmup
Key each line twice SS.

1 When Jorg moves away, quickly place five dozen gloves in the box.
2 Flight 372 leaves at 10:46 a.m. and arrives in Omaha at 9:58 p.m.
3 I obtain unusual services from a number of celebrated decorators.
4 She may sign an authentic name and title to amend this endowment.

| 1 | 2 | 3 | 4 | 5 | 6 | 7 | 8 | 9 | 10 | 11 | 12 | 13 |

55b
Timed Writings
1. Key one 3' timing.
2. Key one 5' writing. Strive for control.

  all letters

	gwam	3'	5'

Reports are one of the best means by which busy executives — 4 | 2 | 26
at any level of a business can keep well informed. The pertinent — 8 | 5 | 29
data in reports can be used to solve a wide variety of problems — 13 | 8 | 31
that arise, make any changes that may be required, analyze — 16 | 10 | 34
results, and make precise, timely decisions. — 19 | 12 | 36

The quality of the plans and decisions made on the basis of — 23 | 14 | 39
the information found in reports depends in large measure on how — 28 | 17 | 41
well the reports are produced. A good report is a thorough and — 32 | 19 | 43
objective summary of all pertinent facts and figures. If reports — 36 | 22 | 46
are not well produced, the firm will surely suffer. — 40 | 24 | 48

3' | 1 | 2 | 3 | 4
5' | 1 | 2 | 3

APPLICATIONS

55c-d1
Edit Table
1. Open **Research Building** from the data files; save as **55c-d1**.
2. Edit the table as marked.
3. Change row height to .3" and center text vertically in the cell.
4. Resave; print.

RESEARCH BUILDING PROJECT STATUS *Center and Bold Title*

Job	Description	Date Completed
A & E Design Work	Plans completed	September 25, 2003
Building Permits	Submit plans *for city review*	October 14, 2003
Construction *Bids*	Prepare bid documents	November 8, 2003

 Add row

Award Bid   *Select final bid*   *January 10,*

To add notations to an envelope:

1. Click the **Add to Document** button; click **View**, **Print Layout** to switch to Print Layout View.

2. Position the insertion point on line 1.3". Click the **Right Align** button. Key the mailing notation, i.e., **SPECIAL DELIVERY**.

3. Position the insertion point on line 1.5". Key the recipient's notation—i.e., **CONFIDENTIAL**—at the left margin. Save and print.

DRILL 1   ENVELOPE WITH NOTATIONS

1. Open **66c-drill1**. Save as **67d-drill1**.

2. Generate an envelope for this letter.

3. In Print Layout View, key the mailing notation **SPECIAL DELIVERY** at the right on line 1.3".

4. Key the recipient notation **PERSONAL** on line 1.5" at the left margin.

5. Save and print the envelope only.

APPLICATIONS

67e-d1
Modified Block Letter
with Notations

1. Format the modified block letter; use mixed punctuation.

2. Add the mailing notation **CERTIFIED** and the reference line **Re: Order No. S3835**.

3. Move the last paragraph to the end of the letter and format as a postscript; save as **67e-d1**. Generate an envelope. Save as **67e-d1a**.

	words
Current date|CERTIFIED|Dr. Carol Metzger, Instructor|Merritt Business	15
College|319 North Jackson St.|Jacksonville, FL 32256-0319|Dear Dr.	32
Metzger:	34

Your TIME+ personal manager software was shipped to you this morning by next-day air service. We realize that your time is valuable, and installing incorrect software is not a good use of your time. However, we are glad to learn that your students benefited from your demonstration of the software.

48
62
77
91
94

Easy-to-follow instructions for installing the new software over the current software are enclosed. You will also note on your copy of the invoice that you were billed originally for the TIME software. The TIME+ software is $99 more; however, we are pleased to provide it at no extra cost to you.

109
124
139
155

An additional bonus for choosing TIME+ is the monthly newsletter, *Managing Time with TIME+.* You should receive your first copy by the first of the month.

168
183
186

Sincerely yours,\|Ms. Veronica Scrivner\|Customer Service Manager\|xx\| Enclosure\|c Eric Shoemaker

198
204

67e-d2
Edit Letter

1. Open **67e-d1** and save it as **67e-d2**.

2. Reformat as a block letter with open punctuation.

3. Save and print the letter.

55c-d2
Edit Report

1. Key the report; DS.
2. Use approximately a 2" top margin; add the title **Foundation Property in South Carolina**; center, bold.
3. Make the edits shown in the table; DS the table.
4. Save as **55c-d2** and print; leave the document open.

The Foundation owns both in-state and out-of-state property. However, the bulk of the property is located within the state. In-state property is divided into three regions—Coastal, Midlands, and Other. The following chart shows the distribution of the property by region:

Property Location and Value *Bold*		
South Carolina Regions *Bold and Center headings*	Value of Property in Region	Percentage of Total Property
Coastal Region *Set right align tab at 3.5"*	$18,325,000	53%
Midlands Region	12,650,000	36% *Center align*
Other Regions—In-State	3,840,000	11%

The total value of the property is $34,815,000. More than half of the property is located in the Coastal region. The next largest concentration is in the Midlands region.

The property values are based on the appraisal price at the time of acquisition. Properties are acquired by gift or purchase. Current market value of the property is significantly higher than the value at the time of acquisition.

Special Letter Parts

Additional special features help communicate clear and effective messages. Learn the purpose of these features.

A **reference line** such as Re: Order No. R1084 directs the reader to source documents or to files. Do not confuse a reference line with a subject line; the purposes are different. Key the reference line a DS below the letter address.

> Route 2, Box 332
> Natchez, MS 39120-1452
> DS
> Re: Order No. R1084
> DS
> Dear Mr. Allison
>
> Demand for two of the items (Stock Nos. 3856C and 9257D) that you ordered has been so great that we've had to place

A **mailing notation** such as FACSIMILE, OVERNIGHT, CERTIFIED, SPECIAL DELIVERY, or REGISTERED provides a record of how the letter was sent. Other notations such as CONFIDENTIAL or PERSONAL indicate how the recipient should treat the letter.

Key special notations in ALL CAPS at the left margin a DS below the dateline. On the envelope, key notations that affect postage right-aligned below the stamp (about line 1.3"). Key envelope notations that pertain to the recipient below the return address.

> April 2, 200-DS
> CONFIDENTIAL
> DS
> Dr. Spencer A. Blakeney
> Golden Triangle Clinic
> P.O. Box 10984
> Tullahoma, TN 37388-1267
>
> Dear Dr. Blakeney

> December 14, 200-
> DS
> CERTIFIED
> DS
> Attention Division 2 Manager
> Clinard Security Services
> 207 Hollyhill Ave.
> Downers Grove, IL 60515-0357
>
> Ladies and Gentlemen

> Dwight Reed
> 389 Highway 17
> Maysville, KY 41056-2332
>
>
>
> CERTIFIED
>
> Attention Division 2 Manager
> Clinard Security Services
> 207 Hollyhill Ave
> Downers Grove IL 60515-0357

55c-d3
Edit Report

1. Save the open document (**55c-d2**) as **55c-d3**.
2. Reformat the report SS; DS between ¶s; do not indent.
3. Change to leftbound report; 1.5" left and 1.0" right margins.
4. SS the table; place a blank line before and after the title of the table.
5. Add a row at the bottom of the table; in column 2 add the total, **$34,815,000**; and in column 3, **100%**.
6. Delete the extra returns at the top of the page so that the title is on the first line; center the page.
7. Resave; print and close the document.

55c-d4
Leftbound Report

1. Open **Meade** from the data files.
2. Change format to a leftbound report.
3. Format title on first page and reference page using all caps, bold, and 14-point font. Position both for an approximate 2" top margin.
4. Make sure all ¶s are indented on the DS report.
   Format all side headings using bold type. Capitalize main words in all side headings.
5. Use the Keep with next feature to ensure that headings remain with the text that follows them and that the table is not separated from its title or divided on two pages.
6. Number pages at the top right margin; do not show number on first page.
7. Preview and check to see that all of the instructions above have been applied properly. Make any necessary corrections.
8. Save as **55c-d4** and print. Leave the document open.

55c-d5
Unbound Report

1. Save the open document (**55c-d4**) as **55c-d5**.
2. Reformat the report as an unbound report, SS. Remove all paragraph indentions.
3. Use 6-point spacing after paragraphs and side headings.
4. Change the font for all titles and headings to Arial.
5. Use the Keep with next feature to ensure that headings remain with the text that follows them and that the table is not separated from its title or divided on two pages.
6. Preview and check to see that all of the instructions above have been applied properly. Make any necessary corrections.
7. Resave and print.

SKILLBUILDING

55d
Skill Builder

Use the remaining class time to build your skills using the Skill Builder module within *Keyboarding Pro*.

Letters with Special Features

67a
Warmup
Key each line twice, striving for good technique.

alphabet 1 Liz Bowhanon moved very quickly and just played exciting defense.
figures 2 I fed 285 cats, 406 dogs, 157 birds, and 39 rabbits at a shelter.
1st/2nd fingers 3 Jimmy or Vick sent my fur hat this summer, but I did not need it.
easy 4 An authentic ivory tusk may be key to the ancient island rituals.

| 1 | 2 | 3 | 4 | 5 | 6 | 7 | 8 | 9 | 10 | 11 | 12 | 13 |

67b
Timed Writings
Key two 1' writings at your top rate. Key two 3' writings at a controlled rate working for good accuracy.

  all letters

gwam 1' | 3'

Technical, human, and conceptual skills are three types   12 4 35
of skills all supervisors are expected to have. The skills are   25 8 40
quite different, and they vary in importance depending on the level   37 12 44
of the supervisor in an organization. Technical skills   50 16 48
refer to knowing how to do the job. Human skills relate to   62 20 52
working with people and getting them to work as a team. Concep-   74 25 56
tual skills refer to the ability to see the big picture as well   87 29 60
as how all the parts fit together.   94 31 63

1' | 1 | 2 | 3 | 4 | 5 | 6 | 7 | 8 | 9 | 10 | 11 | 12 | 13 |
3' | 1 | 2 | 3 | 4 |

67c
Letter Part Drills

1. Key a 30" writing on each drill, keying each line as quickly as possible.

2. Press ENTER the correct number of times between letter parts.

3. DS and key the drill again as many times as possible before the time expires.

Drill A
Current date

4

Dr. J. K. Villivakkam
1000 Honey Tree Dr.
Starkville, MS 39759-1000

Dear Dr. Villivakkam:

Drill B
Sincerely,

4

Ms. Janice A. Minor
Sales Manager

xx

Enclosures

c   J. Thomas Dixon

Edit Documents

SKILLBUILDING

56a
Warmup
Key each line twice SS.

alphabet	1	Jacki might analyze the data by answering five complex questions.
figures	2	Memo 67 asks if the report on Bill 35-48 is due the 19th or 20th.
double letters	3	Aaron took accounting lessons at a community college last summer.
easy	4	Hand Bob a bit of cocoa, a pan of cod, an apricot, and six clams.

| 1 | 2 | 3 | 4 | 5 | 6 | 7 | 8 | 9 | 10 | 11 | 12 | 13 |

56b
Technique Builder
Key each pair of lines 3 times.
Key at a controlled rate.

First row

5 Zam name bank man came exam cave band comb six mine vent back van
6 Zack came back excited; Max made a banner for a vacant zinc mine.

Home row

7 sad lass lag had gag laggard fax hulk salad sales flask glass has
8 Dallas Klass had a jello salad; Ada asked for a large salad also.

Third row

9 were pot toy pew wept you quit power quip peer tower or rope wire
10 Terry wrote Troy for help after a power tower guide wire was cut.

56c
Timed Writings
Build/Assess Straight-Copy Skill

1. Take one 3' timed writing.
2. Take one 5' timed writing.

  all letters

	gwam	3'	5'

For many years, readers who had chosen a particular book had 4 | 2
just one question to answer. Do you want to purchase a hardcover 8 | 5
or a paperback book? It was assumed that books would be purchased 13 | 8
from a retail outlet, such as a bookstore. Currently, books are 17 | 10
being marketed and sold online. The book itself, however, is still 22 | 13
printed on paper. 23 | 14

With the technology that is on the market today, a third 27 | 16
alternative, the electronic or the so-called e-book, is emerging. 31 | 19
E-books are sold in digitized form. The book must be read from the 36 | 21
web site on a computer or on a special device designed for reading 40 | 24
e-books. Many publishers are experimenting with electronic books, 45 | 27
but only a few well-known ones have moved into the e-book market 49 | 29
in a major way. Most e-book companies are small organizations that 54 | 32
are willing to take a risk to make a profit. 56 | 34

The cost of producing and selling books in digital form is 60 | 36
far less than it is in paper form. The result is that books 65 | 39
that appeal to small markets are now feasible in digital form. The 69 | 41
cost was too great in print form. Many publishers have two key 73 | 44
concerns about the e-book market. The first is that a large number 78 | 47
of readers still are not comfortable reading from electronic media 82 | 49
for long time periods. The second factor is that they worry about 87 | 52
copyright protection. Many are very aware of the problems the music 91 | 55
industry experienced in this area. 94 | 56

3' | 1 | 2 | 3 | 4 |
5' | 1 | 2 | 3 |

66d-d2
Modified Block Letter

1. Key the following letter in modified block style with mixed punctuation.
2. Create a subject line. Use appropriate spacing and supply any missing letter parts.
3. Save the letter as **66d-d2** and print.

Sarah Atkinson | 1234 Elm Ln. | Bronx, NY 10466-1234

Thank you for your interest in our dogs. As you know, there are two varieties of collies. The rough-coated collie and the smooth-coated collie both make excellent family pets.

Our kennel, Quality Collies, regularly has rough-coated collies available. We generally have smooth-coated puppies available only in the spring.

Enclosed is a photograph of our most recent litter. You will certainly agree that these quadruplets are adorable. Contact our office (555-0198) Monday through Saturday to arrange a time for you to visit our kennel and see these exquisite puppies for yourself.

Sincerely yours | Sally Moss, Owner | Enclosure

66d-d3
Modified Block Letter

1. Open **66c-drill1**. Remove Mr. Bucciantini as the recipient of the letter. Instead, use the attention line **Marketing Department**.
2. Read the letter and create an appropriate subject line.
3. Add a blind copy notation to **Candice Kinneer** and **James O'Brien**.
4. Preview the letter. Change the font size to 11 point to make the letter fit on one page; assume the letterhead is 1.5" deep.
5. Save it as **66d-d3** and print. Did the letter fit on one page?

66d-d4
Modified Block Letter

1. Open **66Global** from the data files.
2. Read the letter and create an appropriate subject line. Make adjustments so that the letter fits on one page.
3. Save the letter as **66d-d4**.
4. Generate an envelope and add it to the letter. Save it as **66d-d4a**.

56d-d1
Edit Memo with Bullets

1. Open **Trail Design** from the data files. Save as **56d-d1**.
2. Position the first line of heading correctly.
3. Search for *sights* and replace with *sites* each time it occurs.
4. Add bullets to the list of sites.
5. Make other edits shown and add reference initials.
6. Proofread carefully and preview the document.
7. Print and resave it.

To: Trail design task force

From: Dianne Gibson

Date: Current

Subject: Trail design

Thanks for participating in the Trail Design meeting last week. We did make a tremendous amount of progress on this fun project. Specific sights were designated for the components of phase one of the Environmental learning center complex and the first trail loop. Tentative sights were located for the phase two components including the conference center.

Ken provides us with a new lay out of the property showing the following sights that were designated during the visit.

Main Entrance
Parking lot area
Environmental Learning Center
General shelter buildings
Outdoor linear classrooms
First trail loop with key interpretative sights designated
Sustainability exhibit sights

Please review these sights to make sure that the layout and documentation interprets the groups wishes properly. Once we recieve feed back from every one Ken needs to finalize the design documents.

Our timeframe requires us to have finalized concept documents within two weeks to turn over to the architects. The architects will develop the construction documents needed to obtain the necessary permits.

Monica A. Carter
Communication Consultant
100 Main St.
Clinton, MS 39056-0503

July 11, 200-

Attention line
Attention Office Manager
Professional Document Designs, Inc.
9345 Blackjack Blvd.
Kingwood, TX 77345-9345

Ladies and Gentlemen: **Mixed punctuation**

Subject line
Subject: Modified Block Style Letters

Modified block format differs from block format in that the date, complimentary close, and the writer's name and title are keyed at the center point.

Paragraphs may be blocked, as this letter illustrates, or they may be indented 0.5" from the left margin. We suggest using block paragraphs so that an additional tab setting is not needed.

We recommend that you use modified block style only for those customers who request it. Otherwise, we urge you to use block format, which is more efficient. Please refer to the model documents in the enclosed *Communication Experts Format Guide*.

Sincerely,   **Mixed punctuation**

Monica A. Carter
Communication Consultant

xx

Enclosure

bc   Lyndon David, Account Manager   **Blind copy notation—not on original**

Modified Block Letter with Mixed Punctuation

1. Open **Master Plan** from the data files. Save as **56d-d2**.
2. Center the main heading, format in bold, 16-point Arial type. Position main heading at about 2".
3. Number pages at top right margin; do not show number on the first page.
4. Format Level 1 headings with bold, 14-point Arial type. Format Level 2 headings with bold, 12-point Arial type.
5. Use 6-point spacing after paragraphs.
6. Ensure that headings are not separated from the paragraphs that follow.
7. Open **55c-d3**; select the *Property Location and Value* table and copy it; then paste it after the second paragraph in this report. Delete the blank line before and after the table title.
8. Make all edits shown below. Add text that is in script to the document.
9. Proofread and edit carefully. Check to see that you have made all edits and followed all instructions.
10. Print and resave.

Master Plan for Foundation Properties

The Midlands University Foundation properties are categorized into four classifications: Coastal Property, Midlands Property, other in-state property, and out-of-state property. The Foundation acquires property by purchasing it or by accepting gifts from donors desiring to support Midlands University.

Insert → *Generally, the Foundation retains coastal properties for research and environmental education purposes and properties in the Midlands area for future development and use by Midlands University. Usually, properties in the other two categories are held only if they are likely to appreciate significantly; otherwise, they are sold and the proceeds are used to support various University needs. Currently, no out-of-state property is being held.*

Insert table here.

Coastal Properties   *Level 1 Heading*

seven
Currently the Foundation owns ~~a number of~~ different tracts of land in the Coastal Region valued at $18,325,000. Decisions on the future use of five of the tracts are pending. The master plan contains specific plans for only two of the tracts the Marshall tract and the Richardson tract.
∧ em dash

Envelopes

Word will automatically copy the letter address from the letter on the screen to the envelope (**Tools, Letters and Mailings, Envelopes and Labels**).

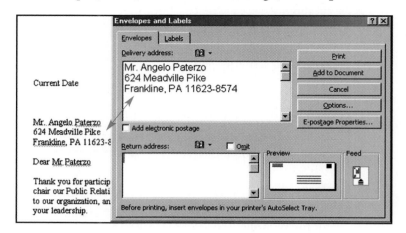

If the return address is not preprinted on the envelope, it is necessary to key a return address. When you complete the information for the envelope, you can either print the envelope, or choose **Add to Document** and print the envelope followed by the letter.

DRILL 1   MODIFIED BLOCK LETTER

1. Open **64Hightower** from the data files.

2. Change the letter to modified block style with mixed punctuation (colon after the salutation and a comma after the complimentary closing). (Do not indent paragraphs.)

3. Position the date so that the letter is formatted attractively on the page. Be sure that if a letterhead were present, the dateline would not print in this area.

4. Add or adjust letter parts and spacing between parts as needed.

5. Save it as **66c-drill1**.

DRILL 2   ENVELOPE

1. Open **66c-drill1**.

2. Generate an envelope for the letter.

3. Attach the envelope to the letter.

4. Save the document as **66c-drill2**.

APPLICATIONS

66d-d1
Modified Block Letter

1. Key the modified block letter on page 257 with mixed punctuation. Note that it includes an attention line, subject line, and blind copy notation.

2. Center the page vertically.

3. Save the letter as **66d-d1**. Preview the letter to be sure the vertical placement is appropriate if a letterhead were present. Print.

4. Add a blind copy notation for Mr. David, save, and reprint.

5. Create an envelope and attach it to the letter. Save the job again as **66d-d1a**.

The Marshall Tract   *Level 2 Heading*

The Marshall tract consists of over 1,200 acres of environmentally sensitive coastal property. Approximately one-half of the tract consists of wetlands with a conservation and preservation easement one the property. A portion of the remaining property has endangered species, including the red cockaded woodpecker. An eagle nest has also been spotted on the property.

Insert

The master plan calls for the retention of the property because of its potential for research and environmental education. The short-term plans call for the establishment of a system of nature trails and boardwalks and the development of a parking area for visitors. Long-term plans specify the design and construction of a research and learning center.

The Richardson Tract   *Level 2 Heading*

The Richardson tract consists of an entire barrier island that is used for research purposes. The property currently has a very basic research and education center. The gift agreement severely restricts development of facilities on the island; therefore, it is not likely to be highly developed at any point in the future.

Midlands Properties   *Level 1 Heading*

The Midlands portfolio of property consists of more than sixty individual parcels of land. Approximately 60 percent of the land was purchased and 40 percent was received as gifts. The land is valued at $12,650,000.

The Wheeler Tract   *Level 2 Heading*

A decision has been made to sell this property. Currently, the property is being surveyed and a new appraisal has been ordered. The property will be ~~put~~ placed on the market as soon as the survey and appraisal have been completed.

The Blossom Tract   *Level 2 Heading*

The Foundation contracted to have infrastructure *work completed before turning the tract over to Midlands University for development.*

SKILLBUILDING

66a
Warmup
Key each line twice SS.

alphabet	1	The Lake View magazine of junior boxers may have clean equipment.
figures	2	She found 4,721 cats, 9,038 kittens, and 56 frightened bluebirds.
shift key	3	Mr. Paul Wilkes called Ms. Angie Pace on Friday, March 15 in OH.
double letters	4	Bill looked down the hall for a happy bookkeeper named Jill Mill.

| 1 | 2 | 3 | 4 | 5 | 6 | 7 | 8 | 9 | 10 | 11 | 12 | 13 |

66b
Timed Writing
Key one 3' writing and one 5' writing.

  all letters

gwam 3' 5'

The technology used in offices today requires employees to be flexible and to be willing to learn new ways to accomplish the work that they do. Too often workers try to adapt the new technology to the old procedures rather than modify the way they do work to maximize the advantages of the technology. Although most people think they can adapt to change very easily, the truth is that change is very frustrating for most people. The majority of the changes in offices caused by technology are difficult to make because many things have to change at the same time. A change in hardware or software requires changes in the way work is done as well as learning to use the new software or hardware. These changes might be easier to implement if they could be made gradually rather than simultaneously.

3'	5'
4	2 34
8	5 37
12	7 39
17	10 42
21	13 45
25	15 47
30	18 50
34	20 53
39	23 55
43	26 58
47	28 60
51	31 63
53	32 64

3' | 1 | 2 | 3 | 4 |
5' | 1 | 2 | 3 |

DOCUMENT DESIGN

66c

Modified Block Letter Review

The only difference between the block and modified block style letters is the placement of the dateline, complimentary close, and the writer's name and title. These lines begin at the horizontal center of the page. See the modified block letter on page 257. Note that it applies mixed punctuation.

Begin the letter by setting a left tab at the center of the page. Determine the center by dividing the line length by two (6" ÷ 2" = 3"). Set a left tab at 3".

Press TAB before keying the dateline, complimentary close, name, and title of the sender.

Note: If the letter has already been keyed and you are changing it to modified block format, select the entire document and then set the tab.

DOCUMENT DESIGN

LESSON 57

SKILLBUILDING

57a
Warmup
Key each line twice SS.

alphabet	1	Max Biqua watched jet planes flying in the azure sky over a cove.
figures	2	Send 105 No. 4 nails and 67 No. 8 brads for my home at 329 Annet.
3d row	3	We two were ready to type a report for our quiet trio of workers.
easy	4	Pamela owns a big bicycle; and, with it, she may visit the docks.

| 1 | 2 | 3 | 4 | 5 | 6 | 7 | 8 | 9 | 10 | 11 | 12 | 13 |

57b
Timed Writings
Take one 3' and one 5' timing on the paragraphs.

  all letters

gwam 3' | 5'

	3'	5'
Voting is a very important part of being a good citizen.	4	2
However, many young people who are eligible to vote choose not	8	5
to do so. When asked to explain or justify their decision, many	12	7
simply shrug their shoulders and reply that they have no particular	16	10
reason for not voting. The explanation others frequently give is	21	13
that they just did not get around to going to the voting polls.	25	15
A good question to consider concerns ways that we can motivate	29	18
young people to be good citizens and to go to the polls and to vote.	34	21
Some people approach this topic by trying to determine how satisfied	39	23
people are who do not vote with the performance of their elected	43	26
officials. Unfortunately, those who choose not to vote are just as	48	29
satisfied with their elected officials as are those who voted.	52	31
One interesting phenomenon concerning voting relates to the	56	34
job market. When the job market is strong, fewer young people vote	61	36
than when the job market is very bad. They also tend to be less	65	39
satisfied with their elected officials. Self-interest seems to	69	41
be a powerful motivator. Unfortunately, those who do not choose	74	44
to vote miss the point that it is in their best interest to be a	78	47
good citizen.	79	47

3' | 1 | 2 | 3 | 4 |
5' | 1 | 2 | 3 |

APPLICATIONS

57c
Assessment

 Continue

 Check

With CheckPro: When you complete a document, proofread it, check the spelling, and preview for placement. When you are completely satisfied, click the **Continue** button to move to the next document. You will not be able to return and edit a document once you continue to the next document. Click the **Check** button when you are ready to error-check the test. Review and/or print the document analysis results.

Without CheckPro: Key the documents in sequence. When time has been called, proofread all documents again and identify errors.

1. Key the following letter in block letter style with open punctuation. Supply a complimentary closing.
2. Position letter attractively on the page. Save as **65e-d3**. Print.

	words
May 15, 200-|Attention Frequent Flyer Service Center|Atlanta	14
International Airport|P.O. Box 84410|Department 129|Atlanta, GA	27
30320-8441|Ladies and Gentlemen	33
Request for Redemption of Frequent Flyer Award	43
Please redeem an award of 30,000 miles from my frequent flyer account	57
#2521-70442. Award #D731 is being redeemed as a round-trip ticket to	71
Honolulu, Hawaii, with a departure on Thursday, August 15, and a return	84
on Monday, August 19, 200-. Flight information is listed below:	99

		words
Thursday, August 15	**Monday, August 19**	106
Depart Jackson, Mississippi	Depart Honolulu, Hawaii	116
7:10 a.m.	6:05 p.m.	120
Flight #5315	Flight #178	125

	words
Please mail a certificate to the business address listed on the letterhead.	140
Your agent, Azida Hamff, has instructed me to submit this certificate to	155
an airline agent by June 15 to receive my airline tickets. I will be sure to	168
follow these instructions and look forward to benefiting from my first fre-	183
quent flyer award.	189
Dr. Frances Hamilton, Professor|xx|bc Robert Heflin, Travel Department	203

1. Key the following block letter for **Alexandria H. Skiwski, Technical Manager**.
2. Add any missing letter parts. Send a copy to **Todd West, Account Manager**.
3. Save as **65e-d4**. Print.

	words
Current date	Mr. Jamie Kurman, Jr.	P.O. Box 7390	Counderspot, PA	15
16315-0985	Dear Mr. Kurman:	Scanner Recommendations	24
Your assessment, Mr. Kurman, is right on target. The payback period for a	39
scanner would be about six months. We are pleased to provide you with our	54
recommendations.	58
Your test generation software handles both text and graphics; therefore, an	73
intelligent OCR should be purchased. The enclosed analysis provides speci-	88
fications, price information, and our recommendations for both the scanner	103
and the software.	107
Please call us at 1-800-555-0139 to schedule a demonstration of the OCR	121
scanner. We look forward to hearing from you.	131
closing	149

1. Open **Site Assessment** from the data files, and make the following edits:
   - Format as unbound report, SS; 6-point spacing after paragraphs.
   - Center title, apply bold, 14-point Arial type. Position heading at about 2" and add an extra blank line after the heading.
   - Format side headings in bold.
   - Use Find and Replace to find *Theme*, and replace it with *Community* each time it occurs.
2. Insert page numbers at the upper-right margin; do not show on first page.
3. Use Keep with next feature to ensure that headings are kept with the paragraphs below them.
4. Preview; make sure headings are not left alone at the bottom of a page.
5. Proofread, save as **57c-d1**, and print.

1. Reformat the report as a leftbound report; DS; indent paragraphs.
2. Key the table shown below making the edits indicated; position it below the last paragraph of the report. If the entire table does not fit at the bottom of the page, place it on the next page.

Site Costs *Center, bold, 14 pt. type*			
Cost Category	**Westlake**	**Southside** *Center column heads*	**Woodcreek**
Land	$720,000	$630,000	$676,000
Infrastructure	175,000	210,000	180,000
Total	$805,000	$840,000	$856,000

Left-align first column

3. Preview; make sure headings are not left alone at the bottom of a page.
4. Proofread, save as **57c-d2**, and print.

65e-d1
Block Letter with Subject Line and Copy Notation

1. Format the following letter in block style with open punctuation. Use your judgment in centering the letter attractively on the page.
2. Add the subject line **Volusia Community Goals Conference—January 30**.
3. Send a copy of the letter to the lead facilitator mentioned in the letter.
4. Save as **65e-d1**. Print.

	words
January 10, 200- | The Honorable Alice Vinicki | P.O. Box 249 | Volusia,	13
FL 32174-3852 | Dear Senator Vinicki	20

Your positive response to deliver the keynote address at the Volusia	34
Community Goals Conference on Saturday, January 30, was received	47
with much excitement by the Goals Conference Planning Committee.	60
Thank you, Senator Vinicki, for your commitment to this community	74
effort. Mr. Roger Bourgeois, director of the United Planning Institute,	88
is the lead facilitator of the goals conference and will introduce you at the	104
opening session beginning at 9 a.m. in the Vinicki Exhibit Hall of	117
the Volusia Convention Center.	124

Hotel accommodations have been made for you at the Riverside Suites	137
for Friday, January 29; confirmation is enclosed. Mr. Bourgeois and I	151
will meet you at the hotel restaurant at 7:30 a.m. for breakfast and	165
to escort you to the convention center. A copy of the conference program	180
and an outline of the issues to be discussed in the various breakout	194
groups are also enclosed for your review.	202

We look forward to your address and to your being a key player in our	216
goals conference.	220

Respectfully yours | Ms. Le-An Nguyen, President | Chamber of Commerce |	234
xx | Enclosures	236

65e-d2
Block Letter with Subject Line and Blind Copy Notation

1. Format the following letter in block style with open punctuation. Center the letter vertically on the page.
2. Add an appropriate subject line. Save as **65e-d2** and print.
3. Add a blind copy notation for Carol Winstead and print the copy for Ms. Winstead.

	words
January 10, 200- | Ms. Denise McWhorter | HandPrints, Inc. |	11
92 E. Cresswell Road | Selden, NY 11784 | Dear Ms. McWhorter	24
Booth 24, your first choice had been reserved for you	35
for the annual craft fair on May 15-17. You booth was ex-	46
treme popular last year and we are very please to have you	59
participate in the fair again this year.	67
Our standard agreement from is inclosed. Please sign	78
the form and return it to us by April 15. Your booths will	90
have a large table and a minimum of two chair. If you need	102
any thing else for the booth please let us know prior to the	114
opening of the fair.	119
Sincerely | Ms. Jennifer A. Reed | resident | xx | Enclosure	129

1. Key the memo shown below.
2. Send the memo to the **Planning Commission** from the **Community Park Site Committee**. Use the current date, and send a copy of the memo to **Mayor Charles Morgan**.
3. Use the report title from **57c-d1** as the subject of the memo.
4. Proofread, print, and save it as **57c-d3**.

The Community Park Site Committee has completed its assessment of the potential sites for the new park. Our report is attached.

The Committee unanimously recommends that the Westlake site be used for the new park. The Woodcreek site was considered acceptable, but it is not as desirable as the Westlake site. The Southside site was the least desirable of the three sites.

Please contact us if you have any questions.

1. Key the following letter in block format. Use the current date and sign your name.
2. Save it as **57c-d4**.

Ms. Margaret C. Worthington
4957 Mt. Elon Church Road
Hopkins, SC 29061-9837

Dear Ms. Worthington

The Planning Commission has authorized me to contact you to discuss the possible purchase of the 120-acre site that we discussed with you for the new Community Park. When we spoke with you yesterday, you indicated that you would be available to meet with us any afternoon next week. If it is still convenient, we would like to meet with you on Wednesday afternoon at 2:00 at the site.

Earlier you indicated that you had a recent survey and an appraisal of the property. We would appreciate it if you could have those documents available for the meeting.

If this time is not convenient, please call my office and leave a message so that I may reschedule the meeting. We look forward to working with you.

Sincerely

65d

An **attention line** is used to direct a letter to a specific individual, position, or department within an organization. It is keyed as the first line of the letter address. Whenever an attention line is used, the correct salutation is *Ladies and Gentlemen*.

Attention Accounting Department
Chou and Chou Furniture Company
First St. and First Ave.
Olympia, WA 99504-6480

A **subject line** provides the reader with a short description of the purpose of the letter. It is placed between the salutation and the body of the letter. Double-space before and after the subject line. The subject line may be keyed using initial caps or all caps. It may be preceded by the word *subject*.

Dear Mr. Jones:

Subject: Projected Sales Figures

The sales figures for the first quarter have been released.

A **copy notation** is used to indicate that someone other than the receiver will get a copy of the letter. It is keyed a double space below the reference initials or the enclosure notation (if there is one). Key **c** to indicate copy; then press TAB and key the name(s).

John Mastrangelo, President

xx

Enclosure

c   Norman Elswick
         Sheila Solari

A **postscript**, often used to emphasize information, is keyed a double space below the last notation in a letter. It is not necessary to begin with *PS*. Do not indent the postscript unless paragraphs in the letter are indented.

John Mastrangelo, President

xx

Enclosure

Use modified block for whenever

A **blind copy notation** indicates that a person(s) is receiving a copy of the letter without the addressee's knowledge. A blind copy notation is keyed a double space after the reference initials, enclosure notation, or copy notation (if any). The blind copy notation appears on copies, but not on the original.

John Mastrangelo, President

xx

Enclosure

bc   Norman Elswick
          Sheila Solari

Appears on copies, but not on the original

Module 7: Checkpoint

Self-Assessment

Evaluate your understanding of this project by answering the questions below.

1. The _____ feature removes text or an image from a document and places it on the Clipboard.
2. The _____ feature enables you to locate multiple uses of a word or phrase and substitute a different word or phrase for it each time it occurs.
3. The_____ is a tool that allows you to look up words and replace them with a synonym.
4. A special character that is the equivalent of two hyphens joined with no spaces is a(n) _____ dash.
5. A special character that is the equivalent of one hyphen and a space is a(n) _____ dash.
6. Use the _____ function to format a one-page document with the same amount of space in the top and bottom margin.
7. The ✂ symbol is most likely to be found on one of the _____ fonts.
8. The character effect _____ positions small text above the line of writing.
9. Drag-and-drop editing allows you to move text within the _____ .
10. To position an extra blank line (6 point) after each paragraph automatically, use the _____ function.

Performance Assessment

Document 1
Edit Report

1. Open **Sampling Plan** from the data files. Make the edits listed below.
   - Format title: center, bold, Arial 16-point font
   - Format first two side headings: bold, Arial 14-point font and the last two side headings: bold, Arial 12-point font
   - Search for *athlete* and replace with *student athlete* each time it occurs.
   - Key your name below the last line of type; right-align it; insert the date below your name.
   - Format paragraphs with 6-point spacing after paragraphs; center the page.
2. Save the document as **checkpoint7-d1**.

Document 2
Memo

1. Format the memo. Save as **checkpoint7-d2**.
2. Send the message To: **Student Athletes** From: **Jan Marks, Faculty Athletics Representative** Date: **Current** Subject: **Exit Interview**

In accordance with NCAA bylaws, the enclosed survey is sent to you as a student athlete who has completed your eligibility to compete in college athletics. This survey gives you an opportunity to share your opinions about your experience both as a student and as an athlete.

Please complete the survey and return it to me in the enclosed self-addressed envelope within two weeks. We urge you to be honest with your responses. The information is used to improve the athletics experience for future students. Your coach does not have access to this information, and your responses will be treated confidentially.

We appreciate your sharing your thoughts with us.

SKILLBUILDING

65a
Warmup
Key each line twice SS.

alphabet	1	The dizzy boxer's mad opponent jabbed quickly with his fat glove.
figures	2	I received 128 books, 7,349 magazines, and 560 newspapers yearly.
1st/2nd fingers	3	Prepare for the future by studying, working, and playing at home.
shift key	4	Mr. Sam Keatley gave the letters and memos to Ms. Charlene Jones.

| 1 | 2 | 3 | 4 | 5 | 6 | 7 | 8 | 9 | 10 | 11 | 12 | 13 |

65b
Skillbuilding
Key each group 3 times; work at a controlled rate.

double letters	5	Janna allowed me to borrow her oval office to answer my messages.
	6	Cobb swallowed the big blue pills with a tall glass of green tea.
	7	Will you commit some time this summer to vacuum for Miss Ferraez?
direct reaches	8	June and I received a number of calls from NYCE Mutuals Thursday.
	9	The brave youngster doubts his cute brown bunny can run and jump.
	10	Bryce bragged about his decision to build huge muscles by summer.
adjacent reaches	11	Yulana was to polish the three silver trays, sweep, and mop well.
	12	Some of the people hoped to quit working by three this afternoon.
	13	Polly was quick to offer her opinions and to make fast decisions.

COMMUNICATION

65c
Compose Journal Entry

1. In a new document, key your name at the left margin and insert the date using the Date and Time feature on the line below. Compose a paragraph that answers the following questions:

   - Why do you think business letters include the date at the beginning of the letter?
   - Why would companies require a common style for business letters, i.e., block letter style with open punctuation?
   - What personal business letters will you be required to write in the months ahead?
   - How do you think this module will assist you in preparing those letters?

2. Save as **65c** and print.

DOCUMENT DESIGN

65d

Special Letter Parts

In Lesson 64, you reviewed the standard letter parts that are present in each business letter. Other special features may be included, depending on the needs of the document. When special parts are added to a letter, they cause the letter to move down farther on the page. If you center the page vertically, always preview the letter to be sure that it is not positioned too high on the page.

Graphic Essentials

- Enhance document format with graphics and text color.
- Create multicolumn newsletters.

LESSON 58 — Skillbuilding and Graphics

SKILLBUILDING

58a
Warmup
Key each line twice.

alphabet	1	Dave Cagney alphabetized items for next week's quarterly journal.
figures	2	Close Rooms 4, 18, and 20 from 3 until 9 on July 7; open Room 56.
upward	3	Toy & Wurt's note for $635 (see our page 78) was paid October 29.
easy	4	The auditor is due by eight, and he may lend a hand to the panel.

| 1 | 2 | 3 | 4 | 5 | 6 | 7 | 8 | 9 | 10 | 11 | 12 | 13 |

58b
Technique Builder
Key each set of lines 3 times; work at a controlled rate.

adjacent reaches	5	art try pew sort tree position copy opera maker waste three draft
	6	sat coil riot were renew forth trade power grope owner score weed
one hand	7	ad null bar poll car upon deed jump ever look feed hill noon moon
	8	get hilly are employ save phony taste union versa yummy wedge fed
balanced hand	9	aid go bid dish elan glen fury idle half jamb lend make name slam
	10	oak pay hen quay rush such urus vial works yamen amble blame pale

58c
Timed Writings
1. Key three 1' writings.
2. Key two 2' writings. Try to maintain your best 1' rate.

  all letters

	gwam	1'	2'
Good plans typically are required to execute most tasks		11	6 50
successfully. If a task is worth doing, it is worth investing		24	12 56
the time that is necessary to plan it effectively. Many people		37	18 62
are anxious to get started on a task and just begin before they		49	25 69
have thought about the best way to organize it. In the long run,		63	31 75
they frequently end up wasting time that could be spent more		75	37 81
profitably on important projects that they might prefer to tackle.		88	44 88

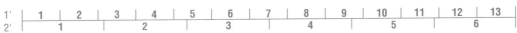

1' | 1 | 2 | 3 | 4 | 5 | 6 | 7 | 8 | 9 | 10 | 11 | 12 | 13 |
2' | 1 | 2 | 3 | 4 | 5 | 6 |

1. Format the following letter in block style with open punctuation. Since this letter is short, align it at the vertical center of the page.

2. Add your reference initials. Save as **64d-d2** and print.

Current date ↓4

Ms. Alice Noe
4723 Glacier Dr.
Selden, NY 11784-4723 ↓2

Dear Ms. Noe ↓2

Due to an unavoidable change in his schedule, Dr. Skyler will be unavailable to see patients during the first week in November. Since your next regularly scheduled appointment is during this week, we would like to give you the opportunity to reschedule your appointment for a later date. If rescheduling your appointment is impossible, we will be glad to make arrangements for you to see one of the other physicians in the medical group. ↓2

We apologize for any inconvenience. Please call our office at 555-0102 as soon as possible to reschedule your appointment. ↓2

Sincerely yours ↓4

Frederick Limerick
Office Manager ↓2

1. Format the letter in block style and open punctuation; center vertically. Send the letter from yourself to **Sylvia Gianchin, Redmon Publishers, 5280 Circle Pt., Long Beach, CA 90840-0792**.

2. Add letter parts and apply correct spacing. Do not include reference initials since you are both the originator and the typist. Save as **64d-d3** and print.

The Institute for Appalachian Studies will be having a seminar this spring entitled "Women of the Mountains". Elizabeth Sugerfoot, author of *Rural Life in Modern Appalachia*, will be our keynote speaker, and we know that the attendees will be clamoring for her exciting book. Enclosed is our purchase order with shipping instructions for 100 copies.

If you have questions regarding this order, please call me between 10 a.m. and 2 p.m. on Thursday or Friday. We will need these books delivered to the convention center during the first week of December. The center will be able to store them until the seminar, but they will not have storage space available before the first week in December.

Sincerely yours

Student Name, Coordinator

Clip art, pictures, AutoShapes, and other images are graphic elements that enhance documents such as announcements, invitations, reports, and newsletters. In this lesson, you will work with clip art and drawing tools.

Clip Art

Microsoft Word (and other applications such as *Excel*, *PowerPoint*, and *Publisher*) provides a collection of pictures, clip art, and sounds that can be added to documents. Additional clips are available online. You can also add your own clips to the collection. The clips are organized into different collections to simplify finding appropriate clip art. The Clip Organizer adds keywords to enable you to search for various types of clip art. You also have the option of selecting the collection and viewing thumbnail sketches (small pictures) of the various clip art available in each category. Once clip art has been inserted into a document, you can size it, copy and paste it, wrap text around it, or drag it to other locations.

To insert clip art:

1. Click **Insert** on the menu bar, click **Picture**, and then click **Clip Art**.

2. In the Task Pane Search text box, key the type of clip art to search for such as rabbit, baseball, or roses; then click **Search**.

TIP

Another option for inserting clip art is to display the Drawing toolbar (**View, Toolbars, Drawing**), and click the **Insert Clip Art** button.

3. When the results are displayed, use the scroll bar to view the thumbnail sketches. When you find the desired clip art, point to the image to display a down arrow at the right of the image, click the down arrow, and then click **Insert**. (*Option:* Click the clip art image.)

4. To display a collection of clip art from various places, choose one of the options under Other Search Options on the Task Pane.

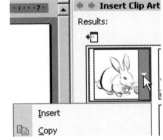

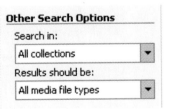

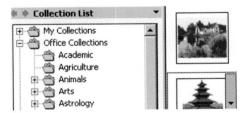

Punctuation Style

Letters may use either open punctuation or mixed punctuation. **Open punctuation** uses no punctuation after the salutation or complimentary closing. **Mixed punctuation** adds a colon after the salutation and a comma after the complimentary closing.

Word Processing Tips for Letters

Dateline: Begin the dateline at about 2" as shown on the status line. Due to variations in fonts, you may not be able to work exactly at 2". You may also center the letter vertically on the page as long as there is at least 0.5" below the letterhead. (If longer letters are centered vertically, the dateline or letter address may print in the letterhead area.) Short letters look better centered on the page.

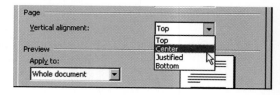

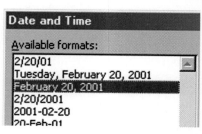

Use the Date and Time feature to insert the date. Use the Month, day, year format; do not select Update automatically (**Insert**, **Date and Time**).

Margins: Use default margins.

Reference Initials: *Word* automatically capitalizes your reference initials. To format them in lowercase, click the smart tag above your initials and choose **Undo Automatic Capitalization**.

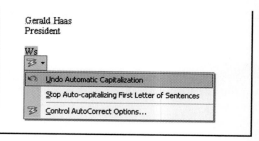

DRILL 1   BLOCK LETTER

1. Open **64Hightower** from the data files.

2. Add or adjust letter parts as needed, including the date.

3. Make the necessary adjustments so that all the lines begin at the left margin and the spacing between the letter parts is correct.

4. Position the date so that the letter is formatted attractively on the page. Be sure that if a letterhead were present, the dateline would not print in this area.

5. Save the letter as **64c-drill1**.

APPLICATIONS

64d-d1
Block Letter

1. Key the block letter on the previous page with open punctuation. Position the date line at approximately 2" (if necessary, deselect Update automatically).

2. Change the *xx* to your initials. Be sure that your initials are both lowercase.

3. Save the document as **64d-d1** and print.

To move or size clip art:

1. Select the clip art.

2. Position the insertion point over one of the handles. When the pointer turns to a double-headed arrow, drag the lower-right handle down and to the right to increase the size; drag it up and to the left to make it smaller. Drag a corner handle to maintain the same proportion.

To move clip art:

1. Select the clip art.

2. Click the **Text Wrapping** button on the Picture toolbar. Then choose **Tight** (or one of the text-wrapping options) from the drop-down list. The sizing handles change to white.

3. Position the arrow pointer on the clip art until a four-headed arrow displays. Click and drag the clip art to the desired location.

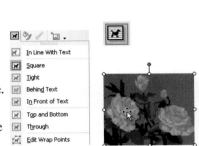

DRILL 1   CLIP ART

1. Search for roses in the clip art gallery, and insert the clip art into a new document.

2. Increase the size of the clip art to approximately double its size. Use the Horizontal and Vertical Rulers to guide you.

3. Move it to the center of the page near the top margin.

4. Create the folder **Module 8 Keys**, and save the document as **58b-drill1** in this folder. Save all exercises for Module 8 in this folder.

Text Color

A simple way to enhance the appearance of a document is to change the color of the text. For example, when creating a club meeting announcement, use club colors to attract attention, e.g., blue and gold.

To change the color of text:

1. Select the text you want to change.

2. Click the arrow next to the **Font Color** button on the Formatting toolbar. Then select the desired color.

   Note: To select the most recently used color, click the **Font Color** button.

DRILL 2   TEXT COLOR

1. Open **meeting** from the data files.

2. Change the main heading to Gill Sans Ultra Bold font and change text color to blue.

3. Add an appropriate clip art that would attract attention to the prize being awarded. Size and place the image attractively.

4. Save as **58d-drill2**.

Letterhead

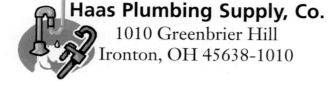

Haas Plumbing Supply, Co.
1010 Greenbrier Hill
Ironton, OH 45638-1010

Dateline September 22, 200- ↓ 4

Letter address Ms. Charise Rossetti
Rt. 3, Box 49A
St. Albans, WV 25177-4900 ↓ 2

Salutation Dear Ms. Rossetti ↓ 2

All of the employees at Haas Plumbing Supply are pleased that you are doing an internship at our company headquarters. One of your duties will be to assist Mr. Joseph Burns in preparing the daily correspondence. We know that your training at Highview Community College has prepared you well for this task. ↓ 2

Body Remember that the correspondence our customers receive from us is one of the ways that they evaluate our effectiveness as a business. Our outgoing letters must be as perfect as we can make them in layout, content, grammar, and punctuation. This will impress upon our customers that we have a company-wide commitment to excellence. ↓ 2

Enclosed is a sample company letter for your review. If you have any questions, contact me or your supervisor, Mr. Burns. Again, we are glad to have you working in our organization. ↓ 2

Sincerely yours ↓ 4 **Complimentary Close**

Writer's Name Gerald Haas
Title President ↓ 2

Reference initials xx ↓ 2

Enclosure notation Enclosure

Block Letter with Open Punctuation

Paragraph Borders and Shading

Borders and shading can be added to paragraphs, pages, or selected text. Various line styles, weights, and colors can be applied to borders. Shading can be applied in a variety of colors and patterns.

> This paragraph illustrates a block border with a 1-point black line. The shading for the paragraph is 10% gray fill.

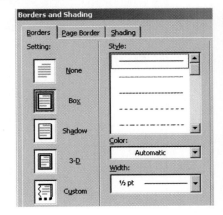

To apply a paragraph border:

1. Click in the paragraph or select the text to be formatted with a border.
2. Click **Borders and Shading** on the Format menu, and then click the **Borders** tab.
3. Select the type of border, line style, color, and width; then click **Apply to Paragraph** and **OK**.

To apply shading:

1. Click in the paragraph or select the text to be shaded.
2. Click **Borders and Shading** on the Format menu, and then click the **Shading** tab.
3. Select the fill and pattern, and then apply them to the paragraph.

DRILL 3   **BORDERS AND SHADING**

Key the paragraph at the right. Then apply a ½-point red, double-line box border and pale blue shading to the paragraph. Save as **58d-drill3**.

> This paragraph is formatted with a ½-point red, double-line box border and pale blue shading.

Page Borders

Attractive page borders can also be added to pages using various line styles, weights, and colors.

To apply a page border:

1. Choose **Format**; then **Borders and Shading**.
2. Click the **Page Borders** tab; then choose a setting, e.g., **Box**. Choose the desired line style, line color, and line width. Click **OK**.
3. Close the document and save your changes.

64c
Basic Letter Review

Business Letter Review

The following letter parts are basic to all business letters. Review the block-format model letter on page 248. In a block-style letter, all lines begin at the left margin.

Letter Parts

Businesspeople expect to see standard letter parts arranged in the proper sequence. The standard parts are listed below. Other parts may be included.

Letterhead. Stationery printed at the top with the company name, logo, full address, and other elements such as trademark symbols, phone numbers, fax numbers, and e-mail address. As a general rule, allow 1.5" for the letterhead.

Dateline. The date is the month (spelled out), day, and year that the letter is prepared. Remember that letters may be used as legal documents, so correctness of the date is very important. Press ENTER four times after the date. The dateline should be positioned about 0.5" below the letterhead. Therefore, position the date about 2" (press ENTER six times). If the letter is short (two paragraphs or about 100 words), center the page vertically.

Letter address. The complete address of the recipient of the letter. The letter address usually includes the personal title, first name, and last name of the recipient followed by the company name, street address, and city, state, and ZIP Code. Press ENTER twice after the letter address.

Salutation. The word *Dear* followed by the personal title and last name of the recipient (*Dear Mr. Nibert*; *Dear Professor Glenn*). Use the first name of the recipient only if there is a close relationship between the sender and recipient (*Dear Sue*). Press ENTER twice after the salutation.

Body. The text that makes up the message of the letter. Single-space the paragraphs and double-space between paragraphs. Press ENTER twice after the last paragraph.

Complimentary closing. A phrase used to end a letter. Capitalize only the first letter. Press ENTER four times after the complimentary close to allow space for a written signature.

Name and title of writer. Key the first and last name of the sender. The sender's personal title (Dr., Ms., Mrs., Mr.) may be included if the first name does not clearly indicate gender (e.g., Ms. Lee Jones). Use a comma to separate the title if it's on the same line as the name. Do not use a comma if the title is on a separate line. Press ENTER twice after the name or title.

> *William Karlet, Coordinator*   or   *William Karlet*
> *Coordinator*

Reference initials. When the letter is keyed for another person who is the originator of the letter, the typist includes his/her initials in lowercase below the signature line. In the textbook, *xx* is a reminder to key your reference initials. If the originator of the letter also keys the letter, reference initials are not included. Press ENTER twice after the reference initials if additional letter parts follow.

Enclosure notation. An enclosure notation indicates that something is included in the envelope with the letter. Read each letter and add an enclosure notation if needed. The notation may include a description of the items.

> *Enclosure*   or   *Enclosure: Application form*   or   *Enclosures: 3*

1. Open **58d-drill3**. Save as **58d-drill4**.

2. Add a page border that is dark red and ½ point.

3. Save and print.

APPLICATIONS

58e-d1
Report with Graphics

1. In a new document, format the main heading, **Trend Analysis Report**, using Arial Black font, 36 point, and indigo text color.
2. Create a subheading below the heading by keying **Market Trends** using 20-point font and adding indigo shading to the paragraph.
3. Key the bulleted list.
4. Search for clip art using the keyword **academic** and add an appropriate piece of clip art centered below the five paragraphs.
5. At the bottom of the page, key in 18-point script font **Understanding our community to prepare for our future!**
6. Save the document as **58e-d1**, and print a copy.

Trend Analysis Report

Market Analysis

- The population in the metropolitan area is growing both in the college's service area and in the demographic segments that represent the greatest market enrollment.

- The metropolitan area continues to add employment opportunities at a growth rate of 22 percent, but the area economy suffers from some of the same insecurities about the future as do other areas.

- Information technology is creating more customer potential and new demands for the delivery of coursework as well as generating new opportunities for competitors to enter this educational market.

- The pace of change is forcing people at all levels of the economy to learn new skills at the same time people are being asked to work harder—and sometimes hold more than one job.

- The new school improvement plan has not taken shape as quickly as anticipated, but a move toward mastering skills and testing for proficiencies—not rote knowledge—is gaining momentum.

Letter and Memo Mastery

- Format block and modified block letters with special features.
- Create e-mail and format interoffice memos.
- Use memo templates for efficiency.
- Prove keyboarding skills.

LESSON 64

Block Letter Format

SKILLBUILDING

64a
Warmup
Key each line twice SS.

alphabet	1	Judging by that quick quiz quality, were my extra videos helpful?
1st/2nd fingers	2	Using a good browser to connect to the Internet will please Benny.
figure/symbol	3	Their new garden (10' wide x 23' long) will cost 48% of $13,695.72.
long words	4	Expect physiological or psychological reactions to unusual works.

| 1 | 2 | 3 | 4 | 5 | 6 | 7 | 8 | 9 | 10 | 11 | 12 | 13 |

64b
Timed Writings
Take a 1' writing on each paragraph and a 3' writing on both paragraphs.

  all letters

gwam 1' | 3'

Do you ever "goof off" for an hour or more with a television program or a visit on the telephone and realize later that you haven't actually enjoyed your leisure? Each nagging little vision of homework or chores to be completed always seems to result in taking the edge off your pleasure. And then you must hurriedly complete whatever you postponed. Why do so many people end up rushing around in a frenzy, trying to meet their deadlines?

First, do not waste time feeling guilty. Check with your friends who always seem ready for a good time but are also ready for unexpected quizzes. Learn their secrets to managing time. Knowing that there are sixty seconds in every minute and sixty minutes in each hour, you can schedule your activities into the time available. Second, learn to set priorities. You can achieve your plans and enjoy your leisure as well.

12	4
25	8
38	13
51	17
64	21
76	25
88	29
12	33
25	38
37	42
50	46
63	50
76	55
85	58

1' | 1 | 2 | 3 | 4 | 5 | 6 | 7 | 8 | 9 | 10 | 11 | 12 | 13 |
3' | 1 | 2 | 3 | 4 |

Skillbuilding and Newsletters

SKILLBUILDING

59a
Warmup
Key each line twice.

alphabetic	1	Jimmy Favorita realized that we must quit playing by six o'clock.
figure	2	Joell, in her 2001 truck, put 19 boxes in an annex at 3460 Marks.
double letter	3	Merriann was puzzled by a letter that followed a free book offer.
easy	4	Ana's sorority works with vigor for the goals of the civic corps.

| 1 | 2 | 3 | 4 | 5 | 6 | 7 | 8 | 9 | 10 | 11 | 12 | 13 |

59b
Technique Builder
Key each set of lines three times; work at a controlled rate.

adjacent reaches	5	Is assessing potential important in a traditional career program?
	6	I saw her at an airport at a tropical resort leaving on a cruise.
direct reach	7	Fred kicked a goal in every college soccer game in June and July.
	8	Ned used their sled on cold days and my kite on warm summer days.
double letters	9	Bobby Lott feels that the meeting at noon will be cancelled soon.
	10	Pattie and Tripp meet at the swimming pool after football drills.

59c
Timed Writings
Take two 3' writings.

  all letters

	gwam	3'	5'

Surrogate grandparents and pet therapy might not be the types   4 | 2

of terms that you expect to find in a medical journal, but they are   9 | 5

concepts that are quite popular with senior citizens. Two of the   13 | 8

most common problems experienced by senior citizens who do not live   18 | 11

with or near a family member are loneliness and the craving to feel   22 | 13

needed and loved.   23 | 14

    Senior citizens who are healthy and who are stable mentally   27 | 16

often can have a high-quality relationship with deprived children   32 | 19

who do not have grandparents of their own. They often have time to   36 | 22

spare and the desire to give these needy children extra attention   41 | 24

and help with their school work and other needs. At first, it may   45 | 27

seem that children gain the most from relationships with seniors.   49 | 30

However, it soon becomes evident that the surrogate grandparents   54 | 32

tend to benefit as much or even more than the children.   57 | 34

| 3' | 1 | 2 | 3 | 4 |
| 5' | 1 | 2 | 3 |

63e

Opposite-Hand Combinations
Concentrate as you key each line for accuracy.

TIP
Key fluently, without rushing.

br/rb
15 break barb brawn orbit brain carbon brakes barbecue brazen barber
16 Barbara Brady brought us a new brand of barbecue to eat at break.

ce/ec
17 cease decide cent collect cell direct cedar check center peck ice
18 Cecil recently received a check for his special barbecue recipes.

mu/um
19 mull dumb must human mud lumber mulch lump mumps slump music fume
20 Bum Muse must have dumped too much muddy mulch on the bumpy lawn.

nu/un
21 nut sun fun nurse gun sinus number punch nuzzle pound lunch until
22 Uncle Gunta, a nurse, was uneasy about numerous units unionizing.

gr/rg
23 grade merge grand purge great large grab organ green margins gray
24 Margo, our great grandmother, regrets merging those large groups.

ny/yn
25 Wayne any shyness many agony balcony Jayne lynx penny larynx myna
26 Wayne and Jayne fed many skinny myna birds on that sunny balcony.

63f

Timed Writings
Take one 5' writing. Strive for good control.

  all letters

	gwam	1'	5'

The job market today is quite different than it was a few | 12 | 2
years ago.   The fast track to management no longer exists. | 24 | 5
Entry-level managers find that it is much more difficult to | 36 | 7
obtain a promotion to a higher-level position in management than | 49 | 10
it was just a few years ago.   People who are in the market for | 61 | 12
new jobs find very few management positions available.   In fact, | 74 | 15
many managers at all levels have a difficult time keeping their | 87 | 17
current management positions.   Two factors seem to contribute | 99 | 20
heavily to the problem.   The first factor is the trend toward | 112 | 22
self-managed teams.   The second factor is that as companies | 124 | 25
downsize they often remove entire layers of management or an | 136 | 27
entire division. | 140 | 28

Layoffs are not new;   but, what is new is that layoffs are | 12 | 30
affecting white-collar workers as well as blue-collar workers. | 24 | 33
Coping with job loss is a new and frustrating experience for many | 38 | 35
managers.   A person who has just lost a job will have concerns | 50 | 38
about personal security and welfare, and the concerns are com- | 63 | 40
pounded when families are involved.   The problem, however, is | 75 | 43
more than just an economic one.   Job loss often damages an in- | 87 | 45
dividual's sense of self-worth.   An individual who does not have | 100 | 48
a good self-concept will have a very hard time selling himself | 112 | 50
or herself to a potential employer. | 120 | 52

1' | 1 | 2 | 3 | 4 | 5 | 6 | 7 | 8 | 9 | 10 | 11 | 12 | 13 |
5' | | 1 | | | 2 | | | 3 | |

Columns

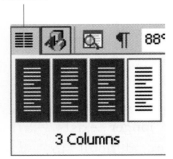

3 Columns

Columns

Text may be formatted in multiple columns on a page to make it easier to read. A newsletter, for example, is usually formatted in columns. Typically, newsletters are written in an informal, conversational style and are formatted with **banners** (text that spans multiple columns), newspaper columns, graphic elements, and other text enhancements. In newspaper columns, text flows down one column and then to the top of the next column. A simple, uncluttered design with a significant amount of white space is recommended to enhance the readability of newsletters.

To create columns of equal width:

1. Click the **Columns** button on the Standard toolbar.

2. Drag to select the number of columns. Using this method to create columns will format the entire document with columns of equal widths.

Column format may be applied before or after keying text. If columns are set before text is keyed, use Print Layout View to check the appearance of the text. Generally, column formats are easier to apply after text has been keyed.

Occasionally, you may want certain text (such as a banner or headline) to span more than one column.

To format a banner:

1. Select the text to be included in the banner.

2. Click the **Columns** button, and drag the number of columns to one.

To balance columns:

To balance columns so that all columns end at the same point on the page, position the insertion point at the end of the text to be balanced and insert a **Continuous section break (Insert, Break, Continuous, OK)**.

To force the starting of a new column:

1. Position the insertion point where the new column is to start.

2. From the Insert menu, choose **Break**.

3. Click **Column break**.

DRILL 1   SIMPLE COLUMNS

1. Open **Training** from the data files. Save it as **59d-drill1**.
2. Click **Columns** and format the document in three even columns. Preview to see how it looks.
3. Format the same document in two columns and balance the columns. Preview to check the appearance.

4. Select the heading **Productivity Enhancement Program**; click **Columns** and select one column. Double space below the heading. Apply 24 point. Center-align the heading. Save again and close.

63d-d1
Editing Review

1. Position the main heading at approximately 2" and key the text below.

2. Save as **63d-d1**. Print. Leave the document on the screen and continue with **63d-d2**.

Looking for a new computer? ← *caps, bold, center, 22-point font*
DS
Fewer and fewer buyers are buying a new desktop computer when the time comes to replace their old one. Laptops have become the "way to go," as the price gap between the 2 has gotten smaller. The decrease in price has resulted in consumers shedding their 60-pound desktop computers in favor of the smaller, lighter laptop computers.

What are consumers looking for in a laptop computer?

- Batteries with a longer life—laptop computers that can be used away from a power outlet as long as possible.

- Powerful microprocessors—with advances in technology, consumers want laptops that have more processing power to meet the requirements of the high-end applications that are becoming more and more common.

- DVD players—with more and more software becoming available on DVDs, users are requiring the ability to play DVDs and *burn* DVDs on the laptop.

Since battery life is a major concern for consumers, manufacturers have been developing some power-saving steps on laptops that can extend the battery time. Axiom has created SlowDoze, which drops the speed of the processor when it is running on battery power. JumpStart shuts down the processor during periods of inactivity, and instantly turns it back on when it is necessary.

Visit our Web site for more information ← *bold, italics, center, 16-point font*

http://www.laptops-r-us.com ← *bold, center, red, 18-point font*

63d-d2
Editing Review

1. Open **63d-d1**.
2. Change the left and right margins to 1".
3. Spell out the number 2 in the first paragraph.
4. Italicize *SlowDoze* and *JumpStart* in the last paragraph.
5. Change the bullets to numbers.
6. Save as **63d-d2**. Print.

Wrap Text Around Graphics

When graphic elements are included in documents such as newsletters, text usually wraps around the graphic.

To wrap text around graphics:

1. Insert the graphic; then place the insertion point over the graphic and right-click.

2. Select **Format picture** to display the Format Picture dialog box.

3. Click the **Layout** tab, and select the desired wrapping style (**Square**).

4. Click the desired alignment (**Right**), and then click **OK**.

DRILL 2   WRAP TEXT AROUND GRAPHIC

1. Open **Productivity** from the data files. Save as **59d-drill2**.

2. Go to the end of the document and select the graphic. Change handles to moving handles (click the **Text Wrapping** icon on the Picture toolbar; click **Square**).

3. Move the graphic and position it before the paragraph that begins with *Integration*. Work patiently.

4. Wrap the text around the graphic using square wrapping and center alignment.

   a. Right-click the graphic. Select **Format Picture**.

   b. Click the **Layout** tab, and select **Square** wrapping and **Center** alignment.

5. If the graphic moves to the left column, drag it back so it is positioned above the *Integration* paragraph. Be sure it is center aligned.

6. Preview and print when you are satisfied.

APPLICATIONS

59e-d1
Newsletter

1. Key the newsletter shown on the next page. Use .5" left and right margins, and apply what you have learned.

2. Key the main heading, **Arena Update**, using Albertus Extra Bold, 48 point, and dark red text color.

3. Insert clip art files, as shown in the newsletter. You may substitute any appropriate clip art you find if you cannot find the same images. Wrap the text around the graphics.

4. Use 18-point Albertus Medium type for the internal headings in the newsletter.

5. Balance columns so that all columns end at about the same place.

6. Create a double-line page border that is dark red and 1 ½ point.

7. Save the document as **59e-d1**.

Skillbuilding and Editing Review

SKILLBUILDING

63a
Warmup
Key each line twice SS.

alphabet 1 We analyzed why my quick proxy fight was not over the objectives.
figures 2 Follow players number 18, 92, 40, and 57 to room 36 for more fun.
shift key 3 Mr. Jeff Smith called Ms. Helene Snow on Monday, April 15, in NY.
easy 4 He puts half the money he earns into the boxes and half in banks.

| 1 | 2 | 3 | 4 | 5 | 6 | 7 | 8 | 9 | 10 | 11 | 12 | 13 |

63b
Technique Builder
Improve keyboarding technique.
Key at a controlled rate.

home row 5 A lad has been hard at work all day; Sal and Dallas had to help.
6 Sally and Jill also had Les Fasladd fill the large salad dishes.

third row 7 Take Wes to the plane to see if Patty is ready for a quick tour.
8 Ray and Roy took a trip to walk with two pretty twins in Queens.

first row 9 Vic and Ben came to show Manny the excellent new victory banner.
10 Benny is excited about the new banners that help bring in money.

right hand 11 Start grading the tests before the exercises for Ted and Saddie.
12 Dale and Dave are trading recipes for salsa, salads, and cookies.

left hand 13 Pay Kip for the many long hours he put in joining the old lines.
14 Jill likes how my mom opens up her home to many homeless people.

| 1 | 2 | 3 | 4 | 5 | 6 | 7 | 8 | 9 | 10 | 11 | 12 | 13 |

63c
Timed Writings
Take two 3' writings. Strive for good control.

 all letters

gwam 3' 5'

If you wish to advance in your career, you must learn how to make good decisions. You can develop decision-making skills by learning to follow six basic steps. The first three steps help you to see the problem. They are identifying the problem, analyzing the problem to find causes and consequences, and making sure you define the goals that your solution must meet.

Now, you are ready to solve the problem with the last three steps. They include finding alternative solutions to the problem, analyzing each of the alternatives carefully to locate the best solution, and putting the best solution into action. Once you have implemented a plan of action, check to make sure that it meets all of your objectives. If it does not, then determine if the problem is with the solution or with the way it is being implemented. Always keep all options open.

4 | 2 | 37
8 | 5 | 39
13 | 8 | 42
17 | 10 | 44
21 | 13 | 47
25 | 15 | 49
29 | 17 | 52
33 | 20 | 54
37 | 22 | 57
41 | 25 | 59
46 | 27 | 62
50 | 30 | 64
54 | 33 | 67
57 | 34 | 69

3' | 1 | 2 | 3 | 4 |
5' | 1 | 2 | 3 |

Arena Update

Get Your Shovels Ready!

The architects have put the final touches on the arena plans and the groundbreaking has been scheduled for March 18. Put the date on your calendar and plan to be a part of this exciting time. The Groundbreaking Ceremony will begin at 5:00 at the new arena site. After the ceremony, you will join the architects in the practice facility for refreshments and an exciting visual presentation of the new arena. The party ends when we all join the Western Cougars as they take on the Central Lions for the final conference game.

Cornerstone Club Named

Robbie Holiday of the Cougars Club submitted the winning name for the new premium seating and club area of the new arena. Thanks to all of you who submitted suggestions for naming the new club. For his suggestion, which was selected from over 300 names submitted, Robbie has won season tickets for next year and the opportunity to make his seat selection first. The Cornerstone Club name was selected because members of our premium clubs play a crucial role in making our new arena a reality. Without the financial support of this group, we could not lay the first cornerstone of the arena.

Cornerstone Club members have first priority in selecting their seats for both basketball and hockey in a specially designated section of the new arena. This section provides outstanding seats for both basketball games and hockey matches. Club members also have access to the Cornerstone Club before the game, during halftime, and after the

game. They also receive a parking pass for the lot immediately adjacent to the arena. If you would like more information about the Cornerstone Club and how you can become a charter member of the club, call the Cougars Club office during regular business hours.

What View Would You Like?

Most of us would like to sit in our seats and try them out before we select them rather than look at a diagram of the seating in the new arena. Former Cougar players make it easy for you to select the perfect angle to watch the ball go in the basket. Mark McKay and Jeff Dunlap, using their patented Real View visualization software, make it possible

for you to experience the exact view you will have from the seats you select. In fact, they encourage you to try several different views. Most of the early testers of the new seat selection software reported that they came in with their minds completely made up about the best seats in the house. However, after experiencing several different views with the Real View software, they changed their original seat location request.

62d-d1
Document with Bullets

1. At about 2.1", center and bold the heading **PROTECT YOUR COMPUTER**; then strike ENTER twice before keying the paragraphs below.
2. Align-justify the first and last paragraphs.
3. Use **Increase Indent** to indent the bulleted items to 1"; align the numbered paragraphs at the left margin.
4. Right-align your name and the current date DS below the last paragraph; save as **62d-d1** and print.

Connecting your PC to the Internet means that you need to have antivirus software and a firewall. Not having this protection is similar to leaving the front door of your home open when you go away on vacation, just inviting anyone in. You might be lucky and not have any intruders, but there is still the risk.

Some ways that you can help keep your computer safe and protected are:

- install a firewall on every computer
- use a firewall that is bidirectional
- use an antivirus software

There are two types of firewalls that can be installed to provide your computer with adequate protection. Choose the one that will best suit your needs.

1. **Hardware firewalls.** A hardware firewall needs to be installed between the terminal or network and the Internet. The firewall can be set to block or allow all packets passing in and out through various ports. Hardware firewalls are much preferred over software firewalls because they do not impede the end user. The major disadvantage of a hardware firewall is the cost; it can easily cost thousands of dollars.

2. **Software firewall.** A software firewall is much less expensive and often can be downloaded from the Internet free of charge. Software firewalls are often loaded on computers used in the home and small businesses.

Once you have installed your virus software and firewall, make sure that you get the updates and patches to the software on a regular basis. This is extremely important with the virus software, as new viruses are constantly being created. Most virus software are updated weekly, but some are updated as often as daily.

Student Name
Current date

62d-d2
Edit Document

1. Open **62d-d1**.
2. Change the paragraphs to DS; tab at the beginning of each ¶. SS the bulleted lines and the numbered paragraphs.
3. Align the numbered paragraphs at .5" (select the ¶s and click the **Increase Indent** button twice).
4. Change the heading to 14-point font and delete one hard return above the heading to make the document fit on one page. Save as **62d-d2**. Print.

1. Key the text below; SS between numbered items.

2. Create two columns of equal width; balance the columns so that both columns end at about the same point.

3. At the right of two of the numbered items, insert an appropriate graphic. Wrap text around the graphics using squaring wrapping and right alignment; size the graphic appropriately.

4. Save as **59e-d2**.

TIPS ON CULTURE AND CUSTOMS

North American business executives need knowledge of customs and practices of their international business partners. The following suggestions provide an important starting point for understanding other cultures.

1. Know the requirement of hand shaking. Taking the extra moment to shake hands at every meeting and again on departure will reap benefits.

2. Establish friendship first if important for that culture. Being a friend may be important first; conducting business is secondary. Establish a friendship; show interest in the individual and the family. Learn people's names and pronounce them correctly in conversation.

3. Understand the meaning of time. Some cultures place more importance on family, personal, and church-related activities than on business activities. Accordingly, they have longer lunches and more holidays. Therefore, they place less importance on adherence to schedules and appointment times.

4. Understand rank. Protocol with regard to who takes precedence is important; i.e., seating at meetings, speaking, and walking through doorways. Do not interrupt anyone.

5. Know the attitudes of space. Some cultures consider 18 inches a comfortable distance between people; however, others prefer much less. Adjust to their space preferences. Do not move away, back up, or put up a barrier, such as standing behind a desk.

6. Understand the attitude of hospitality. Some cultures are generous with hospitality and expect the same in return. For example, when hosting a party, prepare a generous menu; finger foods would be considered "ungenerous."

7. Share their language appropriately. Although the business meeting may be conducted in English, speak the other language in social parts of the conversation. This courteous effort will be noted.

Skillbuilding and Editing Review

SKILLBUILDING

62a
Warmup
Key each line twice SS.

alphabet	1	With zeal the boy quickly jumped over the x-ray, avoiding a fall.
figures	2	Invoice #13579 for $24.80 will be released on or before 06/15/03.
adjacent reaches	3	Were we going to open the voice track before we check any others?
easy	4	I will call you this week to see if you can act in our new plays.

| 1 | 2 | 3 | 4 | 5 | 6 | 7 | 8 | 9 | 10 | 11 | 12 | 13 |

62b
Technique Builder
Improve keyboarding technique.
Key each pair of lines 3 times.
Key at a controlled rate.

| az | 5 | Zen and Ozzie zealously played the anthem in the Aztec Jazz band. |
| | 6 | Batz went to Phoenix, Arizona to take a math quiz that he missed. |

| by | 7 | Boyd drove by the Blue Bayou to bypass the road block at the Bay. |
| | 8 | By daybreak, Mary will stop by to bake a birthday cake for Jayne. |

| cx | 9 | Please carry the X-ray from exit C to exit X for Cece and Xavier. |
| | 10 | Carol can meet Xian at the exit doors following the movie Exodus. |

| dw | 11 | Don walked the dog at dawn when he dwelled in his downtown condo. |
| | 12 | Did Dwight drive Wendy to the new drive-in or the new drive-thru? |

| figures | 13 | The 12 teams spent $3,489.00 on groceries for the 567 boy scouts. |
| | 14 | Judy's 13 puzzles had 60,789 pieces, but 524 pieces were missing. |

| 1 | 2 | 3 | 4 | 5 | 6 | 7 | 8 | 9 | 10 | 11 | 12 | 13 |

62c
Timed Writings
Take two 1' writings and two 3'
writings at your control rate.

  all letters

gwam 3'

One of the most important skills needed for success on the   4 | 42
job is listening.   However, this is a skill that takes hours of   8 | 46
practice.   You can maximize your effectiveness by learning and   12 | 50
using techniques for effective listening.   People can listen two   17 | 55
or three times faster than they can talk.   Use the difference be-   21 | 59
tween the rate at which a person speaks and the rate at which you   25 | 63
can listen to review what the person has said and to identify the   30 | 68
main ideas communicated.   This active style of listening helps   34 | 72
you avoid the tendency to tune in and out of a conversation.   38 | 76

3' | 1 | 2 | 3 | 4 |

SKILLBUILDING

60a
Warmup
Key each line twice.

alphabetic	1	Jayne Cox puzzled over workbooks that were required for geometry.
figures	2	Edit pages 308 and 415 in Book A; pages 17, 29, and 60 in Book B.
one hand	3	Plum trees on a hilly acre, in my opinion, create no vast estate.
easy	4	If they sign an entitlement, the town land is to go to the girls.

| 1 | 2 | 3 | 4 | 5 | 6 | 7 | 8 | 9 | 10 | 11 | 12 | 13 |

60b
Timed Writings
Take one 3' and one 5' writing at your control level.

  all letters

gwam 3' | 5'

	3'	5'
What is a college education worth today? If you asked that	4	2
question to a random sample of people, you would get a wide range of	9	5
responses. Many would respond that you cannot quantify the worth of	13	8
a bachelor's degree. They quickly stress that many factors other	18	11
than wages enhance the quality of life. They tend to focus on the	22	13
benefits of sciences and liberal arts and the appreciation they	26	16
develop for things that they would never have been exposed to if	31	18
they had not attended college.	33	20
Data show, though, that you can place a value on a college	37	22
education—at least in respect to wages earned. Less than twenty	41	25
years ago, a high school graduate earned only about fifty percent	45	27
of what a college graduate earned. Today, that number is quite	50	30
different. The gap between the wages of a college graduate and	54	32
the wages of a high school graduate has more than doubled in the	58	35
last twenty years.	59	36
The key factor in economic success is education. The new	63	38
jobs that pay high wages require more skills and a college degree.	68	41
Fortunately, many high school students do recognize the value of	72	43
getting a degree. Far more high school graduates are going to	76	46
college than ever before. They know that the best jobs are jobs	81	48
for knowledge workers and those jobs require a high level of skill.	85	51

3' | 1 | 2 | 3 | 4 |
5' | 1 | 2 | 3 |

APPLICATIONS

60c
Assessment

 Continue

 Check

With CheckPro: When you complete a document, proofread it, check the spelling, and preview for placement. When you are completely satisfied with the document, click the **Continue** button to move to the next document. You will not be able to return and edit a document once you continue to the next document. Click the **Check** button when you are ready to error-check the test. Review and/or print the document analysis results.

Without CheckPro: On the signal to begin, key the documents in sequence. When time has been called, proofread the document again and identify errors.

61e-d1
Document with Tabs

1. Center the main heading **NEW COMPUTER LAB HOURS** at about 2"; then DS and key the text below.
2. Set left tabs at 1.25" and 3.25" to key the columns of text. Save as **61c-d1** and print.

State budget cuts and reduction of revenue to our district require that the computer lab, located on the first floor of the Business/CIS building, reduce the number of hours of operation.

The new lab hours will be effective beginning Monday, May 1, 200-.

Monday	9:00 a.m. to 8:00 p.m.
Tuesday	10:00 a.m. to 9:00 p.m.
Wednesday	8:30 a.m. to 7:30 p.m.
Thursday	9:00 a.m. to 3:00 p.m.
Friday/Saturday	Closed

Please announce the new lab hours to all your students so they can adjust their schedules accordingly. The new hours will be posted on the lab doors and on the sign-in terminals.

61e-d2
Edit Document

TIP
Review "Proofreaders' Marks" in the Reference Guide.

1. Open **61e-d1**. Change the paragraphs to DS. The column text remains SS. Insert a tab at the beginning of each paragraph.
2. Change the closing hour on Thursday to 9:00 p.m. Delete Friday/Saturday.
3. Move the line beginning with "The new lab hours . . ." and the columns of text to a DS below the last paragraph.
4. Search for the word *lab* and replace it with *laboratory*. Save as **61e-d2**.

61e-d3
Document with Proofreaders' Marks

1. Set 2" side margins; then key the copy below. Make the changes as shown.
2. Create a 2-column, 5-row table a DS below the last ¶, and key the column text shown in **61e-d1**.
3. Center the document vertically on the page. Save as **61e-d3**.

I have received numerous complaints from staff members over the past few weeks regarding their telephone messages. I was told that the phone messages contained misspelled names of callers, wrong telephone numbers, and the date and time the message was taken was not filled in. It is important that our sales and support staff recieve complete and acurate telephone messages. The telephone company will be providing a Customer Service Seminar from 9:00 - 12:00 on Friday, May 15th in conference room 2. Please arrage for all your office staff to be present. *I have arranged for switchboard coverage during these hours.*

1. Key a newsletter using the information that follows.

2. Set page margins for a 1" top margin and .5" side margins.

3. Key the document. Use 12-point Times New Roman for body text.

4. Format the document using two equal columns with .5" spacing between columns.

5. Create a banner heading using Comic Sans MS font, 26 point, and indigo text color.

6. Create a paragraph border around the last paragraph. Choose 5% gray shading and 2 $1/4$-point solid dark red shadow border.

7. Create a triple-line page border that is dark red and $1/2$ point.

8. Insert an appropriate clip art and center it at the bottom of the second column.

9. Preview, save as **60c-d1**, and print.

LEAGUE BASKETBALL RULES
Fourth Grade Division

1. Games consist of four 6-minute quarters. If necessary, two overtime periods are added. After two overtimes, teams will enter into a free throw shootoff.

2. Four players must be present to start a game and must arrive at least five minutes before game time.

3. An intermediate-sized ball and an eight-foot goal are used.

4. Games are half court, and each team must take it back after change of possession. When possession changes, the new offensive team will take the ball out of bounds in the back court. Each team receives three time-outs per game.

5. The clock runs continuously except for (1) the last two minutes of the fourth quarter, (2) during one-and-one free throws when the ball is handed to the shooter for the first shot, (3) during two-shot free throws when the ball is handed to the shooter for the second shot, and (4) for unusual delays according to the referee.

6. Players are limited to the same number of field goals per the grade of the league (three for third, four for fourth, etc.). However, players can make an unlimited number of free throws. Only shooting fouls result in free throws with the exception of one-and-ones after the seventh team foul.

7. All offensive players must be involved in the game. Too much one-on-one will result in an "isolation" violation.

8. All defenses must be player-to-player, but double-teaming is allowed within the three-point line. Within the lane, all defenders can go after the ball. Players may switch after picks or help if a defender loses his player.

9. Players are fouled out after committing five personal fouls.

10. Three-point shots and dunking are not allowed in this league.

For more detailed information on ball handling, passing, positions, shooting, defense, and offense, visit http://www.eteamz.com/basketball/instruction.

Ryan O'Bryant, Coach

Drill Practice

Key each set of drills 3 times; then repeat the timed writing on the previous page.

1st finger

5 fog the turn for yet gun bright got gut nor just fun you give Bob
6 burns turn fern fight found girl granny from Juan hunt minute him
7 The brave boy found his neighbor giving Juan taffy to go hunting.

2nd finger

8 ice ore keep kind kitten echo dickens chicken I kneel nick icicle
9 Pat saw pop swap pizza with Adam as he zipped past the pool hall.
10 Ike etched kittens, chickens, and icicles on Dee's knee with ink.

3rd and 4th fingers

11 swap zone we poll was lap pa asp zap wad sap saw wax papa sow wow
12 as pax own sass is well all pan will ax sew pot Paul few loop Pam
13 Debra averages six fewer servings of sweet dessert during Easter.

left hand

14 crazed bass averages dessert cedar badger affect braggart detects
15 beware greatest feet effects gag faster bazaar assess drawers ads
16 grease estate carafe awarded exerted get careers agrees beads ear
17 In my opinion, today anyone can play pool or monopoly with Jimmy.

right hand

18 honk million kimono pumpkin yolk poplin oil lumpy homily hoop lip
19 pill nylon million puppy uphill yoyo ninny opinion lion polio mum
20 Jimmy minimum pupil holly imply kinky monopoly pool union you ohm
21 Their neighbor's mangy dog and lame duck slept by a box of rocks.

balanced hand

22 neighbor papa tight shantytown usual worn downtown fork ensign am
23 coalfield ape fishbowl disorient ivory giant leprosy neurotic may
24 problem rogue whale theory ornament quench mandible jangle mentor
25 Their big naughty dog would torment us and ambush the wheelchair.

| 1 | 2 | 3 | 4 | 5 | 6 | 7 | 8 | 9 | 10 | 11 | 12 | 13 |

COMMUNICATION

61d

Standard Procedures for Proofreading and Saving a Document

1. Use Spelling and Grammar to check spelling when you have completed the document.
2. Proofread the document on-screen to be sure that it makes sense.
3. Preview the document, and check the overall appearance.
4. Create a new folder for each module to hold the exercises keyed in the module (**Module 10 Keys**).
5. Save the document with the exercise or drill name (**61e-d1**) in the module folder.
6. Print the document.
7. Compare the document to the source copy (textbook), and check that text has not been omitted or added. Revise, save, and print if necessary.

Module 8: Checkpoint

1. To insert clip art, choose _____ from the Insert menu.
2. To move clip art, you must first click the Text Wrapping button on the _____ toolbar.
3. A(n) _____ arrow is needed to move clip art.
4. A(n) _____arrow is needed to size clip art.
5. To change text color, click _____ on the Formatting toolbar.
6. Text columns that flow down one column to the top of the next column are known as _____ columns.
7. To force the starting of a column, choose Break from the _____ menu.
8. To balance columns so that all columns end at the same point, insert a(n) _____ at the end of the text.
9. To add a page border to a page, choose _____ from the Format menu.
10. Page borders can be added using various _____ styles, weights, and colors.

Performance Assessment

Document 1
Newsletter

1. Open **Safety Net** from the data files.
2. Change the side margins for the entire document to .75".
3. Format the main heading, *The Safety Net*, using Arial Black font, 48 point, and dark blue text color.
4. Format the document in two equal-sized columns with lines between columns.
5. Insert a picture of a handheld cell phone positioned at the left side of the column after the cell phone is mentioned in the text.
6. Insert a picture of an individual at a computer workstation after the ergonomics seminar has been introduced.
7. Adjust the newsletter so that it will fit on one page with balanced columns.
8. Print and save the document as **checkpoint 8d-1**.

Skillbuilding and Editing Review

- Improve keyboarding skills.
- Review setting and changing margins.
- Review inserting bullets and numbering.
- Review alignment.
- Review using indent.
- Review using font attributes.

LESSON 61

Skillbuilding and Editing Review

SKILLBUILDING

61a
Warmup
Key each line twice SS.

alphabet	1	Quickly quiz veterans for kinds of whims and big jig experiences.
figures	2	Why add 17%, 26%, and 47%, when others (380, 95) will do as well?
adjacent	3	Miss too many meetings called for noon and you will need to call.
easy	4	Do you see the new dog and cats that play in the yard each night?

| 1 | 2 | 3 | 4 | 5 | 6 | 7 | 8 | 9 | 10 | 11 | 12 | 13 |

61b
Timed Writings
Key two 1' writings at your top rate.
Key two 1' writings at your control rate.

 all letters

gwam 2'

Most men and women in executive positions accept travel as a 6 | 50
part of corporate life. At the same time, executives try to keep 13 | 57
time spent on the road to a minimum. Top management usually 19 | 63
supports the efforts to reduce travel time as long as effective- 25 | 70
ness is not jeopardized. One of the reasons for support is that 32 | 76
it is quite expensive for executives to travel. Other reasons 38 | 82
are that traveling can be tiring and frequently causes stress. 44 | 89

2' | 1 | 2 | 3 | 4 | 5 | 6 |

Selkirk Communications

- Apply keying, formatting, and word processing skills.
- Work independently and with few specific instructions.

Selkirk Communications

Selkirk Communications is a training company that is relocating its office from Spokane, Washington, to Nelson, Canada. As an administrative assistant, you will prepare a number of documents using many of the formatting and word processing skills you have learned throughout Lessons 26 to 60. Selkirk Communications uses the block letter format and unbound report style. Before you begin, add Selkirk Communications as autotext so that you do not have to key it repeatedly.

Document 1

Invitation

Format this document attractively. Use a 20-point font for the main heading and add a special text effect. Use a different font for the callouts (Place, Time, etc.), and 14-point font for the text.

Use a fancy bullet for the bulleted list. Position the document attractively on the page. Save it as **mod9-d1**.

OPEN HOUSE

Place:	Selkirk Communications 1003 Baker Street Nelson BC V1L 5N7
Time:	1:00-4:00 p.m.
Date:	Saturday and Sunday, April 27 and 28

Selkirk Communications is excited to open its tenth international communications office in downtown Nelson. Please plan to attend our open house.

Come in and meet our friendly staff and learn how we can help meet your training needs. Selkirk Communications specializes in:

- Customized Web-based learning programs designed to meet your needs
- Instructor-led training in our classroom or your facility
- Newsletters designed to meet your needs
- Authorized training center for Microsoft Office
- Oral and written communication refresher courses

Level 3

Mastering Document Design

OBJECTIVES

DOCUMENT DESIGN SKILLS
To format business correspondence with special features.

To enhance report formats with elements that add structure, provide a consistent image, and increase readability.

To format tables, forms, and financial documents.

WORD PROCESSING SKILLS
To apply many of the basic competencies.

COMMUNICATION SKILLS
To produce error-free documents and apply language arts skills.

KEYBOARDING
To improve keyboarding speed and accuracy.

Document 2

Memo with Table

Prepare this memo to the staff.

List the words in the table in alphabetical order. Use 10% blue shading in the first row.

Save the memo as **mod9-d2**.

TO:	All Staff, Spokane Branch
FROM:	Marilyn Josephson, Office Manager
SUBJECT:	American vs. Canadian Spelling
DATE:	Current

All correspondence addressed to our Canadian office should now include Canadian spelling. Some of the differences are shown in the following table. We will need to get a list of other words that differ as well.

U.S. Spelling	Canadian Spelling
counseling	counselling
honor	honour
endeavor	endeavour
defense	defence
center	centre
check (meaning money)	cheque
color	colour
marvelous	marvellous
labor	labour
theater	theatre

Document 3

Letter

Use Find and Replace to find and replace any words that should be changed to Canadian spellings.

Save the letter as **mod9-d3**.

Current date | Chamber of Commerce | 225 Hall Street | Nelson BC V1L 5X4 | CANADA | Ladies and Gentlemen

Selkirk Communications will be relocating its headquarters from Spokane, Washington, to downtown Nelson on April 1. We are an international communications company offering the following services:

1. Written and oral communications refresher workshops
2. Customized training onsite, in our training center, or Web-based learning programs
3. Mail-order newsletters
4. Computer training on popular business software
5. Individualized or group training sessions

I would like to attend the Nelson Chamber of Commerce meeting in March to share some of the exciting ways we can help Chamber members meet their training needs. Is there time available for us on your March agenda? Please contact Anthony Baker, public relations coordinator, at our Nelson office at (604) 555-0193.

Selkirk Communications will be holding an open house during the month of April, and we will be inviting you and the Nelson community to attend. We look forward to becoming actively involved with the business community of Nelson.

Yours truly | Richard R. Holmes, President

Internet Activities 2

Explore Search Engines

To find information on the World Wide Web (WWW), the best place to start is often a search engine. Search engines are used to locate specific information. Just a few examples of search engines are AltaVista, Excite, Google, AskJeeves, Lycos, and Yahoo.

 To go to a search engine, click on the **Search** button on your Web browser. (Browsers vary.)

DRILL

1. Go to the search engines on your browser. Click on the first search engine. Browse the hyperlinks available such as Maps, People Finder, News, Weather, Stock Quotes, Sports, Games, etc. Click each search engine and explore the hyperlinks.

2. Conduct the following search using Dogpile, a multithreaded search engine that searches multiple databases;

   a. Open the Web site for Dogpile (http://www.dogpile. com).

   b. In the Search entry box, key the keywords **American Psychological Association** publications; click **Go Fetch**.

3. Pick two of the following topics and search for each using three of your browser's search engines. Look over the first ten results you get from each search. Which search engine gave you the greatest number of promising results for each topic?

aerobics	antivirus software	career change
censorship	college financing	teaching tolerance

Activity 4

Search Yellow Pages

Searching the Yellow Pages for information on businesses and services is commonplace, both in business and at home. Let your computer do the searching for you the next time.

DRILL

1. Open the search engine dogpile.com. Click **Yellow Pages**.

2. Determine a city that you would like to visit. Assume you will need overnight accommodations. Use the Yellow Pages to find a listing of hotels in this city.

3. Your best friend lives in (*you provide the city*); you want to send him/her flowers. Find a listing of florists in this city.

4. You create a third scenario and find listings.

Document 4
Memo

Prepare this memo. Use Find and Replace to find and replace any words that should be changed to Canadian spellings. Save the memo as **mod9-d4**.

TO: Marilyn Smith, Public Relations Media Assistant | **FROM:** Anthony Baker, Public Relations Coordinator | **DATE:** Current | **SUBJECT:** Electronic Presentation

Richard Holmes has been invited to introduce our company at the March 15 meeting of the Nelson Chamber of Commerce. Please prepare a 20-minute electronic presentation for this meeting by extracting the key points from Richard's speech, which is attached.

As you prepare the presentation, remember these key points:

- Write phrases, not sentences, so that listeners focus on the key points.
- Use parallel structure and limit wraparound lines of text.
- Create *builds* to keep the audience alert.
- Add transitions between slides (suggest fade in and out).
- Add graphics and humor—we want them to remember us.

Please have the presentation ready for Richard to review by February 24. After he has made his revisions and the presentation is final, print the presentation as a handout. | xx | Attachment

Document 5
Table

Format this list of purchases as a table. Center the column headings and the data in column 1.

Calculate the total price for each item; then calculate the final total in cell D7. Save the table as **mod9-d5**.

Quantity	Description	Unit Price	Total Price
2	Posture back task chair	265.00	
2	Under-desk keyboard manager	54.00	
1	10 pack Zip 100 disks	99.95	
1	Carton laser paper (5,000 sheets, 20 lb.)	47.50	
2	Laser address labels, #5168	24.95	
	Total		

Document 6
Letter

Prepare this letter to order supplies. Copy the table you created in Document 5 into the letter. Use the current date and add an appropriate salutation.

Insert another row in the table just before the Total with this information: **2 external Zip drives at $89.99 each.** Recalculate the total.

Save the letter as **mod9-d6**.

West Coast Office Supplies
3245 Granville Street
Vancouver BC V6B 5S8

Please ship the following items, which are listed in your current office supplies catalogue.

Insert the table here (Document 5)

Please bill this to our account number 4056278. This order is urgent; therefore, ship it overnight by Loomis.

Yours truly

Allan Burgess, Purchasing Agent

Document 7
Multi-page Report with Table

Open **steeringcommittee** from the data files. Add the text at the right to the end of the document.

Watch closely for any errors that may not be marked. Check for words that need to be changed to Canadian spelling.

Number the pages at the top right.

Prepare a title page. The report was prepared for **Nelson Chamber of Commerce by Richard R. Holmes, President**. Date the report March 15.

Save the report as **mod9-d7**, and save the title page as **mod9-d7a**.

Recommended facilitators include: *teamleaders and* *(set this up as a table)* *the following*

Team	Team Leaders	Facilitators
Education	Dale Coppage, Nelson BC	Ellen Obert, Spokane WA
Youth Services	Lawrence Riveria, Portland, OR	Jack Jones, Vancouver BC
Recreation	Bradley Greger, Nelson BC	Carolos Pena, Calgary AB
Economic Development	Jon Guyton, Nelson BC	Harvey Lewis
Crime	Monica Brigham, Toronto ON	Shawn McNullan, NC

DS After the first breakout sessions, participants will join for lunch in the H. L. Calvert Union Building. The Steering Committee recommends that Mayor Alton johnson address the topic of meeting educational challenges of the *#* next century. A repeat of the morning breakout sessions will begin at 1:00 *a.m.* This repeat will allow participants to contirube to anicher topic. ~~In~~ *During* the closing session breakout facilitators will present the goals and plans to the audience.

Sponsors

The Steerting Committee has discussed the sponsorhsip of a goals conference with a number of partners in the Nelson area. The following organizations have agreed to serve as sponsors: Nelson Economic Development Foundation, Bank of Canada, Northeast Bottling Company, ~~and~~ Bank of Nelson, and Farthington's Clothiers.

Summary

The Steering Committee strongly recommends this goals conference. The committee will be avilable at the Camber *h* of commerce meeting to answer any questions.

Document 8
Agenda

Format the agenda as a table. Apply the **Table Normal** format. Save it as **mod9-d8**.

Goals Conference Agenda *→ all caps*

9:30 a.m. - 9:45 a.m.	Welcome
9:45 a.m. - 10:15 a.m.	Opening Remarks
	Overview of Community Quality Initiative
	Purpose of Goals Conference
	Process
	Introduction of Community Leaders and Chamber Officers
10:15 a.m. - 10:35 a.m.	Refreshment Break
10:35 a.m. - 12 noon	Breakout Sessions *— get these from the report; alphabetize*
12 noon - 1:00 p.m.	Lunch
	Speaker on Educational Challenges of the 21st Century
1:00 p.m. - 2:30 p.m.	~~Goals Setting Workshops~~ *Breakout Sessions*
2:30 p.m. - 2:45 p.m.	Refreshment Break
2:45 p.m. - 4:00 p.m.	Presentation of Goals

Reference Guide

Capitalize

1. First word of a sentence and of a direct quotation.

   We were tolerating instead of managing diversity.
   The speaker said, "We must value diversity, not merely recognize it."

2. Names of proper nouns—specific persons, places, or things.

   Common nouns: continent, river, car, street
   Proper nouns: Asia, Mississippi, Buick, State St.

3. Derivatives of proper nouns and geographical names.

   American history   English accent
   German food   Ohio Valley
   Tampa, Florida   Mount Rushmore

4. A personal or professional title when it precedes the name or a title of high distinction without a name.

   Lieutenant Kahn   Mayor Walsh
   Doctor Welby   Mr. Ty Brooks
   Dr. Frank Collins   Miss Tate
   the President of the United States

5. Days of the week, months of the year, holidays, periods of history, and historic events.

   Monday, June 8   Labor Day   Renaissance

6. Specific parts of the country but not compass points that show direction.

   Midwest   the South   northwest of town

7. Family relationships when used with a person's name.

   Aunt Helen   my dad   Uncle John

8. Noun preceding a figure except for common nouns such as line, page, and sentence.

   Unit 1   Section 2   page 2   verse 7   line 2

9. First and main words of side headings, titles of books, and works of art. Do not capitalize words of four or fewer letters that are conjunctions, prepositions, or articles.

   Computers in the News   Raiders of the Lost Ark

10. Names of organizations and specific departments within the writer's organization.

    Girl Scouts   our Sales Department

Number Expression

General guidelines

1. Use **words** for numbers *one* through *ten* unless the numbers are in a category with related larger numbers that are expressed as figures.

   He bought three acres of land. She took two acres.
   She wrote 12 stories and 2 plays in the last 13 years.

2. Use **words** for approximate numbers or large round numbers that can be expressed as one or two words. Use **numbers** for round numbers in millions or higher with their word modifier.

   We sent out about three hundred invitations.
   She contributed $3 million dollars.

3. Use **words** for numbers that begin a sentence.

   Six players were cut from the ten-member team.

4. Use **figures** for the larger of two adjacent numbers.

   We shipped six 24-ton engines.

Times and dates

5. Use **words** for numbers that precede o'clock (stated or implied).

   We shall meet from two until five o'clock.

6. Use **figures** for times with a.m. or p.m. and days when they follow the month.

   Her appointment is for 2:15 p.m. on July 26, 2000.

7. Use **ordinals** for the day when it precedes the month.

   The 10th of October is my anniversary.

Money, percentages, and fractions

8. Use **figures** for money amounts and percentages. Spell out cents and percent except in statistical copy.

   The 16% discount saved me $145; Bill, 95 cents.

9. Use **words** for fractions unless the fractions appear in combination with whole numbers.

   one-half of her lesson   5 1/2   18 3/4

Addresses

10. Use **words** for street names First through Tenth and **figures** or ordinals for streets above Tenth. Use **figures** for house numbers other than **one**. (If street name is a number, separate it from house number with a dash.)

    One Lytle Place   Second Ave.   142—534 St.

Punctuation

Use an apostrophe

1. To make most singular nouns and indefinite pronouns possessive (add **apostrophe** and **s**).

   computer + 's = computer's   Jess + 's = Jess's
   anyone's   one's   somebody's

2. To make a plural noun that does not end in s possessive (add **apostrophe** and **s**).

   women + 's = women's   men + 's = men's
   deer + 's = deer's   children + 's = children's

3. To make a plural noun that ends in s possessive. Add only the **apostrophe**.

   boys + ' = boys'   managers + ' = managers'

4. To make a compound noun possessive or to show joint possession. Add **apostrophe** and **s** to the last part of the hyphenated noun.

   son-in-law's   Rob and Gen's game

5. To form the plural of numbers and letters, add **apostrophe** and **s**. To show omission of letters or figures, add an **apostrophe** in place of the missing items.

   7's   A's   It's   add'l

Use a colon

1. To introduce a listing.

   The candidate's strengths were obvious: experience, community involvement, and forthrightness.

2. To introduce an explanatory statement.

   Then I knew we were in trouble: The item had not been scheduled.

Use a comma

1. After an introductory phrase or dependent clause.

   After much deliberation, the jury reached its decision. If you have good skills, you will find a job.

2. After words or phrases in a series.

   Mike is taking Greek, Latin III, and Chemistry II.

3. To set off nonessential or interrupting elements.

   Troy, the new man in MIS, will install the hard drive. He cannot get to the job, however, until next Friday.

4. To set off the date from the year and the city from the state.

   John, will you please reserve the center in Billings, Montana, for January 10, 2000.

5. To separate two or more parallel adjectives (adjectives could be separated by and instead of a comma).

   The loud, whining guitar could be heard above the rest.

6. Before the conjunction in a compound sentence. The comma may be omitted in a very short sentence.

   You must leave immediately, or you will miss your flight. We tested the software and they loved it.

7. Set off appositives and words of direct address.

   Karen, our team leader, represented us at the conference.
   Paul, have you ordered the CD-ROM drive?

Use a hyphen

1. To show end-of-line word division.

2. In many compound words—check a dictionary if unsure.
   - Two-word adjectives before a noun:

     two-car family
   - Compound numbers between twenty-one and ninety-nine.
   - Fractions and some proper nouns with prefixes/suffixes.

     two-thirds   ex-Governor   all-American

Use italic or underline

1. With titles of complete literary works.

   College Keyboarding   *Hunt for Red October*

2. To emphasize special words or phrases.

   What does *professional* mean?

Use a semicolon

1. To separate independent clauses in a compound sentence when the conjunction is omitted.

   Please review the information; give me a report by Tuesday.

2. To separate independent clauses when they are joined by conjunctive adverbs (*however*, *nevertheless*, *consequently*, etc.).

   The traffic was heavy; consequently, I was late.

3. To separate a series of elements that contain commas.

   The new officers are: Fran Pena, president; Harry Wong, treasurer; and Muriel Williams, secretary.

Use a dash

1. To show an abrupt change of thought.

   Invoice 76A—which is 10 days overdue—is for $670.

2. After a series to indicate a summarizing statement.

   Noisy fuel pump, worn rods, and failing brakes—for all these reasons I'm trading the car.

Use an exclamation point

After emphatic interjections or exclamatory sentences.

Terrific!   Hold it!   You bet!   What a great surprise!

Proofreading procedures

Proofread documents so that they are free of errors. Error-free documents send the message that you are detail-oriented and a person capable of doing business. Apply these procedures after you key a document.

1. Use Spelling.
2. Proofread the document on screen to be sure that it makes sense. Check for these types of errors:
   • Words, headings, and/or amounts omitted.
   • Extra words or lines not deleted during the editing stage.
   • Incorrect sequence of numbers in a list.
3. Preview the document on screen using the Print Preview feature. Check the vertical placement, presence of headers or footers, page numbers, and overall appearance.
4. Save the document again and print.
5. Check the printed document by comparing it to the source copy (textbook). Check all figures, names, and addresses against the source copy. Check that the document style has been applied consistently throughout.
6. If errors exist on the printed copy, revise the document, save, and print.
7. Verify the corrections and placement of the second printed copy.

Proofreaders' marks

Add horizontal space	#	Lowercase	/ or lc
Align	‖	Bold	~~~
Capitalize	Cap or ≡	Close up	⌒
Delete		Insert	∧
Insert quotation marks	∨ ∨	Underline or italic	——
Let it stand; ignore correction	… or stet		
Move left		Move right	
Move up		Move down	
Paragraph	¶	Spell out	sp
Transpose	or tr		

Word division

With the use of proportional fonts found in current word processing packages, word division is less of an issue. Occasionally, however, you will need to make decisions on dividing words, such as when using the Columns function. The following list contains generally accepted guidelines for dividing words.

1. Divide words between syllables only; therefore, do not divide one-syllable words.
2. **Short words:** Avoid dividing short words (five letters or fewer).
   area   bonus   since   ideal
3. **Double consonants:** Divide words with double consonants between the double letters unless the root word ends with the double letters. In this case, divide after the second consonant.
   mis-sion   trim-ming   dress-ing   call-ing
4. **One-letter syllables:** Do not divide after a one-letter syllable at the beginning of a word or before a one- or two-letter syllable at the end of a word; divide after a one-letter syllable within a word.
   enough   abroad   starter   friendly
   ani-mal   sepa-rate   regu-late
5. **Two single-letter syllables:** Divide between two single-letter syllables within a word.
   gradu-ation   evalu-ation
6. **Hyphenated words:** Compound words with a hyphen may be divided only after the hyphen.
   top-secret   soft-spoken   self-respect
7. **Figures:** Avoid dividing figures presented as a unit.
   #870331   190,886   1/22/02
8. **Proper nouns:** Avoid dividing proper nouns. If necessary, include as much of the proper noun as possible before dividing it.
   Thomas R./Lewiston   not Thomas R. Lewis/ton
   November 15,/2002   not November/ 15, 2002

Addressing procedures

The envelope feature inserts the delivery address automatically if a letter is displayed. Title case, used in the letter address, is acceptable in the envelope address. An alternative style for envelopes is uppercase with no punctuation.

Business letters are usually mailed in envelopes that have the return address preprinted; return addresses are printed only for personal letters or when letterhead is not available. The default size of *Word* is a size 10 envelope (4 1/8" by 9 1/2"); other sizes are available using the Options feature.

When preparing an envelope using an electronic typewriter, follow the spacing guidelines below:

Small envelope. On a No. 6 3/4 envelope, place the address near the center—about 2 inches from the top and left edges. Place a return address in the upper left corner.

Large envelope. On a No. 10 envelope, place the address near the center—about line 14 and .5" left of center. A return address, if not preprinted, should be keyed in the upper left corner (see small envelope).

An address must contain at least three lines; addresses of more than six lines should be avoided. The last line of an address must contain three items of information: (1) the city, (2) the state, and (3) the ZIP Code, preferably a 9-digit code.

Place mailing notations that affect postage (e.g., REGISTERED, CERTIFIED) below the stamp position (line 8); place other special notations (e.g., CONFIDENTIAL, PERSONAL) a DS below the return address.

Folding and inserting procedures

Large envelopes (No. 10, 9, 7 3/4)

Step 1	Step 2	Step 3

Step 1: With document face up, fold slightly less than 1/3 of sheet up toward top.

Step 2: Fold down top of sheet to within 1/2" of bottom fold.

Step 3: Insert document into envelope with last crease toward bottom of envelope.

Small envelopes (No. 6 3/4, 6 1/4)

Step 1	Step 2	Step 3

Step 1: With document face up, fold bottom up to 1/2" from top.

Step 2: Fold right third to left.

Step 3: Fold left third to 1/2" from last crease and insert last creased edge first.

Window envelopes (full sheet)

Step 1	Step 2	Step 3

Step 1: With sheet face down, top toward you, fold upper third down.

Step 2: Fold lower third up so address is showing.

Step 3: Insert document into envelope with last crease toward bottom of envelope.

Two-letter state abbreviations

Alabama, AL	Florida, FL	Kentucky, KY	Montana, MT	Ohio, OH	Texas, TX
Alaska, AK	Georgia, GA	Louisiana, LA	Nebraska, NE	Oklahoma, OK	Utah, UT
Arizona, AZ	Guam, GU	Maine, ME	Nevada, NV	Oregon, OR	Vermont, VT
Arkansas, AR	Hawaii, HI	Maryland, MD	New Hampshire, NH	Pennsylvania, PA	Virgin Islands, VI
California, CA	Idaho, ID	Massachusetts, MA	New Jersey, NJ	Puerto Rico, PR	Virginia, VA
Colorado, CO	Illinois, IL	Michigan, MI	New Mexico, NM	Rhode Island, RI	Washington, WA
Connecticut, CT	Indiana, IN	Minnesota, MN	New York, NY	South Carolina, SC	West Virginia, WV
Delaware, DE	Iowa, IA	Mississippi, MS	North Carolina, NC	South Dakota, SD	Wisconsin, WI
District of Columbia, DC	Kansas, KS	Missouri, MO	North Dakota, ND	Tennessee, TN	Wyoming, WY

Letter parts

Letterhead. Company name and address. May include other data.

Date. Date letter is mailed. Usually in month, day, year order. Military style is an option (day/month/year: 17/1/02).

Letter address. Address of the person who will receive the letter. Include personal title (*Mr., Ms., Dr.*); name, professional title, company, and address.

Salutation. Greeting. Corresponds to the first line of the letter address. Usually includes name and courtesy title; use *Ladies and Gentlemen* if letter is addressed to a company name.

Body. Message. SS; DS between paragraphs.

Complimentary close. Farewell, such as *Sincerely.*

Writer. Name and professional title. Women may include a personal title.

Initials. Identifies person who keyed the document (for example, *tr*). May include identification of writer (*ARB:trt*).

Enclosure. Copy is enclosed with the document. May specify contents.

Copy notation. Indicates that a copy of the letter is being sent to person named.

Block letter (open punctuation)

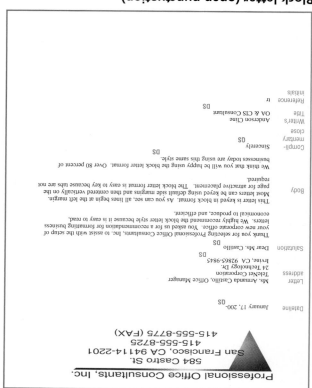

Professional Office Consultants, Inc.
584 Castro St.
San Francisco, CA 94114-2201
415-555-8725   415-555-8775 (FAX)

Dateline — January 17, 200-

Letter address — Ms. Amanda Castillo, Office Manager
TeleNet Corporation
24 Technology Dr.
Irvine, CA 92865-9845

Salutation — Dear Ms. Castillo

Body — Thank you for selecting Professional Office Consultants, Inc. to assist with the setup of your new corporate office. You asked us for a recommendation for formatting business letters. We highly recommend the block letter style because it is easy to read.

This letter is keyed in block format. As you can see, all lines begin at the left margin. Most letters can be keyed using default side margins and then centered vertically on the page for attractive placement. The block letter format is easy to key because tabs are not required.

We think that you will be happy using the block letter format. Over 80 percent of businesses today are using this same style.

Complimentary close — Sincerely

Writer's Title — Anderson Cline
OA & CIS Consultant

Reference initials — tr

Modified block letter (mixed punctuation)

IMAGE MAKERS
5131 Moss Springs Road
Columbia, SC 29209-4768
(803) 555-0127

October 27, 200-

Ms. Mary Bernard, President
Bernard Image Consultants
4927 Stuart Ave.
Baton Rouge, LA 70808-3519

Dear Ms. Bernard:

The format of this letter is called modified block. Modified block format differs from block format in that the date, complimentary close, and the signature lines are positioned at the center point.

Paragraphs may be blocked, as this letter illustrates, or they may be indented from the left margin. We suggest you block paragraphs when you use modified block style so that an additional tab setting is not needed. However, some people who use modified block format prefer indented paragraphs.

Although modified block format is very popular, we recommend that you use it only for those customers who request this letter style. Otherwise, we urge you to use block format, which is more efficient, as your standard style.

Both formats are illustrated in the enclosed *Image Makers Format Guide.* Please note that the block format is labeled "computer compatible."

Sincerely,

Patrick R. Ray
Communication Consultant

tr

Enclosure — Enclosure

Copy notation — c Scot Carl, Account Manager

Letter placement table

Length	Dateline position	Margins
Short: 1-2 ¶s	Center page	Default
Average: 3-4 ¶s	Center page or 2.1"	Default
Long: 4+ ¶s	2.1" (default + 6 hard returns)	Default

Default margins or a minimum of 1".

Envelope

IMAGE MAKERS
5131 Moss Springs Rd.
Columbia, SC 29209-4768

Ms. Mary Bernard, President
Bernard Image Consultants
4927 Stuart Avenue
Baton Rouge, LA 70808-3519

Personal business letter

Scott T. Fischer
1001 Hogan Street, Apt. 216A • Mobile, AL 36617-1001 • (334) 555-0103 • sfischer@cu.edu

August 13, 200- QS

Mr. Coleman Stanberry
Financial News
706 Kentwood Street
Honolulu, HI 96822 DS

Dear Mr. Stanberry DS

My bachelor's degree with double majors in graphic design and information technology and my graphic design work experience in the United States and Japan qualify me as a junior graphic designer for your international newspaper. DS

As a result of my comprehensive four-year program, I am skilled in the latest office suite as well as the current versions of desktop publishing and graphics programs. In addition, my excellent research and writing skills played a very important role in the Cother University Design Award I received last month. Being able to locate the right resources and synthesize that data into useful information for your readers is a priority I understand well and have practiced in my positions at the Cother University College Alumni Office and the Cother University Library. DS

My technical and communication skills were applied as well as I worked as the assistant director and producer of the *Cother University Alumni News*. I understand well the importance of meeting deadlines and also producing a quality product that will increase newspaper sales. Additionally, my intern experience in Japan provides me with a global view of international business and communication. DS

After you have reviewed the enclosed résumé as well as my graphic design samples located on my Web page at http://www.netdoor.~sfischer, I would look forward to discussing my qualifications and career opportunities with you at *Financial News*. DS

Sincerely QS

Scott T. Fischer DS

Enclosure

Special letter parts/features

Attention line. Directs the letter to a specific title or person within the company. Positioned as the first line of letter address; the salutation is *Ladies and Gentlemen.*

Company name. Company name of the sender is keyed in ALL CAPS a DS below complimentary close.

Enumerations. Hanging indent format; block format may be used if paragraphs are not indented.

Mailing notation. Provides record of how the letter was sent (FACSIMILE, CERTIFIED, REGISTERED) or how the letter should be treated by the receiver (CONFIDENTIAL). DS below date.

Postscript. Used to emphasize information; DS below last line of copy.

Reference line. Directs the reader to a source document such as an invoice. DS below letter address.

Return address. Sender's address in a personal business letter. The return address may be keyed immediately above the date or personal letterhead stationery may be used as shown at the left.

Second-page heading. Addressee's name, page number, date arranged in block format about 1" from the top edge. Second sheet is plain paper of the same quality as letterhead.

Subject line. Indicates topic of the letter; DS below salutation at left margin. It may be keyed in ALL CAPS or cap-and-lowercase.

Samantha's Fashions
422 Main St.
Wichita, KS 67202-1304 • (316) 125-3342

March 15, 200-

Attention Fashion Buyer
Amason Fashion Mart
4385 Felten Dr.
Hays, KS 67601-2863 DS

Ladies and Gentlemen DS

FALL FASHION CAMPAIGN DS

The demand for two of the items that were sent last week was

Attention line/Subject line

Your order should be shipped via Pony Express within the next two weeks.

Thank you for your order; we appreciate your business.

Sincerely DS

STYLES BY REX QS

Ms. Ellen Turnquist
General Manager

rt

Company name

MUSIC BY MAIL
3716 Rangely Dr.
New Haven, CT
06513-2257
(203) 156-8975

March 15, 200- DS

CERTIFIED MAIL DS

Mr. John West, Buyer
Tatnal Music Center
4385 Dove Ave.
Rigby, ID 83442-1244 DS

Re: Order No. R-3855 DS

Dear Mr. West

The items that you ordered last week were sent by overnight

Mailing notation/Reference line

.5"

Mr. Jason Artis
Page 2
April 9, 200- DS

You will need to perform the following steps:

1. Review the sample projects and proposed guidelines.
2. Determine the specific responsibilities of the project manager and put these in writing.

Thank you, Mr. Artis, for your cooperation. It is always a pleasure working with you.

Very truly yours

Second-page heading
Enumerated items (hanging indent format)

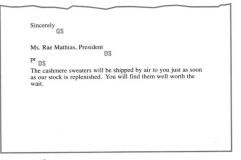

Turner Roofing Co.
10318 Rearview Ave.
Dayton, OH 45029-1927

CERTIFIED MAIL

Mr. Jack Brown
Quality Training Associates
28 Revina Drive
Atlanta, GA 30346-9105

Envelope with mailing notation

Sincerely QS

Ms. Rae Mathias, President DS

pr DS

The cashmere sweaters will be shipped by air to you just as soon as our stock is replenished. You will find them well worth the wait.

Postscript

Standard memo

Tab (1" from left margin)

1.5"

TO: Executive Committee
DS
FROM: Colleen Marshall
DS
DATE: November 8, 200-
DS
SUBJECT: Site Selection
DS

Please be prepared to make a final decision on the site for next year's Leadership Training Conference. Our staff reviewed the students' suggestions and have added a few of their own. The following information may be helpful as you make your decision:
DS
1. New York and San Francisco have been eliminated from consideration because of cost factors.
DS
2. New Orleans is still open for consideration even though we met there three years ago. New Orleans has tremendous appeal to students.
DS
3. Charleston, San Antonio, and Tampa were suggested by students as very desirable locations for the conference.
DS
Site selection will be the first item of business at our meeting next Wednesday. I'm attaching various hotel brochures for each site.
DS
xx
DS
Attachments

Standard memo with distribution list

Tab (1" from left margin)

1.5"

TO: Team Leaders
DS
FROM: Form Paragraph Task Force
DS
DATE: Current
DS
SUBJECT: Initial Meetings with Task Force
DS

The task force assigned the responsibility for developing form paragraphs to use in key departments of our company plans to work in your department beginning two weeks from today. Please assign two representatives from your department to coordinate the work with us.
DS
The procedure that the Executive Committee asked us to follow is to collect samples of typical correspondence, meet with departmental representatives to collect additional information, and then to prepare a draft of the form paragraphs for review. After we receive your feedback on the draft copy, we will schedule a meeting to finalize the paragraphs.
DS
Matthew Redfern has been assigned as the task force coordinator for your department. Please direct all communications about the project to him.
DS
xx
DS
Distribution List:
Nestor Garcia, Claims
Roberta Layman, Underwriting
Rosa Romero, Agency Services
Diana Wang, Business Services

Personal business letter

Current date

[The return address may be keyed immediately above the date, or you may create a personal letterhead as shown here.]

Janna M. Howard
587 Birch Cir.
Clinton, MS 39056-0587
(601) 555-4977

Mrs. Linda Chandler
Financial News
32 North Cruz St.
Hot Springs, AR 71913-0032

Dear Mrs. Chandler

My college degree in office systems technology and my graphics design job experience in the United States and Taiwan qualify me to function well as a junior graphic designer for your newspaper.

As a result of my comprehensive four-year program, I am skilled in the most up-to-date office suite packages as well as the latest version of desktop publishing and graphics programs. In addition, I am very skilled at locating needed resources on the information highway. In fact, this skill played a very important role in the design award that I received last month.

My technical and communication skills were applied as I worked as the assistant editor and producer of the *Cotner Alumni News*. I understand well the importance of meeting deadlines and also in producing a quality product that will increase newspaper sales.

After you have reviewed the enclosed resume, I would look forward to discussing my qualifications and career opportunities with you at *Financial News*.

Sincerely

Janna M. Howard

Enclosure

Resume

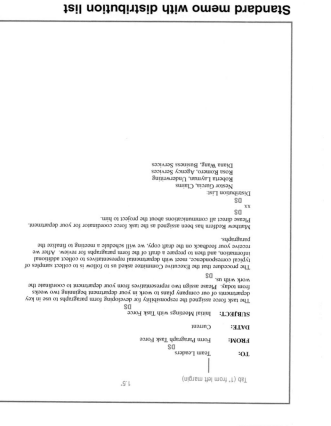

JANNA M. HOWARD

Permanent Address	Temporary Address (May 30, 2000)
587 Birch Cir.	328 Fondren St.
Clinton, MS 39056-0587	Orlando, FL 32801-0328
(601) 555-4977	(407) 555-3834

CAREER OBJECTIVE   To obtain a graphic design position with an opportunity to advance to a management position.

EDUCATION   *B.S. Office Systems Technology*, Cotner University, Mobile, Alabama. May 1998. Grade-point average: 3.8/4.0. Serve as president of Graphic Designers' Society.

SPECIAL SKILLS
Environments: *Microsoft Windows®* and *Macintosh®*
Application software: *Microsoft Office Professional/Windows 95®*, *PageMaker®*, *CorelDraw!*, *Harvard Graphics®*
Internet: *Netscape®*, *Mosaic®*
Keyboarding skill: 70 words per minute
Foreign language: Chinese
Travel: Taiwan (two summers working as graphic design intern)

EXPERIENCE
Cotner University Alumni Office, Mobile, Alabama. Assistant editor and producer of the *Cotner Alumni News*, 1997 to present.
• Work 25 hours per week.
• Design layout and production of six editions.
• Meet every publishing deadline.
• Received the "Cotner Design Award."

Cotner Library, Mobile, Alabama. Student Assistant in Audiovisual Library, 1996-1997.
• Worked 20 hours per week.
• Created *Audiovisual Catalog* on computerized database.
• Processed orders via computer.
• Prepared monthly and yearly reports using database.
• Edited and proofed various publications.

REFERENCES   Request portfolio from Cotner University Placement Office.

Standard unbound report

Margins: *Top* 2" for first page and reference page; 1" for succeeding pages; *Side* 1" or default; *bottom* 1".

Spacing: *Educational reports:* DS, paragraphs indented .5". *Business reports:* SS, paragraphs blocked with a DS between.

Page numbers: Second and subsequent pages are numbered at top right of the page. DS follows the page number.

Main headings: Centered; ALL CAPS; 14 pts.

Side headings: Bold; main words capitalized; DS above and below.

Paragraph headings: Bold; capitalize first word, followed by a period.

NOTE: Styles may also be used for headings.

Report documentation

Internal citations: Provides source of information within report. Includes the author's surname, publication date, and page number (Bruce, 2002, 129).

Footnotes: References cited in a report are often indicated within the text by a superscript number (. . . story.[1]) and a corresponding footnote with full information at the bottom of the same page where the reference was cited.

Bibliography or references: Lists all references, whether quoted or not, in alphabetical order by authors' names. References may be formatted on the last page of the report if they all fit on the page; if not, list on a separate, numbered page.

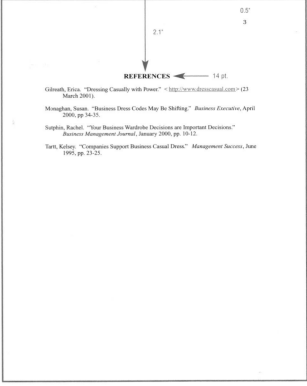

Reference page

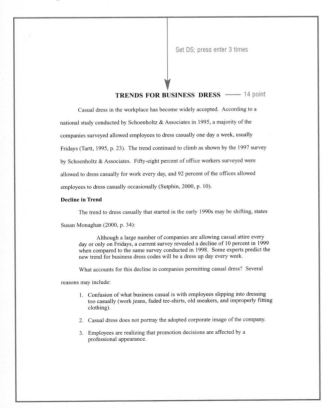

First page of unbound report

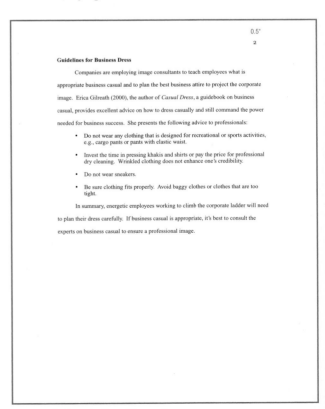

Second page of unbound report

Title page—leftbound

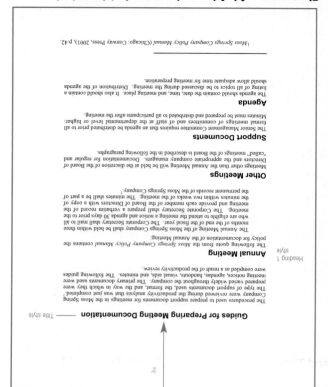

GUIDES FOR PREPARING MEETING DOCUMENTATION

Prepared for
Mr. Justin Markland
Executive Vice President

Prepared by
(Your name)
Administrative Manager

Current date

First page of leftbound report (with styles)

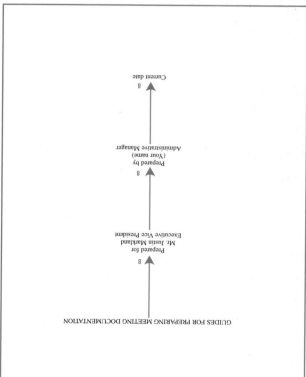

Guides for Preparing Meeting Documentation — Title style

The procedures used to prepare support documents for meetings in the Moss Spring Company were reviewed during the productivity analysis that was just completed. The type of support documents used, the format, and the way in which they were prepared varied widely throughout the company. The primary documents used were meeting notices, agendas, handouts, visual aids, and minutes. The following guides were compiled as a result of the productivity review.

Annual Meeting — Heading 1 style

The following quote from the *Moss Springs Company Policy Manual* contains the policy for documentation of the Annual Meeting.

The Annual Meeting of the Moss Springs Company shall be held within three months of the end of the fiscal year. The Corporate Secretary shall mail to all who are eligible to attend the meeting a notice and agenda 30 days prior to the meeting. The Corporate Secretary shall prepare a verbatim record of the meeting and provide each member of the Board of Directors with a copy of the minutes within two weeks of the meeting. The minutes shall be a part of the permanent records of the Moss Springs Company.[1]

Other Meetings

Meetings other than the Annual Meeting will be held at the discretion of the Board of Directors and the appropriate company managers. Documentation for regular and "called" meetings of the Board is described in the following paragraphs.

Support Documents

The Senior Management Committee requires that an agenda be distributed prior to all formal meetings of committees and of staff at the departmental level or higher. Minutes must be prepared and distributed to all participants after the meeting.

Agenda

The agenda should contain the date, time, and meeting place. It also should contain a listing of all topics to be discussed during the meeting. Distribution of the agenda should allow adequate time for meeting preparation.

[1]*Moss Springs Company Policy Manual* (Chicago: Conway Press, 2001), p.42.

Table of contents—leftbound

TABLE OF CONTENTS

DS

iii

Reference Page

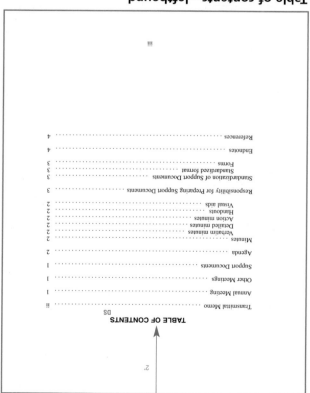

References

Altig, Scott. *Effective Meetings*. Philadelphia: Bay Publishing Co., 2001.

Maslin, Cameron. cmaslin@ProdCon.com. "Enhancing Productivity." The Moss Springs Company." E-mail to Patrick Demetrio, pdemetrio@wm.sc.edu 15 April 2001.

Moss Springs Company Policy Manual. Chicago, 2001.

FUNCTION SUMMARY

Function	Menu Command	Keyboard Shortcut	Toolbar Button
Alignment: Left, Center, Right, Justify	Format, Paragraph, Indents and Spacing tab		▤ ▤ ▤ ▤
AutoCorrect	Tools, AutoCorrect Options		
AutoFormat	Table, AutoFormat		
Autoshapes	Drawing toolbar		AutoShapes ▾
Borders: Page	Format, Borders and Shading		
Borders: Paragraph	Format, Borders and Shading, Border tab, Apply to Paragraph		
Bullets	Format, Bullets and Numbering		▤
Clip Art and Images	Insert, Picture, Clip Art		▣
Columns: Create	Click Columns button or Format, Columns		▦
Copy	Edit, Copy	Shift + F2	▣
Date and Time	Insert, Date and Time		
Double-underline	Format, Font, Underline style		
Envelopes and Labels	Tools, Letters and Mailings, Envelopes and Labels		
Font: Color	Format, Font		A ▾
Footnotes/Endnotes	Insert, Reference, Footnote, Insert. Move the insertion point before the reference and use Tab to indent it.		
Footnotes: Edit	Double-click on the reference number; select reference number to delete footnote.		
Forms: Text Form Field	Forms toolbar		abl
Forms: Check Box Form Field	Forms toolbar		☑
Forms: Drop-Down Form Field	Forms toolbar		▤
Graphic: Wrap Text	Select graphic, Format, Format Picture; Layout tab select wrapping style.		
Graphic: Size	Select graphic; drag resize handle. Double-click graphic; Format picture dialog box, choose Size tab; enter dimensions.		
Hanging Indent	Format, Paragraph, Indents and Spacing tab	Ctrl + T	
Headers and Footers	View, Headers and Footers		
Hyperlink: Remove	Right-click hyperlink; then click Remove Hyperlink		
Indent	Format, Paragraph, Indents and Spacing tab		▤ Increase Indent ▤ Decrease Indent
Insert File	Insert, File, locate file		

FUNCTION SUMMARY

Function	Menu Command	Keyboard Shortcut	Toolbar Button
Keep with Next	Format, Paragraph, Line and Page Breaks tab		
Landscape	File, Page Setup, Margins tab		
Merge	Tools, Letters and Mailings, Mail Merge Wizard		
Merge: Labels	Tools, Letters and Mailings, Mail Merge Wizard, Labels		
Numbering	Format		⊞
Nonbreaking Space	Insert, Symbol, Special Characters		
Page Numbers	Insert, Page Numbers		
Page Number: Change Format	Page Number dialog box, choose position; click Format to change number format		
Paste Function	Table, Formula		
Protect Document	Tools, Protect Document, Forms		🔒
Section Breaks	Insert, Break		
Save As Web Page	File, Save as Web Page		
Shading	Format, Borders and Shading, Shading tab		⬚▾
Spelling and Grammar	Tools, Spelling and Grammar	F7	✓
Styles: Apply	Click down arrow on Style button and make selection.		Normal ▾
Symbols	Insert, Symbols		
Tables: Create	Insert, Table		⊞
Tables: Merge or split	Select cells, click the Merge Cells or Split Cells button on the Tables and Borders toolbar.		⊟ ⊞
Tables: Total Column	Click in cell; then click the AutoSum button on the Tables and Border toolbar.		Σ
Tab: Decimal	Format, Tabs		
Tab: Leader	Format, Tabs, Option 2		
Tab: Underline	Format, Tabs, Option 4		
Tabs: Set	Format, Tabs or Horizontal Ruler; set Tab Alignment, click Ruler.		
Template	File, New, General Templates		
Template: Save as	File, Save as, click drop list and choose Document Template as the type of file.		
Text Orientation	Click in table cell, Format, Text Direction		
Undo	Edit, Undo	CTRL + Z	↶▾
Widow/Orphan Control	Format, Paragraph, Line and Page Breaks tab		
Wizard	File, New, Templates		
WordArt	Drawing Toolbar, Insert WordArt button; choose style; type text; select font, size, and style; click OK.		◢

INDEX